## WORLD ECONOMIC PROFILE

| COUNTRY | GDP | | | LABOR FORCE | | |
|---|---|---|---|---|---|---|
| | SERVICE | INDUSTRY | AGRICULTURE | SERVICE | INDUSTRY | AGRICULTURE |
| Argentina | 59.3% | 32.2% | 8.5% | 76.0% | 23.0% | 1.0% |
| Austrralia | 71.3% | 24.9% | 3.8% | 75.0% | 21.4% | 3.6% |
| Austria | 65.8% | 32.5% | 1.7% | 67.0% | 27.5% | 5.5% |
| Azerbaijan | 33.7% | 60.5% | 5.8% | 48.6% | 12.1% | 39.3% |
| Bahamas | 90.0% | 7.0% | 3.0% | 90.0% | 5.0% | 5.0% |
| Bahrain | 41.5% | 58.0% | 0.5% | 20.0% | 79.0% | 1.0% |
| Belarus | 51.0% | 39.7% | 9.3% | 51.3% | 34.7% | 14.0% |
| Belgium | 74.7% | 24.5% | 0.8% | 73.0% | 25.0% | 2.0% |
| Canada | 69.6% | 28.4% | 2.0% | 79.0% | 19.0% | 2.0% |
| China | 40.5% | 48.6% | 10.9% | 33.2% | 27.3% | 39.5% |
| Cuba | 74.8% | 20.9% | 4.3% | 60.6% | 19.4% | 20.0% |
| Czech Rep. | 62.2% | 35.0% | 2.8% | 56.2% | 40.2% | 3.6% |
| Denmark | 73.1% | 25.7% | 1.2% | 72.9% | 24.2% | 2.9% |
| Ecuador | 57.6% | 35.6% | 6.8% | 70.4% | 21.3% | 8.3% |
| Egypt | 49.2% | 37.7% | 13.1% | 51.0% | 17.0% | 32.0% |
| Ethiopia | 43.0% | 13.2% | 43.8% | 10.0% | 5.0% | 85.0% |
| Finland | 65.8% | 30.8% | 3.4% | 69.9% | 25.6% | 4.5% |
| France | 78.9% | 19.0% | 2.1% | 71.8% | 24.4% | 3.8% |
| Germany | 72.0% | 27.1% | 0.9% | 67.8% | 29.8% | 2.4% |
| Ghana | 37.5% | 25.2% | 37.3% | 29.0% | 15.0% | 56.0% |
| Greece | 75.6% | 20.5% | 3.9% | 65.1% | 22.5% | 12.4% |
| Hong Kong | 92.3% | 7.6% | 0.1% | 91.6% | 8.0% | 0.4% |
| Hungary | 62.4% | 34.2% | 3.4% | 62.6% | 32.4% | 5.0% |
| India | 62.5% | 20.0% | 17.5% | 34.0% | 14.0% | 52.0% |
| Israel | 65.4% | 32.0% | 2.6% | 82.0% | 16.0% | 2.0% |
| Italy | 72.9% | 25.0% | 2.1% | 65.1% | 30.7% | 4.2% |
| Jamaica | 64.7% | 29.6% | 5.7% | 64.0% | 19.0% | 17.0% |
| Japan | 75.3% | 23.1% | 1.6% | 67.6% | 27.9% | 4.5% |
| S. Korea | 57.6% | 39.4% | 3.0% | 67.7% | 25.1% | 7.2% |
| Kyrgyzstan | 53.4% | 15.9% | 30.7% | 39.5% | 12.5% | 48.0% |
| Lebanon | 76.2% | 18.7% | 5.1% | N/A | N/A | N/A |
| Mexico | 61.3% | 34.6% | 4.1% | 59.1% | 25.8% | 15.1% |
| Morocco | 48.6% | 32.6% | 18.8% | 44.6% | 19.9% | 35.5% |
| New Zealand | 69.7% | 25.8% | 4.5% | 74.0% | 19.0% | 7.0% |
| Norway | 52.7% | 45.1% | 2.2% | 76.0% | 21.1% | 2.9% |
| Pakistan | 54.9% | 24.3% | 20.8% | 36.6% | 20.4% | 43.0% |
| Poland | 67.3% | 28.1% | 4.6% | 53.4% | 29.2% | 17.4% |
| Portugal | 72.8% | 24.3% | 2.9% | 60.0% | 30.0% | 10.0% |
| Singapore | 73.2% | 26.8% | 0.0% | 77.4% | 22.6% | 0.0% |
| Switzerland | 64.5% | 34.0% | 1.5% | 73.2% | 22.9% | 3.9% |
| Taiwan | 75.2% | 23.1% | 1.7% | 58.0% | 36.9% | 5.1% |
| Thailand | 43.7% | 44.0% | 12.3% | 37.1% | 20.3% | 42.6% |
| Turkey | 64.7% | 25.9% | 9.4% | 45.8% | 24.7% | 29.5% |
| Ukraine | 58.8% | 31.2% | 10.0% | 56.4% | 24.2% | 19.4% |
| United Kingdom | 75.0% | 23.8% | 1.2% | 80.4% | 18.2% | 1.4% |
| United States | 76.9% | 21.9% | 1.2% | 76.8% | 22.6% | 0.6% |
| Venezuela | 61.4% | 34.6% | 4.0% | 64.0% | 23.0% | 13.0% |
| Vietnam | 38.7% | 39.9% | 21.4% | 25.5% | 18.9% | 55.6% |
| West Bank | 81.0% | 14.0% | 5.0% | 68.0% | 15.0% | 17.0% |
| Yemen | 51.1% | 39.2% | 9.7% | N/A | N/A | N/A |

Source: *The World Factbook 2009* (Washington, DC: Central Intelligence Agency, 2009). **https://www.cia.gov/library/publications/the-world-factbook/**, accessed 28 April, 2010.

*Services Marketing, 4e* by Bateson and Hoffman highlights sustainability, global and technological service issues.

# Sustainability and Services in Action

1. The Origins and the Growth of "Green"
2. The Triple Bottom Line
3. Airline Industry Practices
4. The Top 10 Motivators for Consumers to Recycle
5. LEED Ratings: Process Standards in Green Technology
6. The Cost of Going Green
7. Starbuck's Subtle Promotion about Its Environmental Mission
8. Colleges and Universities on the Cutting-edge of Creating Green Servicescapes
9. Florida's Green Lodging Program
10. How Complicated Can It Be to Throw Garbage Away?
11. TerraPass: Enhancing Satisfaction with Social Conscience
12. Certified 'Green': Enhancing Perceptions of Service Quality
13. TreeHugger Has Issues with Delta Sky: The Green Issue
14. Being "Green" Increases Loyalty in Banking
15. Developing a "Green" Culture: Sustainable Business Practices for Hotels

# Global Services in Action

1. Sweden's ICEHOTEL: One Very Cool Experience!
2. Charity.com
3. Ski Dubai
4. Consumer Tipping Behavior: To Tip or Not to Tip—That Is the Question
5. DHL GlobalMail: International Post Made Easy
6. Ethnic Pricing...Is This Ethical?
7. Personal Selling Approaches around the World
8. An Extraordinary Servicescape in the Caribbean: The Katitche Point Great House
9. Dell Offshore Tech Support: Lost in Translation
10. Customer Service Expectations Vary among Cultures
11. Benchmarking Customer Satisfaction throughout the World
12. American versus European Expectations and Perceptions of Airline Service Quality
13. Service Failures and Recovery Strategies: A Chinese Perspective
14. Singapore Airlines Experiences Rare Backlash from Customers
15. International Considerations for Service Cultures

# E-Services in Action

1. Trip advisor: A Traveler's Best Friend
2. Game, Set, Match.com
3. Social Networking: The New Face of Personal Sources of Information
4. Self-check-out: Why Consumers Might Stay Away?
5. Verizon Enterprise Solutions Group: Teaming Up with Health Care
6. Turbocharged Software Sets Airline Pricing 75,000 Times a Day!
7. The Growth of Personal Communications via Social Media
8. Google.com's Servicescape: "61, Getting a Bit Heavy, Aren't We?"
9. Where Employees Go Online to Sound Off!
10. Mastering the Self-check-out Lane at the Grocery Store
11. Enhancing Online Customer Satisfaction
12. The Seven Dimensions of E-Qual
13. Who Done It? Customer Attributions for Online Service Failures
14. I Heart Zappos
15. Zappos' Core Values that Drive Its Service Culture

# Services Marketing

**FOURTH EDITION**

**JOHN E. G. BATESON**
*Independent Consultant*

**K. DOUGLAS HOFFMAN**
*Professor of Marketing,*
*University Distinguished Teaching Scholar*
*Colorado State University*

SOUTH-WESTERN
CENGAGE Learning

Australia • Brazil • Japan • Korea • Mexico • Singapore • Spain • United Kingdom • United States

## SOUTH-WESTERN
### CENGAGE Learning™

**Services Marketing, Fourth Edition**

**John E. G. Bateson and
K. Douglas Hoffman**

Vice President of Editorial, Business:
Jack W. Calhoun

Editor-in-Chief: Melissa Acuña

Acquisitions Editor: Mike Roche

Developmental Editor: Daniel Noguera

Editorial Assistant: Kayti Purkiss

Senior Marketing and Sales Manager:
Bill Hendee

Marketing Coordinator: Sara Greber

Content Project Management:
PreMediaGlobal

Media Editor: John Rich

Production Technology Analyst:
Starratt Scheetz

Website Project Manager:
Jack Litten, LEAP

Manufacturing Coordinator:
Miranda Klapper

Print Buyer: Arethea Thomas

Production Service: PreMediaGlobal

Copyeditor: Ann Archambault

Senior Art Director: Stacy Jenkins Shirley

Cover Designer: Patti Hudepohl

Cover Image: Shutterstock

Photo Credits:

B/W Image: Getty Images/Hisham Ibrahim

Cover Image: Shutterstock Images/Tiberius
Dinu

Printed in Canada

1 2 3 4 5 6 7 14 13 12 11 10

For product information and technology assistance, contact us at
**Cengage Learning Customer & Sales Support, 1-800-354-9706.**

For permission to use material from this text or product,
submit all requests online at **www.cengage.com/permissions**.
Further permissions questions can be emailed to
**permissionrequest@cengage.com**.

Exam*View*® is a registered trademark of eInstruction Corp. Windows is a registered trademark of the Microsoft Corporation used herein under license. Macintosh and Power Macintosh are registered trademarks of Apple Computer, Inc. used herein under license.

© 2008 Cengage Learning. All Rights Reserved.

Library of Congress Control Number: 2010929753

International Edition:

ISBN 13: 978-0-538-47645-4

ISBN 10: 0-538-47645-1

Cengage Learning International Offices

**Asia**
www.cengageasia.com
tel: (65) 6410 1200

**Brazil**
www.cengage.com.br
tel: (55) 11 3665 9900

**Latin America**
www.cengage.com.mx
tel: (52) 55 1500 6000

**Represented in Canada by
Nelson Education, Ltd.**
tel: (416) 752 9100/(800) 668 0671
www.nelson.com

**Australia/New Zealand**
www.cengage.com.au
tel: (61) 3 9685 4111

**India**
www.cengage.co.in
tel: (91) 11 4364 1111

**UK/Europe/Middle East/Africa**
www.cengage.co.uk
tel: (44) 0 1264 332 424

Cengage Learning is a leading provider of customized learning solutions with office locations around the globe, including Singapore, the United Kingdom, Australia, Mexico, Brazil, and Japan. Locate your local office at: **cengage.com/global**

For product information: **www.cengage.com/international**
Visit your local office: **www.cengage.com/global**
Visit our corporate website: **www.cengage.com**

AVAILABILITY OF RESOURCES MAY DIFFER BY REGION. Check with your local Cengage Learning representative for details.

*For Dori, Lorna, Jonathan, and Thomas*
**John Bateson**

*To Brittain, Emmy, Maddy, and my parents*
**Doug Hoffman**

# Preface

The primary objective of *Services Marketing* is to provide materials that not only introduce the student to the field of services marketing, but also acquaint the student with specific customer service issues. In addition to traditional business knowledge, the business world now demands increasing employee competence in developing effective service processes, constructing meaningful servicescapes, customer satisfaction and service quality measurement, as well as service recovery skills that are essential in growing and sustaining the existing customer base.

## Approach

Following the same philosophical approach used in earlier editions, the fourth edition of *Services Marketing* purposely examines the use of services marketing as a competitive weapon from a broadened perspective. Consequently, we view services marketing not only as a marketing tool for service firms, but also as a means of competitive advantage for those companies that market products on the tangible side of the product continuum. As a result, business examples used throughout the text reflect a wide array of firms representing the nine service economy supersectors, including education and health services, financial activities, government, information, leisure and hospitality, professional and business services, transportation and utilities, wholesale and retail trade, and other services—as well as firms that produce tangible products.

Ultimately, the *service sector* is one of the three main categories of a developed economy—the other two being *industrial* and *agricultural*. Traditionally, economies throughout the world tend to transition from an *agricultural economy* to an *industrial economy* (e.g., manufacturing, mining, etc.) to a *service economy*. The United Kingdom was the first economy in the modern world to make this transition. Several other countries including the United States, Japan, Germany, and France have made this transition, and many more will join this group at an accelerated rate.

We continue to live in interesting times! The increased rate of transformation from an agricultural to a manufacturing to a service-based economy has generally been caused by a highly competitive international marketplace. Simply stated, goods are more amenable to international trade than services, thereby making them more vulnerable to competitive actions. In other words, countries that industrialized their economies first eventually come under attack by other countries that are newly making the transition from an agricultural to an industrial economy. These "newcomer" countries offer lower production costs (especially labor), which is attractive to industry. Consequently, as industrial sectors flow from one country to the next, the countries they abandon begin to rely more heavily on the growth of their service sectors as the mainstay of their economies. This whole process repeats itself over and over as other less-developed countries enter the fray, consequently facilitating the transformation from agriculture to industrial to service-based economies.

## Structure of the Book

*Services Marketing* is divided into three main sections.

### Part I: An Overview of Services Marketing

Part I concentrates on defining services marketing and discusses in detail the fundamental concepts and strategies that differentiate the marketing of services from the marketing of tangible goods. The primary objective of Part I is to establish a core knowledge base that will be built upon throughout the remainder of the text.

Chapter 1, *Understanding the Service Experience*, provides an introduction to the field of services marketing. It establishes the importance of the service sector in the world economy and the need for services marketing education. Chapter 2, *Traditional Service Supersectors and Ethical Considerations*, provides an overview of the service sector and focuses on the nine service industry supersectors and the most substantial changes taking place within the service sector. In addition, Chapter 2 takes an in-depth look at ethics in the service sector. Because of the differences between goods and services, unique opportunities arise that may encourage ethical misconduct. Chapter 3, *Unique Discrepancies between Goods and Services*, focuses more deeply on the differences between goods and services—namely intangibility, inseparability, heterogeneity, and perishability—and their corresponding managerial implications. Possible solutions to minimize the negative consequences of these unique service characteristics are also discussed.

Thus far, Chapters 1, 2, and 3 introduce the fundamentals of the service experience, provide an overview of service industries and ethical considerations, and detail the unique challenges associated with the marketing of services. The remainder of this text is organized around the framework provided in Figure 3.5. The consumer must be at the heart of services marketing, and Chapter 4, *Consumer Decision Making in Services Marketing*, focuses on building your understanding of the behavior of service consumers as they select service providers and evaluate their satisfaction with the service they have received. Chapter 4 provides concepts and frameworks that permeate the rest of this book as service firms adapt their marketing mixes to reflect the changing needs of their customers.

### Part II: The Tactical Services Marketing Mix

One of the most basic ideas in marketing is the marketing mix. The marketing mix represents the levers that the organization controls. These levers can be used to influence consumers' choice processes as well as their evaluation of service satisfaction. The traditional marketing mix is often expressed as the four Ps—product, place, price, and promotion. As Figure 3.5 illustrates, due to the fundamental differences between goods and services, the services marketing mix can be redefined and expanded, offering the three additional marketing mix variables of *process*, the physical environment, and *people*.

Given the importance of the services marketing mix, Part II of this text focuses on *The Tactical Services Marketing Mix*, spotlighting the marketing mix variables that must be the most modified when competing in service marketing environments. More specifically, Chapter 5 hones in on a *Focus on Service Processes*; Chapter 6 examines *Considerations for Services Pricing*; Chapter 7 investigates *Effective Service Promotions*; Chapter 8 addresses *Managing the Servicescape and Other Physical Evidence*; and Chapters 9 and 10 explore the "people issues" surrounding services marketing, including *People as Strategy: Managing Service Personnel* and *People as Strategy: Managing Service Consumers*, respectively.

### Part III: Implementing Successful Service Strategies

Marketing's role with the rest of the organization is the theme for Part III of the book, which focuses on *Implementing Successful Service Strategies*. Marketing is at the heart of

AVAILABILITY OF RESOURCES MAY DIFFER BY REGION. Check with your local Cengage Learning representative for details.

each of these strategies, but their execution is dependent on harnessing all of the functions: Operations, Human Resources, and Marketing. As such, Chapter 11, *The Essentials of Customer Satisfaction Measurement*, expands the consumer behavior chapter to explore how it is possible to satisfy a customer in a particular service experience and how to measure and manage satisfaction. Chapter 12, *Service Quality: Identifying and Rectifying the Gaps*, builds upon Chapter 11 and increases our understanding of how consumers evaluate services and the longer-term concept of service quality. Due to the complexity of the various relationships that comprise a typical service encounter, service failures are inevitable; but because of inseparability, it is often possible to recover from a failure situation during the service encounter. Chapter 13 discusses how to successfully master the art of *Managing Service Failures and Implementing Effective Recovery Strategies*.

Given the current competitive situation among many service firms, Chapter 14 deals with *Strategies for Facilitating Customer Loyalty and Retention* as an important strategy for service firms to consider seriously. Finally Chapter 15, *Pulling the Pieces Together: Creating a World-Class Service Culture*, examines the role of marketing within the service organization. It juxtaposes the industrial management model and the market-focused model, and shows how important the latter is for a service business. This final chapter also discusses the key components of creating a world-class service culture.

## What's New in the Fourth Edition?

**New 15-Chapter Version:** The fourth edition of Bateson and Hoffman has been streamlined to fit perfectly with semester or quarter university schedules. As a result of this revision, Bateson and Hoffman (4e) provides an effectively integrated service marketing textbook that incorporates online, global, sustainability, and ethical considerations within one text while providing the latest in service marketing concepts and practices.

**New Opening Chapter Quotes:** Every chapter begins with a managerially oriented, thought-provoking quote directly pertinent to the chapter's content. Quotes such as "Washrooms will always tell if your company cares about its customers"; and "The bitterness of poor quality is remembered long after the sweetness of low price has faded from memory" set the practical application tone for each chapter.

**Revised Learning Objectives:** Learning objectives establish the framework for every chapter, enabling instructors to more effectively organize their class lectures. In addition, past students have found the learning objectives useful for organizing class notes as they study for essay-oriented exams.

**Significantly Revised Chapters:** Every chapter has been updated and/or significantly revised to deliver the latest in service marketing concepts and practices. Most significantly, chapters pertaining to the introduction of service marketing, managing employees, managing service customers, implementing service recovery programs, understanding service supersectors and ethical considerations, and creating a world-class service culture have undergone the greatest transformations.

**New Opening Vignettes:** Every chapter opens with a brand new vignette which spotlights service issues in real companies. These real-life situations draw readers in and set the stage for the chapter topics. The vignettes represent a variety of firms, as well as relevant customer service issues, including: Netflix, Ticketmaster, Frontier Airlines, Vail Resorts, Harrah's, Google, Geico, "Dinner in the Sky", and RateMyProfessor.com.

**Introducing Sustainability and Services in Action Box Features:** Every chapter contains a new box feature dedicated to Sustainability and Services in Action. As perhaps the first services marketing textbook to incorporate sustainability throughout the text, Bateson and Hoffman specifically address sustainable services marketing practices across a variety of industries throughout the globe. Despite the intangible nature of service products, the companies that produce these services are among the world's largest consumers of the earth's natural resources. Industries and topics include: hotels, banking, airlines, restaurants, universities, LEED rating systems, the cost of going green, TerraPass, Tree-Hugger, consumer motivations to recycle, the triple bottom line, and more.

**Revised Global Services in Action Box Features:** In response to the growth of service economies throughout the world, Bateson and Hoffman (4e) provides box features of international services marketing practices in every chapter. These features demonstrate the often subtle adjustments to international services marketing strategy that are necessary to become a world-class service organization. Companies and concepts featured include: Ski Dubai, Katitche Point Great House, Singapore Airlines, ethnic pricing, Chinese perspectives on service failures, personal selling approaches around the world, international considerations for creating world-class service cultures, and many more.

**Revised E-Services in Action Box Features:** Featured in every chapter, E-Services in Action boxes highlight the dynamic nature of online service marketing practices. Examples of companies and topics include: Zappos.com; Match.com; Google.com; social media sites such as Facebook, Twitter, and LinkedIn; online airline pricing; and the ins and outs of self-check-out options.

**Revised End-of-Chapter Review Questions:** Every chapter concludes with 10 review questions that are intentionally written to further reinforce students' understanding and application of chapter content. Answers for review questions are provided in the Instructor's Manual for adopters.

**Revised Marginal and End-of-Chapter Glossaries:** Key terms, provided in every chapter, are highlighted within the text and defined in the adjacent margin. For student study purposes, key terms are again presented collectively at the end of each chapter in order of appearance and defined in the end-of-chapter glossary.

**New End-of-Chapter Cases:** The fourth edition of Bateson and Hoffman contains a new set of end-of-chapter cases that further illustrate, deepen, and extend the concepts developed in each chapter. These cases, purposely brief in nature but long on application and representing a variety of service industries, provide students with an opportunity to further internalize services marketing concepts. Answers for end-of-chapter cases are provided in the Instructor's Manual for adopters.

**New YouTube Video Library:** Especially prepared for adopters, Bateson and Hoffman (4e) provides over 50 video links that illustrate key service concepts that are cross referenced by chapter. The videos, a mix of humorous and serious, bring services marketing practices alive in the classroom, creating a much more interactive atmosphere for learning.

**Updated Instructors Manual:** The updated Instructors Manual provides updated chapter outlines, PowerPoint slides, the answers to all end-of-chapter review questions and cases, as well as an updated test bank.

## Instructors' Resources

The instructor resources for *Services Marketing*, 4e provide a variety of valuable resources for leading effective classroom discussions and assessing student learning.

### Instructor Support Website

The Instructor Support website provides access to downloadable supplements such as Instructor's Manual, Test Bank, and PowerPoint Slides. The URL for the Instructor Support website is **www.cengage.com/international**.

- The Instructor's Manual for *Services Marketing*, 4e includes a summary of the goals of each chapter, detailed lecture outlines, key terms and definitions, answers to discussion questions, case teaching notes, and other resources to reduce lecture preparation time.

- The Test Bank has been expanded to include an abundant number of multiple-choice questions and new short answer essay questions.
- PowerPoint lecture slides highlight the key concepts of each chapter.
- Exam*View*® (Windows/Macintosh) Computerized Testing allows the instructor to create, deliver, and customize tests in minutes with this easy-to-use assessment and tutorial system.

## Student Resources

### Student Support Website

The Student Support Website (**www.cengage.com/international**) enriches the learning experience with a variety of interactive tools and web resources such as Flash Cards, Interactive Quizzes, PowerPoint slides, and more.

## Acknowledgements

We would like to extend our heartfelt thanks to the good folks at Cengage, many of whom we have had the pleasure of knowing for a number of years through our other text projects. Special thanks to Jack Calhoun, Vice President of Editorial Business; Melissa S. Acuña, Editor-in-Chief; Mike Roche, Executive Acquisitions Editor; and Daniel Noguera, Developmental Editor for generating and maintaining the level of support and enthusiasm associated with this project throughout the entire process.

Additional thanks are extended to Mary Stone, Project Manager; Stacy Shirley, Senior Art Director; Deanna Ettinger, Photo Manager; Jaime Jankowski, Photo Researcher; John Rich, Media Editor; Miranda Klapper, Frontlist Buyer; Mardell Glinski-Schultz, Text Permissions Manager, and everyone at PreMediaGlobal for putting the project together–no small task!

We would also like to thank Holly Hapke of University of Kentucky for revising the Instructor's Manual, Test Bank, and PowerPoint Slides. Thank you, Holly!

Special thanks to Colorado State University Honor Students Shawna Strickland and Ashley Tevault for their contributions to the chapter opening vignettes and Services in Action Box features. It was a great experience to involve students in the development of this fourth edition. Good luck to both of you as you begin your respective masters programs abroad!

Finally, we would also like to thank the Cengage sales force for supporting this project. We truly appreciate your efforts in bringing this package to the marketplace and we offer our assistance in support of your efforts.

These first three editions have benefited greatly from the quality of reviewers' comments. We are very appreciative of the insightful comments of the following colleagues:

Nancy Sirianni, Arizona State University

Nadia Pomirleanu, University of Central Florida

Doug Cords, California State University

Melissa St. James, California State University

Olivia Lee, Saint Cloud State University

Kim Nelson, University of Arizona

Ronald Goldsmith, Florida State University

Mohan Menon, University of South Alabama

Cheryl Brown, University of West Georgia

Bacy Dong, University of Missouri

Roxanne Stell, Northern Arizona University

In closing, we hope that you enjoy the book and your services marketing class. It will likely be one of the most practical courses you will take during your college career. Education is itself a service experience. As a participant in this service experience, you are expected to engage in class discussions. Take advantage of the opportunities provided to you during this course, and become an integral component of the education production process. Regardless of your major area of study, the services marketing course has much to offer.

We would sincerely appreciate any comments or suggestions you care to share with us. We believe that this text will heighten your sensitivity to services; and because of that belief, we leave you with this promise: We guarantee that after completing this book and your services marketing course, you will never look at a service experience in the same way again. This new view will become increasingly frustrating for most of you, as you will encounter many experiences that are less than satisfactory. Learn from these negative experiences, relish the positive encounters, and use this information to make a difference when it is your turn to set the standards for others to follow. As apostles of services marketing, we could ask for no greater reward.

John E. G. Bateson
The Hale, Wendover, Bucks,
HP22 6QR
United Kingdom
**john@johnbateson.net**

K. Douglas Hoffman
Professor of Marketing
University Distinguished
Teaching Scholar
Marketing Department
Colorado State University
Fort Collins, Colorado 80523
**Doug.Hoffman@colostate.edu**

# About the Authors

John E. G. Bateson is an independent consultant and company chairman. Previously, he was Group Chief Executive of the SHL Group, the global leader in psychometric testing for jobs. SHL was listed on the London Stock Exchange. In 2006, Dr Bateson lead a management buyout of the company. He was a senior vice president with Gemini Consulting and a Member of the Group Executive Committee of the Cap Gemini Group. He was associate professor of marketing at the London Business School, England, and a visiting associate professor at the Stanford Business School. Prior to teaching, he was a brand manager at Lever Brothers and marketing manager at Philips.

Dr. Bateson holds an undergraduate degree from Imperial College, London, a master's degree from London Business School, and a doctorate in marketing from the Harvard Business School. He has published extensively in services marketing literature, including the *Journal of Marketing Research*, *Journal of Retailing*, *Marketing Science*, and *Journal of Consumer Research*. He is also the author of *Managing Services Marketing: Text and Readings* (South-Western) and *Marketing Public Transit: A Strategic Approach* (Praeger).

Dr. Bateson was actively involved with the formation of the services division of the American Marketing Association. He served on the Services Council for four years, and has chaired sessions of the AMA Services Marketing Conference. He also serves on the steering committee of the Marketing Science Institute.

K. Douglas Hoffman is Professor of Marketing, Everitt Companies Teaching Scholar, and University Distinguished Teaching Scholar at Colorado State University. He received his BS from The Ohio State University, and his MBA and DBA from the University of Kentucky. Doug's teaching experience at the undergraduate and graduate levels spans nearly 25 years, during which he held tenure track positions at Colorado State University, the University of North Carolina at Wilmington, and Mississippi State University. In addition, Doug has taught as a visiting professor at the Helsinki School of Business and Economics (Helsinki, Finland), the Institute of Industrial Policy Studies (Seoul, South Korea), Thammasat University (Bangkok, Thailand), and Cornell-Nanyang Technological University (Singapore).

Professor Hoffman is an accomplished scholar in the services marketing area. In addition, he has written numerous journal and conference proceedings articles on teaching scholarship that have appeared in a variety of publication outlets. His teaching scholarship has also expanded into the co-authorship of three textbooks, including *Services Marketing*, 4e, published by Cengage. He has received numerous teaching awards at the college, university, and national discipline levels, including the prestigious Board of Governors Excellence in Undergraduate Teaching Award. He was also named University Distinguished Teaching Scholar in 2007—a lifetime appointment. Professor Hoffman was named editor of *Marketing Education Review* in 2010.

Doug's current research and consulting activities are primarily in the areas of sales/service interface, customer service/satisfaction, service failure and recovery, and services marketing education.

# Contents in Brief

# Contents

---

## PART III   Implementing Successful Service Strategies

---

# Services Marketing

# An Overview of Services Marketing

The marketing of services differs from the marketing of goods. The bundle of benefits delivered to customers is derived from the service experience that is carefully created by the service organization.

**Chapter 1**
*Understanding the Service Experience*

**Chapter 2**
*Traditional Service Supersectors and Ethical Considerations*

**Chapter 3**
*Unique Discrepancies between Goods and Services*

**Chapter 4**
*Consumer Decision Making in Services Marketing*

*Services Marketing* is divided into three main sections:

- *Part I: An Overview of Services Marketing (Chapters 1–4);*
- *Part II: The Tactical Services Marketing Mix (Chapters 5–10); and*
- *Part III: Implementing Successful Service Strategies (Chapters 11–15)*

Part I, An Overview of Services Marketing, concentrates on defining services marketing and discusses in detail the fundamental concepts and strategies that differentiate the marketing of services from the marketing of tangible goods. Part I also introduces the service supersectors and discusses ethical issues as they relate to the field of services marketing. Finally, Part I concludes with a discussion pertaining to how consumers of services make purchase decisions, focusing once again on the primary differences between goods and services. The primary objective for Part I is to establish a core knowledge base that will be built upon throughout the remainder of this text.

CHAPTER **1**

# Understanding the Service Experience

## CHAPTER OBJECTIVES

After reading this chapter, you should be able to:

- Understand the basic differences between goods and services.

- Develop an appreciation for how service can be used as a competitive advantage for both intangible and tangible products

- Appreciate the factors that create the customer's service experience and why it is important to manage the overall experience.

- Comprehend the driving forces behind the importance of the study of services marketing.

This chapter provides an introduction to the field of services marketing. As such, this chapter introduces the basic differences between goods and services and highlights the importance of managing the customer's overall service experience. In addition, this chapter establishes the importance of the service sector in the global economy, introduces the concept of technologically-based e-services, and discusses the need to develop sustainable service business practices.

### "STOP TRYING TO BE PERFECT AND START BEING REMARKABLE!"

Seth Godin has written several terrific books about how businesses can set themselves apart from the competition. Two personal favorites are *The Purple Cow* and *The Big Moo*. *The Purple Cow* was inspired by a drive through the French countryside. Seth noted the beauty of the scenery that was populated with equally beautiful dairy cows. However, after seeing the same sights hour after hour as they were being repeated over and over again, the drive began to get a bit monotonous. Seth thought "what would truly be remarkable would be to see a 'purple cow.'" Clearly, a purple cow would truly stand out from the crowd!

Courtesy of Penguin Group USA

Ironically, Seth Godin's experience in the French countryside parallels today's business environment. There are a lot of great companies out there, but they have become boring. These companies rarely take chances, rarely excel at anything in particular, and are often run by CEOs who are so afraid to take risks that they require a belt and suspenders to keep their trousers in place. What today's businesses really need is to develop ideas and concepts that are truly remarkable—"Purple Cows!"

Upon reading *The Purple Cow*, 33 of the world's business leaders wrote one- to three-page essays on what they found to be remarkable. This collection of essays titled, "*The Big Moo*," provides the underlying principles of developing a remarkable business and/or living a remarkable life. Stories such as "Harry Houdini was a Lousy Magician," "Tuesdays with Shecky," "They Say I'm Extreme," and "Bob Wears Panty Hose" provide keen insights into the world of being remarkable. *The Big Moo*, remarkable in and of itself, has waived its copyright—readers are encouraged to make as many copies as they like. In addition, all profits from the sale of the book are donated to charities. The admirable mission of *The Big Moo* is to spread the word and "remarkabalize" business.

What do *The Purple Cow* and *The Big Moo* have to do with services marketing? Given the interpersonal nature of services, delivering a great service experience to customers can make all the difference in the world. Excelling at service transforms the mundane into the realm of the remarkable, whether it is excelling at the delivery of the core service or taking the time to add an extra touch that the competition rarely provides.

The pages that follow provide the keys for delivering a truly remarkable service experience. As you will soon discover, effectively and efficiently managing a service experience is a complicated yet fascinating undertaking. However, the same complexities that comprise a service encounter also provide opportunities to deliver a truly exceptional service experience that benefits consumers, employees, the organization, and society itself. Welcome to the fourth edition of *Services Marketing*!

# Introduction

Services are everywhere we turn, whether it be travel to an exotic tourism destination, a visit to the doctor, a church service, a trip to the bank, a meeting with an insurance agent, a meal at our favorite restaurant, or a day at school. More and more countries, particularly the so-called industrialized countries, are finding that the majority of their gross domestic products are generated by their service sectors. However, the growth of the service sector does not just lie within traditional service industries such as leisure and hospitality services, education and health services, financial and insurance services, and professional and business services. Traditional goods producers such as automotive, computer, and numerous other manufacturers are now turning to the service aspects of their operations to establish a differential advantage in the marketplace as well as to generate additional sources of revenue for their firms. In essence, these companies, which used to compete by marketing "boxes" (tangible goods), have now switched their competitive focus to the provision of unmatched, unparalleled customer services.

Ample evidence exists which documents this transition from selling "boxes" to service competition. Traditional goods-producing industries such as the automotive industry are now emphasizing the service aspects of their businesses such as low APR financing, attractive lease arrangements, bumper-to-bumper factory warranties, low maintenance guarantees, and free shuttle services for customers. Simultaneously, less is being heard about the tangible aspects of vehicles such as acceleration, and vehicle styling. Similarly, the personal computer industry promotes in-home repairs, 24-hour customer service, and leasing arrangements; and the satellite television industry is now boasting the benefits of digital service, pay-per-view alternatives, and security options to prevent children from viewing certain programming.

Overall, this new "global services era" is characterized by:

- *economies and labor force figures that are dominated by the service sector;*
- *more customer involvement in strategic business decisions;*
- *products that are increasingly market-focused and much more responsive to the changing needs of the marketplace;*
- *the development of technologies that assist customers and employees in the provision of services;*
- *employees who have been provided with more discretionary freedom to develop customized solutions to special customer requests and solve customer complaints on the spot with minimal inconvenience; and*
- *the emergence of new service industries and the "**service imperative**" where the intangible aspects of the product are becoming more and more the key features that differentiate products in the marketplace.*

**service imperative**
Reflects the view that the intangible aspects of products are becoming the key features that differentiate products in the marketplace.

It is clear that the service sectors in many countries are no longer manufacturing's poor cousin. Services provide the bulk of the wealth and are an important source of employment and exports for many countries. In addition, there are countless examples of firms using the service imperative to drive their businesses forward to profit and growth. Many of these are highlighted in the *Services in Action* boxes located throughout the remainder of the text. As world economies continue to transform themselves, the service boom looks set to continue.

## What Is a Service?

Admittedly, the distinction between goods and services is not always perfectly clear. In fact, providing an example of a pure good or a pure service is very difficult, if not impossible. A pure good would imply that the benefits received by the consumer contained no elements supplied by service. Similarly, a pure service would contain no tangible elements.

In reality, many services contain at least some tangible elements, such as the menu selections at a Rain Forest Café, the bank statement from the local bank, or the written policy from an insurance company. Also, most goods at least offer a delivery service. For example, simple table salt is delivered to the grocery store, and the company that sells it may offer innovative invoicing methods that further differentiate it from its competitors.

The distinction between goods and services is further obscured by firms that conduct business on both sides of the fence. For example, General Motors, the "goods" manufacturing giant, generates a significant percent of its revenue from its financial and insurance businesses, and the car maker's biggest supplier is Blue Cross-Blue Shield, not a parts supplier for steel, tires, or glass as most people would have thought.[1] Other examples include General Electric and IBM, generally thought of as major goods producers, who now generate more than half of their revenues from services. The transition from goods producer to service provider can be found to varying degrees throughout much of the industrial sector. One of the world's largest steel producers now considers its service-related activities to be the dominate force within its overall business strategy.[2]

**goods** Objects, devices, or things.

**services** Deeds, efforts, or performances.

**product** Either a good or a service.

Despite the confusion, the following definitions should provide a sound starting point in developing an understanding of the differences between goods and services. In general, **goods** can be defined as *objects, devices, or things*, whereas **services** can be defined as *deeds, efforts, or performances*.[3] Moreover, we would like to note that when the term "**product**" is mentioned, for our purposes, it refers to both goods and services and is used in such a manner throughout the remainder of this text. Ultimately, the primary difference between goods and services is the property of *intangibility*. By definition,

Although a service such as education is intangible dominant, tangibles such as buildings and open spaces are frequently used to differentiate one education setting from another.

**scale of market entities** The scale that displays a range of products along a continuum based on their tangibility ranging from tangible dominant to intangible dominant.

**tangible dominant** Goods that possess physical properties that can be felt, tasted, and seen prior to the consumer's purchase decision.

**intangible dominant** Services that lack the physical properties that can be sensed by consumers prior to the purchase decision.

intangible products lack physical substance. As a result, intangible products face a host of services marketing problems that are not always adequately solved by traditional goods-related marketing solutions. These differences are discussed in detail in Chapter 3, Unique Discrepancies between Goods and Services.

## The Scale of Market Entities

An interesting perspective regarding the differences between goods and services is provided by the scale of market entities.[4] The **scale of market entities** presented in Figure 1.1 displays a continuum of products based on their tangibility where goods are **tangible dominant** and services are **intangible dominant**. The core benefit of a tangible dominant product typically involves a physical possession that contains service elements to a lesser degree. For example, an automobile is a tangible dominant product that provides transportation. As the product becomes more and more tangible dominant, fewer service aspects are apparent. In contrast, intangible dominant products do not involve the physical possession of a product and can only be experienced. Like the automobile, an airline provides transportation, but the customer does not physically possess the plane

**FIG-1.1** Scale of Market Entities

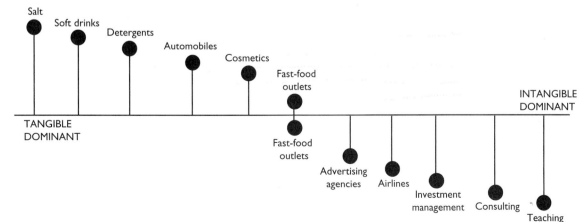

Source: Adapted from G. Lynn Shostack, "Breaking Free from Product Marketing," *The Journal of Marketing* (April 1977), p. 77.

itself. The airline customer experiences the flight; consequently, service aspects dominate the product's core benefit and tangible elements are present to a lesser degree. In comparison, fast food businesses, which contain both a goods (e.g., the food) and service component (e.g., a service provider takes the customer's orders, another service provider cooks the food, the food is then personally presented to the customer) fall in the middle of the continuum.

The scale of market entities reveals two important lessons. First, there is no such thing as a pure good or pure service. Products seemingly are a bundle of tangible and intangible elements that combine to varying degrees. Second, the tangible aspects of an intangible dominant product and the intangible aspects of a tangible dominant product are an important source of product differentiation and new revenue streams. For example, businesses that produce tangible dominant products and ignore, or at least forget about, the service (intangible) aspects of their product offering are overlooking a vital component of their businesses. By defining their businesses too narrowly, these firms have developed classic cases of **service marketing myopia**. For example, the typical family pizza parlor may myopically view itself as being in the pizza business and primarily focus on the pizza product itself. However, a broader view of the business recognizes that it is providing the consumer with a reasonably priced food product in a convenient format surrounded by an experience that has been deliberately created for the targeted consumer. Interestingly, adding service aspects to a product often transcends the product from a commodity into an experience, and, by doing so, increases the revenue producing opportunities of the product dramatically.

For example, when priced as a raw *commodity*, coffee beans are worth little more than $1 per pound.[5] When processed, packaged and sold in the grocery store as a *good*, the price of coffee jumps to between 5 and 25 cents a cup. When that same cup is sold in a local restaurant, the coffee takes on more *service* aspects and sells for $1 to $2 per cup. However, in the ultimate act of added value, when that same cup of coffee is sold within the compelling *experience* of a five-star restaurant or within the unique environment of a Starbucks, the customer gladly pays $4 to $5 per cup. In this instance, the whole process of ordering, creation and consumption becomes "a pleasurable, even theatrical" experience. Hence, economic value, like the coffee bean, progresses from *commodities* to *goods* to *services* to *experiences*. In the above example, coffee was transformed from a raw commodity valued at approximately $1 per pound to $4 to $5 per cup—a markup as much as 5,000 percent!

## The Molecular Model

The molecular model is another useful tool for expanding our understanding of the basic differences between goods and services. A **molecular model** is a pictorial representation of the relationship between the tangible and intangible elements of a firm's operation.[6] One of the primary benefits obtained from developing a molecular model is that it is a management tool that offers the opportunity to visualize the firm's entire bundle of benefits that its product offers customers. Figure 1.2 depicts two molecular models which continue our earlier discussion concerning the differences between automobile ownership (tangible dominant) and purchasing an airline ticket (intangible dominant). As previously discussed, airlines differ from automobiles in that consumers typically do not physically possess the airline. Consumers in this case purchase the core benefit of transportation and all the corresponding tangible (denoted by solid-lined circles) and intangible benefits (denoted by dashed-lined circles) that are associated with flying. In contrast, a consumer who purchases an automobile primarily benefits by the ownership of a physical possession that renders a service—transportation.

**service marketing myopia** Condition of firms that produce tangible products and overlook the service aspects of their products

**molecular model** A conceptual model of the relationship between the tangible and intangible components of a firm's operations.

**FIG-1.2** The Molecular Model

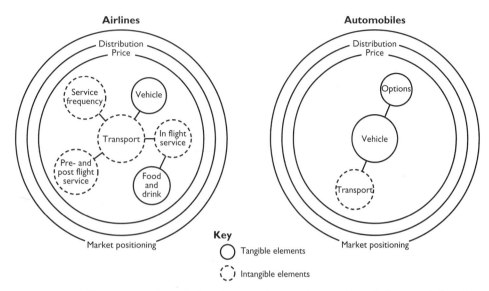

Source: Adapted from G. Lynn Shostack, "Breaking Free from Product Marketing," *The Journal of Marketing* (April 1977), p. 76.

The diagrams provided in Figure 1.2 are oversimplifications of the bundle of benefits that ultimately comprise the airline experience and car ownership. From a managerial perspective, an elaboration of these models would identify the tangible and intangible product components that need to be effectively managed. For example, the successful airline experience is not just determined by the safe arrival of passengers to their selected destinations. The airline molecular model could easily be expanded to include:

- *long-term and short-term parking (intangible element)*
- *shuttle services (intangible element)*
- *rental car availability (intangible element)*
- *flight attendants (tangible elements)*
- *gate attendants (tangible elements)*
- *baggage handlers (tangible elements)*

Similarly, the automobile model could be expanded to include:

- *salespersons on the showroom floor (tangible element)*
- *financing arrangements (intangible element)*
- *finance manager (tangible element)*
- *maintenance and repair services (intangible element)*
- *mechanics and service representatives (tangible elements)*

The overriding benefit obtained by developing molecular models is the appreciation for the intangible and tangible elements that comprise most products. Once managers understand this broadened view of their products, they can do a much better job of understanding customer needs, servicing those needs more effectively, and differentiating their product-offering from competitors. The molecular model also demonstrates that consumers' service "knowledge" and goods "knowledge" are not obtained in the same manner. With tangible dominant products, goods "knowledge" is obtained by focusing in on the physical aspects of the product itself. In contrast, consumers evaluate intangible dominant products based on the *experience* that surrounds the core benefit of the product. Hence, understanding the importance and components of the service experience is critical.

© Mike Baldwin / Cornered

"As you can see from the flow chart, the problem stems from a lack of direction."

The servuction model provides the direction necessary for service companies to create a compelling service experience.

## Framing the Service Experience: The Servuction Model

Due to the intangible nature of service products, service knowledge is acquired differently than knowledge pertaining to goods. For example, consumers can sample tangible dominant products such as soft drinks and cookies prior to purchase. In contrast, a consumer cannot sample an intangible dominant product such as a haircut, a surgical procedure, or a consultant's advice prior to purchase. Hence, service knowledge is gained through the experience of receiving the actual service itself. Ultimately, when a consumer purchases a service, he or she is actually purchasing an experience!

**benefit concept** The encapsulation of the benefits of a product in the consumer's mind.

All products, whether goods or services, deliver a bundle of benefits to the consumer.[7] The **benefit concept** is the encapsulation of these tangible and intangible benefits in the consumer's mind. For a tangible dominant good such as Tide laundry detergent, for example, the core benefit concept might simply be cleaning. However for other individuals, it might also include attributes built into the product that go beyond the mere powder or liquid, such as cleanliness, whiteness, and/or motherhood (it's a widely-held belief in some cultures that the cleanliness of children's clothes is a reflection upon their mother). The determination of what the bundle of benefits comprises—the benefit concept purchased by consumers—is the heart of marketing, and it transcends all goods and services.

In contrast to goods, services deliver a bundle of benefits through the experience that is created for the consumer. For example, most consumers of Tide laundry detergent will never see the inside of the manufacturing plant where Tide is produced. Customers will most likely never interact with the factory workers who produce the detergent or with the management staff that directs the workers. In addition, customers will also generally not use Tide in the company of other consumers. In contrast, restaurant customers are physically present in the "factory" where the food is produced; these customers do interact with the workers who prepare and serve the food as well as with the management staff that runs the restaurant. Moreover, restaurant customers consume the service in the presence of other customers where they may influence one another's service experience. One particularly simple but powerful model that illustrates factors that influence

**FIG-1.3** The
**Servuction Model**

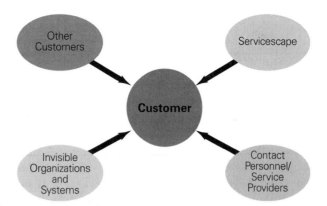

Source: Adapted from E. Langeard, J. Bateson, C. Lovelock, and P. Eiglier, *Marketing of Services: New Insights from Consumers and Managers,* Report No 81-104, (Cambridge, MA: Marketing Sciences Institute, 1981).

the service experience is the servuction model depicted in Figure 1.3. The **servuction model** consists of four factors that directly influence customers' service experiences:

**servuction model** A
model used to illustrate
the four factors that
influence the service
experience, including
those that are visible to
the consumer and
those that are not.

**1.** The Servicescape (visible)
**2.** Contact personnel/service providers (visible)
**3.** Other customers (visible)
**4.** Organizations and systems (invisible)

The first three factors of the servuction model are plainly visible to customers. In contrast, organizations and systems, although profoundly impacting the customer's experience, are typically invisible to the customer.

## The Servicescape

**servicescape** The use
of physical evidence
to design service
environments.

The term **servicescape** refers to the use of physical evidence to design service environments. Due to the intangibility of services, customers often have trouble evaluating the quality of service objectively. As a result, consumers rely on the physical evidence that surrounds the service to help them form their evaluations. Hence, the servicescape consists of *ambient conditions* such as room temperature and music; *inanimate objects* that assist the firm in completing its tasks, such as furnishings and business equipment; and *other physical evidence* such as signs, symbols, and personal artifacts such as family pictures and personal collections. The use of physical evidence varies by the type of service firm. Service firms such as hospitals, resorts, and childcare centers often use physical evidence extensively as they design facilities and other tangibles associated with the service. In contrast, service operations such as express mail drop-off locations use limited physical evidence. Regardless of the variation in usage, all service firms need to recognize the importance of managing the servicescape, because of its role in:

- *Packaging the service*
- *Facilitating the service delivery process*
- *Socializing customers and employees*
- *Differentiating the firm from its competitors*

Given the importance of the servicescape in creating the customer's experience, Chapter 8 is entirely devoted to this important topic.

## Contact Personnel/Service Providers

Another important aspect of the customer's experience involves the contact personnel and service providers that directly interact with customer. Technically speaking, **contact personnel** are employees—other than the primary service provider—who briefly interact with the customer. Typical examples of contact personnel are parking attendants, receptionists, and hosts and hostesses. In contrast, **service providers** are the primary providers of the core service, such as a waiter or waitress, dentist, physician, or college instructor.

Unlike the consumption of goods, the consumption of services often takes place where the service is produced (e.g., dentist's office, restaurant, and hairstylist) or where the service is provided at the consumer's residence or workplace (e.g., lawn care, house painter, janitorial service). Regardless of the service delivery location, interactions between consumers and contact personnel/service providers are commonplace. As a result, service providers have a dramatic impact on the service experience. For example, when asked what irritated them most about service providers, customers have noted seven categories of complaints:

- *Apathy:* What comedian George Carlin refers to as DILLIGAD—Do I look like I give a damn?
- *Brush-off:* Attempts to get rid of the customer by dismissing the customer completely ... the "I want you to go away" syndrome
- *Coldness:* Indifferent service providers who could not care less what the customer really wants
- *Condescension:* The "you are the client/patient, so you must be stupid" approach
- *Robotism:* When the customers are treated simply as inputs into a system that must be processed
- *Rulebook:* Providers who live by the rules of the organization even when those rules do not make good sense
- *Runaround:* Passing the customer off to another provider, who will simply pass them off to yet another provider.[8]

Service personnel perform the dual functions of interacting with customers and reporting back to the internal organization. Strategically, service personnel are an important source of product differentiation. It is often challenging for a service organization to differentiate itself from other similar organizations in terms of the benefit bundle it offers or its delivery system. For example, many airlines offer similar bundles of benefits and fly the same types of aircraft from the same airports to the same destinations. Therefore, their only hope of a competitive advantage is from the service level—the way things are done. Hence, the factor that often distinguishes one airline from another is the poise and attitude of its service providers. Singapore Airlines, for example, enjoys an excellent reputation due in large part to the beauty and grace of its flight attendants. Other firms that hold a differential advantage over competitors based on personnel include the Ritz Carlton, IBM, and Disney Enterprises. Given the importance of service providers and other contact personnel, Chapter 9 is devoted to human resource topics that directly impact a service firm's personnel.

## Other Customers

Ultimately, the success of many service encounters depends on how effectively the service firm manages its clientele. A wide range of service establishments such as restaurants, hotels, airlines, and physicians' offices serve multiple customers simultaneously. Hence, other customers can have a profound impact on an individual's service

**contact personnel**
Employees other than the primary service provider who briefly interact with the customer.

**service providers** The primary providers of a core service, such as a waiter or waitress, dentist, physician, or college instructor.

Paul Simcock/Creatas/Jupiter Images

The service experience is often described as a "shared experience" where "other customers" can dramatically impact the outcome of the one another's overall experience.

**other customers**
Customers that share the primary customer's service experience.

experience. Research has shown that the presence of **other customers** can enhance or detract from an individual's service experience.[9] The influence of other customers can be *active* or *passive*. Examples of other customers actively detracting from one's service experience include unruly customers in a restaurant or a night club, children crying during a church service, or theatergoers carrying on a conversation during a play. Some passive examples include customers who show up late for appointments, thereby delaying each subsequent appointment; an exceptionally tall individual who sits directly in front of another customer at a movie theater; or the impact of being part of a crowd, which increases the waiting time for everyone in the group.

Though many customer actions that enhance or detract from the service experience are difficult to predict, service organizations can attempt to manage the behavior of customers so that they coexist peacefully. For example, firms can manage waiting times so that customers who arrive earlier than others get first priority, clearly target specific age segments to minimize potential conflicts between younger and older customers, and provide separate dining facilities for smokers and customers with children. A more detailed explanation of how "other customers" impact the service experience and strategies for managing "other customers" is presented in Chapter 10.

## Invisible Organization and Systems

Thus far, the servuction model suggests that the benefits derived by the service customer are influenced by the interaction with: (1) the servicescape; (2) contact personnel and/or service providers; and (3) other customers. The benefits service consumers receive are therefore derived from an interactive process that takes place throughout the service experience. Of course, the visible components that comprise the servuction model cannot exist in isolation, and indeed, they have to be supported by invisible components that tie together the organization and its systems. For example, UPS attributes much of the firm's success to the behind-the-scenes activities that the customer seldom sees, including 12 mainframes capable of computing 5 billion bits of information every second; 90,000 PCs; 80,000 hand-held computers to record driver deliveries; the nation's largest private cellular network; and the world's largest BD-2 database designed for package tracking and other customer shipping information.[10]

**invisible organization and systems** That part of a firm that reflects the rules, regulations, and processes upon which the organization is based.

**Invisible organization and systems** reflect the rules, regulations, and processes upon which the organization is based. As a result, although rules, regulations, and processes are invisible to the customer, they have a very profound effect on the consumer's service

Emanuele Biondi/Tips Italia/PhotoLibrary

Although a customer may never see what is going on in a restaurant's kitchen, this important aspect of the "invisible organization and system" will ultimately impact the customer's dining experience.

experience. The invisible organization and systems determine factors such as information forms to be completed by customers, the number of employees working in the firm at any given time, and the policies of the organization regarding countless decisions that may range from the substitution of menu items to whether the firm accepts identification cards for senior citizens' discounts. In contrast to goods that are primarily evaluated based on *outcomes* (e.g., Does the automobile start when I turn the key?), services are evaluated both on *process* and *outcomes* (e.g., My flight to Chicago was an enjoyable experience. I arrived to my destination on time, the service was great, and the employees were very helpful!). The invisible organization and systems drive the service firm's processes. Given the importance of process in the creation of service experiences, Chapter 5 is devoted to issues pertaining to the development of service processes.

Ultimately, the four components of the servuction model combine to create the experience for the consumer, and it is the experience that creates the bundle of benefits that the consumer receives. Creating "experiences" for customers is not a new idea. Entertainment industry entities such as Disney have been doing it for years. Others, particularly in the hospitality sector, have recently picked up on the idea and have introduced "experience" product concepts such as the Hard Rock Café, Planet Hollywood, and the Rainforest Café. The question facing many other types of service providers is how to transform their own operations into memorable experiences for the customer.

Finally, the most profound implication of the servuction model is that it demonstrates that consumers are an integral part of the service process. Their participation may be active or passive, but they are always involved in the service delivery process. This has a significant influence on the nature of the services marketing tasks and provides a number of challenges that are not typically faced by goods' manufacturers.

# Why Study Services?

There are a number of reasons why the study of services marketing is important. Thus far, we have already discussed how consumers evaluate services differently than goods and how service marketers must effectively manage the experiential aspects of the service product. We have also discussed the importance of utilizing service as a differential advantage for tangible-dominant products. Additional reasons to study services marketing include: (1) the growth of the global service economy in terms of contributions to Gross Domestic Products (GDP); (2) the growth of the global service workforce; (3) the emergence of technologically based e-services that have transformed many service industries; and (3) the importance of developing sustainable services marketing business practices.

## The Growth of the Global Service Economy

The *service sector* is one of the three main categories of a developed economy—the other two are *industrial* and *agricultural*. Traditionally, economies throughout the world tend to transition from an *agricultural economy* to an *industrial economy* (e.g., manufacturing, mining, etc.) to a *service economy*. The United Kingdom was the first economy in the modern world to make this transition. Several other countries including the United States, Japan, Germany and France have made this transition, and many more are expected to do so at an accelerated rate.

We live in interesting times! The increased rate of transformation from an agricultural to a manufacturing to a service-based economy has generally been caused by a highly competitive international marketplace. Simply stated, goods are more amenable to international trade than services, thereby, marking them more vulnerable to competitive actions. In other words, countries that industrialized their economies first eventually come under attack by other countries that are newly making the transition from an agricultural to an industrial economy. These "newcomer" countries offer lower production costs (especially labor) which attract industry. Consequently, as industrial sectors flow from one country to the next, the countries they abandon begin to more heavily rely on the growth of their service sectors as the mainstay of their economies. This whole process repeats itself over and over again as other less developed countries enter the fray, consequently facilitating the transformation from agriculture to industrial to service-based economies—which in turn has created economic growth throughout the world.

Worldwide economic growth has further fueled the growth of the service sector, as increasing prosperity means that companies, institutions, and individuals increasingly become willing to trade money for time and to buy services rather than spend time doing things for themselves. Higher disposable incomes have led to a proliferation of personal services, particularly in the entertainment sector. Growth has meant an increase not only in the overall volume of services, but in the variety and diversity of services offered (See Figure 1.6. for a breakdown of U.S. Service Supersectors and their respective contributions to GDP)

The end result has been phenomenal growth in service industries, shown clearly in Worldwide GDP (see Figure 1.4). All developed economies now have large service sectors; and Japan, France, and Great Britain have service economies at least as developed as that of the United States. However, leading the pack with service economies that account for approximately 90 percent of their country's GDP are Hong Kong and the Bahamas.

**FIG-1.4** Worldwide Gross Domestic Product: Composition by Service Sector

| COUNTRY | % | COUNTRY | % |
|---|---|---|---|
| 1. Hong Kong | 92.3 | 11. Belgium | 74.7 |
| 2. Bahamas | 90 | 12. Singapore | 73.2 |
| 3. West Bank | 81 | 13. Denmark | 73.1 |
| 4. France | 78.9 | 14. Italy | 72.9 |
| 5. United States | 76.9 | 15. Portugal | 72.8 |
| 6. Lebanon | 76.2 | 16. Germany | 72 |
| 7. Japan | 75.4 | 17. Australia | 71.3 |
| 8. Taiwan | 75.2 | 18. New Zealand | 69.7 |
| 9. United Kingdom | 75 | 19. Canada | 69.6 |
| 10. Cuba | 74.8 | 20. Poland | 67.3 |

Source: **https://www.cia.gov/library/publications/the-world-factbook/geos/bf.html**

**FIG-1.5** Worldwide Gross Domestic Product: Composition by Service Labor Force

| COUNTRY | % | COUNTRY | % |
|---|---|---|---|
| 1. Hong Kong | 91.6 | 11. New Zealand | 74 |
| 2. Bahamas | 90 | 12. Switzerland | 73.2 |
| 3. Israel | 82 | 13. Belgium | 73 |
| 4. United Kingdom | 80.4 | 14. Denmark | 72.7 |
| 5. Canada | 79 | 15. France | 71.8 |
| 6. Singapore | 77.4 | 16. Ecuador | 70.4 |
| 7. United States | 76.6 | 17. Finland | 69.9 |
| 8. Argentina | 76 | 18. Germany | 67.8 |
| 9. Norway | 76 | 19. South Korea | 67.7 |
| 10. Australia | 75 | 20. Austria | 67 |

Source: **https://www.cia.gov/library/publications/the-world-factbook/geos/bf.html**

## The Growth of the Global Service Labor Force

Throughout the world, the growth and shifting of employment from agriculture to manufacturing to services is evident (see Figure 1.5). The service industries not only have grown in size, but along the way they also have absorbed all the jobs shed by traditional industries, such as agriculture, mining, and manufacturing. The U.S. Bureau of Labor Statistics expects service occupations to account for more than 96 percent of all new job growth for the period 2002-2112.[11] And the same pattern is being repeated in much of the world.

In 1900, 30 percent of the United States' workforce was employed in the service sector; by 2009, service industries employed nearly 79 percent. At the same time, the proportion of the workforce engaged in agriculture declined from 42 percent to just .6 percent.[12] In 1948, 20.9 million persons were employed in goods production of all kinds in America, and 27.2 million persons were employed in services. By the mid-1990s, employment in goods production was 19.9 million (with no increase in more than two decades), whereas service employment had risen to 81.1 million—far more than the total number of persons employed in all sectors 30 years earlier.[13]

Even these numbers conceal the true contribution of services to economic growth, because service employees on direct payroll of goods companies are counted as industrial employees. The service division of IBM, one of the largest worldwide service organizations, is counted as being in the goods, not the service sector, because the government

**FIG-1.6** U.S. Gross
Domestic Product
Composition
by Industry Sector

| INDUSTRY SECTOR: | % CONTRIBUTION | INDUSTRY SECTOR: | % CONTRIBUTION |
|---|---|---|---|
| Agriculture, forestry, fishing, and hunting | 1.0 | Information | 4.4 |
| Mining | 2.3 | Finance, insurance, real estate, rental, and leasing | 20.0 |
| Utilities | 2.1 | Professional and business services | 12.7 |
| Construction | 4.1 | Educational services, health care, and social assistance | 8.1 |
| Manufacturing | 11.5 | Arts, entertainment, recreation, accommodation, and food service | 3.8 |
| Wholesale Trade | 5.7 | Other services | 2.3 |
| Retail Trade | 6.2 | Government | 12.9 |
| Transportation & Warehousing | 2.9 | | |

Source: **http://www.bea.gov/industry**

views IBM's core business as computers and electronics. In contrast, IBM views itself as a major service provider in the "business solutions" industry. A truer picture can be obtained by looking at the combination of persons employed formally in the services sector—such as independent architectural or accounting firms—and the persons employed in those same jobs but working for firms based in the goods sector.[14]

One of the consequences of this change has been a change in the shape of the workforce itself. For example, the bulk of new jobs created in America over the last 30 years have been white-collar jobs in higher-level professional, technical, administrative, and sales positions. Experts monitoring the American economy note that as services have replaced goods as the most dominant force in the economy, "human capital" has replaced physical capital as the important source of investment. "Americans must unshackle themselves from the notion that goods alone constitute wealth, whereas services are nonproductive and ephemeral. At the same time, they should act on Adam Smith's understanding that the wealth of a nation depends on the skill, dexterity, and knowledge of its people."[15]

Given the importance of the global service economy both in terms of contributions to GDP and the worldwide growth of the service labor force, this text provides box features in every chapter that highlight service marketing business practices throughout the world (see Global Services in Action). Titled, "Global Services in Action," these box features highlight companies and concepts such as ethnic pricing, Ski Dubai, DHL Global Mail, global tipping behavior, customer satisfaction expectations among various cultures, and many more.

## The Emergence of E-Service(s)

In its purest form, *technology* represents the application of science to solve problems and to perform tasks. Phenomenal developments in technology—particularly the Internet, have led to fundamental changes in service marketing strategy. Nearly 15 years ago (approximately 1996), the obsession with the Internet began. Thousands of businesses,

## GLOBAL SERVICES *IN ACTION*

### Sweden's ICEHOTEL: One Very Cool Experience!

Transportation and accommodation are two of the most easily recognized industries within the services sector. Think about how many times you have stayed in a hotel, whether in or outside the United States. Do you think of some sort of generic experience, in which every room is somewhat similar and the customer service always feels the same? Many hotels attempt to break these perceptions; however, unfortunately for the majority of us, such luxury treatment is far beyond our financial means.

Take, for instance, the ICEHOTEL in Sweden, settled in the famous Swedish Lapland region. The hotel is built seasonally out of huge blocks of ice and tightly packed snow, creating a true winter wonderland for its guests. Promoted by the hotel as a "mindboggling art project," the structure and all internal features are built entirely of ice. Thick furs cover ice beds and bar stools, and guests are provided coats and capes upon entry. Rooms available include suites and basic single rooms, for a base price of approximately $400 to $1,000 per night. Excursions are also available, including dog sledding, snowmobiling, and skiing.

Visitors do not come to the ICEHOTEL for basic overnight needs; they come to experience a truly unique opportunity. Elaborate shows in an ice theater are held, especially in 2009 when the hotel celebrated its 20th anniversary. Corporations receive incentives to host conferences and retreats at the hotel; packages including rooms, meals, and excursions are all available for purchase, usually on a weekly basis. Availability, given the seasonal nature of the business, is limited due to high demand.

Whether you are sleeping on your ice bed or having a cool drink in the ice bar (served, of course, in a glass made of ice), this hotel experience is one for the record books. Slightly different every year, the ICEHOTEL strives to provide as unique an experience to its guests as possible. No two stays are alike, even for the most loyal of customers.

Source: **http://www.icehotel.com**

---

customers, employees, and partners got wired to one another and began conducting business processes online—also known as *e-business*. Eventually, more and more customers (business and household) became wired and formed a critical mass. Through repeated usage, customer trust has dramatically increased, and the net has become a viable means for revenue production and economic growth for service and goods producers alike. Ultimately, e-business has shifted the power in the marketplace from sellers to buyers. Customers have more choices, more information, and have become increasingly demanding. Accordingly, service marketers have had to become more accessible, more responsive, and more innovative to meet the involving needs of the marketplace.

The growth of online business has been truly phenomenal. In 2009, 1.7 billion people representing 25.6 percent of the world's population had access to the Internet (see Figure 1.7). In contrast, in 2002, 531 million people, representing 8.5 percent of the world's population, had access to the Internet. Within North America, 252.9 million people (74.2 percent of the population) are Internet users.[16] As of 2008, U.S. online retail sales were expected to reach $204 billion, with most of the sales being generated by three product categories—apparel ($26.6 billion), computers (23.9 billion), and automobiles ($19.3 billion). Overall, retail sales have been clicking along with double digit annual growth rates even through recessionary periods.[17]

**e-service** An electronic service available via the net that completes tasks, solves problems, or conducts transactions.

***What are E-Services?***    What exactly are e-services? According to Hewlett-Packard, "an **e-service** is an electronic service available via the net that completes tasks, solves

**FIG-1.7** Worldwide Internet Users by World Regions

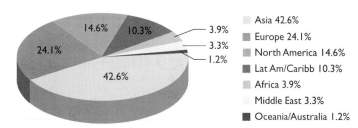

**World Internet Users by World Regions**

- Asia 42.6%
- Europe 24.1%
- North America 14.6%
- Lat Am/Caribb 10.3%
- Africa 3.9%
- Middle East 3.3%
- Oceania/Australia 1.2%

Source: Internet World Stats – **www.internetworldstats.com/stats.htm**, 1,733,933,741 Internet users for September 30, 2009, Copyright © 2009, Miniwatts Marketing Group.

**self-service technologies** Technologically based services that help customers help themselves.

problems, or conducts transactions. E-services can be used by people, businesses, and other e-services and can be accessed via a wide range of information appliances." E-services that are available today include your local bank's online account services, ATMs, UPS package tracking service, Schwab's stock trading services, Travelocity's online purchasing options, a grocery store's self-check-out option, and the list could go on and on. Today, e-services have become more commonly known as **self-service technologies**.

Proponents of self-service technologies (SSTs) frequently boast that "the best service is self-service!" Consequently, companies should operate under the philosophy "help thy customer, help thyself." Ideally, SSTs are purposely created to automate routine interactions between customers and providers with the goal of providing convenience and efficiency to both parties.[18] When these are developed and implemented successfully, consumers love self-service technologies.[19] With respect to airlines, customers can easily compare prices of alternative providers, book their own tickets, select their own seats, and preprint boarding passes to bypass check-in procedures. Ultimately, consumers often enjoy the convenience, speed, and ease of using self-service technologies as compared to traditional assisted services. Service industries that employ self-service technologies include: auto rental chains, banks, insurance companies, hotels, movie rental chains and theatres, and a variety of other retail operations.

SSTs are great when they work; however, when something goes wrong and consumers are unable to successfully navigate SST menus, self-service technologies can become a major source of customer dissatisfaction. Simply consider a service provider's automated phone answering system that does not respond or does not provide the consumer the desired option. In one instance, a hospital's automated phone system provided callers with a multitude of options. Astoundingly, the option that stated "If this is an emergency…" was the ninth option! In some cases, customers view advances into SSTs as a purposeful strategy for the company to distance itself from its customers. As a result, service firms employing SSTs must carefully consider the customer's overall experience. A self-service must provide the customer a benefit (i.e., convenience, and opportunity to customize, cost-savings, time-savings, etc.) in order to be implemented successfully. A self-service technology that is implemented purely to decrease the operating cost of the firm will most likely not be well-received.

E-service plays a critical role in the transformation of the customer's online experience that progresses over time from a functional experience to a more personalized experience. In essence, e-service humanizes the net by providing various customer service activities while simultaneously reducing the online firm's operating costs. Examples include electronic order confirmations, package tracking services, electronic wallets, co-browsing, live text chats, merchandise return services, and collaborative filtering.[20]

## E-SERVICES *IN ACTION*

### Tripadvisor: A Traveler's Best Friend

So, you're going on a cruise! How did you choose the line, cabin, and excursions? Did you seek out recommendations from friends and family? Perhaps you looked up reviews on **www.cruisecritic.com** before making your final choice. As a part of TripAdvisor, LLC, Cruise Critic is just one website in a conglomerate that attracts nearly 36 million unique monthly visitors seeking the best possible holiday. Booking Buddy and Seat Guru are also part of TripAdvisor, as is the host site itself. Whether you are seeking the best travel or accommodation fares, hotel or restaurant recommendations, or cruise reviews, TripAdvisor has it all—and it's free!

Aside from the consumer-specific benefits provided, TripAdvisor also gives businesses the opportunity to advertise to their specific target markets. Graphical advertising opportunities are available on a cost-per-click basis. This service, combined with the travel advisory sites the company hosts, has resulted in multiple awards and accolades from the industry. Some of the key features that have earned this recognition are as follows:

- **Flight Search with Fees Estimator**—largest inventory of flights
- **Top Values Index**—value-based hotel search engine
- **Restaurants**—over 551,000 restaurants with 2 million+ ratings and reviews
- **Gas Tank Gateways**—vacation destinations one tank of gas or less away from home
- **Quick Guides**—downloadable guides to hotels, restaurants, and attractions in 13,000+ of the most popular global destinations

- **Traveler Network**—connection to industry experts and fellow travelers
- **Video**—allows users to post vacation videos and marketers to post promotional clips
- **Content Distribution**—allows travel businesses to post TripAdvisor content on their own sites
- **Saves**—allows users to save reviews to a personalized folder for ease of search
- **Maps**—mashups provide hotel information, including price, availability, and popularity
- **Inside Pages**—allows users to contribute to travel guides
- **goLists**—provides users with travel lists submitted by other users
- **Advanced Hotel Selection Tool**—provides search options for an area's most popular hotels
- **Candid Photos**—provides photos from attractions and cites across the world, while allowing users to post their own
- **Hotel Popularity Index**—worldwide hotel ranking system based on web content
- **Check Rates**—pricing comparison and availability
- **TripWatch**—provides customized email alerts on users' preferred hotels, attractions, and destinations
- **Weekend Getaway Guides**—free, weekly email guide personalized per zip code with weekend travel information

Source: **www.tripadvisor.com**

Given the importance of the role of technology in the provision of services, this text provides box features in every chapter that highlight the role of e-services in the service sector (see E-Services in Action.). Titled, "E-Services in Action," these box features highlight companies and concepts such as Google, Zappos, Match.com, Verizon, social networking sites such as Facebook, LinkedIn, and Twitter, and many more.

### Serving it Up Green: Sustainability Comes to Services

In recent years, much research has been done on the concept of sustainability. Business practitioners have been particularly interested in ways to make production of goods more sustainable and "green." However, up until recently, research has primarily focused on making goods more sustainable. Little has been done in the area of services.

People think of many different things when they hear the word "sustainability." Most people tend to associate the term with being "green" and protecting the environment.

**sustainability** The ability to meet current needs without hindering the ability to meet the needs of future generations in terms of economic, environmental, and social challenges.

However, in broadest terms, sustainability simply means the capacity to endure. More specifically, **sustainability** is defined as "the ability to meet current needs without hindering the ability to meet the needs of future generations in terms of economic, environmental, and social challenges".[21] Hence, sustainability is closely related to the concept of social responsibility.

Why would a service provider want to embrace sustainable practices? The upfront costs of a sustainability program can be extremely expensive in terms of both money and resources. A company may end up focusing too closely on the upfront costs to implement sustainability practices to see the long-term benefits. Doing so may result in the belief that going green is not worth it. This opinion has regained significant strength since the economic crisis. However, in the long run, making a commitment to being more sustainable can benefit a company in more ways than one.

Regardless of whether or not a company makes a good or provides a product, when making the argument for sustainability a company must be able to demonstrate the benefits in financial terms. Companies will be unable to fund sustainability efforts in the future without seeing some sort of payback. Therefore, it is best to make a case for corporate sustainability when the social good can overlap with business opportunity.[22] This overlap is known as the "*sweet spot.*" By being able to identify this area of overlap, executives will then be able to make the case to shareholders, thus gaining support for the strategy. An example can be seen in Unilever's Project Shakti in India. The project seeks to train thousands of women in rural India to sell the company's personal hygiene products to the country's virtually untapped rural market. The project is sustainable in that it hopes to understand how to do business with poor people, thus raising them out of poverty. The plan is also a business opportunity in that it creates a market where there previously was none.

Pursuing sustainable business practices allows companies to find not only areas of improvement, but also a source of competitive advantage. There are four areas in which a company can achieve such aims: *eco-efficiency, environmental cost leadership, beyond compliance leadership, and eco-branding.*[23]

- *Eco-efficiency* focuses on the concept of the "double dividend." Companies that attempt to reduce wastes and inefficiencies within the system see positive results both financially and environmentally.
- *Environmental cost leadership* involves developing a radical innovation that will allow the company to be more environmentally friendly while maintaining cost competitiveness.
- *Beyond compliance leadership* involves companies wanting to increase their sustainability efforts, but also wanting these efforts to be acknowledged by the public. These companies often spend money on environmental certifications, such as LEEDS building certifications. The first-movers in an industry in this case have the greatest advantage. Those who take the first initiative are seen as innovative, while the rest of the companies within the industry are forced to follow suit.
- *Eco-branding strategies* focus on the use of marketing differentiation based on the environmental attributes (e.g., organic, vegan, or fair-trade status) of products. There are three basic prerequisites that often exist for firms to successfully execute this approach: consumers must be willing to pay for the costs of ecological differentiation;reliable information about product's environmental performance must be readily available to the consumer; and the differentiation must be difficult to imitate by competitors.

Given the importance of sustainable operating practices from both an environmental and business perspective, this text provides box features in every chapter that highlight sustainable business practices in the service sector (see Sustainability and Services in Action.).

## SUSTAINABILITY AND SERVICES *IN ACTION*

### The Origins and Growth of "Green"

When considering the "green" movement, many associate it with current trends surrounding sustainability. The origins of the movement, however, have been around since the Industrial Revolution, between the 17th and 19th centuries. The time was defined by unprecedented technological, industrial, and scientific progress that lead to a population explosion among the most industrialized nations. Such booms in the industry and the demand for products resulted in overuse of natural resources, increased waste, and poor working conditions.

The "green" movement reignited in the 1950s and '60s, when consumers became increasingly aware of the impact of global consumption on the environment. Closer to home, American highways, rivers and lakes were becoming increasingly polluted. For example, it was not uncommon to drive behind someone on the highway and watch as they threw trash (e.g., cans, bottles, lunch sacks, cigarette butts, etc.) out their car windows. As another example, the Cuyahoga River located near Akron, Ohio, literally caught fire when an oil slick that covered the surface of the water ignited. The original Keep America Beautiful campaign came about in 1953, composed of a conglomerate of American businesses, nonprofit organizations, government agencies, and concerned consumers. Still in operation, and now the largest community improvement organization in the United States, KAB focuses on litter prevention, the waste hierarchy (reduction, reuse, and recycling of waste), and community beautification. KAB's most recognizable symbol is the "Crying Indian" commercial which ran in the 1970s, depicting a Native American as he observed a polluted American society where once were untouched native lands (see **http://www.youtube.com/watch?v=j7OHG7tHrNM**).

In the 1970s, companies went on the defensive in response to stricter environmental policies. The barrage of new laws led to the creation of Earth Day in 1970 and contributed to the instigation of the first United Nations environmental conference held in Stockholm in 1972. The movement changed hands in the '80s and '90s, transferring from governmental reign to industry and consumer control. Social change began to occur, supporting the advancement of the movement. Though it suffered a setback after the September 11 attacks, when social concern shifted to national security, the public has again claimed sustainability as its own. The Sustainability and Services in Action boxes that are featured throughout the remainder of the text provide specific information about service industries and their transformation into sustainable business practices.

Students will learn about sustainable business practices within the hotel, banking, airline, university, and restaurant industries. In addition, other box items feature concepts or specific companies such as TerraPass, TreeHugger, Starbucks, the LEEDS building certification, motivations to recycle, as well as the origins and growth of the "green" movement.

# Summary

Services permeate every aspect of our lives; consequently, the need for services marketing knowledge is greater today than ever before. When defining services, the distinction between goods and services is often not perfectly clear. In general, goods are defined as objects, devices, or things, whereas services are defined as deeds, efforts, or performances. Very few, if any, products can be classified as pure services or pure goods. The scale of market entities and the molecular model illustrate how products vary according to their tangibility.

When a consumer purchases a service, he or she purchases an experience. The four components of the servuction model create the experience for the consumer—the servicescape, service providers/contact personnel, other customers, and the invisible organization and systems. In turn, the service experience that is created delivers a bundle of benefits to the consumer. In contrast to the production of goods, the servuction model demonstrates that service consumers are an integral part of the service production process.

There are a number of reasons why the study of services marketing is important: (1) consumers evaluate services differently than goods and service marketers must effectively manage the experiential aspects of the service product; (2) services can be effectively used as a differential advantage for tangible-dominant products; (3) the growth of the global service economy in terms of contributions to Gross Domestic Products (GDP) has increased dramatically; (4) the growth of the global service workforce has also increased accordingly; (5) the emergence of technologically based e-services have transformed many service industries; and (6) knowledge is needed in the area of developing sustainable services marketing business practices.

## Key Terms

service imperative, p. 4
goods, p. 4
services, p. 4
product, p. 4
scale of market entities, p. 5
tangible dominant, p. 5
intangible dominant, p. 5

service marketing myopia, p. 6
molecular model, p. 6
benefit concept, p. 8
servuction model, p. 9
servicescape, p. 9
contact personnel, p. 10
service providers, p. 10

other customers, p. 11
invisible organization and systems, p. 11
e-service, p. 16
self-service technologies, p. 17
sustainability, p. 19

## Review Questions

1. Define the following terms: goods, services, products.
2. What can be learned from the service imperative?
3. Why is it difficult to distinguish between many goods and services? Use the scale of market entities and the molecular model concepts to explain your answer.
4. Utilizing the servuction model, describe your classroom experience.
5. How would your servuction model, discussed in the question above, change as you describe the experience at a local restaurant?
6. How does the organization and systems dimension of the servuction model differ from the other three dimensions? What is the purpose of the organization and systems dimension?
7. As you consider the table that provides Worldwide GDP information, a mix of countries comprise the top 10 service economies. These countries sometimes differ greatly, yet still generate large service economies. Please explain.
8. Discuss the keys to delivering effective self-service technologies.
9. Describe online services that help humanize the online experience.
10. Discuss the four approaches to utilizing sustainability as an effective business positioning strategy.

## Notes

1. "The Final Frontier," *The Economist*, (February 20, 1993), p. 63.
2. Organization for Economic Co-Operation and Development (OECD) (2000), *The Service Economy, STI: Business and Industry Policy Forum Series*, p.10
3. Leonard L. Berry, "Services Marketing Is Different," *Business Magazine* (May-June 1980), pp. 24–29.
4. This section adapted from G. Lyn Shostack, "Breaking Free from Product Marketing," *Journal of Marketing* 41 (April 1977), pp. 73–80.
5. Joseph B. Pine II and James H. Gilmore, *The Experience Economy* (Boston: Harvard Business School Press, 1999).
6. G. Lyn Shostack, pp. 73–80.
7. This section adapted from John E. G. Bateson, *Managing Services Marketing*, 2nd ed. (Fort Worth, TX: The Dryden Press, 1992), pp. 8–11.
8. Ron Zemke and Kristen Anderson, "Customers from Hell," *Training* (February 1990) pp. 25–31.
9. For more information, see Charles L. Martin, "Consumer-to-Consumer Relationships: Satisfaction

with Other Consumers' Public Behavior," *Journal of Consumer Affairs,* 30, 1, (1996), pp. 146–148; and Stephen J. Grove and Raymond P. Fisk, "The Impact of Other Customers on Service Experiences: A Critical Incident Examination of Getting Along," *Journal of Retailing,* 73, 1, (1997), pp. 63–85.

10. Jim Kelley, "From Lip Service to Real Service: Reversing America's Downward Service Spiral," *Vital Speeches of the Day,* 64, 10, (1998), pp. 301–304.

11. See **www.bls.gov** for more information pertaining to the growth of U.S. service supersectors.

12. Ibid.

13. *Statistical Abstract of the United States,* 1993.

14. Eli Ginzberg and George J. Vojta, "The Service Sector of the U.S. Economy," *Scientific American,* 244, 3, (March 1981), pp. 31–39.

15. Ibid.

16. **http://www.internetworldstats.com/stats.htm**, accessed 31 January, 2010.

17. **http://www.paymentsnews.com/2008/04/us-online-retai.html**, accessed 31 January, 2010.

18. **http://knowledge.wpcarey.asu.edu/article.cfm?articleid=1624**, accessed 31 January, 2010.

19. **http://searchcio.techtarget.com/tip/0,289483, sid182_gci1252698,00.html**, accessed 31 January, 2010; and **http://www.jazdhotels.com/hotelworld-networkmarketplace/research/Penn-Center-Systems.htm?contentSetId=40003768**, accessed 31 January, 2010.

20. Rafi A. Mohammed, Robert J. Fisher, Bernard J. Jaworski, and Aileen Cahill, *Internet Marketing: Building Advantage in a Networked Economy,* (Boston: McGraw-Hill Irwin, 2002). Zemke and Connellan, e-Service, AMACOM.

21. Lisa Cooling, "On the Front Line of Social Responsibility and Sustainability." *Inside Supply Management,* 20,1 (2009), 22. Web. 27 September, 2009.

22. Adrienne Fox, "Corporate social responsibility pays off: by being good corporate citizens, companies can woo top talent, engage employees and raise productivity," *HR Magazine,* August 2007, n. pag. Web. 3 November, 2009. **http://findarticles.com/p/articles/mi_m3495/is_8_52/ai_n20525141/?tag= content;col1**, accessed 1 February, 2010.

23. Orsato, Renato J. "Competitive Environmental Strategies: When Does it Pay to Be Green?" *California Management Review,* 48, 2, (2006), pp. 127–143.

# The Twins' First Service Encounter

Our day began at 5:20 a.m. Hurricane Felix was predicted to hit the Carolina coast by the end of the afternoon, and I, like most of the other folks in southeastern North Carolina, had spent much of the previous day preparing the house for the upcoming storm. However, my wife and I had one extra concern that the others did not. My wife was six months pregnant with twins, and the prospect of spending lots of time in the car in the attempt to remove ourselves from harm's way was not particularly attractive. We had decided to wait until after my wife's doctor appointment at 9 a.m. to make a decision on whether we should leave or stay at home and ride out the storm. We never made it to the doctor's appointment.

At 5:20 a.m., I was awakened by the fear in my wife's voice. Her water had broken, and the twins that were due on November 16 had apparently made up their collective minds that they were going to be born 13 weeks early. As first-time parents, we understood that our next move would be to go to the hospital; however, we were unsure as to the best mode of transportation given our particular situation. We had been informed by doctors that multiple-birth pregnancies were high-risk pregnancies, and every precaution should be taken. We quickly called the hospital and asked for advice. The hospital suggested that my wife take a shower, shave her legs, pack some essentials, and that it would be appropriate for us to drive ourselves to the hospital. Too stressed out to take any chances, we passed on the shower advice, quickly threw some things together, and drove to the hospital immediately.

## The Emergency Department

Upon our arrival at the hospital, we drove to the emergency entrance, and I quickly exited the car to find a wheelchair. I was immediately confronted by a security guard who had been previously engaged in a casual conversation with another gentleman. I was informed that I could not leave my car in its current position. In response, I informed the security guard that I needed a wheelchair and would move the car after I was able to move my wife inside. The security guard pointed his finger in the direction of the wheelchairs. I grabbed the first wheelchair I could get my hands on and headed back out the sliding doors to assist my wife. At this point, the security guard informed me that I had grabbed a juvenile-sized wheelchair. I headed back inside and grabbed a much larger wheelchair. I returned to the car, assisted my wife into the wheelchair, and headed back inside. The security guard, while continuing with his other conversation, instructed me to leave my wife with the triage nurse in the emergency department so that I could move my vehicle. I said goodbye to my wife and went to move the vehicle. When I returned,

Source: Originally printed as: K. Douglas Hoffman, "Rude Awakening, " *Journal of Health Care Marketing,* Summer 1996, 16, 2, pp. 14-22.

the security guard informed me that they had taken my wife to the maternity ward, located on the third floor.

My wife's encounter with the triage nurse was apparently short and sweet. The triage nurse had called for an orderly to move my wife to the maternity ward. On her way to the third floor, the orderly asked my wife whether she was excited about having the baby. She responded that she was scared to death because she was only six months pregnant. The orderly replied that there was "no way [she was] having a baby that early that [would] survive."

## The Maternity Ward

As I exited the elevator on the third floor, I headed for the nurses' station to inquire about my wife's current location. I was greeted by several smiling nurses who escorted me to my wife's room. On my way to the room, I met another nurse who had just exited my wife's room. This nurse pulled me aside and informed me of the orderly's remarks. She continued to assure me that what he said was not only inappropriate, but more importantly, inaccurate. She also informed me that my wife was very upset and that we needed to work together to help keep her calm. This particular nurse also informed us that she herself had given birth to a premature child, who was approximately the same gestational age as ours, a couple of years earlier.

By this time, it was between 6 and 6:30 a.m. The resident on duty entered the room and introduced himself as Dr. Baker. My wife gave me this puzzled and bewildered look. The clinic where my wife is a patient consists of five physicians who rotate their various duty assignments. Dr. Baker is one of the five. However, Dr. Baker was 30 to 40 years older than the resident who had just introduced himself as Dr. Baker. What had happened was that the resident was nervous and had introduced himself as Dr. Baker rather than as Dr. Baker's assistant. Realizing and embarrassed by his mistake, he reintroduced himself and informed us that Dr. Baker was the physician on call, and that he was being contacted and kept informed of my wife's condition.

The resident left the room and soon reappeared with an ultrasound cart to check the positions of the babies. This time he was accompanied by a person I assumed to be the senior resident on duty. For the next 30 minutes or so, I watched the junior resident attempt to learn how to use the ultrasound equipment. He consistently reported his findings to us in sentences that began with, "I think...." Several times during this period my wife voiced her concern over the babies' conditions, and the location of Dr. Baker. We were reassured by the residents that Dr. Baker was being kept informed and were told that being upset was not going to help the babies' conditions. After about 30 minutes, I informed both residents that despite their advice for us to stay calm, they were not exactly instilling a lot of confidence in either one of us. The senior resident took over the ultrasound exam at this time.

Dr. Baker arrived at the hospital somewhere between 7 and 7:30 a.m. He apologized for not being there earlier and mentioned that he was trying to help his wife prepare for the ensuing hurricane. Sometime during this same time period, it was shift change time for the nurses and also for Dr. Baker. New nurses were now entering the room, and now Dr. Johnson was taking over for Dr. Baker. By approximately 8 a.m., Dr. Baker had pulled me aside and informed me that after conferring with Dr. Johnson, they had decided that if my wife's labor subsided, she would remain in the hospital for seven to 10 days, flat on her back, before they would deliver the babies. It was explained that with each passing day, the babies would benefit from further development. The lungs were of particular concern.

Upon being admitted to the maternity floor, my wife had immediately been hooked up to an EKG to monitor contractions. Due to the small size of the babies, the contractions were not severe. However, as far as my wife and I could tell, the interval between contractions was definitely getting shorter. Being first-time parents, we were not overly alarmed by this since we figured we were in the hospital and surrounded by healthcare providers.

Between 8 and 8:30 a.m., two other nurses entered the room with lots of forms for us to complete. Since we were having twins, we needed duplicates of every form. The forms covered the basics: names, addresses, phone numbers, social security numbers, and insurance information. These were all the same questions that the hospital had sent to us weeks earlier, which we had completed and returned. The nurses asked us the questions, we supplied the information, and they wrote the responses.

By 8:30 a.m., Dr. Baker was informing me that due to one baby's breach position, they would deliver the babies by caesarean section. Wondering whether the schedule had been moved up from a week to 10 days, I asked when he thought this would be happening. He replied: "In the next hour or so." He then commented that labor had not subsided and that Dr. Johnson would be delivering the babies.

As my wife was being prepared for the operating room, I stood in the hallway outside her room. I noticed another physician limping down the hall with one foot in a cast and a crutch underneath one arm. He stopped outside my wife's room and began to examine her medical charts. He introduced himself as Dr. Arthur (he had broken his foot while attempting to change a tire). Dr. Arthur was the neonatologist, which meant nothing to me at the time. I eventually figured out that my wife had her set of doctors and that my unborn children had their own set of healthcare providers. Dr. Arthur asked to speak to my wife and me together. This is when he told us that 90 percent of babies such as ours survive and that 90 percent of those survivors develop normally. He was a calm, pragmatic individual who encouraged us to ask questions. He continued to explain that the babies would spend their next few months in the hospital's Neonatal Intensive Care Unit (NICU) and that, if all went well, we could expect to take them home within two weeks of their due date (November 16, 1995).

By 9 a.m., all hell had broken loose. My wife had dilated at a quicker pace than had been anticipated … the contractions had indeed been occurring at more frequent intervals. Some orderlies and nurses grabbed my wife's bed and quickly rolled her down the hall to the delivery room. I was thrown a pair of scrubs and told to put them on. I was further told that they would come back and get me if they were able. For 10 to 12 very long minutes, I sat on a stool in an empty hospital room by myself, watching The Weather Channel track Hurricane Felix. The volume on the television had been muted, and the only thing I could hear was a woman screaming from labor in the next room. Suddenly, a nurse popped her head in the door and said that a space had been prepared for me in the delivery room.

## The Delivery Room

As I entered the delivery room, I was overwhelmed by the number of people involved in the process. Myself included, I counted 12 "very busy" people. I was seated next to my wife's head. She had requested to stay awake during the procedure. My wife asked me whether the man assisting Dr. Johnson was the junior resident. Sure enough, I looked up to see the junior resident wearing a surgical gown and mask with a scalpel in his hand. I lied and told her, "No."

Suddenly, we realized that we had not finalized our choices for names. Somehow, what we couldn't decide despite months of discussion, we decided in 30 seconds. Our first baby girl, Emma Lewis (Emmy), was born at 9:15 a.m. Emmy weighed 2 pounds and was 14.5 inches long. Our second baby girl, Madeline Stuart (Maddy), was born at 9:16 a.m. and weighed 2 pounds, 2 ounces, and also measured 14.5 inches long. Both babies were very active at birth, and their faint cries reassured my wife and me that they had at least made it this far.

Upon being delivered from their mother, the babies were immediately handed to Dr. Arthur and his staff, who had set up examination stations in the delivery room. Each baby had her own team of medical personnel, and I was encouraged by Dr. Arthur, who hopped on one foot across the delivery room, as I watched him examine the girls. The neonatal staff examining the girls "ooohed and aaahed," and almost in a competitive manner compared measurements about which baby had better vitals in various areas. Dr. Arthur then suggested that I follow the girls to the NICU to watch further examinations. He also made sure that my wife got a good look at both babies before they were wheeled out of the delivery room in their respective incubators. My wife and I said our goodbyes, and I was told I could see her again in the recovery room in about 20 to 30 minutes.

## The Recovery Room

The recovery room and the delivery room are contained within the maternity ward on the third floor of the hospital. The NICU is located on the fourth floor, which is designated as the gynecological floor. The staff on the third floor is geared for moms and babies. The staff on the fourth floor, outside the NICU, is geared for women with gynecological problems.

After receiving the "so far, so good" signals from both my wife's and my babies' doctors, I was permitted to rejoin my wife in the recovery room. It was a basic hospital room with the exception that a nurse was assigned to the room on a full-time basis. One of the hospital volunteers from the maternity floor had taken pictures of each of the babies and taped them to the rails of my wife's hospital bed. The nurses of the third floor maternity ward asked my wife whether she would like a room on the fourth floor so that she could be closer to her babies when she was ready to start walking again. She agreed and spent the next four days in a room on the fourth floor.

Hurricane Felix stayed out to sea and moved up the coastline, missing us completely.

## The Fourth Floor

My wife's private room on the fourth floor was small, dingy, and dirty. From an emotional standpoint, the staff on the fourth floor were not prepared to deal with our situation. In fact, one nurse, after discussing the situation with my wife, asked whether we were going to have the babies transported to a major university medical center three hours away.

My wife's quality of care on the fourth floor was sporadic. Some of the nurses were good and some were inattentive—slow to respond to the patient's call button and blaming nurses on other shifts when medications and other scheduled or promised care (e.g., providing the patient with a breast pump) were not provided on a timely basis. Although it might seem trivial to many, the breast pump represented my wife's primary contribution to the care of her babies. It was the only thing she could control. Everything else was out of her hands. My wife was instructed to begin pumping as soon as she felt able, yet due to her location away from the maternity ward, obtaining a breast pump was difficult and became a sore point for my wife.

After receiving a courtesy call by the hospital's patient representative, my wife expressed her concerns. Shortly thereafter, personnel were changed, the quality of care improved, and we were moved to a much larger room on the third afternoon.

# The Neonatal Intensive Care Unit

The NICU (pronounced "nick-u") is located in an isolated area of the fourth floor. The primary purpose of the NICU is to provide care for premature babies and for full-term babies requiring special care. The number of babies cared for each day throughout our stay typically averaged 12.

Emmy and Maddy spent approximately seven weeks in the NICU. The staff made every effort to explain the purpose of every piece of machinery and every tube that seemed to cover the babies' bodies. I was repeatedly told that I could and should ask questions at any time and that the staff understood that it was an overwhelming amount of information. Hence, it was understandable and acceptable to ask the same questions day after day. The staff had made signs welcoming each of the babies in bright neon colors and taped them above each of their stations. For ease of access, the girls had not yet been placed in incubators. They lay in what looked like large in/out baskets with raised borders. We celebrated weeks later when they finally had enough tubes removed so that they could be moved into incubators —what we called "big-girl beds."

During the first three days, I walked into the NICU to find baby quilts at each of the girls' stations. A local group called Quilters by the Sea had sewn the quilts; apparently they regularly provide the quilts for infants admitted to the NICU. For some reason that I still cannot explain today, the fact that someone outside the hospital who I did not know cared about my girls touched me deeply. The signs the staff had made and the babies' patchwork quilts humanized all the machines and tubes. Somehow, I was no longer looking at two premature infants—I was looking at Emmy and Maddy.

Throughout the girls' stay in the NICU, the quality of care delivered was primarily exceptional. The staff not only excelled at the technical aspects of their jobs but also were very good in dealing with parents. Some of the personal touches included numerous pictures of each of the girls for us to take home, homemade birthday cards with pictures from the girls for Mom and Dad on their birthdays, baby stickers on their incubators, and notes of encouragement from staff when a milestone, such as when weighing 3 pounds, was achieved. We arrived one day and found pink bows in the girls' hair. The nurses even signed Emmy's and Maddy's names on the foot cast worn by the baby boy in the next incubator.

Parental involvement in the care of all the infants was encouraged, almost demanded. I had somehow managed never to change a diaper in my life (I was 35 years old). I was threatened, I think jokingly, that the girls would not be allowed to leave the NICU until I demonstrated some form of competency with diaper changes, feedings, and baths. The primarily female staff made me feel at times that my manhood was at stake if I was not able to perform these duties. Personally, I think they all wished they'd had the same chance to train their husbands when they'd had their own babies. I am now an expert in the aforementioned activities.

As for the babies' progress, some days were better than others. We celebrated weight gains and endured a collapsed lung, blood transfusions, respirators, alarms caused by bouts with apnea and bradycardia, and minor operations. Throughout the seven weeks, many of the staff and three neonatologists became our friends. We knew where one another lived, we knew about husbands, wives, boyfriends, and kids. We also heard a lot about the staff's other primary concern–scheduling.

# The Grower Room

Sometime after the seventh week, we "graduated" from the NICU and were sent to the Grower Room. The Grower Room acts as a staging area and provides the transition between the NICU and sending the babies home with their parents. Babies who are transferred to the Grower Room no longer require the intensive care provided by the NICU but still require full-time observation. As the name indicates, the Grower Room is for feeding and diaper changing, administering medications, and recording vital statistics—basic activities essential for the growth and development of infants. The Grower Room held a maximum of four infants at any one time.

The Grower Room was located in a converted patient room located in the back corner of the second floor, which is designated as the pediatric floor of the hospital. In general, the Grower Room was staffed by one pediatric nurse and visited by the neonatologists during rounds. As parents who were involved in the care of their babies, being transferred to the Grower Room meant that we had to establish new relationships with another set of healthcare providers all over again.

Compared with the "nurturing" culture we had experienced in the NICU, the Grower Room was a big letdown. One of the first nurses we were exposed to informed us that the nurses on the second floor referred to the Grower Room as "The Hole," and that sooner or later they all had to take their turn in "The Hole." We asked the reasons for such a name, and the nurse explained that because the room was stuck back in the corner, the rest of the staff seldom allowed the "grower nurse" to take a break, and because of the constant duties involved, the grower nurse could never leave the room unattended. It was also explained that some of the nurses simply did not feel comfortable caring "for such small little babies." We quickly found that this attitude had manifested itself in a lack of supplies specifically needed for smaller babies, such as premature-sized diapers and sheepskin rugs inside the incubators.

Furthermore, it became quickly apparent that friction existed between the NICU and the Grower Room. The Grower Room was very hesitant to request supplies from the NICU, and on several occasions would delay informing the NICU that an occupancy existed in the Grower Room. The reason for delay was so that the Grower Room nurse could catch up on other duties and avoid having to undertake the additional duties involved in admitting new patients. The "successful delay" would pass on these activities to the nurse taking the next shift. Apparently, the friction was mutual, since one of the nurses in the NICU commented to us on the way out of the NICU, "Don't let them push you around down there. If you don't think they're doing what they should, you tell them what you want them to do."

When the Grower Room was in need of supplies for our babies and others, I (on more than one occasion) volunteered to ask for supplies from the NICU. Although my foraging attempts were successful, I definitely got the feeling that there was some reluctance on both sides for me to do this. I suspected that the Grower Room nurses did not want to ask for any favors, and the NICU staff felt that it was not their job to keep the Grower Room stocked with supplies. Moreover, I suspect that the NICU and the Grower Room operate from different budgets. Stocking the Grower Room is not one of the objectives of the NICU's budget. However, from my side, my babies needed supplies, and I did not care about either department's budget.

After a few dark days, we established new relationships with the Grower Room personnel and became very involved with the care of our babies. After spending seven weeks in the NICU, we felt more familiar with each baby's personal needs than some of the Grower Room staff were. Recognizing our level of involvement, most of the staff looked forward to our visits since it meant less work for them. By now, we had learned to ask lots of questions, to double check that medications had been provided, and to develop a working relationship with Grower Room personnel. Looking back, it was almost as if we and the Grower Room staff trained each other. At the conclusion of our Grower Room experience, my wife and I felt that we had met some good people, but also that the quality of the experience was far lower than what we had grown accustomed to in the NICU.

## Nesting

Once the babies had "graduated" from the Grower Room, our last night in the hospital was spent "nesting." Friends of ours joked that this must have involved searching for twigs, grass, and mud. The nesting rooms were located on the second floor of the hospital, in the same general location as the Grower Room. Nesting allows the parents and the babies to spend a night or two together in the hospital before they go home. During the nesting period, parents are solely responsible for all medications, feedings, and general care of the infants. The nesting period allows the parents to ask any last-minute questions and to smooth the transition from, in our case, nine weeks of hospital care to multiple infant care at home.

The nesting room itself was a small patient room that consisted of one single bed and a fold-out lounge chair. By now, the babies had been moved from their incubators to open, plastic bassinets that were wheeled into the room with us. Each baby remained attached to a monitor that measured heart and breathing rates. To say the least, space was limited, but for the first time in nine weeks, the four of us were alone as a family.

Throughout the 22 hours we nested, we were frequently visited by neonatologists, nurses who continued to take the babies' vital signs, the babies' eye doctor, social workers who were assigned to all premature baby cases, hospital insurance personnel, and a wonderful discharge nurse who was in charge of putting everything together so that we could get out the door. Nine weeks to the day after we had entered the hospital, we took our two 4-pound babies home.

## Discussion Questions

1. Based on the scale of market entities, is health care tangible dominant or intangible dominant? Please explain.
2. Using the servuction model as a point of reference, categorize the factors that influenced this service encounter.
3. Develop a molecular model for this hospital.
4. Discuss corrective actions that need to be taken to ensure that a patient's subsequent service experience will run more smoothly.

# CHAPTER 2
# Traditional Service Supersectors and Ethical Considerations

The purposes of this chapter are twofold. First, this chapter provides students with a broad understanding of the wide array of service industries that comprise the service sector. More specifically, descriptions and employment projections of each of the nine service supersectors are introduced. The second objective of this chapter is to introduce the very important topic of ethical issues in services marketing.

Jack Affleck/Alamy

Service marketers as well as service customers often face unique ethical issues that merit discussion.

## VAIL RESORTS: HEADS UP—KNOW THE CODE, IT'S YOUR RESPONSIBILITY!

The service sector is comprised of nine supersectors such as the Leisure and Hospitality supersector. As should be the case with all service marketers, Leisure and Hospitality service providers have an ethical and social responsibility to enhance society's welfare—including the welfare of its customers, employees, stockholders, and surrounding communities. Many leading service companies actively embrace their responsibility to society and conduct business in an ethical manner. Vail Resorts is an example of one such company.

Like many other service encounters, winter skiing on the Colorado slopes is a shared experience where skiers enhance and detract from one another's skiing experience. Vail Resorts, the owners and operators of Vail, Beaver Creek, Keystone, Breckenridge and Heavenly ski resorts, recognize the potential threat that skiers pose to one another. Consequently, Vail Resorts has recognized its responsibility to its guests and aggressively promotes skier safety.

There are many different kinds of winter sports enthusiasts enjoying the ski slopes of the Rocky Mountains. In addition to traditional alpine skiers, snow-boarders, telemark skiers, blade skiers, ski bikers, cross-country skiers, skiers with disabilities, and skiers with specialized equipment share the slopes. The needs and abilities within and among each group often greatly differ. In addition to showing courtesy to one another and using good common sense, Vail Resorts has developed "Your

Responsibility Code." Vail Resorts hopes that, by its guests following the code and sharing the responsibility of safety, everyone will have a great experience.

The Responsibility Code is highly visible in and around Vail Resorts properties. Posted prominently in lodges, on ski maps, and even on the support posts of ski lifts, the code reads as follows:

*Your Responsibility Code:*

- *Always stay in control and be able to stop or avoid persons or objects.*
- *People ahead of you have the right of way; it's your responsibility to avoid them.*
- *Do not stop where you obstruct a trail or are not visible from above.*
- *Whenever starting downhill or merging on a trail, look uphill and yield to others.*
- *Always use devices to help prevent runaway equipment.*
- *Observe all posted signs and warnings. Keep off closed trails and out of closed areas.*
- *Prior to using any lift, you must have the knowledge and ability to load, ride and unload safely.*

In addition to skier safety programs, Vail Resorts demonstrates its commitment to social responsibility in a number of other ways that protect the surrounding environment, including waste reduction, recycling, chemical management and educational programming. Keystone Resorts' environmental statement typifies Vail Resorts' commitment to the environment:

*Keystone Resort is entrusted with the stewardship of lands in the beautiful Rocky Mountains and the White River National Forest. We promote renewable energy, resource conservation, recycling, wildlife habitat preservation and environmental education. Please help us by sharing in this responsibility:*

- *Pack it in, pack it out.*
- *Carpool and use public transportation.*
- *Reduce, Reuse, and Recycle.*
- *Share the mountain. Respect all posted closures.*
- *Spread the word.*

Source: **http://mediaguide.snow.com/info/vri/safety.asp**, accessed 15 December, 2009; and **http://www. keystoneresort.com/explore-keystone/environmental-initiatives.aspx**, accessed 15 December, 2009.

## Introduction

For students seeking a career in services marketing, the first half of this chapter provides a broad overview of the nine service supersectors that comprise the service economy, including education and health services, financial activities, government, information, leisure and hospitality, professional and business services, transportation and utilities, wholesale and retail trade, and other services. The nine service supersectors illustrate the diversity of activities within the service sector, yet at the same time allow for similarities to be identified among service occupations.

In addition, this chapter's opening vignette pertaining to Vail Resorts provides an example of how one service organization attempts to conduct daily business practices in a responsible manner. In general terms, *social responsibility* is the collection of marketing philosophies, policies, procedures, and actions intended to enhance society's welfare.[1] Ethics are embedded within a firm's social responsibility. Over the past decade, integrating ethics into the business curriculum has reemerged as an important topic of discussion among marketing educators and practitioners. Originally, business ethics was generally taught as a single course; however, many business schools now believe that business ethics should be taught across the curriculum, and that ethical issues as they relate to each topic area should be discussed in greater detail.[2]

Because of the unique opportunities that exist for ethical misconduct in service organizations, students of services marketing courses in particular should be made aware of the issues surrounding ethical decision making. Although the majority of service organizations providers fulfill their duties ethically, infamous service providers such as Enron, WorldCom, and an ever growing list of entertainment and sports personalities have provided recent evidence that not all service providers may be trustworthy.

## What Is the Service Economy?

**service economy**
Includes the "soft parts" of the economy consisting of nine industry supersectors.

For students truly interested in services marketing, it would seem that the most basic question would be: *What is the service economy, and what opportunities exist within the various service sectors?* It is generally accepted that the **service economy** includes the "soft parts" of the economy consisting of nine industry supersectors: education and health services, financial activities, government, information, leisure and hospitality, professional and business services, transportation and utilities, wholesale and retail trade, and other services. Figures 2.1 and 2.2 provide an overview of the nine service supersectors in terms of composition of the service sector and past, present, and future employment trends.[3]

For students interested in pursuing a career in services marketing, the U.S. Bureau of Labor Statistics (**www.bls.gov**) provides an overview of each of the nine supersectors as well as a career guide. The career guide contains a description of the industries in each supersector along with information about working conditions, current and projected employment, occupations, and wages. A brief description of each supersector as classified in the United Sates is provided below. (Service sectors in other countries may be classified differently based on government recordkeeping practices.)

The service sector is booming! As a result, many employees are reinventing themselves and beginning new careers in one of the nine service supersectors.

**FIG-2.1** The U.S.
Service Economy
(Employment
Growth Projections
2006–2016)

| SERVICE SECTOR | RELATED ACTIVITIES: | EMPLOYMENT PROJECTIONS* |
|---|---|---|
| **Wholesale and Retail Trade** Wholesale trade Retail trade | Sales to Businesses | +7% |
| | Automobile Dealers | +11% |
| | Clothing, Accessory, and General Merchandise Stores | +7% |
| | Grocery Stores | +1% |
| **Transportation and Utilities** | Air Transportation | +7% |
| | Truck Transportation and Warehousing | +15% |
| | Utilities | −6% |
| **Information** | Broadcasting | +9% |
| | Internet Services and Data Processing | +14% |
| | Motion Picture and Video Industries | +11% |
| | Publishing | −7% |
| | Software Publishers | +32% |
| | Telecommunications | +5% |
| **Financial Activities** | Banking | +4% |
| | Insurance | +7% |
| | Securities, Commodities, and other Investments | +46% |
| **Professional & Business Services:** | Advertising and Public Relations Services | +14% |
| | Computer Systems Design and Related Services | +38% |
| | Employment Services | +19% |
| | Management, Scientific, and Technical Consulting Services | +78% |
| | Scientific Research and Development Services | +9% |
| **Education & Health Services:** | Child Day Care Services | +34% |
| | Educational Services | +11% |
| | Health Care | +22% |
| | Social Assistance | +59% |
| **Leisure & Hospitality** | Arts, Entertainment, and Recreation | +31% |
| | Food Services and Drinking Places | +11% |
| | Hotels and Other Accommodations | +14% |
| **Government** | Advocacy, Grantmaking, and Civic Organizations | +13% |
| | Federal Government | −4.6% |
| | State and Local Government | +8% |
| **Other services** | Providing services including repair, personnel care, dating, pet services, and parking | NA |

*Projections are expected growth through year 2016. When combined with non-service industries (many of which expect significant declines), overall projected growth is +11%.
Source: **www.bls.gov/oco/cg/cgs014.htm**

## Education and Health Services

The education and health services supersector consists of two subsectors: (1) the educational services subsector; and (2) the health care and social assistance subsector. The educational services sector includes schools, colleges, universities and training centers. Since education is mandatory until at least age 16 in all 50 states, one in four Americans are currently enrolled in educational institutions. Accordingly, educational services,

**FIG-2.2** Past, Present & Future: U.S. Service Supersector Employment

| SERVICE INDUSTRY | PERCENT OF EMPLOYMENT (1996) | PERCENT OF EMPLOYMENT (2006) | PERCENT OF EMPLOYMENT (PROJECTED 2016) |
|---|---|---|---|
| Education and Health Services | 10.1 | 11.8 | 13.5 |
| Financial Activities | 5.2 | 5.6 | 5.8 |
| Government | 14.5 | 14.6 | 14.1 |
| Information | 2.2 | 2.0 | 2.0 |
| Leisure & Hospitality | 8.0 | 8.7 | 9.0 |
| Professional and Business Services | 10.0 | 11.7 | 13.0 |
| Transportation and Utilities | 3.4 | 3.4 | 3.3 |
| Wholesale and Retail Trade | 14.6 | 14.1 | 13.4 |
| Other Services | 4.0 | 4.1 | 4.3 |
| **Total** | **72.0** | **76.0** | **78.4** |

Source: **www.bls.gov/oco/cg/cgs014.htm**

including both public and private institutions, are the second largest employment industry, accounting for 13.3 million jobs. Half of all educational service jobs are teaching jobs that require at least a bachelor's degree. Master's and doctoral degrees are required for many higher-education and administrative positions. Job opportunities in this field look promising, as expected retirements in the near future are forecasted.

The health care and social assistance sector is comprised of health services such as hospitals, nursing care facilities, physician's offices and home health care services. In turn, social assistance includes individual and family services, vocational rehabilitation services, community food and housing, and emergency and other relief services. Health services are currently the largest industry in the private sector, providing 14 million jobs. Moreover, seven of the top 20 fastest-growing occupations are in health care. Overall, employment projections for the education and health services supersector forecast employment will increase by 3 million jobs over the period 2006–2016, making it the highest projected growth of any industry supersector. The health care industry consists of 580,000 establishments with offices of physicians, dentists, and other health practitioners accounting for nearly 77 percent of establishments. Somewhat surprisingly, hospitals only comprise 1 percent of all establishments but employ 35 percent of all health care workers. Most health care workers occupy positions that require less than a four year degree, while other health care workers, such as surgeons and anesthesiologists, are highly educated.

With respect to social assistance, workers such as home health aides, personal and home care aides, and social and human service assistants occupy some of the fastest-growing occupations in the United States. Job opportunities in these areas are forecasted to be plentiful due to job turnover and growth of employment. Average earnings for this subsector of the service economy are low, due to a large number of part-time workers and low paying jobs.

## Financial Activities

The financial activities supersector consists of the banking and insurance subsector, as well as securities, commodities and other investments. The banking subsector is comprised of establishments primarily engaged in protecting money and valuables and providing loans, credit, and payment services. Employment in banking is expected to increase by 4 percent between 2006 and 2016. Major trends in banking include: (1) two out of every three workers in the banking industry are office and administrative support workers; (2) future opportunities for bank tellers and office and administrative support are forecasted due to the large number of jobs available and frequent turnover; and (3) management positions are typically filled by experienced, technologically savvy, professional personnel.

The insurance subsector is comprised of firms that provide clients protection against financial loss for a variety of incidents such as fire, auto accidents, theft, medical expenses, storm damage, disability and death. Employment in the insurance industry is expected to increase by 7 percent between 2006 and 2016. Major trends in insurance include: (1) office and administrative personnel are typically high school educated while occupations in sales, managerial, and professional jobs are filled by college educated personnel; (2) medical and health insurance are the two fastest-growing areas within the insurance industry; and (3) future job growth is limited by corporate downsizing, automated technologies, and the increasing use of direct mail, telephone, and Internet sales methods.

The securities, commodities, and other investments subsector manage the issuance, purchase, and sale of financial instruments. Employment in this subsector is expected to increase by a staggering 46 percent between 2006 and 2016. This dramatic increase in employment is attributed to the growing need for investments and securities to fuel the global marketplace, as well as the increase in need for financial advice. Most workers in this subsector have either an associate's or a bachelor's degree. Moreover, due to the earning potential of successful employees in this field, competition for jobs within this subsector will be intense.

## Government

The government supersector consists of three subsectors: advocacy, grantmaking, and civic organizations; the federal government; and state and local government. The advocacy, grantmaking, and civic organizations subsector is comprised of a multitude of enterprises typically referred to as the not-for-profit sector. These organizations have impacted practically everyone's life in the United States and range from museums to little league baseball

Perhaps surprisingly, 9 out of 10 U.S. Federal Government employees work at locations outside the Washington D. C. area.

## GLOBAL SERVICES *IN ACTION*

### Charity.com

Charitable giving has been part of the American way of life for quite some time. Companies provide programs to match their employees' charitable giving, organizations fundraise for charitable programs, and people purchase gifts for families in need during the holidays. What once was restricted locally has, with the Internet revolution, exploded globally. People can purchase a goat online for a family in Africa or provide a monetary donation to fund an underprivileged child's education. The multitude of websites offering consumers ways to provide overseas aid can become immense for users to navigate. Charity.com, a non-profit organization, strives to provide information about different options for charitable giving in one convenient location.

The site lists charities by category, including Addiction, Criminal Justice, Disaster Relief, Education, Firefighters & Police, Human Rights, Peace, Seniors, and many more. It also provides a search option, through which visitors can locate charities via category, keyword, and region. Descriptions of the charities are provided, including identification number, name, address, phone and fax numbers, email addresses, and URLs. Brief descriptions of the charity's general operations are also included. Only certain charities can be donated to immediately online, and these charities are listed together with easy-to-use donation links and contact information.

Charities can submit their information for review by the site, which will then be added to the database once approved. Charities of the Month are also chosen, and a catalog of the past winners is provided, dating back to the site's inception in 2003. Detailed descriptions of the charities, and options by which the public can donate, are provided.

This website crosses international boundaries, allowing people in the United States to reach out to charities worldwide. It provides a platform for these charities to gain recognition and credibility, thus increasing their operations through greater donations as a result of the publicity. Finally, it serves as an advertising service for charities and companies wishing to gain further notice in collaboration with the site. With all of these features, Charity.com is an ultimate online service provider.

Source: **www.charity.com**

to homeless shelters to symphonies. In addition, other not-for-profit agencies are focused on global concerns (see Global Services in Action). For the period 2006–2016, employment is projected to increase by 13 percent. This subsector employed approximately 1.2 million personnel in 2006, and future job growth is projected due to a large number of job openings resulting from employment growth, employee turnover, and low paying wages.

The federal government is the United States' largest single employer with 1.8 million civilian employees. Perhaps surprisingly, 9 out of 10 federal employees work at locations outside the Washington, D.C. area. The main function of the federal government is to produce public services and provide a broad array of services relating to areas such as defense, veteran affairs, homeland security, treasury, justice, agriculture, the interior, health and human services, transportation, commerce, state, labor, energy, housing and urban development, and education. Projected employment within the federal government is projected to decrease by 4.6 percent throughout the 2006–2016 timeframe. Only Homeland Security is projected to increase employment within this subsector. In turbulent economic periods, potential workers often seek the stability of a federal government paid occupation.

The third subsector, state and local governments, provide services such as utilities, courts of law, education, health care, transportation, and public safety. Local governments employ twice as many workers as the state government where professional and service occupations account for more than half of all jobs. At the local government level, firefighters and law enforcement account for the largest occupations. When compared to the private sector, one of the biggest advantages to working for state and local governments is the employer-provided benefits. Employment in this subsector is projected to increase by eight percent between 2006 and 2016.

## Information

The information supersector consists of establishments that produce and distribute information and cultural products, provide the means to distribute or transmit these products and/or process data. Major players in this supersector include the publishing industries (both traditional and Internet publishing), the motion picture and sound recording industries, the broadcasting industries, the telecommunication industries, Internet service providers and web search portals such as Match.com (see E-Services in Action), data processing industries, and information services industries. Although wide in scope, the information supersector modestly employs about 2.6 percent of all employment and accounts for 1.9 percent of all establishments. However, within the information supersector, software publishers are currently the fastest-growing industry in the economy, with a projected growth rate of 32 percent for the 2006–2016 period.

## E-SERVICES *IN ACTION*

### Game, Set, Match.com

Ah, the dating game. People across the globe from every walk of life have been playing it for centuries. Trends in this timeless game, however, are rapidly changing. Gone are the days of village matchmakers and fertility festivals, though some countries still keep these traditions alive on a novelty basis, and here are the days of cyber relationships. Studies conducted by Harris Interactive and eHarmony reveal that 19.4% of newlyweds (between the ages of 20 and 54) polled in 2008 were matched by dating websites. Of these online matchmakers, multiple web ranking services cite Match.com as the industry leader.

Match.com was launched in early 1995 as one of the pioneers in the industry. Now, the site has grown to host over 15 million users in multiple countries worldwide, and is considered the best and largest dating service in the United States. Subscribers pay to be included in the Match.com database, a membership which includes access to other users, relationship advice from industry experts, a customizable profile page, self discovery quizzes, search features, and an initial compatibility profile. This last is perhaps the most important, as the information provided on the profile is used to identify each user's most eligible matches. Match.com also provides a method of safe communication between matches, and gives users the opportunity to accept or deny other users' advances.

Now, just how much do users pay to maintain their profiles and partake of the membership perks? The going rates are $19.95 for month-to-month purchase, $39.95 for three months, and $59.95 for six months. Further, Match.com guarantees that, if a user doesn't find a match within six months, an additional six months of the service will be provided free of charge. A three-day trial period including limited features is also available for interested users to test the service.

Success stories abound on Match.com. People worldwide have found their fiancés, spouses, and partners on the website. Even company employees have found successful relationships using the dating service. Match.com and its competitors are part of one of the most interesting, complicated, and controversial services that the age of the Internet has created. Can one find love through a computer screen? According to 15 million people, it's at least worth a try.

Sources:
1. Pickel, Janet. "More and more couples finding connections online." *The Patriot-News.* 12, February 2009. <http://www.pennlive.com/midstate/index.ssf/2009/02/more_and_more_couples_finding.html>.
2. www.match.com
3. MatchMaking Service: http://www.matchmaking-service.net/match-review/

Food services and drinking places provide many young people with their first job. More than one in five employees within the food service and drinking establishments are between the ages of 16 to 19.

## Leisure and Hospitality

The leisure and hospitality sector is comprised of three subsectors: the arts, entertainment, and recreation subsector; food services and drinking places; and hotels and other accommodations. The arts, entertainment, and recreation sector includes establishments that: (1) produce, promote, or participate in live performances, events, or exhibits intended for public viewing; (2) preserve and exhibit objects and sites of historical, cultural, or educational interest; and (3) operate facilities that provide amusement, hobby, and leisure time interests. Essentially, any activity that occupies an individual's leisure time, with the exception of viewing motion pictures and video rentals, is part of this subsector. More than 40 percent of the workforce within this subsector has no formal education beyond high school. Although earnings are low and workers tend to be part-time and/ or seasonal, employment in this subsector is projected to increase by 31 percent due to rising consumer incomes, more leisure time, and growing interest in the health benefits provided by physical fitness.

Food services and drinking places range from fast food franchises to fine dining and also include cafeterias, caterers, bars, and food service contractors. Food services and drinking places provide many young people with their first jobs. More than one in five employees within the food service and drinking establishments subsector are between the ages of 16 and 19. Compared with all other industries, this is a five-fold increase. In addition, two out of five employees work part time—twice the proportion of other industries. Employment is projected to increase by 11 percent over the 2006–2016 timeframe, as many workers leave these jobs which in turn creates many job opportunities. Nearly three out of five workers are cooks, waitresses and waiters.

Hotels and other accommodations account for two-thirds of all leisure and hospitality employment and include establishments built for: customers visiting friends and family, customers on business, and customers on vacations where the hotel is the final destination. For example, resort hotels and casino hotels are now popular vacation destinations. Similar to food services, hotels employ numerous first-time workers who are often employed on a seasonal and/or part-time basis. Based on the projected growth of the industry in general, jobs are projected to increase at a rate of 14 percent.

## Professional and Business Services

The professional and business services supersector is comprised of advertising and public relations services; computer systems design and related services; employment services, management, scientific, and technical consulting services; and scientific research and development services. Consulting is the fastest growing service and one of the highest paid. The projected growth rate for the consulting industry is 78 percent for the 2006–2016 time period. Twenty-one percent of all workers are self-employed and approximately 74 percent have a bachelor's or higher degree. Computer systems and design also offers an attractive employment growth rate projection at 38 percent, and remains one of the 20 fastest-growing industries in the nation. Nearly 500,000 jobs are expected to be added between 2006 and 2016.

Due to the glamour associated with the industry, advertising and public relations services typically obtain more job seekers than there are jobs to offer. Twenty percent of jobs in this industry are located in New York and California, which employees 25 percent of the industry workers. Job growth projections are 14 percent; however, job seekers should be aware that layoffs are common due to lost accounts, budget cuts, or when agencies merge.

Employment services provide temporary workers to business which gives many workers an entry into the workforce. In addition, employment services assist employers in locating suitable employees and provide human resource services to clients. Growth within this subsector has slowed, but still offers a 2006–2016 projected growth of 19 percent.

Finally, scientific research and development services develop the technologies of tomorrow that will change the face of how we do business and how we live our lives. Given its scientific nature, 58 percent of all jobs in this subsector are characterized as professional and related occupations. This is one of the highest paying industries across all supersectors. Job opportunities are best for scientists and engineers who have obtained doctoral degrees. Projected employment growth for this subsector is a modest 9 percent.

## Transportation and Warehousing and Utilities

As its name implies, the transportation and warehousing and utilities supersector consists of three subsectors: (1) air transportation; (2) truck transportation and warehousing; and (3) utilities. Perhaps no other sector of the economy has experienced more turbulence in recent times than air transportation. Between 2001 and 2004, U.S. air travel has experienced the negative impacts of recession, terrorism, and pandemic concerns such as SARS and H1N1. Despite its bumpy road, air travel remains one of the most popular forms of transportation. Major trends for this subsector include better job prospects for those working for regional or low-cost providers; most jobs involve employment pertaining to ground operations; and at least a bachelor's degree is preferred for most pilot and flight attendant jobs. Pilots with seniority are among the highest paid workers in the country. Projected employment for 2006–2016 is 7 percent.

The truck transportation and warehousing subsector consists of a variety of activities that provide a link between manufacturers and consumers, such as generalized and specialized freight trucking, warehousing and storage. While truck drivers and driver/sales workers occupy 45 percent of all jobs in this subsector, job opportunities are best for truck drivers and diesel mechanics. Projected employment growth is 15 percent; however, employment fluctuates dramatically with the economy.

The utility subsector comprises establishments that provide the following services: electricity, natural gas, steam, water, and sewage removal. Given the diversity of these services, expertise in one field may not easily transfer to another utility. Employment projections forecast that nearly half of current utility workers will retire within the next 10 years, resulting in many more job opportunities than the 6 percent growth forecasted. Utility workers are typically well-paid compared to other industries, and potential employees with college or technical degrees will have the best opportunities.

### Wholesale and Retail Trade

The wholesale and retail trade supersector consists of the wholesale trade subsector and the retail trade subsector which include: automobile dealers; clothing, accessory, and general merchandise stores; and grocery stores. Wholesale trade includes establishments that wholesale merchandise (generally without transformation) and provide services related to the sale of merchandise to other businesses. Most wholesalers are small, employing fewer than 20 workers, 7 out of 10 of whom work in office and administrative support, sales, or transportation and material moving occupations. A high school education is sufficient for most jobs within the wholesaling subsector.

In comparison, the retail trade subsector includes establishments that retail merchandise (generally without transformation) and provide services related to the sale of merchandise to final consumers. Employment in automotive sales is projected to grow at 11 percent; however, employment opportunities fluctuate greatly based on the economy. Compared to other industries, weekly wages are high and job opportunities are particularly promising for automotive service technicians who have completed formal training.

Employment opportunities will also be available in the clothing, accessory, and general merchandise stores subsector. Eighty-four percent of job opportunities in this subsector revolve around sales and administrative support jobs. Most jobs do not require a formal education, consequently, the workforce is often comprised of employees who are working their first job. Although employment projections are a modest 7 percent, ample jobs are available as large numbers of employees typically transfer to other industries or leave the workforce altogether, resulting in numerous job openings.

Grocery stores are an interesting lot, with major chains such as Publix, Wegmans, and Whole Foods making the upper echelon of *Fortune* magazine's Best Places to Work in America list for several consecutive years.[4] The grocery store subsector offers another great opportunity for young people as 16 to 24-year-olds occupy one-third of all grocery store jobs. Many of these jobs are part-time and one-half of all jobs in this subsector are comprised of cashiers and stock clerks. Although the projected employment growth rate for 2006–2016 is projected at 1 percent, numerous jobs are available due the industry's large size and a high employee turnover rate.

### Other Services

The "other services" supersector is a "catch-all" for all the services that do not neatly fit into the preceding eight supercenter categories. Consequently, the other services supersector includes a myriad of establishments that are in engaged in a variety of activities including equipment and machinery repair, promoting or administering religious activities, drycleaning and laundry service, personal care, death care, pet care, photofinishing, temporary parking services, and dating services. The other services supersector accounts for approximately 3.3 percent of all employment and 12.6 percent of all establishments. Employment projections for the 2002–2012 period indicate a 15.7 percent increase.[5]

The nine service supersectors illustrate the diversity of activities within the service economy. However, one of the major themes of this text is to convey the message that service sectors should not be studied as separate entities (such as banking, transportation, business services, health care, and food service firms). Seemingly too often, companies diminish their own chances to develop truly innovative ideas by only examining the practices of competitors within their own industries. Many service industries share common service delivery challenges and therefore would benefit from sharing their knowledge with each other. Unfortunately, many service firms look only to firms within their own industry for guidance. For example, banks look to other banks, insurance companies look to other insurance companies, and so on. This myopic approach slows the progress of truly unique service innovations within each of the respective industries.

One needs only to consider the advances that hospitals could make if they borrowed concepts from restaurants and hotels instead of relying on other hospitals for innovative service ideas. Similarly, many service jobs, such as a bank teller and an airline gate agent, who on the surface seem quite different, actually perform similar tasks and experience many of the same customer-related challenges throughout a typical day. Consequently, lessons that have been learned in the front-lines of banking operations may be of value to those who work the front-lines of the airline industry.

## Service Sector Concerns: Materialismo Snobbery

**materialismo snobbery** Belief that without manufacturing there will be less for people to service and so more people available to do less work.

Although the service economy is growing in leaps and bounds, not everyone is rejoicing.[6] **Materialismo snobbery** reflects the attitude that only manufacturing can create real wealth, and that all other sectors of the economy are parasitic and/or inconsequential. Materialismic individuals believe that without manufacturing, there will be little for people to service. As a result, more people will be available to do less work, driving wages down and subsequently decreasing the standard of living in the United States. Ultimately, materialismo snobbery supports the belief that the continued shift to a service economy will jeopardize the American way of life.

Similar concerns were voiced in the United States more than 160 years ago, when the economy was shifting from agriculture to manufacturing. In 1850, 50 years after industrialization, 65 percent of the population was connected to farming. During this period, many experts voiced great concern over workers leaving the farms to work in the factories. The concerns centered on the same type of logic: If the vast majority of the population left the farms, what would the people eat? Today, less than 1 percent of the U.S. labor force is involved in farming operations.[7] This small but mighty workforce provides such a surplus of food that the federal government provides price supports and subsidies to keep the farms in business. Apparently, the concerns regarding the shift to manufacturing were unwarranted. In fact, the shift lead to economic growth. Similarly, with advances in technology and new management practices, the need no longer exists to have as many people in manufacturing as we had in the mid 1900s. Manufacturing is not superior to services. The two are interdependent. In fact, half of all manufacturing workers perform service-type jobs.[8]

**dichotomization of wealth** The rich get richer and poor get poorer.

Another criticism of the service economy pertains to the dichotomization of wealth among service workers. In the United States, 80 percent of the population has experienced a decrease in real income over the past 20 years. In contrast, the wealthiest 5 percent has seen an increase of 50 percent, and the top 1 percent has seen a doubling in income.[9] Although experts disagree, some believe that the poor wages paid by some service industries, along with the shift of the economy away from manufacturing, will lead to a further **dichotomization of wealth**—the rich will get richer and the poor will get poorer. Without a doubt, the service sector has a lot of low-paying jobs.[10] For individuals under the age of 30, service jobs pay 25 percent less than manufacturing jobs. Some experts believe that as the manufacturing sector continues to decline, the supply of labor available for service jobs will increase, driving service wages even lower.

However, not everyone in services is poorly paid. For example, in the finance and wholesale trade subsectors, salaries are much closer to manufacturing wages. Moreover, an increasing number of service personnel are highly skilled and employed in knowledge-based industries. In fact, more than half the U.S. labor force is currently employed in either the production, storage, retrieval, or dissemination of knowledge. Furthermore, the fastest-growing service sector employment opportunities are in finance, insurance, property, and business services—occupations that require educated personnel.[11] Overall, service wages seem to be catching up with wages obtained via manufacturing employment, and clearly service occupations exist that earn much more money than their manufacturing counterparts.[12]

The final concern over wages associated with service employment is a real concern, and illustrates the continuation of traditional industrial management practices. "Most service enterprises consist of a well-paid brain trust and poorly paid support staff—$500-an-hour lawyers and $10-an-hour secretaries."[13] This is an important point to consider. Throughout the world, some of the most important people in a service organization, in terms of customer first impressions and key sources of information for customers, are the least respected and least paid individuals in their respective organizations—secretaries, receptionists, host/hostesses, classroom teachers, nurses, etc. This makes absolutely no sense! Why should a poorly paid and disrespected employee tout the excellence of a company that treats its own employees so shabbily? Successful service firms recognize the importance of front-line personnel and treat them accordingly.

## Ethical Considerations for Services Marketers

The second half of this chapter is dedicated to the important topic of services marketing ethics. Unique circumstances occur in the service sector creating an ethical environment worth examination and discussion. The following discussion presents a variety of ethics-related topics as they pertain specifically to the service sector. More specifically, these topics include: (1) consumer vulnerability in services marketing; (2) issues that create ethical conflict; (3) factors influencing ethical decision making; (4) the effects of ethical misconduct; and (5) strategies for controlling ethical behavior.

Note that in this chapter, we do not intend to "preach" what we think is right or wrong. Such a decision is left to the discretion of the individual student. Unfortunately, as you will live to learn, the appropriateness and/or public acceptance of your decisions and/or behavior are usually decided on the evening news or even popular talk shows such as "Oprah," "Ellen," or "Nancy Grace." Our objective primarily is to provide you with food for thought, to encourage **ethical vigilance**—paying close attention to whether one's actions (individual or organizational) are right or wrong—and to facilitate class discussions about an important subject that is often overlooked.

## What Are Ethics?

In general, **ethics** are commonly defined as: (1) "a branch of philosophy dealing with what is good and bad and with moral duty and obligation;" and (2) "the principles of moral conduct governing an individual or group."[14] **Business ethics** comprises moral principles and standards that guide behavior in the world of business.[15] For example, some organizations actively pursue a "triple bottom line" that takes into account not only the firm's economic prosperity, but also includes goals and objective pertaining to environmental issues and advancements, and social justice and equality movements as the firm conducts its daily operations (see Sustainability and Services in Action).

The distinction between an ordinary decision and an ethical one is that values and judgments play a critical role in ethical decisions. In contrast, ordinary decisions are generally decided utilizing a set of preordained acceptable rules.

In general, the public's view about business ethics is not overwhelmingly positive.[16] According to a Business Week/Harris poll, 46 percent of respondents believed that the ethical standards of businesspeople were only average. In addition, 90 percent of respondents believed that white-collar crime was somewhat or very common. Another survey reported that the majority of Americans believe that many businesspeople regularly

**ethical vigilance** Paying close attention to whether one's actions are "right" or "wrong," and if ethically "wrong," asking why you are behaving in that manner.

**ethics** A branch of philosophy dealing with what is good and bad and with moral duty and obligations; the principles of moral conduct governing an individual or group.

**business ethics** The principles of moral conduct that guide behavior in the business world.

## SUSTAINABILITY AND SERVICES *IN ACTION*

### The Triple Bottom Line

As sustainability takes hold of the business world, the service industry is adopting a concept known as the triple bottom line. This "refers to an organization's commitment to economic, environmental, and social progress." Coined in 1994 by John Elkington, this concept has become the imperative business practice of the 21st century. In order to adhere to the principle, companies must consider current economic prosperity, environmental issues and advancements, and social justice and equality movements.

Creating policies to help support and improve these ideals can reap huge benefits for service companies. Ethical practices, transparency, and an environmental focus are becoming increasingly important in creating a firm's image. This presentation is vital to increase the trust and investment of stakeholders, retention of employees, and loyalty of customers. Bob Willard, a former IBM Canada executive, cites seven benefits for companies pursuing a sustainability philosophy:

1. Enhanced recruitment
2. Higher retention of top talent
3. Increased employee productivity
4. Reduced expenses in operations for manufacturing goods
   a. Reducing the materials, energy, and resources used for each product
   b. Redesign of operations
   c. Reusing and recycling
5. Reduced expenses in commercial sites
   a. Improved waste handling
   b. Water conservation
   c. Reduced office space and less business travel
   d. Lower landscaping costse.
   e. Energy efficiencies
6. Increased revenue and market share
7. Reduced risk and easier financing
   a. Easier to attract investors
   b. Less risk from governmental and legislative changes

Source: Tevault, Ashley. "Serving it up Green: Examination of Sustainability in the Service Sector." Colorado State University Honors Program Senior Thesis. 12 November 2009.

engage in ethical misconduct. In fact, 76 percent of respondents in yet another study believe that the decline in moral standards in the United States is a direct result of the lack of business ethics practiced daily. Perhaps even more damaging are the results of a survey of business practitioners themselves: 66 percent of executives surveyed believe that businesspeople will occasionally act unethically during business dealings, while another 15 percent believe that ethical misconduct occurs often in the business sector.

## The Opportunity for Ethical Misconduct in Services Marketing

Opportunities for ethical misconduct within the service sector can be attributed predominantly to the intangibility, heterogeneity, and inseparability dimensions inherent in the provision of services.[17] As will be discussed in much greater detail in Chapter 3,

"WE NAMED HIM 'ENRON' BECAUSE HE SHREDS EVERYTHING."

Most service firms conduct business in an ethical manner; however, there have been a few corporations who have not played by the rules…and eventually paid a very heavy price.

*intangibility* complicates the consumer's ability to evaluate objectively the quality of service provided; *heterogeneity* reflects the difficulty in standardization and quality control; and *inseparability* reflects the human element involved in the service delivery process. All three dimensions contribute to consumer vulnerability to and reliance upon the service provider's ethical conduct during the service encounter.

In more specific terms, consumer vulnerability to ethical misconduct within the service sector can be attributed to several sources including:[18]

- *Services are characterized by few search attributes.*
- *Services are often specialized and/or technical.*
- *Some services have a significant time lapse between performance and evaluation.*
- *Many services are sold without guarantees and warranties.*
- *Services are often provided by boundary-spanning personnel.*
- *Variability in service performance is somewhat accepted.*
- *Reward systems are often outcome-based as opposed to behavior-based.*
- *Customers are active participants in the production process.*

### Few Search Attributes

As will be discussed in Chapter 4 (Consumer Decision Making in Services Marketing), *search attributes* can be determined prior to purchase and include such attributes as touch, smell, visual cues, and taste. However, due to the intangibility of services, consumers lack the opportunity to physically examine a service before purchasing it. Consequently, consumers have little prepurchase information available to help them make an informed, intelligent decision. Hence, consumers of services often must base their purchase decisions on information provided by the service provider.

### Technical and Specialized Services

Many services are not easily understood and/or evaluated; consequently, the opportunity exists easily to mislead consumers. Evaluating the performance of professional service providers is particularly intriguing. As a consumer, how do you know whether your doctor, lawyer, broker, priest, or minister is competent at his or her job? Often, our evaluations of these people are based on their appearance, the furniture in their offices, and whether they have pleasant social skills. In other words, in the absence of information that they can understand, customers often resort to evaluating information that surrounds the service as opposed to the core service itself when forming evaluations.

### Time Lapse between Performance and Evaluation

The final evaluation of some services such as insurance and financial planning is often conducted only at a time in the distant future. For example, the success or failure of retirement planning may not be realized until 30 years after the original service transaction is conducted. Hence, service providers may not be held accountable for their actions in the short run. This could lead to a scenario where unethical service providers may maximize their short-term gains at the expense of consumers' long-term benefits.

### Services Sold without Guarantees and Warranties

Another opportunity for ethical misconduct in the service sector results from few meaningful guarantees and warranties. Consequently, when the consumer experiences difficulties with an unscrupulous provider, there are few or no means of seeking quick retribution. For example, what are your options if you get a bad haircut—glue, a new hat?

### Services Performed by Boundary-Spanning Personnel

**boundary-spanning personnel** Personnel who provide their services outside the firm's physical facilities.

Many service providers deliver their services outside their firm's physical facilities. In doing so, these types of service providers expand the boundary of a firm beyond the firm's main office. Service providers such as painters, lawn-care specialists, paramedics, and carpet cleaners are typical examples. Because of the physical distance from the main office inherent in the role of **boundary-spanning personnel**, these particular service providers often are not under direct supervision and may act in a manner inconsistent with

Siri Stafford/Stone/Getty Images

Service providers who are not under direct supervision and perform services in or at the homes of customers have more opportunity to engage in ethical misconduct.

organizational objectives. Hence, the opportunity to engage in ethical misconduct without repercussions from upper management increases.

### Accepted Variability in Performance

Another opportunity for ethical misconduct within the service sector is provided via the *heterogeneity* inherent in the provision of services. Due to heterogeneity, standardization and quality control are difficult to maintain throughout each individual service delivery transaction. Many services are customized, requiring different skills of the service provider, and often consumers are exposed to different providers within the same firm. The bottom line is that variability in performance is unavoidable.

### Outcome-Based Reward Systems

The reward system of an organization often dictates the behavior of its employees, and it does not take employees long to figure out the shortest route to the most money. Hence, the reward system of an organization may encourage, albeit unintentionally, the unethical conduct of its employees. For example, straight commissions and quotas reinforce activities that are directly linked to making the sale while discouraging nonselling activities such as maintaining the store, stocking shelves, and spending an inordinate amount of time fielding customer questions.

### Consumer Participation in Production

On the surface, one would think that the more the consumer is involved in the service encounter, the less the opportunity exists for the service provider to engage in ethical misconduct. However, service exchanges may be jeopardized by coercive influence strategies used by the service provider. The consumer's involvement in the service delivery process enables a service provider to try to influence the consumer through fear or guilt to agree to a purchase the consumer would otherwise decline. An auto mechanic who makes a statement such as, "I wouldn't want my family riding around in a car that has brakes like these," is a typical example of the type of influence a service provider can have on a customer. Moreover, due to the consumer's input into the production process, the consumer often accepts much of the responsibility for less-than-satisfactory service transactions. Consumers often feel that they didn't explain themselves clearly enough and will accept much of the blame to avoid a confrontation with the service provider. In fact, conflict avoidance is one of the major reasons customers do not complain to service providers. This situation further removes service providers from taking responsibility for their own actions and provides yet another opportunity to engage in unethical behavior.

## Issues That Create Ethical Conflict

The types of ethical issues service providers encounter are not always unique to the service sector. This can be accounted for by the mix of products and customer service involved in a multitude of different businesses. Figure 2.3 contains a sample of the many types of ethical issues that are encountered in the business world. Through surveying their personnel, individual companies can determine the specific ethical issues that pertain to their firm. The most typical issues that managers and/or employees will face while conducting business include:[19]

- *Conflict of interest*
- *Organizational relationships*
- *Honesty*

- *Fairness*
- *Communication*

## Conflict of Interest

**conflict of interest** The situation in which a service provider feels torn between the organization, the customer, and/or the service provider's own personal interest.

Service providers are often in close proximity to customers during the provision of services. Consequently, the service provider may experience **conflicts of interest** as the service provider/customer relationship develops and friendships are formed. In such a situation, the service provider may feel torn between the organization, the customer, and/or the service provider's own personal interest. For example, insurance personnel may coach friends and family members on how to complete the necessary forms in order to obtain a less expensive rate. In this situation, the customer benefits (via lower rates), the employee benefits (via "the sale"), but the organization suffers (by failing to obtain the proper premium amount).

## Organizational Relationships

**organizational relationships** Working relationships formed between service providers and various role partners such as customers, suppliers, peers, subordinates, supervisors, and others.

Service providers form working **organizational relationships** with a variety of role partners, including customers, suppliers, peers, subordinates, supervisors, and others. The information gained via these relationships is often highly sensitive. For example, most people would not want their priest to reveal the contents of their confession or their doctor telling others of their medical problems. Because of the sensitivity of information, ethical service providers are required to maintain confidentiality in relationships to meet their professional obligations and responsibilities. In contrast, unethical service providers may use the information acquired from organizational relationships for their own personal gain. Ivan Boesky, one of Wall Street's top arbitragers, was charged with insider

**FIG-2.3** Types of Ethical Issues Encountered by Businesses

| TYPES OF ETHICAL ISSUES ENCOUNTERED BY BUSINESS | |
|---|---|
| Honesty | Accuracy of books, records |
| Conflict of interest | Privacy of employee records |
| Marketing, advertising issues | Political activities and contributions |
| Environmental issues | Misuses of company assets |
| Discrimination by age, race, or sex | Corporate governance |
| Product liability and safety | Issues |
| Codes of ethics and self-governance | Ethical theory |
| Relations with customers | Ethics in negotiation |
| Bribery | Relations with local communities |
| Rights of and responsibilities to shareholders | Plant closing and layoffs |
| Whistleblowing | Employee discipline |
| Kickbacks | Use of others' proprietary information |
| Insider trading | Relations with U.S. government representatives |
| Antitrust issues | Relations with competitors |
| Issues facing multinationals | Employee benefits |
| Relations with foreign governments | Mergers and acquisitions |
| Ethical foundations of capitalism | Drug and alcohol abuse |
| Workplace health and safety | Drug and alcohol testing |
| Managing an ethical environment | Intelligence gathering |
| Relations with suppliers and subcontractors | Leveraged buyouts |
| Use of company proprietary information | |

trading activities by the Securities and Exchange Commission (SEC). Boesky allegedly made millions from obtaining information concerning company takeovers before the public announcements of the takeovers were made. Once Boesky learned of a takeover, he would purchase large blocks of stock that he later sold at huge profits. In exchange for the names of other inside traders, Boesky plead guilty to one charge of criminal activity and agreed to pay $100 million in penalties. He also served three years in jail. The old adage that "knowledge is power" is often embraced by those who engage in ethical misconduct.

### Honesty

Honesty is a partner of truthfulness, integrity, and trustworthiness. Examples of dishonesty in customer service include promising to do something for a customer but having no intention of delivering on the promise or stating that a service has been performed when, in fact, it has not. Honesty issues may also cover selected business strategies utilized by service firms to manage consumer expectations. For example, a typical practice at some restaurants today is to purposely estimate waiting times in excess of the actual expected waiting times. If customers are seated before expected, they feel they are getting better service. Do you think this practice is ethical? Other honesty issues involve: (1) respecting the private property of clients while services are provided in the clients' homes and places of business; (2) performing services as promised at the designated time; (3) providing accurate billing for services delivered; and (4) providing clients with accurate information even if it means the loss of a sale.

### Fairness

Fairness is an outcome of just treatment, equity, and impartiality. Clients should be treated equitably, and deals based on favoritism should be avoided. In addition, service discrimination issues should also be addressed. Do men receive better service compared with women, or vice versa? Are well-dressed persons served better than blue jean-clad clients? Does a client's race or general appearance affect the level of service provided?

### Communication

Ethical issues also arise through the communication that the service organization releases to the public. Communication may range from mass advertising to warranty information to interpersonal communication between the service provider and the customer. Ethical misconduct stemming from communication may include making false claims about the superiority of the company's services, making false claims about competitive offerings, and/or making promises the company knowingly understands it cannot keep.

## The Effects of Ethical Misconduct

Service organizations should stress the importance of ethical conduct by employees for several reasons. First, in terms of social responsibility, service organizations should be required to act in a manner that is in the best interest of society. Secondly, employees forced to deal with ethical issues on a continuing basis frequently suffer from job-related tension, frustration, anxiety, ineffective performance (i.e., reduced sales and reduced profits), turnover intentions, and lower job satisfaction.[20] One only needs to witness Toyota's dilemma regarding the recall of millions of automobiles to see first-hand the impact of covering up mistakes.

In addition to the personal effects of ethical misconduct, the organization as a whole suffers. Ethical improprieties have also been linked to customer dissatisfaction (loss of sales), unfavorable word-of-mouth publicity for the organization, and a negative public image for the entire industry.[21]

# Controlling Ethical Decision Making

The adverse effects of unethical decision making may lead service firms to try to control the ethical behavior of their employees in a number of ways. Suggestions for controlling and managing ethical behavior include:[22]

- *Employee socialization*
- *Standards of conduct*
- *Corrective control*
- *Leadership training*
- *Service/product knowledge*
- *Monitoring of employee performance*
- *Building long-term customer relationships*

## Employee Socialization

**employee socialization** The process through which an individual adapts and comes to appreciate the values, norms, and required behavior patterns of an organization.

**Employee socialization** refers to the process through which an individual adapts and comes to appreciate the values, norms, and required behavior patterns of an organization. Ethical issues such as cheating, payment of bribes, and lying may be defined through socialization of organizational values and norms. These values and norms may be transmitted via new employee orientation sessions and subsequent formal meetings to address new issues and reinforce past lessons.

Service organizations can also convey organizational values and norms through communications such as company newsletters and advertising. For example, Delta Airlines has been commended for its advertising that depicts very helpful, friendly, and happy employees who exert discretionary effort to assist the airline's customers. The ads not only appeal to customers, but also help define for Delta employees their role within the company and the types of behavior the company expects and rewards.

## Standards of Conduct

**code of ethics** Formal standards of conduct that assist in defining proper organizational behavior.

As part of the socialization process, formal standards of conduct can be presented to service employees through a **code of ethics**. Research indicates that employees desire codes of ethics to help them define proper behavior, thereby reducing role conflict and role ambiguity.[23] Although developing a code of ethics does not guarantee subsequent employee ethical behavior, it is an important early step in the process of controlling ethical decision making.

## Corrective Control

**corrective control** The use of rewards and punishments to enforce a firm's code of ethics.

For the service firm's code of ethics to be effective, the conditions set forth in it must be enforced. Enforcement of the code of ethics may be accomplished through **corrective control**, the use of rewards and punishments. Service providers who are rewarded (or not punished) for unethical behavior will continue practicing it. Interestingly, research indicates that employees of firms that have codes of ethics are more prone to believe that violators of ethical codes should be punished.

## Leadership Training

Due to the apparent effects of *differential association* upon ethical decision making, service organizations need to stress to their leaders the importance of those leaders' own behavior and its influence upon subordinates. Leaders must be examples of the standards of ethical conduct. They need to understand that employees faced with ethical decision making often emulate the behavior of their supervisors. This is particularly true of young employees, who tend to comply with their supervisors to demonstrate loyalty.

### Service/Product Knowledge

Service firms need to constantly train all employees concerning the details of what the service product can and cannot provide. Due to the complex nature of many service offerings and an ever-changing business environment, service firms cannot afford to assume that employees completely understand the ramifications of new service/product developments. A few service industries understand the social responsibility of keeping employees informed. For example, the insurance industry now requires continuing education of its sales agents.[24]

### Monitoring of Employee Performance

Another possible method of controlling ethical decision making is the measurement of employee ethical performance. This approach involves comparing behaviors utilized in obtaining performance levels against organizational ethical standards. Service firms may monitor employee performance by either observing employees in action or by utilizing employee questionnaires regarding ethical behavior. Results obtained from monitoring should be discussed with the employees to alleviate any ambiguities in the employees' minds about the appropriate actions to take when questionable situations arise.

### Stress Long-Term Customer Relationships

Service providers must build trusting relationships between themselves and their customers to promote a long-term, mutually beneficial relationship.[25] Ethical marketing practices provide the basis from which such trust-based relationships are formed. Many unethical decisions that are made emphasize the short-run benefits that the decision provides. For example, a service provider may mislead a customer in order to make a quick sale. Service firms who properly socialize their employees should stress the importance of building long-term relationships. Service firms whose employees are oriented toward a long-term customer relationship should be able to minimize the frequency of unethical decision making.

## Summary

It is generally accepted that the service economy includes the "soft parts" of the economy consisting of nine industry supersectors: education and health services, financial activities, government, information, leisure and hospitality, professional and business services, transportation and utilities, wholesale and retail trade, and other services. The *service sector* is one of the three main categories of a developed economy—the other two being *industrial* and *agricultural*. Traditionally, economies throughout the world tend to transition themselves from an *agricultural economy* to an *industrial economy* (e.g, manufacturing, mining, etc.) to a *service economy*.

The nine service supersectors illustrate the diversity of activities within the service economy. Many service industries share common service delivery challenges and therefore would benefit from sharing their knowledge with each other. Despite the continued growth and dominance of the service sector, some are quick to criticize the service economy. *Materialistic* individuals believe that without manufacturing, there will be little for people to service.

This chapter also presented an overview of ethics as they apply to the service sector.

Service consumers are particularly vulnerable to ethical misconduct for a variety of reasons. For example, services possess few search attributes and therefore are difficult to evaluate before the purchase decision has been made; services are often technical and/or specialized, making evaluation by the common consumer even more difficult; many services are sold without warranties and/or guarantees and are often provided by unsupervised boundary-spanning personnel. In addition, reward systems that compensate service personnel are often based on results as opposed to the behaviors utilized to achieve those results. Other factors contributing to consumer vulnerability include the time lapse that occurs for some services between service performance and customer evaluation (e.g., financial planning, life insurance, etc.), the inherent variation in service performance, and the consumer's willingness to accept the blame for failing to effectively communicate his or her wishes to the service provider.

The most common ethical issues involve conflict of interest, confidentiality in organizational relationships, honesty, fairness, and the integrity of the firm's communications efforts. Employees forced to deal with ethical issues on a continuous basis frequently suffer from job-related tension, frustration, anxiety, ineffective performance, turnover intention, and low job satisfaction. In addition to the personal effects of ethical misconduct, the organization as a whole is likely to suffer as well. Ethical improprieties have been linked to customer dissatisfaction, unfavorable word-of-mouth publicity, and negative public images for an entire industry.

Organizations have utilized a number of strategies that attempt to control the ethical behavior of employees, including employee socialization, the development and enforcement of codes of ethics, leadership training, service/product knowledge training, monitoring employee performance, and education of employees regarding the benefits of long-term customer relationships.

## Key Terms

service economy, p. 32
materialismo snobbery, p. 41
dichotomization of wealth, p. 41
ethical vigilance, p. 42
ethics, p. 42

business ethics, p. 42
boundary-spanning
    personnel, p. 45
conflict of interest, p. 47
organizational relationships, p. 47

employee socialization, p. 49
code of ethics, p. 49
corrective control, p. 49

## Review Questions

1. Rank and discuss the projected growth rates of the nine service supersectors. What do you believe is driving the growth of the three most highly ranked supersectors?

2. Explain how a service supersector can have minimal projected growth yet still have many job opportunities available.

3. Go to **http://www.bls.gov/iag/leisurehosp.htm** and click on the Hotel and Other Accommodations Career Guide link found at the bottom of the scrolled page. Discuss working conditions, current and projected employment, occupations, and earnings as they related to the hotel industry.

4. Compare changing from an agricultural economy to an industrial economy with moving from an industrial economy to a service economy.

5. Discuss the difference between ethics and social responsibility.

6. How does the public feel about the ethical behaviors of businesspeople?

7. What type of company has more difficulties controlling the ethical behavior of its employees—a centralized firm or a decentralized firm? Please explain.

8. Explain how reward systems impact ethical behavior.

9. Discuss the relationship between a "Code of Ethics" and "corrective control."

10. Describe the relevance of a "search attribute" as it applies to service marketing ethics.

# Notes

1. K. Douglas Hoffman et al., *Marketing Principles & Best Practices*, 3rd ed. (Mason, OH: Thomson* Southwestern, 2006), p. 68.

2. Mary L. Nicastro, "Infuse Business Ethics into Marketing Curriculum," *Marketing Educator*, 11, 1, (1992), p. 1.

3. Materials for this section were obtained from **www.bls.gov** accessed 17 December, 2009.

4. **http://money.cnn.com/magazines/fortune/best-companies/2009/full_list/**, accessed 14 December, 2009.

5. 2006–2016 figures are not available for "other services."

6. Michael E. Raynor, "After Materialismo…," *Across the Board*, (July–August 1992), pp. 38–41.

7. **https://www.cia.gov/library/publications/the-worldfactbook/geos/us.html**, accessed 17, December 2009.

8. "Wealth in Services," *The Economist*, (February 20, 1993), p. 16.

9. Raynor, "After Materialismo…," p. 41.

10. "The Manufacturing Myth," *The Economist*, (March 19, 1994), p. 92.

11. "The Final Frontier," *The Economist*, (February 20, 1993), p. 63.

12. Robert W. Van Giezen, "Occupational Pay in Private Goods and Service Producing Industries." *Compensation and Working Conditions Online*, 1, 1, (June 1996).

13. Raynor, "After Materialismo…," p. 41.

14. *Webster's New Ideal Dictionary* (Springfield, MA: G. & C. Merriam Co., 1973), p. 171.

15. O. C. Ferrell and John Fraedrich, *Business Ethics* (Boston, MA: Houghton Mifflin, 1991), p. 5.

16. Gene R. Laczniak and Patrick E. Murphy, *Ethical Marketing Decisions* (Needham Heights, MA: Allyn and Bacon, 1993), p. 3.

17. Valerie A. Zeithaml, A. Parasuraman, and Leonard L. Berry, "Problems and Strategies in Services Marketing," *Journal of Marketing*, 49, 2, (1985), pp. 33–46.

18. K. Douglas Hoffman and Judy A. Siguaw, "Incorporating Ethics into the Services Marketing Course: The Case of the Sears Auto Centers," *Marketing Education Review* 3, 3 (1993), pp. 26–32.

19. Ferrell and Fraedrich, *Business Ethics*, pp. 22–29.

20. Orville C. Walker, Gilbert A. Churchill, and Neil M. Ford, "Where Do We Go from Here: Selected Conceptual and Empirical Issues Concerning the Motivation and Performance of the Industrial Sales Force," *Critical Issues in Sales Management: State-of-the-Art and Future Research Needs*, G. Albaum and G. A. Churchill, eds. (Eugene, OR: College of Business Administration, University of Oregon, 1979).

21. Ronald W. Vinson, "Industry Image Stuck in Downcycle," *National Underwriter Property & Casualty-Risk & Benefits Management*, (January 7, 1991), pp. 25–29.

22. Ferrell and Fraedrich, *Business Ethics*, pp. 137–150.

23. Sandra Pelfrey and Eileen Peacock, "Ethical Codes of Conduct are Improving," *Business Horizons* (Spring 1991), pp. 14–17.

24. C. King, "Prof. Challenges Industry to Face Ethical Issues," *National Underwriter Life & Health-Financial Services*, (August 16, 1990), pp. 15–16.

25. Lawrence A. Crosby, Kenneth R. Evans, and Deborah Cowles, "Relationship Quality in Services Selling: An Interpersonal Influence Perspective," *Journal of Marketing*, (July 1990), pp. 68–81.

# The Conundrum: Sears Auto Centers

The field of business ethics is particularly intriguing. On one hand, businesses must make a profit in order to survive. The survival of the firm provides employees' salaries with which employees feed their families and educate their children, thereby leading to the betterment of society. In addition, company profits and employee salaries are taxed, the funds from which furnish the support for various governmental programs. On the other hand, business profits should not be obtained by any means necessary. A tradeoff must exist between the firm's desire for profits and what is good for individuals and society.

Sears Auto Centers found themselves in a controversial position as they pondered such tradeoffs. It is generally agreed that the marketing concept states that the goal of most for-profit organizations is to recognize and satisfy customer needs while making a profit. Such was the goal of Edward Brennan, chairman of Sears, Roebuck and Company. Under his leadership, market research studies were conducted on customer automotive repair needs. Subsequently, Sears established a preventive maintenance program that instructed the auto repair centers to recommend repair/replacement of parts based on the mileage indicated on the odometer. Concurrently, sales quotas were established for Sears' 850 auto repair centers. Meeting or exceeding these quotas earned bonus money for the service personnel and provided management with an objective means of evaluating employee performance.

The new sales incentive program required the sale of a certain number of repairs or services, including alignments, springs, and brake jobs, every eight hours. Service employees were also able to qualify for bonus money by selling a specified number of shock absorbers or struts for every hour worked. The objective of this program was to meet customer needs while increasing the profits of the auto service centers.

After the program was put into place, the automotive unit became the fastest-growing and most profitable unit in recent Sears history. However, a growing number of consumer complaints were lodged against Sears. These complaints sparked investigations by the states of California, New Jersey, and Florida into practices at Sears auto service centers. The state of California alleged that Sears consistently overcharged its customers an average of $223 for unnecessary repairs or work that was never done. Sears contends that its auto centers were merely servicing vehicles based on the manufacturer's suggested maintenance schedule. Moreover, Sears maintains that its failure to make these suggestions for improvements would neglect the safety of the consumer. Consequently, the

Source: Lawrence M. Fisher, "Sears Auto Centers Halt Commissions After Flap," *The New York Times*, 1992, pp. D1, D2; Gregory A. Patterson, "Sears' Brennan Accepts Blame for Auto Flap,' *The Wall Street Journal*, 1992, p. B1; "Systematic Looting," *Time*, June 22, 1992, pp. 27, 30; and Tung Yin, "Sears Is Accused of Billing Fraud at Auto Centers," *The Wall Street Journal*, June 12, 1992, pp. B1, B5.

dilemma for Sears employees concerning what is good for customers and what is good for the company becomes muddled.

## Discussion Questions

1. What properties inherent in auto repair services contribute to consumer vulnerability?
2. What types of ethical issues are involved with this case?
3. Describe the consequences of Sears Auto Center's behavior?
4. What strategies would you suggest to help control future problems?

CHAPTER **3**

# Unique Discrepancies between Goods and Services

## CHAPTER OBJECTIVES

After reading this chapter, you should be able to:

- **Understand the characteristics of intangibility, inseparability, heterogeneity, and perishability.**

- **Discuss the marketing challenges associated with intangibility and their possible solutions.**

- **Describe the marketing challenges created by inseparability and their possible solutions.**

- **Explain the marketing challenges associated with heterogeneity and their possible solutions.**

- **Identify the marketing challenges created by perishability and their possible solutions.**

- **Consider the impact of intangibility, inseparability, heterogeneity, and perishability on marketing's relationship to other functions within the service organization.**

- **Appreciate the organization of the remainder of this text**

This chapter discusses the basic differences between goods and services, the marketing problems that arise due to these differences, and possible solutions to the problems created by these differences.

### THE BED WARS AND PILLOW SKIRMISHES

The intangibility of the core service benefit often makes it difficult for customers to objectively evaluate

Ghislain & Marie David de Lossy/Digital Vision/Jupiter Images

the quality of service and/or compare service alternatives. As a result, customers rely on the physical evidence that surrounds the core benefit to assist in forming service evaluations. Hence, the effective management of physical evidence by service firms is key to establishing service differentiation.

Service differentiation through the purposeful use of physical evidence has been long exemplified by the lodging industry through the effective management of facility exterior, facility interior, and other tangibles associated with the hotel experience. Interestingly, the latest battleground in physical differentiation has become the bed itself. With the introduction of the "Heavenly Bed" in 1999, Westin Hotels ushered in a new movement in the hotel industry to "move away from the institutional feel of some rooms and give guests more luxurious accommodations." Westin was on a quest to build the best bed in the industry. The end result was a custom-made Simmons mattress decked out with down blankets, sheets with high thread counts, a comforter, a duvet and five pillows—"enough to make other hotel beds feel like rock slabs." At first, rivals scoffed at Westin's new bedding strategy. First, the $30 million price tag seemed a bit extravagant and second the linens were white—"what was Westin thinking?" However, opinions changed quickly as Westin and the Heavenly Bed racked up multiple business rewards including "improved guest satisfaction, higher room rates, better revenue-per-available-room and an avalanche of publicity." In addition, overall cleanliness scores increased even though Westin even admits all it did extra was "add the bed." Since the Heavenly Bed's introduction, Westin has sold over 7,000 beds to its enamored customers. Westin's next move involved the introduction of Heavenly Cribs which placed 2,000 new cribs in 300 plus hotels at an investment (note, Westin does not refer to costs, but investments) of $1 million.

Given Westin's success, other hotels are taking initiative and responding to the "Heavenly Bed" with their own luxury packages. Hotels including Radisson and Hampton Inn are investing thousands of dollars in new beds and bedding for their guests. Marriott International has perhaps undertaken the most ambitious investment in the "Battle of the Beds" with the replacement of 628,000 beds in 2005. Beds will be changed in eight different Marriott lodging brands including Fairfield Inn, Courtyard by Marriott, Renaissance Hotels, Marriott Hotels and JW Hotels and Resorts. The project will cost an estimated $190 million and will use 30 million yards of fabric. JW Marriott Jr., Marriott CEO, notes, "This initiative draws on the finest designs and service traditions at our best hotels worldwide to position each of our brands as the most luxurious in their segment."

Marriott's intent is not to move out of their current market position dominated by their eight lodging brands; however, Marriott wishes to be known as "best in class" in each of the various segments. This move is consistent with the message that is routinely delivered to Marriott's associates, "Marriott brands are about selling a rewarding experience, not just selling a hotel room. Our guests indicate that the room is their oasis, so we must ensure their oasis provides a thoroughly superior experience!"

More recently, hotels are reinforcing their overall bed-based sleep initiatives and are now providing guests with a selection of an array of pillows. A typical pillow menu may include buckwheat sleep pillows, Mediflow water pillows, Isotonic 4 position pillows, Tri-core cervical support pillows, butterfly pillows, Conforel body pillows, and neck support pillows, just to name a few. Given all of the improvements in comfort, guests may never come out of their rooms!

Source: **www.comforthouse.com/hotelpillows.html**, accessed 4 December, 2009; **http://www.travelandleisure.com/articles/battle-of-the-beds/1**, accessed 4 December 2009. "Marriott to Replace 628,000 Hotel Beds" **www.usatoday.com**, accessed 2 May 2005; "Waking Up to the Marketing Potential of a Good Night's Sleep," *Advertising Age*, (April 18, 2005) 76, Issue 16, 16; No Author Listed, "Heavenly Bed for Babies," *Lodging Hospitality*, (September 15, 2001) 57, Issue 12, 9.

# Introduction

In the beginning, the work toward accumulating services marketing knowledge and establishing services marketing as a legitimate subfield of marketing was slow. In fact, it was not until 1970 that services marketing was even considered an academic field. It then took 12 more years before the first international conference on services marketing was held in the United States in 1982.[1] Many simply felt that the marketing of services was not significantly different from the marketing of goods. Markets still needed to be segmented, target markets still needed to be sought, and marketing mixes that catered to the needs of the firm's intended target market still needed to be developed. However, since those early days, a great deal has been written regarding specific differences between goods and services and their corresponding marketing implications. The majority of these differences are primarily attributed to four unique characteristics—*intangibility, inseparability, heterogeneity, and perishability.*[2]

Services are said to be *intangible* because they are performances rather than objects. They cannot be touched or seen in the same manner as goods. Rather, they are experienced, and consumers' judgments about them tend to be more subjective than objective. *Inseparability* of production and consumption refers to the fact that whereas goods are first produced, then sold, and then consumed, services are sold first and then produced and consumed simultaneously. For example, an airline passenger first purchases a ticket and then boards a plane, consuming the in-flight service as it is produced.

*Heterogeneity* refers to the potential for service performance to vary from one service transaction to the next. Services are produced by people; consequently, variability is inherent in the production process. This lack of consistency cannot be eliminated as it frequently can be with goods. Finally, *perishability* means that services cannot be saved; unused capacity in services cannot be reserved, and services themselves cannot be inventoried.[3] Consequently, perishability leads to formidable challenges relating to the balance of supply and demand.

This chapter focuses on each of the four unique characteristics that differentiate the marketing of services from the marketing of goods. Because services fall in many places along the continuum that ranges from tangible dominant to intangible dominant, as described by the scale of market entities in Chapter 1, the magnitude and subsequent impact that each of these four characteristics has on the marketing of individual services will vary.

Today, the field of services marketing is thriving both in terms of academic research and in the number of services marketing courses taught throughout the world. Services marketing, which was once thought subordinate to goods marketing, is now considered by prominent scholars to be "THE" dominant force in marketing.[4] Marketers who embrace this **service-dominant logic** believe that the primary role of marketers is to deliver service. Consequently, goods are simply a means of rendering a service to the customer. For example, automobiles manufactured by BMW provide transportation, an Apple iPod provides entertainment, and the treadmills at 24 Hour Fitness health clubs provide a means of exercise. Clearly, services marketing's place within the field of marketing has been substantially elevated compared to those early years, and rightly so!

**service-dominant logic** Philosophical viewpoint that the primary role of marketers is to deliver service. Consequently, goods are simply a means of rendering a service to the customer.

# Intangibility: The Mother of All Unique Differences

Of the four unique characteristics that tend to distinguish goods from services, intangibility is the primary source from which the other three unique characteristics emerge. As discussed in Chapter 1, services are defined as performances, deeds, and efforts; whereas, goods are defined as objects, devices, and things. As a result of their **intangibility**, services cannot be seen, felt, tasted, or touched in the same manner as tangible goods. For example, compare the differences between purchasing a movie ticket and purchasing a pair of shoes. The shoes are tangible goods, so the shoes can be objectively evaluated before the actual purchase. You can pick up the shoes, feel the quality of materials from which they are constructed, view their specific style and color, and actually put them on your feet and sample the fit. After the purchase, you can take the shoes home, and you now have ownership and the physical possession of a tangible object.

**intangibility** A distinguishing characteristic of services that makes them unable to be touched or sensed in the same manner as physical goods.

In comparison, consider the purchase of a service such as a movie to be enjoyed at a local cinema. In this instance, the customer purchases a movie ticket which entitles the consumer to an experience. Because the movie experience is intangible, it is subjectively evaluated. For example, consumers of services must rely on the judgments of others who have previously

**FIG-3.1** Marketing
Challenges
and Solutions
Pertaining to
Intangibility

| CHARACTERISTIC | RESULTING MARKETING CHALLENGES | POSSIBLE SOLUTIONS |
|---|---|---|
| Intangibility | Services cannot be inventoried | The use of tangible clues to help "tangibilize" the service |
| | Services lack patent protection and can be easily copied | Use personal sources of information to market services |
| | Services are difficult to display and/or explain to customers | Create a strong organizational image |
| | The pricing of services is difficult | Utilize an activity-based costing approach |

experienced the service for prepurchase information. Because the information provided by others is based on their own sets of expectations and perceptions, opinions will differ regarding the value of the experience. For example, if you ask five moviegoers what they thought about the film *Avatar*, they are likely to voice widely divergent opinions ranging from "I loved it!" to "I hated it!" After the movie, the customer returns home with a memory of the experience and retains the physical ownership of a ticket stub only.

## Marketing Challenges Created by Intangibility

As a result of the intangibility of services, a number of marketing challenges arise that are not normally faced when marketing tangible goods. More specifically, these challenges include the lack of service inventories, the lack of patent protection, the difficulties involved in displaying and communicating the attributes of the service to its intended target market, and the special challenges involved in the pricing of services. The following paragraphs address these challenges and offer possible solutions to minimize their effects. A summary of issues pertaining to intangibility is presented in Figure 3.1.

*Lack of Service Inventories*   Because of their intangibility, services cannot be inventoried. As a result, supplies of services cannot be stored as buffers against periods of high demand. For example, physicians cannot produce and store medical examinations to be used at a later date; movie seats that are not sold for the afternoon matinee cannot be added to the theater for the evening show; and the Auto Club cannot inventory roadside service to be distributed during peak periods of demand during hazardous driving conditions. Consequently, customers are commonly forced to wait for desired services, and service providers are limited in how much they can sell by how much they can produce. The bottom line is that the inability to maintain an inventory translates into constant supply and demand problems for services. In fact, the lack of service inventories presents so many challenges to marketers that it has earned its own name—*perishability*.

*Services Lack Patent Protection*   Due to their intangible nature, services cannot be patented. What is there to patent? Human labor and effort are not protected. Firms sometimes advertise that their processes are patented; however, the reality is that the tangible machinery involved in the process is protected, not the process itself. Therefore, an important challenge faced by the lack of patent protection is that new or existing services may be easily copied. Consequently, it is difficult to maintain a firm's differential service advantage over attentive competitors for long periods of time.

*Services Are Difficult to Display and/or Communicate*   The promotion of services presents yet another set of special challenges to the service marketer and is discussed in greater detail in Chapter 7. The root of the challenge is this: How do you get customers to take notice of your product when they cannot see it? As an example, consider the insurance industry. Insurance is a complicated product for many people. As customers, we cannot see it, we are unable to sample it prior to purchase, and many of us do not understand it. Insurance seems to cost an awful lot of money, and the benefits of its purchase are not realized until some future time, if at all. In fact, if we do not use it, we are supposed to consider ourselves lucky. Why should spending thousands of dollars a year on something the customer never uses make them feel lucky? To say the least, due to intangibility, the task of explaining your product's merits to consumers is often challenging.

***Services Are Difficult to Price*** Typically, a tangible product's price is often based on cost-plus pricing. This means that the firm selling the product calculates the cost of producing the product and adds a predetermined markup to that figure. The challenge involved in the pricing of services is that, due to intangibility, there is no cost of goods sold! Ultimately, the primary cost of producing a service is labor.

As an example, let's say you are very competent in the field of principles of marketing. Taking notice of your expertise in the field, a student who is struggling with his marketing assignments wants to hire you as a tutor. What would you charge per hour? What are your costs involved?

Based on feedback from other services marketing classes faced with this example, students usually begin laughing and indicate that they would engage in price-gouging and charge fellow students $100 per hour. After reality sets in, students quickly realize how difficult it is to place a value on their time. Specific considerations usually emerge, such as how much money the tutor could make doing something else and the opportunity costs associated with not being able to do something else instead of tutoring. Typically, the consensus is that the tutor should charge something comparable to the fees charged by other tutors. The problem with this response is that it still does not answer the original question, that is, how was this competitive-based price originally calculated?

## Possible Solutions to Challenges Caused by Intangibility

Over the years, marketing practitioners have implemented a number of strategies in the attempt to offset or minimize the marketing challenges posed by intangibility. These strategies include the use of tangible clues to help "tangibilize" the service, the use of personal sources of information to help spread word-of-mouth communications about service alternatives, and the creation of strong organizational images to reduce the amount of perceived risk associated with service purchases. Although marketers may not be capable of totally eliminating the challenges posed by intangibility, strategies such as these have provided innovative solutions for many service industries.

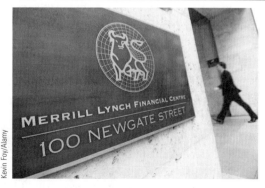

Service organizations such as insurance companies or investment firms often use tangible symbols such as company mascots to "tangibilize" their service offering to current and potential customers.

**physical evidence/ tangible clues** The physical characteristics that surround a service to assist consumers in making service evaluations, such as the quality of furnishings, the appearance of personnel, or the quality of paper stock used to produce the firm's brochure.

***Utilize Tangible Clues***  Given the absence of tangible properties, services are evaluated differently when compared to goods. In many instances, in the absence of a physical product, consumers look to the **physical evidence** or tangible clues that surround the service to assist them in making service evaluations. **Tangible clues** may include such evidence as the quality of furniture in a lawyer's office, the appearance of the personnel in a bank, and the quality of paper used for an insurance policy. Tangible clues are also often used in services advertising. Returning to the insurance example, the major challenge of an insurance firm is to communicate to consumers in a 30-second television commercial what the specific firm has to offer and how the firm is different from every other insurance firm under the customer's consideration. One strategy embraced by many service firms is to use some form of tangible clues in advertising. Prudential uses "the rock" and promises "rock-solid protection." Allstate shows us "helping hands" and promises that "you're in good hands with Allstate." The list goes on and on—Merrill Lynch has "the bull," Nationwide promotes "blanket-wide protection," Kemper has "the cavalry," Travelers utilizes "the umbrella," Geico has the "gecko," Aflac has the "duck," and Transamerica promotes the shape of its office building as "the power of the pyramid." The lesson that all these companies have learned over time is that the services they sell are abstract to the consumer and therefore difficult for the average consumer to understand. The answer to this challenge was to provide tangible clues that were easily understood by the public and directly related to the bundle of benefits the services provided. For example, State Farm's credo of "Like a good neighbor, State Farm is there" reinforces the firm's commitment to looking after its clients when they are most in need.

**personal sources of information** Sources such as friends, family, and other opinion leaders that consumers use to gather information about a service.

***Utilize Personal Sources of Information***  Because consumers of services lack any objective means of evaluating services, they often rely on the subjective evaluations relayed by friends, family, and a variety of other opinion leaders. For example, when moving to a new town and seeking a family physician, consumers will often ask coworkers and neighbors for referrals. Hence, in purchasing services, *personal sources* of information become more important to consumers than *nonpersonal sources* such as the mass media (e.g., television, radio, Yellow Pages, etc.).

**Personal sources of information** such as friends, family and other opinion leaders are sources of word-of-mouth communications (*aka: viral marketing*) that consumers use to gather information about services. One strategy often used to *stimulate* word-of-mouth advertising is to offer incentives to existing customers to tell their friends about a firm's offerings. Apartment complexes often use the incentive of a free month's rent to encourage tenants to have their friends rent vacant units. Service firms sometimes simulate personal communication while using the mass media. Mass media advertising that features customer testimonials *simulates* word-of-mouth advertising and can be very effective. Examples include hospital advertisements featuring former patients who have successfully recovered from major surgery and are now living normal and happy lives. Other examples include insurance companies that feature victims of hurricanes, fires and earthquakes who are grateful for their insurance protection when they needed it most. In more recent times, web-based social networks have emerged as a key sources of information as customers share their personal experiences with a variety of service businesses (see E-Services in Action).

***Create a Strong Organizational Image***  Another strategy utilized to minimize the effects of intangibility is to create a strong organizational image. Because of intangibility and the lack of objective sources of information to evaluate services, the amount of perceived risk associated with service purchases is generally greater than their goods counterparts. In an attempt to combat the higher levels of perceived risk, some service firms have spent a great deal of effort, time, and money in developing a nationally recognized organizational image. A well-known and respected corporate image lowers the level of

---

## E-SERVICES *IN ACTION*

## Social Networking: The New Face of Personal Sources of Information

Perhaps some of the most widely used services on the Internet are social networking websites. They have gained incredible popularity both for consumers and companies in recent years, becoming a forum for companies to identify their target markets, conduct market research, and investigate consumer behavior. Some of the most widely used and fastest growing sites include Facebook.com, Twitter.com, and LinkedIn.com.

### Facebook.com

Facebook has risen to the top of the social networking hierarchy and, according to the statistics posted by the site, it has more than 300 million active users. It is estimated that over 8 billion minutes worldwide are spent on Facebook on a daily basis. The site can be translated into over 70 languages, and approximately 70 percent of users live outside the United States. Over 1 million businesses from 180 countries have created and hosted Platform applications, which are utilized by over 70 percent of Facebook users. The Facebook Platform is a unique service that allows companies to integrate with the website through advertisements and interactive applications in an effort to reach their target market.

### Twitter.com

Recently, both consumers and companies have taken to advertising their lives and business moves through short status updates on Twitter.com. It seems that every celebrity, reality TV star, and major brand has a Twitter account. Some businesses have even taken to using the networking site as an opportunity to create connections with potential partners and competitors. The site attributes its roaring success to the simplicity of its use and construction. Users answer one simple question, "What's happening?" and submit updates through a variety of media, including mobile web, instant messaging, third parties, or online. The site boasts millions of daily users, with the user base rapidly increasing.

### LinkedIn.com

For companies and prospective employees seeking to create networking relationships with each other, there is no better forum than LinkedIn. With over 50 million users in more than 200 countries, the networking possibilities are nearly limitless. The latest published facts indicate that executives from every Fortune 500 company are LinkedIn members. Membership allows individuals to create a vast array of contacts for both individual and company support. Entry level employees can identify and receive mentorship from experienced professionals, senior managers can connect with industry peers, and businesses can recruit new talent.

Sources: 1. **www.facebook.com**; 2. **www.twitter.com**; 3. **www.linkedin.com**

---

perceived risk experienced by potential customers and, in some instances, lowers the reliance on personal sources of information when making service provider choices. As an example, the consumer who is moving to a new town may bypass personal referrals and automatically seek out the nearest State Farm agent for home and auto insurance needs based on the firm's organizational image. In this case, the national firm, through image development and subsequent brand awareness, has developed a differential advantage over small, local firms of which the consumer may be unaware.

Organizational image is usually the result of the firm's own positioning strategy in the marketplace. Typical positioning strategies include leadership in areas such as price, innovation, service, personnel, and convenience. Over the last several years, sustainability has become the new battleground for firms that wish to differentiate themselves from the competition. For example, airlines, which many consumers believe are a commodity (no substantial differences among competing alternatives), have embraced the idea of sustainable business practices both because the airlines believe it is inherently a good idea, and also because the airline understands that a substantial number of customers believing that "all other things being equal" will select an airline that is associated with sustainable business practices (see Sustainability and Services in Action).

---

# SUSTAINABILITY AND SERVICES *IN ACTION*

## Airline Industry Practices

Incorporating sustainable practices into services is a challenging task for any service provider, but perhaps especially so for the airline industry. Some consumers have chosen to use alternate modes of transportation in an effort to reduce the already heightened levels of fuel use in the industry. For many consumers, however, avoiding air travel is simply out of the question. Thus, multiple carriers have made attempts to reduce their carbon footprints and increase their brand appeal. Following are some of the ways in which airline carriers have made efforts towards sustainability.

### Virgin America

1. Installation of winglets on all planes to increase fuel efficiency.
2. Experimentation with biofuels in an effort to increase the number of flights exclusively powered by biofuels.
3. Recycling program in place, with expectations to eliminate 50 percent of the company's waste by 2012.
4. Provision of only fair trade coffee onboard.
5. Providing options to consumers to offset their carbon footprtints.

### Continental

1. $16 billion investment in the last decade to replace fleet with more efficient planes.
2. Installation of winglets, reducing emissions by up to 5 percent.
3. Using single engine taxiing, engine washing, and ground vehicles powered by electricity (as opposed to combustion engines).
4. 13 full-time staff environmentalists to "work with engine manufacturers, design green terminals, and track carbon emissions and chemical recycling daily."

### JetBlue

1. Organic food options and carbon offsets available with ticket purchases.
2. Utilization of methane recapture processes.
3. Efforts such as super-efficient lighting and green building techniques at headquarters, recycled cooking oil, paperless ticketing, and recycled oil filters.

Source: Tevault, Ashley. "Serving it up Green: Examination of Sustainability in the Service Sector." Colorado State University Honors Program Senior Thesis. 12 November 2009.

---

**activity-based costing (ABC)** Costing method that breaks down the organization into a set of activities, and activities into tasks, which convert materials, labor, and technology into outputs.

*Utilize Activity-based Costing* Traditional cost accounting practices, which were designed to monitor raw material consumption, depreciation, and labor, offer little in helping service managers understand their own cost structures. A more useful approach, **activity-based costing (ABC)**, focuses on the resources consumed in developing the final product.[5] Traditionally, overhead in most service firms has been allocated to projects based on the amount of direct labor charged to complete the customer's requirements. However, this method of charging overhead has frustrated managers of specific projects for years.

Activity-based costing focuses on the cost of activities by breaking down the organization into a set of activities and activities into tasks, which convert materials, labor, and technology into outputs. These tasks are thought of as "users" of overhead and are identified as *cost drivers*. The firm's past records are used to arrive at cost-per-task figures that are then allocated to each project based on the activities required to complete the project. In addition, by breaking the overall overhead figure into a set of activities that are driven by cost drivers, the firm can now concentrate its efforts on reducing costs and increasing profitability.

# Inseparability: The Interconnection of Service Participants

**inseparability** A distinguishing characteristic of services that reflects the interconnections among the service provider, the customer involved in receiving the service, and other customers sharing the service experience.

One of the most intriguing characteristics of the service experience involves the concept of inseparability. **Inseparability** reflects the interconnection among the service provider, the customer involved in receiving the service, and other customers sharing the same service experience. Unlike the goods manufacturer, who may seldom see an actual customer while producing the good in a secluded factory, service providers are often in constant contact with their customers and must construct their service operations with the customer's physical presence in mind. This interaction between customer and service provider defines a **critical incident** and represents the greatest opportunity for both gains and losses in regard to customer satisfaction and retention.

**critical incident** A specific interaction between a customer and a service provider.

## Marketing Challenges Created by Inseparability

The inseparable nature of services poses a number of unique challenges for marketing practitioners. First, in many instances, the execution of the service often requires the physical presence of the service provider. As a result, service providers require different skill sets, such as interpersonal skills, while a manufacturing worker may never actually interact with a customer. Second, the customer's involvement in the service delivery process presents a number of other challenges. Customers often dictate the type of service to be delivered, the length of the service delivery process, and the cycle of service demand. As a result, customer involvement often jeopardizes the overall efficiency of the service operation. Third, services are often a shared experience among a number of customers. Consequently, problems arise as customers adversely influence one another's service experience. Finally, inseparability presents a number of challenges pertaining to the mass production of services. A single service provider can only produce a finite amount of service. In addition, only so many customers can travel to one physical location to consume a specific service provided by a specific provider. A summary of challenges and potential solutions pertaining to inseparability is provided in Figure 3.2.

***The Service Provider Is Physically Connected to the Service***    For the production of many services to occur, the service provider must be physically present to produce

Claudiobaba/iStockphoto.com

Unlike the goods manufacturer who may seldom see an actual customer, service providers often produce their services in close physical proximity to their customers. As a result, services are often characterized by inseparability.

**FIG-3.2** Marketing
Challenges
and Solutions
Pertaining to
Inseparability

| CHARACTERISTIC | RESULTING MARKETING CHALLENGES | POSSIBLE SOLUTIONS |
|---|---|---|
| Inseparability | The service provider is physically connected to the service | Strategic selection and training of public contact personnel |
| | The customer is involved in the production process | Effectively managing consumers |
| | "Other customers" are involved in the production process | The use of multisite locations |
| | The mass production of services is especially challenging | |

and deliver the service. For example, dental services require the physical presence of a dentist or hygienist, medical surgery requires a surgeon, and in-home services such as carpet cleaning require a service provider to complete the work.

Because of the intangibility of services, the service provider becomes a tangible clue on which at least part of the customer's evaluation of the service experience becomes based. As tangible clues, service providers are particularly evaluated based on their use of language, clothing, personal hygiene, and interpersonal communication skills. Many service firms have long appreciated the impact that public contact personnel have on the firm's overall evaluation. For example, wearing uniforms or conforming to dress codes is often required of service employees to reflect professionalism. Other service firms such as restaurants often place their most articulate and attractive personnel in public contact positions such as wait staff, host/hostess, and bartender. Personnel who do not have these skills and traits are often employed in areas that are invisible to the consumer, such as the kitchen and dish room areas.

Further complicating the service encounter, face-to-face interactions with customers make employee satisfaction crucial. Without a doubt, employee satisfaction and customer satisfaction are directly related. Dissatisfied employees who are visible to customers will translate into lower consumer perceptions of the firm's performance. The importance of employee satisfaction within service firms cannot be overemphasized. Customers will never be the number one priority in a company where employees are treated poorly. Employees should be viewed and treated as internal customers of the firm. This issue is discussed in much greater detail in Chapter 9.

***Customers Are Involved in the Production Process***    The second defining characteristic of inseparability is that the customer is involved in the production process. The customer's involvement in the production process may vary from: (1) a requirement that the customer be physically present to receive the service, such as in dental services, a haircut, or surgery; (2) a need for the customer to be present only to start and stop the service, such as in dry cleaning and auto repair; and (3) a need for the customer to be only mentally present, such as in participation in college courses that are transmitted via the Internet. Each scenario reflects a different level of customer contact, and as a result each service delivery system should be designed differently.

Overall, as customer contact increases, the efficiency of the operation decreases. More specifically, the customer has a direct impact on the type of service desired, the length of the service delivery process, and the cycle of service demand. Attempting to balance consumer needs with efficient operating procedures is a delicate art.

With regards to the cycle of demand, restaurants would be more efficient if consumers would smooth their demands for food throughout the day as opposed to eating primarily during specific time periods corresponding to breakfast, lunch, and dinner hours. As one frustrated, senior citizen McDonald's employee told one of the authors of this text, "These people [the customers] would get better service if they all didn't show up at the same time!" Further complications arise as consumers also dictate the nature or type of service needed. This is particularly frustrating for health care workers who provide services to waiting emergency room patients. Every patient has a different need, some needs are more immediate than others, and you never know what the next patient who walks or is rolled in via wheel chairs and gurneys through the emergency room doors will need. Obviously, this scenario is frustrating for waiting patients, and the care for "less needy" patients is further delayed. Finally, even when consumer needs are the same, some consumers ask more questions and/or need more attention than others, thereby affecting the length of demand. As a result, fixed schedules are difficult to adhere to without delays. This scenario explains why doctor appointments seldom begin at their appointed time.

Throughout the customer's interaction with the service provider, the customer often provides inputs into the service production process. As such, the customer often plays a key role in the successful completion of the service encounter. For example, a patient who feels ill must be able to accurately describe his or her symptoms to a physician to receive proper treatment. Not only must the symptoms be described accurately, but the patient also must take the recommended dosage of medicines prescribed. In this case, the customer (the patient) becomes a key player in the service production process and can directly influence the outcome of the process itself. Failure of the patient to follow recommended instructions will likely lead to a dissatisfactory service experience.

One final issue directly related to the consumer's presence in the service factory concerns the appearance of the service factory itself. Service factories, be they restaurants, hospitals, museums, or universities, must be built with consumers' presence in mind. Consequently, the service factory not only provides the service, but in and of itself becomes a key tangible clue in the formation of consumer perceptions regarding service quality. The design and management of the service factory is discussed in much greater detail in Chapter 8, Managing the Servicescape and Other Physical Evidence.

***"Other Customers" Are Involved in the Production Process***   The presence of "other customers" during the service encounter is the third defining characteristic of inseparability. Because production and consumption occur simultaneously, several customers often share a common service experience. This "shared experience" can be negative or positive. The marketing challenges presented by having other customers involved in the production process generally reflect the negative aspects of their involvement. Restaurants once again provide an ideal setting for examples of negative events, including smokers violating the space of nonsmokers and vice-versa, families with young children sharing the same space with adult couples seeking a quiet dining experience, drunk customers interacting with sober patrons, and the occasional lovers' quarrel that spills over into the aisles. Overall, the primary challenge concerns effectively managing different market segments with different needs within a single service environment. Such will be the case as cell phone use is eventually approved on airlines. Some passengers will see the addition of this service as overwhelmingly positive while others will view it as noise pollution and extremely irritating.

The impact of "other customers" is not always negative. On the positive side, audience reaction in the form of laughter or screams of terror often enhances level of emotion at a movie theater. Similarly, a crowded pub may facilitate the opportunity for social interaction, and a happy crowd may make a concert an even more pleasurable event. As social creatures, humans tend to frequent places of business and feel more comfortable in

**"other customers"** The term used to describe customers that share a service experience.

places that have other customers in them. In fact, the lack of other customers may act as a tangible clue that the impending experience may be less than satisfactory. For example, if given the choice of dining at one of two new restaurants, would you select a restaurant that had no cars in the parking lot, or would you choose a restaurant down the street with a full parking lot?

***The Mass Production of Services Presents Special Challenges***   One final obstacle presented by inseparability is how to mass produce services successfully. The problems pertaining to mass production are twofold. First, because the service provider is directly linked to the service being produced, an individual service provider can produce only a limited supply. Consequently, the question arises: How does one provider produce enough service product to meet the demand of the mass market? The second problem directly relates to the consumer's involvement in the production process. Consumers interested in a particular provider's services would have to travel to the provider's specific location. For example, if a sports enthusiast would like to experience snow skiing in the desert, he or she would have to personally travel to the Middle East to experience the wonders of Ski Dubai (see Global Services in Action).

### Possible Solutions to Challenges Created by Inseparability

Similar to the solutions proposed for intangibility, marketing practitioners have developed a number of strategies in the attempt to offset or minimize the marketing challenges posed by inseparability. These strategies include: (1) an increased emphasis

## GLOBAL SERVICES *IN ACTION*

### Ski Dubai

Imagine what activities you would enjoy on vacation in Dubai. Perhaps you would sunbathe on one of the world renowned beaches, take a safari, or tour the impressive surrounding sand dunes. Of anything you might do, going skiing (not the water kind) would probably be the furthest thing from your mind. But Ski Dubai has provided that very service in the desert country: an artificially made, indoor ski resort.

At Ski Dubai, visitors can ski, snowboard, and even toboggan all year round on the indoor slopes furnished with real snow. The resort boasts 22,500 square meters of snow-covered terrain, including five runs of varying difficulty and a "Freestyle Zone" created solely for snowboarders to practice their stunts. The resort also contains several themed restaurants, an exclusive retail shop, expert Snow School instructors, and a quad-chairlift.

Visitors purchase Slope Passes upon arrival, which include a jacket, trousers, skis and ski boots or a snowboard and snowboard boots, ski poles, disposable socks, and helmets for children. Admission to the park costs approximately the equivalent of USD $ 27.23, though time on the slopes must be purchased in addition. Prices for ski time vary from $50 to $82, with discounts for children, groups, or corporate events. Additional charges include group or private lessons, consults with ski experts, meals in the themed restaurants, or items from the retail shop.

As the only resort with such amenities in the area, Ski Dubai provides an exclusive experience for its visitors. It is the prime example of a unique service through the delivery of an intangible and unforgettable experience. Nowhere else in the Middle East can consumers ski down a black level slope, make snow angels, or learn to snowboard. Ski Dubai was the first resort to offer these services, and it remains the only location where consumers can partake in these wintery activities in the Middle East.

Source: Ski Dubai, **http://www.skidxb.com/English/Default.aspx**

placed on the selection and training of public contact personnel to ensure that the right types of employees are in the right jobs; (2) the implementation of consumer management strategies that facilitate a positive service encounter for all consumers sharing the same service experience; and (3) the use of multisite locations to offset the mass production challenges posed by inseparability.

***Strategic Selection and Training of Public Contact Personnel***    Contact personnel, unlike goods, are not inanimate objects and, being human, they exhibit variations in behavior that cannot be controlled by the service process. Moreover, the attitudes and emotions of contact personnel are visible to the customer and can affect the service experience for better or worse. Surly or unhappy employees can affect both customers with whom they come into direct contact and other employees as well. On the other hand, a bright, highly motivated employee can create a more pleasant service experience for everyone who comes into contact with that person.[6]

As a result of the frequency and depth of interactions between service providers and consumers, *selection* of service personnel with superior communication and interpersonal skills is a must. In addition, *training* personnel once they are on the job is also necessary. For example, consider the training needs of UPS, which handles more than 3 billion packages and 5.5 percent of the United States' GNP annually. The behind-the-scenes activities of hiring, training, and rewarding employees is directly related to how well customers are served. UPS believes in building trust and teamwork, and making employees loyal to the company's mission. The company spends more than $300 million a year on training, paying full-time drivers (on average) more than $50,000 a year, and surveying its employees for service-improving suggestions.[7]

Too often, newly hired employees are left to fend for themselves and placed in front of customers with little or no training. Consequently, it should come as no surprise to learn that a large percentage of consumer complaints about service focuses on the action or inaction of ill-prepared employees. Even when training has been received, the content of training often misses the mark. Critics of service quality have focused on "robotic" responses by staff and on staff who have been trained in using the technology associated with the business, but not in dealing with different types of customers. Experts in service quality believe that employees must also be trained in "soft" management skills such as

www.CartoonStock.com

ACCORDING TO THE SURVEY, RETENTION IS HELPED BY TRAINING AND MONEY...THERE'S NO MENTION OF CHAINING STAFF TO THEIR DESKS

Employee retention is directly related to customer satisfaction; however, there are right ways and a wrong ways to retain good employees reliability, responsiveness, empathy, assurance, and managing the tangibles that surround the service.

***Effectively Manage Consumers*** The problems created by inseparability can also be minimized through effective **consumer management.** The goal of effectively managing consumers that share a service experience is to minimize the negative aspects and maximize the positive aspects of "other customers." Separating smokers from nonsmokers is an example of one way to minimize the impact of other customers. Sending a patient insurance forms and information about office procedures before the patient arrives may help control the length of the service encounter. Restaurant reservation systems may help smooth out demand created by an overabundance of customers. Finally, providing delivery services may eliminate the need for many consumers to be physically present within a service factory, thereby increasing the firm's operating efficiencies and improving delivery speed. Encouraging the positive aspects of the presence of "other customers" is also possible. Encouraging classroom participation makes classes more enjoyable for everyone. In addition, encouraging group waits where customers talk to one another and occupy each other's time can make that time much more enjoyable than solo waits. The management of service consumers is discussed in much greater detail in Chapter 10, People as Strategy: Managing Service Consumers.

***Develop Multisite Locations*** To offset the effects of inseparability pertaining to challenges associated with centralized mass production, service firms that mass produce do so by setting up multiple locations. Typical examples include H & R Block accounting services, Hyatt Legal Services, Marriott Hotels, and a myriad of banking and insurance institutions. **Multisite locations** serve at least two purposes. First, because the consumer is involved in the production process, multisite locations limit the distance the consumer must travel to purchase the service. Second, each multisite location is staffed by different service providers, each of whom can produce their own supply of services to serve their local market. Ultimately, multisite locations act as **factories in the field.** Without them, every consumer who desired legal services would have to travel to a single location that housed all the lawyers in the country plus all their clients for that day. Obviously, this is not practical or realistic.

The use of multisite locations is not without its own set of special challenges. Each site is staffed by different service providers who have their own personalities and their own sets of skills. For example, every H & R Block tax representative does not have the same personality and same set of skills as the founder, Henry Block. The differences in personnel are particularly troublesome for service firms attempting to establish a consistent image by providing a standardized product. The variability in performance from one multisite location to another and even from one provider to another within a single location leads us to the next special unique characteristic of services—heterogeneity.

## Heterogeneity: The Variability of Service Delivery

One of the most frequently stressed differences between goods and services is **heterogeneity**—the variation in consistency from one service transaction to the next. Service encounters occur in real time, and consumers are often physically present in the service factory, so if something goes wrong during the service process, it is too late to institute quality control measures before the service reaches the customer. Indeed, the customer (or other customers who share the service experience with the primary customer) may be part of the quality problem. If, in a hotel, something goes wrong during the night's stay, that lodging experience for a customer is bound to be affected; the manager cannot logically ask the customer to leave the hotel, re-enter, and start the experience from the beginning.

---

**consumer management** A strategy service personnel can implement that minimizes the impact of "other customers" on each individual customer's service experience (e.g., separating smokers from nonsmokers in a restaurant).

**multisite locations** A way service firms that mass produce combat inseparability, involving multiple locations to limit the distance the consumers have to travel and staffing each location differently to serve a local market.

**factories in the field** Another name for multisite locations.

**heterogeneity** A distinguishing characteristic of services that reflects the variation in consistency from one service transaction to the next.

Heterogeneity, almost by definition, makes it impossible for a service operation to achieve 100 percent perfect quality on an ongoing basis. Manufacturing operations may also have problems achieving this sort of target, but they can isolate mistakes and correct them over time, since mistakes tend to reoccur at the same points in the process. In contrast, many errors in service operations are one-time events; the waiter who drops a plate of food in a customer's lap creates a service failure that can be neither foreseen nor corrected ahead of time.[8]

Another challenge heterogeneity presents is that not only does the consistency of service vary from firm to firm and among personnel within a single firm, but it also varies when interacting with the same service provider on a daily basis. For example, some McDonald's franchises have helpful and smiling employees, whereas other McDonald's franchises employ individuals who are less helpful. Not only can this be said for different franchises, but the same is true within a single franchise on a daily basis because of the mood swings of individuals.

## Marketing Challenges Created by Heterogeneity

The major challenges presented by heterogeneity translate into the fact that service standardization and quality control are difficult to achieve. Why is this so? Because of the inseparability characteristic previously discussed, you now know that in many instances the service provider must be present to provide the service. Firms such as financial institutions employ a multitude of front-line service providers. As an individual, each employee has a different personality and interacts with customers differently. In addition, each employee may act differently from one day to the next as a result of mood changes as well as numerous other factors. As an example, many students who work as wait staff in restaurants frequently acknowledge that the quality of interaction between themselves and customers will vary even from table to table. Hotel desk clerks, airline reservationists, and business-to-business service personnel would respond similarly.

The marketing problems created by heterogeneity are particularly frustrating. A firm could produce the best product in the world, but if an employee is having a "bad day," a customer's perceptions may be adversely affected. The firm may never have another opportunity to serve that customer. Returning to our McDonald's example, the franchisee may pay $1,000,000 for the franchise and the right to sell a "proven product." However, the real secret to each individual franchise's success is the 16-year-old behind the counter who is interacting with customers and operating the cash register. Can you imagine the franchisee who has just spent $1,000,000 for the franchise trying to sleep at night while thinking that his or her livelihood depends on the "kid" behind the counter? It does!

## Possible Solutions to Challenges Caused by Heterogeneity

Solutions proposed to offset the challenges posed by heterogeneity could be considered complete opposites of one another. On one hand, some service firms use the heterogeneous nature of services to provide customized services. In this case, the service offering is tailored to the individual needs of the consumer. The second possible solution is to develop a service delivery system that standardizes the service offering—every consumer receives essentially the same type and level of service. Each of these opposing strategies encompasses a different set of advantages and disadvantages. A summary of issues pertaining to heterogeneity is provided in Figure 3.3.

**customization** Taking advantage of the variation inherent in each service encounter by developing services that meet each customer's exact specifications.

***Pursue a Customization Strategy***  One possible solution to the problems created by heterogeneity is to take advantage of the variation inherent in each service encounter and customize the service. **Customization** develops services that meet each customer's individual needs. Producers of goods typically manufacture the good in an environment that

**FIG-3.3** Heterogeneity: Marketing Challenges and Possible Solutions

| CHARACTERISTIC | RESULTING MARKETING CHALLENGES | POSSIBLE SOLUTIONS |
|---|---|---|
| Heterogeneity | Service standardization and quality control are difficult to achieve | Pursue a customization strategy |
| | | Pursue a standardization strategy |

is isolated from the customer. As such, mass-produced goods do not meet individual customer needs. However, because both the customer and the service provider are involved in the service delivery process, it is easier to customize the service based on the customer's specific instructions.

Note that there are tradeoffs associated with a customized service. On one hand, if everything is provided exactly to the customer's specifications, the customer ends up with a service that meets his or her specific needs; however, the service will take longer to produce and will be more costly to provide. Consequently, pursuing a customization strategy enables the provider to charge higher retail prices, which can potentially lead to higher profit margins for the provider. Providers pursuing a customization strategy typically focus on profit margins on a per-customer basis as opposed to achieving profits through a mass volume or turnover strategy.

The downside of providing customized services is threefold. First, customers may not be willing to pay the higher prices associated with customized services. Second, the speed of service delivery may be an issue. Customized services take extra time to provide and deliver, and the customer may not have the luxury of waiting for the final service product. Finally, customers may not be willing to face the uncertainty associated with customized services. Each customized service is different, so the customer is never sure exactly what the final product will be until it is delivered. So, do customers prefer customized services over standardized services? Intuitively, most believe that customers would prefer customized products; however, the answer is, "It depends." If price, speed of delivery, and consistency of performance are issues, the customer will probably be happier with a standardized service.

***Pursue a Standardization Strategy***    Standardizing the service is a second possible solution to the marketing challenges created by heterogeneity. The goal of **standardization** is to produce a consistent service product from one transaction to the next. Service firms can attempt to standardize their service through intensive training of their service providers. Training certainly helps reduce extreme variations in performance. However, even with all the training in the world, employees ultimately will continue to vary somewhat from one transaction to the next. One way to eliminate this variance is to replace human labor with machines.

A financial institution's automatic teller machine (ATM), an automated car wash, and web-based services such as procuring airline tickets, hotel reservations, or digital music files are prime examples of standardized services that appeal to consumers' convenience-oriented needs. When using an ATM for banking services, consumers key in their service request by answering a series of predetermined automated prompts and the service is then provided accordingly. This type of system minimizes the amount of customer contact and variations in quality during the order and delivery processes.

On the positive side, standardization leads to lower consumer prices, consistency of performance, and faster service delivery. However, some consumer groups believe that standardization sends the message that the firm does not really care about individual consumer needs and is attempting to distance itself from the customer. Perceived

**standardization** The goal of standardization is to produce a consistent service product from one transaction to the next.

distancing is particularly an issue as organizations are increasingly replacing human labor with machines, such as automated phone services that are programmed to respond with, "your call is very important to us"—does anyone really believe this anymore? In many instances, customers become increasingly frustrated when forced to select from a menu of phone prompts and to interact with voice recognition software that is far from perfect. Of course, standardization and customization do not have to be mutually exclusive and presented as all-or-nothing propositions. Numerous companies, particularly in the travel and tourism arena, provide a standardized core product and allow consumers to select options to semi-customize their final outcome. For example, customers booking an airline flight on Travelocity select their destination, day of travel, time of travel, seat location, and can arrange hotel and rental car accommodations that suit their individual needs.

## Perishability: Balancing Supply and Demand

**perishability** A distinguishing characteristic of services in that they cannot be saved, their unused capacity cannot be reserved, and they cannot be inventoried.

The fourth and final unique characteristic that distinguishes goods from services is perishability. **Perishability** reflects the challenge that services cannot be saved, their unused capacity cannot be reserved, and they cannot be inventoried. Unlike goods that can be stored and sold at a later date, services that are not sold when they become available cease to exist. For example, hotel rooms that go unoccupied for the evening cannot be stored and used at a later date; airline seats that are not sold cannot be inventoried and added on to aircraft during the holiday season when airline seats are scarce; and service providers such as dentists, lawyers, and hairstylists cannot regain the time lost from an empty client appointment book.

The inability to create an inventory presents profound difficulties for marketing services. When dealing with tangible goods, the ability to create an inventory means that production and consumption of the goods can be separated in time and space. In other words, a good can be produced in one locality in Asia and transported for sale in another country around the globe. Similarly, a good can be produced in January and not released into the channels of distribution until June. In contrast, most services are consumed at the point of production. Education is consumed as it is produced; the same is also true for psychiatric services, religious services, and a host of other service products.

The existence of inventory also greatly facilitates quality control in goods-producing organizations. Statistical sampling techniques can be used on warehouse stock to select individual items for testing, to the point of destruction if necessary (e.g., automobile crash tests). The sampling process can be set up to ensure minimum variability in the quality of product prior to its release for distribution. Once again, the same cannot be said for services as statistical sampling for quality-control purposes prior to the service reaching the customer is not an option. Quality-control systems also provide numerical targets against which managers can work. It is thus possible for Procter & Gamble to produce tens of millions of packages of Tide laundry detergent that are essentially identical. In contrast, when you purchase a room at a hotel, you are likely to experience a wide range of factors that may influence your good night's sleep. Issues such as air conditioning, plumbing, and noisy neighbors factor into the hotel guest's experience.

Finally, in goods-producing businesses, inventory performs the function of separating the marketing and the production departments. In many organizations, tangible products are actually sold at a transfer price from one department to another within the same company. The two parts of the firm have what amounts to a contract for quality and volumes. Once this contract has been negotiated, each department is able to work relatively independently of the other. In service firms, however, marketing and operations must constantly interact with each other—because of the inability to inventory the service product.[9]

## Marketing Challenges Caused by Perishability

Without the benefit of carrying an inventory, matching demand and supply within most services firms is a major challenge. In fact, because of the unpredictable nature of consumer demand for services, the only likely way that supply perfectly matches demand is by accident! For example, as a manager, try to imagine scheduling cashiers at a grocery store. Although we can estimate the times of the day that the store will experience increased demand, that demand may fluctuate widely within any 15-minute interval. Now try to imagine forecasting demand for a hospital's emergency ward, an entertainment theme park, or a ski resort. Demand can be "guesstimated" but will rarely be exact. Clearly, consumer demand for many services at any given time is unpredictable. The lack of inventories and the need for the service provider to provide the service lead to several possible demand and supply scenarios. In contrast to their service-producing counterparts, manufacturers of goods could more easily adapt to these scenarios through selling or creating inventories. A summary of issues pertaining to perishability is provided in Figure 3.4.

***Demand Exceeds Supply of Service Available***   Within this scenario, consumer demand simply outpaces what the firm can supply, which results in long waiting periods and, in many cases, unhappy customers. Business may be lost to competitors as waiting times become too excessive for consumers to endure. Ironically, in cases of consistent excess consumer demand, consumers may continue to attempt to patronize a firm out of curiosity and/or the social status obtained by telling others of their experience: "We finally got in to see the show!"

***Demand Exceeds Optimal Supply of Service Available***   In many instances, the consequences associated with demand exceeding optimal supply may be worse than when demand exceeds maximum available capacity. By accepting the customer's business by beginning the service (e.g., being seated at a busy restaurant), the firm implicitly promises to provide the same level of service that it always provides, regardless of the number of customers being served. For example, it seems that airlines typically staff flights with the same number of flight attendants regardless of the number of tickets actually sold. However, when demand exceeds optimal levels, the service provided is generally at inferior levels. As a result, customer expectations are not met, and customer dissatisfaction and negative word-of-mouth publicity results.

**FIG-3.4** Perishability: Marketing Challenges and Possible Solutions

| CHARACTERISTIC | RESULTING MARKETING CHALLENGES | POSSIBLE SOLUTIONS TO MANAGE DEMAND | POSSIBLE SOLUTIONS TO MANAGE SUPPLY |
|---|---|---|---|
| | Demand exceeds supply of service available | Utilize creative pricing strategies to shift demand | Use part-time employees to increase supply of service |
| | Demand exceeds optimal levels of supply | Implement a reservation system | Share capacity with other providers |
| Perishability | Lower demand than optimal supply levels | Shift demand to complimentary services | Prepare for expansion in advance |
| | | Utilize nonpeak demand periods to prepare for peak periods of demand | Utilize third parties to increase sources of supply |
| | | | Increase customer participation |

When demand exceeds optimal supply levels, the temptation is to accept the additional business. However, in many instances the firm's personnel and operations are not up to the task of delivering service effectively beyond optimal demand levels. For example, suppose that a landscaper became very successful in a short time by providing high-quality services to upscale customers. As the word spread to other potential clients, demand for the landscaper's time dramatically increases. As the landscaper's firm expands to serve new clients via the purchase of new equipment and hiring new personnel, the landscaper quickly discovers that he is losing control over the quality of service delivered by his own business. His new personnel simply do not provide the same level of service that his original customer base had grown accustomed to receiving. Over time, the landscaper may lose his new clients as well as his old clients as a result of the decline of his reputation. In this particular scenario, the service traits of perishability, inseparability, and heterogeneity can all be seen to present their challenges to the service provider.

***Lower Demand than Optimal Supply Levels***    As we discussed earlier, providing the exact number of grocery store cashiers needed at any given time is a challenge for most store managers. One solution would be to staff each line with a full-time cashier; however, this strategy would result in an inefficient deployment of the firm's resources. During times when demand is below optimal capacity, resources are underutilized (e.g., cashiers are standing around) and operating costs are needlessly wasted.

***Demand and Supply at Optimal Levels***    The optimal scenario is to have demand match supply. This scenario describes the situation in which customers do not wait in long lines and employees are utilized to their optimal capacity. Because services cannot be stored, a buffer to ease excess demand cannot be developed. Moreover, service providers are not machines and cannot produce a limitless supply. Consequently, service demand and supply rarely balance. Customers do at times experience lengthy waits, and service providers are sometimes faced with no one to serve.

## Possible Solutions to Challenges Created by Perishability

Because service demand and supply balance only by accident, service firms have developed strategies that attempt to adjust supply and demand to achieve a balance. The strategies presented below are possible solutions to overcome the difficulties associated with the perishability of services.[10] The first group of strategies concerns the management of the firm's demand. This discussion is followed by a second group of strategies that focuses on managing supply.

Opening multisite locations such as branch offices enables a service provider to overcome the mass production challenges posed by the service characteristic of perishability.

**creative pricing** Pricing strategies often used by service firms to help smooth demand fluctuations, such as offering "matinee" prices or "early bird specials" to shift demand from peak to nonpeak periods.

*Demand Strategy: Utilizing Creative Pricing Strategies to Smooth Demand*   **Creative pricing** strategies are often used by service firms to help smooth demand fluctuations. For example, offering price reductions in the form of "early bird specials" and "matinees" have worked well for restaurants and movie theaters, respectively. Price-conscious target markets, such as families with children, are willing to alter their demand patterns for the cost savings. At the same time, service firms are willing to offer price reductions to attract customers during nonpeak hours, thereby making their operations more efficient. By shifting demand to other periods, the firm can accommodate more customers and provide better service during periods in which demand previously has been (1) turned away because of limited supply, and (2) not served as well as usual because demand surpassed optimal supply levels.

Creative pricing has also been used to target specific groups such as senior citizens, children and their parents (families), and college students. This type of pricing strategy has not only helped smooth fluctuating demand but has also aided in separating diverse target markets from sharing the same consumption experience at the same time. For example, by providing family-type specials during late afternoon and early evening hours, a restaurant significantly reduces the amount of potential conflict between its "family customers" and its "adult-only customers," who generally dine later in the evening. Price incentives have also been recently used to persuade customers to use the company's website. Customers who are willing to place their orders on the Internet may do so 24 hours a day, 7 days a week. Increasing website usage reduces demand for personal service during regular business hours.

**reservation system** A strategy to help smooth demand fluctuations in which consumers ultimately request a portion of the firm's services for a particular time slot.

*Demand Strategy: Implement a Reservation System*   Another common strategy used to reduce fluctuations in demand is to implement a **reservation system** by which consumers ultimately reserve a portion of the firm's services for a particular time slot. Typical service firms that use reservation systems include restaurants, hotels, airlines, rental car agencies, hair care salons, doctors of all varieties, golf courses (tee times), and day spas. On the plus side, reservations reduce the customer's risk of not receiving the service and minimize the time spent waiting in line for the service to be available. Reservation systems also allow service firms to prepare in advance for a known quantity of demand. Consequently, the customer and the firm benefit from improved service.

Despite the advantages of a reservation system, a host of disadvantages accompanies this strategy. First, someone must maintain the reservation system, which adds additional cost to the operation. Next, customers do not always show up on time or sometimes fail to show up at all. As a result, the operation ends up with unused services and lost revenues. For example, a common strategy for some golfers (particularly young and single) is to reserve a tee time at two or three different golf courses at two or three different times on the same day. Depending on their whims and which golf course they decide to play that particular day, the golfers choose which tee time to use, leaving the other two golf courses holding the tee for a foursome that is not going to show up. Given that the greens fee for an 18-hole round with riding cart averages at least $50, the golf course has just lost $200 that it could have otherwise collected by filling the spot with another foursome.

Another drawback of reservation systems is that they offer the customer an implied guarantee that the service will be available at a specified time, thereby increasing the customer's expectation. All too often, this implied guarantee is not met. For example, customers with early appointments may show up late, causing a chain reaction of delayed appointments for the rest of the day. Similarly, the rate at which restaurant tables turn over is difficult to determine and further compounded by the size of the party sitting at a table compared with the size of the party waiting for a table. In addition, medical doctors schedule as many as four patients at the same appointment time in an attempt to serve patient demand. Despite the use of reservation systems, customers may still end up waiting and become even more unhappy (compared with a "first come, first serve" system) because of the implied promise made by the reservation system.

**complimentary services** Services provided for consumers to minimize their perceived waiting time, such as driving ranges at golf courses, arcades at movie theaters, or reading materials in doctors' offices.

*Demand Strategy: Shift Demand to Complimentary Services*   Companies can also buffer the challenges associated with perishability by developing **complimentary services** that directly relate to the core service offering. A lounge in a restaurant is a typical example of a complimentary service that not only provides the space to store customers while they wait, but also provides the restaurant with an additional source of revenue. Similarly, golf courses often provide putting greens for their customers as a form of complimentary service. Although free of charge to customers, the putting green occupies the customer's time, minimizing their perceived waiting time. The end result is more satisfied customers. Other complimentary services that have been developed to help manage demand include driving ranges at golf courses, arcades at movie theaters, reading materials in doctors' offices, and televisions in the waiting areas of hospital emergency rooms.

**nonpeak demand development** A strategy in which service providers use their downtime to prepare in advance for peak periods or by marketing to a different target markets that follow different demand pattern than the firm's traditional market segment.

*Demand Strategy: The Effective Use of Nonpeak Demand Periods*   Developing nonpeak demand can also modify the effects of perishability. **Nonpeak demand development** utilizes service downtime to prepare in advance for peak periods, and/or to market to different market segments with different demand patterns. Consequently, nonpeak demand development can reduce the effects of perishability in two ways. First, employees can be cross-trained during nonpeak demand periods to perform a variety of other duties to assist fellow personnel (e.g., dishwashers may trained to set up and clear tables) during peak demand periods. In addition, although services cannot be stored, the tangibles associated with the service (such as salads at a restaurant) can be premade and ready prior to the service encounter. Advance preparation activities such as these free personnel to perform other types of service when needed.

Second, nonpeak demand can also be developed to generate additional revenues by marketing to a different market segment that has a different demand pattern than the firm's traditional segment. For example, golf courses have filled nonpeak demand by marketing to housewives, senior citizens, and shift workers (e.g., factory workers, nurses, students, and teachers) who use the golf course during the morning and afternoon hours—traditionally slow periods during weekdays. These groups exhibit different demand patterns than traditional golfers, who work from 8 a.m. to 5 p.m. and demand golf course services in the late afternoons, early evenings, and on weekends.

*Supply Strategy: Utilize Part-Time Employees*   In addition to managing consumer demand, the effects of perishability can also be minimized through strategies that make additional supply available in times of need. One such supply strategy is the use of part-time employees to assist during peak demand periods. Retailers have successfully used part-time employees to increase their supply of service during the holidays for years.

The advantages of employing part-time workers as opposed to adding additional full-time staff include lower labor costs and a flexible labor force that can be employed when needed and released during nonpeak periods. On the negative side, using part-time employees sometimes causes consumers to associate the firm with lower job skills and lack of motivation and organizational commitment. Such traits subsequently lead to dissatisfied customers. However, these disadvantages appear most commonly in organizations that staff their operations with part-time workers on a full-time basis, as opposed to those employing part-time employees only during peak demand periods.

**capacity sharing**
Strategy to increase the supply of service by forming a type of co-op among service providers that permits co-op members to expand their supply or service as a whole.

*Supply Strategy: Capacity Sharing*   Another method of increasing the supply of service is **capacity sharing,** forming a type of service co-op with other service providers, which permits the co-op to expand its supply of service as a whole. For example, many professional medical service providers are combining their efforts by sharing the cost and storage of expensive diagnostic equipment. By sharing the cost, each service firm can supply forms of service it may not otherwise be able to provide because of the prohibitive costs associated with purchasing such equipment. In addition, the funds saved through cost sharing are freed to spend on additional resources such as equipment, supplies, and additional personnel, expanding the supply of service to consumers even further. Surgery centers and other medical group practices offer typical examples of capacity sharing in application.

**expansion preparation**
Planning for future expansion in advance and taking a long-term orientation to physical facilities and growth.

*Supply Strategy: Prepare in Advance for Expansion*   Although the strategy of **expansion preparation** does not provide a "quick fix" to the supply problems associated with perishability, it may save months in reacting to demand pressures, not to mention thousands of dollars in expansion costs. In the effort to prepare in advance for expansion, many service firms are taking a long-term orientation with regard to constructing their physical facilities.

For example, one local airport terminal was built with future expansion in mind. This terminal was built on a isolated portion of the airport property, where no adjoining structure would interfere with future growth. All plumbing and electrical lines were extended to the ends on both sides of the building and capped, making "hook-ups" easier when expansion becomes a reality. Even the road leading to the terminal was curved in the expectation that new terminal additions will follow along this predetermined pattern.

**third parties** A supply strategy in which a service firm uses an outside party to service customers and thereby save on costs, personnel, etc.

*Supply Strategy: Utilization of Third Parties*   A service firm can also expand its supply of a service through use of third parties. Service organizations frequently use **third parties** to service customers and thereby save on costs, personnel, etc. Travel agencies are a typical example. Travel agents provide the same information to customers as an airline's own representatives. This third-party arrangement, however, enables the airline to reduce the number of personnel it employs to make flight reservations and lets it redirect the efforts of existing personnel to other service areas. The cost savings associated with using third parties is evidenced by the airlines' willingness to pay commissions to travel agencies for booking flights.

Note that although the use of third parties increases the supply of service, this type of arrangement may expose customers to competitive offerings as well. As a result, a tradeoff does exist. Many third parties, such as travel agents, represent a variety of suppliers. A customer who intended to book a flight on British Airways may end up taking a Lufthansa flight because of a more compatible flight schedule and/or a less expensive fare. This type of competitive information would not have been available if the customer had called British Airways directly to make the flight reservation.

**customer participation**
A supply strategy that increases the supply of service by having the customer perform part of the service, such as providing a salad bar or dessert bar in a restaurant.

*Supply Strategy: Increase Customer Participation*   Another method for increasing the supply of service available is to have the customer perform part of the service. For example, in many fast-food restaurants, **customer participation** means giving customers a cup and expecting them to fill their own drink orders. In other restaurants, customers make their own salads at a "salad bar," dress their own sandwiches at the "fixings bar," prepare plates of food at the "food bar," and make their own chocolate sundaes at the "dessert bar."

Without a doubt we are performing more and more of our own services every day. We pump our own gas, complete our own bank transactions at automatic teller machines, and bag our own groceries at local supermarkets. In fact, one of the major advantages of a website is that it enables customers to help themselves, or at least be more prepared when they request help from service personnel. However, although self-service does free employees to provide other services, a number of advantages and disadvantages are associated with customer participation. The willingness of customers to provide their own service is generally a function of convenience, price, and customization. For example, automatic teller machines offer the customer the convenience of 24-hour banking, bagging groceries is generally accompanied by faster check-out processes, and Dell provides customers the opportunity to configure their own personal computer order to their own individual specifications.

In contrast, customer participation may also be associated with a number of disadvantages that predominantly concern loss of control. In many instances, the more the customer becomes a major player in the production of the service, the less control the service firm is able to maintain over the quality of the service provided. For example, the physician who instructs a patient to administer his own medicine relinquishes control over the outcome of the prescribed care. Quality control may also suffer as a result of confused customers who decrease the efficiency of the operating system. Customer confusion in a self-service environment is likely to affect not only the outcome of the confused customer's service, but also the delivery process of "other customers" who are sharing that customer's experience. For example, customers who are standing in line behind a customer who is using an ATM for the first time experience the effects of the new customer's learning curve.

The loss of quality control may also be accompanied by the loss of control over operating costs. Self-service, particularly in the food industry, is associated with waste as a result of abuse of the system. Customers may take more food than they would normally order and then consume or share food with nonpaying friends. Finally, increasing customer participation may be interpreted by some as the service firm's attempt to physically distance itself from the customer. As a result, the image of an uncaring, unresponsive, and out-of-touch firm may develop, driving many customers away to full-service competitors. Hence, the tradeoff is apparent. While increasing customer participation frees service providers to offer additional services and may provide the customer with increased convenience, opportunities for customization, and reduced prices, this strategy may also create unhappy customers who are forced to fend for themselves.

## The Structure of This Text

This chapter has outlined the key factors that distinguish services marketing from goods marketing, and has highlighted challenges that are unique to service marketers. Due to the characteristics of intangibility, inseparability, heterogeneity, and perishability, marketing plays a very different role in service-oriented organizations than it does in pure goods organizations. As a result of these four unique service characteristics, this chapter has shown how closely the different components of the Servuction model presented in Chapter 1 are interwoven. The *invisible and visible parts of the organization*, the *contact personnel* and the *physical environment*, the organization and its customers, and indeed the customers themselves are all bound together by a complex series of relationships. Consequently the marketing staff must maintain a much closer relationship with the rest of the service organization than is customary in traditional goods-producing companies. The philosophy of the operations department being solely responsible for producing the product, the human resources department being solely responsible for employees, and the marketing department being responsible for issues solely relating to the customer does not work well within a service firm. Service firms that excel understand the interrelationships among these core functional areas and work together to create a seamless service experience for the customer.

## An Overview of Services Marketing

Thus far, Chapters 1, 2 and 3 have introduced the fundamentals of the service experience, provided an overview of service industries and ethical considerations, and detailed the unique challenges associated with the marketing of services. The remainder of this text is organized around the framework provided in Figure 3.5. At the heart of services marketing must be the consumer and Chapter 4 (Consumer Decision Making in Services Marketing) focuses on building your understanding of the behavior of service consumers as they select service providers and then evaluate their satisfaction with the service that they have received. Chapter 4 provides concepts and frameworks that permeate the rest of this book as service firms adapt their marketing mixes to reflect the changing needs of their customers.

## The Tactical Services Marketing Mix

One of the most basic ideas in marketing is the marketing mix. The marketing mix represents the levers that the organization controls. These levers can be used to influence consumers' choice processes as well as their evaluation of service satisfaction. The traditional marketing mix is often expressed as the 4 Ps—product, place, price, and promotion. As Figure 3.5 illustrates, due to the fundamental differences between goods and services presented in this chapter, the Services Marketing Mix can be redefined and

**FIG-3.5** Overview of Services Marketing Chapters

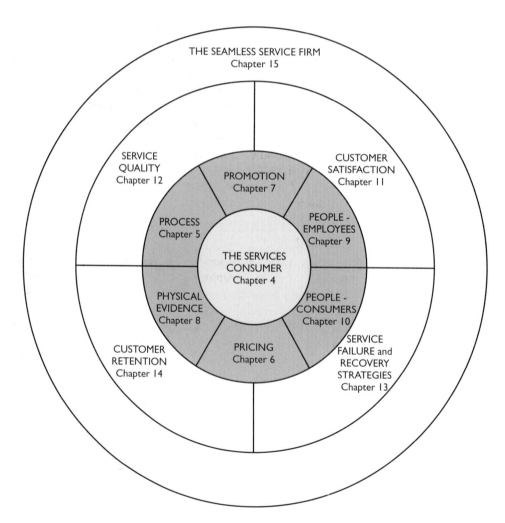

expanded offering the three additional marketing mix variables of *process*, the *physical environment*, and *people*.

Given the importance of the services marketing mix, Part 2 of this text focuses upon *The Tactical Services Marketing Mix* and on the marketing mix variables that must be the most modified for competing in service marketing environments. More specifically, Chapter 5 hones in on the *Focus on Service Processes*; Chapter 6 examines the *Considerations for Services Pricing*; Chapter 7 investigates *Effective Service Promotions*; Chapter 8 addresses *Managing the Servicescape and Other Physical Evidence;* and Chapters 9 and 10 explore the people issues surrounding services marketing, including *Managing Service Personnel* and *Managing Service Consumers* respectively.

### Implementing Successful Service Strategies

Marketing's role with the rest of the organization is the theme for Part 3 of the book, which focuses on *Implementing Successful Service Strategies.* Marketing is at the heart of each of these strategies but their execution is dependent on harnessing all of the functions: Operations, Human Resources, and Marketing. As such, Chapter 11, *The Essentials of Customer Satisfaction Measurement*, expands the consumer behavior chapter to explore how it is possible to satisfy a customer in a particular service experience and how to measure and manage satisfaction. Chapter 12, *Service Quality: Identifying and Rectifying the Gaps*, builds upon Chapter 11 and increases our understanding of how consumers evaluate services and the longer-term concept of service quality. Due to the complexity of the various relationships that comprise a typical service encounter, service failures are inevitable, but because of inseparability it is often possible to recover from a failure situation during the service encounter. Chapter 13 discusses how to successfully master the art of *Managing Service Failures and Implementing Effective Recovery Strategies.*

Given the current competitive situation among many service firms, Chapter 14 deals with *Strategies for Facilitating Customer Loyalty and Retention* as an important strategy for service firms to seriously consider. Finally, Chapter 15 *(Pulling the Pieces Together: Creating a World-Class Service Culture)* examines the role of marketing within the service organization. It juxtaposes the industrial management model and the market focused model, and shows how important the latter is for a service business. This final chapter also discusses the key components of creating a world class service culture.

## Summary

The major differences between the marketing of goods and the marketing of services are most commonly attributed to the four distinguishing characteristics—intangibility, inseparability, heterogeneity, and perishability. This chapter has discussed the marketing challenges presented by these four characteristics and described possible solutions that minimize their impact on service firms.

Intangibility means that services lack physical substance and therefore cannot be touched or evaluated like goods. The marketing challenges associated with intangibility include difficulties in communicating services to consumers, pricing decisions, patent protection, and storage of services for future use. Strategies developed to offset the challenges posed by intangibility include the use of tangible clues, organizational image

development, the development of personal sources of information that consumers access when selecting service providers, and the use of activity-based costing procedures.

Inseparability reflects the interconnection between service providers and their customers. Unlike the producers of goods, service providers engage in face-to-face interactions with their customers, who are directly involved in the service production process. Strategies developed to minimize the challenges of inseparability include the selective screening and thorough training of customer contact personnel, the implementation of strategies that attempt to manage customers throughout the service experience, and the use of multisite facilities to overcome the inseparability difficulties associated with centralized mass production.

Heterogeneity pertains to the variability inherent in the service delivery process. The primary marketing problem associated with heterogeneity is that standardization and quality control are difficult for a service firm to provide on a regular basis. Service firms typically react to heterogeneity in two diverse directions. Some firms try to standardize performance through intensive training or by replacing human labor with machines. In contrast, other firms take advantage of the variability by offering customized services that meet individual customer needs. Neither strategy is universally superior, because customer preference for customization versus standardization is dependent on price, speed of delivery, and consistency of performance.

Perishability refers to the service provider's inability to store or inventory services. Services that are not used at their appointed time cease to exist. Moreover, because services cannot be inventoried, the few times that supply matches demand often occur by accident. A variety of strategies have been developed to try to offset the potential problems created by perishability. Some strategies attack the problems by attempting to manage demand, while others attempt to manage supply. Demand management strategies include creative pricing strategies, reservation systems, staging demand through complimentary services, and developing nonpeak demand periods. Supply management strategies include using part-time employees, capacity sharing, third-party utilization, increasing customer participation in the production process, and preparing in advance for future expansion to reduce the response time in reaction to demand increases.

Due to the challenges posed by intangibility, inseparability, heterogeneity, and perishability, marketing plays a very different role in service-oriented organizations than it does in pure goods organizations. The philosophy of the operations department being solely responsible for producing the product, the human resources department being solely responsible for employees, and the marketing department being responsible for issues solely relating to the customer does not work well within a service firm. The four characteristics presented in this chapter that distinguish the marketing of goods from the marketing of services provide ample evidence that the invisible and visible parts of the organization, the contact personnel, the physical environment, and the organization and its customers are bound together by a complex set of relationships. As a result, marketing must maintain a much closer relationship with the rest of the service organization than is customary in a traditional goods manufacturing organization.

## Key Terms

service-dominant logic, p. 57
intangibility, p. 57
physical evidence/tangible
  clues, p. 60
personal sources
  of information, p. 60
activity-based costing (ABC), p. 62
inseparability, p. 63
critical incident, p. 63

"other customers", p. 65
consumer management, p. 68
multisite locations, p. 68
factories in the field, p. 68
heterogeneity, p. 68
customization, p. 69
standardization, p. 70
perishability, p. 71
creative pricing, p. 74

reservation system, p. 74
complimentary services, p. 75
nonpeak demand development,
  p. 75
capacity sharing, p. 76
expansion preparation, p. 76
third parties, p. 76
customer participation, p. 76

## Review Questions

1. Briefly describe how the unique service characteristics of intangibility, inseparability, heterogeneity and perishability apply to your educational experience in your services marketing class.
2. Discuss why the pricing of services is particularly difficult in comparison with the pricing of goods.
3. What strategies have the insurance industry utilized in its attempt to minimize the effects of intangibility? Of the companies that have actively attempted to minimize the effects, have some

companies done a better job than others? Please explain.
4. Discuss the pros and cons of having the customer involved in the production process.
5. Discuss the reasons why the centralized mass production of services is challenging.
6. What is meant by the term "other customers" and why is their influence so much greater for services compared to goods?

7. Why are standardization and quality control difficult to maintain throughout the service delivery process?

8. Which is better for consumers: (1) a customized service or (2) a standardized service? Please explain.

9. What are the limitations associated with a service firm's inability to maintain inventories?

10. A number of supply and demand strategies were presented as possible solutions to offset the challenges created by the perishability of services. (1) Discuss the major objective of demand strategies in comparison to supply strategies. (2) To which group of strategies does "increasing consumer participation" belong? (3) How does "increasing consumer participation" solve potential problems caused by the perishability of services?

## Notes

1. Leonard L. Berry and A. Parasuraman, "Building a New Academic Field—The Case of Services Marketing," *Journal of Retailing* 69 (Spring 1993), 1, 13.

2. The framework for this chapter was adapted from Figures 2 and 3 in Valerie A. Zeithaml, A. Parasuraman, and Leonard L. Berry, "Problems and Strategies in Services Marketing," *Journal of Marketing* 49 (Spring 1985), 33–46. For a more in-depth discussion of each of the problems and strategies associated with services marketing, consult Figures 2 and 3 in this article for the appropriate list of references.

3. Adapted from John E. G. Bateson, *Managing Services Marketing,* 3rd ed. (Fort Worth, TX.: The Dryden Press, 1995), 9.

4. David Ballyntyne and Richard J. Varey, "The Service-Dominant Logic and the Future of Marketing," *Journal of the Academy of Marketing Science* 36, no. 1 (March 2008), 11–14.

5. Beth M. Chaffman and John Talbott, "Activity-based Costing in a Service Organization," *CMA Magazine* (December 1990/January 1991), pp. 15–18.

6. Bateson, *Managing Services Marketing,* p. 9.

7. Jim Kelley, "From Lip Service to Real Service: Reversing America's Downward Service Spiral," *Vital Speeches of the Day* 64, no. 10 (1998), 301–304.

8. Bateson, *Managing Services Marketing,* p. 18.

9. Ibid., 11–13.

10. The framework and materials for this section were adapted from W. Earl Sasser, "Match Supply and Demand in Service Industries," *Harvard Business Review* (November/December 1976), 133–140.

# Online Air Travel: Expedia, Orbitz, and Travelocity Lead the Pack

In more traditional times, booking an airline ticket involved one of three basic options. First, a customer could call the airline directly to speak to a customer service representative. The second option involved speaking to a travel agent over the phone or visiting with a travel agent at the local travel agent's office. The third option required traveling to the local airport to purchase the ticket from a ticketing agent. All three of these options still exist today; however, many customers have opted to purchase their airline tickets from web-based services such as Expedia, Orbitz, and Travelocity. In addition, the airline's own websites such as united.com, singaporeair.com, and lufthansa.com have become popular methods to purchase airline tickets.

There are many benefits for offering and purchasing tickets for sale via the web. From the company's perspective, the web offers an additional distribution outlet that not only makes tickets more available to the public but also provides an additional means to communicate the firm's promotional messages. Given the web's self-service nature, additional ticket sales are obtained without the aid of customer service representatives, which in turn lowers the firm's overall labor cost. For those customers that use the web for purely informational purposes, but still prefer to transact business with a "live" customer service representative, the web facilitates the efficiency of the purchase. After reviewing potential options on the web and conferring with family members and/or business associates, customers are more specific regarding their ticketing requests, increasing the speed in which the transaction can be completed.

Customers also enjoy a number of benefits from using web-based services to purchase airline tickets. First, web-based services are typically readily available. There are no busy signals, no being placed on "hold" or waiting in line for one's turn. Second, web-based services such as Expedia, Orbitz, and Travelocity all display a number of competing options in terms of price, schedule, and number of layovers for the same destination. In fact, new travel sites such as Kayak.com will display the search results from as many as five travel search engines simultaneously. Consequently, the customer's information search abilities are greatly enhanced. Customers can also easily obtain information regarding the type of aircraft to be flown, select seat locations, and redeem frequent flyer miles if desired. Moreover, many of these services also provide ancillary services such as opportunities to purchase flight insurance, hotel and rental car accommodations, and even show tickets to select locations.

Sources: **www.kayak.com; www.travelocity.com; www.expedia.com; and www.orbitz.com**, accessed 4 December, 2009.

## Discussion Questions

1. Does the service characteristic of intangibility change once a service is placed on the web? Please explain. How can a service provider "tangibilize' their service on the web?

2. Does the service characteristic of inseparability change once a service is placed on the web? Please explain.

3. Does the service characteristic of heterogeneity change once a service is placed on the web? Please explain.

4. Does the service characteristic of perishability change once a service is placed on the web? Please explain.

5. Why would an airline, such as Southwest Airlines, not participate with online travel search engines such as Expedia, Orbitz, and Travelocity?

# CHAPTER 4

# Consumer Decision Making in Services Marketing

## CHAPTER OBJECTIVES

After reading this chapter, you should be able to:

- Appreciate the value of models that attempt to explain how consumers process information.

- Discuss the six steps that comprise the consumer decision process model.

- Understand the special considerations of service purchases as they pertain to the *prepurchase*, *consumption*, and *postpurchase* stages of the consumer decision process model.

- Describe three theories that attempt to explain the consumer's postpurchase evaluation with regards to customer satisfaction.

In this chapter we discuss consumer decision process issues as they relate to the purchase of services.

### FRONTIER AIRLINES: A WHOLE DIFFERENT ANIMAL

Denver-based Frontier Airlines understands its customers and competitive situation very well. Frontier accepts that it cannot compete effectively against United Airlines for business travelers flying in and out of Denver, Colorado. United is simply too big, has far more planes, and flies to too many destinations multiple times throughout the day. So who are Frontier's primary customers?

Rick Wilking/Reuters/Landov

Frontier's primary customers are the price-sensitive, non-business travelers who purchase plane tickets for vacations or to visit friends and family. Who primarily purchases the tickets for these types of trips? In a word, women. These same women often have kids in tow who can also have a say in airline ticket purchase decisions. Never underestimate the influential power of children. It has been estimated that 4 to 12 year olds influence the spending of nearly $700 billion a year in the U.S.

Based on Frontier's understanding of its consumer decision making processes, the airline focuses on what it calls "one comfortable class of service"—coach. To begin, most of Frontier's jets are much newer, on average a decade newer, than its competitors. As a result, the interiors of the aircraft are in excellent condition which positively influences passenger safety perceptions. Second, Frontier offers one inch to two inches more legroom than most other airlines which might not sound like much, but it truly makes a difference, especially when traveling with children. Third, Frontier's in-flight entertainment system offering 24 channels of live DIRECTV® in each seatback is a life saver when it comes to keeping the kids occupied. Finally, Frontier's Emmy-award winning advertising campaign featuring unique animal images such as Grizwald the Bear, Jack the Rabbit, and Larry the Lynx that adorn the tails of 60 different Frontier aircraft were intentionally designed to be very family friendly.

In fact, the airline has video that documents mothers and children peering through terminal jetways to catch a glimpse of which one of Frontier's namesake animals is proudly displayed on the tail of today's flight. Further evidence of the success of Frontier's use of animal mascots was provided during a five-week advertising campaign that allowed customers to vote on a name for a new animal mascot. The company's website collected over one million votes that were cast online which netted increased traffic to the airline's site by 50 percent compared with the previous year.

Frontier further caters to its customers now by offering three different classes of coach seating: Economy, Classic, and Classic Plus. *Economy* seating offers the lowest price for passengers if the customer is willing to make some concessions. For example, passengers flying economy receive seat assignments at check-in, are charged $20 for their first checked bag and $30 for their second checked bag, and DIRECTV® is available for purchase. In contrast, *Classic* seating offers advanced seating assignments, first and second checked bags are free, free DIRECTV®, frequent flyer passengers rewarded with 125 percent EarlyReturns Mileage and a two-for-one lift ticket at Winter Park or Copper Mountain ski resorts. Finally, *Classic Plus* offers a fully-refundable ticket, advanced seat assignment, stretch seating (where available), priority boarding, first and second checked bags are free, free DIRECTV®, free snacks and beverages, 150 percent EarlyReturns Mileage, and the two-for-one lift ticket at Winter Park or Copper Mountain. Ultimately, the three classes of seating allow customers to customize their own decisions regarding price and service options as opposed to being offered a standardized service product from the airline.

For its efforts, Frontier Airlines has been voted the "Best Low Cost Carrier" by the readers of *Business Traveler* magazine, and one of the Top Five Domestic Airlines by readers of *Travel & Leisure* magazine. Given Frontier's understanding of its customers and the adaptations it has made to its service product to suit the needs of its target market, the airline truly lives up to its marketing slogan, "a whole different animal."

Source: **http://www.usatoday.com/travel/columnist/grossman/2007-02-25-frontier-airlines_x.htm**, accessed 13 November, 2009.

## Introduction

Consumer orientation lies at the heart of the marketing concept.[1] As marketers, we are required to understand our consumers and to build our organizations around them. As Jeff Bezos of Amazon.com puts it, "We see our customers as invited guests to a party,

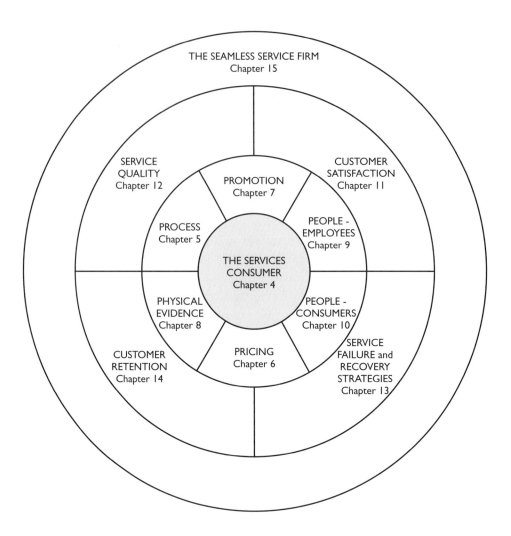

and we are the hosts. It's our job everyday to make every important aspect of the customer experience a little bit better."[2] Understanding consumers and improving the experience is particularly important for services, which in many instances still tend to be operations-dominated rather than customer-oriented. Case in point: Richard Branson, best known for his Virgin brand of over 360 companies, explains, "I never get the accountants in before I start up a business. It is done on gut feeling, especially if I can see that they [the operations-dominant accountants] are taking the mickey out of the consumer."[3] Given today's economic and competitive environment, it is more important than ever to understand consumers, how they choose among alternative services offered to them, and how they evaluate these services once they have received them.

Throughout the three primary stages of the consumer decision making—*prepurchase, consumption* and *postpurchase evaluation*—the consumer must be using a process or model to make his or her decision. Although a variety of models have been developed and are discussed in this chapter, it is important to point out that no model is wholly accurate. The consumer's mind is still closed to us; it is a "black box" that remains sealed. We can observe inputs to the box and the decisions made as a result, but we can never know how the act of processing inputs (information) truly happens.

Why, then, bother with such models? Whether marketing managers like it or not, every time they make marketing decisions, they are basing their decisions on some model of how the consumer will behave. Quite often these models are implicit and seldom shared with others, representing, in effect, the marketing manager's own experience. However, every time a price is changed, a new product is launched, or advertising appears, some assumption has been made about how the consumer will react.

The purpose of this chapter is to discuss the consumer decision process as it relates to the purchase of services. Due to the unique characteristics of services, differences exist between the way consumers make decisions regarding services versus goods. This chapter has been constructed in two sections. The first section is a broad overview of the consumer decision-making process. It provides a summary of the process and its applications to marketing decisions. The second section of the chapter is dedicated to specific considerations pertaining to the consumer decision-making process as it relates to services.

## The Consumer Decision Process: An Overview

To market services effectively, marketing managers need to understand the thought processes used by consumers during each of the three stages of the **consumer decision process**: the prepurchase choice among alternatives, the consumer's reaction during consumption, and the postpurchase evaluation of satisfaction (see Figure 4.1). Although we can never truly know the thought process used by the individual when making that choice, the consumer decision process helps to structure our thinking and to guide our understanding regarding consumer behavior. Let's begin this discussion by focusing on the prepurchase stage of the consumer decision process model which includes the phases of stimulus, problem awareness, information search, and evaluation of alternatives.

### The Prepurchase Stage: The Stimulus

The prepurchase stage of the consumer decision process refers to all consumer activities occurring before the acquisition of the service. This stage begins when an individual receives a **stimulus** that incites a consumer to consider a purchase.[4] The stimulus may be a commercial cue, a social cue, or a physical cue. **Commercial cues** are the result of promotional efforts. For example, a consumer may be exposed to a commercial about a local college. As a result, the individual may begin to assess his or her current situation in life and the possibility of enrolling at a university to pursue a university degree. Similarly, **social cues** are obtained from the individual's peer group or from significant others. For example, watching friends leave for college in the fall, or watching peers who have completed college degrees being promoted at work may incite an individual to consider furthering his or her own education. Finally, the stimulus may also be the result of a **physical cue** such as thirst, hunger, or various other biological cues. Hypothetically, an individual may enroll in a university as a response to a biological need to find a suitable

### Margin glossary

**consumer decision process** The three-step process consumers use to make purchase decisions; includes the prepurchase stage, the consumption stage, and the postpurchase evaluation stage.

**stimulus** The thought, action, or motivation that incites a person to consider a purchase.

**commercial cue** An event or motivation that provides a stimulus to the consumer and is a promotional effort on the part of the company.

**social cue** An event or motivation that provides a stimulus to the consumer, obtained from the individual's peer group or from significant others.

**physical cue** A motivation, such as thirst, hunger, or another biological cue that provides a stimulus to the consumer.

**FIG-4.1** Consumer Decision Process Model

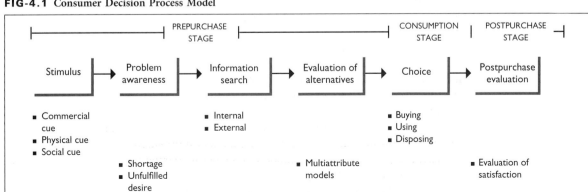

partner for marriage and to begin a family, or may begin to think more seriously about pursuing a college degree as they age. Upon receipt of a stimulus, the consumer begins to think about the product category (in this case a university education), and to assess their current situation by transitioning into the problem awareness phase of the prepurchase stage of consumer decision making. Managers of service firms can effectively utilize cues to stimulate customer decision making regarding their respective product categories. For example, in the hopes of promoting an eco-friendly environment, a public service announcement such as "each of us uses approximately an 110-foot-tall Douglas fir tree in paper and wood products per year" may provide the commercial cue necessary to influence changes in consumer behavior (See Sustainability and Services in Action).

## SUSTAINABILITY AND SERVICES *IN ACTION*

### The Top 10 Motivators for Consumers to Recycle

As the green movement takes hold, what can you as a consumer do to contribute to environmental health? The easy answer, as we all know, is to recycle. However, before consumers are willing to spend the time, effort, and money to begin a recycling plan, they need to be motivated to do so. It's one thing to talk about the green movement and what we as consumers can do to change it; it's another thing entirely to demonstrate an individual's impact on energy usage.

Of the many facts listed by the Oberlin College Recycling Program, here are the Top 10 Motivators for Consumers to Recycle:

1. **Paper makes an impact**. More than 56 percent of the paper consumed in the United States during 2007 was recovered for recycling—an all-time high. This impressive figure equals nearly 360 pounds of paper for each man, woman, and child in America.
2. **One spill can impact millions**. One gallon of used motor oil can contaminate 1 million gallons of water.
3. **Running water = light bulbs**. Letting your faucet run for five minutes uses about as much energy as letting a 60-watt light bulb run for 14 hours.
4. **You are 100 feet tall**. Each of us uses approximately one 100-foot-tall Douglas fir tree in paper and wood products per year.
5. **One aluminum can could power your house for a day**. Recycling one aluminum can saves enough energy to run a 100-watt bulb for 20 hours, a computer for three hours, or a TV for two hours.
6. **Styrofoam: the one trick pony of recycling**. Styrofoam is un-recyclable; you can't make it into new Styrofoam. The industry wants you to assume it is. The only way to combat this is to avoid purchasing it.
7. **Glass never wears out**. Glass can be recycled forever. We save over a ton of resources for every ton of glass recycled—1,330 pounds of sand, 433 pounds of soda ash, 433 pounds of limestone, and 151 pounds of feldspar.
8. **Recycling saves trees, space, and energy**. Recycling one ton of paper saves 17 mature trees, 7,000 gallons of water, three cubic yards of landfill space, two barrels of oil, and 4,100 kilowatt-hours of electricity—enough energy to power the average American home for five months.
9. **Recycle to make clothes**. Twenty-six recycled PET bottles equals a polyester suit. Five recycled PET bottles make enough fiberfill to stuff a ski jacket.
10. **Rubber bounces back efficiently**. Producing one pound of recycled rubber versus one pound of new rubber requires only 29 percent of the energy.

Source: "Recycling Facts." Oberlin College Recycling Program. *Oberlin College & Conservatory*. 2008. **http://www.oberlin.edu/recycle/facts.html**

## The Prepurchase Stage: Problem Awareness

**problem awareness**
The second phase of the prepurchase stage, in which the consumer determines whether a need exists for the product.

**Problem awareness** occurs when consumers realize that they need to do something to get back to a normal state of comfort. During the problem awareness phase of consumer decision making, the consumer examines whether a need or want truly exists for the product category. Ultimately, needs are unsatisfactory conditions of the consumer that prompt him or her to an action that will make the condition better. In contrast, wants are desires to obtain more satisfaction than is absolutely necessary to improve an unsatisfactory condition. Accordingly, problem awareness may be based on a **shortage** (a need) or on an **unfulfilled desire** (a want). For example, if the consumer is motivated by a commercial cue to pursue a college degree and is not currently enrolled in a university, then a shortage exists. In contrast, if the consumer is currently enrolled in a university and no longer values that particular institution but still would like to complete their degree at an another university, then an unfulfilled desire exists. Finally, if the consumer does not recognize a shortage or unfulfilled desire the decision process stops at this point. Otherwise, the decision process continues as the consumer seeks to resolve their current problem and proceeds on to the information search phase of consumer decision making. Managers that better understand consumer needs and wants more fully appreciate the motivations of the consumer for seeking their product category in the first place. Communication messages that reinforce these motivations, such as a college billboard that states, "Tired of Working in that Same Old Job?" further motivate consumers to take definitive actions to return to a normal state of comfort.

**shortage** The need for a product or service due to the consumer's not having that particular product or service.

**unfulfilled desire** The need for a product or service due to a consumer's dissatisfaction with a current product or service.

**information search** The phase in the prepurchase stage in which the consumer collects information pertaining to possible alternatives.

## The Prepurchase Stage: Information Search

**awareness set** The set of alternatives of which a consumer is aware.

The awareness of a problem demands a solution from the individual, and usually implies that a potential purchase will ensue. The individual searches for alternatives during the information search phase of the prepurchase stage. As the name implies, during the **information search** phase, the consumer collects information regarding possible alternatives that will ultimately resolve the consumer's problem. It is clear that in all consumer decision making, consumers seldom consider all feasible alternatives. Instead, they have a limited list of options chosen on the basis of past experience, convenience, and knowledge. This list is often referred to by theorists as the **awareness set**—the set of alternatives of which a consumer is aware. This list of alternatives is further narrowed down at the time of actual decision making. Alternatives that the consumer actually remembers at the time of decision making are referred to as the **evoked set**. Of the brands in the evoked set, those considered unfit (e.g., too expensive, too far away, etc.) are eliminated right away. The remaining alternatives are termed the **consideration set**.

**evoked set** Alternatives that the consumer actually remembers at the time of decision making.

**consideration set** Of the brands in the evoked set, those considered unfit (e.g., too expensive, too far away, etc.) are eliminated right away. The remaining alternatives are termed the consideration set.

Returning to our college selection example, when considering alternatives, the consumer may first engage in an internal search. An **internal search** accesses the consumer's own memories about possible alternative colleges. In this example, the previous knowledge may be based on the proximity to a local college, information obtained while watching local sporting events, or listening to older family members reminisce about their own college experiences. An internal search is a passive approach to gathering information. The internal search may be followed by an **external search**, which would involve the collection of new information obtained via campus visits, talking to friends, and/or reading specific magazines that rate universities on an annual basis. Based on internal and external search processes the consumer works their way through a possible broad range of alternatives and narrows their search from an awareness set to an evoked to a final consideration set of alternatives. Managers that understand consumer information search processes have a much better chance of strategically locating information and making information easily accessible to consumers. In turn, this greatly improves

**internal search** A passive approach to gathering information in which the consumer's own memory is the main source of information about a product.

**external search** A proactive approach to gathering information in which the consumer collects new information from sources outside the consumer's own experience.

**evaluation of alternatives** The phase of the prepurchase stage in which the consumer places a value or "rank" on each alternative.

**nonsystematic evaluation** Choosing among alternatives in a random fashion or by a "gut-level feeling" approach.

**systematic evaluation** Choosing among alternatives by using a set of formalized steps to arrive at a decision.

**linear compensatory approach** A systematic model that proposes that the consumer creates a global score for each brand by multiplying the rating of the brand on each attribute by the importance attached to the attribute and adding the scores together.

the odds of the service provider being included in the consumer's consideration set of alternatives.

## The Prepurchase Stage: Evaluation of Alternatives

Once relevant information has been collected from both internal and external sources, the consumer arrives at a consideration set of alternative solutions to resolve the recognized problem. The possible solutions are considered in the **evaluation of alternatives** phase of the consumer decision process. This phase may consist of a **nonsystematic evaluation** of alternatives, such as the use of intuition—simply choosing an alternative by relying on a "gut-level feeling"—or it may involve a **systematic evaluation** technique, such as a multi-attribute choice model. Such systematic models utilize a set of formalized steps to arrive at a decision.

Marketing theorists have made extensive use of multi-attribute models to simulate the process of evaluating products.[5] According to these models, consumers employ a number of attributes or criteria as basic references when evaluating a service. For example, consumers may compare alternative universities based on location, tuition, admission requirements, academic reputation, degree programs, and sports programs. Consumers compute their preference for the service by summing the scores of the service on each individual attribute.

Within the evaluation of alternatives phase of the decision process, consumers are assumed to create a matrix similar to the one shown in Figure 4.2 to compare alternatives. The example in the table is the choice of a university for an undergraduate degree. Across the top of the table are two types of variables. The first is the consideration set of alternatives to be evaluated. As previously mentioned, this consideration set will, for various reasons, be less than an exhaustive list of all possible choices; in this example it includes CSU, OSU, UK, and MSU. The second type of variable is the importance weight with which the consumer ranks the various attributes that comprise the vertical axis of the table. For example, in Figure 4.2, the consumer weights location and tuition as the most important attributes, followed by academic reputation and degree programs, followed by admission requirements and sports programs. To complete the table, the consumer rates each alternative on each attribute based on his or her expectations of each attribute. For example, this particular consumer gives CSU top marks for location, lower marks for tuition and academic reputation, still lower marks for admission requirements and degree programs, and even lower marks for sports programs.

Given such a table, various choice processes have been suggested with which the consumer can use the table to make a decision. The **linear compensatory approach** proposes that the consumer create a global score for each brand by multiplying the rating

**FIG-4.2** Multi-attribute Choice Model for Evaluating Alternative Universities

| | CONSIDERATION SET OF UNIVERSITY ALTERNATIVES | | | | |
|---|---|---|---|---|---|
| **ATTRIBUTES** | **CSU** | **OSU** | **UK** | **MSU** | **IMPORTANCE WEIGHTS** |
| Location | 10* (10)** | 8(10) | 8(10) | 7(10) | 10 |
| Tuition | 9(10) | 7(10) | 7(10) | 8(10) | 10 |
| Admission Requirements | 8(8) | 8(8) | 8(8) | 8(8) | 8 |
| Academic Reputation | 9(9) | 10(9) | 8(9) | 8(9) | 9 |
| Degree Programs | 8(9) | 9(9) | 9(9) | 8(9) | 9 |
| Sports Programs | 7(8) | 10(8) | 10(8) | 8(8) | 8 |
| Totals | 463 | 465 | 447 | 422 | |

*Rankings range from 1 (lowest) – 10 (highest)

**Numbers in parentheses are the weights for each criterion

of the alternative on each attribute by the importance weight attached to the attribute and adding the scores together. CSU would score 10 × 10 (location) plus 9 × 10 (tuition) plus 8 × 8 (admission requirements), and so on. The university with the highest score, in this example OSU, is then chosen.

**lexicographic approach** A systematic model that proposes that the consumer make a decision by examining each attribute, starting with the most important, to rule out alternatives.

Another type of multi-attribute approach that has been suggested is the **lexicographic approach**. This approach describes so-called "lazy decision makers" who try to minimize the effort involved. They look at each attribute in turn, starting with the most important, and try to make a decision. The individual whose preferences are shown in Figure 4.2 would look first at location and rule out OSU, UK, and MSU. Thus, a different decision rule results in a different choice: CSU under the lexicographic model and OSU under the linear compensatory model.

Given the popularity of multi-attribute models, it is no surprise that they have been used to describe and explain the consumer's service decision processes. The merit of these models lies in their simplicity and explicitness. The attributes identified cover a wide range of concerns related to the service experience, and they are easily understood by service managers. For example, analyzing consumer multi-attribute models provides at least five valuable pieces of information:

1. A list of alternatives that are included in the consideration set.
2. The lists of attributes that consumers consider when making purchase decisions.
3. The importance weights attached to each attribute.
4. Performance beliefs, reflected by ratings, associated with a particular firm.
5. Performance beliefs, reflective by ratings, associated with the competition.

The tasks for management when using these models are relatively straightforward. For example, advertising can be used to stress a particular attribute on which the firm's service appears to be weak in the mind of consumers. A college may have had a poor academic reputation in the past, but advertising may change consumer perceptions by featuring the school's accomplishments. If necessary, competitive advertising can also be used to try and reduce the attribute scores obtained by competitors.

## The Consumption Stage: Choice

Thus far, we have discussed the prepurchase stage of the consumer decision process, which described the stimulus, problem recognition, information search, and evaluation of alternatives phases. An important outcome of the prepurchase stage is a decision to purchase one of the alternatives under consideration. During this consumption stage, the consumer may make a *store choice*—deciding to purchase from a particular outlet, or a *nonstore choice*—deciding to purchase from a catalog, the Internet, or a variety of mail-order possibilities. This decision is accompanied by a set of expectations about the performance of the product to be purchased. In the case of goods, the consumer then uses the product and disposes of any solid waste remaining. The activities of buying, using, and disposing are grouped together and labeled the **consumption process**.[6]

**consumption process** The activities of buying, using, and disposing of a product.

Understanding consumers' choice or purchase alternatives is important for managerial decision making. For example, banking services traditionally were only available at a centrally-located bank. Over the years, consumers have now become accustomed to conducting banking activities electronically via ATMs or online banking, or at grocery stores through branch banks that are physically located conveniently within the store itself.

## The Postpurchase Stage: Postpurhase Evaluation

Once a purchase has been made and as the product, whether a service or a good, is being consumed, postpurchase evaluation takes place. During this stage, consumers may

**cognitive dissonance**
Doubt in the consumer's mind regarding the correctness of the purchase decision.

experience varying levels of **cognitive dissonance**—doubt that the correct purchase decision has been made. Marketers often attempt to minimize the consumer's cognitive dissonance by reassuring the customer that the correct decision has been made. Strategies to minimize cognitive dissonance include aftersale contact with the customer, providing a reassuring letter in the packaging of the product, providing warranties and guarantees, and reinforcing the consumer's decision through the firm's advertising. For example, learning through the university's advertising that the college of choice has been nationally recognized by *U.S. News & World Report* would positively reinforce the consumer's enrollment decision. Simply stated, postpurchase evaluation is all about customer satisfaction, and customer satisfaction is the key outcome of the marketing process. Ultimately, customer satisfaction is achieved when consumers' perceptions meet or exceed their expectations. Customer satisfaction is an end in and of itself, but typically leads to customer loyalty and retention, which generates positive word-of-mouth recommendations, which lead to increased sales and profitability.

During the evaluation process of the postpurchase stage, multi-attribute models can once again be utilized. For this process, the choices of universities are replaced by two columns termed perception score and expectation score. The perception score for each attribute is obtained by the consumer after enrollment. Hence, the perception score reflects what the consumer actually believes has happened based on their own personal experience. The expectation score for each attribute was obtained from Figure 4.2 which reflected the consumer's expectations prior to actually attending the university selected.

The satisfaction score is then derived by creating a global score of the comparisons between perceptions and expectations weighted by the importance of each attribute. This is shown in Figure 4.3.

In this example, the customer chose OSU by using the multi-attribute choice matrix shown in Figure 4.2 and based on the linear compensatory approach. The expected levels on each attribute are, therefore, taken from that matrix. In reality, the tuition was increased, and the school did not live up to its academic reputation. The consumer, therefore, downgraded his evaluation on those attributes. Perceptions greater than expectations result in a positive satisfaction score and customers are said to be *delighted*. Perceptions equal to their expectations result in a satisfaction score of zero and customers are said to be *satisfied*. Perceptions less than expectations result in a negative satisfaction score and, as is the case for this example, customers are *dissatisfied* with their selection of OSU.

**FIG-4.3** University Selection: A Post Purchase Evaluation for OSU

| ATTRIBUTES | PERCEPTION SCORE[1] | EXPECTATION SCORE[2] | SATISFAC-TION SCORE[3] | CUSTOMER EVALUATION | IMPORTANCE WEIGHTS |
|---|---|---|---|---|---|
| Location | 8(10) | 8(10) | 0 | Satisfied | 10 |
| Tuition | 5(10) | 7(10) | −20 | Dissatisfied | 10 |
| Admission Requirements | 8(8) | 8(8) | 0 | Satisfied | 8 |
| Academic Reputation | 8(9) | 10(9) | −18 | Dissatisfied | 9 |
| Degree Programs | 10(9) | 9(9) | +9 | Delighted | 9 |
| Sports Programs | 10(8) | 10(8) | 0 | Satisfied | 8 |
| Totals | 436 | 465 | −29 | Dissatisfied | |

[1]Perception scores based on the student's actual experience.
[2]Expectation scores for OSU obtained from original multi-attribute model in Figure 4.2.
[3]Satisfaction Score = Perception − Expectation.

# Special Considerations Pertaining to Services

Although the consumer decision process model applies to both goods and services, unique considerations arise with respect to service purchases. Many of these special considerations can be directly attributed to the unique service characteristics of intangibility, inseparability, heterogeneity and perishability. The considerations addressed in this part of the chapter help in developing a deeper understanding of consumer behavior as it relates to the purchase of services.

## Prepurchase Stage Considerations: Perceived Risk

In contrast to consumers when purchasing goods, consumers of services tend to perceive a higher level of risk during the prepurchase decision stage. The concept of perceived risk as an explanation for customer purchasing behavior was first suggested in the 1960s.[7] The central theory is that consumer behavior involves risk in the sense that any action taken by a consumer will produce consequences that he or she cannot anticipate with any certainty, and some of which are likely to be unpleasant. Consequently, perceived risk is proposed to consist of two dimensions:

- *Consequence, the degree of importance and/or danger of the outcomes derived from any consumer decision.*
- *Uncertainty, the subjective possibility of the occurrence of these outcomes.*

Medical surgery provides an excellent example of how consequence and uncertainty play a major role in service purchases. With respect to uncertainty, the consumer may have never undergone surgery before and therefore has no idea what to expect. Moreover, even though the surgeon has performed the operation successfully hundreds of times in the past, the patient is not guaranteed that this particular surgery will end with the same successful outcome. Furthermore, uncertainty is likely to increase if the patient lacks sufficient knowledge prior to the operation concerning specific details of the surgery and its after effects. As for consequences, the consequences of a poor decision regarding surgery could be life threatening.

*Types of Risk*   As the idea of consumer perceived risk developed, five types of perceived risk were identified that were common in many purchase situations, based on five different kinds of outcomes: financial, performance, physical, social, and psychological.[8] **Financial risk** assumes that financial loss could occur if the purchase goes wrong or fails to operate correctly. **Performance risk** relates to the idea that the item or service purchased will not perform the task for which it was purchased. The **physical risk** of a purchase can emerge if something does go wrong, inflicting injury on the purchaser. **Social risk** suggests that there might be a loss of personal social status associated with a particular purchase (e.g., a fear that one's peer group will react negatively—"Who bought this?"). As perhaps a striking example of social risk, studies are now finding that users of self-checkout technologies such as those found at grocery stores feel a lot of pressure to perform as others wait patiently behind them to complete their transaction (See E-Services in Action). **Psychological risk** pertains to the influence of the purchase upon the individual's self-esteem. For example, an individual may not patronize certain theatre or sporting events because they are not consistent with their self-image.

*Risk and Standardization*   Much of the heightened level of perceived risk can be attributed to the difficulty in producing a standardized service product. In Chapter 3, we introduced the concept of heterogeneity. Because a service is an experience involving highly complex interactions, it is, not surprisingly, very difficult to replicate the experience from customer to customer or from day to day.[9] As a result, the customer may find

---

**financial risk** The possibility of a monetary loss if the purchase goes wrong or fails to operate correctly.

**performance risk** The possibility that the item or service purchased will not perform the task for which it was purchased.

**physical risk** The possibility that if something does go wrong, injury could be inflicted on the purchaser.

**social risk** The possibility of a loss in personal social status associated with a particular purchase.

**psychological risk** The possibility that a purchase will affect an individual's self-esteem.

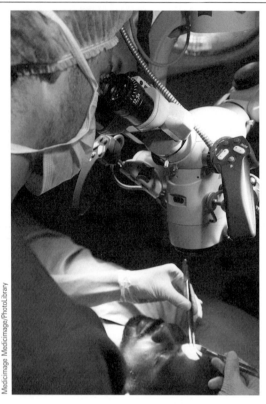

Medicimage Medicimage/PhotoLibrary

Elective surgery poses many risks for clients including financial, performance, physical, social and psychological risks.

it difficult to predict precisely the quality of service he or she will buy. The fact that the local State Farm Insurance agent works well with your neighbor does not guarantee that this same insurance agent will have exactly the same relationship with you. Perceived risk, therefore, tends to be higher for purchasing services in contrast to the purchase of goods.

***Co-Producer Risk***   The involvement of the consumer in the "production process of services" is another source of increased perceived risk. Co-producer risk is directly related to the concept of inseparability. Dental services provides a great example of the consumer's involvement in the production process. Unlike goods, which can be purchased and taken away, services cannot be taken home and used in private, where the buyer's mistakes will not be visible. Instead, the consumer must take part in the ritual of the service itself. To be part of such a process and not to know exactly what is going on clearly increases the uncertainty about the consequences, particularly the physical consequences of being involved in a service encounter such as dental care, or the social consequences of doing the "wrong" thing, such as wearing the wrong type of clothing to an important dinner party held at an upscale restaurant in the presence of other guests.

***Risk and Information***   Others have argued that the higher levels of risk associated with service purchases is due to the limited information that is readily available before the consumer makes the purchase decision. For example, the economics literature suggests that goods and services possess three different types of attributes:[10]

- ***Search attributes***—attributes that can be determined prior to purchase.
- ***Experience attributes***—attributes that can be evaluated only during and after the production process.

**search attributes**
Product attributes that can be determined prior to purchase.

**experience attributes**
Product attributes that can be evaluated only during and after the production process.

## E-SERVICES *IN ACTION*

### Self Checkout: Why Consumers Might Stay Away

Consider why you would want to use a self checkout kiosk at a grocery store. Would it be to reduce your waiting time or speed up the transaction? Would you prefer to avoid potentially negative interaction with employees? Or, would you like to avoid the "impulse buy" products lining traditional checkout lines to remove yourself from temptation? No matter the reason, people usually choose the self checkout options to improve their overall experience. Researchers have found, however, that the self checkout option has an opposite effect in many cases.

Grocery stores have been using self checkout kiosks since 1992, and consumer reactions to them have been varied. It is easy to see why stores have implemented them: they reduce labor costs and minimize potential conflicts by limiting interaction between consumers and employees. Customers' reactions, however, have raised questions about the best way to implement the technology.

An article published by AOL describes consumer behaviors towards self checkout options as "stage fright"; in other words, people avoid them when there are too many other customers assembling. People simply do not appreciate looking dumb or stupid, so confidence levels drop when the pressure of the waiting masses builds. This leads to consumers opting out of using self checkout, even if the traditional checkout lines are much longer. Discomfort levels also rise when items such as condoms are in the general vicinity of the kiosks. Further, off-putting interaction can increase due to emotions such as impatience, frustration, and anger on behalf of other consumers. All of these factors combine to have a negative impact on the consumer's self checkout experience.

So, the question remains as to how managers and companies can improve the consumer self checkout experience in an effort to cater to consumer behaviors. Researchers note that it is best to have the self checkout area somewhere with lower traffic and neutral products. The lack of peer pressure from other consumers will soothe users, while the neutral products create a welcoming environment. The hope is that these elements will increase consumer confidence and empower people to utilize self checkout kiosks to a greater extent.

Source: Cardona, Mercedes. "Self-checkout machines cause 'stage fright' in shoppers." *DailyFinance*. (30 October 2009), **http://www.dailyfinance.com/2009/10/30/self-checkout-machines-cause-stage-fright-in-shoppers/**

**credence attributes**
Product attributes that cannot be evaluated confidently even immediately after receipt of the good or the service.

- *Credence attributes*—attributes that cannot be evaluated confidently, even immediately after receipt of the good or service.

Search attributes typically consist of tangibles that can be evaluated prior to purchases. For example, when purchasing an automobile, the buyer can see the automobile, sit in it and fiddle with all of gadgets new automobiles frequently offer, and take the vehicle for a test drive. The same cannot be said for most services. Because of the intangible nature of services, it is often extremely difficult for consumers to objectively evaluate a service prior to its purchase. Services thus have very few search attributes.

A large proportion of the properties possessed by services (e.g., the friendliness of the flight attendants of a particular airline or the skill level of a hairstylist) can be discovered by consumers only during and after the consumption of the service; these are referred to as experience attributes. Moreover, some of the properties of many services cannot be assessed even after the service is completed; these are called credence attributes. For example, how do you know whether your psychologist or tax accountant is really any good or not? In cases such as these, the customer often lacks the specialized or technical knowledge to make an informed evaluation. All in all, due to the properties of intangibility (which limit search attributes), inseparability (which increases credence attributes), and the variation in quality provided by service personnel, services tend to be characterized by experience and credence attributes, which in turn reduce the amount of prepurchase information available to consumers, increasing their perceived risk.

***Risk and Brand Loyalty***   If we start with the premise that consumers do not like taking risks, it would seem obvious that they will try, whenever possible, to reduce risk during the purchase process. One strategy is to be brand- or store-loyal.[11] Brand loyalty is based on the degree to which the consumer has obtained satisfaction in the past. If consumers have been satisfied in the past with their supplier of service, they have little incentive to risk trying someone or something new. For example, satisfied clients of Citigroup may see little reason to switch their loyalty to another financial service provider.

Having been previously satisfied in a high-risk purchase, a consumer is less likely to experiment with a different provider. Consequently, maintaining a long-term relationship with the same service provider, in and of itself, helps reduce the perceived risk associated with the purchase. This is why it is common to observe consumers acquiring services from the same physician, dentist, and hairstylist over long periods of time.

Brand loyalty may also be higher with regard to purchasing services, due to the limited number of alternative choices available. This is particularly true of professional services, where acceptable substitutes may not be available. Finally, brand loyalty may also be higher for services due to the **switching costs** that can accrue when changing from one service provider to another. A wide array of switching costs can be accrued, depending on the service product involved. Consider, for example, the switching costs involved in changing from one brand of canned vegetables to another compared with the switching costs involved in changing banks. Typical switching costs include:

**switching costs** Costs that can accrue when changing one service provider to another.

- *Search costs*—the time costs associated with seeking out new alternatives.
- *Transaction costs*—the monetary costs associated with first-time visits, such as new x-rays when changing dentists.
- *Learning costs*—costs such as time and money that are associated with learning new systems, such as new versions of software packages.
- *Loyal customer discounts*—discounts that are given for maintaining the same service over time, such as accident-free auto insurance rates. Such discounts are sacrificed when switching from one supplier to the next.
- *Customer habit*—costs associated with changing established behavior patterns.

"I'm torn between brand loyalty & changing trends in the consumer experience."

www.CartoonStock.com

In general, consumers of services tend to be more brand loyal than the consumers of goods. Brand loyalty reduces service consumers levels of perceived risk.

- *Emotional costs*—the emotional turmoil that one may experience when severing a long-term relationship with a provider. Emotional costs are particularly high when a personal relationship has developed between the client and the provider.
- *Cognitive costs*—costs in terms of the time it takes simply thinking about making a change in service providers.

## Prepurchase Stage Considerations: The Importance of Personal Sources of Information

Another special consideration during the prepurchase stage is the importance of personal sources of information. Research has shown that in the area of communications, personal forms such as word-of-mouth references and information from opinion leaders are often given more importance than company-controlled communications, such as mass advertising. A reference from a friend becomes more important when the purchase to be made has a greater risk. For example, a visit to a new hairdresser can be stressful because the outcome of the service will be highly visible. That stress can be reduced by a recommendation from someone in whose judgment the consumer trusts. The consumer will then feel more confident about the outcome.

Similarly, evidence suggests that opinion leaders play an important role in the purchase of services. An opinion leader in a community is an individual looked to for advice. Within the perceived-risk framework, an opinion leader can be viewed as a source of reduced social risk. A woman who visits a hairdresser for the first time may feel uncertain about the quality of the outcome. However, she might be reassured by the fact that the friend who recommended the service is widely known to have good judgment in such matters and will convey this to others in their mutual social group. In this way, the opinion leader's judgment partially substitutes for the consumer's own.

In addition to reducing perceived risk, the importance of personal sources of information to service consumers is relevant for a number of other reasons. Due to the intangibility of services, mass media is not as effective in communicating the qualities of the service compared with personal sources of information. For example, would you feel comfortable purchasing services from a medical physician featured in a television advertisement? Moreover, would it be feasible for the physician to adequately describe medical procedures during a 30-second television spot? Overall, personal sources of information become more important as objective standards for evaluation decrease and as the complexity of the service product being marketed increases.

Other reasons that consumers rely to such a great extent on personal sources of information is that nonpersonal sources may simply not be available. Professional restrictions or negative attitudes regarding the use of mass advertising within certain service sectors reduce its use as a communication, too. Alternatively, many service providers are small and lack the resources or knowledge to advertise effectively. How many marketing or communications classes do you suppose your dentist or physician enrolled in while attending college? Most have no idea what a target market, positioning strategy, or marketing mix really entails. Regardless of their training and subsequent status, professional service providers are operating businesses and must effectively compete in order to maintain their livelihoods. The bottom line is that many professional service providers either lack the knowledge or feel uncomfortable marketing their services.

## Prepurchase Stage Considerations: Fewer Alternatives to Consider

In comparison with goods, another difference for service marketers to consider is that consumers of services tend to evaluate a smaller number of alternative sources of supply during the prepurchase stage. This situation occurs for a variety of reasons. First, each service provider tends to offer only one brand. For example, Geico Insurance sells only one brand of insurance—Geico. Similarly, your dentist provides only one brand of dental care. In contrast, consumers shopping for a blender generally have many brands to consider at each retail location.

The second reason the consideration set tends to be smaller pertains to the number of establishments providing the same service. Services tend to have a smaller number of outlets providing the same service. For example, a market area can support only so many psychologists, dentists, and medical doctors. In comparison, similar goods tend to be available in many locations. The difference between the distribution of goods and services relates directly to the diversification of the product mix. Retailers of goods sell many products under many brand names, thereby earning their revenues through many different sources. Due to the diversified product mix, the same goods are available at many locations. In contrast, the survival of the service firm often depends upon selling only one brand of service.

A third reason consumers consider fewer service alternatives relates to the lack of available prepurchase information. Consumers of services simply are not aware of as many service alternatives and/or do not choose to undertake the time-consuming task of obtaining information from competing service providers. In contrast, consumers of goods often simply look at what is on the store's shelves and can compare prices as well as a number of other factors such as ingredients, construction quality, feel, and size.

### Prepurchase Stage Considerations: Self-Service as a Viable Alternative

The final, but important, difference between goods and services in the prepurchase choice stage of the consumer decision process is that self-provision often becomes a viable alternative for such services as lawn care, fence installation, housekeeping, painting, and a number of other services. In comparison, consumers rarely consider building a refrigerator over purchasing one from a local retailer. Consequently, many service providers must consider the customer's own self-provision as a viable competitor in the marketplace.

### Consumption Stage Considerations

The consumption of goods can be divided into three activities: buying, using, and disposing. The three activities occur in a definite buy-use-dispose order, and have clear boundaries between them. The customer buys a box of detergent at a supermarket, uses it at home in the washing machine, and disposes of the empty box after the detergent is used up.

This scenario does not apply to the consumption of services, however. First of all, no clear-cut boundary or definite sequence exists between the acquisition and the use of services because there is no transfer of ownership. Because of the prolonged interactions between the customer and the service provider, the production, acquisition, and use of services become entangled and appear to be a single process.[12] Furthermore, the concept of disposal is irrelevant because of the intangibility and experiential nature of services.

Without a doubt, the consumption stage is more complex for services in comparison with that of goods. As discussed in the first chapter, the benefits bought by a service customer consist of the experience that is delivered through the four dimensions of the servuction model. Even when a service is rendered to something that the consumer owns, such as a car, rather than to the individual's person, the service production/consumption process often involves a sequence of personal interactions (face-to-face or by telephone) between the customer and the service provider.[13]

Interactions between the service customer and the company's facilities and personnel are inevitable. It is from these interpersonal and human-servicescape interactions that the service experience is acquired.[14] Perhaps the most important outcome of these interactions is the contradiction of the idea that postchoice evaluation occurs only at a certain point in time after use.[15] The difference in how goods and services are evaluated can be explained in the following manner. The use of goods is essentially free from any kind of direct marketer influence. For example, the manufacturer of the breakfast cereal that you ate this morning had no interaction with you whatsoever. Hence, consumers of goods can choose when, where, and how they will use a good. On the other hand, service firms play an active role in customer consumption activities because services are produced and consumed simultaneously.

No service can be produced or used with either the consumer or the service firm absent. Due to the extended service delivery process that is common with services, many believe that the consumer's postchoice evaluation occurs both *during* and *after* the use of services rather than only afterward. In other words, consumers evaluate the service while they are experiencing the service encounter during the consumption stage as well as during the postpurchase stage.

From a marketer's point of view, this opens up the prospect of being able to directly influence that evaluation. Hence, the restaurant manager who visits diners' tables and asks, "How is your dinner this evening?" can catch problems during the consumption stage and change consumer evaluations in a way that the manufacturer of a packaged good cannot. The bottom line for managers is to recognize that consumer evaluation of service occurs both during the service delivery process and after consumption. This insight, in turn, increases the importance of developing and effectively managing the consumer's overall service experience.

## Postchoice Considerations

The postpurchase evaluation of services is a complex process. It begins soon after the customer makes the choice of the service firm he or she will be using and continues throughout the consumption and postconsumption stages. The evaluation is influenced by the unavoidable interaction of a substantial number of social, psychological, and situational variables. Service satisfaction relies not only on the properties of the four elements of the servuction system—contact personnel, inanimate environment, other customers, and internal organization systems—but also on the synchronization of these elements in the service production/consumption process.

The success or failure of a service transaction can be at least partly attributed to management's ability or inability to manipulate the customer experience as the output of a collection of interpersonal interactions (client versus client, client versus employee) and human-servicescape interactions (employee versus working environment and supporting facilities, customer versus service environment and supporting facilities). Ultimately, managers would like to better understand postchoice considerations to gain additional insight into how consumer satisfaction/dissatisfaction evaluations are formed. A number of proposed models attempt to describe the process by which consumers evaluate their purchase decisions.

***Postchoice Models: The Expectancy Disconfirmation Theory***    How does service satisfaction arise during the consumption and postpurchase stages? A number of approaches have been suggested, but perhaps the simplest and most powerful is the **expectancy disconfirmation theory**. The basic concept behind this explanation is straightforward. Consumers evaluate services by comparing expectations with perceptions. If the perceived service is better than or equal to the expected service, then consumers are satisfied. Hence, ultimately customer satisfaction is achieved through the effective management of customer perceptions and expectations.

It is crucial to point out that this entire process of comparing expectations with perceptions takes place in the mind of the customer. It is the perceived service that matters,

**expectancy disconfirmation theory** The theory proposing that consumers evaluate services by comparing expectations with perceptions.

not the actual service. One of the best examples that reinforces this issue of managing perceptions involves a high-rise hotel. The hotel was receiving numerous complaints concerning the time guests had to wait for elevator service in the main lobby. Realizing that, from an operational viewpoint, the speed of the elevators could not be increased, and that attempting to schedule the guests' elevator usage was futile, management installed mirrors in the lobby next to the elevator bays. Guest complaints were reduced immediately—the mirrors provided a means for the guests to occupy their waiting time. Guests were observed using the mirror to observe their own appearance and the appearance of others around them. In reality, the speed of the elevators had not changed; however, the perception was that the waiting time was now acceptable.

It is also feasible to manage expectations in order to produce satisfaction without altering in any way the quality of the actual service delivered. Motel Six, for example, by downplaying its service offering in its cleverly contrived advertising, actually increases consumer satisfaction by lowering customer expectations prior to purchase. The firm's advertising effectively informs consumers of both what to expect and what not to expect: "A good clean room for $49.99…a little more in some places…a little less in some others…and remember…we'll leave the light on for you."[16] Many customers simply do not use services such as swimming pools, health clubs, and full-service restaurants that are associated with the higher-priced hotels. Economy-minded hotels, such as Motel Six, have carved out a niche in the market by providing the basics. The result is that customers know exactly what they will get ahead of time and are happy not only with the quality of the service received, but also with the cost savings.

***Postchoice Models: The Perceived-Control Perspective***    Another explanation that assists in describing the postpurchase stage is the **perceived-control perspective**. Over the years, the concept of control has drawn considerable attention from psychologists. They argue that in modern society, in which people no longer have to bother about the satisfaction of primary biological needs, the need for control over situations in which one finds oneself is a major force driving human behavior.[17] Rather than being treated as a service attribute, as implied by multi-attribute models, perceived control can be conceptualized as a superfactor—a global index that summarizes an individual's experience with a service. The basic premise of this perspective is that during the service experience, *the higher the level of control over the situation perceived by consumers, the higher their satisfaction with the service will be.* A similar positive relationship is proposed between service providers' experience of control and their job satisfaction.

**perceived-control perspective** A model in which consumers evaluate services by the amount of control they have over the perceived situation.

When consumers perceive that they are in control, or at least that what is happening to them is predictable, customer satisfaction increases.

In a slightly different way, it is equally important for the service firm itself to maintain control of the service experience. If the consumer gets too much control, the economic position of the firm may be affected as consumers tip the value equation in their favor, even to an extent that the firm may begin to lose money. On the other hand, if the service employees take complete control, consumers may become unhappy and leave. Even if this does not happen, the operational efficiency of the firm may be impaired.

To better understand the control perspective, services can be thought of as a consumer's giving up cash and control to the service provider in exchange for benefits, with each party seeking to gain as much advantage as possible. The concept of control consists of two types of control—behavioral and cognitive. *Behavioral control*, the ability to control what is actually going on, is only part of the idea. Research shows that *cognitive control* is also important. Thus, when consumers perceive that they are in control, or at least that what is happening to them is predictable, the effect can be the same as that achieved by behavioral control. In other words, it is the perception of control, not the reality that is most important.

Managerially, this concept raises a number of interesting ideas. The first idea raised is the value of the information given to consumers during the service experience in order to increase consumers' sense that they are in control and they know what will happen next. This is particularly important for professional service firms, which often assume that simply having a "good outcome" will make their clients happy—they forget that their clients may not have heard from them for more than a month and are frantic due to the lack of contact and little or no information. It is equally important to an airline that delays a flight after passengers have boarded but fails to let them know what is happening or how long the delay will be. In both situations, customers will feel that they have lost control over the situation, which eventually tends to result in customer dissatisfaction.

Moreover, according to the perceived-control perspective, if a firm is due to make changes in its operation that will have an impact on consumers, it is important that those consumers be forewarned. If they are not, they may perceive themselves to be "out of control" and become dissatisfied with the service received to the extent that they change providers.

The control perspective raises interesting issues about the tradeoff between predictability and choice. Operationally, one of the most important strategic issues pertaining to the perceived-control perspective is the amount of choice (customization) to give the consumer. Because both choice (customization) and predictability (standardization) can contribute to a sense of control, it is crucial to determine which is the more powerful source of control for the consumer in each particular service setting.

### Postchoice Models: The Script Perspective—All the World's a Stage and All the People Players

A number of theories in psychology and sociology can be brought together in the ideas of a *script*. The **script perspective** proposes that rules, mostly determined by social and cultural variables, exist to facilitate interactions in daily repetitive events, including a variety of service experiences.[18] These rules shape the participants' expectations in these types of interactions. Furthermore, the rules must be acknowledged and obeyed by all participants if satisfactory outcomes are to be generated. For example, patrons of a fine dining restaurant will have behavioral expectations of their waiter consistent with the service setting. Similarly, the waiter will have expectations of the patrons' behavior as well. If one participant deviates from the rules, the other co-actors in the service setting will be uncomfortable. Therefore, a satisfied customer is unlikely given a dissatisfied service provider, and a dissatisfied customer is unlikely given a satisfied service provider. Consequently, the principle idea proposed by script theory is that in a service encounter, customers follow scripts, and their satisfaction is a function of **script congruence**—whether the actual scripts performed by customers and staff are consistent with the expected scripts.

**script perspective**
Argues that rules, mostly determined by social and cultural variables, exist to facilitate interactions in daily repetitive events, including a variety of service experiences.

**script congruence**
Occurs when the actual scripts performed by customers and staff are consistent with the expected scripts.

## GLOBAL SERVICES *IN ACTION*

### Consumer Tipping Behavior: To Tip or Not to Tip—That is the Question

Imagine you're in China, and you've just ordered dinner at a fancy restaurant. The food is excellent, and the service is stellar. Naturally, you leave a large tip to indicate your pleasure with the experience. How would you react if the server confronted you, angry and insulted, and attempted to give your money back?

Sure, this seems like an unlikely situation, but you'd be surprised. Many Asian countries currently look down on tipping, and European tipping rules have a much lower percentage than is recognized here in the United States. Where you might tip 20 percent for outstanding service in Colorado, you would instead tip 5 percent to 10 percent at a pub in Dublin, Ireland. But the real tip is that American tipping practices exercised in foreign countries are changing global opinions on tipping. Though China hadn't fully accepted the practice by the 2008 Olympics, it was becoming more common in business settings.

The biggest thing, though, for American travelers to remember is that many countries put service charges on their bills. Make sure to check your bill before you pay; there is no need to tip if a service charge has been applied. Also, a hotel concierge is the best resource for local tipping policies, although asking servers is always an option. It is important to remember that keeping an open mind and pleasant manner will inspire service providers across the globe to assist you willingly.

Source:   **http://www.azcentral.com/arizonarepublic/business/articles/0914biz-tipping0914.html?&wired, accessed 19 November, 2009.**

The key managerial implications of script theory are: (1) to design scripts for the service encounter that are acceptable and capable of fulfilling the needs of both the customers and the service providers; and (2) to communicate these scripts to both customers and employees so that both have realistic perceptions and expectations of their roles as well as those of their partners in their interactions. Failure to effectively communicate scripts can lead to awkward and disappointing moments for customers and providers alike. For example, in many cultures, tipping a provider for good service is expected and customary; however, in other cultures tipping may be viewed as an insult. Without the appropriate tipping script, customers who travel the globe often struggle with the question "To Tip or Not to Tip" (See Global Services in Action).

In closing, the expectancy disconfirmation model, the perceived-control perspective, and the script perspective may not totally reflect reality, but because they are the result of much research in marketing and psychology, they at least allow us to make logical deductions about consumer behavior when making marketing decisions. Moreover, since all the models to be described have both strengths and weaknesses, they should be considered complementary rather than mutually exclusive. For example, all three models deal with different but complementary aspects of consumer expectations and perceptions. Managerial insights can be developed more effectively through a combination of these various perspectives as we continue to learn about consumer decision processing.

## Summary

This chapter has presented consumer decision process issues as they relate to service consumers. The consumer decision process model consists of three main stages: the prepurchase stage, the consumption stage, and the postpurchase stage. The prepurchase stage consists of the events that occur prior to the consumer's acquisition of the service and includes stimulus reception, problem awareness, information search, and evaluation of alternatives. The outcome of the prepurchase stage is a choice that takes place during the consumption stage. The consumption stage includes the activities of buying, using, and disposing of the product. The postpurchase stage refers to the process by which the consumer evaluates his or her level of satisfaction with the purchase.

Although the consumer decision process model applies to both goods and services, unique considerations arise with respect to services in each of the three stages. With regard to the prepurchase stage considerations, consumers of services: (1) perceive higher levels of risk to be associated with the purchase; (2) tend to be more brand loyal; (3) rely more heavily on personal sources of information; (4) tend to have fewer alternatives to consider; and (5) often include self-provision as a viable alternative.

The consumption stage is more complex for services in comparison with that of goods as the production, acquisition, and use of services become entangled in a single process. Moreover, due to the extended service delivery process, many believe that the consumer's postchoice evaluation occurs both during and after, rather than only after, the use of services. From a marketer's point of view, this provides the opportunity to directly influence the consumer's evaluation during the service delivery process. Because of the client/company interface, the service provider is able to catch problems and positively influence evaluations in a way that the manufacturer of a packaged good cannot.

Similarly, the postpurchase evaluation of services is also a complex process. The evaluation process begins soon after the customer makes the choice of the service firm he or she will be using and continues throughout the consumption and postconsumption stages. The evaluation is influenced by the unavoidable interaction of a substantial number of social, psychological, and situational variables. Service satisfaction relies not only on the technical quality of the service and the four elements of the servuction system (contact personnel, inanimate environment, other customers, and internal organizational systems), but also on the synchronization of these elements in the service production/consumption process.

Models that assist in our understanding of the consumer's postpurchase evaluation process include the expectancy disconfirmation model, the perceived control perspective, and the script perspective. In short, the expectancy disconfirmation model defines satisfaction as meeting or exceeding customer expectations. The perceived-control perspective proposes that during the service experience, the higher the level of control over the situation perceived by consumers, the stronger their satisfaction with the service. Finally, the script perspective proposes that in a service encounter, customers perform scripts, and their satisfaction is a function of "script congruence"—whether the actual scripts performed by customers and staff are consistent with the expected scripts. Models such as these help us understand how consumer evaluations are processed, and indicate areas where service marketers can focus their efforts in pursuit of the ultimate goal of providing customer satisfaction.

# Key Terms

consumer decision process, p. 87
stimulus, p. 87
commercial cue, p. 87
social cue, p. 87
physical cue, p. 87
information search, p. 89
problem awareness, p. 89
shortage, p. 89
unfulfilled desire, p. 89
awareness set, p. 89
evoked set, p. 89
consideration set, p. 89
internal search, p. 89

external search, p. 90
evaluation of alternatives, p. 90
nonsystematic evaluation, p. 90
systematic evaluation, p. 90
linear compensatory approach, p. 90
lexicographic approach, p. 91
consumption process, p. 91
cognitive dissonance, p. 92
financial risk, p. 93
performance risk, p. 93
physical risk, p. 93
social risk, p. 93

psychological risk, p. 93
search attributes, p. 94
experience attributes, p. 94
credence attributes, p. 95
switching costs, p. 96
expectancy disconfirmation theory, p. 99
perceived-control perspective, p. 100
script perspective, p. 101
script congruence, p. 101

## Review Questions

1. In general terms, discuss the purpose of consumer behavior models like the consumer decision process model depicted in Figure 4.1.
2. Why do consumers of services perceive higher levels of risk associated with their purchases compared to goods purchases?
3. Discuss the different types of risk.
4. Define and discuss the following terms: search attributes, experience attributes, and credence attributes. Which type(s) of attributes most accurately apply to services? Explain.
5. Regarding multi-attribute models, what is the difference between the linear compensatory approach and the lexicographic approach?

6. Who is typically more brand loyal—a consumer of goods or a consumer of services? Please explain.
7. Discuss the reasons why personal sources of information tend to be more important for consumers of services.
8. Discuss the managerial implications of the client-company interface during the consumption stage.
9. What is a script and how does it relate to the manner in which customer satisfaction evaluations are formed?
10. Explain the relevance of the perceived-control model as it relates to the postconsumption stage.

## Notes

1. John E. G. Bateson, *Managing Services Marketing: Text and Readings*, 2nd ed. (Fort Worth, TX: The Dryden Press, 1992), p. 93.
2. **http://www.woopidoo.com/business_quotes/customer-quotes.htm**, *accessed 20 November, 2009.*
3. Ibid.
4. Adapted from Michael Levy and Barton A. Weitz, *Retailing Management* (Homewood, IL: Irwin, 1992), pp. 117–154.
5. Adapted from John E. G. Bateson, *Managing Services Marketing*.
6. F. Nicosia and R. N. Mayer, "Toward a Sociology of Consumption," *Journal of Consumer Research*, 3, 2, (1976), pp. 65–75.
7. D. Guseman, "Risk Perception and Risk Reduction in Consumer Services," *Marketing of Services*, J. Donnelly and William R. George, eds., (Chicago: American Marketing Association, 1981), pp. 200–204; and R. A. Bauer, "Consumer Behavior as Risk Taking," in *Dynamic Marketing for a Changing World*, ed. R. S. Hancock (Chicago: American Marketing Association, 1960), pp. 389–398.
8. L. Kaplan, G. J. Szybilo, and J. Jacoby, "Components of Perceived Risk in Product Purchase; A Cross-Validation," *Journal of Applied Psychology* 59 (1974): pp. 287–291.
9. D. Guseman, "Risk Perception," pp. 200–204.
10. Adapted from John E. G. Bateson, *Managing Services*.

11. Zeithaml, Valerie A., "How Consumer Evaluation Processes Differ between Goods and Services," in *Marketing of Services*, J. Donnelly and William R. George, eds., (Chicago: American Marketing Association, 1981), pp. 191–199.
12. Bernard Booms and Jody Nyquist, "Analyzing the Customer/Firm Communication Component of the Services Marketing Mix," *Marketing of Services*, J. Donnelly and W. George, eds., (Chicago: American Marketing Association, 1981), p. 172; and Raymond Fisk, "Toward a Consumption/Evaluation Process Model for Services," *Marketing of Services*, p. 191.
13. Christopher H. Lovelock, "Classifying Services to Gain Strategic Marketing Insights," *Journal of Marketing*, 47, (Summer 1983), pp. 9–20.
14. Alan Andrasen, "Consumer Research in the Service Sector," *Emerging Perspectives on Services Marketing*, L. Berry, G. L. Shostack, and G. Upah, eds., (Chicago: American Marketing Association, 1982), pp. 63–64.
15. Raymond Fisk, "Toward a Consumption/Evaluation Process Model for Services," *Marketing of Services*, J. Donnelly and W. George, eds., (Chicago: American Marketing Association, 1981), p. 191.
16. **http://www.motel6.com**, accessed 20 November, 2009.
17. John E. G. Bateson, "Perceived Control and the Service Encounter," *The Service Encounter*,

John A. Czepiel, Michael R. Solomon, and Carol F. Suprenant, eds., (Lexington, MA: Lexington Books, 1984), pp. 67–82.

18. Ruth A. Smith and Michael Houston, "Script-based Evaluations of Satisfaction with Services," *Emerging*

*Perspectives in Services Marketing*, L. Berry, G. L. Shostack, and G. Upah, eds., (Chicago: American Marketing Association, 1982), pp. 59–62.

Al Marshall, ACU National

# CASE 4

# Mariano Ferreyra's Choices

Airline travel for the typical traveller involves time spent in a small seat in a confined space in order to get to the final destination. It also involves getting to the airport by a certain time, checking in with tickets and bags, going through security, waiting for flight boarding, boarding the flight, and experiencing in-flight service. At the final destination it involves disembarking from the plane, proceeding through immigration and customs (if it is an international flight), waiting to collect the bags, collecting the bags from the luggage belt, and then leaving the airport. All in all a number of activities are involved, with the customer and airport, airline and government personnel all performing a number of services.

These activities and 'service performances' can vary somewhat depending on whether the flight is domestic or international, the duration of the flight, and the class of travel that the traveller has paid for. Many consumers have views about airlines and the whole experience of airline travel, and these inform and guide their decision making.

Mariano Ferreyra works for an international software company with offices in a number of Australian capital cities. Part of his job involves quite a lot of travel interstate within Australia, especially between his company's head office in Sydney and Melbourne, Brisbane and Adelaide. He also is part of a new product development team, comprised of employees from a number of offices around the world. As such, he is twice-yearly required to attend meetings at several of the design centres that the company has in Europe. For his domestic and international trips, Mariano is allowed to choose which airlines he wants to fly, providing that the ticket prices are judged to be 'fair and reasonable'. He tends to do his own research and make his own bookings, rather than going through a corporate travel agency. He used to deal with them a lot but as travel services have moved online, Mariano has found that it is quite easy to do himself (and make the choices himself).

For his trips to the interstate offices within Australia, he prefers to fly on discount airlines like Virgin Blue and Jetstar rather than on Qantas. He feels the same when he flies within Europe, preferring easyJet and brands like Ryanair over European national carriers like British Airways, Air France and Lufthansa. However, when it comes to long-distance international travel, Mariano prefers to fly on full-service airlines like Qantas or Air New Zealand.

## Short-Haul Decision Making

Mariano does not know much about Tiger Airways, so he does not check that airline's website when looking to fly interstate (he needs to know a bit more about them before he does this). He usually finds that Jetstar and Virgin Blue are quite a bit cheaper than Qantas regarding the destinations that he needs to fly to. In fact, recently he stopped checking the Qantas site, restricting his choice to the two discount carriers. He 'just knows' that Qantas will be more expensive, and can't justify this to himself (or the company) when the flight duration is a maximum of an hour or two between Sydney and Melbourne, Melbourne and Brisbane, or Sydney and Adelaide. Sure, it's a bit of a pain having to pay for food on the flights with the discount carriers, and some of the other restrictions that apply, but the higher price on the full-service carrier is not worth it, in Mariano's view.

Qantas has lost market share in the domestic market since the launch of Virgin Blue a few years ago, and fought back by launching Jetstar. The more recent launch (and growth) of Tiger Airways is expected to further damage its market share. Launching Jetstar as its discount carrier has worked well, though ideally Qantas would like to acquire the business of consumers like Mariano on the Sydney, Melbourne, Brisbane and Adelaide legs that Mariano flies domestically (and which are the key domestic business routes for Qantas). How to do this when many potential passengers like Mariano are price-sensitive is a major challenge.

Of the two carriers in Mariano's consideration set, nowadays Jetstar is his preferred carrier. He feels the seats are a bit bigger than they are on Virgin Blue, and he is a Qantas Club member so he can use the Qantas Club lounge before the flight (and get a snack and a drink there). He also perceives that being owned by Qantas means that Jetstar planes are pretty safe.

Were it not for his Qantas Club membership, Mariano might be more open to considering Virgin Blue. The perceived bigger seats and greater safety on Jetstar are important to him as perceived rational attributes, but his Qantas Club membership is important to him for both what it rationally offers him, and for its emotional value. Being a member and being able to use the lounges makes him feel good, and a bit different from the other passengers using Jetstar. Since he really has to fly on a discount airline for interstate work, being able to use the Qantas Club lounges is a kind of compensation!

Mariano knows that not having Tiger Airways in his consideration set is something he has to change. It reputably has inexpensive flights and a growing route network, and Mariano believes that the customer service (bookings, check-in, baggage handling, in-flight, etc.) is probably at least comparable to Jetstar and Virgin Blue. To date, though, he has not seen any marketing communications for Tiger, and knows no-one who has flown on the airline. He may check the airline's website in the future, but really needs to know a lot more about this airline than the website alone may be able to deliver!

Virgin Blue, while still being in Mariano's consideration set, is really the second choice. This is despite the fact that the airline advertises extensively to keep its brand name and product offerings 'top of mind' among consumers; its prices compare favourably to Jetstar's prices; and it offers regular flights to the cities where Mariano's company has its interstate offices. Furthermore, it now offers airport lounges in an attempt to match the key competitor's offerings, and in order to appeal more to business travellers like Mariano Ferreyra.

When Mariano flies within Europe, it is generally for work also. These flights, like the ones on Australia's eastern seaboard, typically are no longer than two hours in duration. Initially Mariano just flew on the European national carriers that the corporate travel agent in Sydney booked him on. He had a preference for British Airways since it has an extensive route network within Europe, a quality reputation, and it is a full-service carrier with a standard baggage allowance, in-flight beverage and food service, and other standard service offerings. Furthermore, on his British Airways flights Mariano felt safe, and an added bonus was the ability to use his Qantas Club membership card for access to British Airways Club lounges. This gave him a special feeling, even though he always flies economy class, and it helps make him feel better about being so far away from home.

However, after a friend told him about easyJet, and after visiting the easyJet website a couple of years ago and hearing good things about the company, he decided to book a flight. The airline was so much cheaper on the route that he needed to fly than British Airways or other full-service carriers like Air France, that it seemed a 'no brainer' to try it. The experience was good, with an easy Internet booking, an on-time departure, a modern aircraft, cabin announcements in both English and the language of the destination being flown to, reasonable prices for the food and beverages available in-flight, a smooth takeoff and landing, and (aside from having to pay) no problems with the baggage. He has used easyJet ever since, and it was in fact convenient to be able to visit the airline's website and do all his own bookings at home in Australia. This might be possible with the European national carriers, but Mariano really is not too sure.

As noted earlier, the other brand in his European consideration set is Ryanair, which (though he has never flown the airline) Mariano perceives as a direct competitor to easyJet, with really reasonable prices and an extensive route network within Europe. He had heard that the chief executive (Michel O'Leary) was very entrepreneurial, and that (like easyJet) the airline fleet is pretty new (one of Mariano's 'tests' for how safe airlines are likely to be). On the downside, he read a news story that made international headlines, claiming that Michael O'Leary had been considering charging Ryanair passengers to use the toilets in-flight. While Mariano is prepared to pay for items like baggage, food and beverages, he really thinks that this is going too far! In his mind, what will be next – seatbelts? Most recently he has heard that passengers booking tickets on this airline have had to pay to print out their own tickets, and that this is a necessary precondition in order to be able to check in, and that they might also have to pay to check in. This too seems to Mariano to be going too far. Accordingly, he has resolved to only really consider easyJet for his flights within Europe in the future, and to use Ryanair as a 'back up'.

## Long-Haul Decision Making

In terms of actually getting to Europe for his new product-development meetings, Mariano normally chooses Qantas or Air New Zealand. The prices on both of these are reasonable, he can collect airline points with both (having both One World and Star Alliance memberships), he perceives both as safe airlines (notwithstanding some recent media stories about Qantas incidents), and the in-flight service in terms of cabin staff, food, beverages and entertainment is reasonable. Importantly, Mariano feels psychologically and socially comfortable. He recognises the interiors of the aircraft, the cabin crew and pilots 'speak the same language', there are generally some 'local' entertainment options in the entertainment system, the food choices are generally known, and the airlines are long established, employing typically experienced staff, in his opinion. Importantly, too, as he is a Qantas Club member, Mariano can use the lounge facilities before the long flights to Europe. While he flies economy, being able to use the lounges makes him feel kind of special!

There are, however, a number of other airlines that Mariano may like to fly on (some of which he has already flown on) when he goes overseas. These include Singapore Airlines, JAL (Japan Airlines) and Emirates. He has flown on Singapore Airlines a number of times. He likes the fact that it claims to have the youngest aircraft fleet in the world (this makes him feel safer); he also likes the KRIS World entertainment system, which gives him lots of entertainment options on the very long flights between Australia and Europe; the polite in-cabin service; and the classy Singapore Girl advertising! While never having flown JAL, Mariano imagines that the planes are well serviced, that the cabin staff are highly attentive, and that the food is good. Emirates is, however, the one he really wants to fly with next time he goes to Europe (assuming the airfare is competitive with Qantas, and carriers like Air New Zealand). Mariano just sees this airline as setting a high standard across a whole range of fronts, and believes that even economy class passengers like himself are treated really well on Emirates. Dubai, too, would be an interesting stopover on the long haul to or from Europe.

In contrast to this, however, he also has a 'mental list' of airlines that he would definitely not want to fly with, either for short-haul (domestic or international) or long-haul travel. These include Aeroflot, Garuda and, while he would in any case be highly unlikely to ever need to fly with them, Air Comoros (after seeing a recent news story about this airline's maintenance of its planes and a recent crash it had!). This makes it very difficult for these airlines to acquire customers like Mariano, since (apart from their route networks) they are simply not in his consideration set, even though they are in his evoked (known) set. In order to move from the former to the latter, they need to enhance their reputations, and they can only do this by working on both their brand images and their service offerings. Both require a substantial investment of financial, technical and human resources.

Mariano also would take some convincing and might need to do some personal research before he would book and fly on a number of airlines that he simply does not know much about. These include Philippine Airlines, Hawaiian Airlines and Eva Air, even though the airfares offered by these airlines are often more-competitively priced than those of Qantas or Air New Zealand. It is hard to evaluate these airlines when you have not personally experienced their services, and you don't know anyone else who has either. Travel agents were one source of information, and Mariano trusts the corporate travel agent, but at the same time is finding that as travel services like airlines, hotel and rental car companies move their businesses online, he is dealing less and less with the corporate travel agent, and is instead researching and doing all the bookings himself. Typically, therefore, he sticks with what he knows and has experienced.

## Discussion Questions

1. Services marketing is different from the marketing of tangible products in a number of ways. Using the example of the airline industry (both domestic and international), illustrate some of the difficulties involved in marketing services to a potential passenger like Mariano.

2. Outline some of the challenges facing Virgin Blue and Tiger Airways in getting Mariano to develop a preference for flying with them. What two or three key services marketing (or marketing communications) initiatives would you recommend?

3. Mariano does fly Qantas on long-haul international flights to Europe, and he is a Qantas Club member, yet it does not have him as a domestic customer on its flights. What, if anything, could Qantas do to acquire him as a customer on its key domestic routes?

4. Mariano appears to be looking for different service experiences with his short-haul domestic flights and his long-haul international flights. Consider why this is the case, and what implications this has for the services marketing mix. Illustrate this for three of the seven Ps.

5. How has online technology impacted on the consumer's knowledge about airline services and airline quality, and what challenges and opportunities does it pose to both discount and full-service airlines seeking to win business from potential customers?

6. Make a list of the criteria that Mariano uses to evaluate service performance, whether he has flown on an airline or not, and then rank these criteria in likely order of importance to Mariano. Consider what criteria he is not using that could be important to other consumers.

# The Tactical Services Marketing Mix

Michael Runkel/SuperStock

Ski Dubai offers the world's largest snow park consisting of 3000 square meters of snow. The entertainment venue offers a classic example of how the tactical service marketing mix can be effectively managed to create a world class service experience.

Part II is dedicated to topics that pertain to managing the service experience. Due to consumer involvement in the production of services, many challenges for management occur that rarely, if ever, need to be considered in the production of goods. In this part, you will learn about the strategic issues that affect both the marketing mix and the components of the servuction model including process, pricing, promotion, physical evidence and people (employee and customer) issues.

CHAPTER **5**

# Focus on Service Processes

## CHAPTER OBJECTIVES

After reading this chapter, you should be able to:

- Compare and contrast the four stages of operational competitiveness.

- Appreciate the relationship between operations and marketing as it pertains to developing service delivery systems.

- Describe the types of operational models that facilitate operational efficiency.

- Consider the challenges associated with applying operational efficiency models to service organizations and recommend strategies that overcome some of these difficulties.

- Explain the art of service blueprinting as it relates to the design of service delivery operations.

- Discuss the role of complexity and divergence as it relates to new service product development

The main objective in this chapter is to familiarize students of services marketing with operations concepts, and explain the strategic importance of balancing operations and marketing functions in service operations.

### NET FLIX PROCESS: RIP, SORT, AND REPEAT

Consider for a moment how people traditionally went about renting movies. The consumer had to fulfill multiple steps, beginning with locating a rental store, driving to the store, searching movie titles for desirability and availability, paying for the movie, driving back home to watch the movie, driving back to the rental store to return the movie, and ending with a drive back home after returning the movie. In the event of a faulty product, the consumer had to repeat the process all over again. Now, however, we have the incredible processes pioneered by Netflix, a company that has given a facelift to the film rental business.

Brian Snyder/Reuters /Landov

The most important aspect of the unique Netflix process is the Internet-based ordering, shipping, and return system. Consumers simply access their online account, select movies for their queue, and wait for post delivery. After viewing the DVD, consumers repackage the disc and drop it back in the mailbox—no additional postage necessary. No longer must consumers drive into town to select or return a movie; instead, they walk as far as their mailboxes and the rest is handled for them.

The entire hidden inspection, sorting, and resending process is designed to deliver the highest quality service to the consumer. Once the discs are scanned upon arrival at one of the firm's 58 distribution centers, an automatic receipt email is sent to the individual customer and the next disc in their queue is flagged. Employees then inspect the discs by hand; they verify titles, look for physical damage, and remove problem discs from the process. The discs are then hand cleaned and sorted into bins, which are taken to a unique machine that Netflix itself designed for speed, efficiency, and quality. "The Stuffer" repackages and records the discs and either sends them immediately to the mail sorter for posting to their next destination, or places them in inventory. Netflix typically ships 2.2 million discs a day to its over 10 million customers!

Netflix has created a process that is truly an art. Consumers see only the final product, and are relieved the hassle of the messy steps in between. Further, the quality assurance practices used by the company strive to deliver the highest value product to each consumer. Perhaps the beauty of the process is the customer's blissful unawareness of the expansive process necessary to execute the service. Clearly, if the customer has no idea what's happening behind the scenes, then they have never encountered a problem that would make them start thinking about it in the first place! In short, Netflix has done its job well, and its major competitive advantage is all in its processes.

Source: Horowitz, Etan, "Rip, Sort, Repeat: Netflix Process Is Speedy, Efficient, Impressive," *Orlando Sentinel*, August 19, 2009. Used with permission of the Orlando Sentinel, copyright 2009.

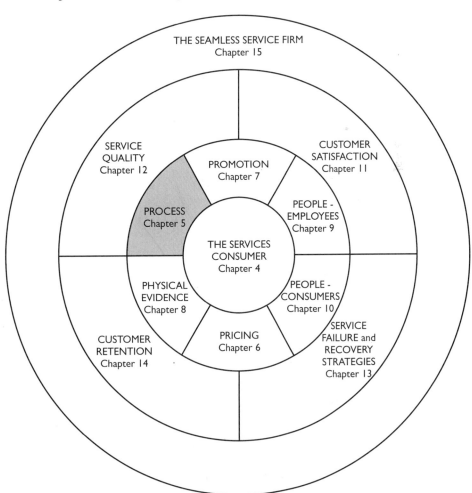

# Introduction

Unlike the "Rip, Sort, Repeat" process that enables Netflix to keep its customers at arm's length and away from their sorting operations, many service customers find themselves as integral components of most service production processes. The customer's participation in the process may be active (e.g., exercising at the local health club to become more physically fit) or passive (e.g., patrons viewing a theatrical production), but customers are often physically present during the service production process. Given the customer's physical presence during the service encounter, it is clear that if the process within the service factory (the place where the service is produced) changes, consumer scripts will have to change as well. To understand this point more fully, simply think about what it is like to cash a check inside a bank as opposed to using the bank's ATM—two different processes that achieve the same final goal requiring customers to follow two completely different scripts. Finally, and perhaps most importantly, students should recognize the importance of process strategy in the customer's overall service experience. Given the consumer's involvement within the service encounter, the consumer's evaluation of the encounter is often based as much on the process as the final outcome.

This chapter highlights the tradeoffs between the search for operational efficiency and the need to create marketing effectiveness. With regards to service operations, many of the traditional methods typically recommended for increasing operational effectiveness cannot be implemented without impacting the customer or employees. As such, changes made to increase the service operation's efficiency can often downgrade the final service product. This chapter focuses on the positive things marketing can achieve to help improve the efficiency of service operations.

# Stages of Operational Competitiveness

Without a successful service delivery process, the service firm will meet its final demise as customers become frustrated over the level of poor service delivered. For example, a

"Still getting the hang of laser surgery?"

The importance of having good service processes in place prior to serving customers.

hotel may have the best location and the best rooms on the market, but if it takes guests forever to check in and out of their rooms, restaurants are not properly stocked, and housekeeping services are dismal, the hotel will eventually lose all existing and potential customers.

Service firms seeking to construct a service process to improve operational effectiveness can choose from a large range of operational options. Strategically, the service firm can choose to use its operations as the key component of its competitive strategy, or view its operations as a necessary evil to complete day-to-day tasks. The manner in which "operational competitiveness" is embraced by various service firms can be described by four stages:[1]

1. Available for Service
2. Journeyman
3. Distinctive Competencies Achieved
4. World-Class Service Delivery

## Stage 1: Available for Service

Operations for a firm at this level of competitiveness are viewed as a "necessary evil." Operations are at best reactive to the needs of the rest of the organization and deliver the service as specified. As its mission, the operations department attempts primarily to avoid mistakes. Back office support is minimized to keep costs down. Technological investment is also minimized, as is investment in training for front-line personnel. Management designs skill out of the work done by these personnel, leaving little room for any discretionary effort, and pays minimum wage whenever possible.

A basic example of "available for service" would be an individual who sells local concert tickets online via their own website. Customers place orders, and the business simply fulfills the customer orders as they are received. In this case, operations are reactive to customer requests, the major goal is to send the correct ticket to the correct individual, and the complexity of the operation is kept to a minimum.

## Stage 2: Journeyman

The motivation to jump to Stage 2 of operational competitiveness is often provided by the arrival of competition. The service firm may find that it is no longer enough just to have a basic operation that works. The firm must now seek feedback from its customers on the relative costs and perceived qualities of the service to seek improvements in the service delivery process. At this point, the operations department becomes much more outward-looking, and often becomes interested in benchmarking its operations relative to the competition. Consider, for example, the changes Blockbuster Inc. began to consider once Netflix entered the market.

The introduction of technologically based systems for firms at this stage tends to be justified based on the cost savings possible. For example, the introduction of self checkout systems at grocery stores assists in reducing labor costs. Within the "journeyman" stage of operational competitiveness, the emphasis shifts from controlling workers to managing processes. As such, employees often are given procedures to follow, and management focuses on ensuring that these procedures are followed. This is much like how an employee handbook at a casual dining restaurant such as Olive Garden or Outback Steakhouse outlines specific processes for employee appearance and time-based steps for interacting with customers. The motivation for employees to follow the handbook is reinforced by managers who assess employee performance, set work schedules, and determine pay levels.

### Stage 3: Distinctive Competence Achieved

Upon entering Stage 3 of operational competitiveness, operations have reached a point where they continually excel, reinforced by the personnel management function and systems that support the customer focus. By this time, the firm has mastered the core service and understands the complexity of changing current operations. Within Stage 3, technology is no longer seen as a source of cost efficiencies alone, but also as a way of enhancing the effectiveness of service to customers. Consequently, the transition from Stage 2 to Stage 3 involves a philosophical change of balancing efficiency with effectiveness.

In addition to the philosophical change of heart, perhaps the second biggest change pertains to the workforce and in the nature of front-line management. Within Stage 3, front-line workers are allowed to select from alternative procedures, and are not obligated to treat all customers in a uniform manner regardless of the customer's request. Stage 3 of operational competitiveness encourages front-line management to listen to customers and become coaches and facilitators to front-line workers.

### Stage 4: World-Class Service Delivery

Stage 4 of operational competitiveness offers "world-class service delivery." To sustain this level of performance, operations not only have to continually excel, but also become fast learners and adapt to competitive offerings and customers' ever evolving needs. Within Stage 4, technology is seen as a way to "break the mold" – to do things competitors cannot do. For example, DHL Global Mail has instituted a process that has made it a leader in international mail services (See Global Services in Action).

When offering "world-class service delivery," the workforce itself must be a source of innovators, not just robots following a standardized process. To achieve this, the front-line supervisors must go beyond coaching to mentoring. As mentors, they need to be accountable for the personal development of the workforce so that employees can develop the skills necessary for the service firm to evolve.

Overall, as service firms transition through the four stages of operational competitiveness, the transformation from "Available for Service" to "World-Class Service Delivery" highlights the fact that operations management problems in services cannot be solved by the operations personnel alone. As pointed out by the four stages noted above, the search for operations efficiency can be crucial to long-term competitiveness. However, operational efficiency must be balanced with the effectiveness of the system from the customer's point of view. Figure 5.1 provides a quick glimpse into the major tradeoffs between

E-tailer, Amazon.com, distinguishes itself from its competitors by employing processes that result in a world class service delivery system.

**FIG-5.1** Major Design Trade-offs in High- and Low-Contact Systems

| DECISION | HIGH-CONTACT SYSTEM | LOW-CONTACT SYSTEM |
|---|---|---|
| Facility location | Operations must be near the customer. | Operations may be placed near supply, transportation, or labor. |
| Facility layout | Facility should accommodate the customer's physical and psychological needs and expectations. | Facility should enhance production. |
| Product design | Environment as well as the physical product define the nature of the service. | Customer is not in the service environment so the product can be defined by fewer attributes. |
| Process design | Stages of production process have a direct immediate effect on the customer. | Customer is not involved in the majority of processing steps. |
| Scheduling | Customer is in the production schedule and must be accommodated. | Customer is concerned mainly with completion dates. |
| Production planning | Orders cannot be stored, so smoothing production flow will result in loss of business. | Both backlogging and production smoothing are possible. |
| Worker skills | Direct workforce makes up a major part of the service product and so must be able to interact well with the public. | Direct workforce need have only technical skills. |
| Quality control | Quality standards are often in the eye of the beholder and, hence, variable. | Quality standards are generally measurable and, hence, fixed. |
| Time standards | Service time depends on customer needs, so time standards are inherently loose. | Work is performed on customer surrogates (e.g., forms), and time standards can be tight. |
| Wage payments | Variable output requires time-based wage systems. | "Fixable" outputs permits output-based wage systems. |
| Capacity planning | To avoid lost sales, capacity must be set to match peak demand. | Storable output permits setting capacity at some average demand level. |
| Forecasting | Forecasts are short-term, time oriented. | Forecasts are long-term, output oriented. |

Source: Richard C. Chase, "Where Does the Customer Fit in a Service Operation?" *Harvard Business Review* (November–December 1978), pp. 137–142. Reprinted by permission of *Harvard Business Review*. Copyright © 1978 by the President and Fellows of Harvard College.

efficiency and effectiveness when developing operations for low-customer-contact versus high-customer-contact services.

Frequently, from a pure operational perspective, it is easy to view the customer as a constraint: "If all these customers didn't always show up at the same time, we could provide much better service!" Such a negative perspective ignores a golden opportunity. The physical presence of service customers within the service operation can be used to help, not hinder operations. Such a positive view, does however, require that traditional operations personnel recognize the importance of the goals of their marketing counterparts—to enhance the effectiveness of the customer's service experience. Just as important, such a view also requires that marketing personnel have an intimate knowledge of the operations system and its challenges. It is not enough to propose new service offerings to be delivered through existing operational systems. Marketers who excel at providing world-class service recognize that the impact of offering new services through existing operational systems must be considered prior to introducing new services to the customer.[2]

## GLOBAL SERVICES *IN ACTION*

### DHL GlobalMail: International Post Made Easy

Not that long ago, efficient and expeditious mailing was one of the biggest barriers to international trade. Today, however, with the development of a uniquely tailored delivery process, it's as easy as hopping online and clicking a few buttons. DHL GlobalMail has designed a process that begins at the customer's door and ends at the specified destination. A simple online ordering process or a quick phone call is all it takes to quickly connect to over 220 countries.

DHL promotes their service as a partnership with their customers, working together to create lasting relationships by delivering the highest quality possible. To begin, DHL will retrieve the letters, magazines, packages, and any other item to be mailed directly from the business. Then items to be mailed are immediately taken to a sorting facility, which uses an electronic sorting and tracking process to redirect packages to the appropriate distribution facility. Once the mail has arrived in the one of 40+ distribution centers closest to the final destination, it is taken over by local carriers and delivered with the regular post. This entire process is clearly illustrated on the GlobalMail page of the company website, which features a detailed video specifically designed for customer comprehension.

Not only does DHL use this unique process, which effectively creates positive relationships both with their own customers and the countries in which they do business, but it also sets a standard of excellence for customer service. The tracking system used to identify packages across the globe is easily accessible to consumers online. At any time, a customer can check the status of his or her delivery. Further, DHL verifies the mailing addresses on the mailings at the sorting center; if the address is incorrect, a corrected label is affixed and an email notification of the change is sent to the customer.

As globalization trends step in and eliminate many trade barriers, companies will find the advanced processes that DHL uses to be highly beneficial; when coupled with stellar customer service standards, it is no wonder that the firm has established a highly successful global enterprise.

Source: DHL GlobalMail, **http://us.dhlglobalmail.com/expedited-mail-process-details.aspx**.

# Marketing and Operations: Balance is Critical

One way of viewing the relationship between marketing and operations in a service firm is to think of it as marrying the consumers' needs with the technology and manufacturing capabilities of the firm. As is the case with most marriages, a successful union between operations and marketing will obviously involve compromises, since the consumers' needs can seldom be met completely and economically.

In a service firm, establishing a balance between marketing and operations is critical! Significant aspects of the service operation are the product that creates the experience that delivers the bundle of benefits to the consumer. For example, a restaurant experience is not based solely on the quality of the food. The physical environment and interactions with contact personnel throughout the experience also greatly influence consumer perceptions of the quality of service delivered. A successful compromise between operations efficiency and marketing effectiveness is, therefore, that much more difficult to achieve. Consequently, success in services marketing demands a much greater understanding of the constraints and opportunities posed by the firm's operations.

To introduce these complexities, in this chapter we first adopt the perspective of an operations manager and ask, "What would be the ideal way to run the service delivery system from an operations perspective?" The impact on marketing and the opportunities for marketing to assist in the creation of this ideal are then developed.

As pointed out in Chapter 1, the key distinctive characteristic of services is that the service product is an experience. The service experience is created by the operating system of the firm's interaction with the customer. Thus, the operating system of the firm, in all its complexity, is the service product. For a marketing manager, this imposes constraints on the strategies that can be employed, but it also presents new and challenging opportunities for improving the profitability of the firm.

Chapter 4 provided one base on which to build an understanding of the product design problem for services. An understanding of consumer behavior has always been a necessary condition for successful marketing. One way of viewing the product design process is to think of it as the process of combining such an understanding with the technological and manufacturing skills of the organization. Consequently, to be an effective services marketer, a knowledge of consumer behavior is not sufficient in itself to produce economically successful products. Successful managers require a keen understanding of operations and human resource concepts and strategies as well.

As we discussed in Chapter 3, it is possible for goods producers to separate the problems of manufacturing and marketing by the use of inventory. Even so, there are many areas of potential conflict, as can be viewed in Figure 5.2. Although the issues are

**FIG-5.2 Sources of Cooperation/Conflict Between Marketing and Operations**

| PROBLEM AREA | TYPICAL MARKETING COMMENT | TYPICAL MANUFACTURING COMMENT |
|---|---|---|
| 1. Capacity planning and long range sales forecasting | "Why don't we have enough capacity?" | "Why didn't we have accurate sales forecasts?" |
| 2. Production scheduling and short-range sales forecasting | "We need faster response. Our lead times are ridiculous." | "We need realistic customer commitments and sales forecasts that don't change like wind direction." |
| 3. Delivery and physical distribution | "Why don't we ever have the right merchandise in inventory?" | "We can't keep everything in inventory." |
| 4. Quality assurance | "Why can't we have reasonable quality at reasonable costs?" | "Why must we always offer options that are too hard to manufacture and that offer little customer utility?" |
| 5. Breadth of product line | "Our customers demand variety." | "The product line is too broad— all we get are short, uneconomical runs." |
| 6. Cost control | "Our costs are so high that we are not competitive in the marketplace." | "We can't provide fast delivery, broad variety, rapid response to change, and high quality at low cost." |
| 7. New product introduction | "New products are our lifeblood." | "Unnecessary design changes are prohibitively expensive." |
| 8. Adjunct services such as spare parts, inventory support, installation, and repair | "Field service costs are too high." | "Products are being used in ways for which they weren't designed." |

Source: Reprinted by permission of *Harvard Business Review*. An exhibit from "Can Marketing and Manufacturing Coexist?" by Benson P. Shapiro (September/October 1977), p. 105. Copyright © 1977 by the President and Fellows of Harvard College; all rights reserved.

characterized as conflicts, they can be reconceptualized as opportunities. In each area it is clear that a better integration of marketing and operations could yield a more efficient and profitable organization. For example, a firm that is considering the decision of expanding its product line or focusing solely on one product can be seen as a compromise between the heterogeneous demands of consumers and the operations demand of homogeneity. If marketing managers have their way, too many products will probably be developed, and the operation will become inefficient. As long as this is compensated for by higher prices, a successful strategy can be implemented. In contrast, if the operations people have their way, the customer would have one product to select from, which is a less attractive option. However, as long as this is compensated for by lower costs and hence lower prices, a successful strategy can emerge.

Ultimately, marketing and operations are in a tug-of-war that should be resolved by compromise. In the service sector, the possible areas of conflict or compromise are much broader because the operation itself is the service product. Again, there is no single solution since operational efficiency and marketing effectiveness may often push in opposite directions.

By its very nature, this chapter is purposely meant to be operations oriented rather than marketing oriented. To polarize the issues surrounding marketing and operations even further, the perspective adopted in this chapter is that of the operations manager. Consequently, the remaining focus of this chapter is on the requirements for operational efficiency and the ways that marketing can help achieve those requirements. Finally, we would like to stress that in the drive for competitive advantage in the marketplace, marketing goals and objectives may in the end mean less operational efficiency. This is particularly true for high-contact service firms. As the amount of customer contact increases, the likelihood that the service firm will operate efficiently decreases. In the end, the service customers ultimately determine:

- *the type of demand,*
- *the cycle of demand, and*
- *the length of the service experience.*

Meanwhile, the service firm loses more and more control over its daily operations. It's the nature of the service business.

## In a Perfect World, Service Firms Would Be Efficient

**technical core** The place within an organization where its primary operations are conducted.

**perfect-world model** J. D. Thompson's model of organizations proposing that operations' "perfect" efficiency is possible only if inputs, outputs, and quality happen at a constant rate and remain known and certain.

From an operations manager's perspective, establishing process that operate a service firm at peak efficiency would be the ideal situation. J. D. Thompson's *perfect-world model* provides us the direction needed to achieve this ultimate goal. However, in reality, peak efficiency is often unattainable. The *focused factory* and *plant-within-a-plant* concepts provide managers with alternative strategies that enhance the efficiency of the firm while taking into consideration marketing effectiveness.

### Thompson's Perfect-World Model

The starting point for this discussion is the work of J. D. Thompson.[3] Thompson, long ago, introduced the idea of a **technical core**—the place within the organization where the primary operations functions are conducted. In the service sector, the technical core consists of kitchens in restaurants, service bays in auto dealerships, back work areas at dry cleaners, and surgical rooms in a hospital. Thompson proposed in his **perfect-world model** that in order to operate efficiently, a firm must be able to operate "*as if the market will absorb the single kind of product at a continuous rate and as if the inputs flowed* *continuously at a steady rate and with specified quality."* At the center of his argument was the idea that uncertainty creates inefficiency. In the ideal situation, the technical core is able to operate without uncertainty on both the input and output side, thereby creating many advantages for management.

The absence of uncertainty means that decisions within the core can become programmed and that individual employee decision making can be replaced by rules. The removal of individual discretion means that jobs are "deskilled" and that a lower quality of labor can be used, resulting in lower labor costs. Alternatively, the rules can be programmed into machines and labor replaced by automation. Because output and input can be fixed through the use of inventories, it is simple to plan production and run at the high levels of utilization needed to generate the most efficient operations performance.

All in all, a system without uncertainty is easy to control and manage. Performance can be measured using objective standards. And since the system is not subject to disturbances from the outside, the causes of any operations-related problems are also easy to diagnose.

## The Focused Factory Concept

**focused factory** An operation that concentrates on performing one particular task in one particular part of the plant; used for promoting experience and effectiveness through repetition and concentration on one task necessary for success.

Obviously, such an ideal world as proposed by Thompson is virtually impossible to create, and even in goods companies the demands of purchasing the inputs and marketing's management of the outputs have to be traded off against the ideal operations demands. In goods manufacturing, this tradeoff has been accomplished through the **focused factory**.[4] The focused factory focuses on a particular job; once this focus is achieved, the factory does a better job because repetition and concentration in one area allow the workforce and managers to become effective and experienced in the task required for success. The focused factory broadens Thompson's perfect-world model in that it argues that focus generates effectiveness as well as efficiency. In other words, the focused factory can meet the demands of the market better whether the demand is low cost through efficiency, high quality, or any other criterion.

## The Plant-within-a-Plant Concept

**plant-within-a-plant (PWP)** The strategy of breaking up large, unfocused plants into smaller units buffered from one another so that each can be focused separately.

The idea of a focused factory can be extended in another direction by introducing the **plant-within-a-plant (PWP)** concept. Because there are advantages to having production capability at a single site, the plant-within-a-plant strategy introduces the concept of breaking up large, unfocused plants into smaller units buffered from one another so that they can each be focused separately.

**buffering** Surrounding the technical core with input and output components to buffer environmental influences.

In goods manufacturing, the concept of **buffering** is a powerful one. "Organizations seek to buffer environmental influences by surrounding their technical core with input and output components."[5] A PWP can thus be operated in a manner close to Thompson's perfect-world model if buffer inventories are created on the input and output sides. On the input side, the components needed in a plant can be inventoried and their quality controlled before they are needed; in this way, it can appear to the PWP that the quality and flow of the inputs into the system are constant. In a similar way, the PWP can be separated from downstream plants or from the market by creating finished goods inventories. Automobile manufacturers are good examples. Finished goods are absorbed downstream by an established retail dealership system that purchases and holds the manufacturer's inventory in regional markets until sold to the final consumer.

**smoothing** Managing the environment to reduce fluctuations in supply and/or demand.

**anticipating** Mitigating the worst effects of supply and demand fluctuations by planning for them.

The alternatives proposed by Thompson to buffering are smoothing, anticipating, and rationing. Smoothing and anticipating focus on the uncertainty introduced into the system by the flow of work; **smoothing** involves managing the environment to reduce fluctuations in supply and/or demand; and **anticipating** involves mitigating the worst effects

**rationing** Direct allocations of inputs and outputs when the demands placed on a system by the environment exceed the system's ability to handle them.

of those fluctuations by planning for them. Finally, **rationing** involves resorting to triage when the demands placed on the system by the environment exceed its ability to handle them. Successful firms preplan smoothing, anticipating, and rationing strategies so that they can be more efficiently implemented in times of need.

## Applying Efficiency Models to Service Firms

The application of operations concepts to services is a bumpy road. The problem can be easily understood by thinking about the servuction model presented in Chapter 1. From an operational point of view, the key characteristics of the model are that the customer is an integral part of the process and that the system operates in real time. Because customers are often inseparable from the operation, the system can be (and often is) used to customize the service for each individual. Consequently, as the amount of customer contact increases within a service operation, the efficiency of the operation itself decreases.

To put it bluntly, the servuction system itself is an operations nightmare. In most cases it is impossible to use inventories on the input and output sides of the operations and impossible to decouple production from the customer. Instead of receiving demand at a constant rate, the system is linked directly to a market that frequently varies from day to day, hour to hour, and even minute to minute (see E-Services in Action). This creates massive problems in capacity planning and utilization—the fundamental building blocks of managing supply and demand. In fact, in many instances the only time supply and demand match up in service firms happens purely by accident. For example, when are there exactly enough wait staff to serve restaurant customers, when are there exactly enough doctors and nurses to serve hospital patients, and when are there exactly enough tax accountants to serve clients? There are times when supply and demand do balance, but due to the unpredictable ebb and flow of customers, a balance is achieved only by accident.

It is clear, by their very nature, services do not meet the requirements of Thompson's *perfect-world model*. The closest the servuction model comes to this ideal state is the part of the system that is invisible to the customer. Even here, however, the customization taking place may introduce uncertainty into the system. Provided that all customization can take place within the servuction system itself, then the part invisible to the customer can be run separately. It can often be located in a place different from the customer contact portion of the model.[6] However, when customization cannot be done within the servuction system, uncertainty can be introduced into the back office.

Frances Roberts/Alamy

The servuction system itself is an operations nightmare! Customers do not arrive one at a time to be immediately processed. All too often, customers arrive in bunches resulting in wait times that are not characteristic of a peak efficiency model.

Instead of "the single kind of product" desired by the perfect-world model, the service system can be called upon to make a different customized "product" for each customer. Indeed, one could argue that since each customer is different and is an integral part of the process, and since each experience or product is unique, the uncertainty about the next task to be performed is massive.

The Thompson model requires inputs that flow continuously, at a steady rate, and at a specified quality. Consider the inputs to the servuction system: the physical environment, contact personnel, other customers, and the individual customer. The physical environment (servicescape) may remain constant in many service encounters, but the other three inputs are totally variable, not only in their quality, but also in their rate of arrival into the process.

Moreover, contact personnel are individuals, not inanimate objects. They have emotions and feelings and, like all other people, are affected by things happening in their lives outside of the work environment. If they arrive in a bad mood, this can influence their performance throughout the day. And that bad mood directly influences the customer, since the service worker is a visible part of the experience being purchased.

Customers can also be subject to moods that can influence their behavior toward the service firm and toward one another. Some moods are predictable, like the mood when a home team wins and the crowds hit the local bars. Other moods are individual, specific, and totally unpredictable until after the consumer is already part of the servuction system.

Finally, customers arrive at the service firm at unpredictable rates, making smoothing and anticipation of incoming demand difficult. One minute a restaurant can be empty, and in the next few minutes, it can be full. One need only consider the variability of demand for cashiers in a grocery store to understand the basics of this problem. Analysis of demand can often show predictable peaks that can be planned for in advance, but even this precaution introduces inefficiency since the firm would ideally prefer the customers to arrive in a steady stream. Worse still are the unpredictable peaks. Planning for these peaks would produce large amounts of excess capacity at most times—lots of cashiers standing around waiting for the peak rush to begin. The excess would strain the entire system, undermining the experience for customer and contact personnel alike.

## Operations Solutions for Service Firms

Within the operations management and marketing literatures of the past decade, a growing list of strategies has emerged regarding overcoming some of the problems of service operations. These strategies can be classified into five broad areas:

1. isolating the technical core;
2. production-lining the whole system;
3. creating flexible capacity;
4. increasing customer participation; and
5. moving the time of demand.

***Isolating the Technical Core*** Isolating the technical core proposes the clear separation of the servuction system (the part of the service operation where the customer is present), which is characterized by a high degree of customer contact, from the technical core. Once separation is achieved, different management philosophies should be adopted for each separate unit of operation. In other words, let's divide the service firm into two distinct areas—high customer contact, and no/low customer contact—and operate each area differently. For example, consider a restaurant where high customer contact takes place in the dining and bar areas and low customer contact takes place in the kitchen area separate from the customer.

Plush Studios/Bill Reitzel/Blend Images/Jupiter Images

The use of physical barriers, such as a well-placed counter in a service establishment, enable service providers to separate high contact areas where effectiveness is maximized from the technical core where operational efficiency is the major goal.

In high customer contact areas, management should focus on optimizing the experience for the consumer. Conversely, once the technical core (no/low contact area) has been isolated, it should be subjected to traditional production-lining approaches.[7] In sum, high-contact systems should sacrifice efficiency in the interest of the customer, but low-contact systems need not do so.[8]

Isolating the technical core argues for minimizing the amount of customer contact with the system. "Clients … pose problems for organizations … by disrupting their routines, ignoring their offers for service, failing to comply with their procedures, making exaggerated demands and so forth."[9] Thus, operating efficiency is reduced by the uncertainty introduced into the system by the customer.[10]

**decoupling** Disassociating the technical core from the servuction system.

Examples of **decoupling** the technical core from high-contact areas include suggestions from operations experts such as handling only exceptions on a face-to-face basis, with routine transactions as much as possible being handled by telephone or, even better, by mail or e-mail—mail or e-mail transactions have the great advantage of being able to be inventoried.[11] In addition, the degree of customer contact should be matched to customer requirements, and the amount of high-contact service offered should be the minimum acceptable to the customer.[12] Overall, operational efficiency always favors low-contact systems, but effectiveness from the customer's point of view may be something completely different.

At this point, the need for marketing involvement in the approach becomes clear, as a decision about the extent of customer contact favored by the customer is clearly a marketing issue. In some cases, a high degree of customer contact can be used to differentiate the service from its competitors; in such cases, the operational costs must be weighed against the competitive benefits. Consider the competitive advantages that a five-star restaurant has over a fast-food franchise.

Conversely, in some situations, the segment of the firm that the operations group views as the back office is not actually invisible to the customer. For example, in some financial services, the teller operation takes place in the administrative offices. Operationally, this means that staff members can leave their paperwork to serve customers only when needed. Unfortunately, customers view this operationally efficient system negatively. A customer waiting to be served can see a closed teller window and observe staff who apparently do not care because they sit at their desks without offering to assist the customer. However, the reality is that these tellers may be very busy, but the nature of the administrative work is such that they may not give this impression to customers.

Even if it is decided that part of the system can be decoupled, marketing has a major role in evaluating and implementing alternative approaches. Any change in the way the servuction system works implies a change in the behavior of the customer. For example, a switch from a personal service to online banking clearly requires a massive change in the way the customer behaves in the system.

Sometimes decoupling the system to become more efficient does not go over well with customers. For example, in its effort to make its tellers use their time more efficiently, First National Bank of Chicago made national news when it started charging customers a $3.00 fee for speaking with a bank teller. The bank's Chicago competition quickly created promotional messages featuring "live tellers" and giving away "free" money at their teller windows. Even Jay Leno, from NBC's "The Tonight Show" got in on the act: "Nice day isn't it? … That'll be $3.00 please. Huh? What? Who? … That'll be another $9.00 please."[13]

*Production-Lining the Whole System*    A second possible solution to tackle the operations problems of service firms involves production-lining the whole system. The **production-line approach** involves the application of hard and soft technologies to both the "front" and "back" of the service operation.[14] **Hard technologies** involve hardware to facilitate the production of a standardized product. Similarly, **soft technologies** refer to rules, regulations, and procedures that should be followed to produce the same result. This kind of approach to increasing operational efficiency is relatively rare, and, indeed, fast-food firms provide a classic example in which customization is minimal, volume is large, and customer participation in the process is high.

Generating any kind of operational efficiency in such a high-contact system implies a limited product line. In the case of fast food, the product line is the menu. Moreover, customization must be kept to a minimum since the whole operating system is linked straight through to the consumer. The primary problem is how to provide efficient, standardized service at some acceptable level of quality while simultaneously treating each customer as unique.[15] Past attempts to solve this problem illustrate its complexity. Attempts at forms of routine personalization such as the "have-a-nice-day" syndrome have had positive effects on the perceived friendliness of the service provider but adverse effects on perceived competence. Consequently, an apparently simple operations decision can have complex effects on customer perceptions.

Production-lining the whole system applied to fast food also depends for its success on a large volume of customers being available to take the standardized food that is produced. Since the invisible component is not decoupled and food cannot be prepared to order, the operating system has to run independently of individual demand and assume that, in the end, aggregate demand will absorb the food produced. This is why premade sandwiches are stacked in bins as they wait to be absorbed by future demand in the marketplace.

Such an operating system is extremely demanding of its customers, who must preselect what they want to eat. They are expected to have their order ready when they reach the order point. They must leave the order point quickly and carry their food to the table. Finally, in many cases, these same customers are expected to bus their own tables.

*Creating Flexible Capacity*    The third method to effectively manage service operations is used to minimize the effects of variable demand by creating flexible capacity (supply).[16] For example, consider how Verizon has increased the capacity for the UMass Memorial Healthcare system through the implementation of their SONET Services. SONET Services provides the hospital with the ability to communicate with physicians and healthcare professionals without being in the same place at the same time (see E-Services in Action).

**production-line approach** The application of hard and soft technologies to a service operation in order to produce a standardized service product.

**hard technologies** Hardware that facilitates the production of a standardized product.

**soft technologies** Rules, regulations, and procedures that facilitate the production of a standardized product.

## E-SERVICES *IN ACTION*

### Verizon Enterprise Solutions Group: Teaming Up with Healthcare

Verizon Enterprise Solutions Group provides network solutions for large businesses, government and education customers across the United States. As a business entity, the solutions group employs more than 7,800 employees and generated approximately $6 billion in 2004 business unit revenues. Verizon Enterprise Solutions Group products and services include voice services, voice and data customer premises equipment, managed network services, and a vast array of data services. Key target markets include finance, education, health care and the government.

One of the more intriguing solutions projects has been Verizon's interaction with UMass Memorial Healthcare, the largest healthcare system in Massachusetts. Thanks to a recent $9.6 million agreement between the healthcare system and Verizon, medical specialists will now collaborate in the diagnosis and care of patients through the use of high-speed, broadband services. Manage SONET Services allows patient histories and diagnostic data to be viewed simultaneously at the healthcare system's three campuses, four community hospitals and other care facilities. SONET Services provides the hospital with the ability to communicate with physicians and healthcare professionals without being in the same place at the same time. Patient privacy is also ensured.

Verizon Enterprise Solutions Group also offers Telemedicine Solutions to the healthcare industry. Telemedicine Solutions can literally place physicians and other key medical personnel in patient homes and other critical places. Physicians can now communicate with paramedics while en route to the hospital and oversee procedures in an operating room without being physically present. Telemedicine Solutions utilize picture archiving and communications systems that provide information to multiple users at the same time regardless of their locations.

The ultimate goals of all Verizon healthcare solutions are to increase patient access to healthcare services, provide faster service delivery, improve patient outcomes, and reduce healthcare costs. In the meantime, Verizon Enterprise Solutions Group generates an increasingly significant amount of revenue for the firm.

Source: **http://www22.verizon.com/enterprisesolutions/Default/Index.jsp**, accessed 9 April, 2009.

However, even in this area, strategies that start as common-sense operational solutions have far-reaching marketing implications as these new initiatives come face-to-face with the service firm's customer base. For example, a few of the strategies to create flexible capacity mentioned in Chapter 3 included (1) using part-time employees; (2) cross-training employees so that the majority of employee efforts focus on customer-contact jobs during peak hours; and (3) sharing capacity with other firms.

Although these strategies are fairly straightforward from an operational point of view, consider their marketing implications. Part-time employees appear to be a useful strategy since they can be used to provide extra capacity in peak times without increasing the costs in off-peak times. There are, however, a number of marketing implications. For example, part-time employees may deliver a lower quality service than full-time workers; their dedication to quality may be less, as their training will probably be. They are used at times when the operation is at its busiest, such as holiday seasons or during tourist seasons, when demand is fast and furious, and this may be reflected in their attitudes of frustration, which can be highly visible to customers, negatively influencing customer perceptions of the quality of service delivered.[17]

In a similar way, the other two possible solutions for creating flexible capacity also have major marketing implications. First, focusing on customer contact jobs during peak demand presupposes that it is possible to identify the key part of the service from the customer's point of view. Secondly, the dangers of sharing capacity are numerous. For example, the television classic "Cheers" provided ample examples of the problems associated with the upscale and upstairs customers of Melville's Restaurant as they mixed with Cheers everyday clientele such as Norm and Cliff. Confusion may be produced in the customer's mind over exactly what the service firm is doing (e.g., who is their target market?) and this could be particularly critical during changeover times when customers from two different firms share the same facility, each group with different priorities and different behavior scripts. For example, a recent MBA student described his grand-mother's confusion with her favorite local ice cream shop that sold ice cream during the day and then transformed into a gay nightclub in the evenings.

***Increasing Customer Participation***   A fourth approach to managing service operations involves increasing the customer's involvement with the service operation itself. For example, service firms wishing to obtain LEED Certification for sustainability business practices are encouraged to sit down and work with LEED volunteers before beginning operations (see Sustainability and Services in Action). The essence of increasing customer participation is to replace the work done by the employees of the firm with work done by the customer.[18] Unlike the other strategies discussed, which focus on improving the efficiency of the operation, this approach primarily focuses on reducing the costs associated with providing the service to the customer. This strategy, too, has its tradeoffs.

Consider for a moment our earlier discussions about consumer behavioral scripts. Increasing consumer participation in the service encounter requires a substantial modification of the consumer's script. Moreover, as greater customer participation is required, customers are called upon to take greater personal responsibility for the service they receive. For example, the automatic teller machine (ATM) is seen by many operations personnel as a way of saving labor. In fact, the substitution of human labor with machines is a classic operations approach, and the ATM can definitely be viewed in that light. From a customer's point of view, such ATMs provide added convenience in terms of the hours during which the bank is accessible. However, it has been shown that for some customers, an ATM represents increased risk, less control of the situation, and a loss of human contact.[19]

Such a switching of activities to the customer clearly has major market implications since it changes the whole nature of the product received. Such changes in the customer's script, therefore, require much customer research and detailed planning prior to introducing any schemes to further involve customer participation in the service delivery process.

## Moving the Time of Demand to Fit Capacity

Finally, yet another strategy utilized to optimize the efficiency of service operations is the attempt to shift the time of demand to smooth the peaks and valleys associated with many services. Perhaps the classic example of this problem is the mass transit system that needs to create capacity to deal with the rush hour and, as a consequence, has much of its fleet and labor idle during non-rush hours. Many mass transit authorities have attempted to reduce the severity of the problem by inducing customers through discounts and giveaways to travel during non-rush periods. Once again, operations and marketing become intertwined. Smoothing demand is a useful strategy from an operations point of view; however, this strategy fails to recognize the change in consumer behavior needed to make the strategy effective. Unfortunately, because much of the travel on the mass transit system derives from demand based on consumer work schedules, little success in the effort to reallocate demand can be expected.[20]

## SUSTAINABILITY AND SERVICES *IN ACTION*

### LEED Ratings: Process Standards in Green Technology

The green initiative has truly taken the nation by storm, but many are left wondering what it truly means to be a green institution. The Leadership in Energy and Environmental Design (LEED) Rating Systems by the U.S. Green Building Council (USGBC) has established a means by which to truly test the environmental impact of construction projects. LEED ratings focus on six main components:

1. Sustainable site development
2. Water savings
3. Energy efficiency
4. Materials selection
5. Indoor environmental quality
6. Innovation & Design Process

The rating system is developed by LEED committees, which are composed of volunteers from various areas within the building and construction industry. The actual rating process is carried out by the Green Building Certification Institute (GBCI) and begins with the planning of the construction process. A strategy team of GBCI representatives and the major participants in the construction project will meet to review plans to define the goals and LEED rating desired. Throughout the construction process, resources for continuing to meet LEED standards are offered to managers of the project. Further education can also be attained from GBCI to ensure the continued success of the project, while online support is provided to help with the extensive documentation processes. The LEED rating system is based on a possible 69 points, and LEED designation levels are as follows:

| Level | Points |
|-------|--------|
| Platinum | 52-69 |
| Gold | 39-51 |
| Silver | 33-38 |
| Certified | 26-32 |

The service offered by the GBCI allows companies to achieve a multitude of benefits, all of which are obtained only through following the strict processes outlined. From the beginning application phase to the final certification, GBCI works closely with each management team to find the best possible LEED rating for the project. Though a standardized basic process is used for every undertaking, customization is necessary to deliver the highest quality support service and rating attainment for each project. In a way, LEED ratings are process approval standards which indeed demonstrate a company's dedication to environmental wellbeing.

Source: LEED Rating Systems, **http://www.usgbc.org/DisplayPage.aspx?CMSPageID=222**.

## The Art of Blueprinting

One of the most common techniques used to analyze and manage complex production processes in pursuit of operational efficiency is flowcharting. Flowcharts identify:

- *the directions in which processes flow;*
- *the time it takes to move from one process to the next;*
- *the costs involved with each process step;*

- *the amount of inventory buildup at each step; and*
- *the bottlenecks in the system.*

**blueprinting** The flowcharting of a service
operation.

The flowcharting of a service operation, commonly referred to as **blueprinting**, is a useful tool not only for the operations manager but for the marketing manager as well.[21]

Because services are delivered by an interactive process involving the consumer, the marketing manager in a service firm needs to have a detailed knowledge of the operation. Blueprinting provides a useful systematic method for acquiring that knowledge. Blueprints enable the marketing manager to understand which parts in the operating system are visible to the consumer and hence part of the servuction system—the fundamental building blocks of consumer perceptions.

Identifying the components of an individual firm's servuction system turns out to be more difficult than it first appears. Many firms, for example, underestimate the number of points of contact between them and their customers. Many forget or underestimate the importance of telephone operators, secretarial and janitorial staff, or accounting personnel. The material that follows describes the simple process of flowcharting these numerous points of contact. Service flowcharts, in addition to being useful to the operations managers, allow marketing managers to better understand the servuction process.

The heart of the service product is the experience that delivers the bundle of benefits to the customer. This "experience" can occur in a building or in an environment created by the service firm, such as the complex environments created at Disney World, Epcot Center, and Universal Studios. In other instances, such as lawn care, the service interaction takes place in a natural setting. In the end, it is the process itself that creates the experience that delivers the benefits desired by the consumer. Designing that process, therefore, becomes key to the product design for a service firm.

The interactive process that is visible to consumers develops their perceptions of reality and defines the final service product. However, as the servuction model discussed in Chapter 1 demonstrated, the visible part of the operations process, with which the consumer interacts, must be supported by an invisible process.

The search for operational efficiency is not unique to service firms, but it does pose some interesting problems. A change in the service operation may be more efficient, but it may also change the quality of interaction with the consumer. For example, for many years now, students at many universities can now register for classes through automated telephone or online services. This type of operation offers increased efficiency but sometimes minimizes the quality of the student/advisor interaction. In the end, a detailed blueprint provides a means of communication between operations and marketing, and can highlight potential problems on paper before they occur in realtime.

## An Example of a Simple Blueprint[22]

Figure 5.3 shows a simple process in which, for now, it is assumed that the entire operation is visible to the customer. It represents the blueprint of a cafeteria-style restaurant and specifies the steps involved in getting a meal. In this example, each process activity is represented by a box. In contrast to a goods manufacturer, the "raw materials" flowing through the process are the customers. Due to the intangibility of services, there are no inventories in the process, but clearly, inventories of customers form at each step in the process while they wait their turn to proceed to the next counter. A restaurant run in this manner would be a single long chain of counters with customers progressing along the chain and emerging after paying, such as a Western Sizzlin' or Golden Corral. In Figure 5.3, the cost figure by each stage represents the cost of providing personnel to service each counter.

**FIG-5.3** Blueprint for Cafeteria-Style Restaurant

| | Appetizer counter | Salad counter | Hot-food counter | Dessert counter | Drinks counter | Cashier |
|---|---|---|---|---|---|---|
| | $8/hr | $8/hr | $8/hr | $8/hr | $8/hr | $10/hr |
| Number of stations | I | I | I | I | I | I |
| Activity time | 15 sec | 30 sec | 60 sec | 40 sec | 20 sec | 30 sec |
| Process time | 15 sec | 30 sec | 60 sec | 40 sec | 20 sec | 30 sec |
| Maximum output/hr | 240 | 120 | 60* | 90 | 180 | 120 |

*Bottleneck      Service cost per meal = $\dfrac{50}{60}$ = $0.83

**service cost per meal**
The labor costs associated with providing a meal on a per-meal basis (total labor costs/maximum output per hour).

**process time** Calculated by dividing the activity time by the number of locations at which the activity is performed.

**activity time** The time required to perform one activity at one station.

**stations** A location at which an activity is performed within a service blueprint.

**maximum output per hour** The number of people that can be processed at each station in one hour.

To calculate the **service cost per meal**, or the labor costs associated with providing the meal on a per-meal basis, the following calculations are made:

First, the **process time** is calculated by dividing the **activity time** (the time required to perform the activity) by the number of **stations**, or locations performing the activity. In our example, the process and activity times are the same because only one station is available for each activity.

Second, the **maximum output per hour** for each location is calculated based on the process time. Simply stated, the maximum output per hour is the number of people that can be served at each station in an hour's time. For example, the process time at the salad counter is 30 seconds. This means that two people can be processed in a minute, or 120 people (two people × 60 minutes) in an hour. Another easy way to calculate the maximum output per hour is to use the formula: 60(60/process time). In our example, the salad counter calculation would be 60(60/30) = 120.

Finally, to calculate the service cost per meal, total labor costs per hour of the entire system are divided by the maximum output per hour for the system (service cost per meal = total labor costs/maximum output per hour). Total labor costs per hour are calculated simply by adding the hourly wages of personnel stationed at each counter. In our example, total labor cost per hour equals $50.00 ($8 + $8 + $8 + $8 + $8 + $10). Maximum output per hour is determined by selecting the lowest maximum output calculated in the second step. Hence, the service cost per meal in our example is $50.00/60 customers, or $0.83 per meal.

Why would you use the lowest maximum output per hour? This step is particularly confusing for some students. The lowest maximum output in the system is the maximum number of people who can be processed through the entire system in an hour's time. In our example, 240 customers can be processed through the appetizer counter in an hour; however, only 120 customers can be processed through the salad counter in the same amount of time. This means that after the first hour, 120 customers (240 − 120) are still waiting to be processed through the salad counter. Similarly, only 60 customers can be processed through the hot-food counter in an hour's time. Since 60 is the lowest maximum output per hour for any counter in the system, only 60 customers can actually complete the entire system in an hour.

## The Service Operations Manager's Perspective

The first thing the blueprint does is provide a check on the logical flow of the whole process. Clearly, a service blueprint makes it immediately apparent if a task is being performed out of sequence. At this point, we shall place a constraint on our example system that the cashier's station is fixed and cannot be moved to another point in the process. All other stations can be moved and resequenced.

**bottlenecks** Points in the system at which consumers wait the longest periods of time.

Once the different steps have been identified, it is relatively easy to identify the potential **bottlenecks** in the system. Bottlenecks represent points in the system where consumers wait the longest periods of time. In Figure 5.3, the hot-food counter is an obvious bottleneck since it represents the longest process time—the time to process one individual through that stage. A balanced production line is one in which the process times of all the steps are the same and inventories or, in our case, consumers flow smoothly through the system without waiting for the next process.

To solve this particular bottleneck problem, we could consider adding one extra station, in this case an extra counter, to the hot-food stage. The process time would drop to 30 seconds (60 seconds divided by 2). The bottleneck would then become the dessert counter, which has a process time of 40 seconds and a maximum turnover rate of 90 persons per hour. Costs would go up by $8.00 per hour since we added an additional hot-food counter; however, the service cost per meal would go down to $0.64 per meal. These changes are illustrated in Figure 5.4.

The creative use of additional counters and staff may produce a model such as that shown in Figure 5.5, which combines certain activities and uses multiple stations. This particular layout is capable of handling 120 customers per hour compared with the original layout presented in Figure 5.3. Although labor costs rise, the service cost per meal falls because of the increase in the number of consumers who are processed through the system in a shorter period of time. Further changes to this particular setup would be fruitless. Adding counters at the bottlenecks created by both the dessert/drinks and cashier counters would actually increase the service cost per meal from $0.48 ($58.00/120 meals) to $0.50 ($68.00/137.14 meals).

**FIG-5.4** Modified Blueprint for Cafeteria-Style Restaurant

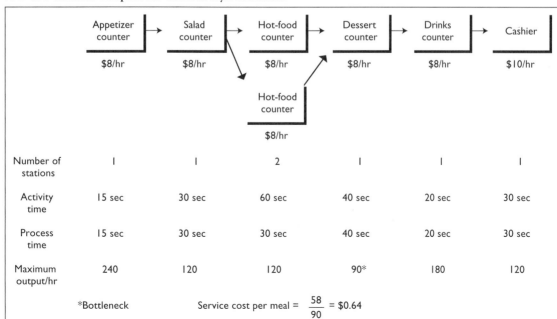

|  | Appetizer counter | Salad counter | Hot-food counter | Dessert counter | Drinks counter | Cashier |
|---|---|---|---|---|---|---|
|  | $8/hr | $8/hr | $8/hr | $8/hr | $8/hr | $10/hr |
|  |  |  | Hot-food counter |  |  |  |
|  |  |  | $8/hr |  |  |  |
| Number of stations | 1 | 1 | 2 | 1 | 1 | 1 |
| Activity time | 15 sec | 30 sec | 60 sec | 40 sec | 20 sec | 30 sec |
| Process time | 15 sec | 30 sec | 30 sec | 40 sec | 20 sec | 30 sec |
| Maximum output/hr | 240 | 120 | 120 | 90* | 180 | 120 |

*Bottleneck          Service cost per meal = $\dfrac{58}{90}$ = $0.64

**FIG-5.5** Alternate Blueprint for Cafeteria-Style Restaurant

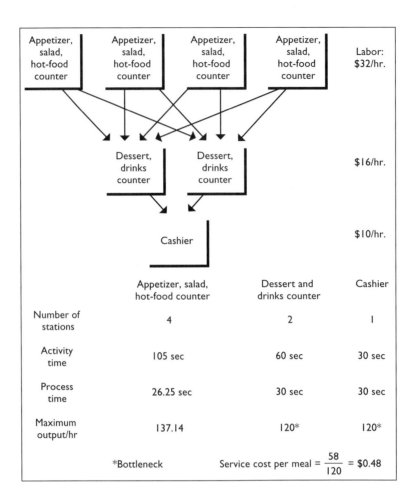

| | Appetizer, salad, hot-food counter | Dessert and drinks counter | Cashier |
|---|---|---|---|
| Number of stations | 4 | 2 | 1 |
| Activity time | 105 sec | 60 sec | 30 sec |
| Process time | 26.25 sec | 30 sec | 30 sec |
| Maximum output/hr | 137.14 | 120* | 120* |

*Bottleneck          Service cost per meal $= \dfrac{58}{120} = \$0.48$

## The Service Marketing Manager's Perspective

A marketing manager dealing with the process illustrated in Figure 5.3 has some of the same problems as the operations manager. The process as defined is designed to operate at certain production levels, and these are the service standards that customers should perceive. But if the process is capable of processing only 60 customers per hour, there may be a problem. For example, lunch customers who need to return to work quickly might purchase their lunches at a competing restaurant that serves its customers more efficiently. Also, it is clear that the bottleneck at the hot-food counter will produce lengthy, possibly frustrating, waits within the line.

The marketing manager should immediately recognize the benefits of changing the system to process customers more effectively. However, the blueprint also shows the change in consumer behavior that would be required in order for the new system to operate. In Figure 5.3, the consumer goes from counter to counter, has only one choice at each counter, will probably have to wait in line at each counter, and will definitely have to wait longer at the hot-food counter. Moreover, the wait at each stage will certainly exceed the time spent in each activity. In the process proposed in Figure 5.5, the consumer visits fewer stations but is frequently faced with a choice between different stations. Clearly, depending on the format chosen, the behavior script to be followed by consumers will be different. In addition, the restaurant itself will look completely different.

The use of the blueprinting approach allows the marketing and operations personnel to analyze in detail the process that they are jointly trying to create and manage. It can easily highlight the types of conflict between operations and marketing managers and provide a common framework for their discussion and a basis for the resolution of their problems.

## Using Service Blueprints to Identify the Servuction Process

Blueprints may also be used for a different purpose. Consider Figure 5.6, which shows a much more detailed blueprint for the production of a discount brokerage service. This chart is designed to identify the points of contact between the service firm and the customer. The points above the line are visible to the consumer, and those below are invisible. In assessing the quality of service received, according to the servuction model, the customer refers to the points of contact when developing perceptions regarding the value of service quality received.

To illustrate, consider the customers to be proactive rather than reactive. Consider them as worried individuals looking for clues that they have made the right decision rather than as inanimate raw materials to which things are done. The points of contact are the clues that develop the servuction process.

Besides illustrating a more complicated process, Figure 5.6 has a number of added features. First, each of the main features is linked to a target time. In the top right corner, for example, the time to mail a statement is targeted as five days after the month's end. In designing a service, these target times should initially be set by marketing, and they should be based on the consumers' expected level of service. If the service is to be offered in a competitive marketplace, it may be necessary to set standards higher than those of services currently available. Once the standards have been set, however, the probability of achieving them must be assessed. If the firm is prepared to invest enough, it may be feasible to meet all of the standards developed by marketing; doing so, however, affects the costs and, therefore, the subsequent price of the service. The process should, then, be an interactive one.

Figure 5.6 also highlights the potential **fail points**, "F." Fail points have three characteristics:

1. the potential for operations malfunction is high;
2. the result of the malfunction is visible to consumers; and
3. a system malfunction is regarded by consumers as particularly significant.

## A Marketing or an Operations Blueprint?

Although the idea of a blueprint is attractive to both marketing and operations, it may well be that a marketing blueprint should be prepared in a different way. The blueprints we have discussed so far have an internal focus—although they identify clearly the tangible points of contact with the client, they start from the organization and look outward.

An alternative way to develop a blueprint would be to start from consumer scripts. Consumers, individually or in groups, would be asked to describe the process or steps they follow in using a service. Obviously, such an approach cannot cover the invisible part of the service firm, but it can provide a much better understanding of the points of contact. The process as described by the consumer may differ greatly from that perceived by the firm.

Consumers asked to describe a flight on USAir, for example, might start with their experience with the travel agent. They might then describe the process of getting to the airport, parking, and entering the terminal. If the signs for USAir and the entrance to its specific terminal are confusing, this will be reflected in consumers' perceptions of the airline. A parking lot that is littered, poorly lit, and inhabited by vagrants will also deter customers. Although the airline may not have direct control over these points of contact, it could be a wise investment for the airline to use its own staff to improve the parking

**fail points** Points in the system at which the potential for malfunction is high and at which a failure would be visible to the customer and regarded as significant.

**FIG-5.6** Flowchart of a Discount Brokerage Service

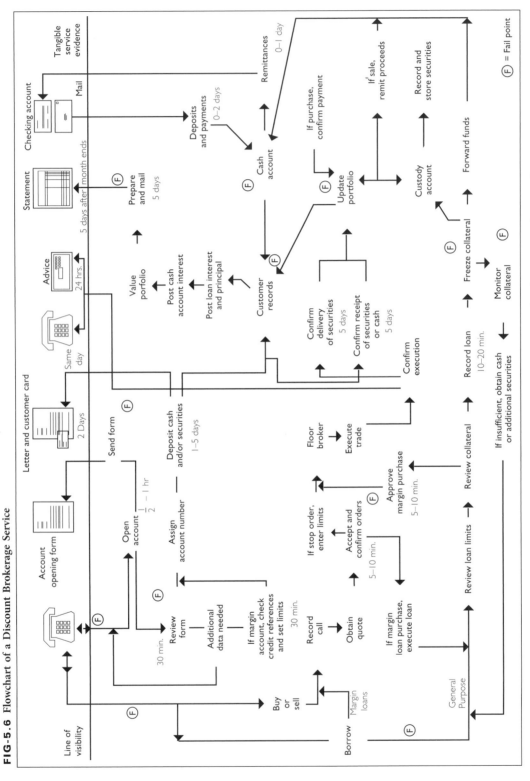

Source: G. Lynn Shostack, "Service Design in the Operating Environment," pp. 27–43, 1984, reprinted with permission from *Developing New Services*, William R. George and Claudia Marshall, eds., published by American Marketing Association, Chicago, IL 60606.

lot. McDonald's long ago learned the value of removing the litter not only from its own property but also from the adjoining roadways. McDonald's recognized that their customers' experiences began long before they entered the actual restaurant.

## Constructing the Service Blueprint[23]

The first step in the design of a service blueprint is to elicit scripts from both employees and consumers. The primary objective of this task is to break down the service system into a sequence of events followed by both parties. Too often, management makes the mistake of developing a **one-sided blueprint** based on its own perception of how the sequence of events should occur. This one-sided approach fails to recognize that consumer perceptions, not management's, define the realities of the encounter. Similarly, employee scripts are equally important in identifying those parts of the service system not observable to the consumer. Hence, both scripts are necessary to develop a successful blueprint.

Script theory suggests that consumers possess purchasing scripts that guide their thinking and behavior during service encounters. The scripts contain the sequence of actions that consumers follow when entering a service interaction. Experts believe that "these action sequences, or cognitive scripts, guide the interpretation of information, the development of expectations, and the enactment of appropriate behavior routines."[24]

Similarly, service employees also have scripts that dictate their own behavior during interactions with the customer. **Convergent scripts**, those that are mutually agreeable, enhance the probability of customer satisfaction and the quality of the relationship between the customer and the service operation. **Divergent scripts** point to areas that need to be examined and corrected because consumer expectations are not being met and evaluations of service quality could decline.

Obtaining consumer and employee scripts is a potentially powerful technique for analyzing the service encounter. Scripts provide the dialogue from which consumer and employee perceptions of the encounter can be analyzed and potential or existing problems identified. Overall, scripts provide the basis for:

- *planning service encounters;*
- *setting goals and objectives;*
- *developing behavioral routines that maximize the opportunities for a successful exchange; and*
- *evaluating the effectiveness of current service delivery systems.*

The procedure used to develop **two-sided blueprints** is to present employees and customers with a script-relevant situation, such as the steps taken to proceed through an airline boarding experience. Respondents are requested to note specific events or activities expected in their involvement in the situation. In particular, employees and consumers are asked to pay special attention to those contact activities that elicit strong positive or negative reactions during the service encounter. **Script norms** are then constructed by grouping together commonly mentioned events and ordering the events in their sequence of occurrence.

To facilitate the process of identifying script norms, the blueprint designer can compare the frequency of specific events mentioned by each of the groups. The value of this process is the potential recognition of gaps or discrepancies existing between employee and consumer perceptions. For example, consumers may mention the difficulties associated with parking, which employees may not mention since many report to work before the operation is open to customers.

The second step of the blueprint development process is to identify steps in the process at which the system can go awry. By asking employees and customers to further

**one-sided blueprint** An unbalanced blueprint based on management's perception of how the sequence of events *should* occur.

**convergent scripts** Employee/consumer scripts that are mutually agreeable and enhance the probability of customer satisfaction.

**divergent scripts** Employee/consumer scripts that "mismatch" and point to areas in which consumer expectations are not being met.

**two-sided blueprint** A blueprint that takes into account both employee and customer perceptions of how the sequence of events actually occurs.

**script norms** Proposed scripts developed by grouping together events commonly mentioned by both employees and customers, and then ordering those events in their sequence of occurrence.

focus on events that are important in conveying service (dis)satisfaction, fail points can be isolated. The consequences of service failures can be greatly reduced by analyzing fail points and instructing employees on the appropriate response or action when the inevitable failure occurs.

After the sequence of events/activities and potential fail points have been identified, the third step in the process involves specifying the timeframe of service execution. The major cost component of most service systems relates to the time required to complete the service; consequently, standard execution time norms must be established.

Once the standard execution times of the events that make up the service encounter have been specified, the manager can analyze the profitability of the system, given the costs of inputs needed for the system to operate. The resulting blueprint allows the planner to determine the profitability of the existing service delivery system as well as to speculate on the effects on profitability when changing one or more system components. Consequently, the service blueprint allows a company to test its assumptions on paper and minimize the system's shortcomings before it imposes the system on customers and employees. The service manager can test a prototype of the delivery system with potential customers and use the feedback to modify the blueprint before testing the procedure again.

## Blueprinting and New-Product Development: The Roles of Complexity and Divergence

Blueprints may also be used in new-product development. Once the process has been documented and a blueprint has been drawn, choices can be made that will produce "new" products. Although the processes in Figures 5.3, 5.4 and 5.5 are for the same task, from the consumer's point of view they are very different. The three blueprints define alternatives that are operationally feasible; the choice between which of the three to implement is for marketing to decide.

Strategically, the decision may be to move the line separating visibility and invisibility. Operationally, arguments have been made for minimizing the visible component by isolating the technical core of the process. From a marketing point of view, however, more visibility may create more differentiation in the mind of the consumer. For example, a restaurant can make its kitchen into a distinctive feature by making it visible to restaurant patrons. This poses constraints on the operational personnel, but it may add value in the mind of the consumer.

**complexity** A measure of the number and intricacy of the steps and sequences that constitute a process.

**divergence** A measure of the degrees of freedom service personnel are allowed when providing a service.

New-product development within service firms can be implemented through the introduction of complexity and divergence.[25] **Complexity** is a measure of the number and intricacy of the steps and sequences that constitute the process—the more steps, the more complex the process. **Divergence** is defined as the degrees of freedom service personnel are allowed when providing the service. As an example, Figures 5.7 and 5.8 illustrate the blueprints for two florists who differ dramatically in their complexity and divergence. Although they perform equivalent tasks from an operations viewpoint, they can be very different from a marketing viewpoint and, therefore, constitute new products.

Figure 5.7 presents a traditional florist. The process, as in our restaurant example in Figure 5.3, is linear and involves a limited number of steps and so is low in complexity. However, the generation of flower arrangements under such a system calls for considerable discretion or degrees of freedom to be allowed the florist at each stage—in the choice of vase, flowers, and display—and produces a heterogeneous final product. The system is, therefore, high in divergence.

**FIG-5.7** Park Avenue Florist

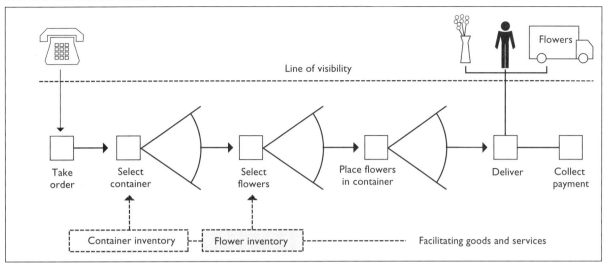

Source: G. Lynn Shostack, "Service Positioning through Structural Change," *Journal of Marketing*, 51, (January 1987), pp. 34–43. Reprinted by permission of the American Marketing Association.

**volume-oriented positioning strategy** A positioning strategy that reduces divergence to create product uniformity and reduce costs.

**niche positioning strategy** A positioning strategy that increases divergence in an operation to tailor the service experience to each customer.

**specialization positioning strategy** A positioning strategy that reduces complexity by unbundling the different services offered.

**unbundling** Divesting an operation of different services and concentrating on providing only one or a few services in order to pursue a specialization positioning strategy.

Figure 5.8 provides the blueprint for a second florist that has attempted to standardize its final product. Because the objective of this system is to deskill the job, the system is designed to generate a limited number of standardized arrangements. The divergence of the system is therefore reduced, but to achieve this, the complexity of the process is increased significantly.

In developing products in the service sector, the amount of manipulation of the operation's complexity and divergence are the two key choices. Reducing divergence creates the uniformity that can reduce costs, but it does so at the expense of creativity and flexibility in the system. Companies that wish to pursue a **volume-oriented positioning strategy** often do so by reducing divergence. For example, a builder of swimming pools who focuses on the installation of prefabricated vinyl pools has greatly reduced the divergence of his operations. In addition to lowering production costs, reducing divergence increases productivity and facilitates distribution of the standardized service. From the customer's perspective, reducing divergence is associated with improved reliability, availability, and uniform service quality. However, the downside of reduced divergence is the lack of customization that can be provided to individual customers.

On the other hand, increasing divergence creates flexibility in tailoring the experience to each customer, but it does so at increased expense, and consumer prices are subsequently higher. Companies wishing to pursue a **niche positioning strategy** do so through increasing the divergence in their operations. For example, our pool builder may increase the divergence of his operation by specializing in the design and construction of customized pools and spas that can be built to resemble anything from a classical guitar to an exclamation point! Profits, under this scenario, depend less on volume and more on margins on each individual purchase. The downside of increasing divergence is that the service operation becomes more difficult to manage, control, and distribute. Moreover, customers may not be willing to pay the higher prices associated with a customized service.

Reducing complexity is a **specialization positioning strategy** often involving the **unbundling** of the different services offered. Hence, our hypothetical pool builder may restrict himself to the installation of a single type of prefabricated pool and divest operations that were focused on supplemental services, such as pool maintenance and repair as

**FIG-5.8** Florist Services: Alternative Design

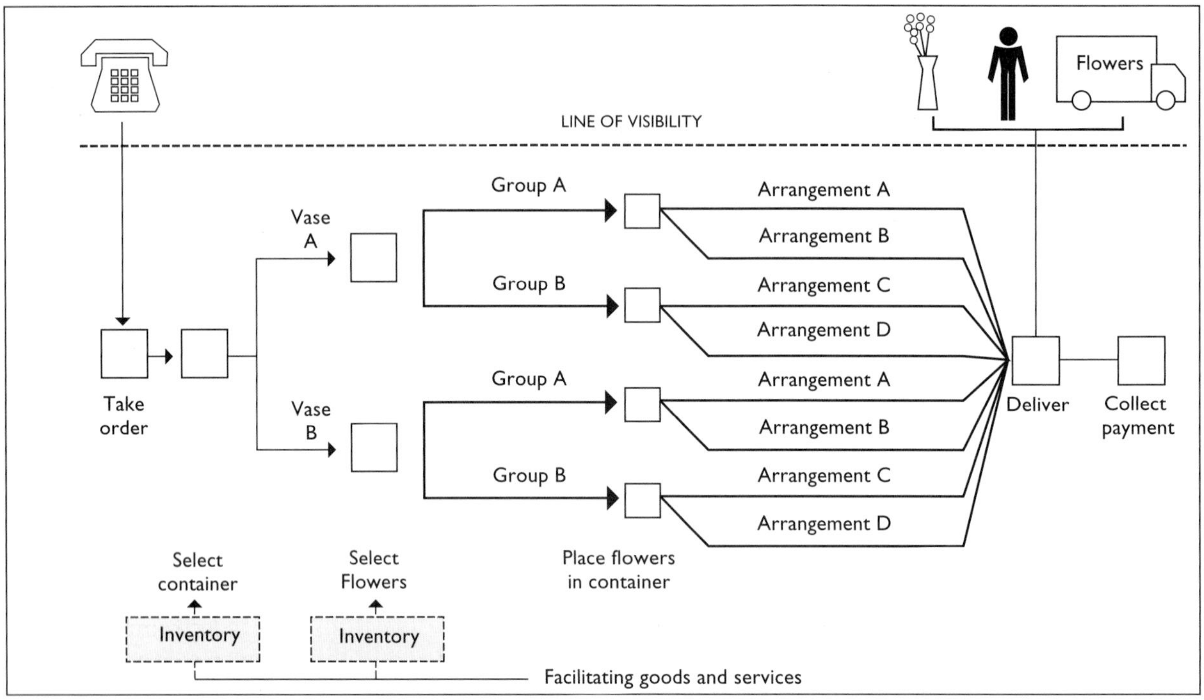

Source: G. Lynn Shostack, "Service Positioning through Structural Change," *Journal of Marketing*, 51, (January 1987), pp. 34–43. Reprinted by permission of the American Marketing Association.

well as the design of pools and spas. The advantages associated with reduced complexity include improved control over the final product and improved distribution. However, risks are involved if full-service competitors offering one-stop convenience continue to operate. The full-service competitor appeals to consumers wishing to work with a provider that offers a number of choices.

**penetration strategy** A positioning strategy that increases complexity by adding more services and/or enhancing current services to capture more of a market.

Increasing complexity is utilized by companies that pursue a mass market or **penetration strategy**. Increasing complexity translates into the addition of more services to the firm's offering, as well as the enhancement of current ones. Within this scenario, our pool builder would offer customized pools and spas and a wide variety of prefabricated vinyl pools. In addition to installation, other services such as general pool maintenance and repair would be offered. Firms pursuing a penetration strategy often try to be everything to everybody and often gloss over individual consumer needs. Moreover, when providing such a broad range of services, the quality of the provider's skills are bound to vary depending upon the task being performed, leaving some customers less than satisfied. Hence, firms that increase the complexity of their operations by offering enhanced and/or additional services run the risk of becoming vulnerable to companies that pursue more specialized types of operations.

## Summary

The primary objective of this chapter was to highlight the idea that for a service firm to be successful, its marketing and operations departments must work together. In a broad sense, one could view the functions of marketing and operations as the marriage of consumers' needs with the technology and manufacturing capabilities of the firm. This marriage entails many compromises that attempt to balance operational efficiency with the effectiveness of the system from the consumer's point of view. To be effective, operations personnel must recognize the importance of their marketing counterparts, and vice versa.

Firms operating at peak efficiency are free from outside influences and operate as if the market will consume the firm's production at a continuous rate. Uncertainty creates inefficiency. Hence, in an ideal situation, the technical core of the firm is able to operate without uncertainty on either the input or output side. Although the attempt to operate at peak efficiency is a worthy goal, it likely represents an unrealistic objective for most service firms. The production of most services is an operations nightmare. Instead of receiving demand at a constant rate, service firms are often linked directly to a market that frequently varies from day to day, hour to hour, and even minute to minute. Service customers frequently affect the time of demand, the cycle of demand, the type of demand, and the duration of many service transactions.

Plans to operate at peak efficiency must be altered to cope with the uncertainties inherent in service operations. Strategies that attempt to increase the efficiency of the service operation by facilitating the balance of supply and demand include minimizing the servuction system by isolating the technical core; production-lining the whole system utilizing hard and soft technologies; creating flexible capacity; increasing customer participation; and moving the time of demand to fit capacity.

Service blueprints can be developed that identify the directions in which processes flow and parts of a process that may both increase operational efficiency and enhance the customer's service experience. Operational changes made to the service blueprint often require changes in consumer behavior and, in some instances, lead to new service products. New service development is achieved through the introduction of complexity and divergence. Reducing divergence standardizes the service product and reduces production costs, whereas increasing divergence enables service providers to tailor their products to individual customers. Similarly, reducing complexity is consistent with a specialization positioning strategy, while increasing complexity is appropriate for firms pursuing a penetration strategy.

## Key Terms

technical core, p. 120
perfect-world model, p. 120
focused factory, p. 121
plant-within-a-plant (PWP), p. 121
buffering, p. 121
smoothing, p. 121
anticipating, p. 121
rationing, p. 122
decoupling, p. 124
production-line approach, p. 125
hard technologies, p. 125
soft technologies, p. 125

blueprinting, p. 129
service cost per meal, p. 130
process time, p. 130
activity time, p. 130
stations, p. 130
maximum output per
   hour, p. 130
bottlenecks, p. 131
fail points, p. 133
one-sided blueprint, p. 135
convergent scripts, p. 135
divergent scripts, p. 135

two-sided blueprints, p. 135
script norms, p. 135
complexity, p. 136
divergence, p. 136
volume-oriented positioning
   strategy, p. 137
niche positioning strategy, p. 137
specialization positioning
   strategy, p. 137
unbundling, p. 137
penetration strategy, p. 138

## Review Questions

1. Why is developing an effective process strategy particularly important for service firms?

2. Discuss the role of technology as a service firm transitions itself through the four stages of operational competitiveness.

3. Explain how the inability to inventory services on the input and output sides of the technical core affects the operational efficiency of most service firms.

4. Compare Thompson's perfect-world model to the focused factory and plant-within-a-plant concepts.

5. What is buffering? How do the strategies of anticipating, smoothing, and rationing relate to buffering?

6. Discuss some specific examples of how the customer's involvement in the service encounter influences the operational efficiency of the average service firm.

7. What does it mean to isolate the technical core of a business?

8. Provide examples of hard and soft technologies and explain their relevance to this chapter.

9. Discuss the steps for developing a meaningful blueprint.

10. What are the tradeoffs associated with increasing/decreasing divergence and increasing/decreasing complexity?

# Notes

1. Richard B. Chase and Robert H. Hayes, "Beefing Up Operations in Service Firms," *Sloan Management Review*, (Fall 1991), pp. 15–26.

2. Much of this chapter is adapted from Chapters 3 and 4 of John E. G. Bateson, *Managing Services Marketing*, 2nd ed. (Fort Worth, TX: The Dryden Press, 1992), pp. 156–169, 200–207.

3. J. D. Thompson, *Organizations in Action* (New York: McGraw-Hill, 1967).

4. W. Skinner, "The Focused Factory," *Harvard Business Review*, 52, 3, (May-June 1974), pp. 113–121.

5. Thompson, *Organizations in Action*, p. 69.

6. R. J. Matteis, "The New Back Office Focuses on Customer Service," *Harvard Business Review* 57, (1979), pp. 146–159.

7. Matteis, "The New Back Office."

8. These extensions of the customer contact model are developed in Richard B. Chase, "The Customer Contact Approach to Services: Theoretical Base and Practical Extensions," *Operations Research*, 29, 4, (July-August 1981), pp. 698–706; and Richard B. Chase and David A. Tansik, "The Customer Contact Model for Organization Design," *Management Service* 29, 9, (1983), pp. 1037–1050.

9. B. Danet, "Client-Organization Interfaces," *Handbook of Organization Design*, 2nd ed., P. C. Nystrom and W. N. Starbuck, eds. (New York: Oxford University Press, 1984), p. 384.

10. These studies employed the critical incident technique to look at service encounters that fail. See Mary J. Bitner, Jody D. Nyquist, and Bernard H. Booms, "The Critical Incident Technique for Analyzing the Service Encounter," *Service Marketing in a Changing Environment*, Thomas M. Block, Gregory D. Upah, and Valerie A. Zeithaml, eds., (Chicago: American Marketing Association, 1985), pp. 48–51.

11. Chase, "The Customer Contact Approach."

12. For a detailed description, see Richard B. Chase and Gerrit Wolf, "Designing High Contact Systems: Applications to Branches of Savings and Loans," Working Paper, Department of Management, College of Business and Public Administration, University of Arizona.

13. Chad Rubel, "Banks Should Show that They Care for Customers," *Marketing News*, (July 3, 1995), p. 4.

14. T. Levitt, "Production-line Approach to Services," *Harvard Business Review* 50, 5, (September-October 1972), pp. 41–52.

15. Carol F. Suprenant and Michael Solomon, "Predictability and Personalization in the Service Encounter," *Journal of Marketing*, 51, (April 1987), pp. 86–96.

16. W. Earl Sasser, "Match Supply and Demand in Service Industries," *Harvard Business Review* 54, 5, (November-December 1976), pp. 61–65.

17. Benjamin Schneider, "The Service Organization: Climate is Crucial," *Organizational Dynamics*, (Autumn 1980), pp. 52–65.

18. See also J. E. G. Bateson, "Self-Service Consumer: An Exploratory Study," *Journal of Retailing*, 61, 3, (Fall 1986), pp. 49–79.

19. Ibid.

20. Christopher H. Lovelock and Robert F. Young, "Look to Consumers to Increase Productivity," *Harvard Business Review*, (May-June 1979), pp. 168–178.

21. G. Lynn Shostack, "Service Positioning through Structural Change," *Journal of Marketing*, 51, (January 1987), pp. 34–43.

22. Bateson, *Managing Services*, pp. 200–207.

23. K. Douglas Hoffman and Vince Howe, "Developing the Micro Service Audit via Script Theoretic and Blueprinting Procedures," *Marketing Toward the Twenty-First Century*, Robert L. King, ed., (University of Richmond: Southern Marketing Association, 1991), pp. 379–383.

24. Thomas W. Leigh and Arno J. Rethans, "Experience with Script Elicitation within Consumer Making Contexts," *Advances in Consumer Research*, V. 10, Alice Tybout and Richard Bagozzi, eds., (Ann Arbor, MI: Association for Consumer Research, 1983), pp. 667–672.

25. Shostack, "Service Positioning," pp. 34–43.

# Build-A-Bear Workshops: Calculating the Service Cost per Bear

Service firms can strategically view their operations along a continuum ranging from necessary evil to the other extreme, where operations are viewed as a key source of competitive advantage. Clearly, Build-A-Bear Workshops have used their world-class service delivery systems to create a compelling service experience for its customers. Build-A-Bear Workshops offer an experience-based business model where customers and their children, grandchildren, nieces, nephews or friends can make and accessorize their own teddy bears. Given the option of purchasing a bear off the shelf at a the local discount toy store or accompanying a child to a Build-A-Bear Workshop where they can be personally involved in creating the bear as a family, many customers are enthusiastically opting for the latter choice.

Build-A-Bear Workshop is the only national company that provides a make-your-own stuffed animal interactive entertainment retail experience. The company opened its first store in St. Louis in 1997, and as of October 2009 operated 400 stores, including company-owned stores in the United States, Puerto Rico, Canada, United Kingdom, Ireland, and France and franchise stores in Europe, Asia, Australia, and Africa. In addition to Build-A-Bear Workshops, the company has also introduced make-your-own Major League Baseball mascot in stadium locations and Build-A-Dino Stores. The company has also teamed up with prominent zoos and the Rain Forest Café and offers customers the opportunity to make stuffed animals that are unique to these specific locations. Since 1997, the company has sold tens of millions of stuffed animals making Build-A-Bear Workshop the global leader in the teddy bear business.

Build-A-Bear's competitive advantage has been its service delivery system, consisting of the clever process of *Choose Me, Hear Me, Stuff Me, Stitch Me, Fluff Me, Name Me, Dress Me, and Take Me Home.* As described by the company's website (www.buildabear .com), the process of making a teddy bear flows as follows:

Choose Me—guests select from a variety of bears, dogs, cats, bunnies, monkeys and a series of limited edition offerings.

Hear Me—guests then select from several sound choices that are placed inside their new stuffed friend. Examples of sounds include giggles, growls, barks, meows, and recorded messages such as "I Love You" and songs like "Let Me Call You Sweetheart."

Stuff Me—guests with the help of master Bear Builder associates fill their new stuffed friends with just the right amount of stuffing for customized huggability. Each guest then selects a satin heart, makes a wish, and places the heart inside their new furry friend.

Sources:

1. **www.buildabear.com**, accessed 28 October, 2009.
2. **http://media.corporate-ir.net/media_files/irol/18/182478/FactSheet_010709.pdf**, accessed 28 October, 2009.

Stitch Me—stuff friends are stitched up, but not before a store associate places a bar-code inside the stuffed animal so that if lost, the furry friend can be reunited with its owner. The company believes that thousands of bears have been returned to their owners through their exclusive Find-A-Bear ID tracking program.

Fluff Me—guests are now able to fluff their new friends to perfection with the use of cool-air hair dryers and brushes at the purposely designed bear spa.

Name Me—guests stop at the Name me computer where they enter their names and the birth date and name of their new friend. Guests can then select between customized birth certificates or a story that incorporates the owner's name and the stuffed animal's name. Guests can either select English or Spanish.

Dress Me—guests are now directed to the bear apparel boutique where Pawsonal Shoppers help guests select from hundreds of choices the perfect outfit and accessories for their new friend.

Take Me Home—guests end their experience at the Take Me Home station where they receive their customized birth certificate or story and a Buy Stuff Club Card to apply toward future purchases. Finally, each new furry friend is placed within a Club Condo carrying case which is specifically designed as a handy travel carrier and new home.

As testament to the effectiveness of Build-A-Bear Workshop's extraordinary delivery system, the company has received numerous awards such as *ICSC "2004 Hot Retailer Award"* and was named *National Retail Federation's International 2001 Retail Innovator of the Year—Global Winner*. In 2008, the company's founder and CEO, Maxine Clark, was named one of *The 25 Most Influential People in Retailing* by Chain Store Age. In 2006, Clark was inducted into the Junior Achievement National Business Hall of Fame.

As a manager of a local Build-A-Bear Workshop, Laura Gray was wondering about the service costs associated with making each bear (or other type of animal friend). Store associates, known as master Bear Builder associates, shared the experience with customers at each stage of the bear-making process and were paid $10 per hour. Laura further estimated the average activity time for each stage of the bear-making process:

| BUILD-A-BEAR PROCESS STEPS | ACTIVITY TIMES (SECONDS)* |
|---|---|
| Choose Me | 180 |
| Hear Me | 60 |
| Stuff Me | 90 |
| Stitch Me | 60 |
| Fluff Me | 120 |
| Name Me | 120 |
| Dress Me | 240 |
| Take Me Home | 60 |

*Activity times used in this case are hypothetical

## Discussion Questions

1. Construct a service blueprint for the bear-making process indicating (1) the stages in the process; (2) the directional flow of the process; (3) labor cost for each stage in the process; (4) the number of stations per stage; and (5) the activity time for each process stage.

2. Based on the information provided in question 1, calculate (1) the number of customers that can complete the bear-making process in an hour; (2) the average service cost per bear; and (3) identify the bottleneck in the current process.

3. Develop a solution that minimizes the negative impact of the bottleneck and improves the number of customers that can make a bear in an hour. (1) What is your suggestion to improve the bottleneck situation? (2) Upon implementing your solution, how many customers can now build a bear in an hour? (3) What is the new service cost per bear?

4. Discuss your next step in increasing the efficiency of the bear-making process. What are the managerial (practical) implications of taking additional steps to decrease the service cost per bear?

## CHAPTER OBJECTIVES

After reading this chapter, you should be able to:

- Discuss the concept of perceived value as it pertains to comparing total customer cost to total customer value.

- Understand the special considerations of service pricing as they relate to cost, demand, customer, competitor, profit, product, and legal considerations.

- Discuss the pros and cons of using cost-based pricing in service pricing decisions.

- Discuss the circumstances under which price segmentation is most effective.

- Explain satisfaction-based, relationship, and efficiency approaches to pricing and provide examples of service firms that are using each of these pricing.

# CHAPTER 6
# Considerations for Services Pricing

The purpose of this chapter is to discuss pricing as a strategic decision in overall service strategy. More specifically, the major objectives of this chapter are to familiarize you with the special considerations pertaining to service pricing decisions and to introduce emerging pricing practices within the service sector.

AP Photo/Paul Sakuma

## SPRINGSTEEN, PEARL JAM AND OTHERS UPSET OVER TICKETMASTER PRICING POLICIES

Ticketmaster Entertainment, Inc. sells and distributes tickets to live venues such as arenas, stadiums, and theaters throughout the world and is the world's largest ticket seller. Ticketmaster, serving as an agent, sells tickets on behalf of promoters, teams, bands, and venues. As such, Ticketmaster does not set ticket prices or determine seating locations. The company makes its money by adding service fees to the tickets customers purchase and by the fees promoters pay Ticketmaster for selling and distributing tickets. According to the company's website, Ticketmaster's stated goal is "to make your purchasing experience easy, efficient and equitable, so we can get you on your way to live events as quickly as possible."

While many customers would agree that using Ticketmaster's services is easy and efficient, many would also agree that Ticketmaster's pricing policy is not very equitable. First, there are the "extra charges" that can include service charges, building facility charges, processing charges, and shipping charges (including E-ticket Convenience Charges, or Will Call Charges). Based on an example posted on Wikipedia, a Britney Spears ticket that originally cost $56 ended up costing $72.60 after Ticketmaster added its "service fees," including a $4.10 processing charge, a $3.50 facility charge (which is actually determined by the venue, and not Ticketmaster—nonetheless customers blame Ticketmaster for this charge as well), and a $9 convenience charge for a total of $16.60 in service charges representing nearly 30 percent of the ticket's original price. Consequently, tickets for a family of four would cost nearly $67 in extra fees.

In addition to the service fees, many are upset with Ticketmaster's lack of competition. For many, Ticketmaster is viewed as monopolistic—a situation where customers have few alternatives but to pay to Ticketmaster whatever the company feels is "equitable." Ticketmaster's pricing policy has raised the ire of fans and performers alike. For example, Pearl Jam took Ticketmaster to court, claiming that the company was monopolistic and for the company's refusal to lower its service fees to keep tickets affordable. Ticketmaster eventually won the lawsuit, and Pearl Jam responded by cancelling its concert tour. In more recent times, Ticketmaster has proposed a merger with Live Nation (one of only a few competitors) which has raised more than a few eyebrows about anti-trust issues. Bruce Springsteen has been quoted to say that he is "furious" about the possible merger, and goes on to say, "…the one thing that would make the current ticket situation even worse for the fan than it is now would be Ticketmaster and Live Nation coming up with a single system, thereby returning us to a near monopoly situation in music ticketing."

In early 2009, Ticketmaster's selling and pricing approaches came under close scrutiny with Grateful Dead fans that resulted in a lawsuit. In addition to Ticketmaster's original sales operation, the company also owns TicketsNow, which offers resale services. According to the lawsuit, New Jersey resident Michael Kelly "used Ticketmaster to buy four Grateful Dead tickets with a face value of $398 and was routed to the TicketsNow website, which charged him $829.15 for seats." The complaint continues: "Within literally moments of tickets going on sale by Ticketmaster, and often less than one minute later for high-demand events, those tickets are being offered for resale in the secondary market by TicketsNow at greatly inflated prices." Given Ticketmaster's relationship with TicketsNow, the U.S. Justice Department and the Federal Trade Commission as well as Canada's Competition Bureau are looking into these charges.

Sources:

1. **http://www.denverpost.com/business/ci_12373583?source=rss**, accessed 23 October, 2009.
2. **http://en.wikipedia.org/wiki/Ticketmaster**, accessed 23 October, 2009.
3. **http://www.ticketmaster.com/h/purchase.html**, accessed 23 October, 2009.
4. **http://www.wired.com/epicenter/2009/02/would-a-ticketm/**, accessed 23 October, 2009.

# Introduction

Of the traditional marketing mix variables, price has the most direct effect on profitability and is the most easily controlled element of the marketing mix.[1] However, despite its importance and ease of use, the development of effective pricing strategies remains perhaps the most elusive concept in business today. Pricing is often a perplexing issue for practitioners and researchers alike. Consider the following sample of expressed opinions regarding pricing practices over the last 50 years that reflect both the confusion and frustration associated with pricing decisions:

> …pricing policy is the last stronghold of medievalism in modern management…
> [Pricing] is still largely intuitive and even mystical in the sense that the intuition is often the province of the big boss.[2]

> …perhaps few ideas have wider currency than the mistaken impression that prices are or should be determined by costs of production.[3]

> …for marketers of industrial goods and construction companies, pricing is the single judgment that translates potential business into reality. Yet pricing is the least rational of all decisions made in this specialized field.[4]

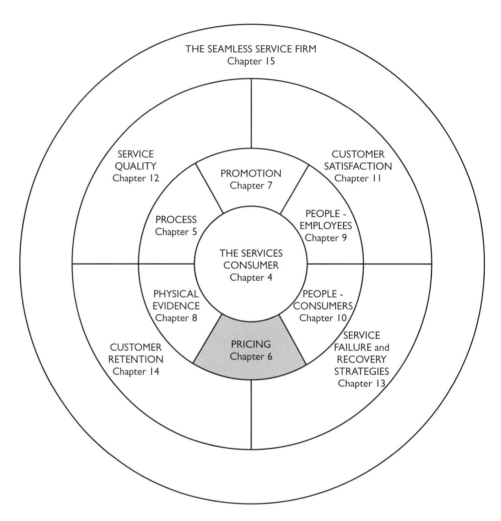

*...many managing directors do not concern themselves with pricing details; some are not even aware of how their products are priced.*[5]

*...pricing is approached in Britain like Russian roulette—to be indulged in mainly by those contemplating suicide.*[6]

*Perhaps it is reasonable that marketers have only recently begun to focus seriously on effective pricing. Only after managers have mastered the techniques of creating value do the techniques of capturing value become important.*[7]

Today, price remains one of the least researched and mastered areas of marketing. Research and expertise pertaining to the pricing of services is particularly lacking. As a result, this chapter focuses on special considerations with regards to service pricing decisions and discusses service pricing practices that are in use today.

## What Does It Mean to Provide Value?

As we begin our discussion on the pricing of services, it is important first to understand the fundamentals of the ideal of providing value to the service firm's customers, clients, patients, etc. Often, both service providers and service customers incorrectly assume that value is calculated simply by comparing the value of the core service provided (e.g., medical care, transportation, sporting event) to the money spent to obtain the service.

The value of a service goes beyond simply comparing the service product to its monetary price. Value also includes service, personnel, and image aspects which when maximized increases the total value of the service experience.

**monetary cost** The actual dollar price paid by the consumer for a product.

**time costs** The time the customer has to spend to acquire the service.

**energy costs** The physical energy spent by the customer to acquire the service.

**psychic costs** The mental energy spent by the customer to acquire the service.

Ultimately, the buyers' perceptions of value represent a tradeoff between the perceived benefits of the service to be purchased and the perceived sacrifice in terms of the total costs to be paid (see Figure 6.1). Total customer costs include more than just the **monetary cost** paid for the service. Other costs include **time costs**, **energy costs**, and **psychic costs**, which reflect the time and trouble the customer has to endure to acquire the

**FIG-6.1** Buyer's Perception of Value

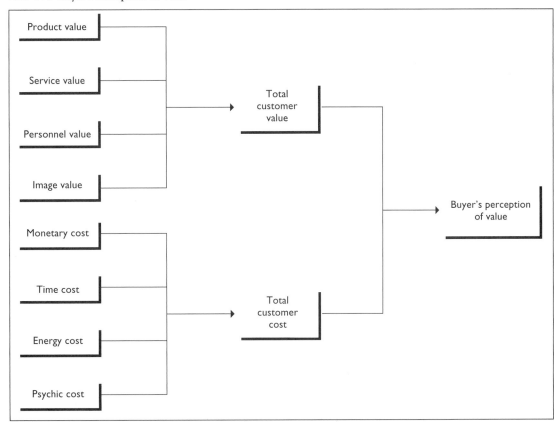

Source: Philip Kotler, *Marketing Management: Analysis, Planning, Implementation, and Control*, 9th ed. (Englewood Cliffs, NJ: Prentice-Hall, 1997), 1997, p. 37. Print and Electronically reproduced by permission of Pearson Education, Inc., Upper Saddle River, New Jersey.

**product value** The worth assigned to the product by the customer.

**service value** The worth assigned to the service by the customer.

**personnel value** The worth assigned to the service-providing personnel by the customer.

**image value** The worth assigned to the image of the service or service provider by the customer.

service. Similarly, total customer value extends beyond **product value** and includes **service value**, **personnel value**, and **image value**.[8]

For example, a customer who wishes to purchase an airline ticket must pay the *monetary cost* for the right to board the plane and travel to their destination. This particular customer selected a direct flight to her destination which reduced her overall travel time (*time cost*) and allowed her to spend more time at the beach. Moreover, this customer selected an airline that offered curbside check-in at the airport, which reduced the amount of physical labor (*energy cost*) necessary to carry her luggage. Finally, the customer purchased her ticket from a well-established airline, which minimized her safety concerns (*psychic cost*).

In exchange for the monetary price of the ticket, the customer boarded a modern jet that was equipped with very comfortable seats and a variety of nicely appointed modern conveniences (*product value*). The flight attendants were very friendly and very knowledgeable (*personnel value*). In addition, the airline offered a number of food and beverage options in addition to a very flexible cancellation policy in case the trip needed to be postponed (*service value*). Finally, her friends were impressed by her choice of airline, given the airline's reputation as a top-notch provider of air travel services (*image value*).

Overall, if the signal sent by total customer cost is an indicator of sacrifice relative to value, then price will have a negative or repelling effect and may reduce demand. If the signal sent by the price is an indicator of benefit or value, then price will be an attractor and may increase demand. Because of the perceived connection between cost and benefit, buyers have both lower and upper price thresholds. For example, buyers might be discouraged from buying when the price is perceived to be too low simply because they see a low price as an indicator of inferior quality.

Consumers exchange their money, time, and effort for the bundle of benefits the service provider offers. Economic theory suggests that consumers will have a reservation price that captures the value they place on these benefits. As long as the total cost to the consumer is lower than the reservation price, he or she will be prepared to buy. For example, if the cost of going "green" is less than the perceived benefits obtained, home buyers are willing to pay the additional costs for eco-friendly improvements (see Sustainability & Services in Action). Consequently, if the consumer can purchase the service for less than the reservation price, a consumer's surplus will exist. The eight dimensions of value described above provide direction for how service firms can differentiate themselves from competitors.

## Special Considerations of Service Pricing

The ultimate pricing decision faced by most firms is determining a price that sells the service while at the same time offering a profitable return. Despite the fact that companies can literally spend billions of dollars developing their images, establishing brand preference, and creating a differential advantage in the minds of consumers, these same companies often "blink" (lower their own prices) or become paralyzed (do nothing) when faced with competitors offering lower prices.[9] The end result is that the firm becomes obsessed with "setting prices" as opposed to engaging in "strategic pricing" activities. "The difference between price setting and strategic pricing is the difference between reacting to market conditions and proactively managing them."[10] The literature suggests that strategic pricing decisions should be based on cost, demand, customer, competitive, profit, product, and legal considerations.[11] While these market conditions are the same for goods and services, the content of the considerations differ. The discussion that follows highlights these key differences. Figure 6.2 provides a summary of the key considerations.

## SUSTAINABILITY AND SERVICES *IN ACTION*

### The Cost of Going Green

Becoming "green" seems like a worthwhile goal, but is going eco-friendly really worth the cost? For those offering green design services for home construction, the answer seems to be "it depends." On the consumer-side, 90 percent of potential home buyers said they would pay an extra $5,000 for a home that uses less energy or incorporates eco-friendly materials that help protect the earth. In reality, the cost of going green typically adds 10 to 30 percent to home construction prices that may not be necessarily recouped when it comes time to resell the home. However, recouping the costs of going green can come in other ways besides resale values. For example, the most common reasons homeowners and buyers go green included the following:

**You can save energy—and money.** It turns out the typical home loses 15 to 20 percent of its heating or air-conditioning from poorly designed air ducts. Given the high cost of energy, taking steps to reduce the amount of energy leakage is not only good from an eco-friendly point of view, but also makes good economic sense. However, while retaining energy that is currently escaping makes good sense, creating your own energy through the use of solar panels is quite a different story. Panels are expensive to install and recouping their costs may take years.

**You can save your lungs.** Did you know that indoor air is two to five times more polluted than outdoor air? Who knew? It seems that paints, stains, and glues that are used to construct homes contain volatile organic compounds (VOCs) that release chemicals as they dry and continue to do so for years. Consequently, incorporating environmentally friendly materials with low VOCs may save customers money by cutting down on healthcare costs. VOCs aggravate allergies and asthma and can cause nausea and headaches. Ironically, the more tightly one's house is sealed, the worse the problem. The cost for installing a mechanical ventilation system which circulates fresh air into the house ranges from $500 to $2,000.

**You can save the planet.** Not everyone can be a superhero and save the planet in some dramatic fashion; however, we can all work on leaving a smaller carbon footprint. Green home buyers wishing to do their part to save the planet commonly use recycled building materials, reduce water consumption via low-flow toilets, low-flow faucets and showerheads, and rainwater filtration systems, and utilize sustainable natural products such as bamboo flooring, wool carpeting, and cotton insulation. Although these practices may reduce a home buyer's psychic cost, monetary costs do increase with each green initiative.

Source:   **http://money.cnn.com/magazines/moneymag/moneymag_archive/2007/01/01/8397399/index .htm**, accessed 23 October, 2009.

## Cost Considerations

Compared to their goods-producing counterparts, service firms encounter a number of unique cost considerations that need to be addressed when formulating service pricing strategy. First, service pricing is often not finalized until after provision. Consequently, the consumer experiences greater price uncertainty. Second, since services have no cost of goods sold (nothing tangible was produced), cost-based pricing is more difficult for services. Third, many service industries are often characterized by a high fixed cost to variable cost ratio which leads to further pricing challenges. Finally, the mass production of services leads to limited economies of scale.

***Consumers May Not Know the Actual Price They Will Pay for a Service until after the Service Is Completed***   Although consumers can usually find a base price to use as a comparison during prepurchase evaluation, many services are customized during

**FIG-6.2** Unique Differences Associated with Service Prices

| Cost Considerations | |
|---|---|
| D1: | Cost-oriented pricing is more difficult for services. |
| D2: | With many professional services (and some others), the consumers may not know the actual price they will pay for the service until the service is completed. |
| D3: | Services tend to be characterized by a high fixed cost to variable cost ratio. |

| Demand Considerations | |
|---|---|
| D4: | The demand for services tends to be more inelastic than the demand for goods. |
| D5: | Due to the implicit bundling of services by consumers, cross-price elasticity considerations need to be examined. |
| D6: | Price discrimination is a viable practice to manage demand and supply challenges. |
| D7: | Economies of scale tend to be limited. |

| Customer Considerations | |
|---|---|
| D8: | Price tends to be one of the few cues available to consumers during prepurchase. |
| D9: | Service consumers are more likely to use price as a cue to quality. |
| D10: | Service consumers tend to be less certain about reservation prices. |

| Competitive Considerations | |
|---|---|
| D11: | Comparing prices of competitors is more difficult for service consumers. |
| D12: | Self-service is a viable competitive alternative. |

| Profit Considerations | |
|---|---|
| D13: | Price bundling makes the determination of individual prices in the bundle of services more complicated. |
| D14: | Price bundling is more effective in a services context. |

| Product Considerations | |
|---|---|
| D15: | Compared to the goods sector, there tend to be many different names for price in the service sector. |
| D16: | Consumers are less able to stockpile services by taking advantage of discount prices. |
| D17: | Product-line pricing tends to be more complicated. |

| Legal Considerations | |
|---|---|
| D18: | The opportunity for illegal pricing practices to go undetected is greater for services than goods. |

delivery. Consumers may not know the exact amount they will be charged until after the service is performed. For example, a patient may know what a doctor's office visit costs, but may not know what she charges for lab work, x-rays, and other ancillary services. Similarly, a client may know how much an attorney charges for an hour of work, but may not know how many hours it will take to finalize a will. In contrast to goods which are typically produced, purchased, and consumed (in this specific order), services often are first purchased, then produced and consumed simultaneously. The final bill is not presented to the customer until the service has already been provided. Consequently, the final price is sometimes the last piece of information revealed to the customer. Service firms wishing to reduce the perceived risk associated with consumption of services should consider making additional efforts to increase the transparency of costs to customers.

***Cost-Based Pricing Is Often More Difficult for Services***   Many service managers experience difficulties in accurately estimating their costs of doing business. This difficulty arises for several reasons. First, when producing an intangible product, cost of goods sold is either a small or nonexistent portion of the total cost. For example, what is the cost of goods sold for a marketing professor to provide a one-hour seminar to a local business on the pricing of services? Since nothing tangible is produced, there is little to no cost of goods sold! Second, cost-based pricing for services is often more difficult because labor needs are challenging to forecast accurately in many service settings due, in part, to fluctuating demand. Third, workforce turnover is typically high in many service industries. This, coupled with the fact that finding good personnel is an ongoing challenge, leads to further difficulty in estimating the costs associated with a particular service encounter. These factors make what is often considered the most common approach to pricing, cost-oriented pricing, difficult at best for service firms. Consequently, the difficulties associated with controlling and forecasting costs are a fundamental difference between goods and services pricing.

***Many Services Are Typically Characterized by a High Fixed to Variable Cost Ratio*** The United Parcel Service (UPS) is a prime example. On the retail side of the business, the company maintains 3,400 UPS Stores, 1,100 Mail Boxes Etc., 1,000 UPS Customer Centers, 17,000 authorized outlets, and 45,000 UPS Drop Boxes. Packages and documents collected at these retail sites are then funneled to 1,748 operating facilities, where they are distributed to a delivery fleet consisting of 88,000 package cars, vans, tractors, and motorcycles, 270 UPS Jet Aircraft, and 304 chartered aircraft. As a result of this infrastructure, the company handles more than 3 billion packages and 5.5 percent of the United States' GDP annually.[12] In comparison to UPS's massive **fixed costs**, the **variable costs** associated with handling one more package are practically nil.

> **fixed costs** Costs that are planned and accrued during the operating period regardless of the level of production and sales.

> **variable costs** Costs that are directly associated with increases in production and sales.

The airline industry is another typical example of a service with a high fixed cost to variable cost ratio. The three major costs to an airline are cost of the fleet, labor, and jet fuel. Fleet and labor costs are primarily fixed, whereas fuel costs are variable. Perhaps more importantly, fuel costs are beyond an airline's control; however, the airline has some influence over the other two expenses. In order to increase profits, airlines can sell more tickets, reduce costs, or both. In the attempt to sell more tickets, airlines engage in price discounting, which is virtually always matched by their competition. The net result is that the airline cost structure has stayed the same while industry revenues steadily decrease. In other words, the net result is a greater loss for the airline. In the end, the winners of any price war within the airline industry will be the providers with the lowest cost structures. For example, Frontier Airlines' break-even load factor is approximately 55 percent—55 percent of available seats need to be filled on average of every flight for the airline to break even. In contrast, United Airlines break-even load factor is approximately 91 percent. Clearly, Frontier and other discount airlines are better positioned to withstand the competitive pressures of a price war.[13]

The challenges faced by businesses that have a high fixed cost to variable cost ratio are numerous. First, what prices should be charged to individual customers? For example, the airline industry commonly changes 75,000 prices a day (See E-Services in Action). How should the firm sell off unused capacity? For example, should an airline sell 20 unsold seats at a reduced rate to customers who are willing to accept the risk of not reserving a seat on the plane prior to the day of departure? Does selling unused capacity at discounted rates alienate full-fare paying customers? How can companies offer reduced prices to sell off unused capacity without full-fare paying customers shifting their buying patterns?

***Service Economies of Scale Tend to Be Limited*** Due to the service characteristics of inseparability and perishability, the consumption of services is not separated by time and physical space. For example, consider the daily operations of a dental office. Inventory cannot be used to buffer demand, and the physical presence of patients and providers is frequently necessary for a transaction to take place. Consequently, service providers often produce services on demand rather than in advance. Therefore, it is

---

## E-SERVICES *IN ACTION*

## Turbocharged Software Sets Airline Pricing 75,000 Times a Day!

Have you ever checked airline pricing online and found a great deal, and then came back to actually book the ticket an hour later, only to find that the price was no longer available? It's as if the company tracked your online behavior, and then set you up to pay a higher price—it's very frustrating! "In reality, the airlines use sophisticated computers and software that predicts ticket demand the way 'models' predict the weather." When ticket demand is predicted to increase, airline ticket prices increase as well—and may do so several times a day.

This is how the system works. For example, let's say that Continental Airlines launches about 2,000 flights a day. Each flight charges between 10 to 20 different prices depending on time of advance purchase, day of the week, refundability, third-party charges, and cabin class (just to name a few of the factors that ultimately impact airline pricing strategy). Given this scenario, this one airline may have nearly 7 million prices posted in the market that may change several times a day based on the prices of other airlines.

A joint fare-publishing enterprise called ATPCO is charged with collecting all the major airlines' pricing (except Southwest) and then publishing all of these fares back to the airlines and other reservation services. ATPCO used to collect this information once a day and report findings back the next day and were closed on the weekends. As a result, an airline could change its pricing once a day and competitors could find out the next day what changes had been made to the industry's pricing. Today, ATPCO accepts price changes three times a day and once each on Saturday and Sunday. Consequently, fare changes that used to be filed five times a week are now filed 17 times a week. Between proactive price changes and competitors reacting to those price changes, airlines collectively change prices on average 75,000 times a day. On a very active day, airline prices can change as much as 400,000 times a day. In order to keep track of all the changes and make on the spot pricing decisions, airlines utilize what they refer to "turbocharged software" that facilitates the management of their pricing strategy.

Source: **http://www.fastcompany.com/magazine/68/pricing .html**, accessed 23 October, 2009.

---

**economies of scale**
Based on the idea of the more you produce, the cheaper it is to produce it...the cheaper it is to produce it, the cheaper it can be sold...the cheaper it can be sold, the more it is sold...the more it is sold, the more it can be produced (and so on and so forth).

difficult for service providers to achieve the cost advantages traditionally associated with **economies of scale**—based on the idea of the more you produce, the cheaper it is to produce it...the cheaper it is to produce it, the cheaper it can be sold...the cheaper it can be sold, the more it is sold...the more it is sold, the more it can be produced (and so on and so forth). Moreover, since many services are also customized to individual customer specifications, the act of customization limits the amount of work that can be done in advance of a customer's request for service and further limits potential cost advantages obtained through traditional economies of scale.

In closing, it should also be mentioned that although costs are an important consideration in establishing pricing strategy, pricing experts would agree that their role in setting the final price is often overemphasized.[14] Without a doubt costs are paramount in determining the firm's profitability; however, service firms that overemphasize the role of cost in setting final prices are limited by their internal focus, and tend to under-price their services in the market. Firms that rely solely on costs to set prices fail to look externally at the market and extract the full value that customers place on the services offered. For example, tickets for popular sporting events and Broadway shows are often quickly purchased by brokers who resell these same tickets for five to 10 times the original asking price. In cases such as this, the additional profits go to the resellers, not to the businesses that created the value in the first place and priced their tickets for the purpose of covering their costs. Service firms that are able to extract the full value from the market also take into account external market factors such as demand considerations.

## Demand Considerations

Service firms that are better able to extract the full value from the market take into account external market factors such as demand considerations. There are a number of demand considerations that differentiate the pricing of services from the pricing of goods. First, demand for services tends to be more inelastic. Cost increases are often simply passed along to consumers. Second, consumers of services often implicitly bundle prices. For example, the demand for food services at a theme park may be impacted by the price of the theme park's hotel and ticket prices. Consequently, the cross-price elasticity of services should be taken into careful consideration. Finally, due to the supply and demand fluctuations inherent in services, price discrimination strategies should also be investigated.

***Demand for Services Tends to Be More Inelastic***   In general, consumers of services are more willing to pay higher prices if doing so reduces their level of perceived risk. Perceived risk is a function of consequence (the degree of importance and/or danger associated with the purchase) and uncertainty (the variability in service performance from customer to customer or from day to day). The service characteristics of intangibility, inseparability, heterogeneity, and perishability contribute greatly to heightened levels of perceived risk.

Experts in the field suggest 10 factors that can play a major role in influencing customer price sensitivity. The 10 price sensitivity factors include:

- *Perceived Substitute Effect*
- *Unique Value Effect*
- *Switching Cost Effect*
- *Difficult Comparison Effect*
- *Price-Quality Effect*
- *Expenditure Effect*
- *End-Benefit Effect*
- *Shared-Cost Effect*
- *Fairness Effect*
- *Inventory Effect*

Figure 6.3 provides an overview of each of the 10 price sensitivity factors and their proposed relationships to price sensitivity. Successful strategic pricing considers the impact of each of these 10 factors on final pricing decisions. Clearly, price sensitivities will vary across different types of services, but in general the demand for services tends to be **inelastic**. Different groups of consumers will likely weigh the importance of each price sensitivity factor differently. Service firms must assess which of the factors are more salient to their target market's purchasing decisions.

***Cross-Price Elasticity Considerations Need to Be Examined***   Consumers of services often implicitly bundle prices. In other words, consumers may figure that the total cost of going to the movies includes the tickets and refreshments. Therefore, total revenues may be maximized by carefully considering the cross-price elasticities of the total product offering. This is particularly true in cases where the price of the core service offering influences the demand of supplemental services. **Cross-price elasticity** of demand measures the responsiveness of demand for a service relative to a change in price for another service. If this relationship is negative (e.g., as the price of Product A increases, the demand for Product B decreases), then the two services are said to be **complementary**. For example, as the price of movie tickets continue to increase, customers may offset the price increase by purchasing less popcorn and soda. If the relationship is positive (e.g., as the price of Product A increases, the demand for Product B increases), then the

**inelastic demand** The type of market demand when a change in price of service is greater than a change in quantity demanded.

**cross-price elasticity** A measure of the responsiveness of demand for a service relative to a change in price for another service.

**complements** The effect of cross-price elasticity in which an increase in the price of Product A decreases the demand for Product B.

**FIG-6.3** Factors Influencing Customer's Price Sensitivity

| PRICE SENSITIVITY FACTORS: | PROPOSED RELATIONSHIP |
|---|---|
| Perceived Substitute Effect | Price sensitivity increases when the price for service "A" is higher than the price of perceived substitutes. |
| Unique Value Effect | Price sensitivity increases as the unique value of service "A" is perceived to be equal or less than the unique value of perceived substitutes. |
| Switching Costs Effect | Price sensitivity increases as switching costs decrease. |
| Difficult Comparison Effect | Price sensitivity increases as the difficulty in comparing substitutes decreases. |
| Price-Quality Effect | Price sensitivity increases to the extent that price is not used as a quality cue. |
| Expenditure Effect | Price sensitivity increases when the expenditure is large in terms of dollars or as a percentage of household income. |
| End-Benefit Effect | The more price-sensitive consumers are to the end benefit, the more price-sensitive they will be to services that contribute to the end benefit. |
| Shared-Cost Effect | Price sensitivity increases as the shared costs with third parties decreases. |
| Fairness Effect | Price sensitivity increases when the price paid for similar services under similar circumstances is lower. |
| Inventory Effect | Price sensitivity increases as the customer's ability to hold an inventory increases. |

**substitutes** The effect of cross-price elasticity in which an increase in the Price of Product A increases the demand for Product B.

two services may be **substitutes**, and consumption of one is at the expense of the consumption of the other. For example, as the price of movie tickets increases, the demand for substitute services such as Blockbuster and Netflix movie rentals increases.

Multi-product considerations dominate many service industries such as business services, personal services, professional services, and the hospitality industry. The golf industry provides a prime example of the effects of cross price elasticities. Consumers have different price sensitivities for greens fees, cart fees, range fees, and food and beverage expenses. If consumers perceive the price of admission (greens fees) as a good value, they are likely to purchase additional products such as riding carts, practice range balls, and food and beverages which in turn produce more revenue for the firm. In contrast, if the price of admission is perceived as low in value, consumer price sensitivities for supplemental services are likely to increase. Consumers often forgo some or all of these additional services in order to keep their total expenses in line. In effect, the higher price of admission often leads to overall lower consumer expenditures and reduces the revenue

Spencer Grant/PhotoEdit

Price discrimination is a viable practice in the movie industry due to differences in the demand elasticities held by customers and the need for movie theatres to balance demand and supply for its motion pictures.

**price discrimination**
The practice of charging different customers different prices for essentially the same service.

stream for the firm. If this is the case, the service firm is much better off keeping admission prices low and making additional margins from complementary products.

*Price Discrimination Is a Viable Practice to Manage Demand and Supply Challenges*    **Price discrimination** involves charging customers different prices for essentially the same service. For example, some international airlines charge different prices for

## GLOBAL SERVICES *IN ACTION*

### Ethnic Pricing...Is this Ethical?

The practice of *ethnic pricing*, giving discounts to people of certain nationalities, has long been routine in countries such as India, China, and Russia. Other countries also offer ethnic pricing but are not very public about it due to ethical and legal ramifications. According to a recent *Wall Street Journal* article, airline passengers throughout Europe can obtain discount fares on airline tickets based on the origin of their passport or those of their employers. Brendan McInerney, a passenger attempting to book a Lufthansa flight to Japan, accidently learned of the practice and was not too happy about it. His wife could fly to Japan for 1,700 marks; however, Mr. McInerney's ticket was priced at 2,700 marks! The reason given by the airline: Mr. McInerney is an American while his wife is Japanese. The airline eventually capitulated, and Mr. McInerney was given the same fare after he complained.

**EXAMPLES OF SOME ETHNIC DISCOUNTS**

| AIRLINE | ROUTE | NORMAL PRICE | "ETHNIC PRICE" |
|---------|-------|--------------|----------------|
| Lufthansa | Frankfurt-Tokyo | $1,524 | $960 |
| Lufthansa | Frankfurt-Seoul | 1,524 | 903 |
| British Airways | Istanbul-London | 385 | 199 |

Note: Taxes, landing fees not included.
Source: Travel Agents.

Lufthansa does not deny its involvement with ethnic pricing. Dagmar Rotter, a spokesperson for the airline, states that the airline is only reacting to the competition from the national carrier of Japan that also flies out of Germany. "The others started it...we only offer it [ethnic pricing] after the market forced us to do so."

Other European airlines such as Swissair, and Air France also practice ethnic pricing. Swissair offers "guest-worker" fares to passengers from Turkey, Portugal, Spain, Greece, and Morocco flying to these same destinations. However, it does not offer discount fares to Japanese flying to Japan. A Swissair spokesperson argues that if the discounts were not provided to the "guest-workers" from Southern Europe and the Mediterranean rim, they would never be able to afford to go home to visit their families. Similarly, Air France offers discounted rates to citizens of Viet Nam, China, South Korea, and Japan, but only for its flights that are departing from Germany. An Air France spokesperson notes..."in Germany everybody seems to be doing it...it seems to be something very specific to the German market."

British Airway's involvement was readily apparent when it offered its travel package: "Ho, Ho, Ho" for British citizens in Turkey. "Short of stuffing, need some pork sausages, fretting about Christmas pud? Not to worry--show your British passport and you can take 48 percent of normal fares to Britain."

U.S. airlines were quietly involved in ethnic pricing until the practice was barred in 1998. A spokesperson for Lufthansa in New York noted that ethnic pricing could not occur in the United States "because it is discriminatory."

Source: Brandon Mitchener, "Ethnic Pricing Means Unfair Air Fares," *Wall Street Journal*, (December 5, 1997), pp. B1, B14. Reprinted by permission of The Wall Street Journal. Copyright © 1997 Dow Jones & Company, Inc. All Rights Reserved Worldwide.

the same flights based on the passengers' ethnicity (see Global Services in Action). This unique aspect of service pricing relates to both the perishability and simultaneous production and consumption of services. Price discrimination is a viable practice in service industries due in part to differences in the demand elasticities held by customers and the need of the organization to balance demand and supply for its service products.

The viability of price discrimination is enhanced by the fact that in some services customers readily accept that prices often drop significantly before the opportunity to sell the service passes completely (e.g., last minute concert tickets). In other service settings, consumers have become quite accustomed to different customers paying different amounts for the same service (e.g., airfares). In addition, online services such as priceline.com have now emerged which allow consumers to name their own price for airline tickets and car rentals. Service providers accept these proposals in order to cover at least some portion of their fixed costs. Some revenue is deemed better than no revenue in these situations.

Effective price segmentation benefits consumers and providers alike. Consumers often benefit from options that offer lower prices, and providers are often able to manage demand and increase capacity utilization. As a result, pricing is called upon to try to smooth demand in two ways:

- *Creating new demand in off-peak, low-capacity utilization periods.*
- *Flattening peaks by moving existing customers from peaks to less busy times.*

In order to engage in an effective price segmentation strategy, the following six criteria should be met:[15]

1. *Different groups of consumers must have different responses to price.* If different groups of consumers have the same response to price changes, then the price segmentation strategy becomes counterproductive. For example, for years movie theaters have offered matinees at a reduced fee. This strategy helped the theater create demand for unused capacity during the day, and also helped to smooth demand during the evening shows. Moreover, this approach has attracted additional market segments such as families with children and individuals on fixed incomes, who may not otherwise attend the higher-priced evening shows. This strategy has been effective because the price change did not create the same response for everyone. If most consumers had shifted their demand to the afternoon shows at lower rates, the movie theater would have overutilized capacity in the afternoons and would be generating lower total revenues for the firm.

2. *The different segments must be identifiable, and a mechanism must exist to price them differently.* Effective price segmentation requires that consumer segments with different demand patterns be identifiable based on some readily apparent common characteristics such as age, family-life cycle stage, gender, and/or educational status. Discriminating based on a convoluted segmentation scheme confuses customers and service providers, who must implement the strategy. Common forms of segmentation identification for a price discrimination strategy based on age include college ID card holders, AARP card holders, and drivers' licenses.

3. *No opportunity should exist for individuals in one segment who have paid a low price to sell their tickets to those in other segments.* For example, it does the movie theater little good to sell reduced-price seats in the afternoon to buyers who can turn around and sell those tickets that evening to full-paying customers. Sometimes you just can't win! A local municipal golf course was trying to do "the right thing" by offering its senior citizen customers coupon books for rounds of golf priced at a reduced rate. Soon after the promotion began, some senior citizen customers were

seen in the parking lot selling their coupons at a profit to the golf course's full-price customers.

4. ***The segment should be large enough to make the exercise worthwhile.*** The time and effort involved in offering a price segmentation scheme should be justified based on the return it generates to the business. Having little or no response to the firm's effort signals that either consumers are uninterested, eligible customers are few, or the firm's price discrimination offer is off its mark.

5. ***The cost of running the price segmentation strategy should not exceed the incremental revenues obtained.*** The objectives of engaging in price segmentation efforts may be to reduce peak demand, fill periods of underutilized capacity, increase overall revenues, or achieve nonprofit issues, such as making a service available to individuals who otherwise may not be able to take advantage of the services the firm offers. If the cost of running the price segmentation strategy exceeds the returns produced, management needs to reconsider the offering.

6. ***The customers should not be confused by the use of different prices.*** Phone companies and electric utilities often offer customers reduced rates that are based on the time of usage. Frequently, however, these time-related discounts change as new promotions arise. Customers caught unaware of the change often end up paying higher rates than expected, which negatively impacts customer satisfaction. In the past, phone companies, particularly cell phone service providers, offered higher-priced "peak rates" and lower-priced "nonpeak rates" that varied by day and throughout the day. Customers had to be aware at all times which rate they will be paying in order to take advantage of this particular type of pricing strategy. In the end, these types of pricing strategies confused and often frustrated customers.

## Customer Considerations

Customer considerations take into account the price the customer is willing to pay for the service. In comparison to goods, the price of the service tends to be one of the few search attributes available to consumers for alternative evaluation purposes. As a result, the price of the service is often used as a quality cue—the higher the price, the higher the perceived quality of the service. Services that are priced too low may very well be perceived as inferior in quality and bypassed for more expensive alternatives. Finally, service customers tend to be less certain about reservation prices.

***Price Tends to Be One of the Few Cues Available to Consumers during Prepurchase*** Due to the intangible nature of services, services are characterized by few search attributes. Search attributes are informational cues that can be determined prior to purchase. In contrast, the tangibility of goods dramatically increases the number of search attributes available for consumers to consider. For example, the style and fit of a suit can be determined prior to purchase. In contrast, the enjoyment of a dinner is not known until after the experience is complete.

Pricing research has noted that the informational value of price decreases as the number of other informational cues increases. Similarly, others have found consumer reliance on price to be U-shaped. Price is heavily used if few cues are present, loses value as more cues become present, and then increases in value if consumers are overwhelmed with information.[16]

**signpost items** Items that customers frequently purchase and are very well aware of typical prices.

Further research suggests using **signpost items** to form an impression of overall service firm prices. Signpost items are items that customers frequently purchase and are very well aware of typical prices. Smart firms price signpost items at competitive prices because customers use these items to benchmark the value of other services that the firm offers. For example, a health club may offer personal trainer services for an additional fee. If the health club happens to sell bottles of water and sodas in a vending machine in the health club at competitive prices, the soda and water become signpost items that convey to health club members that the personal trainer rates must be competitive as well.[17]

***Service Consumers Are More Likely to Use Price as a Cue to Quality***   Service providers must also consider the message the service price sends to customers. Much work has been devoted to understanding whether price can be an indicator of quality. Some studies that have been performed seem to imply that consumers can use price to infer the quality of the product they are considering. Conflicting studies seem to indicate that they cannot. For example, classic studies in the field have presented customers with identical products, such as pieces of carpet, priced at different levels. The respondents' judgment of quality seemed to indicate that quality followed price. However, very similar studies later found little relationship between price and perceived quality.[18]

Price plays a key informational role in service consumer decision processes. Decision theory suggests that consumers will use those cues that are most readily available in the alternative evaluation process to assess product quality. Due to the importance of its role, price should be a dominant cue for consumers attempting to evaluate service quality prior to purchase. Studies suggest that price is more likely to be used as a cue to quality under the following conditions:

- *when price is the primary differential information available;*
- *when alternatives are heterogeneous; and*
- *when comparative price differences are relatively large.*

Clearly, these conditions exist in many service purchase scenarios.

**reservation price** The price a consumer considers to capture the value he or she places on the benefits.

***Service Consumers Tend to Be Less Certain about Reservation Prices***   A consumer's **reservation price** is the maximum amount that the consumer is willing to pay for a product. Ultimately, a consumer's reservation price for a service determines whether a purchase or no purchase decision is made. If the reservation price exceeds the price charged for the service, the consumer is more inclined to purchase that particular service. However, if the reservation price is lower than the actual price charged, then the consumer is precluded from purchasing that particular service offering.

Research has noted the lack of service consumer certainty regarding reservation prices. Consumers' reservation prices are determined in part by their awareness of competitive prices in the market. For some services, the lack of pricing information available and the lack of purchasing frequency may lead to less certainty regarding the reservation price of the service under consideration.[19]

## Competitive Considerations

Service pricing strategy is affected by two unique competitive considerations. First, comparing prices of service alternatives is often difficult, which may make competitive-based pricing a less-important consideration for services compared to goods. In addition, a unique competitor must be considered when pricing services—the self-service consumer. Consumers are often willing to provide self-service to save money and customize the end result among other perceived advantages.

***Comparing Prices of Competitors Is More Difficult for Service Consumers***   Actual price information for services tends to be more difficult for consumers to acquire than for goods. Further, when service price information is available to consumers, it also tends to be more difficult to make meaningful comparisons between services. For example, although base service prices can sometimes be determined in advance,

Unlike goods, self-service is a viable competitive alternative. Customers may select to perform their own personal services and forgo the expense of hiring a service provider.

competing services are not sold together in retail stores the way that many competing goods are in supermarkets, discount, or department stores. Consumers either have to visit geographically separated service firms in person or contact them to compare prices. With regards to services, comparative shopping requires more time and effort.

***Self-Service Is a Viable Competitive Alternative*** One result of the inseparability of production and consumption for services is the possibility of the customer actively participating in the service delivery process, commonly referred to as self-service options. The availability of self-service options has an effect on customer perceptions of the service. Initially, self-service options invariably provided the service customer with some form of price reduction (e.g., self-service gasoline). Today, the literature suggests that service customers often are seeking other benefits besides lower prices when purchasing self-service options. These benefits might include: greater convenience, more control, less human contact, faster service time, greater efficiency, and greater independence. Self-service options must be considered in the formation of pricing strategy.

## Profit Considerations

**price bundling** The practice of marketing two or more products and/or services in a single package at a single price.

Price bundling often increases the profit opportunities for service firms. Compared to goods, services are more amenable to price bundling; however price bundling makes the determination of individual prices in the bundle of services more complicated. **Price bundling** involves pricing a group of services at a price that is below their cost if bought

"YEAH, BUT LOOK AT THE MONEY WE SAVED BY YOUR ACTING AS YOUR OWN ATTORNEY."

The downside of self-service.

separately. For example, a ski lodge located in the Rocky Mountains may bundle a guest room, dinner, ski tickets and ski lessons. In general, price bundles are perceived as a better value for the customer and typically generate additional revenues for the selling firm.

***Price Bundling Makes the Determination of Individual Prices in the Bundle of Services More Complicated*** Bundling, the practice of marketing two or more goods and/or services for a single price, is a useful strategic pricing tool that can help services marketers achieve several different strategic objectives. However, it also complicates the alternative evaluation process for consumers. Consumers experience difficulty when attempting to calculate how much each component of the bundle is contributing to the total cost. For example, a consumer evaluating available alternatives for a trip to Jamaica might have a hard time comparing the costs associated with an all-inclusive hotel package bundled with airfare and transfers to a traditional pay-as-you-go vacation alternative.

***Price Bundling Is More Effective in a Service Context*** A wide variety of services make use of price bundling as a strategic approach to pricing. Many service organizations bundle their own service offerings together, as when a doctor combines diagnostic tests with physical examinations. Other service organizations choose to form strategic alliances with other firms and bundle services that each provides. For example, the travel industry bundles hotel charges, airline tickets and transfer services into a single price. Regardless of the form or type of bundling, this strategy essentially creates a new service that can be used to attract new customers, cross-sell existing customers, or retain current customers. Bundling has proliferated in the service sector primarily because of high fixed/variable cost ratios, the degree of cost sharing, and the high levels of interdependent demand. For example, the demand for a hotel restaurant is directly related to the demand for hotel rooms.

## Product Considerations

Service pricing strategy recognizes three unique service product considerations. First, price is called by many different names in the service sector. As a result, price may be perceived differently in some sectors compared to others. Second, since service products are unable to be inventoried, service consumers should be less price sensitive and less prone to delay their purchases until a better price is offered some time in the future. Finally, the common practice of price lining used for tangible products makes less sense to service consumers.

***Compared to the Goods Sector, There Tend to Be Many Different Names for Price in the Service Sector*** One of the interesting aspects of pricing in a service context involves the many different names used to express price in different service industries. For example, in the financial services industry the term "price" is rarely, if ever, used. Instead, customers pay service charges, points, and commissions. Similarly, travelers pay airfares or bus fares, apartment dwellers pay rent, hotel occupants are charged a room rate, and the list goes on and on.

Upon further examination, many of the terms used for price in the service sector incorporate the benefit(s) customers receive. For instance, customers pay fares for the benefit of transportation, rents and room rates for occupancy, and service charges for processing requests. Is price by any other name, still a price, or does incorporating the benefit into the term used for price alter consumer perceptions and influence price sensitivities?

***Consumers Are Less Able to Stockpile Services by Taking Advantage of Discount Prices*** Retail pricing researchers note that pricing policies and strategies can have a direct impact on inventory decisions and planning.[20] Goods are often discounted to

**forward buying** When retailers purchase enough product on deal to carry over until the product is being sold on deal again.

**product-line pricing** The practice of pricing multiple versions of the same product or grouping similar products together.

reduce over-abundant inventories. Consumers take advantage of the discounts and often engage in forward buying. **Forward buying** enables consumers to build their own inventories of goods, and reduces the amount of defections to competitive brands. In contrast, services cannot be stored. Consequently, service consumers cannot stockpile service offerings. When consumers need or want a service, they must pay the prevailing price.

*Product-Line Pricing Tends to Be More Complicated*    **Product-line pricing**, the practice of pricing multiple versions of the same core product or grouping similar products together, is widely used in goods marketing. For example, beginner, intermediate, and expert level tennis rackets are generally priced at different price points to reflect the different levels of quality construction. Consumers of goods can more easily evaluate the differences among the multiple versions offered since tangibility provides search attributes. Search attributes assist consumers in making objective evaluations. In contrast, consider the difficulty of real estate consumers when faced with the choices offered by Century 21 Real Estate. The company offers home sellers three levels of service that are priced at increasing commission rates of 6, 7, and 8 percent. Customers, particularly those who sell their homes infrequently, lack the expertise to make an informed decision. The performance levels associated with the three levels of service offered cannot be assessed until after the contract with the real estate agent has been signed and the customer has committed to the commission rate.

Traditionally, product-line pricing provides customers with choices and gives managers an opportunity to maximize total revenues. However, the product-line pricing of services more often than not generates customer confusion and alienation. Industries struggling with the price lining of their services include telecommunications (e.g., AT&T, MCI, and Sprint calling and texting plans), health care (e.g., multiple versions of Blue Cross/Blue Shield plans, HMOs, etc.), and financial services (e.g., multiple types of checking and savings accounts, investment options, etc.).

## Legal Considerations

Finally, when developing pricing strategy, marketers must not only consider what is profitable, but also what is legal. In general, the opportunity to engage in and benefit from illegal pricing practices in the service sector is predominantly attributed to intangibility, inseparability, and heterogeneity. As discussed in Chapter 3, intangibility decreases the consumer's ability to objectively evaluate purchases, while inseparability reflects the human element of the service encounter that can potentially expose the customer to coercive influence techniques.

*The Opportunity for Illegal Pricing Practices to Go Undetected Is Greater for Services Than Goods*    Is it legal for a physician to charge excessive prices for vaccinations during an influenza epidemic, or for repair services to triple their hourly rate to repair homes in neighborhoods damaged by severe weather? In some states there are gouging laws to protect consumers from such practices during special circumstances. However, the special circumstances (e.g., epidemics and severe weather) draw attention to such practices. In contrast, identifying excessive service pricing practices is not as clear for "everyday" types of purchase occasions.

Service consumers are more vulnerable to illegal pricing practices. The pricing implications of service consumer vulnerability are twofold. First, consumer vulnerability and perceived risk are directly related. Consumers feeling particularly vulnerable are willing to pay higher prices for a service if it lowers their perceived risk. Second, dubious service providers that abuse the customer's trust by taking advantage of vulnerable consumers through excessive prices may benefit in the short-term, but once they are discovered, the long-term success of their firms is doubtful. To consumers, the issue is one of fairness and **dual entitlement**. Cost-driven price changes are perceived as fair because they allow sellers to maintain their profit entitlement. In contrast, demand-driven prices are often perceived as unfair. They allow the seller to increase their profit margins purely at the expense of the increasing consumer demand.[21]

# Emerging Service Pricing Strategies

Due to the many special considerations surrounding the pricing of services, traditional pricing strategies such as penetration pricing, competitive pricing, and premium pricing may offer little benefit to service customers or service providers. For example, competitive pricing has led to disappearing profit margins in such industries as car rental, airlines, and health insurance, and to customer confusion and mistrust in industries such as long distance telephone service. At the core of the pricing problem is a lack of understanding of the special considerations in the pricing of services and how consumers use and benefit from the services they are purchasing. Service marketers should create pricing strategies that offer a compromise between the overly complex and the too simplistic, both of which neglect the variations in consumer needs.[22]

To price services effectively, the service firm must first understand what its target market truly values. Three alternative pricing strategies that convey value to the customer include satisfaction-based, relationship, and efficiency pricing (see Figure 6.4).[23]

### Satisfaction-Based Pricing

The primary goal of **satisfaction-based pricing** is to reduce the amount of perceived risk associated with the service purchase and appeal to target markets that value certainty. Satisfaction-based pricing can be achieved through offering guarantees, benefit-driven pricing, and flat-rate pricing.

Service guarantees are quickly becoming a popular way of attracting customers, and are discussed in much greater detail in Chapter 14 as a means of retaining customers.[24] The guarantee assures customers that if they are less than satisfied with their purchase, they can invoke the guarantee and obtain a partial or full refund to offset their dissatisfaction with the service firm. Offering service guarantees signals to customers that the firm is committed to delivering quality services and confident in its ability to do so. Customers often believe that a firm offering service guarantees would not do so unless it was confident in its ability to deliver. In instances where competing services are priced

**FIG-6.4** Satisfaction-based, Relationship, and Efficiency Pricing Strategies

| PRICING STRATEGY | PROVIDES VALUE BY … | IMPLEMENTED AS … |
|---|---|---|
| Satisfaction-based pricing | Recognizing and reducing customers' perceptions of uncertainty, which the intangible nature of service magnifies. | Service guarantees Benefit-driven pricing Flat-rate pricing |
| Relationship pricing | Encouraging long-term relationships with the company that customers view as beneficial. | Long-term contracts Price bundling |
| Efficiency pricing | Sharing with customers the cost saving that the company has achieved by understanding, managing, and reducing thecosts of providing the service. | Cost-leader pricing |

Source: Leonard L. Berry and Manjit S. Yadav, "Capture and Communicate Value in the Pricing of Services," *Sloan Management Review*, (Summer 1996), pp. 41–51.

similarly and options to differentiate one service provider to the next are few, the service guarantee offers a differential advantage.

**benefit-driven pricing**
A pricing strategy that charges customers for services actually used as opposed to overall "membership" fees.

**flat-rate pricing** A pricing strategy in which the customer pays a fixed price and the provider assumes the risk of price increases and cost overruns.

**Benefit-driven pricing** focuses on the aspects of the service that customers actually use. The objective of this approach is to develop a direct association between the price of the service and the components of the service that customers value. For example, on-line computer services typically do not use benefit-driven pricing strategies. This is evident by their practice of charging customers a monthly fee as opposed to billing for the time they actually use online. Innovative online services, such as ESA-IRS and its "pricing for information" program, have introduced benefit-driven pricing and have shifted their marketing focus from keeping customers online to marketing information that is beneficial to their customers.

The concept of **flat-rate pricing** is fairly straightforward. Its primary objective is to decrease consumer uncertainty about the final price of the service by agreeing to a fixed price before the service transaction occurs. With flat-rate pricing, the provider assumes the risk of price increases and overruns. Flat-rate pricing makes the most sense when:

- *the price is competitive;*
- *the firm offering the flat rate has its costs under control and runs an efficient operation; and*
- *the opportunities to engage in a long-term relationship and to generate additional revenues with the customer is possible.*

The United States Postal Service has introduced flat-rate pricing for customers interested in shipping packages across the country. According to USPS, "Shipping shouldn't take a lot of time and guesswork. With Priority Mail Flat-Rate Boxes, if it fits in the box, it ships anywhere in the U.S. for a low flat rate. And no need for those zone maps."[25]

## Relationship Pricing

**relationship pricing**
Pricing strategies that encourage the customer to expand his or her dealings with the service provider.

The primary objective of **relationship pricing** is to enhance the firm's relationship with its targeted consumers. For example, in the banking industry, relationship pricing strategies can be utilized to further nurture the relationship between the bank and its existing checking account customers by offering special savings accounts, deals on safe deposit boxes, and special rates on certificates of deposit. Two types of relationship pricing techniques include long-term contracts and price bundling.

Long-term contracts offer prospective customers price and nonprice incentives for dealing with the same provider over a number of years. UPS recently entered into long-term shipping contracts with Land's End and Ford Motor Company. Because of its customers' long-term commitments, UPS has been able to transform its business with these clients from discrete to continuous transactions. UPS now has operations and personnel dedicated solely to providing services to these specific customers. Since transactions are now continuous, economies of scale have developed, and cost savings that can be passed to the customer plus opportunities for improving the firm's profit performance have emerged.

Since most service organizations provide more than one service, the practice of bundling services has become more common.[26] *Price bundling*, broadly defined, is the practice of marketing two or more services in a single package at a single price. For example, Comcast Cable's Triple Play Offer which bundles HD (high-definition) Cable, Phone, and High-Speed Internet services for one low price is a classic example.[27] Other common bundling examples include hotels offering weekend packages that include lodging, meals, and entertainment options at an inclusive rate, and online travel sites such as Travelocity that offer vacation packages that include air travel, car rental, and hotel accommodations for one single price.[28]

**mixed bundling** Price-bundling technique that allows consumers to either buy Service A and Service B together or purchase one service separately.

In general, services are concerned with **mixed bundling**, which enables consumers to either buy Service A and Service B together or purchase one service separately. The simplest argument for bundling is based on the idea of consumer surplus: Bundling makes it possible to shift the consumer surplus from one to another service that otherwise would have a negative surplus (i.e., would not be purchased). Moreover, mixed bundling offers customers a better value than purchasing services separately.

Three reasons have been suggested for why mixed bundling has a greater value than the sum of the individual parts. First, information theory would argue that the consumer finds value in easy access to information. For example, international guests of a resort hotel in Mexico experience lower information cost when purchasing a one-day excursion sightseeing trip from the hotel than when buying that same one-day excursion directly from the provider of the trip. The concierge at the hotel simply informs the hotel guest about the trips that are available which greatly reduces the guest's information search costs. A second case argues that the bundling of Service B with Service A can enhance a consumer's satisfaction with Service A. For example, the guest experience of the Mexican resort, Moon Palace, may be enhanced due to the numerous one-day sightseeing excursion packages the resort offers its guests. Consequently, guests may have a great day visiting the ruins of the Mayan City of Tulum, which in turn enhances their overall experience with the hotel. The final argument is that the addition of Service B to Service A can enhance the total image of the firm. Hence, the Moon Palace's reputation as a beach destination in Playa del Carmen known for its relaxation, tranquility, and seclusion is enhanced by the day-trip options available to guests who are seeking a more active approach to their vacation. Activities such as zip-lining through a rainforest, snorkeling at XelHa, or taking a nine-mile boat trip to Isla Mujeres (The Island of Women) enhances the resort's reputation as destination that offers something for everyone.

## Efficiency Pricing

**efficiency pricing** Pricing strategies that appeal to economically minded consumers by delivering the best and most cost-effective service for the price.

The primary goal of **efficiency pricing** is to appeal to economically minded consumers who are looking for the best price. "Efficiency pricers almost always are industry heretics, shunning traditional operating practices in search of sustainable cost advantages."[29] Southwest Airlines and its relentless efforts to reduce costs is one such example. Southwest Airlines reduces costs by flying shorter, more direct routes to less-congested, less-expensive airports. No meals are served, passengers are seated on a first-come, first-served basis, and the airline was the first to offer "ticketless" travel on all flights.

Efficiency pricing focuses on delivering the best and most cost-effective service available for the price. Operations are streamlined, and innovations that enable further cost reduction become part of the operation's culture. The leaner the cost structure, the more difficult it is for new competitors to imitate Southwest's success. Understanding and managing costs are the fundamental building blocks of efficiency pricing.

Today, Southwest Airlines continues its price leadership in the airline industry with its Bags Fly Free™ promotion.[30] While many other airlines charge their customers baggage fees for their first (up to $20) and second (up to $30) pieces of luggage in addition to ticket prices, Southwest proudly boasts, "We don't believe in springing unpleasant surprises on our Customers…Take a stand against other airline bag fees. Book a Southwest flight today and save up to $100 roundtrip when your Bags Fly Free™." Readers might also notice that when Southwest speaks of its "Customers," the first letter is capitalized. Symbolically, the capital "C" reflects the importance Southwest places on delivering top-notched, value-based services to its customers.

## Some Final Thoughts on Pricing Services

The pricing services is a complex task. Consumers are purchasing an experience and often feel uneasy about or do not understand what they are paying for. Similarly, service providers do not have a cost of goods sold figure upon which to base their prices. Confused and bewildered, many providers simply look to what the competition is charging, regardless of their own cost structures and competitive advantage. In contrast, successful service providers tend to abide by the following pricing guidelines:[31]

- *The price should be easy for customers to understand.*
- *The price should represent value to the customer.*
- *The price should encourage customer retention and facilitate the customer's relationship with the providing firm.*
- *The price should reinforce customer trust.*
- *The price should reduce customer uncertainty.*

## Summary

Successful service pricing depends on recognizing the value that a customer places on a service and pricing that service accordingly. Customer perceptions of value represent a tradeoff between the perceived benefits obtained from purchasing the product and the perceived sacrifice in terms of cost to be paid. Total customer costs extend beyond monetary costs and include time, energy, and psychic costs. Similarly, total customer value extends beyond product value and includes service, personnel, and image value.

When developing service pricing strategies, managers should take into account a number of considerations including cost, demand, customer, competitive, profit, product, and legal considerations. Figure 6.2 provides a summary of each of these considerations.

Overall, traditional pricing strategies and cost accounting approaches offer little benefit to either service consumers or service providers. Three alternative pricing strategies that convey value to the customer include satisfaction-based, relationship, and efficiency pricing. The primary goal of satisfaction-based pricing is to reduce the perceived risk associated with the purchase of services and to appeal to target markets that value certainty. Satisfaction-based pricing strategies include offering guarantees, benefit-driven pricing, and flat-rate pricing. The goal of relationship pricing is to enhance the firm's relationship with its targeted consumers. Relationship pricing techniques include offering long-term contracts and price bundling. In comparison, efficiency pricing appeals to economically minded consumers and focuses on delivering the best and most cost-effective service for the price. Understanding and managing costs are the fundamental building blocks of efficiency pricing.

## Key Terms

monetary cost, p. 147
time costs, p. 147
energy costs, p. 147
psychic costs, p. 147
product value, p. 148
service value, p. 148
personnel value, p. 148
image value, p. 148
fixed costs, p. 151
variable costs, p. 151

economies of scale, p. 152
inelastic demand, p. 153
cross-price elasticity, p. 153
complements, p. 153
substitutes, p. 154
price discrimination, p. 155
signpost items, p. 157
reservation price, p. 158
price bundling, p. 159
forward buying, p. 161

product-line pricing, p. 161
dual entitlement, p. 162
satisfaction-based pricing, p. 162
benefit-driven pricing, p. 163
flat-rate pricing, p. 163
relationship pricing, p. 163
mixed bundling, p. 164
efficiency pricing, p. 164

# Review Questions

1. It is often suggested that service firms should set their prices based on customers' perceived value of the service. What is value?
2. Discuss the role of costs in setting final prices.
3. Discuss the role of price as an indicator of quality to consumers.
4. Describe the tradeoffs associated with taking hotel reservations from customers who pay lower rates than same-day customers.
5. Should self-service always be rewarded with lower prices? Please explain.
6. Under what conditions is price segmentation most effective?
7. Discuss the basic concepts behind satisfaction-based, relationship, and efficiency pricing.
8. Provide three examples of relationship pricing not addressed in this chapter.
9. Define price bundling and provide three reasons why it makes sense for service firms to engage in price bundling practices.
10. Define flat-rate pricing and provide an explanation for why a service firm may want to pursue a flat-rate pricing strategy.

# Notes

1. David M. Feldman, "Making Cents of Pricing," *Marketing Management,* May/June (2005), pp. 21–25.
2. J. Dean, "Research Approach to Pricing," *Planning the Price Structure,* Marketing Series No. 67, American Marketing Association (1947).
3. J. Backman, *Price Practices and Price Policies* (New York: Ronald Press, 1953).
4. Walker A. W. "How to Price Industrial Products," *Harvard Business Review,* 45, (1967), pp. 38–45.
5. A. Marshall, *More Profitable Pricing* (London, McGraw-Hill, 1979).
6. Chief Executive, "Finding the Right Price Is No Easy Game to Play," *Chief Executive,* (September 1981), pp. 16–18.
7. Thomas T. Nagle and Reed K. Holden, *The Strategy and Tactics of Pricing* (Englewood Cliffs, NJ: Prentice Hall, 1995).
8. Philip Kotler, *Marketing Management*, 8th ed. (Englewood Cliffs, NJ: Prentice-Hall, 1994), p. 38.
9. Robert G. Gross and Ashutosh Dixit, "Customer-Centric Pricing: The Surprising Secret for Profitability," *Business Horizons*, 48, (2005), pp. 483–491.
10. Thomas T. Nagle and Reed K. Holden, *The Strategy and Tactics of Pricing*, 3e (Upper Saddle River, Prentice Hall, 2002) p. 1.
11. K. Douglas Hoffman and L. W. Turley, "Toward an Understanding of Consumer Price Sensitivity for Professional Services," *Developments in Marketing Science*, Charles H. Noble, ed. (Miami, FL: Academy of Marketing Science, 1999) pp. 169–173.
12. UPS website: **http://www.ups.com**, accessed 30 January 2005. "Only Santa Delivers More in One Day than UPS," Press Release (December 13, 2004); **http://pressroom.ups.com/ups.com/us/press_releases/**, accessed 30 January 2005; and John Alden "What in the World Drives UPS?" *International Business* 11 (2), (1998), pp. 6–7+; and Jim Kelley, "From Lip Service to Real Service: Reversing America's Downward Service Spiral," *Vital Speeches of the Day*, 64 (10), (1998), pp. 301–304.
13. Wendy Zellner and Brain Grow, "Waiting for the First Bird to Die," Business Week, Issue 3917, (January 24, 2005), p. 38; Lori Calabro, "Making Fares Fairer," CFO, 18 no. 9 (September 2002), 105–107.
14. Robert G. Gross and Ashutosh Dixit, "Customer-Centric Pricing: The Surprising Secret for Profitability," *Business Horizons*, 48, (2005), pp. 483–491.
15. Adapted from John E. G. Bateson, *Managing Services Marketing*, 2nd ed. (Fort Worth, TX: The Dryden Press, 1992) pp. 357–365.
16. Kent B. Monroe, "Buyers Subjective Perceptions of Price," *Journal of Marketing Research*, 10, (February 1973), pp. 70–80.
17. Eric Anderson and Duncan Simester, "Minding Your Pricing Cues," *Harvard Business Review*, (September 2003), pp. 97–103.
18. Bateson, *Managing Services Marketing*, pp. 338–339.
19. Joseph P. Guiltinan, "The Price Bundling of Services: A Normative Framework," *Journal of Marketing* 51 2, (1987), pp. 74–85.
20. Saroja Subrahmanyan and Robert Shoemaker, "Developing Optimal pricing and Inventory Policies for Retailers Who Face Uncertain Demand," *Journal of Retailing*, (1996) 72 (1), pp. 7–30.
21. Czinkota, et al., *Marketing: Best Practices* (Fort Worth, TX: The Dryden Press, 2000).

22. Leonard L. Berry and Manjit S. Yadav, "Capture and Communicate Value in the Pricing of Services," *Sloan Management Review*, (Summer 1996), pp. 41–51.

23. Ibid.

24. Christopher W. L. Hart, Leonard A. Schlesinger, and Dan Maher, "Guarantees Come to Professional Service Firms," *Sloan Management Review*, (Spring 1992), pp. 19–29.

25. **https://www.prioritymail.com/flatrates.asp**, accessed 25 October, 2009.

26. Joseph P. Guiltinan, "The Price Bundling of Services: A Normative Framework," *Journal of Marketing*, (April 1987), pp. 51, 74–85.

27. **http://www.comcastspecial.com/**, accessed 26 October, 2009.

28. **http://www.travelocity.com/**, accessed 26 October, 2009.

29. Berry and Manjit, "Capture and Communicate Value," p. 49.

30. **http://www.swabiz.com/bagsflyfree/**, accessed 26 October, 2009.

31. Berry and Manjit, "Capture and Communicate Value," p. 49.

# MDVIP: Become a Priority, Not Just a Patient

Faced with the mounting pressure of practicing family medicine, Dr. Charles Ray knew something had to change with how he was running his medical practice. Dr. Ray's current practice consisted of nearly 3,000 patients that he normally saw only when they were already sick. Trained in the areas of preventative medicine, Dr. Ray felt he never really had the opportunity to use his training effectively to prevent illness and promote a healthy lifestyle for his patients before they fell ill. Moreover, due to the increasing number of patients, the average time for each visit was approximately eight minutes, and the appointment schedule was often booked out nearly a week in advance. As a result, sick patients were often waiting seven to 10 days to actually get an appointment. Complicating matters even further, insurance companies often dictated the final fees for many services and paid doctors a fraction of what was actually charged to patients. Over the years, Dr. Ray found himself feeling stressed out over the patient load, his family life was suffering due to the number of nights he was on call, and most importantly, he felt like patients were not getting the quality of care that he was actually able to provide.

Upon attending a medical conference, Dr. Ray learned of a new business model for physicians like himself that was being promoted by a firm named **MD**VIP. **MD**VIP is a network of approximately 300 physicians in 26 states who emphasize preventative, personalized health care. **MD**VIP offers what many call "concierge medical care," where physicians offer individualized health care for an annual fee. The annual fee buys patients a higher level of care, more personalized attention, easier access to physicians, and is paid for in addition to regular medical fees. The business model allows physicians to decrease the size of their practices dramatically and focus on preventative as well acute patient care.

More specifically, physicians who adopt the **MD**VIP patient care business model promise to keep their patients as healthy as possible by providing unprecedented value and services, including:

- *A smaller practice size, which allows time to focus on wellness, prevention, and the best treatment available. In Dr. Ray's case, the size of his practice would be reduced from 3,000 to 600 patients.*
- *An executive annual physical and personalized wellness plan. The executive annual physical is a $2,000 value covered by the patient's annual fee. The personalized wellness plan focuses on preventative healthcare activities in the hope of avoiding healthcare problems before they occur.*

Source: **www.mdvip.com** accessed 23 October, 2009

- *Specialty care from premier hospitals and research facilities in the country, such as Cleveland Clinic, Memorial Sloan-Kettering Cancer Center and UCLA Medical Center, as part of* **MD**VIP's *Medical Centers of Excellence.* **MD**VIP's *Medical Centers of Excellence provide patients additional care for those situations that are beyond the care abilities of the local physician.*
- *Twenty-four hour physician availability and same or next day appointments. Due to the smaller size of the practice, patients can obtain appointments the same day, or, worst case scenario, next day appointments. In addition, patients receive the physicians direct cell phone number for 24/7 access. Each member patient also receives a personalized website that offers a secure messaging feature where patients can contact their physician directly by email. Moreover, adult children under the age of 25 as well as out-of-town guests also have access to the physician for no additional charge.*
- *State-of-the-art technology including your own personal health record CD. The CD is wallet-sized, contains all the individual's personal health information, and can be carried as easily as a credit card. In fact,* **MD**VIP *recommends that its patients carry the medical CD at all times, and suggests placing the CD between an individual's driver's license and insurance card in case of a medical emergency.*
- *Access to other* **MD**VIP *physicians throughout the country for urgent or emergent care to provide patients with piece of mind when they travel. As the network of* **MD**VIP *physicians continues to grow, member patients can access other providers, if necessary, while traveling throughout the country.*

Physicians invited to join the **MD**VIP network are carefully screened to assure patients that they are receiving the "gold standard" in terms of quality of care. The network selects physicians based on their medical expertise and philosophical relationships with their patients. **MD**VIP selects physicians who believe in preventative care and want to emphasize preventative care in their practices.

The annual cost for patients to participate in a **MD**VIP practice is $1,500. The amount may be tax deductible and may be reimbursable through FSAs (Flexible Spending Accounts) or HSAs (Health Savings Accounts). As Dr. Ray considered adopting the **MD**VIP business model, he wondered how his patients would respond.

## Discussion Questions

1. Using the Buyer's Perception of Value presented in Figure 6.1, discuss the value provided by the **MD**VIP business model. Do you believe that **MD**VIP offers a good value to patients?
2. Based on the 10 factors that influence price sensitivity described in the text, select five of these factors and discuss whether patient demand for health care is elastic (patients are typically price sensitive) or inelastic (patients are typically less price sensitive).
3. If Dr. Ray reduces his practice to 600 patients, discuss the pros and cons of three possible strategies for making arrangements for his 2,400 patients that will no longer be his responsibility.
4. Discuss the ethical or social responsibility issues that Dr. Ray faces as he considers signing on with **MD**VIP.

# CHAPTER 7

# Effective Service Promotions

## CHAPTER OBJECTIVES

After reading this chapter, you should be able to:

- Discuss the steps necessary to manage the firm's service communication strategy effectively.

- Understand the special challenges associated with developing service communications.

- Describe specific guidelines for developing service communications.

- Appreciate the special considerations faced by professional service providers and recommend solutions to overcome these challenges.

The purpose of this chapter is to provide an overview of communication strategy as it applies to the marketing of services.

Courtesy of Geico

### GEICO'S GECKO OFFERS A COMMUNICATION STRATEGY OF REASSURANCE IN TROUBLING TIMES

Although it seems for many of us that the U.S. insurance company Geico is a relatively new addition to the major players in the insurance sector such as State Farm, Prudential, and Allstate, the company has actually been around since the 1930s. Founded in 1936 by Leo and Lillian Goodwin, the company originally marketed auto insurance to its primary target markets of federal employees and the top three grades of noncommissioned military officers (Hence, the name GEICO—the Government Employees Insurance Company). The company was based on the idea that if it could lower costs by focusing on specific target markets, it could charge lower premiums and still be profitable. The idea caught on quickly and by the end of 1936 the company had sold 3,700 auto policies and had 12 employees. Approximately 30 years later, GEICO passed the 1 million policyholder mark in 1964.

Today, GEICO is a subsidiary of one of the most profitable organizations in the country—Warren Buffet's Berkshire Hathaway investment firm. Buffet's investment firm provided the financial backing necessary in 1996 that led to GEICO's explosive growth over the past decade and a half. National advertising and direct mail campaigns were launched on an enormous scale and consumers responded in mass. GIECO is now the third largest private-passenger auto insurer in the United States (only State Farm and Allstate are larger) with 9 million auto policyholders insuring more than 16 million vehicles. The company now employs 24,000 associates.

Contributing to the company's success has been the introduction of the GEICO "gecko." GEICO's gecko became an instant advertising phenomenon when introduced during the 1999–2000 television season. Developed by the Martin agency in Richmond, Virginia, the gecko was the result of the mispronunciation of the GEICO name. The gecko with his English accent has become a recognizable, tangible symbol and an advertising icon for the company. The gecko makes special appearances at community events around the country. Gecko merchandise can be purchased by visiting the Gecko Store Online. Items for sales include bobble heads, tattoos, pens, visors, diecast racing cars, and polo shirts among a plethora of other items for the gecko enthusiast. In addition to the gecko, GEICO has strengthened its organizational image over the years by developing complementary communication campaigns featuring cavemen and the "It's So Easy, A Caveman Can Do It!" theme and googly eyes backed by Mysto & Pizzi's compelling remix of "Somebody's Watching Me."

In more recent times, responding to the upheaval of financial markets and the downward spiral in consumer confidence, the gecko has appeared in print ads offering a reassuring message. In these messages, the gecko wears horn-rimmed glasses and describes GEICO as a "financially stable company that is here for the long run," and "a wholly-owned subsidiary of Warren Buffet's Berkshire Hathaway, Inc." A second print ad touts that "Warren Buffet and the gecko. They go together like pie and chips." The ad copy continues, "Since Mr. Buffet's Berkshire Hathaway acquired GEICO in 1996…he and the gecko have seen GEICO grow to become the third-largest auto insurer in the nation." The messages are intended to reassure concerned customers about GEICO's stability. Specifically, the message hits upon Mr. Buffet's deep pockets and Berkshire Hathaway's triple-A rating from Standard and Poor's. According to GEICO's vice president of marketing, "The strategy for this [reassuring customers] is driven by the need to emphasize to people there's a way to save money without risking anything … hitting stability, trust, the right things to be talking about in this environment." GEICO offers a classic illustration that as environmental forces change the course of a company's overall marketing strategy, the service firm's communication strategy should adapt to fit changing business conditions.

Sources:
1. **http://www.geico.com/**, accessed 15 October, 2009.
2. **http://www.nytimes.com/2009/02/19/business/media/19adco.html**, accessed 15 October, 2009.

# Introduction

**communication strategy** Communicates the firm's positioning strategy to its target markets, including consumers, employees, stockholders, and suppliers for the purpose of achieving organizational objectives.

The firm's promotion, or **communications strategy**, informs, persuades, and reminds target markets, including consumers, employees, and stockholders about the firm's goods and services for the purpose of achieving organizational objectives. The term **communications mix** describes the array of communications tools available to marketers that deliver the firm's communication strategy. Just as marketers need to combine the elements of the marketing mix (the 4Ps of product, price, place, and promotion) to produce a marketing program, managers of service firms must also select the most appropriate communication tools to convey their message.

**communication mix** The array of communications tools available to marketers including advertising, personal selling, publicity, sales promotions, and sponsorships.

The tools of the communications mix fall into five broad categories: personal selling; advertising; publicity, sales promotions, and sponsorships. Much like five players on a basketball team, each of the five communication tools excel at their own unique purpose. For example, *personal selling* is the only communication tool that enables two-way

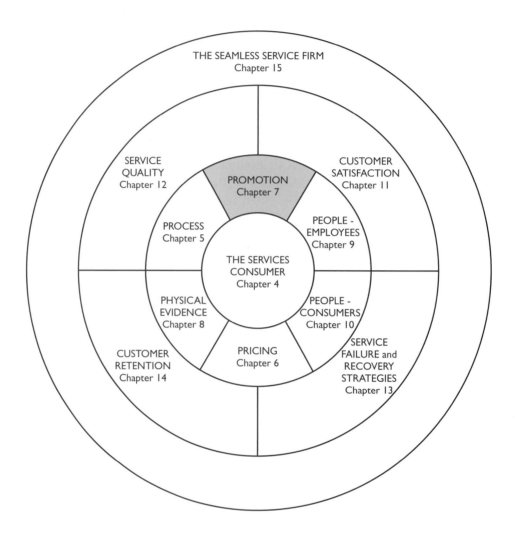

communication between the service provider and the customer. As a result, the service provider can tailor their communication message to each specific customer. As for *advertising*, no other communication tool is faster in creating overall awareness. Moreover, *publicity* is free and typically reported by a third party making it the most credible source of communication information. In turn, the primary strategic advantage of utilizing *sales promotions* is to increase short-term sales. Finally, *sponsorships* allow the service firm to target narrow, but highly desirable target audiences and provide an option for service firms to adapt to consumers' changing media habits—customers are simply not watching that much television anymore, and when they do, advertising is often skipped via technological devices or ignored.

Using more than one communications tool to communicate the same message (known as *integrated marketing communications*) or using any one tool repeatedly increases the chances that existing and potential customers will be exposed to the firm's message, associate it with the firm, and remember it. By reinforcing its message, the firm can ensure that existing customers as well as potential ones become more aware of "who" the firm is and what it has to offer. The firm's communications mix often lays the foundation for subsequent contact with potential consumers, making discussions with consumers easier for the provider and more comfortable for the consumers.

Selecting Target Markets

‖

Establishing Communication Objectives

‖

Setting the Communication Budget

‖

Formulating the Positioning Strategy

‖

Establishing Message and Media Strategies

‖

Monitoring, Evaluating and Controlling the Communication Strategy

# Managing the Service Communication Process

In many ways, the development of a sound communications strategy closely parallels the basic fundamentals of developing an effective marketing strategy—identifying a target market, selecting a positioning strategy, and tailoring a communication mix to the targeted audience that reinforces the desired positioning strategy. Consequently, managing the service communication mix is much more than developing an advertisement, buying a commercial time slot, and sitting back and watching what happens. Marketing as a discipline consists of a number of processes that, when used effectively, increase the likelihood of success for the processes intended purpose. Similarly, service practitioners who adhere to the following service communication process substantially increase their odds of obtaining their communication objectives (see Figure 7.1).

## Selecting Target Markets

**target markets** The market segment that becomes the focus of a firm's marketing efforts.

Developing a communications strategy follows a common pattern whether the firm is producing goods or services. The service firm must first analyze the needs of consumers in the marketplace and then categorize consumers with similar needs into market segments. Each market segment should then be considered based on profit and growth potential and the segment's compatibility with organizational resources and objectives. Segments that become the focus of the firm's marketing efforts become **target markets**.

If you don't particularly like the way lawyers are portrayed on television advertisements, there is probably a good reason—you're not their target market. According to

Peter Samuels/Riser/Getty Images

Women are more likely to initiate a call to a lawyer when automotive-related injuries occur. As a result, law advertising pertaining to personal injury as a result of an automobile related accident should be targeted primarily to females.

Greg Norton, Vice President of Rainmaker Marketing, Inc. in Wilmington, North Carolina, "over one half of the attorney advertisers on television nationwide are sending the wrong message to the wrong audience.[1] In markets all over the country, attorney advertisers are turning off the people they wish to reach." Rainmaker Marketing offers its services to law clients to keep them from making the same mistakes.

Who responds to lawyers who advertise on television? The results may surprise you. For example, research indicates that women make the initial calls to lawyers 60 to 70 percent of the time for automobile injuries (regardless of whether it's a male or female who is injured in the accident). Clearly, attorney advertisements should be created to speak to that female audience, and the message should be "trust." Women are looking for a relationship based on trust when selecting an attorney.

The typical respondents to attorney advertising are blue collar, age 21 to 54, with a ninth to 12th grade education. Younger callers tend to be single wage earners with families consisting of small children. This target audience is very connected to the television, as they obtain 90 percent of their current information from this medium. Women tend to respond immediately to attorney advertising viewed in the morning, but will delay responses in the afternoon until after their favorite shows have ended.

## Establishing Communications Objectives

At the broadest level, the service firm's communication objectives seek to *inform*, *persuade*, and *remind* current and potential customers about the firm's service offerings. Furthermore, the objectives of a firm's communication mix often relate directly to the service offering's stage within its product life cycle (PLC) (see Figure 7.2). In general, the major communication objectives within the introduction and growth stages of the PLC are to inform the customer. Informational communications introduce the service offering and create brand awareness for the firm. Informational communications also encourage trial, and often prepare the way for personal selling efforts to be conducted later.

*"I'm giving you 10,000 free golf balls with my company's logo on them. Since you'll lose every one of them, it'll be good advertising."*

www.CartoonStock.com

Since many service providers own and operate small firms with limited resources, exploring unique approaches to create awareness is a top priority.

**FIG-7.2** Product Life
Cycle Stage and
Communication
Objectives

| PRODUCT LIFE CYCLE STAGE | COMMUNICATION OBJECTIVE | COMMUNICATION TACTICS |
|---|---|---|
| Introduction | Informational | Introduce the service offering. Create brand awareness. Prepare the way for personal selling efforts. Encourage trial. |
| Growth and Maturity | Informational and Persuasive | Create a positive attitude relative to competitive offerings. Provoke an immediate buying action. Enhance the firm's image. |
| Maturity and Decline | Persuasive and Reminder | Encourage repeat purchases. Provide ongoing contact. Express gratitude to existing customer base. Confirm past purchase decisions. |

As professional service providers slowly begin to communicate with the market, informational communications objectives tend to be the first step. Informational communications tend to be less obtrusive than other forms of communication, and, in many ways, the information conveyed often provides a public service to consumers who otherwise might not have access or knowledge of the range of services available. Legal and medical services that engage in communication campaigns are typical examples. Although many of us poke fun at many of the ads that lawyers place on the airways, they do serve their purpose. Many of the clients who contact these services are lower-income, less-educated clients who, by their own admission, have stated that if it were not for the advertisements they would not know where to turn.[2]

Communications objectives during the growth and maturity stages of the PLC tend to lean toward informational and persuasive content. Objectives during this stage include *creating a positive attitude* toward the service offering relative to competitive alternatives, attempting to *provoke an immediate purchase action*, and *enhancing the firm's image*. Professional service organizations often discourage the use of persuasive advertising among their members as it often pits one professional member of the organization against another. For example, it is hard to imagine that one physician would name a competing physician by name and make claims that one physician is better than the other. In general, professional service organizations often believe that members who engage in persuasive communications ultimately cheapen the image of the entire industry. As a result, promotional messages that are primarily information-based are viewed as a more acceptable and tasteful method of promotion. When persuasive approaches are undertaken in the service arena, they are typically less personal and more global in nature. For example, a service firm may claim more expertise or that they have been in business longer than their competition (without mentioning the specific names of competitors).

Communications objectives during the maturity and decline stages of the PLC tend to utilize persuasive and reminder communications. The communications objectives during this phase of the PLC are to influence existing customers to purchase again; to provide ongoing contact with the existing client base in order to remind clients that the firm still values their relationship; and to confirm clients' past purchase decisions, thereby minimizing levels of felt cognitive dissonance. As with informational communications, reminder communications tend to be less obtrusive and more acceptable to professional organizations than persuasive communications.

Finally, the broad categories of informational, persuasive, and reminder objectives are typically undertaken to achieve additional strategic objectives such as *increases in sales*, positive *changes in consumer attitudes*, and *increasing overall consumer awareness* of the firm and its offerings. Furthermore, each objective should be stated in **SMART** terms:

- *S*pecific—objectives should be stated in specific (e.g., sales, awareness, etc.) as opposed to general (let's do a good job this year) terms.
- *M*easurable—objectives should be stated in quantitative terms so that they can be measured (e.g., the objective is to increase sales by 10 percent).
- *A*chievable—objectives should be realistic and reachable. Unrealistic objectives will never be achieved, and may actually discourage as opposed to encourage employee behavior.
- *R*elevant—objectives should be relevant to the people who are undertaking the objectives. Corporate personnel should undertake corporate level objectives, while department personnel should undertake department level objectives.
- *T*ime-bound—Objectives should be stated to be completed within a specific time frame (e.g., six months, one year, etc.)

## Setting the Communications Budget

Once the target market is selected and communication objectives established, the communications budget needs to be set. Budget setting techniques typically are covered in most introductory marketing classes and include the corporate level approaches of *top-down budgeting*, *bottom-up budgeting*, *bottom-up/top-down budgeting*, and *top-down/bottom-up budgeting*. Other budget setting techniques that are more applicable to small service firms include the *percentage-of-sales technique*, the *incremental technique*, the *all-you-can-afford approach*, *competitive parity*, and the *objective-and-task method*.[3] As a refresher, Figure 7.3 provides a brief description for each technique.

Ideally, the communications budget should provide the necessary resources for the service firm to meet its established communication objectives. In other words, the firm's communication objectives should drive the budget. However, a quick review of the majority of budget setting techniques mentioned above provides the insight that it is often the budget that drives which objectives can be achieved and not the other way around. Limiting the budget severely hinders the firm in reaching its communication objectives. As the opening quote in this chapter states, "The business that considers itself immune to the necessity of advertising [communications] sooner or later finds itself immune to business."

**FIG-7.3** An Overview of Communication Strategy Budget Setting Techniques

| BUDGET SETTING TECHNIQUE | DESCRIPTION |
|---|---|
| Top-down Budgeting | Budget is set by upper management. |
| Bottom-Up Budgeting | Budget is set by the product-level or brand manager. |
| Bottom-Up/Top-Down Budgeting | Budget is set by the product-level or brand manager and then revised by upper management. |
| Top-Down/Bottom-Up Budgeting | Budget is set by upper management and then revised by the product-level or brand manager. |
| Percentage-of-Sales Technique | Budget is set based on a percentage of the previous year's sales. |
| Incremental Technique | Budget is increased by a fixed percent every year. |
| All-you-Can-Afford Approach | Budget is set based on what is left over after the firm pays for operating expenses and planned profits. |
| Competitive Parity | Budget is set based on promotional spending behavior demonstrated by the competition. |
| Objective-and-Task Method | Budget is set based on the amount necessary to achieve stated communication objectives. |

## Formulating the Service Firm's Positioning Strategy

**positioning strategy**
How the firm is viewed by consumers relative to its competitors. Positioning strategy speaks to the firm's differential advantage.

The next step in managing the service communication process is to formulate the service firm's positioning strategy. A successful **positioning strategy** communicates to customers how the service firm distinguishes itself from competing alternatives. Starbucks, for example, positions itself as a socially responsible purveyor of coffee (see Sustainability and Services in Action).

---

## SUSTAINABILITY AND SERVICES *IN ACTION*

### Starbucks' Subtle Promotion about Its Environmental Mission

Most of the world's population is well aware of Starbucks dominance as a retail coffee purveyor, but a much smaller portion of the market is likely to have much knowledge about the company's environmentally friendly business practices. Although Starbucks does not deliberately hide its environmental efforts, the company certainly does not openly boast about its numerous efforts as much as it could. Perhaps the less the company openly uses its eco-friendly practices in marketing communications to attract new customers, the more credible its efforts in social responsibility and sustainability become.

To understand more fully Starbucks notable efforts, customers must seek out information under the "about us" tab on the company's website—not a single "peep" is mentioned on the opening web page. For example, in addition to its corporate mission statement, Starbucks commitment to environmentally friendly business practices is demonstrated in a separate environmental mission statement.

### Starbucks' Environmental Mission Statement

Starbucks is committed to a role of environmental leadership in all facets of our business. We fulfill this mission by a commitment to:

    Understanding of environmental issues and sharing information with our partners.
    Developing innovative and flexible solutions to bring about change.
    Striving to buy, sell and use environmentally friendly products.
    Recognizing that fiscal responsibility is essential to our environmental future.
    Instilling environmental responsibility as a corporate value.
    Measuring and monitoring our progress for each project.
    Encouraging all partners to share in our mission.

Accordingly, Starbucks actively attempts to minimize its environmental impact and creates opportunities for environmentally friendly business in a variety of ways. First, the company has adopted purchasing guidelines to buy environmentally friendly products from companies which share their concern for the environment. In addition, the company purchases lead-free ink for paper purchases, engages in paperless administration systems when possible, practices minimal packaging, recycles post-consumer materials, recycles coffee grounds obtained from roasting and extract operations into compost, incorporates energy conservation practices into its retail and manufacturing locations, voluntarily tracks and reduces the company's greenhouse gas emissions, and actively trains employees about Starbucks' commitment to the preservation of the environment. Moreover, the company's "commitment to origins" initiative actively assists "producers, their families and communities, and the natural environment to help promote a sustainable social, ecological, and economic model for the production and trade of coffee."

Sources:
1. **http://www.starbucks.com/mission/**, accessed 15 October, 2009.
2. **http://www.starbucks.com/aboutus/gr.asp**, accessed 15 October, 2009.

**FIG-7.4**
**Differentiation Approaches for Effective Positioning**

| PRODUCT DIFFERENTIATION | PERSONNEL DIFFERENTIATION |
|---|---|
| Features | Competence |
| Performance | Courtesy |
| Conformance | Credibility |
| Durability | Reliability |
| Reliability | Responsiveness |
| Repairability | Communication Style |
| Design (integrates the above) | |

| IMAGE DIFFERENTIATION | SERVICE DIFFERENTIATION |
|---|---|
| Symbols | Delivery (speed, accuracy) |
| Written, audio/visual media | Installation |
| Atmosphere | Customer training |
| Events | Consulting service |
| | Repair |
| | Miscellaneous service |

Source: Adapted from Philip Kotler, *Marketing Management: Analysis, Planning, Implementation, and Control*, 9th ed. (Englewood Cliffs, NJ: Prentice-Hall, 1997), p. 283. Print and Electronically reproduced by permission of Pearson Education, Inc., Upper Saddle River, New Jersey.

Other typical examples of positioning strategies used by both goods and service firms include product differentiation, image differentiation, personnel differentiation, and service differentiation (see Figure 7.4 for additional detail). In the end, despite a firm's best efforts to communicate its desired positioning, it is the customer who ultimately defines the company's positioning strategy. Effective positioning is particularly critical for service firms where intangibility clouds the consumer's ability to differentiate one service provider's offering from the next. For example, one of the challenges faced by international service marketers is developing promotional campaigns that meet the needs of local clientele. In order to customize the promotional plan for the international market, the international marketer must consider issues related to positioning and advertising copy. The most important positioning adaptations are often based on local behavior, tastes, attitudes, and traditions—all reflecting the marketer's need to gain customers' approval. The service product itself may not change at all, only its positioning may need to be adjusted. Consequently, a Marriott property in one location may be positioned as a weekend getaway for adults, while another location in a more conservative country may stress family values in its communication strategy.

**copy** The content of the firm's communication message

Frequently, in support of the service firm's positioning strategy, the **copy** of the communication mix needs to be adjusted to appeal to the international customer. While some communications may share common graphic elements, the copy in the ad will be customized for the local culture. Marriott used similar ads to reach the business traveler in the United States, Saudi Arabia, Latin America, and German-speaking Europe. However, the copy was modified based on the needs of the local consumer. While the common theme, "When You Are Comfortable, You Can Do Anything," was used worldwide, local emphases in the creative approach varied; for example, the Latin version stressed comfort, while the German version focused on results.

Similarly, ads for hotel properties marketed in countries such as Saudi Arabia need to be sensitive to local moral standards. While a global creative approach can be used, the copy and the images used in communications may require some adjusting. For example, if a Western-based Marriott advertisement showed a man and a women embracing with

Through the effective use of its "Ladies and Gentlemen serving Ladies and Gentlemen" communications campaign, the Ritz Carlton has successfully positioned itself as the hotel of choice for both affluent customers and professional service providers.

bare arms visible, this version used around the world may be adjusted for Saudi Arabia to show the man's arm clothed in a dark suit sleeve, and the woman's hand merely brushing his hand. In the end, international service communications should be carefully positioned to fit the needs and expectations of local markets.

## Establishing Message and Media Strategies

Upon developing the service firm's positioning strategy, message content must be created that conveys the positioning strategy to current and potential customers. For example, the Ritz Carlton effectively positions itself as a high-end hospitality provider through its motto, "We are Ladies and Gentlemen serving Ladies and Gentlemen."[4] This is a classic example of using personnel differentiation as a positioning strategy. In addition to creating message content, the message also needs to be effectively delivered to customers via effective media strategies. The effectiveness of media strategies varies based on whether the message is targeted to nonusers or users.

*Media Strategies for Targeting Nonusers*    If the objective is to reach nonusers of the service, then the choice of communications channel is reduced to media advertising, selling performed by a sales force rather than a service provider, public relationships, and sponsorships.

One way of assigning tasks across the array of communications channels is to consider the degree to which the message can be targeted at specific audiences. Media advertising itself varies along this dimension. At the broadcast, "shotgun" level, television advertising can reach a very wide audience but is not especially selective except in the variation of audiences across channels by time of day. For example, based on automobile accident statistics, 50 to 60 percent of all injury-causing accidents occur between Friday morning and Sunday midnight. Two-thirds of all injuries are soft tissue damage that begins to show symptoms 24 to 72 hours after the accident. Consequently, primetime for attorney advertising begins Monday morning and extends through Wednesday afternoon.[5]

In comparison, national print media such as newspapers and magazines offer more selective focus, as they themselves tend to be targeted at more specific segments of consumers. Trade magazines are even more specific in their readership. Direct mail offers the most focused of the impersonal media. Ultimately, the choice between these media must be based on the cost per thousand members of the target audience and the risk and cost of reaching the wrong segments.

When the service provider has a broadly defined audience and little to lose in reaching the wrong segments, television advertising may work out to be the least expensive vehicle on a cost per person basis. However, television and other forms of mass media are unlikely to be efficient for a specialty service such as an upscale restaurant with a tightly defined target audience and a high cost associated with attracting the wrong segment.

Public relations and publicity can be either broad or tightly focused, depending on how they are used. Editorial comment can be solicited in broad or narrow media. Public relations carries with it the advantages and disadvantages of not being paid advertising. On the positive side, it receives more credence by the consumer; on the negative side, it is much more difficult to control. The content may not be designed, or the coverage may be limited.

Both media advertising and public relations and publicity are one-way forms of communication. They cannot respond to consumers' inquiries or tailor the message to the particular characteristics of the receiver. Personal or telemarketing is far more expensive per member of the target audience, but it does offer the flexibility of altering the message during the presentation. If the message is difficult to communicate or a great deal of persuasion is needed, personal communication may be most appropriate. A sales force can be highly targeted and trained to make complex arguments interactively, responding to the inputs of consumers during the process.

***Media Strategies for Targeting Users***   Users can be reached through all the channels discussed above, and they can be further reached by communications through the service provider themselves. Clearly, the role of the service provider is multifaceted. Different providers are called upon to perform different communication functions. These providers and functions have been classified along the following types of service staff:[6]

**type 1 service staff**
Service staff who are required to deal with customers quickly and effectively in "once only" situations where large numbers of customers are present.

**Type 1 service staff** are required to deal with customers quickly and effectively in "once only" transaction-based service encounters where large numbers of customers are present. The exchanges consist of simple information and limited responses to customer requests. Effective communication requires the ability to establish customer relationships very quickly, deal efficiently with customer problems, and convey short, rapid messages that customers can easily understand. Typical examples include front-line personnel at fast-food restaurants or dry cleaners and patient representatives whose job is to obtain and process insurance information.

**type 2 service staff**
Service staff who deal with numerous, often repeat customers in restricted interactions of somewhat longer duration.

**Type 2 service staff** deal with numerous, often repeat customers in restricted interactions of somewhat longer duration. The information provided is mixed—partly simple and partly more complex—and requires some independent decision making on the part of the staff member. Communication in this category requires effective listening skills, the ability to establish trust, interpreting customer information, and making decisions in customer relationships that are often ongoing over a period of time. Communications are generally more intense than in Type 1 situations. Typical examples include relationships with suppliers or customer relationships, such as with a customer who requests floral designs from a florist on a regular basis, a loyal customer of a seamstress/tailor, or an effective waitstaff person at a fine dining establishment.

**type 3 service staff**
Service staff required to have more highly developed communication skills because of more extended and complex interactions with customers.

**Type 3 service staff** are required to have more complex communication skills. Interactions with consumers are repeated over time, extensive flow of communication is required, and communication tasks are complicated and often nonrepeatable. Effective communication requires the ability to listen and process complicated information, to think creatively in face-to-face interactions with consumers, and to provide information in a clear and understandable manner. Typical examples include staff members who are likely to be qualified as professionals.

Any service organization may have employees in one, two, or all three of the above categories. Thus, a bank may have tellers performing Type 1 communications, a loan officer engaged in Type 2, and a commercial loan officer engaged in Type 3. A travel company may have an agent engaged in both Type 2 (when writing tickets and booking arrangements) and Type 3 communications (when planning trips) and a receptionist handling Type 1 communications.

Each type of communication requires a different set of skills from the providers and places different levels of stress on them. It is clearly important that the correct communications role be assigned to the correct person within the organization. Type 1 is predominantly an operations role, whereas Type 3 is a mixed selling and operations role.

When a communication mix that includes the service provider is developed, the final objectives for the staff will probably fall within one of the above categories. However, it is important to recall the position of the employee providing the service. The service provider is not simply a salesperson; he or she is an integral part of the operations process and the experience purchased by the customer. An apparently simple decision—for example, to have a bank teller sell services—can have profoundly negative consequences. It could well be that the decision produces role conflict for the teller. Role/self-conflict could be caused by the tellers' wanting to see themselves not as salespeople but as bankers. Direct conflict between the two roles can arise when the operations role demands fast service and minimization of time spent with each customer but the selling role demands the opposite. In addition, the script may break down for both the service provider and the customer as the teller tries to do something new. The customer may be expecting a brisk, businesslike transaction when suddenly, the teller wants to build rapport by talking about the weather and local sporting events (before starting the sale).

Potentially, such a decision can also diminish operational efficiency as the transaction time per customer rises. This problem is illustrated by the experiences of FedEx before it centralized its telephone customer contact system. In times of peak demand, especially if those times were unpredicted, everyone in the FedEx depots answered telephones, including the field salespersons based at the depots. The result was that the various depot employees changed the service communication from Type 1 to Type 3. It also meant that calls took much longer than usual, and the telephone bottleneck consequently worsened.

## Monitoring, Evaluating and Controlling the Communication Strategy

Once a firm's communication strategy has been launched, managers should monitor reactions to the strategy, evaluate its effectiveness, and make adjustments when necessary. Evaluating the communicating strategy is typically conducted by comparing communication outcomes with previously stated objectives. For example, if the stated objective of the communication strategy is to increase customer awareness by 20 percent over the first four weeks of the communication's campaign, pre-test and post-test surveys pertaining to levels of awareness could assist in verifying the success of the communication strategy. It should be noted that effective communication strategies do not always lead to immediate increases in sales. Many service communications are characterized by a **lagged effect** where demand for many types of services is infrequent, and therefore the success of the campaign may not be realized until a later point in time. For example, many patients only see their dentist once or twice a year, and their physician once a year for an annual physical. Clients may seek out their insurance agent or financial advisor even less frequently. However, even though sales may not immediately increase as a result of the communication strategy, the communications often increase client awareness and facilitate the formation of positive attitudes toward the service provider. Consequently, if at a future point in time, the customer looks to change an existing service provider or seeks out new services, the sales effectiveness of the communication strategy is now realized.

**lagged effect** When demand for the service is infrequent, and therefore the success of the communication strategy may not be realized until a later point in time.

# Special Challenges Associated with the Service Communications Strategy[7]

As established earlier in this text, the marketing of services is unique. Therefore, the development of an effective service communication strategy must take into consideration a number of special challenges not typically faced by goods-producing companies. More specifically, intangibility and inseparability present special challenges that should be considered when developing a communication strategy. First, since services are often consumed as a shared experience with "other customers," *mistargeted communications* may result in the unanticipated consequence of having two diverse target markets responding to the same communication at the same time. Second, service managers should also be aware that the firm's communications are often interpreted as *explicit service promises* that consumers use to base their initial expectations. As a result, service firms should be ready to deliver what is communicated in their promotional messages. Third, since employees often produce the service in close proximity to customers, employees should be considered as *internal customers* who are as much as a target audience as traditional external customers. Finally, in many instances the service providers who produce the service also must sell the service and questions arise concerning the strategic implications of *turning doers into sellers*. When the service provider is engaged in selling activities, the production of the service itself comes to a grinding halt. On the other hand, when the service provider is busy producing services, future customers will not be cultivated, threatening the long-term success of the service operation running without interruption. This ultimately leads to the question, "How should service providers balance the activities of selling and operations?"

## Mistargeted Communications

Segmentation is one of the basic concepts of marketing. In essence, it suggests that a firm's marketing efficiency can be improved by targeting marketing activities at specific groups of consumers who behave differently in some way toward the firm. Although segmentation is applied in both goods and service companies, the consequences of reaching an inappropriate segment with a part of the communication mix are far less serious for goods companies than for services. If the wrong group of consumers buys a particular brand of detergent, for example, it does not really affect the company making the detergent; sales are still being generated. Or a product may have been developed for the youth market, but through some quirk of the advertising execution, the product has attracted some senior citizens. For example, take the Pepsi advertisement that portrayed the youthful effects of Pepsi being delivered to a senior citizens' home by error instead of to the college fraternity house. Let's say that the ad is interpreted by senior citizens that Pepsi will make them feel young again. Clearly, this was not the original intent of Pepsi, which targets the younger generation. Members of the group that misinterpreted the message visit the supermarket, buy the product, and use it in their homes. The negative consequences associated with the elder segment's use of the product are few.

Suppose, however, that some of the wrong segment decides to buy the services of a restaurant. An upscale concept has been developed, but to launch the restaurant, management decides to have a price promotion, and the advertising agency develops inappropriate advertising. Or, through poor management, the advertising is unfocused and produces feature articles in the wrong magazines. The result is that the restaurant gets two types of customers: upscale, middle-aged couples and price-conscious groups of students. The former were the original target, and the latter were attracted by inappropriate marketing tactics. Unfortunately for the restaurant and for many other services, "other customers" are part of the product. The result is that neither segment enjoys the experience because of the presence of the other, and neither type of customer returns. Hence, the consequences of **mistargeted communications** for service firms, because of the shared consumption experience, are clearly more significant than the consequences experienced by traditional goods-producing firms.

**mistargeted communications**
Occurs when the same communication message appeals to two diverse market segments.

## Managing Expectations and Perceptions[8]

The service firm's communication strategy can play a key role in formulating customer expectations about its services. A firm's communications may reinforce pre-existing ideas or they may dramatically alter those ideas and be replaced by a new set of expectations. Expectations can be set by something as explicit as a promise (e.g., "Your food will be ready in five minutes") or as implicit as a behavior pattern that sets a tone (e.g., a cordial greeting upon entering the place of business). Often such expectations are created unwittingly, as when a server promises to "be right back." Such a statement can be viewed both as a binding contract by a customer and as a farewell salutation by the service provider.

In addition to expectations, perception also has many sources. *Technical service quality* is an objective level of performance produced by the operating system of the firm. It is measurable with a stopwatch, temperature gauge, or other measuring instrument. Unfortunately, this is not the level of performance the customer perceives. Perception acts as a filter that moves the perceived service level up or down.

Perception is itself influenced by the same factors that dictate expectations. For example, communications can create warm feelings toward the organization that raises perceived service levels. In comparison, inappropriately dressed and ill-behaving staff can deliver high levels of technical service quality but be poorly perceived by the consumer, who will downgrade the perceived service level.

Many sources of expectations are under the direct control of the firm. Only past experience and competitors' activities cannot be directly influenced in one way or the other. Given such control, the firm must determine what the objectives of the communication mix should be. In the absence of competition, one possible communication objective would be to reduce customer expectations prior to arrival. The reduced expectations would result in higher satisfaction levels, provided that levels of perceived service are maintained. Realistically, communications must also play the more traditional role of stimulating demand. It is inconsistent to think of achieving this by promising average service, even if doing so might minimize customers' expectations (for the few customers who use the service!).

In competitive terms, firms make promises and strive to build expectations that will differentiate them in the marketplace and cause customers to come to them and not to their competitors. The temptation is, therefore, to promise too much and raise expectations to an unrealistic level. It is perhaps fortunate that the variability in services is well known to most consumers and that they, therefore, discount many of the promises made by service firms. When promises are taken seriously, however, the result is often dissatisfied customers.

## Advertising to Employees

The staff of service firms frequently form a secondary audience for any firm's advertising campaign. Clearly, communications seen by the staff, if they empathize with it, can be highly motivating. However, if communications are developed without a clear understanding of the reality of the service provider's role in service delivery, it can imply service performance levels that are technically or bureaucratically impossible; that is, it can set expectation levels unrealistically high. This has a doubly detrimental effect on the staff since: (1) it shows that people who developed the communications (the marketing department) do not understand the business; and (2) it raises the prospect that customers will actually expect the service to operate that way, and the staff will have to tell them that the reality differs from the level of service portrayed in the firm's communications. In both cases, there will be a negative impact on staff motivation, which will, in turn, negatively influence customer satisfaction.

A classic example involved American Airlines. The company developed an advertisement that featured a flight attendant reading a young child a story during the flight. As a result, passengers expected the flight attendants to tend to their children, and flight attendants were upset by the implication that they were supposed to be babysitters in addition to all of their other duties.

The bottom line is that, in order for service firms to succeed, they must first sell the service job to the employee before they sell the service to the customer.[9] For years, communications from Southwest Airlines have shown smiling employees going through great lengths to please the customer. Although the communications are clearly targeted toward customers, they also send a message to employees regarding appropriate role behavior. In the end, service communications not only provide a means of communicating with customers, but also serve as a vehicle to communicate, motivate, and educate employees.[10]

### Selling/Operation Conflicts

Another consideration unique to the service sector is that the individuals who sell the service are often the same people who provide the service. In many instances, the service provider is much more comfortable providing the service than marketing his or her own abilities. However, in some cases, providers become so involved in the communications aspects of their firm that they no longer actively participate in the operations end of the business (see Global Services in Action).

The conflicts associated with selling versus operations are at least twofold. First are the economic considerations. Typically, service providers are paid for providing services and not for time spent on communications activities. Clearly, the provider must engage in marketing activities in order to generate future customers, but the time spent on marketing does not generate revenues for the provider at that particular point in time. Complicating matters further, the time spent on communications activities with potential new customers often occurs while an ongoing project is conducted. This means that the time dedicated to communications activities must be considered when estimating completion dates to current customers. Often the firm's communications efforts must occur while previously sold services are being processed in order to avoid shut-down periods between customer orders.

The second conflict that arises is often role related. Many professional service providers believe that communications activities such as personal selling are not within their areas of expertise, and in some cases beneath them! Consequently, some providers feel uncomfortable with communications activities. The healthcare field in particular has been plagued by this problem through the years. However, increased competition in the healthcare arena has led to recognition of the need for marketing training directed at technical specialists. Many healthcare institutions, particularly the good ones, now embrace the importance of the firm's communication efforts.

# Specific Guidelines for Developing Service Communications

Based on a review of the literature that directly examines the specifics of marketing services, several common themes emerge that create guidelines pertaining to the development of service communications. Over the years, many of these guidelines have been

## GLOBAL SERVICES *IN ACTION*

### Personal Selling Approaches around the World

Service providers not only produce the service but in many cases must also sell the service as well. As one might imagine, some service providers are much more comfortable in engaging in the sales process than others. Complicating matters, as the firm moves its service operations into foreign markets, subtle differences must be taken into consideration. Fortunately, *Sales and Marketing Management* magazine regularly publishes personal selling tips for those conducting business abroad. Some of the more interesting insights include the following:

| COUNTRY | INSIGHT |
| --- | --- |
| Belgium | In the Dutch speaking region of Belgium, group decision-making is the norm. In contrast, in the French speaking region of Belgium, high-level executives make the final decisions. |
| China | Contracts are thought to be the beginning of the relationship, so expect to continue negotiations after the contract has been signed. |
| Columbia | Developing a strong personal relationship and maintaining that relationship throughout negotiations is the key. Changing personnel during the sales process is likely to end the deal. |
| Germany | Sales presentations should be straight to the point keeping information plain and simple (no flashy graphics). German decision makers like lots of facts and figures, so the presentation of pertinent data is key. |
| India | On the one hand, time has little meaning so for those scheduling appointments meeting times need to be flexible. On the other hand, due to the rigid hierarchy, only top executives make key decisions. |
| Mexico | Developing personal relationships with meetings that include breakfast or lunch is typical. Decisions are often based on the personal relationship as opposed to the professional experience of the provider. |
| Peru | Like their Mexican and Columbian counterparts, building a strong personal relationship prior to conducting business is crucial. Peruvians also do not like it when personnel are changed during the sales process. |
| Russia | First meetings are just a formality where the customer assesses the overall credibility of the provider. The provider should be especially warm and friendly during this first meeting. |
| Scotland | Since they are soft-spoken and very private, it often takes time to build a relationship with the Scots. Personal relationships become more friendly once bonds are formed. |
| South Korea | Status rules! Make sure your title is on your business card and that the title of the company representative is at least as high as the customer's title. To do otherwise would be an insult to the South Korean customer. |
| Thailand | Thais are non-confrontational, so personal sales efforts should not attempt to force any issue such as closure of the deal. Within Thai culture, to show anger is a sign of weakness. |

Sources:
1. **www.salesandmarketing.com**, accessed 16 October, 2009.
2. Philip R. Cateora, Mary C. Gilly, and John L. Graham, *International Marketing*, 14th ed., (Boston: McGraw-Hill Irwin, 2009).

developed by service firms as solutions to challenges created by the intangibility, inseparability, heterogeneity, and perishability inherent in service products.

## Develop a Word-of-Mouth Communications Network

Consumers of services often rely on personal sources (e.g., friends, family, co-workers) of information more than nonpersonal sources (e.g., mass media) to reduce the risk associated with a purchase. Given the importance of nonpersonal sources, communications should be developed that facilitate the development of a word-of-mouth network. Communications that feature satisfied customers and promotional strategies that encourage current customers to recruit their friends are typical. Other communication strategies such as presentations for community and professional groups and sponsorship of community and professional activities have also been effective in stimulating word-of-mouth communications. In many ways, today's customers and service firms can access and generate more personal sources of information through the Internet via blogs, social networks, and review and opinion websites such as epinions.com and TripAdvisor.com than any prior generation. Smart consumers use these sources of information to make more informed purchase decisions and "just as smart" service providers are learning to use these sites to drive traffic to their firms (see E-Services in Action).[11]

## Promise What Is Possible

In its most basic form, customer satisfaction is developed by customers comparing their expectations to their perceptions of the actual service delivery process. In times of increasing competitive pressures, firms may be tempted to overpromise in their marketing communications. Making promises the firm cannot keep initially increases customer expectations but subsequently lowers customer satisfaction when those promises are not met.

Two problems are associated with overpromising. First, customers leave disappointed, and a significant loss of trust occurs between the firm and its customers. Moreover, disappointed customers are sure to tell others of their experience, which increases the fallout from the experience. The second problem directly affects the service firm's employees. Working for firms that routinely make false promises places employees in compromising and often confrontational positions. Front-line personnel are left to explain repeatedly to customers why the company cannot keep its promises. Given the link between employee satisfaction and customer satisfaction, creating expectations that cannot be met can have devastating long-term effects.

## Tangibilize the Intangible[12]

Given the intangible nature of services, service products are often abstract in the minds of potential customers. Consequently, one of the principal guidelines for advertising a service is to make it more concrete. Insurance companies face this challenge on a daily basis—how to tangibilize the intangible? One possible solution for many insurance companies has been to utilize tangible symbols to represent their companies. Prudential has "The Rock," Merrill Lynch has "The Bull," and GEICO has "The Gecko." However, no insurance icon has ever been as successful as the Aflac Duck![13]

The Aflac Duck campaign was created by Linda Kaplan Thaler, CEO/chief creative officer and Robin Koval, chief marketing officer/general manager of The Kaplan Thaler Group (KTG) Ltd. Their charge was to increase the public's awareness of the Aflac brand. Aflac's chair and CEO told Thaler, "I don't care what you do, as long as you get people to know the name of this company." The impetus behind the duck campaign was based on KTG's "big bang" theory—"if we allow a little illogic into our thoughts...we can

# E-SERVICES *IN ACTION*

## The Growth of Personal Communications via Social Media

It is a well-established characteristic of services marketing that consumers of services perceive higher levels of risk prior to purchase than their goods-purchasing counterparts. As a result, service consumers often seek out personal (as opposed to nonpersonal) sources of information prior to making purchase decisions. Personal sources of information reduce the buyer's perceived risk. Personal sources of information include word-of-mouth communications and peer recommendations that are now more prevalent than ever thanks to the Internet. Social media (such as social networking, blogs, virtual worlds, and video sharing) are now powerful communication strategy tools that should be considered by service firms. These tools are particularly useful for service marketers given the personal nature of the communication. Examples of the types of the social media tools available are provided below.

| SOCIAL MEDIA TOOLS | EXAMPLES |
|---|---|
| **Communication:** | |
| Blogs | Blogger, Live Journal, Open Diary, TypePad, WordPress, Vox & Expression Engine |
| Micro-Blogging | Twitter, Plurk, Tmblr, Jaiki & fmylife |
| Social Networking | Bebo, Facebook, LinkedIn, MySpace, Orkut, Skyrock, Hi5, Ning & Elgg |
| Social Network Aggregation | NutShellMail & FriendFeed |
| Events | Upcoming, Eventful & Meetup.com |
| **Collaboration:** | |
| Wikis | Wikipedia, PBwiki & Wetpaint |
| Social Tagging | Delicious, StumbleUpon, Google Reader & CiteULike |
| Social News | Digg, Mixx, Reddit & NowPublic |
| Opinion Sites | Epinions & Yelp |
| **Muultimedia:** | |
| Photo Sharing | Flickr, Zoomr, Photobucket, SmugMug & Picasa |
| Video Sharing | YouTube, Vimeo & Sevenload |
| Livecasting | Ustream.tv, Justin tv, Stickam & Skype |
| Audio & Music Sharing | Imeem, The Hype Machine, Last.fm & ccMixter |
| **Reviews & Opinions:** | |
| Product Reviews | Epinions.com & MouthShut.com |
| Business Reviews | Yelp.com |
| Community Q&A | Yahoo! Answers, WikiAnswers, Askville& Google Answers |
| **Entertainment:** | |
| Media & Entertainment Platforms | Cisco Eos |
| Virtual Worlds | Second Life, The Sims Online, Forterra |
| Game Sharing | Miniclip, Kongregate |

Source: **http://en.wikipedia.org/wiki/Social_media**, accessed 16 October, 2009.

Neilson Barnard/Getty Images

The AFLAC duck campaign has helped "tangibilize" the intangible and has been one of the most successful advertising campaigns in services marketing history.

break through the prison of current convention." When pronounced audibly, Aflac sounds like a duck, so why not create a slightly annoying waterfowl (who hates to be ignored) to represent a company that is trying to make a splash in the marketplace?

The Aflac Duck campaign has been an unparalleled success. To begin, Aflac's name recognition grew from 12 percent in January of 2000 to over 90 percent in 2005. Aflac is now the number one provider of guaranteed renewable insurance in the United Sates and Japan. Aflac has a presence in all 50 United States and the U.S. territories. Aflac is actively involved in a number of philanthropic endeavors and has been nationally recognized in "The 100 Best Companies to Work for in America"; the "100 Best Places to Work in IT"; the "50 Best Companies for Latinas"; "America's Most Admired Companies"; and the "100 Best Companies for Working Mothers." In addition to its success in the United States, Aflac insures one in four Japanese households and is the fourth most profitable foreign company operating in any industry in Japan.

In tangibilizing the intangible, the scale of market entities (presented in Chapter 1) should be turned on its end (see Figure 7.5). Tangible dominant market entities—described as concrete by nature—such as perfume utilize image development in their advertising schemes. From a basic viewpoint, perfume is simply liquid scent in a bottle. The customer can pick it up, try it on, and smell the perfume's fragrance. Hence, the perfume is tangible dominant. As with many tangible dominant products, the advertising tends to make it more abstract in order to differentiate one product from another. In contrast, the advertising of intangible dominant products—described as abstract by nature—should concentrate on making them more concrete through the use of physical

**FIG-7.5** The Impact of Intangibility: Different Communication Strategies for Different Types of Products

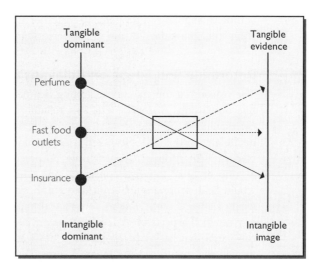

Source: Adapted from G. Lynn Shostack, "Breaking Free from Product Marketing," *The Journal of Marketing* (April 1977).

cues and tangible evidence. Insurance products are already abstract, so it becomes the communication's objective to explain the service in simple and concrete terms. In addition to tangible symbols, other service firms have tangibilized their service offerings by using numbers in their advertisements, such as, "We've been in business since 1925,"or "Nine out of ten customers would recommend us to a friend." Finally, the communication objectives for products in the middle of the scale of market entities often utilize both approaches—abstract and concrete elements. McDonald's, for example, promotes "food, folks, and fun" in its advertisement. Food and folks are concrete, and fun is abstract.

### Feature the Working Relationship between Customer and Provider

As you should well understand by now, service delivery is an interactive process between the service provider and the customer. Because of inseparability, it is appropriate in the firm's communications to feature a company representative and a customer working together to achieve a desired outcome. The tax accounting firm H&R Block's advertising commonly shows a company representative and a customer interacting in a friendly and reassuring manner. Many financial institutions, legal firms, and insurance companies also follow this same model. The advertising of services, in particular, must concentrate not only on encouraging customers to buy, but also on encouraging employees to perform. Clearly, advertising that illustrates the inseparability of the service delivery process should target both the customer and the firm's service personnel.

### Reduce Consumer Fears about Variations in Performance

The firm's marketing communications can also minimize the pitfalls of heterogeneity in the customer's mind. To enhance the perception of consistent quality, the firm's communications should provide some form of documentation that reassures the customer. Typical examples include stating the firm's performance record through numbers as opposed to qualitative testimonials. The use of "hard" numbers in advertisements reduces the consumer's fear of variability and also tangibilizes the service, as mentioned earlier. For example, statements such as 9 out of 10 doctors agree that service "X" is the best, or our company maintains a 98 percent customer satisfaction level helps to reassure customers about the consistency of the firm's performance.

## Determine and Focus on Relevant Service Quality Dimensions

The reasons customers choose among competing services are often closely related to the five dimensions of service quality—reliability, responsiveness, assurance, empathy, and the quality of the tangibles associated with the service—which will be discussed in great detail later in this text. However, it is common that some features are more important to customers than others. For example, 30 percent of today's airline customers list "safety" as one of their top five considerations when choosing an airline.[14] Consequently, it would be appropriate for airlines to emphasize the assurance dimension of service quality by featuring the airline's safety record, maintenance and training programs, as well as any certified aspects of their particular airline operation. One marketing communication campaign that backfired promoted a hotel as one of the tallest hotels in the world. Although this reinforced the tangible dimension of service quality, this particular tangible component was not very important to customers in choosing hotels. In fact, many customers who had even the slightest fear of heights avoided the hotel for fear of being placed on an upper floor. The lesson to be learned is that when developing marketing communications, the content of communications should focus on the features and benefits that really matter to customers.

## Differentiate the Service Product via the Service Delivery Process

A dramatic difference exists between what the service provides and how it is provided. Identifying the various inputs into the process, which contributes to a competitive or quality advantage, and stressing these inputs in the firm's advertising is likely to be a successful approach. For example, on the surface, it appears somewhat difficult to differentiate one tax accountant from the next. However, if we consider the process of obtaining a consultation, which consists of calling to make an appointment, interacting with staff at the front desk, the appearance of the office in the reception area where the client is waiting, the appearance of the accountant's office, the interaction between the client and the accountant, and the payment procedures, several potential areas for differentiation arise. Outlining the various inputs within the service delivery process may indicate key competitive and/or quality advantages that traditionally have been overlooked. As a result, these competitive differences can be stressed in the firm's marketing communications and establish a key positioning strategy in the market.

## Make the Service More Easily Understood

Services can also be more fully explained to potential customers via the communication mix by presenting the service as a series of events. When questioned, consumers often break down the service experience into a series of sequential events. Understanding the sequence permits the service provider to view the service from the customer's perspective. For example, bank customers may first view the external building, parking facilities, landscaping, and cleanliness of the grounds. When entering the bank, customers notice the interior furnishings, odors, music, temperature, and service personnel. While conducting bank transactions, the appearance and demeanor of specific contact personnel become additional quality cues. Hence, perceptions of quality are assessed at each stage of the service encounter. Communication strategies developed from the sequence-of-events perspective consider the customer throughout the process and highlight the firm's strengths in each area.

# Developing Communication Strategies for Professional Service Providers

## Special Considerations for Professional Service Providers

Professional service providers often experience their own distinct challenges that may be tempered by the development of an effective communications program.[15] Specifically, the 10 most frequent problems encountered include:

1. ***Third-Party Accountability.*** Investors, insurance companies, banks, governmental agencies, and even members of their own professions often hold professional service providers accountable for their actions or at least monitor those actions. Creating credibility and projecting the image of a quality firm to third parties can be accomplished through the firm's communications mix, thereby minimizing excessive scrutiny by outside parties. Communication strategies that come to mind include conducting business seminars, giving speeches, and writing trade articles. Business seminars in the professional's area of specialization demonstrate the provider's expertise not only to potential and existing clients, but also to interested third parties, particularly other industry members. Speeches to local civic organizations as well as national conventions spotlight the firm's talents and further enhance the firm's image. Reprints of articles should be included in company newsletters and sent to appropriate audiences.

2. ***Client Uncertainty.*** Many professional services are costly, associated with danger or importance, and, in some cases, technical and specialized, making them difficult for the customer/client to understand. Effective communications can communicate the procedures involved, show the likely outcomes (managing consumer expectations), answer consumers' common questions, and/or minimize consumers' areas of concern. For example, many surgical centers now send patients informational pamphlets or direct patients to video-ready websites that describe and/or illustrate surgical procedures prior to the patient's scheduled appointment.

3. ***Experience Is Essential.*** Effective marketing communications are successful in attracting and maintaining the customer base. The opening of a new doctor's office is not greeted with nearly the same enthusiasm as that of a new restaurant. The more professional the service, the more the service provider's years or quality of experience matters to potential customers. Once again, the value of offering seminars, membership in local organizations, speaking at civic functions or on talk radio programs, and writing articles for local consumption are great icebreakers.

4. ***Limited Differentiability.*** As the level of competition increases among professional service providers, differentiation among providers decreases as they match one another's offerings with comparable alternatives. Marketing communications that differentiate the provider on factors beyond the mere service product itself, such as personnel, customer service, and image, must be communicated to the marketplace to set the provider apart from the crowd (see Figure 7.4).

5. ***Maintaining Quality Control.*** Because the consumer is part of the service production process, he or she ultimately has a large amount of control over the quality of the final outcome. Communication that stresses the importance of following the professional's advice and its relationship to achieving positive outcomes educates the consumer about the importance of his or her own role in the service delivery system. Physicians who need their patients to follow specific diets or exercise plans to improve their health are classic examples.

6. ***Turning Doers into Sellers.*** In many instances, the employment of outside sales representatives to market professional services to clientele is inappropriate and

ineffective. Client uncertainty dictates that the professional provider him/herself must become actively involved in the sales process to reassure clients and minimize their fears. Ultimately, no one should be able to sell the available service better than the provider. However, as discussed earlier, while some providers thrive on making sales, many other providers feel uncomfortable when thrust into the sales spotlight.

7. ***The Challenge of Dividing the Professional's Time between Marketing and Providing Services.*** Directly related to the previous point is the problem associated with the professional provider becoming too involved in the personal selling component of the firm's communication mix. Professionals generate revenues by billing for the time that they are servicing existing customers. Marketing activities not only consume a portion of the professional's billable hours, but the professional does not get paid directly for the time spent conducting marketing efforts. As a result, the professional must decide how much personal time to allocate to marketing activities and how to divide that time between cultivating new prospects, maintaining relationships with existing clients, and involvement in more general public relations work—this is not an easy task.

8. ***Tendencies to Be Reactive Rather than Proactive.*** The pressure of everyday business cuts into the amount of time the professional can devote to marketing activities. Existing customers demand the attention of the provider in the short-run by expecting services to be delivered in an expedient manner. As a result, many professionals find themselves in a reactive mode as they search out new business when existing business transactions end. This creates the unenviable position of attempting to run a business while moving from one client to the next. Often, slack time develops between clients, which negatively affects the cash flow of the operation, not to mention placing increased pressure on the anxious provider and their employee workforce looking for new clients.

   The communication mix should not be based solely on the professional's personal selling efforts. Ongoing communications must work for the provider in a proactive manner while the provider performs everyday activities with existing clientele. The professional can make better use of the time devoted to marketing efforts by focusing on closing the sale, not starting from scratch as the sole individual charged with initiating the sales process.

9. ***The Effects of Advertising Are Unknown.*** In the not-so-distant past, many professional organizations such as those for U.S. lawyers forbid their members to engage in marketing communication activities. However, in 1978, the courts ruled that the ban on marketing communications was unconstitutional, based on the case *Bates v. The State Bar of Arizona.* Despite the ruling, some members of professional societies still frown upon the use of certain communication methods such as traditional advertising.

   Consumer groups are particularly advocating that professional service providers engage in active marketing communications. Consumer advocates believe that an increase in communication efforts will provide consumers with much needed information and increase the level of competition among providers. They also believe that as a result of the increase in competition, prices will fall, and the quality of service will improve. However, service providers such as those in the healthcare arena do not agree. Healthcare providers quickly point to the legal profession and state that increasing communications will likely have a negative impact on their profession's image, credibility, and dignity. In addition, healthcare professionals believe that customer benefits created by increased communications efforts are unlikely. In fact, some state that if consumers believe that health care is expensive now, just wait until the profession has to start covering the costs of its communications efforts. Needless to say, the jury is still out on who is correct. However, as time has passed and as competitive pressures among professional service providers have mounted, the use of marketing communications seems to be becoming more acceptable in general.

10. *Professional Providers Have a Limited Marketing Knowledge Base.* As business students, many of the terms you take for granted, such as market segments, target markets, marketing mix variables, and differentiation and positioning strategies, are totally foreign to many professional service providers. Professional service providers are trained to perform their technical duties effectively. For example, lawyers attend law schools, physicians attend medical schools, dentists attend dental schools, and veterinarians attend veterinary schools. What do all these professional providers have in common when they go into practice for themselves? They all run businesses, yet they have no formal business educational backgrounds.

Due to a limited marketing knowledge base, professional service providers are often tempted to develop the firm's communication mix in isolation, without regard to the firm's overall marketing strategy. Ultimately, the firm's communications mix should be consistent with targeted consumer expectations and synergistic with other elements in the marketing mix.

## Communications Tips for Professional Service Providers[16]

*Turning Current Clients into Company Spokespersons*   Too often, service firms lose sight of their existing clients as they develop a communication mix with the sole purpose of attracting new business. A firm's existing client base is the heart of its business and represents a vast potential for additional revenue. Existing clients are a rich resource of further revenue and offer opportunities for business that can be generated without substantial promotional expenditures, without additional overhead, and frequently without hiring additional personnel. By being constantly on the alert for suggestions and ideas and by discovering the clients' needs and responding to them in a professional and timely manner, professional service providers essentially win over clients, who, in turn, become a perpetual advertisement for the firm. Given the importance of personal sources of information in choosing among service alternatives, having existing clients who sing the praises of your firm to others is an invaluable resource.

**halo effect** An overall favorable or unfavorable impression based on early stages of the service encounter.

*First Impressions Are Everything*   Because of the **halo effect**, early stages of the service encounter often set the tone for consumer evaluations made throughout the service experience. As a result, providers must pay special attention to the initial interactions in the encounter because they are often the most important. First impressions often are believed to establish or deny relationships within the first four minutes of contact.[17] For example, telephone calls need to be answered promptly and politely. During a speech about service excellence, Tom Peters of *In Search of Excellence* fame reported his personal experience with telephone contact personnel at Federal Express. Mr. Peters reported that in 27 of 28 cases, FedEx operators answered the phone on or before the first ring. In fact, Mr. Peters admitted that FedEx may be 28 for 28 since he assumes that he misdialed and hung up the phone on the 28th event. Peters then redialed the number and the phone was answered before the first ring.

Communication cues on which consumers base initial impressions include websites, "yellow page" advertisements, signage, and an easily accessible place of business. Once the client actually arrives, the firm's reception area should be a showplace, complete with tangible clues that reinforce the firm's quality image. Possible tangible clues in the reception area include the name of the firm and its service providers prominently displayed, furnishings that reflect the personality of the business, fresh flowers, a "brag book" that includes letters from happy customers, past company newsletters, provider profiles, and indications of the firm's involvement in the community. Finally, the reception area should be staffed by professional and pleasant customer contact personnel. Despite the importance of first impressions, many firms simply view their reception areas as waiting rooms, making little effort to enhance the aesthetics of these areas. In many cases, these areas are equipped with uncomfortable and unappealing furnishings and staffed by low-paid, poorly trained personnel—a major mistake when one considers the importance of first impressions.

***Create Visual Pathways That Reflect the Firm's Quality*** The firm's printed image includes all printed communication to clients such as correspondence, annual reports, newsletters, and billings. It also includes printed material of general use, such as firm brochures, letterhead, envelopes, and business cards, as well as internal communications—from agendas to checklists, from memos to manuals. Printed materials create a **visual pathway** through which the professional image of the firm can be consistently transmitted.

From the first time the firm's business card is put into a prospective client's hand, through the first letter the client receives, and on through finished reports delivered to the client and final billings, the presentation of printed material makes an impression. With every piece of material the client receives, he or she subconsciously reacts to the quality of paper, reproduction, and binding with which the firm has produced it. And most of all, he or she is responding to the visual images the professional provider has chosen to represent the firm, starting with the logo.

Effective communication of the firm's logo assists the firm in establishing familiarity throughout the market region in which it operates. In addition to identifying the firm, other primary goals of logo development are to simplify and explain the purpose of the organization. In essence, logo development can be viewed as creating a form of hieroglyphic symbol that enables others to quickly identify the professional firm.

Given the lack of a substantial marketing knowledge base, professional service providers should seriously consider engaging the advice of a communications professional. Graphic artists, ad agencies, and public relations firms are typical examples of communications specialists who work with a client to produce the kind of image that will give the firm the individual yet professional identity that successfully positions it in the marketplace. When a logo is designed, it can be printed in various sizes and in reverse. The various forms of the logo can then be easily applied to all manner and style of printed materials. Finally, the firm's choice of stock (paper), typeface, and kind of printing (engraving, offset, or thermograph) will complete the highly professional image of its printed material and create a visual pathway that consistently communicates quality to the client.

**visual pathway** Printed materials through which the professional image of the firm can be consistently transmitted, including firm brochures, letterhead, envelopes, and business cards.

## Establish Regular Communications with Clients

Every letter sent to a client or a colleague is a potential promotional opportunity. Experts suggest taking advantage of this potential from the very beginning of the relationship with the client. Every new client should receive a special letter of welcome to the firm and a sample newsletter that conveys the firm's service concept. The use of standardized letters embossed with the firm's logo, which can be adapted for different circumstances such as welcome letters, thank you's for referrals, and reminder letters of upcoming appointments are also effective. Better yet, handwritten, personalized messages on the firm's note cards provide a personal touch.

The most important piece of regular communication with clients should be the firm newsletter. It can be as simple as an email communication, or an 8½-by-11-inch sheet, typed at the office and photocopied. Or it can be as elaborate as a small booklet, typeset and printed in color on quality stock. Some firms choose to make their newsletters informal bulletins; others prefer to make them polished publications. Regardless of the technique, the newsletter should always have a clean, professional appearance and be filled with information valuable to clientele.

### Develop a Firm Brochure

The firm's brochure is a menu of the its service offering and should be the written showpiece. In addition to providing an overview of available services, firm brochures typically include the firm's history, philosophy, and profiles of personnel. To add to its flexibility, the brochure may be developed with flaps on the inside front and/or back covers for holding supplemental materials or other information that changes from time to time. Personnel profiles featuring printed photographs and biographies are likely candidates for materials that frequently change as employees move from firm to firm. The flaps for supplemental materials also provide the option to customize each brochure for particular clients who desire specific services and will be dealing with specific personnel. The firm brochure is a prime opportunity for the professional service firm to project its uniqueness. Ultimately, the firm brochure should be the kind of product the firm can enthusiastically present to existing and prospective clients.

### An Informed Office Staff Is Vital

Last, but definitely not least, engendering respect and pride in the firm's capability does not stop with external promotion. In fact, it starts internally, and generating a professional image for the benefit of firm staff can be as important as promoting that image to clients. Remember, the staff is in constant, direct contact with clients. Failure to communicate effectively with the firm's staff is readily apparent and quickly erases all other communication efforts to project a quality program.

## Summary

The firm's communications strategy informs, persuades, and reminds target markets, including consumers, employees, and stockholders about the firm's goods and services for the purpose of achieving organizational objectives. In many ways, the development of a sound communications strategy closely parallels the basic fundamentals of developing an effective marketing strategy: identifying a target market, selecting a desired positioning strategy and developing communications that reinforce the firm's positioning strategy. More specifically, service firms that effectively manage their communication strategy engage in a communication process of selecting target markets, establishing communication objectives, setting the communication budget, formulating the positioning strategy, establishing message and media strategies, and monitoring, evaluating, and controlling the communication strategy.

The development of an effective service communication strategy must take into consideration a number of special challenges not typically faced by goods-producing companies. More specifically, intangibility and inseparability present special challenges that should be considered when developing a communication strategy. First, since services are consumed as a shared experience with "other customers," mistargeted communications may result in the unanticipated consequence of having two diverse target markets responding to the same communication at the same time. Second, service managers should also be aware that the firm's communications are often interpreted as explicit promises that consumers use to base their initial expectations. As a result service firms should be prepared to deliver what is stated in their promotional messages. Third, since service employees often produce the service in close proximity to customers, employees should be considered internal customers who are as much a target audience as traditional external customers. Finally, in many instances the service providers who produce the service also must sell the service;

consequently, questions arise concerning the strategic implications of turning "doers into sellers."

Compared to service providers in general, professional service providers often experience distinct challenges that may be tempered by the development of an effective communications program. Specifically, the 10 most frequent problems encountered include third-party accountability, client uncertainty; limited differentiability; maintaining quality control; turning doers into sellers; dividing time between marketing and providing services; tendencies to be reactive rather than proactive; the unknown effects of advertising; and professional service providers tending to have a limited marketing knowledge base.

## Key Terms

communication strategy, p. 171
communication mix, p. 171
target markets, p. 173
SMART, p. 176
positioning strategy, p. 177

copy, p. 178
type 1 service staff, p. 180
type 2 service staff, p. 180
type 3 service staff, p. 180
lagged effect, p. 181

mistargeted
   communications, p. 183
halo effect, p. 193
visual pathway, p. 194

## Review Questions

1. Discuss the process associated with managing an effective communication strategy.
2. Describe the strategic differences among the five elements of the communication mix.
3. Define what it means to develop communication objectives in SMART terms. State three objectives that abide by the SMART guidelines.
4. Compare the communication skills necessary to conduct Type 1, Type 2, and Type 3 transactions. Which type of service staff should a firm recruit?
5. Why is the development of an effective positioning strategy particularly important for service firms?

6. What problems are associated with mistargeted communications? Why do they occur?
7. Why should service employees be considered when developing communications materials?
8. Discuss how insurance companies like Aflac and GEICO make their services more easily understood.
9. What problems arise in turning professional service providers into proactive marketing personnel?
10. Discuss the concept of "visual pathways" and its potential use within a medical practice.

## Notes

1. Gregory Norton, "Marketing Your Practice with Television," FindLaw, http://marketing.lp.findlaw.com/articles/oherron2.html, accessed 26 April 2005.
2. Based on a customer satisfaction study conducted by K. Douglas Hoffman for Rainmaker Marketing's North Carolina Lawyer Referral Service.
3. See, for instance, Louis E. Boone and David L. Kurtz, *Contemporary Marketing*, 8th ed. (Fort Worth, TX: The Dryden Press, 1995).
4. **http://corporate.ritzcarlton.com/en/Careers/WorkingAt.htm**, accessed 14 October, 2009.
5. Gregory Norton, "Marketing Your Practice with Television," FindLaw, http://marketing.lp.findlaw.com/articles/oherron2.html, accessed 26 April, 2005.
6. Bernard H. Booms and Jody L. Nyquist, "Analyzing the Customer/Firm Communication Component of the Services Marketing Mix," *Marketing of Services*, James H. Donnelly and William R. George, eds. (Chicago: American Marketing Association, 1981), pp. 172–177.
7. This section has been modified from William R. George and Leonard L. Berry, "Guidelines for the Advertising of Services," *Business Horizons*, 24, 4, (July-August 1981), pp. 52–56.
8. This section is adapted from John E. G. Bateson, *Managing Services Marketing*, 3rd ed. (Fort Worth, TX: The Dryden Press, 2006), p. 207.
9. W. Earl Sasser and Stephen P. Albeit, "Selling Jobs in the Service Sector," *Business Horizons*, (June 1976), p. 64.

10. George and Berry, "Guidelines for the Advertising of Services."
11. For more information see: Rick E. Bruner, "The Decade in Online Advertising: 1994-2204, DoubleClick website, **www.doubleclick.com**, accessed 27 April 2005.
12. Donna H. Hill and Nimish Gandhi, "Service Advertising: A Framework to Its Effectiveness," *The Journal of Services Marketing* 6, 4, (Fall 1992), pp. 63–77.
13. Sources: www.aflac.com, accessed 26 April 2005; Jerry Fisher, "Duck Season," *Entrepreneur*, 33, 1, (January 2005), p. 67; Fran Matso Lysiak, "Aflac's Quacking Duck Selected One of America's Favorite Ad Icons," *BEST'S REVIEW*, 105, 6, (October 2004), p. 119.
14. Cyndee Miller, "Airline Safety Seen as New Marketing Issue," *Marketing News*, (July 8, 1991), pp. 1, 11.
15. This section adapted from Philip Kotler and Paul N. Bloom, *Marketing Professional Services* (Englewood Cliffs, NJ: Prentice-Hall, 1984), pp. 9–13.
16. This section adapted from Jack Fox, *Starting and Building Your Own Accounting Business* (New York: John Wiley & Sons, 1994).
17. Leonard Zunin and Natalie Zunan, *Contact: The First Four Minutes* (Los Angeles: Nash Publishing, 1972).

# Scouts Australia: A Proud History and the Way Forward

Greg Elliott, Macquarie University

As the centenary of the foundation of the worldwide Scout movement in 1907 approached, Scouts Australia could look forward to an exciting year of celebration, which would continue in 2008 with the official Year of the Scout in Australia. The organisation could feel justifiably proud of its long and distinguished history, its achievements as a movement and those of its individual members, and its position as the largest youth organisation in the world. At the same time, any organisation whose motto is 'Be prepared' would be acutely aware of the uncertainty that the future can bring, and of the danger of complacency. Thus, while it continues to enjoy a preeminent position in the community, like all organisations, Scouts Australia does not take such a position for granted. Also, like all successful organisations, it recognises the need to plan for continued health and growth. Moreover, in recent years there has been evidence that interest in Scouts might be waning in the face of changing community attitudes, the onset of new technology, particularly the Internet, and increasing competition for 'share of mind' of both children and their parents.

## The History of Scouting

The Scout movement was founded by Lord Robert Baden-Powell. In August 1907, he held the first camp for a group of boys on Brownsea Island in the United Kingdom. Baden-Powell was a national hero following his victory in the siege of Mafeking in the Boer War. On returning to the United Kingdom following the war, B-P, as he was known, was encouraged to apply his military training methods to the training of boys, which led to the Brownsea Island camp. Following the success of this camp, B-P was encouraged to begin a fortnightly publication called *Scouting for Boys*, which quickly attracted the attention of the male youth of the United Kingdom. In early 1908, the Scout movement in Australia received widespread community attention following the publication of an article by B-P in a local newspaper. By 1922, the Federal Council of Scout groups had been established, and in 1967 the Scout Association of Australia was incorporated under Royal Charter and an Act of Parliament. Today, the association has around 65000 members: children, adults, boys and men, women and girls (females were first admitted in the 1970s.)

## The Scouting Product

Scouting is a service that is delivered through the scouting program, which aims to prepare young people from the ages of six to 26 to play an active and leading role in the community – to develop life, teamwork and leadership skills through a values-based program known as the Scout Method. While its origins lie in military training and in developing self-reliance, especially in the outdoors, more recently Scouts has recognised that it is in competition with many alternative ways for youth to spend their spare time. These include the Boys' Brigade, Girls' Brigade and Girl Guides, but also organised weekend sport such as football, tennis and surf lifesaving, all of which compete for the attention and weekend time of Australian youth. Beyond these immediate competitors, scouting arguably also competes with the Internet and other unstructured uses of children's spare time. To continue its long, successful history, Scouts needs to constantly evaluate its offer, to refine and enhance its product and its delivery, and to communicate its message in a style and language that is both relevant and appealing.

## Target Markets

Scouting is the largest youth-development organisation in Australia, with over 1600 groups across the country. In this sense, the target market for Scouts Australia might be seen as 'all young people and their parents'. Scouting, in this sense, is universal and inclusive – it's open to both boys and girls in all regions of Australia, including remote communities; youth with special needs; and those from diverse cultural backgrounds, including religious and Indigenous groups. The universal aim of scouting is to encourage the physical, social, intellectual, emotional and spiritual development of young people to enable them to play a constructive role in society as members of local, national and international communities. The key components in achieving these aims are:

- *membership of a local group, which is increasingly self-governing*
- *commitment to Scouts' code of living (the Scout Promise and Law)*
- *a diverse range of attractive, constructive, challenging and fun activities, including indoor and outdoor adventure and exploration*
- *opportunities for leadership*
- *an award scheme that recognises individual participation and achievement.*

Children are eligible to join Scouts from the age of six, when they become Joey Scouts. Over the years they progress to Cub Scouts at the age of eight, Venture Scouts at 15, and, finally, Rovers at 17. All levels of Scouts employ the key scouting methods with increasing self-determination until, in the last two stages, adult Leaders provide advice only.

## Diverse Activities

Beyond the traditional outdoor and camping activities, Scouts are today involved in an increasingly diverse range of activities, including abseiling, climbing, sailing, white-water rafting, the performance arts and overseas travel. Today, individual Scouts who excel in their divisions' activities can take on 'executive' functions within the Scout hierarchy, including its State and national governing bodies, and they may also undertake international travel to visit scouting events in the Asia-Pacific region and around the world. In recent years, Scouts Australia has taken an active role in the development of international scouting, particularly in the Asia-Pacific region. The expertise which Scouts has developed in the education, training and development of its members has resulted in a number of its training programs being formally recognised by government and professional educational and training authorities. In this way, youth members can have their Scouts Australia courses recorded in their school results and adults may also obtain professional training credentials through Scouts. Scouts Australia is continuing to develop its range of accredited courses, especially those in the fields of leadership and adventure activities.

# Scouts' Management

While being an obviously large and successful organisation, there are two aspects of Scouts that influence the scope, intensity and 'style' of its business and management activities. In particular, Scouts is both a volunteer and non-profit organisation. These aspects limit the range and intensity of the organisation's commercial activities. As a non-profit organisation, Scouts does not have access to the substantial commercial funding that would be necessary for any large-scale advertising, recruitment or expansion programs. In particular, Scouts' promotional campaigns are modest by commercial standards and rely on donations and community service announcements. But in spite of its modest financial means, Scouts has managed to portray itself in commercial media as a contemporary, exciting and dynamic organisation. In recent years it has used television, local press, outdoor billboards and cinema to promote its programs. In addition, its national 1-800-SCOUTS number and its website (www. scouts.com.au) have ensured that the organisation has the ability to communicate its message to the widest possible national audience. Like many similar community and sporting organisations, Scouts has sought to supplement its traditional income sources through sponsorships and commercial partnerships, which include co-branding with national marketing companies. With only a modest marketing budget, Scouts has managed to achieve very high levels of community recognition and brand awareness.

Scouts is also a volunteer organisation with only a skeleton staff of professional managers spread across the Australian States and Territories, and with a national executive office. The vast bulk of Scouts' administration is done by volunteers at the local group level, and, while the organisation would clearly cease to function without the contributions of these volunteers, the lack of a large professional management team is a significant constraint on Scouts' commercial and managerial activities. To partially overcome this constraint, Scouts' national management and strategies are complemented by management committees staffed by volunteer Scouts office bearers and business professionals, in fields such as marketing, finance and operations. Beyond its volunteer basis, Scouts Australia is also organised around a 'federated' model in which most of the administration and management is devolved to the State level, where the considerable autonomy is jealously protected. Under such circumstances, parochialism is a constant threat. Thus, the coordination of activities between States, and the development and implementation of national programs, is the responsibility of the national organisation; however, such activities rely for their funding and implementation on the willing participation of the State bodies. This participation cannot be taken for granted.

Reliance on volunteer involvement also creates its own unique ethos and management style, especially since these volunteers are usually deeply committed to the traditional established view of the organisation. Under such circumstances, change does not come quickly or easily. As an example, the recent change in the traditional uniform of Scouts from the familiar militaristic khaki to a more contemporary and fashionable blue shirt and coloured collars created widespread debate and considerable disquiet among the scouting rank-and-file, many of whom would not accept a need for change in what they considered to be the icon image of Scouts. Such a seemingly minor change brought into sharp focus the challenges in managing a volunteer not-for-profit organisation in a changing world in which those whose commitment to the organisation is deepest and whose history in the organisation is longest. These people care most passionately about history, values and traditions, but they may also need to be convinced of the need for the organisation to be renewed and, possibly, to change.

# Recent Results

In 2005/06, the results for Scouts could best be described as 'mixed'. Total Scouts numbers (including youth and adult members) stood at around 60000, making Scouts still comfortably the largest youth organisation in Australia. However, when compared with approximately 63 000 members in 2002, this number represented a substantial decline. Among adult leaders, the situation was even more concerning, with a cumulative decline in numbers from around 16000 in 2002 to around 11000 in 2006. The decline in the number of adult leaders was perhaps the more serious concern, as without leaders, many individual Scouts groups could not continue, and therefore the number of Scouts groups may well decline even though the demand among new members of Scouts may continue to be strong. Membership growth in both youth members and adult leaders was thus identified as the key organisational and marketing priority for Scouts in the immediate future.

Through market research, it was identified that the awareness of Scouts in the broader community remained high and that the image of Scouts was generally positive, also that the Scouts provide a valuable and enjoyable outdoor-oriented learning experience that is relevant to all young people. At the same time, there was also some evidence that Scouts was perceived as somewhat conservative and not necessarily suitable for young adults. These attitudes are reflected in the perceptual map below.

Furthermore, opinion within Scouts membership and management was that attracting new Scouts to the Joeys and Cub ranks was not difficult as the image of the organisation and its program still resonated with these age groups. More difficult than attracting new junior Scouts was the task of retaining and attracting adult leaders, although this was felt to be a common problem among community and sporting organisations. In this context, the usual work demands and increasing community concern over 'stranger danger' have combined to make such volunteer activities less attractive to parents.

**CASE-7.1** Scouts Positioning Within the Competitive Environment

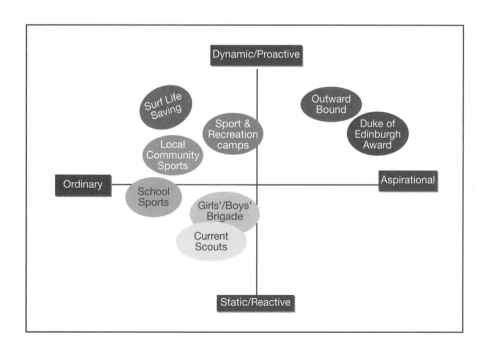

# The Challenge for Scouts' Management

Thus, while the history and achievements of the Scouts movement, and of individual Scouts, gave justifiable cause for pride and satisfaction, it was equally clear that there was no reason for complacency. In particular, the steady decline in membership over the previous five years needed to be arrested. At the same time, new members needed to be recruited, especially adult leaders.

In seeking to arrest the decline, a yet-unanswered question concerned the continued relevance and desirability of the 'core product'. Is the Scouts product still relevant? Is the decline in popularity attributable to a lack of awareness and understanding of scouting among the general public? If so, could the desired turnaround be achieved with a public awareness and education campaign?

Beyond the short-term priority of halting the decline, the opportunities for longer-term growth, such as the development of new 'products' and the movement into new 'markets', also need to be explored. At the same time, any changes to the Scouts' 'product' should attract new members but not alienate loyal and involved current members.

One thing is certain. 'Business as usual' is not an option.

# Discussion Questions

1. Discuss the distinctive characteristics of Scouts that impact (both positively and negatively) on its marketing capabilities?
2. Using the perceptual map, where do you think Scouts should aim to reposition itself? What are the implications for Scouts in this repositioning?
3. From the facts of the case and your knowledge of Scouts, identify 'opportunities' and 'threats' for the organisation – both immediate and longer-term.
4. How would you prioritise these opportunities and threats?
5. Based on the above priorities and the new suggested positioning, outline a brief 'action plan' to respond to these opportunities and threats.

CHAPTER **8**

# Managing the Servicescape and Other Physical Evidence

## CHAPTER OBJECTIVES

After reading this chapter, you should be able to:

- Appreciate the strategic role of physical evidence as it relates to the marketing of service firms.

- Outline the stimulus-organism-response (SOR) model.

- Discuss the major components of the Servicescapes model.

- Describe the managerial use of sensory cues when developing tactical design strategies.

- Compare design considerations for low-contact versus high-contact service firms.

This chapter's purpose is to provide you with an understanding of the importance of the service firm's physical evidence regarding customer perceptions of the quality of services provided.

### DINNER IN THE SKY: ASTONISHING VIEWS THE WORLD WIDE

In 2007, a Belgian events planner and a Dutch crane expert pooled resources to create Dinner in the Sky, a company that offers a unique dining experience to its consumers. Originally pitched to clients as an opportunity to literally float above the competition, Dinner in the Sky became a worldwide phenomenon in the matter of a few short years. Globalization was their plan from the beginning; their company design revolved around the idea of selling their unique crane-hoisted table design and logo rights to partners across the globe. Now, in 2009, the company has partners in approximately 30 countries around the world, including the United States, Latvia, England, Germany, and more. In fact, in January 2009, their parent company reported revenues of about $1.34 million from rights and fees alone.

So what makes Dinner in the Sky worth the hefty premium clients pay for the unique experience? The food could be found in any restaurant, and the level of service from the waitstaff is no better than what can be found in upscale restaurants. Why, then, do people pay thousands of dollars to dine? The servicescape, of course, makes all the difference. Not only are customers given the opportunity to literally dine among the clouds while suspended at 130 feet in the air, they are given the chance to hoist their company logos over the heads of everyone down below. And, since Dinner in the Sky is still a novelty receiving considerable attention from international publications, the interest each dining experience attracts from local press is incredible.

What would you pay to eat next to the Eiffel Tower at sunset in Paris, safely held above the chaotic throng of tourists down below? Or, if the company's next innovation becomes reality, suspended over the Grand Canyon at dizzying heights?

Dinner in the Sky continues to expand their partner base and services offered, including an entertainment option. Want an opera singer or a band on a separate platform, slowly circling your table? You got it. Want a wedding in the sky? You can have that, too. If the parent company's current monetary successes are any indication, Dinner in the Sky will continue to see its global enterprise increase, thanks to a servicescape so unique it is nearly priceless.

Source: Hettie Judah, "A highflying marketing concept goes global," *The New York Times*, (January 9, 2009). **http://www.nytimes.com/2009/01/09/business/worldbusiness/09iht-wbspot10.1.19137553.html?_r=1**. Copyright © 2009 The New York Times. All rights reserved. Used by permission and protected by the Copyright Laws of the United States. The printing, copying, redistribution, or retransmission of the Material without express written permission is prohibited. Accessed 14 September, 2009.
*Pictures are on the company's website:* **http://www.dinnerinthesky.com/**

## Introduction

Managing the firm's physical evidence includes everything tangible, from the firm's physical facilities, to brochures and business cards, to the firm's personnel. A firm's physical evidence influences the consumer's experience throughout the duration of the service encounter. Consider the average consumer's restaurant experience.[1]

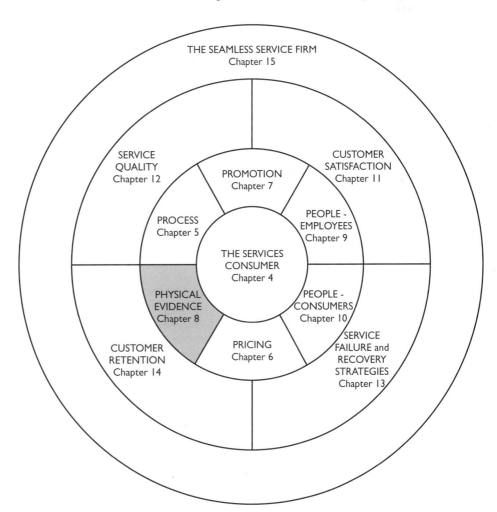

Prior to entering the restaurant, customers begin to evaluate it based on advertising they may have seen on television or in the phone book. As the consumer drives to the restaurant, the location of the restaurant, the ease with which the location can be found, the restaurant's sign, and the building itself, all enter into the consumer's evaluation process. Similarly, the availability of parking spaces, the cleanliness of the parking lot, and the smells that fill the air once the customer steps out of the car affect consumer expectations and perceptions.

Upon entering, the restaurant's furnishings, cleanliness, and overall ambience provide further evidence regarding the quality of the ensuing experience. The appearance and friendliness of the firm's personnel and the ease with which customers can move about and find telephones and restrooms without asking also enters into the consumer's mind.

When seated at a table, the customer notices the stability and quality of the table and chairs, the cleanliness of napkins, silverware, and the table itself. Additional evaluations occur as well: Is the menu attractive? Is it readable or crumbled and spotted with food stains from past customers? How are the waitstaff interacting with other customers? What do the other customers look like?

Once the meal is served, the presentation of the food is yet another indicator of the restaurant's quality. Consumers will make comparisons of the food's actual appearance and the way it is pictured in advertisements and menus. Of course, how the food tastes also enters into the customer's evaluation.

Upon completing the meal, the bill itself becomes a tangible clue. Is it correct? Are charges clearly written? Is the bill clean, or is it sopping wet with spaghetti sauce? Are the restrooms clean? Did the waitstaff personnel say thank you and really mean it?

# The Strategic Role of Physical Evidence

**facility exterior** The physical exterior of the service facility; includes the exterior design, signage, parking, landscaping, and the surrounding environment

**facility interior** The physical interior of the service facility; includes the interior design, equipment used to serve customers, signage, layout, air quality, and temperature.

**other tangibles** Other items that are part of the firm's physical evidence, such as business cards, stationery, billing statements, reports, employee appearance, uniforms, and brochures.

Due to the intangibility of services, service quality is often difficult for consumers to evaluate objectively. As a result, consumers often rely on the tangible evidence that surrounds the service to help them form their evaluations. The role of physical evidence in the marketing of intangibles is multifaceted. When developing servicescapes, physical evidence is comprised of three broad categories: (1) facility exterior; (2) facility interior; and (3) other tangibles. **Facility exterior** includes the exterior design, signage, parking, landscaping, and the surrounding environment. For example, the facility may be built on a mountainside, overlooking a lake. The **facility interior** includes elements such as the interior design, equipment used to serve the customer directly or to run the business, signage, layout, air quality, and temperature. **Other tangibles** that are part of the firm's physical evidence include such items as business cards, stationery, billing statements, reports, employee appearance, uniforms, and brochures.[2]

The extensive use of physical evidence varies by the type of service firm (see Figure 8.1). Service firms such as hospitals, resorts, and child-care facilities often make extensive use of physical evidence in facility design and other tangibles associated with the service. In contrast, service firms such as insurance providers and express mail drop-off locations (e.g., Federal Express) use limited physical evidence. Regardless of the variation in usage, all service firms need to recognize the importance of managing their physical evidence in its multi-faceted role of:

- Packaging *the service;*
- Facilitating *the flow of the service delivery process;*
- Socializing *customers and employees alike in terms of their respective roles, behaviors, and relationships; and*
- Differentiating *the firm from its competitors.*[3]

**FIG-8.1** Variations in Usage of Physical Evidence

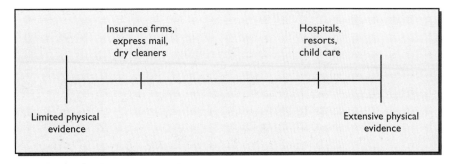

Source: Mary J. Bitner, "Servicescapes: The Impact of Physical Surroundings on Customers and Employees," *Journal of Marketing* 56, 2, (April 1992), p. 60. Reprinted with permission of the American Marketing Association.

For example, the Rain Forest Café, Chili's, T.G.I. Friday's, Cracker Barrel, and a host of other restaurants that are sometimes described as "museums with food" offer food as an interactive experience with the carefully managed physical evidence that comprises the dining environment. With an average floorspace of 23,000 square feet, Rainforest Café venues feature aquariums, live parrots, a waterfall, a mechanical crocodile, fiberglass monkeys, a video screen, a talking tree, and a regularly timed thunderstorm, complete with lightning. The environment theme features strongly in the chain's décor and products. The restaurants make a point of not serving beef from deforested land or fish caught in nets. The talking trees give messages about the environment to customers waiting in line. However, the restaurants place a great deal of focus on their core business, the food, and work to ensure quality in this area.[4]

Ultimately, the firm's exterior, interior elements, and other tangibles create the package that surrounds the service. Promoted as the world's most luxurious hotel, the Al Burj Hotel located in Dubai uses its own unique architecture to package its services.

## Packaging

The firm's physical evidence plays a major role in packaging the service. The service itself is intangible and, therefore, does not require a package for purely functional reasons. However, utilizing the firm's physical evidence to package the service does send quality cues to consumers and adds value to the service in terms of image development. Image development, in turn, improves consumer perceptions of service while reducing both levels of perceived risk associated with the purchase and levels of cognitive dissonance after the purchase.

One example of using physical evidence to package the service involves the Airbus A380. This new jumbo jetliner which weighs 308 tons took Airbus 11 years to build and cost approximately $13 billion. The A380 is 80 feet tall (equivalent to a seven-story building), 239 feet long, boasts a wingspan of 262 feet and can fly approximately 8,000 nautical miles. The A380 can carry up to 840 passengers on two decks, or, if preferred, the space can be redesigned to include shops, a casino, and restaurant on the lower deck with passenger space maintained above.[5]

Ultimately, the firm's exterior, interior elements, and other tangibles create the package that surrounds the service. Similarly, in an online environment, the site's homepage creates the package that surrounds the site's content—and sometimes less of a package is a strategic advantage (See E-services in Action). The firm's physical facility forms the customer's initial impression concerning the type and quality of service provided. For example, Mexican and Chinese restaurants often utilize specific types of architectural designs that communicate to customers their firms' offerings. The firm's physical evidence also conveys expectations to consumers. Consumers will have one set of expectations for a restaurant with dimly lit dining rooms, soft music, and linen tablecloths and napkins and a different set of expectations for a restaurant with cement floors, picnic tables, and peanut shells strewn about the floor.

## Facilitating the Service Process

Another use of the firm's physical evidence is to facilitate the flow of activities that produce the service. Physical evidence can provide information to customers on how the service production process works. Other examples include signage that specifically instructs customers. Menus and brochures explain the firm's offerings and facilitate the ordering process for consumers and providers. Physical structures direct the flow of waiting consumers, and barriers, such as counters at a dry cleaner's, separate the technical core of the business (backroom operations) from the part of the business in which customers take part in the production process.

## Socializing Employees and Customers

**socialization** The process by which an individual adapts to the values, norms, and required behavior patterns of an organization.

Organizational **socialization** is the process by which an individual adapts to and comes to appreciate the values, norms, and required behavior patterns of an organization.[6] The firm's physical evidence plays an important part in the socialization process by conveying expected roles, behaviors, and relationships among employees and between employees and customers. The purpose of the socialization process is to project a positive and consistent image to the public. However, the service firm's image is only as good as the image each employee conveys when interacting with the public.

Physical evidence, such as the use of uniforms, facilitates the socialization of employees toward accepting organizational goals and affects consumer perceptions of the caliber of service provided. Studies have shown that the use of uniforms:

## E-SERVICES *IN ACTION*

## Google.com's Servicescape: "61, Getting a Bit Heavy, Aren't We?"

One of the secrets behind Google's success has been the thoughtful management of its own servicescape. The components of an online servicescape consists of the web page's layout of text and graphics, colors, product depictions, use of flash media, streaming video and audio, and advertisements, just to name a few. In the early days of the Internet, it seemed like the "flashier" the web page, the better. Web page developers were literally in a race to outdo one another for bragging rights. However, in the end, all that really mattered was whether the website effectively served customers.

Google's success story is extraordinary! Google entered the search engine market in 1998, long after its counterparts like Yahoo and Excite. However, Google made three great decisions that eventually led to it being named Global Brand of the Year. First, Google found the right technology for the right price. The company's two young cofounders, Sergey Brin and Larry Page, built their own system from commodity hardware parts and were able to pack in eight times as much server power in the same space as competitors. Second, Google's search strategy is innovative. Instead of being based solely on key word searches, a Google search is based on the site's popularity. As a result, a Google search is directed more by human input than technology. The end result is that users typically received more relevant information.

Google's third great decision provides us all an example of how sometimes "less is more." Motivated by an anonymous user who periodically sent a Google vice president a single number (e.g., 13, 33, 53, 61 [Getting a bit heavy, aren't we?], 37, 28), the VP eventually determined that the user was a human version of a scale, and was actively weighing the number of words used on Google's homepage. Since then Google dedicated itself to keeping its homepage to a minimum. Google uses simple graphics, allows no advertising on its home page, and within its web pages allows only banner advertisements without graphics. Consequently, Google's servicescape downloads faster than competitive offerings and is easier to read since it is less distracting. As of this writing, the current word count is 29 (in case you were wondering).

As a testament to Google's effectiveness, the company performs 250 million searches on its 4 billion and growing web pages a day. Customers can "google" in 88 languages, and many customers are doing just that! Google is the most visited website in the world. Today, it is estimated that one-third of global Internet users visited Google.com yesterday!

Sources:
1. **http://googleblog.blogspot.com/2008/07/what-comes-next-in-this-series-13-33-53.html**, accessed 1 October, 2009;
2. **http://www.alexa.com/siteinfo/google.com**, accessed 1 October, 2009;
3. Judy Strauss, Adel El-Ansary, and Raymond Frost, *E-Marketing*, 4th ed. (Upper Saddle River, NJ: Pearson Prentice Hall, 2006), 241.

- *Aids in identifying the firm's personnel;*
- *Presents a physical symbol that embodies the group's ideals and attributes;*
- *Implies a coherent group structure;*
- *Facilitates the perceived consistency of performance;*
- *Provides a tangible symbol of an employee's change in status (e.g., military uniforms change as personnel move through the ranks); and*
- *Assists in controlling the behavior of errant employees.*[7]

One classic example of how tangible evidence affects the socialization process of employees involves women in the U.S. military. Pregnant military personnel were originally permitted to wear civilian clothing in lieu of traditional military uniforms. However, the military soon noticed discipline and morale problems with these servicewomen as they began to lose their identification with their roles as soldiers. "Maternity uniforms are now standard issue in the Air Force, Army, and Navy, as well as at US Air, Hertz, Safeway, McDonald's, and the National Park Service."[8]

### A Means for Differentiation

The effective management of the physical evidence can also be a source of differentiation. Service differentiation through the purposeful use of physical evidence has been long exemplified by the lodging industry through the effective management of facility exterior, facility interior, and other tangibles associated with the hotel experience. Interestingly, the latest battleground in physical differentiation has become the bed itself. With the introduction of the "Heavenly Bed," Westin Hotels ushered in a new movement in the hotel industry. Over the years, Westin and the Heavenly Bed have racked up multiple business rewards including "improved guest satisfaction, higher room rates, better revenue-per-available-room and an avalanche of publicity." In addition, overall cleanliness scores increased even though Westin admits all it did extra was "add the bed." Since the Heavenly Bed's introduction, Westin has sold over 7,000 beds to its enamored customers.[9]

The appearance of personnel and facilities can also serve as differentiating factors and can have a direct impact on how consumers perceive the firm will handle the service aspects of its business. Numerous studies have shown that well-dressed individuals are perceived as more intelligent, better workers, and more pleasant to engage with in interactions.[10] Similarly, nicely designed facilities will be perceived as having the advantage over poorly designed alternatives.

Differentiation can also be achieved by utilizing physical evidence to reposition the service firm in the eyes of its customers. Upgrading the firm's facilities often upgrades the image of the firm in the minds of consumers, and may also lead to attracting more desirable market segments, which further aids in differentiating the firm from its competitors. On the other hand, note that a too-elaborate facility upgrade may alienate some customers who believe the firm may be passing on the costs of that upgrade to consumers through higher prices. This is precisely why many offices, such as insurance, dental, and medical offices are decorated professionally, but not too lavishly.

## The SOR Model

The science of utilizing physical evidence to create service environments and its influence on the perceptions and behaviors of individuals is referred to as **environmental psychology**. The **stimulus-organism-response (SOR) model** presented in Figure 8.2 was developed by environmental psychologists to help explain the effects of the service environment on consumer behavior.[11] The SOR model consists of three components:

**environmental psychology** The use of physical evidence to create service environments and its influence on the perceptions and behaviors of individuals.

**stimulus-organism-response (SOR) model** A model developed by environmental psychologists to help explain the effects of the service environment on consumer behavior; describes environmental stimuli, emotional states, and responses to those states.

Stimuli within the servicescape, such as lighting, temperature, and music, are interpreted by customers who then behave in a manner consistent with the servicescape.

**FIG-8.2** The Three Components of the SOR Model

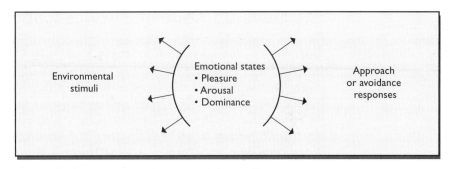

Source: Adapted from Robert J. Donovan and John R. Rossiter, "Store Atmosphere: An Environmental Psychology Approach," *Journal of Retailing* 58 (Spring 1982), p. 42.

**stimuli** The various elements of the firm's physical evidence.

**organism** The recipients of the set of stimuli in the service encounter; includes employees and customers.

**responses (outcomes)** Consumers' reaction or behavior in response to stimuli.

**pleasure-displeasure** The emotional state that reflects the degree to which consumers and employees feel satisfied with the service experience.

**arousal-nonarousal** The emotional state that reflects the degree to which consumers and employees feel excited and stimulated.

**dominance-submissiveness** The emotional state that reflects the degree to which consumers and employees feel in control and able to act freely within the service environment.

**approach/avoidance behaviors** Consumer responses to the set of environmental stimuli that are characterized by a desire to stay or leave an establishment, explore/interact with the service environment or ignore it, or feel satisfaction or disappointment with the service experience.

- *A set of stimuli (sight, sound, touch, taste, and smell);*
- *An organism component (employees/customers who are recipients of stimuli); and*
- *A set of responses or outcomes (approach/avoidance behaviors by employee/customers).*

In a service context, the different elements of the firm's physical evidence, such as exterior, interior design, lighting, and so on, compose the set of stimuli. **Stimuli** are collected through the five senses of sight, sound, touch, taste, and smell and can be effectively managed to create compelling service atmospheres. Once received and interpreted by an individual, the combined stimuli lead to expectations and perceptions about the service firm via the firm's environment. Consequently, even though an individual may have never been to a particular restaurant before, he or she notices that the lights are low and the table napkins are linen. This leads to the perception that the restaurant is of higher caliber and that the food should be good, though expensive.

The **organism** component, which describes the recipients of the set of stimuli within the service encounter, includes employees and customers alike. The **responses** of employees and customers to the set of stimuli are influenced by three basic emotional states: pleasure-displeasure, arousal-nonarousal, and dominance-submissiveness. The **pleasure-displeasure** emotional state reflects the degree to which consumers and employees feel satisfied with the service experience. The **arousal-nonarousal** state reflects the degree to which consumers and employees feel excited and stimulated. The third emotional state, **dominance-submissiveness**, reflects the feelings of control and the ability to act freely within the service environment. Ideally, service firms should utilize physical evidence to build environments that appeal to pleasure and arousal states and avoid creating atmospheres that encourage submissiveness.

Finally, consumer and employee responses to the set of environmental stimuli are characterized as **approach behaviors** or **avoidance behaviors**. Consumer approach and avoidance behaviors and outcomes can be demonstrated in any combination of four ways (employees exhibit similar behaviors):[12]

1. A desire to stay (approach) or leave (avoid) the service establishment.
2. A desire to further explore and interact with the service environment (approach) or a tendency to ignore it (avoidance).
3. A desire to communicate with others (approach) or to ignore the attempts of service providers to communicate with customers (avoid).
4. Feelings of satisfaction (approach) or disappointment (avoidance) with the service experience.

# The Development of Servicescapes[13]

**servicescapes** The use of physical evidence to design service environments.

The term **servicescapes** refers to the use of physical evidence to design service environments. The servicescape framework presented in Figure 8.3 is a comprehensive application of the SOR model that directly applies to the influence of the service firm's physical evidence on consumers' and employees' behaviors. Due to inseparability, the model recognizes that the firm's environment is likely to impact consumers and employees alike. For example, many colleges and universities are leading the way in building environmentally friendly campus buildings (Eduscapes) that are benefiting both students and staff (see Sustainability and Services in Action). However, in the end, the servicescape should be designed to meet the needs of those individuals who spend the most time within the confines of the service firm.

**FIG-8.3** The Servicescapes Model

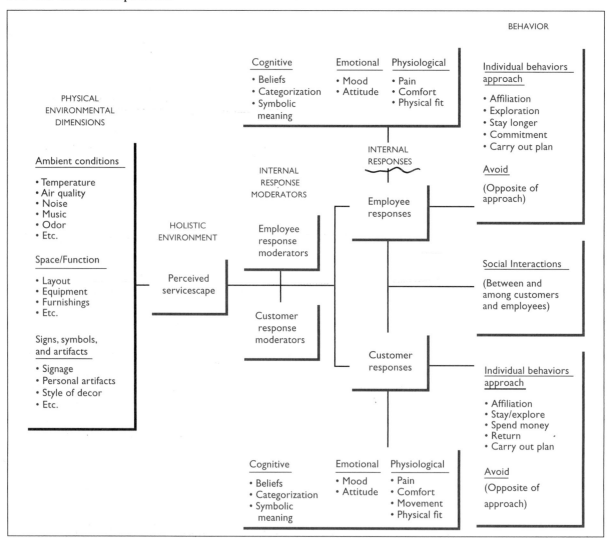

Source: Mary J. Bitner, "Servicescapes: The Impact of Physical Surroundings on Customers and Employees," *Journal of Marketing* 60, no. 2 (April 1992), p. 60. Reprinted with permission of the American Marketing Association.

## SUSTAINABILITY AND SERVICES *IN ACTION*

### Colleges and Universities on the Cutting-edge of Creating Green Servicescapes

Within the United Sates, buildings constructed using conventional methods account for 36 percent of the country's total greenhouse gas emissions, 39 percent of its total carbon dioxide emissions, 71 percent of the country's electricity use, and consume 40 percent of the world's raw materials. As a result, sustainable buildings are "in" and colleges and universities are leading the way in providing the "triple bottom line" of planet, people and profit. Sustainable facilities benefit the planet by using more environmentally friendly products. People benefit by working in environments that lead to lower absenteeism rates and improved productivity. Finally, although eco-friendly buildings are more expensive to build, they also cost less to operate and aid in student recruitment which leads to improved profitability.

Many college and university administrators believe that the educational setting has a social responsibility to promote green alternatives; thereby, making a public statement and setting a good example for students and other constituencies. Examples of eco-friendly college and university servicescape strategies include:

| INSTITUTION | ECO-FRIENDLY SERVICESCAPE STRATEGY |
| --- | --- |
| Santa Clara University | Utilizes carpet tiles made of yarn on a floor that is raised 14 inches to aid in circulating warm and cold air |
| Stanford University | Integrates redwood salvaged from old wine vats into its buildings |
| East Los Angeles College | Proudly displays 5,952 solar panels that produces nearly half of the College's energy needs |
| Yale University | Utilizes a material for a translucent curtain that is known as "frozen smoke" to allow sunlight in but maintains current temperatures. |
| University of Michigan | Floors are constructed with tire rubber and countertops consist of soy flour, newspapers, wheat, and sunflower seeds. In some restrooms, tile consisting of glass from airplane windshields are used. |
| Northern Arizona University | Walls are insulated with thousands of pairs of recycled denim jeans. |
| Warren Wilson College | A converted railroad tank car funnels storm water through one of its buildings. |

The country's most prominent eco-friendly rating system, the Green Building Council's certification in Leadership in Energy and Environmental Design (also known as LEED), has noted a marked uptick in higher education institutions seeking LEED certification. In 2001, there were 42 LEED projects in higher education. In contrast, in June of 2008, 1,497 buildings of higher education were seeking certification. Higher education servicescapes are not only incorporating behind-the-scenes eco-friendly improvements, but are also purposely showcasing their environmentally friendly efforts in very deliberate and visible ways.

Source: **http://www.latimes.com/news/local/la-me-ecocollege7-2008jul07,0,2908946.story**, accessed 1 October, 2009.

### Remote, Self-Service, and Interpersonal Services

As customer involvement in the coproduction of services varies, so should the design of the servicescape. As such, service firms can be characterized as remote, self-service and interpersonal services. Figure 8.4 presents a continuum of facility usage by service type.

In contrast to remote services and self-service, Interpersonal services should construct servicescapes with both the service providers and the customer's physical and psychological needs in mind.

**remote services**
Services in which employees are physically present while customer involvement in the service production process is at arm's length.

**self-services** Service environments that are dominated by the customer's physical presence, such as ATMs or postal kiosks.

**interpersonal services** Service environments in which customers and providers interact.

**FIG-8.4** A Continuum of Facility Use by Type of Service

Some services, such as mail order, coupon-sorting houses, and telephone and utility services are described as **remote services**. In remote services, employees are physically present within the service operation while customer involvement in the service production process is at arm's length. In other words, these services require very little of the customer's physical presence to complete the service. Consequently, facility design should facilitate the employees' overall efforts and enhance employee motivation, employee productivity, and employee satisfaction.

At the other end of the spectrum are services that customers can acquire on their own—**self-services**. Self-service environments are dominated by the customer's physical presence and include services such as ATMs, miniature golf courses, postal kiosks, and self-service car washes. The environment of self-service establishments should be located in conveniently accessible locations and constructed to attract customers and enhance satisfaction.

In contrast to remote and self-service environments, many services such as restaurants, hospitals, hotels, banks, and airlines can be described as **interpersonal services**, where the physical space is shared jointly by consumers and employees (and in some cases like hospitals, the patient's family is also involved and physically present). The

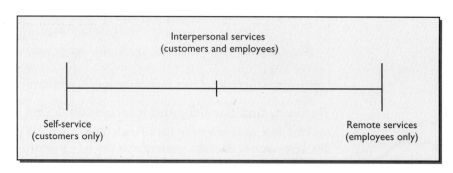

environments of interpersonal services should be developed with the needs of both parties in mind, and should facilitate the social interaction between and among customers and employees. To further illustrate the importance of understanding the coproduction role of the end-user with regard to servicescape design, consider the following decisions with respect to high-contact versus low-contact service firms.[14]

*Facility Location*   The choice location for the firm's service operation depends upon the amount of customer contact that is necessary during the production process. If customers are an integral part of the process, convenient locations located near customers' homes or workplaces will offer the firm a differential advantage over competitors. For example, with all other things being equal, the most conveniently located car washes, dry cleaners, and hairstylists are likely to obtain the most business.

In contrast, low-contact service firms should consider locations that may be more convenient for labor, sources of supply, and closer to major transportation routes. For example, mail-order facilities have little or no customer contact and can actually increase the efficiencies of their operations by locating closer to sources of supply and major transportation alternatives, such as near interstate highways for trucking purposes or airports for overnight airline shipments. In many cases, these types of locations are less expensive to purchase or rent, since they are generally in remote areas where the cost of land and construction is not as expensive as inside city limits where other businesses are trying to locate close to their customers.

*Facility Layout*   In regard to the layout of the service operation, high-contact service firms should take the customers' physical and psychological needs and expectations into consideration. When a customer enters a high-contact service operation, that customer expects the facility to look like something other than a dusty, musty, old warehouse. Professional personnel, clearly marked signs explaining the process, enough room to comfortably move about the facility, and a facility suited for bringing friends and family are among consumer expectations. In contrast, low-contact facility layouts should be designed to maximize employee expectations and production requirements. Clearly, designing facilities for high-contact services is often more expensive than designing for their low-contact counterparts.

*Product Design*   Since the customer is involved in the production process of high-contact services, the customer will ultimately define the product differently from one produced by a low-contact service. In services such as restaurants, which have a tangible product associated with their service offering, the customer will define the product by the physical product itself as well as by the physical evidence that surrounds the product in the service environment. High-contact services that produce purely intangible products such as education and insurance are defined almost solely by the physical evidence that surrounds the service and by the thoughts and opinions of others.

In low-contact services, the customer is not directly involved in the production process, the product is defined by fewer attributes. Consider our mail-order operation in which the customer never physically enters the facility. The customer will define the end product by the physical product itself (a pair of boots), the conversation that took place with personnel when ordering the boots, the quality of the mail-order catalog that featured the boots, the box in which the boots were packaged, and the billing materials that request payment.

*Process Design*   In high-contact operations, the physical presence of the customer in the process itself must also be considered. Each stage in the process will have a direct

**ambient conditions**
The distinctive atmosphere of the service setting that includes lighting, air quality, noise, music, and so on.

**space/function** Environmental dimensions that include the layout of the facility, the equipment, and the firm's furnishings.

**signs, symbols, artifacts** Environmental physical evidence that includes signage to direct the flow of the service process, personal artifacts to personalize the facility, and the style of decor.

**holistic environment** Overall perceptions of the servicescape formed by employees and customers based on the physical environmental dimensions.

**perceived servicescape** A composite of mental images of the service firm's physical facilities.

**economic customers** Consumers who make purchase decisions based primarily on price.

**personalized customers** Consumers who desire to be pampered and attended to and who are much less price sensitive.

**apathetic customers** Consumers who seek convenience over price and personal attention.

**ethical customers** Consumers who support smaller or local firms as opposed to larger or national service providers.

and immediate effect on the customer. Consequently, a set of mini-service encounters and the physical evidence present at each encounter will contribute to the customer's overall evaluation of the service process. For example, a hotel guest is directly involved in the reservation process, the check-in process, the consumption process associated with the use of the hotel room itself, the consumption processes associated with the use of hotel amenities such as the restaurant, pool, and health club, and the check-out process. In contrast, since the customer is not involved with many of the production steps in low-contact services, their evaluation is based primarily on the outcome itself.

## Stage 1: Physical Environmental Dimensions

The servicescapes model depicted in Figure 8.3 consists of five stages and begins by recognizing the set of stimuli that are commonly utilized when developing service environments. In broad terms, the set of stimuli include ambient conditions, space/function, and signs, symbols, and artifacts. **Ambient conditions** reflect the distinctive atmosphere of the service setting and include elements such as lighting, air quality, noise, music, and so on. Environmental dimensions that pertain to the use of **space/function** include elements such as the layout of the facility, equipment, and the firm's furnishings. **Signs, symbols, and artifacts** include signage that directs the flow of the service process, personal artifacts, which lend character and individuality that personalize the facility, and the style of decor, such as southwestern, contemporary, or traditional, to name a few.

## Stage 2: Holistic Environment

Once the physical environmental dimensions noted above are in place, perceptions of the firm's holistic environment are formed. Hence, the **holistic environment** portion of the servicescape model pertains to the perceptions of the servicescape that employees and customers form based on the physical environmental dimensions. In other words, the holistic environment is a perceived overview or image of the firm based on the physical evidence, which is referred to in the model as the **perceived servicescape**. The perceived servicescape is difficult to define precisely, and perceptions of the same establishment will vary among individuals. Essentially, the perceived servicescape is a composite of mental images of the service firm's physical facilities.

Strategically managing the perceived servicescape aids in establishing a positioning strategy that differentiates the firm from competitors and ultimately influences the customer decision process when choosing among competing alternatives. The firm should develop the servicescape with its target market in mind. **Economic customers**, who make purchase decisions based on price, will avoid service establishments that appear too fancy or elaborate based on the perception that such an establishment will be a higher-priced provider. Economic customers tend to be attracted to environments that are simple yet reflect quality, and those that are clean and modern. Oil-change specialists such as the "Jiffy Lube" franchise use this type of environment as does the modern day superpower of retailing, Walmart. In contrast, **personalized customers** desire to be pampered and attended to, and are much less price sensitive when choosing among competing alternative providers. Firms catering to personalized shoppers create environments that reflect the status their customers seek by investing more in items such as marble foyers, glass and brass fixtures, and furnishings that encourage customers to shop at a leisurely pace. Similarly, firms that service **apathetic customers**, who seek convenience, and **ethical customers**, who support smaller or local as opposed to larger or national service providers should create their servicescapes accordingly.

## Stage 3: Internal Response Moderators

**internal response moderators** The three basic emotional states of the SOR model that mediate the reaction between the perceived servicescape and customers' and employees' responses to the service environment.

Customer and employee responses to the firm's servicescape are influenced (moderated) by a number of factors. The **internal response moderators** component of the servicescapes model simply pertain to the three basic emotional states of the SOR model discussed earlier: pleasure-displeasure, arousal-nonarousal, and dominance-submissiveness. The three response moderators mediate the reaction between the perceived servicescape and customers' and employees' responses to the service environment. For example, if a customer desires to remain in a state of nonarousal and spend a nice, quiet evening with someone special, that customer will avoid bright, loud, and crowded service establishments and will be attracted to environments that are more peaceful and conducive to conversation. Similarly, the employees' responses to the firm's environment will also be affected by their own emotional states. Sometimes employees look forward to engaging in conversations with customers. Other days, employees would just as soon minimize conversations and process customers as raw materials on a production line. Response moderators help explain why services are characterized by heterogeneity as the service varies from provider to provider, and even from day to day with the same provider.

## Stage 4: Internal Responses

Thus far, the Servicescape Model proposes that the servicescape consists of a variety of physical environmental dimensions. These dimensions form the individual's overall (holistic) perception of the servicescape. Moreover, the individual's reaction to the servicescape will be moderated by their current emotional state. The next step in the Servicescape Model attempts to describe how individuals respond to the firm's servicescape, which can be described at three different levels: cognitively, emotionally, and physiologically.

**beliefs** Consumers' opinions about the provider's ability to perform the service.

*Cognitive Responses*   Cognitive responses are the thought processes of individuals and, according to the model, include beliefs, categorization, and symbolic meaning. In the formation of **beliefs**, the firm's environment acts as a form of non-verbal communication and influences a consumer's beliefs about the provider's ability to perform the service. For example, if a professor's lectures are difficult to follow in class, a student may attribute this difficulty to the professor's inability to teach or may blame him/herself for an inability to learn the subject. Studies have shown that faced with this type of scenario, the physical environment influences consumers when they are attributing blame.[15] In particular, if the provider's office is in disarray, students are more likely to attribute poor service to the provider. Hence, physical evidence may assist customers with beliefs pertaining to the provider's success, price for services, and competence. Similarly, employees form similar types of beliefs about their own firm based on the overall perceived servicescape.

**categorization** The process of categorizing servicescapes based on previous experiences.

**Categorization** is the second type of cognitive response. Restaurants and nightclubs operate within a number of environments. Some are fine dining establishments, while others cater strictly to local clientele or specific market segments. The process of categorization facilitates human understanding at a quicker pace. Consumers assess the physical evidence via their five senses, quickly categorize the service establishments with existing types of operations and then access the appropriate behavior script for the type of operation and act accordingly. For example, a dimly lit restaurant typically symbolizes a higher caliber of restaurant, and cues customers to talk softly while enjoying their meal.

**symbolic meaning** Meaning inferred from the firm's use of physical evidence.

Individuals also infer **symbolic meaning** from the firm's use of physical evidence. For example, if a nightclub features portraits of James Dean, Jimi Hendrix, Janice Joplin, Kurt Cobain, and others who have followed similar paths, the club evokes a symbolic meaning to its employees and customers. In this instance, the physical evidence may translate into a number of symbols, such as individuality, youthful success, shattered dreams, or other meanings, depending on individual interpretation. Symbolic meaning through the use of physical evidence aids in differentiation and positioning.

**emotional responses**
Feelings that are a result of the servicescape.

*Emotional Responses*    In addition to forming beliefs, individuals will also respond to the firm's physical environment on an emotional level. **Emotional responses** do not involve thinking, they simply happen, often unexplainably and suddenly. Specific songs, for example, may make individuals feel happy or sad, or recreate other past feelings that were associated with the particular piece of music. Scents have similar effects on individuals. Obviously, the goal of effective physical evidence management is to stimulate positive emotions that create atmospheres in which employees love to work and customers want to spend their time and money.

**physiological responses** Responses to the firm's physical environment based on pain or comfort.

*Physiological Responses*    In contrast to cognitive and emotional responses, **physiological responses** are often described in terms of physical pleasure or discomfort. Typical physiological responses involve pain and comfort. Environments in which music is played very loudly may lead to employee and customer discomfort and movement away from the source of the noise. For example, the retail operations of Hollister are known for creating environments that teenagers love and older adults despise. In another example, the lack of a nonsmoking section in an airport may cause some customers difficulty in breathing and further discomfort. Instead of being arousing, environments that are brightly lit may cause eye discomfort. In contrast, a dimly lit restaurant may cause eye strain as customers struggle to read their menus. All these responses determine whether a customer will approach and explore the firm's offerings or avoid and leave the premises to minimize the amount of physiological discomfort. Because of the duration of time spent in the firm's facility, employees might find the physical environment particularly harmful if mismanaged. Adequate work space, proper equipment to get the job done, and appropriate ambient conditions such as temperature and air quality are directly related to employees' willingness to continue to work, their productivity while at work, their job satisfaction, and their positive interactions with coworkers.

## Stage 5: Behavioral Responses to the Environment

**individual behaviors**
Responses to the servicescape that are typically described as approach and avoidance behaviors.

**Individual Behaviors** The Servicescape Model concludes with an individual's behavioral response to the physical environment. Individual behaviors in response to environmental stimuli are characterized as approach and avoidance behaviors. In retail settings, the store's environment influences approach behaviors such as:

- *shopping enjoyment,*
- *repeat visits,*
- *favorable impressions of the store,*
- *money spent,*
- *time spent shopping, and*
- *willingness to stay and explore the store.*

In other instances, environmental stimuli have been purposely managed to discourage unwelcome market segments. For example, some U.S. convenience stores have cleverly used "elevator music" (e.g., Muzak—boring music) outside their stores to repel unwelcome neighborhood gangs that "hang out" in the store's parking lot and deter desired clientele from entering the store. In a more recent case, shopkeepers in New Zealand are purposely playing Barry Manilow music to drive away "mall rats"—more commonly known as "unruly teenagers."[16]

*Social Interactions*    Ultimately, an interpersonal service firm's servicescape should encourage interactions between employees and customers, among customers, and among employees. The challenge in creating such an environment is that often what the customer desires, employees would prefer to forego so that they can complete their tasks with a minimum of customer involvement. Environmental variables such as physical proximity, seating arrangements, facility size, and flexibility in changing the configuration of the servicescape define the possibilities and place limits on the amount of social interaction possible.[17]

Consider the seating arrangements of a Japanese steakhouse, which combines different groups of customers at one table as opposed to traditional seating arrangements in which each party has its own table. Obviously, for better or worse, "community seating" at a Japanese steakhouse encourages interaction among customers. In addition, each table is assigned its own chef who interacts with the customers during the production process. Similar strides have been made in increasing consumer interaction at Max's and Erma's restaurants. Tables are numbered overhead and equipped with phones that enable customers to call one another. Oversized booths at Outback Steakhouse permit the waitstaff to actually sit at the customer's table while explaining the menu and taking dinner orders. This type of approach, while initially awkward to some customers who are not familiar with the practice (a modification to the traditional restaurant script), facilitates the amount of interaction between the waitstaff and their customers, but permits them to stay within the traditional bounds of simply taking and delivering orders.

## Managing the Senses When Creating Servicescapes

When developing the servicescape, the service firm must consider the physical and psychological impact of the atmosphere on customers, employees, and the firm's operations. Just as the firm cannot be all things to all people, the servicescape must make tradeoffs to meet its human resource, marketing, and operations needs. Experts suggest answering the following questions before implementing a servicescape development plan:[18]

1. Who is the firm's target market?
2. What does the target market seek from the service experience?
3. What atmospheric elements can reinforce the beliefs and emotional reactions that buyers seek?
4. How do these same atmospheric elements affect employee satisfaction and the firm's operations?
5. Does the suggested atmosphere development plan compete effectively with competitors' atmospheres?

**size/shape/colors** The three primary visual stimuli that appeal to consumers on a basic level.

**harmony** Visual agreement associated with quieter, plusher, and more formal business settings.

**contrast/clash** Visual effects associated with exciting, cheerful, and informal business settings.

Ultimately, individuals base their perceptions of a firm's facilities on their interpretation of sensory cues. The following section discusses how firms can effectively manage the senses of sight, sound, scent, touch, and taste in creating sensory appeals that enhance customer and employee attraction responses.[19]

### Sight Appeals

The sense of sight conveys more information to consumers than any other sense and, therefore, should be considered the most important means available to service firms when developing the firm's servicescape. Sight appeals can be defined as the process of interpreting stimuli, resulting in perceived visual relationships.[20] On a basic level, the three primary visual stimuli that appeal to consumers are **size, shape, and colors**. Consumers interpret visual stimuli in terms of visual relationships, consisting of perceptions of harmony, contrast, and clash. **Harmony** refers to visual agreement and is associated with quieter, plusher, and more formal business settings. In comparison, **contrast** and **clash** are associated with exciting, cheerful, and informal business settings. Hence, based

Science Faction/SuperStock

Service customers base many of their expectations based on visual cues. What would be your expectations of this service provider's organizational skills and level of professionalism?

on the size, shape, and colors of the visual stimuli utilized and the way consumers interpret the various visual relationships, extremely differing perceptions of the firm emerge. For example, consider how different target markets might respond to entering a "Chucky Cheese" restaurant for the first time. Some segments would find the environment inviting, while others might be completely overwhelmed by too much stimuli.

*Size*    The actual size of the firm's facility, signs, and departments conveys different meanings to different markets. In general, the larger the size of the firm and its corresponding physical evidence, the more consumers associate it with importance, power, success, security, and stability. For many consumers, the larger the firm, the lower the perceived risk associated with the service purchase. Such consumers believe that larger firms are more competent and successful and more likely to engage in service recovery efforts if problems do arise. Still other customers enjoy the prestige often associated with conducting business with a larger, well-known firm.

On the flip side, some customers may view large firms as impersonal and uncaring and seek out smaller, niche firms that they view as more personal, intimate, and friendly. When is bigger not better? When smaller translates into more personal service, that's when! In a time when mergers and acquisitions spawn megabanks that find it difficult to provide personal service to their customers, private boutique banks such as PrivateBank & Trust, PrivateBancorp, Boston Private Financial Holdings and Bryn Mawr Trust are filling the void. Case in point, Chicago developer Patrick F. Daly needed a loan to buy a shopping center but the big national bank that he usually dealt with couldn't track down necessary information fast enough, which jeopardized Daly's deal. Daly quickly called the bank that handled his personal finances, PrivateBank & Trust, a tiny little Chicago-based bank, and within 48 hours received a short-term signature loan for "tens of thousands of dollars." The bank's quick action saved Daly's shopping center deal and earned Daly's respect. "At PrivateBank," he says, "…they make it their business to know your business. They're just very responsive."[21] Hence, depending on the needs of the firm's target market, size appeals differently to different segments.

*Shape*    Shape perceptions of a service firm are created from a variety of sources, such as the use and placement of shelves, mirrors, and windows, and even the design of wallpaper if applicable. Studies show that different shapes arouse different emotions in consumers. Vertical shapes or vertical lines are perceived as "rigid, severe, and lend[ing] a masculine quality to an area. It expresses strength and stability … gives the viewer an up-and-down eye movement … tends to heighten an area, gives the illusion of increased space in this direction."[22] In contrast, horizontal shapes or lines evoke perceptions of relaxation and restfulness. Diagonal shapes and lines evoke perceptions of progressiveness, proactiveness, and movement. Curved shapes and lines are perceived as feminine and flowing. Utilizing similar and/or dissimilar shapes in facility design will create the desired visual relationship of harmony, contrast, or clash. For example, the use of several different shapes in one area might distinguish an area of emphasis.[23]

***Color*** The color of the firm's physical evidence often makes the first impression, whether seen in the firm's brochure, the business cards of its personnel, or the exterior or interior of the facility itself. The psychological impact of color upon individuals is the result of three properties: hue, value, and intensity. **Hue** refers to the actual family of the color, such as red, blue, yellow, or green. **Value** defines the lightness and darkness of the colors. Darker values are called **shades**, and lighter values are called **tints**. **Intensity** defines the brightness or the dullness of the hue.

Hues are classified into warm and cool colors. Warm colors include red, yellow, and orange hues, while cool colors include blue, green, and violet hues. Warm and cool colors symbolize different things to different consumer groups, as presented in Figure 8.5. In general, warm colors tend to evoke consumer feelings of comfort and informality. For example, red commonly evokes feelings of love and romance, yellow evokes feelings of sunlight and warmth, and orange evokes feelings of openness and friendliness. Studies have shown that warm colors, particularly red and yellow, are a better choice than cool colors for attracting customers in retail settings. Warm colors are also said to encourage quick decisions, and work best for businesses where low-involvement purchase decisions are made.

In contrast to warm colors, cool colors are perceived as aloof, icy, and formal. For example, the use of too much violet may dampen consumer spirits and depress employees who have to continuously work in the violet environment. Although cool colors do not initially attract customers as well as warm colors, cool colors are favored when the customer needs to take time to make decisions, such as the time needed for high-involvement purchases. Despite their different psychological effects, when used together properly, combinations of warm and cool colors can create relaxing, yet stimulating atmospheres.

**hue** The actual color, such as red, blue, yellow, or green.

**value** The lightness and darkness of the colors.

**shades** Darker values.

**tints** Lighter values.

**intensity** The brightness or the dullness of the colors.

**FIG-8.5** Perceptions of Colors

| WARM COLORS | | | COOL COLORS | | |
|---|---|---|---|---|---|
| **RED** | **YELLOW** | **ORANGE** | **BLUE** | **GREEN** | **VIOLET** |
| Love | Sunlight | Sunlight | Coolness | Coolness | Coolness |
| Romance | Warmth | Warmth | Aloofness | Restfulness | Shyness |
| Sex | Cowardice | Openness | Fidelity | Peace | Dignity |
| Courage | Openness | Friendliness | Calmness | Freshness | Wealth |
| Danger | Friendliness | Gaiety | Piety | Growth | |
| Fire | Gaiety | Glory | Masculinity | Softness | |
| Sin | Glory | | Assurance | Richness | |
| Warmth | Brightness | | Sadness | Go | |
| Excitement | Caution | | | | |
| Vigor | | | | | |
| Cheerfulness | | | | | |
| Enthusiasm | | | | | |
| Stop | | | | | |

Source: Dale M. Lewison, *Retailing*, 4th ed. (New York: Macmillan, 1991), p. 277.

The value of hues also psychologically affects the firm's customers. Offices painted in lighter colors tend to look larger, while darker colors may make large, empty spaces look smaller. Lighter hues are also popular for fixtures such as electrical face plates, air conditioning vents, and overhead speaker systems. The lighter colors help the fixtures blend in with the firm's environment. On the other hand, darker colors can grab consumers' attention. Retailers are often faced with the problem that only 25 percent of their customers ever make it more than halfway into the store. Some retailers have had some success in attracting more customers farther into the store by painting the back wall in a darker color that attracts the customer's attention.

The intensity of the color also affects perceptions of the service firm's atmosphere. For example, bright colors make objects appear larger than do duller colors. However, bright colors are perceived as harsher and "harder," while duller colors are perceived as "softer." In general, children appear to favor brighter colors, and adults tend to favor softer tones. For firms serving international markets, cultural perceptions of color must be taken into consideration (see Figure 8.6).

***Location***    The firm's location is dependent upon the amount of customer involvement necessary to produce the service. While low-contact services should consider locating in remote sites that are less expensive and closer to sources of supply, transportation, and labor, high-contact services have other concerns. Typically, when evaluating locations for the firm, three questions need to addressed:

First, how *visible* is the firm? Customers tend to shop at places of which they are aware. The firm's visibility is essential in creating awareness. Ideally, firms should be visible from major traffic arteries and can enhance their visibility by facing the direction of traffic that maximizes visibility. If available, preferable sites are set back from the street, permitting customers to gain a broad perspective, while still remaining close enough to permit customers to read the firm's signs.

The second question about a location under consideration pertains to the *compatibility* of the site being evaluated with its surrounding environment. Is the size of the site suitable for the size of the building being planned? More importantly, what other types of businesses are in the area? For example, it would make sense for a law office specializing in healthcare matters to locate close to a major hospital, which is generally surrounded by a number of private medical practices as well.

The third question concerns whether the site is suited for customer *convenience*. Is the site accessible? Does it have ample parking or alternative parking options nearby? Do customers who use mass transit systems have reasonable access to the firm?

***Architecture***    The architecture of the firm's physical facility is often a three-way trade-off among the type of design that will attract the firm's intended target market, the type of design that maximizes the efficiency of the service production process, and the type of design that is affordable. The firm's architecture conveys a number of impressions as well as communicating information to its customers, such as the nature of the firm's business, the firm's strength and stability, and the price of its services. For example, the Katitche Point Greathouse located on the island of Virgin Gorda utilizes its own unique architecture to distinguish itself from other hospitality providers in the Caribbean (See Global Services in Action).

***Signage***    The firm's sign has two major purposes: to identify the firm and to attract attention. The firm's sign is often the first "mark" of the firm the customer notices. All logos on the firm's remaining physical evidence, such as letterhead, business cards, and note cards, should be consistent with the firm's sign to reinforce the firm's image.

**FIG-8.6** Color Perceptions by Culture

| | CHINA | CHEROKEES | EASTERN | EGYPT | INDIA | IRAN | IRELAND | JAPAN | RUSSIA | WESTERN |
|---|---|---|---|---|---|---|---|---|---|---|
| Red | Good luck, celebration, summoning | Success, triumph | Worn by brides | | Purity | | | | Bolsheviks and Communism | Excitement, danger, love, passion, stop, |
| Orange | | | | | | | Religious (Protestants) | | | Halloween (with black), creativity, autumn |
| Yellow | Nourishing | | | Color of Mourning | Merchants | | | | | Hope, hazards, coward |
| Green | Green hats indicate a man's wife is cheating on him, exorcism | | | | Islam | | Symbol of the entire country | Courage | | Spring, new birth, go, Saint Patrick's Day, Christmas (with red |
| Blue | | Defeat, trouble | | | | Color of heaven and spirituality | | | | Depression, sadness, conservative, corporate, "something blue" bridal tradition |
| Purple | | | | | | | | | | Royalty |
| White | | | Funerals | | | | | White carnation symbolizes death | | Brides, angels, good guys, hospitals, doctors, peace (white dove) |
| Black | Color for young boys | | | | | | | | | Funerals, death, Halloween (with orange), bad guys, rebellion |

Source: **http://webdesign.about.com/od/color/a/bl_colorculture.htm**, accessed 5 October, 2009.

## GLOBAL SERVICES *IN ACTION*

### An Extraordinary Servicescape in the Caribbean: The Katitche Point Greathouse

Tired of the same old vacations in the same old hotels? The Katitche Point Greathouse, strategically located on the island of Virgin Gorda in the British Virgin Islands will put a definitive end to your vacation blues. In fact, as you stand on the panoramic horizon pool deck the word "blue" itself takes on an entire new meaning. Go to www.katitchepoint.com and you'll see what we mean as the blue shades of pool water, the Caribbean, and skyline provide a servicescape beyond compare.

The Katitche Point Greathouse is a compound of sorts, or more pleasantly described as a "small holiday village." The "village" comfortably sleeps eight to 10 people and consists of a three-level pyramid-shaped main house, four large bedroom suites, each complete with their own bathroom suite and private verandahs, and a large separate master bedroom suite complete with sitting room and a deep soaking tub that is built into the rocks next to a koi pond. In all, the Katitche Point Greathouse is comprised of 22,000 spacious square feet of living space that offers unobstructed panoramic views of the Caribbean in all directions.

Built in 2000, Katitche Point has received many accolades. *Elle* magazine ranked the Katitche Point Greathouse as the eighth best "deluxe holiday home around the globe." *Vogue* magazine refers to Katitche Point as "A Private Paradise." The United Kingdom's version of *The Travel Channel* featured Katitche Point in a 10-minute long segment on its "Cool Caribbean" series and called the Great House "the most stunning villa they've ever seen." *Barefoot Traveler* featured the Great House's Viking Kitchen and called Katitche Point "the best that life has to offer." These comments and many more like them serve as Katitche Point's primary promotional strategy which is backed up by the website and reinforced by the positive word-of-mouth of fortunate guests.

So, what is the price of this level of luxury? Given the villa's limited capacity and tremendous accommodations, a week's stay at the Katitche Point Greathouse is not inexpensive. Rates start at $17,600 per week for the full facility during the off-season and peak over the Christmas and New Year's season at $26,000 a week. For those that only require the Greathouse plus the separate Master Bedroom suite, prices are reduced by approximately $10,000 per week. A special honeymoon package is also offered for two for $8,500 per week based on availability. All rates include full maid service from 8 a.m. to 4 p.m., pool maintenance, laundry service and a gardener! Gourmet chef and masseuse services are also available upon request for additional fees. Although expensive for most, the Katitche Point Greathouse offers a once in a lifetime experience for many of its guests who will never forget this unimaginable holiday destination.

Sources: **www.katitchepoint.com** and **www.b-v-i.com/baths.htm**, accessed 1 October, 2009 and the fortune of personal experience.

Ideally, signs should indicate to consumers the "who," "what," "where," and "when" of the service offering. The sign's size, shape, coloring, and lighting, all contribute to the firm's projected image.

*Entrance*    The firm's entrance and foyer areas can dramatically influence customer perceptions about the firm's activities. Worn carpet, scuffed walls, unprofessional artwork, torn and outdated reading materials, and unskilled and unkempt personnel form one impression. In contrast, neatly appointed reception areas, the creative use of colors, distinctive furnishings, and friendly and professional staff create a much different, more positive impression. Other tactical considerations include: lighting that clearly identifies the entrance; doors that are easy to open; flat entryways that minimize the number of customers who might trip; nonskid floor materials for rainy days; and doors that are wide enough to accommodate customers with disabilities and large materials being transported in and out of the firm.

*Lighting*    The psychological effects of lighting on consumer behavior are particularly intriguing. Most customer responses to light may have started when parents tucked them in their beds, turned out the lights, and told them it was time to be quiet and go to sleep. Through repetitive conditioning, most individuals' responses to dimly lit rooms is that of relaxation. Lighting sets the mood, tone, and pace of the service encounter. Consumers talk more softly when the lights are low; the service environment is perceived as more formal, and the pace of the encounter slows. In contrast, brightly lit service environments are typically louder, communication exchanges among customers and between customers and employees more frequent, and the overall environment perceived as more informal, exciting, and cheerful.

## Sound Appeals

Sound appeals have three major roles: *mood setter*, *attention grabber*, and *informer*. Proactive methods for purposely inserting sound into the service encounter can be accomplished through the strategic use of music and announcements. Music helps set the mood of the consumer's experience while announcements can be used to grab consumers' attention or inform them of the firm's offerings. Sound can also be a distraction to the consumer's experience; consequently, sound avoidance tactics should also be considered.

*Music*    Studies have shown that background music affects sales in at least two ways. First, background music enhances the customer's perception of the store's atmosphere, which in turn influences the consumer's mood. Second, music often influences the amount of time spent in stores.[24] In one study, firms that played background music in their facilities were thought to care more about their customers.[25]

Studies have shown that in addition to creating a positive attitude, music directly influences consumer buying behavior. Playing faster tempo music increases the pace of consumer transactions. Slowing down the tempo of the music encourages customers to stay longer. Still other studies have indicated that consumers find music distracting when considering high-involvement purchases, but found that listening to music during low-involvement purchases made the choice process easier. Moreover, employees tend to be happier and more productive when listening to background music, which in turn leads to a more positive experience for customers.

Figure 8.7 displays the impact of background music on consumer and provider behavior in a restaurant setting. As can be concluded by the figures, the pace of service

**FIG-8.7 The Impact of Background Music on Restaurant Patrons**

| VARIABLES | SLOW MUSIC | FAST MUSIC |
|---|---|---|
| Service time | 29 min. | 27 min. |
| Customer time at table | 56 min. | 45 min. |
| Customer groups leaving before seated | 10.5% | 12.0% |
| Amount of food purchased | $55.81 | $55.12 |
| Amount of bar purchases | $30.47 | $21.62 |
| Estimated gross margin | $55.82 | $48.62 |

Source: R. E. Milliman, "The Influences of Background Music on the Behavior of Restaurant Patrons," *Journal of Consumer Research*, 13, (September 1986), p. 288; see also R. E. Milliman, "Using Background Music to Affect the Behavior of Supermarket Shoppers," *Journal of Marketing*, (Summer 1982), pp. 86–91.

delivered and the pace of consumer consumption is affected by the tempo of the music. Although the estimated gross margin was higher when the restaurant played slow music, the restaurant should also consider the additional number of tables that would turn if faster-paced music was played throughout the day.

***Announcements***   Another common sound in service establishments is the announcements made over intercom systems, such as to alert restaurant patrons when their tables are ready, to inform airline passengers of their current location, and to page specific employees within the firm. The professionalism with which announcements are made directly influences consumer perceptions of the firm. An example of a bizarre announcement made in a grocery store setting involved a male who requested over the intercom: "Red, what's the price on a box of so and so?" A female then responded for everyone in the store to hear: "Red, my ass!" If this type of announcement had been made in a doctor's or lawyer's office, consider how it would have reflected on the competence of the firm. Speaking of such incidents, now is probably a good time to discuss sound avoidance.

***Sound Avoidance***   When planning the firm's facilities, it is as important to understand the avoidance of undesirable sounds as it is to understand the creation of desirable sounds. Desirable sounds attract customers, and undesirable sounds distract from the firm's overall atmosphere. Within a restaurant setting, sounds that should be strategically masked include those emanating from kitchen, dish room, and restroom areas. Obviously, listening to a toilet flush throughout dinner does little to add to the enjoyment of the customer's dining experience. Other tactics for eliminating unwanted noise include installing durable hallway carpets to eliminate the distracting sounds of clicking heels, strategically placing loud central air conditioning units in areas away from those where the firm conducts the majority of its business, and installing lower ceilings and sound-absorbing partitions so that unwanted sounds can be reduced even further.

## Scent Appeals

The servicescape of the firm can also be strongly affected by scents. When considering scent appeals, as was the case with sound appeals, service managers should pay as much attention to scent avoidance as to scent creation. Stale, musty, foul odors affect everyone and are sure to create negative impressions. Poor ventilation systems that fail to remove odors and poorly located trash receptacles are common contributors to potential odor problems.

On the other hand, pleasurable scents often induce customers to make purchases and can affect the perception of products that don't naturally have their own scent. For example, in one study conducted by Nike, customers examined pairs of gym shoes in two different rooms. One room was completely odor free, and the other was artificially permeated with a floral scent. Results of the study indicated that the floral scent had a direct positive effect on the desirability of the sneakers to 84 percent of the participants.[26] Although this particular example is related to a tangible product, it does seem to indicate that scents do influence consumer perceptions regarding products such as services that do not naturally smell on their own. Experts in scent creation note that a firm should smell like it's supposed to, according to target market expectations. Hospitals should smell clean and antiseptic; and perhaps older, established law firms should even smell a little musty.

### Touch Appeals

The chances of a product's selling increases substantially when the consumer handles the product. But how does one touch an intangible product? Service firms such as mail-order retailers have a tangible component that can be shipped to customers. One of the reasons that nonstore retailing now accounts for 10 percent of all retail sales and is increasing is the liberal return policies that were implemented to increase touch appeals. Spiegel, for example, will send the customer the merchandise for inspection, and, if the customer does not want it, they simply pick up the phone, notify Spiegel, and place the returning product outside the door. Spiegel notifies UPS to pick up the package and pays for all costs associated with the return.

For purer services with a smaller tangible component, touch appeals can be developed through the use of "open houses" where the public has a chance to meet the people providing the service. Shaking hands and engaging in face-to-face communications with potential and existing customers is definitely a form of touch appeal. Clearly, firms engaged in creating touch appeals are perceived as more caring, closer to their customers, and genuinely concerned and interested in their customers' welfare.

### Taste Appeals

Taste appeals, the final sensory cue, are the equivalent of providing the customer with samples. Within the service sector, the usefulness of taste appeals when developing service atmospheres depends upon the tangibility of the service. Service firms such as car washes, dry cleaners, and restaurants may use taste appeals to initially attract customers. While sampling the firm's services, the customer will have the opportunity to observe the firm's physical evidence and form perceptions regarding the firm and its performance capabilities. Consequently, firms that use samples should view this process as an opportunity rather than as catering to a bunch of customers who want something for free. In fact, sampling has become one of the most effective promotional methods, particularly for smaller firms with little brand awareness and minimal promotional budgets.

## Summary

The effective management of physical evidence is particularly important to service firms. Due to the intangibility of services, consumers lack objective sources of information when forming evaluations. As a result, customers often look to the physical evidence that surrounds the service when forming evaluations.

A firm's physical evidence includes, but is not limited to, facility exterior design elements such as the architecture of the building, the firm's sign, parking, landscaping, and the surrounding environment of the firm's location; interior design elements such as size, shape, and colors, the firm's entrance and foyer areas, equipment utilized to operate the business, interior signage, layout, air quality, and temperature; and other physical evidence that forms customer perceptions, including business cards, stationery, billing statements, reports, the appearance of personnel, and brochures.

From a strategic perspective, the importance of managing the firm's physical evidence stems from its ability to: (1) package the service; (2) facilitate the flow of the service delivery process; (3) socialize customers and employees alike in terms of their respective roles, behaviors, and relationships; and (4) differentiate the firm from its competitors.

From a theoretical perspective, the firm's environment influences the behavior of consumers and employees alike, due to the inseparability of many services. When designing the firm's facilities, consideration needs to be given to whether the firm is a remote service, an interpersonal service, or a self-service. The subsequent design should reflect the needs of the parties who are dominating the service production process. Decisions about facility location, layout, product design, and process design in particular may result in different outcomes, depending on whether the customer is actively involved in the production process or not. Figure 8.3 illustrates the servicescape framework that helps us to further understand how individuals are affected by the firm's environmental dimensions, which ultimately leads to approach and/or avoidance behaviors.

Finally, numerous tactical decisions must be made when designing the firm's environment. Individuals base perceptions of the firm's services on sensory cues that exist in the firm's environment. Specific tactical decisions must be made about the creation and sometimes the avoidance of scent appeals, sight appeals, sound appeals, touch appeals, and taste appeals. The design and management of the firm's sensory cues are critical to the firm's long-term success.

## Key Terms

facility exterior, p. 206
facility interior, p. 206
other tangibles, p. 206
socialization, p. 208
environmental psychology, p. 210
stimulus-organism-response (SOR)
    model, p. 210
stimuli, p. 211
organism, p. 211
responses (outcomes), p. 211
pleasure-displeasure, p. 211
arousal-nonarousal, p. 211
dominance-submissiveness, p. 211
approach behaviors, p. 211
avoidance behaviors, p. 211

servicescapes, p. 212
remote services, p. 214
self-services, p. 214
interpersonal services, p. 214
ambient conditions, p. 216
space/function, p. 216
signs, symbols, artifacts, p. 216
holistic environment, p. 216
perceived servicescape, p. 216
economic customers, p. 216
personalized customers, p. 216
apathetic customers, p. 216
ethical customers, p. 216
internal response moderators, p. 217
beliefs, p. 217

categorization, p. 217
symbolic meaning, p. 217
emotional responses, p. 218
physiological responses, p. 218
individual behaviors, p. 218
size/shape/colors, p. 219
harmony, p. 219
contrast/clash, p. 219
hue, p. 221
value, p. 221
shades, p. 221
tints, p. 221
intensity, p. 221

## Review Questions

1. Explain the relationship between physical evidence and formation of customer perceptions and expectations.

2. Discuss the four strategic roles of physical evidence.

3. Discuss the relevance of low-contact versus high-contact service firms with respect to location, layout, product design, and process design decisions.

4. How should the servicescape of a firm that targets ethical shoppers be designed?

5. Discuss how internal response moderators influence the customer's response to the servicescape.

6. Discuss the three types of internal responses to the firm's environment.

7. Describe the impact of music on customer and employee behavior?

8. Develop strategies for a service firm that would enhance the firm's touch and taste appeals.

9. Discuss the use of employee uniforms as physical evidence as they relate to the unique service characteristic of heterogeneity.

10. Go to www.colorquiz.com and complete the quiz. Do you agree or disagree with your psychographic profile that was generated based on your color selections?

## Notes

1. Kristen Anderson and Ron Zemke, *Delivering Knock Your Socks Off Service* (New York: AMACOM, 1991), pp. 27–30.

2. Mary Jo Bitner, "Servicescapes: The Impact of Physical Surroundings on Customers and Employees," *Journal of Marketing* 56 (April 1992), pp. 57–71.

3. Ibid.

4. **www.rainforestcafe.com**, accessed 7 October, 2009.

5. Laurence Frost, "Biggest Bird Takes to the Sky: Airbus A380 Makes Aviation History with Maiden Flights," *The Coloradoan*, (Thursday, April 28, 2005).

6. Edgar Schein, "Organizational Socialization and the Profession of Management," *Industrial Management Review* 9 (Winter 1968), pp. 1–16.

7. Michael R. Solomon, "Packaging the Service Provider," Christopher H. Lovelock, *Managing Services*

*Marketing, Operations, and Human Resources* (Englewood Cliffs, NJ: Prentice-Hall, 1988), pp. 318–324.

8. Ibid.

9. **http://www.travelandleisure.com/blogs/carry-on/ 2009/9/1/westins-heavenly-bed-on-sale**, accessed 7 October, 2009; Matthew Creamer, "Marriott to Replace 628,000 Hotel Beds," **www.usatoday.com**, accessed 2 May 2005; "Waking Up to the Marketing Potential of a Good Night's Sleep," *Advertising Age*, 76, 16, (April 18, 2005), p. 16.

10. Michael R. Solomon, "Packaging the Service Provider," Christopher H. Lovelock, *Managing Services Marketing, Operations, and Human Resources* (Englewood Cliffs, NJ: Prentice-Hall, 1988), pp. 318–324.

11. Avijit Ghosh, *Retail Management*, 2nd ed. (Fort Worth, TX: The Dryden Press, 1994), pp. 522–523.

12. Ibid.

13. Valerie A. Zeithaml and Mary Jo Bitner, *Services Marketing* (New York: McGraw Hill, 1996), p. 528.

14. Richard B. Chase, "Where Does the Customer Fit in a Service Operation?" *Harvard Business Review* (November-December 1978), pp. 137–142.

15. Valerie A. Zeithaml and Mary Jo Bitner, *Services Marketing* (New York: McGraw Hill, 1996), p. 531.

16. **http://www.msnbc.msn.com/id/29474213/**, accessed 7 October, 2009.

17. Valerie A. Zeithaml and Mary Jo Bitner, *Services Marketing* (New York: McGraw Hill, 1996), p. 531.

18. Philip Kotler, "Atmospherics as a Marketing Tool," *Journal of Retailing*, (Winter 1973–1974), p. 48.

19. Dale M. Lewison, *Retailing*, 4th ed. (New York: MacMillan, 1991), pp. 273–283.

20. Ibid.

21. Joseph Weber, "Personal Banking for the Merely Rich," *Business Week*, (May 3, 2004), Issue 3881, 121–123.

22. Kenneth H. Mills and Judith E. Paul, *Applied Visual Merchandising* (Englewood Cliffs, NJ: Prentice-Hall, 1982), p. 47.

23. Kenneth H. Mills and Judith E. Paul, *Create Distinctive Displays* (Englewood Cliffs, NJ: Prentice-Hall, 1974), p. 61.

24. J. Barry Mason, Morris L. Mayer, and J. B. Wilkinson, *Modern Retailing: Theory and Practice*, 6th ed. (Homewood, IL: Irwin, 1993), pp. 642, 643.

25. Ronald E. Milliman, "Using Background Music to Affect the Behavior of Supermarket Shoppers," *Journal of Marketing*, 46, 3, (Summer 1982), pp. 86–91; see also Douglas K. Hawse and Hugh McGinley, "Music for the Eyes, Color for the Ears: An Overview," in *Proceedings of the Society for Consumer Psychology*, David W. Schumann, ed. (Washington, DC: Society for Consumer Psychology, 1988), pp. 145–52.

26. J. Barry Mason, Morris L. Mayer, and Hazel F. Ezell, *Retailing*, 5th ed. (Homewood, IL: Irwin), 1994.

# The Service Is All Part of the CRAIC

Consumers understand brands and know what to expect in themed bars, restaurants, cafe's and adventure playgrounds. They do this by looking at the name and conjuring up the images and associations that the name implies. Similarly the retail outlet's physical evidence or store front can also give clues as to the type of experience the consumer will receive when they step inside. Themed pubs and bars have been in the marketplace for many years and the name, logo and tangible elements clearly let customers know what they can expect. The pub chain 'Walkabout' gives the impression of a laid-back Australian culture. The furnishings are bare and 'sun-bleached' and there are crocodiles hanging from the ceiling and posters alerting us to 'kangaroos crossing' - all the light-hearted fun of an Australian themed bar.

Irish bars are another theme that can be seen in over 53 countries worldwide (Irish Pub Concept 2008). Kitty O'Shea's Paris is France's oldest and most treasured Irish bar. It has a good location at 10 rue des Capucines in the second Arrondissement, which is in the centre of Paris. They say their success is because of their authentic Irish decor and friendly Irish bar staff (**http://kittyosheas.com/kitty_paris.asp**). If you are in Tenerife you could visit the Irish Fiddler and enjoy music 'live' every night of the week. Or call into Murphy's in Japan for Guinness Beef Stew with Bread (winter only!) (**http://en.misawairishpub .com/sb.cgi?cid=7**).

The reason they are the most popular of branded themed bars is not because of the decor or Irish stew - it is because of the Craic. Craic is fun, happiness, laughter, drinking, singing, enjoyment or a combination of some or all of them. And the Irish know how to throw a good party. So the Craic is the intangible experience that many people want from a night out in an Irish bar.

O'Neills is a chain of Irish-themed bars owned by Mitchell and Butlers. They are described as the 'largest Irish bar brand in the world'. And they claim to be the 'heart and soul of the high street' (Mitchell and Butlers, 2008). It is also known that the Irish are friendly, warm-hearted and work hard. Therefore, the service provided in Irish-themed bars must match that of a 'true' Irish bartender who will know your name and choice of drink by the end of your visit.

Sources:

1. Frow, P. and Payne, A. (2007] 'Towards the 'perfect' customer experience', *Brand Management* 15(2): 80-101.

2. Mitchell & Butlers (2008] 'Business Navigator' **http://vvww.mbplc.com/managed_content/components/ navigator/business_nonflash.cfm?section=pubs&pagetype=about&company=oneills**, accessed 20 August, 2008.

3. **www.Guinness-storehouse.com**.

4. **http://kittyosheas.com/kitty_paris.asp**.

5. **http://en.misawairishpub.com/sb.cgi?cid=7**.

Many Irish bars also have the support of two of the major Irish stout brands - Guinness and Murphy's - which has certainly helped promote and sustain Irish theme bars. In fact, the Guinness heritage began with Arthur Guinness brewing dark English beer, porter, as far back as the 1770s. Arthur Guinness's grandson Benjamin took over the family business and introduced the first trademark label for Guinness stout. Guinness, the brand, therefore came into force in 1862 and by the end of the nineteenth century it was being sold across the world. In fact by the end of the twentieth century Guinness was *brewed* in 40 countries such as Nigeria (1962), Cameroon (1970) and Ghana (1971). And whilst Guinness always sells well in Irish bars such as Kitty 0'Sheas, it is actually sold in over 150 countries across the globe (**www.Guinness-storehouse.com**).

Naturally Guinness is very proud of their stout and they put their heart and soul into each of the 10 million glasses of Guinness that are sold every day throughout the world. They care so much for the brand's reputation, its production quality and how it is delivered to the customer that they set up a team of people to ensure that each pint of Guinness is delivered perfectly every time - in every country! Managing the service delivery of Guinness may not seem such a difficult thing to do - but if you were tasked to ensure that every pub, restaurant or hotel worldwide served a perfect pint consistently, I am sure you would agree this is not an easy task.

The 'Perfect Pint Team' was formed to try to ensure that Guinness reached the lips of its consumers perfectly every time they had a drink, wherever they were drinking it. The Perfect Pint Team were a cross-functional team of people who carefully studied the many different 'touch points' of Guinness to ensure that each intermediary that served Guinness understood their role in pouring the perfect pint. One of the main groups of intermediaries were landlords of pubs and bars - be they Irish bars, traditional English pubs or up-scale concept bars. Landlords of pubs and bars were advised that the service quality they provided was vital in serving the perfect pint using a method known as the 'two-part pour'. Landlords were given recognition, therefore, for their important role through training and promotional material. Training materials came via booklets, leaflets and in some cases on-site training. Steve Kenyon and his staff at O'Niells Irish Bar in Huddersfield, West Yorkshire were filmed for a training video of the 'two part pour', how to put an Irish Shamrock in the head of the pint of Guinness, why it takes 117 seconds to pour a pint of Guinness and how to present the 'perfect pint' to the customer. The training video was sent to pubs and bars in Europe that served Guinness. This type of investment in service quality ensured that landlords felt proud of the drink that they were serving to their customers. Within the trade Guinness became sought after and 'famous' because of the investment made in the 'two-part pour system'. However, it was important that customers were advised of the two-part pour system. To advise the customer, extensive above- and below-the-line advertising campaigns were launched to advise customers to be patient whilst waiting for their perfect pint. An advertising slogan created was 'Good things come to those who wait'. The slogan suggests that the waiting time creates anticipation which in turn will make the customer enjoy the product even more once they receive it. The waiting, anticipation and celebration of receiving the 'perfect pint' was and still is shown in TV advertising campaigns. For example, at the end of the 1990s a TV advertising campaign included a man dancing crazily whilst waiting for his perfect pint. The same theme of patience and anticipation is used in the current TV advertisement - The Andean Domino Race. The current advertisement shows a fantastic community spirit where a whole town has collected household items to create a domino race which culminates in the 'perfect pint', made out of 10,000 books. The advertisement suggests that consumers can become emotionally involved in the creation of their perfect pint. Frow and Payne (2007) discovered in their research regarding the 'perfect customer experience' that Guinness's success was all down to the commitment from their intermediaries, i.e. landlords. Londlords the worldover committed themselves to the two-part pour method. So next time you see a Guinness being served, check for the quality of service provided by the intermediaries wherever you are in the world!

## Discussion Questions

1. How and why are intermediary landlords important to Guinness's success?
2. What marketing techniques were used to ensure that landlords were consistent in the service quality they provided to the customer?
3. How was the customer involved in understanding the new service delivery of their pint of Guinness?
4. Consider you are the Marketing Manager for Guinness and you were tasked with ensuring that service quality is upheld at a very large sporting event where Guinness is sponsoring the event. How would you ensure that temporary staff would uphold the quality of the brand?
5. Choose a service organization of your choice and discuss whether the internal communications that Guinness provided for its intermediaries would be sufficient to provide marketing initiatives to service personnel.

## CHAPTER 9

# People as Strategy: Managing Service Personnel

## CHAPTER OBJECTIVES

After reading this chapter, you should be able to:

- Understand the importance of customer facing employees.

- Understand the inherent stresses and strains faced by the typical service employee.

- Define the role that a service employee has to play based upon the service strategy.

- Understand how that role definition can be used to recruit the most appropriate service team.

- Understand how the role definition is at the center and drives all HR systems in a service business.

- Understand the role of management in supporting the "climate for service."

The purpose of this chapter is to help you understand the many challenges associated with managing employees within the service experience. Service businesses, by their very definition, are people businesses, with very few exceptions, and require talented managers who can navigate the thin line between the needs of the organization, its employees, and its customers.

Chris Mueller/Redux

### WEGMANS: THE BEST COMPANY TO WORK FOR IN AMERICA!

Every year *Fortune Magazine* publishes its highly anticipated list of "The 100 Best Companies to Work For." The winner for 2005 may surprise you. It was not a dominant healthcare provider, a giant auto manufacturer, or the world's largest retailer—it was a grocery store! Wegmans—the best company to work for in America!

Who or what is a Wegmans? Wegmans is a privately held supermarket chain that employs over 30,000 employees in its 67 stores located in New York, Pennsylvania, New Jersey and Virginia. Reported revenues for 2004 were $3.4 billion. Newer Wegmans' stores boast 130,000 square feet, which makes Wegmans three times larger than the size of a typical supermarket. Wegmans' operating margins are double what the "big four" (Albertson's, Kroger, Safeway, and Ahold USA) earn, and sales per square foot are 50 percent higher than industry averages.

One of the key secrets to Wegmans' success has been its recognition that the grocery store of tomorrow must become more than just a supermarket and it cannot compete solely on price. The biggest challenge for supermarkets today is that there is no compelling reason to shop there anymore. Grocery stores are viewed as commodities—84 percent of customers believe that traditional grocers are all pretty much the same. As a result, nontraditional grocers such as club stores (Sam's) and discounters (Walmart and Kmart) have been able to gain a stronghold in the market. In 2003, nontraditional grocers controlled 31.3 percent of the grocery market. According to industry experts, that number is expected to grow to nearly 40 percent by 2008. Traditional grocers have responded to the onslaught by cutting prices, which have further lowered already miniscule margins. Between 1999 and 2004, the four largest U.S. grocery chains (Albertson's, Kroger, Safeway, and Ahold USA) reported shareholder returns ranging from -49 percent percent to -78 percent. Labor unrest for several of these chains poses future challenges.

Wegmans has embraced the idea that, in order to compete effectively with the mass merchandisers of the world, grocery shopping should become a compelling experience. Employee comments reflect this notion: "We are taking customers to a place they have not been before." "Going there is not just shopping, it's an event." Creating the Wegman experience has been the result of a keen combination of goods and services and hiring and retaining great personnel. Each Wegman store boasts a huge selection of food products, including amazing assortments of beautifully displayed produce, fresh-baked goods, and other specialty items such as a selection of over 500 cheeses. Other offerings within Wegmans include a child play center, a dry cleaner, a photo lab, a florist, a wine shop, a pharmacy, and a bookstore.

In addition to its compelling array of goods and services, much of the Wegmans experience is derived from its employees and its customers. Of the nearly 7,000 letters the company received in 2004, almost half were requests by customers for Wegmans to open a new location in their town. Wegmans' customers are passionate about their grocery store, which is good news for Wegmans. Customers who are emotionally connected to their grocery stores spend on average 46 percent more than shoppers who are satisfied but do not share a bond with their local supermarket.

Wegmans' relationship with its employees is also legendary. Over the past 20 years, Wegmans has invested nearly $54 million in college scholarships to more than 17,500 full-time and part-time employees. The company promotes from within, and new stores are populated by the best and brightest of existing employees. In addition, Wegmans listens to its employees. Wegmans' Chief of Operations half jokingly comments: "We're a $3 billion company run by 16-year-old cashiers." Hourly wages and annual salaries are at the high end of the market. Wegmans' labor costs run approximately 16 percent of sales compared to the industry average of 12 percent; however, Wegmans' full-time employee turnover rate is 6 percent compared to the industry average of 19 percent. Moreover, nearly 6,000 Wegman employees have 10 years or more service with the firm. According to Chairman Robert Wegman: "I have never given away more than I got back." Clearly, Wegmans provides a tremendous example of how a company can excel through superior operations, legendary employee relations, and great customer service.

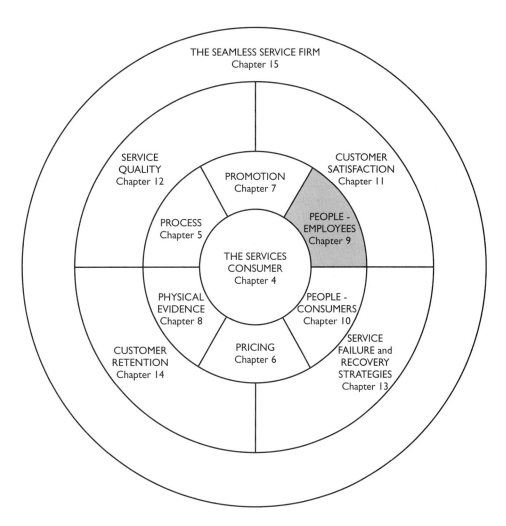

## Introduction

Employee satisfaction and customer satisfaction are clearly related. Let's say it again another way...if you want to satisfy your customers, employee satisfaction is critical! The public face of a service firm is its contact personnel. Part factory workers, part administrators, part servants, service personnel often perform a complex and difficult job.[1] Despite their importance and the complexity of their activities, service personnel are often the lowest paid and least respected individuals in most companies, and often in society. For example, in the healthcare community, the individuals most responsible for patient care and patient perceptions of service quality received are ... the nurses. Who are the lowest paid and least respected individuals in the health care community? The nurses. In the education system, who is most responsible for the day-to-day education of and interaction with students? The classroom teachers. Who in the education system are the least paid and least respected individuals? The classroom teachers. The list goes on and on. Consider any service industry, and look to the individuals who are the most responsible for customer interactions and customer perceptions of quality delivered, and you will most likely see the lowest paid and least respected individuals in the company. It makes no sense!

The quote from Isadore Sharp and the Wegmans' case make the counter argument for investing in service personnel. Their approach can be expressed as *the service-profit chain* shown in Figure 9.1.[2]

**FIG-9.1** The Service-Profit Chain.

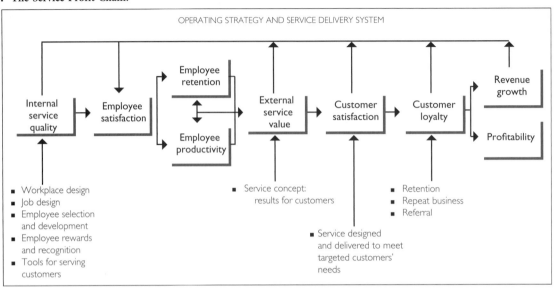

Source: James L. Heskett, Thomas O. Jones, Gary W. Loveman, W. Earl Sasser, Jr., and Leonard A. Schlesinger, "Putting the Service-Profit Chain to Work," *Harvard Business Review* (March–April 1994), 164–174. Reprinted by permission of *Harvard Business Review*. Copyright © 1994 by the President and Fellows of Harvard College.

The links in the chain reveal that employee satisfaction and customer satisfaction are directly proportional. Satisfied employees remain with the firm and improve their individual productivity. Hence employee satisfaction is linked with increases in the firm's overall productivity and decreases in recruitment and training costs. The scale of the recruitment and training costs can be huge for many service businesses. For example, in one year, 119,000 sales jobs turned over within the retail network of the Sears Merchandise Group. The cost of hiring and training each new sales assistant was $900, or more than $110 million in total, a sum that represented 17 percent of Sears' income in that year.[3]

Employee attitudes and beliefs about the organization are often reflected in their behaviors. Because service firms often involve the customer as a co-producer, the effects of human resource practices and policies as well as the organization's climate are visible to customers. A large number of studies show that the employees' perception of the service climate is directly related to the customers' perception of service quality[4].

Customer satisfaction is directly related to customer loyalty, which is demonstrated through repeat purchases and positive word-of-mouth referrals to other customers. The net effects of customer retention are increased revenues and profitability for the firm. For example, various studies have looked at the cost of acquiring new customers versus the cost of retaining an existing one. The ratio quoted by the U.S. Office of Consumer Affairs was five times, but other authors have cited numbers as high as eight times.[5]

Simultaneously, employees are also rewarded for their efforts. The outcomes associated with employee satisfaction—external service values, customer satisfaction, customer loyalty, revenue growth, and increased profitability—reinforce the company's commitment to continually improve internal service quality. As the recipients of internal quality improvements and positive customer responses, employees directly experience the fruits of their efforts. Employee satisfaction is subsequently reinforced, maintaining the integrity of the service-profit chain.

The purpose of this chapter is to focus on the first half of the service-profit chain relating to the employee. First, we will discuss the importance of the front-line service provider in generating a differentiated product and delivering it to satisfied customers. Next, we will look at the stresses and strains inherent in the service provider role and why it requires careful management. We go on to focus on how to create a service climate that will reinforce employees' natural desire to give good service. To do this the tools of HR management need to be integrated around a clear definition of the specific service provider role the firm has chosen. Wegmans has chosen to differentiate itself with excellent customer service. Their competitors have chosen a more industrialized model which, in the extreme, replaces the store team with automated self-service check out. Clearly the HR processes have to be different.

## The Importance of Service Personnel

Today, over 40 percent of the U.S. workforce is employed in selling food; selling merchandise in retail stores; performing clerical work in service industries; cleaning hospitals, schools, and offices; or providing some other form of personal service. These are occupations that accounted for most of the U.S. job growth over the last two decades. Yet, for the most part, these jobs are poorly paid, lead nowhere, and provide little, if anything, in the way of health, pension, and other benefits and other benefits (see Figure 9.2).[6] It's no wonder why *Business Week* recently investigated the question…"Why Service Stinks?"[7]

Strategically, service personnel are an important source of product differentiation. It is often challenging for a service organization to differentiate itself from other similar organizations in the benefit bundle it offers or its delivery system. For example, one extreme

Richard Hutchings/PhotoEdit

Employee satisfaction is the key to customer satisfaction. Nothing will drive customers away faster than employees who are unhappy with their job.

**FIG·9.2** Temp Worker
Facts (U.S.)

- Temps earn an average 40 percent less per hour than full-time workers.
- 55 percent do not have health insurance.
- 80 percent work 35 hours a week.
- 25 percent are under age 25.
- 53 percent are women; in the total workforce, 47 percent are women.
- 60 percent of the women have children under 18.
- 22 percent of the temp workforce is African-American; 11 percent of the total workforce is African-American.

Source: "Temporary workers getting short shrift," *USA Today*, (April 11, 1997), p. B1.

view is that many airlines offer similar bundles of benefits and fly the same types of aircraft from the same airports to the same destinations. Their only hope of a competitive advantage is, therefore, from the service level—the way things are done. Some of this differentiation can come from staffing levels or the physical systems designed to support the staff. Often, however, the deciding factor that distinguishes one airline from another is the attitude of the service providers.[8] Singapore Airlines, for example, enjoys an excellent reputation due, in large part, to the beauty, grace, and service orientation of its flight attendants. Other firms that hold a differential advantage over competitors based on personnel include the Ritz Carlton, IBM, and Disney.[9]

It often seems, however, that front-line personnel, customers, and the service firm itself are in pursuit of different goals representing the classic confrontation between marketing, human resources, and operations. Inevitably, clashes occur that have profound long-term effects on how customers view the organization and how the service providers view customers in subsequent transactions. It is a self-perpetuating nightmare. Cynical service providers turn their clientele into "customers from hell," and nightmarish customers return the favor by eventually wearing down even the best service providers.[10]

In the book *At America's Service*, service personnel behaviors that irk customers the most mirrored similar themes across different industries and organizations. These unsavory behaviors have been classified into seven categories including:

1. Apathy: What comedian George Carlin refers to as DILLIGAD—Do I look like I give a damn?
2. Brush-off: Attempts to get rid of the customer by dismissing the customer completely…the "I want you to go away" syndrome.
3. Coldness: Indifferent service providers who could not care less what the customer really wants.
4. Condescension: The "you are the client/patient, so you must be stupid" approach.
5. Robotism: Where the customers are treated simply as inputs into a system that must be processed.
6. Rulebook: Providers who live by the rules of the organization even when those rules do not make good sense.
7. Runaround: Passing the customer off to another provider, who will simply pass them off to yet another provider.

The quality of service offered by Wegmans and the kind of behaviors described here seem totally incompatible. Clearly the answer is the management. Wegmans has created a management system and climate that encourages its employees to support its differentiated market position. To understand how they have achieved this, it is first important to understand that the front-line service role is not an easy one.

# The Natural Stresses & Strains on Contact Service Personnel

**boundary-spanning roles** The various parts played by contact personnel who perform dual functions of interacting with the firm's external environment and internal organization.

Before discussing how to manage service personnel it is important to understand that by the very nature of the job, being a contact service person is not easy. They are what are called **boundary-spanners**.[11] They sit on the boundary of the organization, interacting both with a firm's external environment, particularly its customers, and its internal organization and structure. They represent the organization and are required to collect the information from the customer needed to perform the service. They are part of the production process but also represent the customer.

**subordinate service roles** The jobs within service organizations where the customer's decisions are entirely discretionary such as waitresses, porters, etc.

Individuals who occupy boundary-spanning roles can be classified along a continuum that ranges from **subordinate service roles** to professional service roles[12]. The subordinate roles are usually subordinate to both the organization and the customer. They are the lowest of the low within the organizational hierarchy. They are also treated as subordinate by customers, often reinforced by signs prominently on display reading "the customer is always right".[13]

**person/role conflict** A bad fit between an individual's self-perception and the specific role the person must play in an organization.

Such boundary spanning roles cause different kinds of stress and strains on the individual. The role they called upon to play may be in conflict with the individual's self perception (**person/role conflict**). Boundary-spanning personnel often are called upon to suppress their personal feelings and are asked to smile and be helpful while feeling miserable and aggressive. This has been termed emotional labor and can certainly cause stresses on an individual.

**organization/client conflicts** Disagreements that arise when a customer requests services that violate the rules of the organization.

More problematic yet are the **conflicts between organization and client**. A customer asks for an extra bread roll but company policy is only one per guest. This is often compounded by the application of common sense ("there are no more guests and the bread will go to waste!"). This is often a fight between organizational efficiency and customer satisfaction, with the contact person in the middle. The bread roll problem appears simple, but what if a bus passenger asks the bus driver to leave the established route and drop them off at home?[14]

The reaction to this kind of conflict is often related to how subordinate the role is within the organization. A low level subordinate service role and a lack of understanding of why the rules were written will often mean the contact person sides with the customer against the organization. In contrast, professional service personnel with their higher

AP Photo/Dima Gavrysh

One of the main sources of conflict in service jobs is person/role conflict. Not everyone can do this job well and not everyone would want to do it! The bottom-line is finding the right fit—the right person for the right job.

status and clearer understanding of the purpose of specific rules and regulations are more able to control what happens.

**inter-client conflicts**
Disagreements between clients that arise because of the number of clients who influence one another's experience.

**Conflicts between clients** arise because many service delivery systems have multiple clients who influence one another's experiences. Because different clients are likely to have different needs, they tend to have completely different scripts for themselves, the contact personnel, and other customers. When customers do conflict, it is usually the boundary-spanning personnel who are asked to resolve the confrontation.

For example, it is the waiter who is generally requested to ask another diner not to smoke in a nonsmoking section. Attempts to satisfy all of the clients all of the time can escalate the conflict or bring the boundary-spanning personnel into the battle. For example, a restaurant customer requesting speedy service and receiving it can cause complaints from other tables about the inequitable levels of service.

Employee reaction and effectiveness in resolving inter-client conflicts appear to be once again related to the level of the employee's role within the organization. Employees in subordinate roles start from the weakest position since they have low status with clients. Clients may simply disregard responses made by subordinate service providers. Professionals may face the same problems; for example, consider the patient in the hospital waiting room, demanding preferential treatment. In a case such as this, however, the professional can invoke his or her status and expertise to resolve the situation.

## Coping Strategies and Implications for Customers

The consequences of role conflict and stress produce dissatisfaction, frustration, and turnover intention in personnel. It may even result in service sabotage. When faced with potential conflict and stress in their jobs, employees attempt a variety of strategies to shield themselves. These manifest themselves as the seven unsavory behaviors described in *At America's Service*. The simplest way of avoiding conflict is to avoid the customers. This is exemplified by the waiter who refuses to notice a customer who wishes to place an order. This allows the employee to increase his or her personal sense of control over the encounter. It would be perceived as "apathy," "brush-off," "coldness," or even "DILLIGAD." An alternative approach is to move into a people-processing mode,[15] where customers are treated as inanimate objects to be processed rather than as individuals. This would be perceived as "roboticism" or "rulebook." This reduces the requirement of the boundary-spanning personnel to associate or empathize with an individual and hence become conflicted.

Boundary-spanning personnel also employ other strategies to maintain a sense of control of the encounter. Physical symbols and furniture are often used to boost the employee's status and, hence, his or her sense of control.[16] Hiding behind a desk is one way of coping with the conflict.

**service sabotage**
Willful and malicious acts by service providers designed to ruin the service.

In the extreme case, the role conflict and ambiguity can lead to acts of **service sabotage**[17]. These acts serve to regain control, or a sense of it, for the service provider. In some cases such sabotage is kept private – smaller portions or bad beer for difficult customers. In other cases it manifests in more public ways, with whole teams of service providers playing games and tricks on each other, through the customers or on customers directly. Clearly this represents a breakdown in the climate for service, but it is much more common than we think. A survey of 182 first line service personnel found that 90 percent accepted behavior with malicious intent to reduce or spoil service.

An alternative strategy employees use to reduce organization/client conflict is to side completely with the customer. When forced to obey a rule with which they disagree, boundary-spanning personnel will proceed to list for the customer all the other things about the organization with which they disagree. In this way, employees attempt to reduce stress by seeking sympathy from the customer.

### The Direct Impact of Marketing on Service Providers' Stresses and Strains.

Marketing can either cause or reduce role stress. Marketing can, without making major strategic changes, help to reduce service employee stress levels, and it's in marketing's best interest to do so. Clearly, unhappy, frustrated, and disagreeing contact personnel are visible to customers and will ultimately affect consumer perceptions of service quality. Customers obviously do not like being ignored by waiters or treated as if they were inanimate objects. If contact personnel attempt to maximize their sense of control over their encounters, it will most likely be at the expense of the amount of control felt by customers. In addition, although customers may sympathize with a service provider's explanation that the organization stops them from providing excellent service, customers will still develop negative perceptions about the organization.

***Reducing Person/Role Conflicts***   Marketing can reduce the conflict between the individual and the assigned role by simply being sensitive and actively seeking input from employees about the issue. A promotional gimmick dreamed up at the head office may look great on paper. For example, a medieval theme day in the hotel almost certainly will have great public relations value, but how will the staff feel when they are called upon to wear strange and awkward (not to mention uncomfortable) costumes? How will these costumes affect the employees' relationships with customers during the service encounter?

Marketing may recommend a change in operating procedure in order to improve the quality of service. However, it is important to ensure that service providers are well trained in the new script. If they are not, they may well become extremely embarrassed in the presence of customers. This situation can be aggravated if the new service is advertised in such a way that the customers are more aware of the new script than the staff.

***Reducing Organization/Client Conflicts***   Similarly, marketing can help reduce conflicts between the organization and its clients. It is crucial, for example, that customer expectations be consistent with the capabilities of the service system. Customers should not ask for services the system cannot provide. Advertising is one of the main causes of inflated expectations, as the temptation is to exaggerate claims in advertising to maximize the impact. Consider, for example, the advertisement that depicted a flight attendant reading a young child a story while the plane was in flight. This was designed to show what a friendly and caring airline they really were. A number of passengers took the advertisement literally, either because they believed it or because they could not resist the temptation, and called upon the flight attendants to read stories to their children. The result was conflict for the cabin crew and far from the caring image the ad was designed to portray.

***Reducing Inter-client Conflicts***   Conflicts between clients can be avoided if the clients are relatively homogeneous in their expectations. Due to the inseparability of services, customers often share their service experiences with other customers. Hence, successful service firms recognize the importance of effective segmentation, which minimizes the chances that two or more divergent groups will share the encounter simultaneously. As long as all the clients share the same script and expect the same standard of service, the chances of inter-client conflicts are much reduced.

## Unleashing Service with the Right Climate

Employees who chose to a take a job as a front-line service provider do not start with the intention of giving bad service. There is a lot of evidence to suggest that, given a free choice, individuals migrate to jobs that will motivate them. People are not motivated to give bad service. The subordinate service provider role does have inherent conflicts within it, but there is no reason that they cannot be resolved.

Service personnel will, however, be influenced by their shared perception of the "practices, procedures and kinds of behaviors that get reward." That shared perception is the "climate" of the organization. The important thing is to create a climate that is supportive of giving good service. Often, however, front-line customer contact jobs are designed to be as simple and narrow as possible so that they can be filled by anyone—in other words, "idiot-proof" jobs. Employers place few demands on employees, selection criteria are minimal, and wages are low.

The result is that fewer and less knowledgeable contact personnel are available, and hence, the customer gets less and lower quality help. Customers vent their feelings of impatience and dissatisfaction on the staff, which, in turn, de-motivates the employees, especially the most conscientious ones, since they are already aware of the poor service they are being forced to give. The best staff leave and are replaced with poorly trained recruits—and the cycle continues.

By comparison when service commitment is high, the service firm displays a passion for doing things directly related to the provision of service. Consider for example, employee comments from The Container Store, recently chosen as the #1 Best Place to Work by *Fortune* magazine.[18]

- *"I love this company because 'Customer Service is #1'!!...All customers can use our phones at any time."*
- *"We grew up with 'family values' and it's rare to find a company with the same values, philosophy, and foundation principles. Going to work is like going to a family reunion everyday."*
- *"Working for this company has made me a better person and certainly made the world a better, more organized place."*
- *"I miss everyone when I go on vacation."*
- *"I will never leave."*

Employees speak often, and favorably, about the service delivery process and the product offered to consumers, as well as about the concern for and/or responsiveness of the firm to customer opinions.

## Creating a Climate for Service

**work facilitation** The provision of the basic infrastructure and technology to enable service providers to deliver the desired service.

**interdepartmental service support:** The support provided by other departments in the service organization that allow a service provider to do their job.

There are three core drivers to create a climate for service: **work facilitation**, **interdepartmental support**, and human resource practices, all of which must minimize the role stress and ambiguity[19]. The first two are the basic service foundations that have to be in place. Service personnel have to be given the capability to deliver good service should they want to. The equipment, processes and, increasingly, the information technology have to be available to do the job (work facilitation). A check-in agent for an airline needs the boarding systems and the boarding card reader to be working. If they do not, the service suffers anyway, but the second order effect is that the provider takes the complaints, becomes de-motivated, and the climate for service suffers. No service employee exists in isolation but they are all dependent on the rest of the service organization. The check-in team can only give service if the plane is available, serviced, fuelled, and crewed. Each other department, flight crew, maintenance, and cabin crew, is critical to the service that the check-in team can provide.

Having laid the foundations for an employee to successfully execute his or her job, the climate can be built in the form of service-orientated HR policies and practices designed to fit the service strategy. If what people get rewarded for is inconsistent with what the managers praise them for, there will be ambiguity and stress. If the avowed strategy is "superior quality" but internal performance measures are all based on cost management then it is unlikely that the right climate will ensue.

Services human resources practices can be broken down into the broad categories shown in Figure 9.3, **the Service HR Wheel**. At the center of the wheel are the objectives for the role. We must first ask what are the role and the climate trying to achieve. Consider the Wegmans case. The company's strategy is based on the proposition that most customers see grocery stores as a commodity. (*"Grocery stores are viewed as commodities – 84 percent of customers believe that traditional grocers are pretty much the same"*). The service provider roles were designed to create a differential advantage in a commoditized world.

Consider, however, two alternative approaches to defining the role of the service provider in the same industry: FedEx and UPS. FedEx was the first service organization to win the coveted Malcolm Baldrige National Quality Award. Behind the blue, white, and red planes and uniforms are self-managed work teams, garnishing plans, and empowered employees seemingly concerned with providing flexible and creative service to customers with varying needs. In contrast, at UPS, we find turned-on people and profits, but we do not find the same levels of empowerment. Instead we find controls, rules, a detailed

**the service HR wheel**
The HR functions that together support the creation of a climate for service.

**FIG-9.3** The Services HR wheel

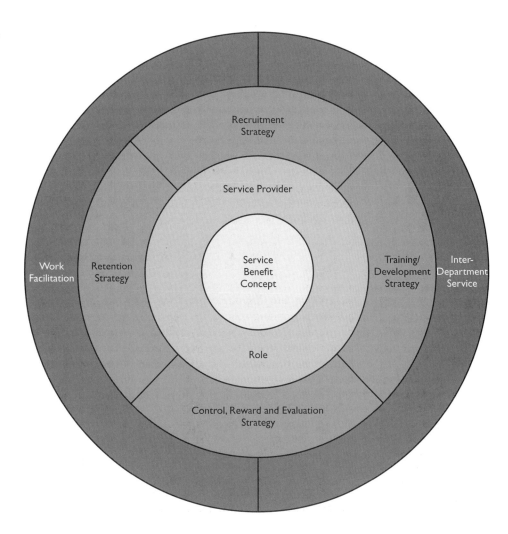

**climate for service**
The shared perception of the service practices, procedures and kind of behaviors that get reward.

union contract, and carefully studied work methods. UPS makes no promises that its employees will bend over backward to meet individual customer needs. However, what we do find are rigid operational guidelines, which help guarantee the customer reliable, low-cost service.[20] Within both organizations there are motivated employees, doing their best to serve their customers and creating a "**climate for service**" perceived and appreciated by the customer.

To set the objectives for the human resources practices, we must therefore define the role of the service providers in terms of the behaviors that should be displayed. A definition of that role starts with the service strategy. Everything begins with the marketing strategy and the benefit concept the organization has chosen as its competitive edge. This determines the system and technology created to support the concept. The technology and the benefit concept define the role of the provider.

A branded service organization that guarantees consistency of product and service across multiple locations will build systems and structure accordingly. McDonald's restaurants' processes and systems are built to standardize service delivery. Their pricing and economics determine the type and cost of the service provider. The behaviors required by the role can be derived and are tightly constrained. Overly friendly staff who talk to the customers and customize the orders are incompatible with the consistency and speed promised. The role of the service provider is part of a tightly designed formula.

As the UPS and FedEx story shows, even within the same industry, different strategies can lead to different solutions. For another example, consider the hotel industry and the potential role definitions for service providers. The industry has segmented itself along the star rating system. Customers have come to expect a certain level of perceived service from a three-star hotel and a different one from a one- or five-star hotel. Equally, customers expect the prices to vary accordingly. The service provider role in a five-star hotel will be defined very differently from a lower level hotel. However at any level of hotel the service strategy chosen by the particular firm can create the same kind of differences as between UPS and FedEx.

At the heart of the services HR wheel is the role that the service provider has to play. This is the set of behaviors that the provider must display, backed up with the necessary skills. Provided the definition is correct, there should be no ambiguity for the employees about what is expected. Their managers and senior managers should all be aligned with their role since it is based on the agreed strategy. Once the role has been defined, it drives the next layer of the wheel: recruiting the right people; developing competent service employees; controlling, rewarding and evaluating service employees; and retaining service employees.

***Recruiting the Right People***　Not everyone is suited to the stress and strains of a boundary-spanning role. Some people, however, thrive on the day-to-day contact and the instant feedback that this brings. Any recruitment strategy should be designed to find the right people for the role as defined. Consider the Australian firm, Krispy Kreme selling their own brand of cream doughnut internationally. In the early days in Australia, the HR team was under pressure to identify new staff who could work within a growing and changing environment while maintaining the company standard in delivering constant quality service across all stores.[21]

They used psychometric tests supplied by the SHL Group, including their customer service questionnaire, followed by an assessment center, which involved candidates participating in simulation exercises. Such assessment approaches are used by blue chip service businesses across the world. Care has to be taken to ensure that the test only discriminates between individuals based on the competence or behaviors required by the job. This improves the quality of hire, but also serves to protect recruiters from claims of discrimination by minorities. After partnering with SHL, Krispy Kreme measured the success of the process and was able to show that unsuccessful hires were reduced by 50 percent.

Consider a different setting, in this case, the Neiman Marcus Retail Group. They were already using psychometric assessment to screen and assess candidates for their large volume store roles. However with the launch of their new Human Resource Information System (HRIS) they wanted to standardize testing across the group, move to remote web-based testing, and have the results integrated into the HRIS.

To create the standard test, SHL defined key competencies, attitudes and behaviors by looking at existing associates who met the criteria of top sales performance and good employment tenure. Following the introduction of a series of screening tests, the results were evaluated by comparing stores pre and post the rollout of the new system. Staff turnover was reduced by 18 percent using the new process compared to the old approach and sales-per-hour per associate increased 15.4 percent. In a tight labor market, the new process also provided a 24-hour interview-to-hire cycle. (To experience these kinds of tests for yourself, visit the practice site at SHL.com.)

Both these organizations recognized that selection is a key part of the recruitment process and that it is possible to find people with the propensity to display the right behaviors or competencies and have the right inclination towards customers. Where the role requires specific abilities, such as the ability to work with numbers as a bank teller, personality tests can be supplemented by ability tests. It is important to realize that selecting the right person for the role has multiple benefits. For the organization, good selection improves the performance of the person in the role and hence productivity and service. Having the right role also reduces the role stress suffered by service providers who may not be suited to the job. This increases their wellbeing and reduces the pathologies caused by role stress for the customer.

**employer brand** The brand that is created in the market for staff, which is analogous to the brand in the customer market.

Part of the recruitment strategy must also be the creation of a suitable "**employer brand**." The firm is not only competing for customers but also for talented people. The value proposition to prospective employees has to be attractive enough to create a pool of candidates big enough to find enough employees with the right competencies. This is no more or less than the application of marketing to the employee market. The communication, branding, and proposition development skills are the same.

***Developing Competent Service Employees***   Training is at the heart of creating satisfied employees and satisfied customers. Training is cumulative and expensive, and hence this

Due to the inseparable nature of service encounters, effective service training involves both technical training and interpersonal training.

strategy has to be combined with a strong focus on employee retention. The development strategy covers everything from recruiting and hiring new employees, to technical training on how to use the infrastructure and technology, to interpersonal training on how to deal with customers, to developmental training preparing the employees for their next role.

Preparing a new employee to operate in their "production" role, maintaining, and upgrading the skills of existing employees is the role of **technical training** and the foundation on which everything is built.[22] Employees need to know how to use the "technology" provided to them, whether it is a sophisticated customer relationship management system in a call center, a complex till in a fast food restaurant, or a pad of paper on which to place orders in a fine dining restaurant. They need to know where they fit in the production process and what is required of them to ensure an efficient process. Using a theatrical analogy, service providers need to know the roles in the play and the script for the production. They also need to understand the role the consumer has to play in the production.

Training new workers around a well-developed script is a widely practiced procedure. Take, for example, the McDonald's approach, which trains new staff in a specific script including:

- *Greeting customers.*
- *Asking for the order (with suggestions for additional items).*
- *Assembling the order (cold drinks first, the hot next, etc.).*
- *Placing various items on the tray.*
- *Placing the tray where the customer can reach it.*
- *Collecting money and giving change.*
- *Saying "thank you" and "come again."*

In most cases, for entry level subordinate staff the script encompasses much of the interpersonal training as well as the technical aspects of the job.

Inadequate investment in technical training produces a cycle of failure. Employees are nervous and ill prepared. They do a bad job and it is visible to the customers. The customers complain and make things worse for the employee. The employee becomes dissatisfied and leaves, wasting all of the investment in training. High turnover costs provoke management to reduce training to try to maintain the profitability.

The more difficult training involves the development of the skills and abilities to handle customers. **Interpersonal training** has to be built upon a strong foundation of technical knowledge.[23] Employees need to be able to run the factory instinctively, saving their energy for dealing with customers. Many methods are used for interpersonal training of subordinate service personnel that were developed for managers. These include sensitivity training, role playing, and behavioral modeling.

Examples of sensitivity training include having new bus drivers spend their first week on the help desk instead of the bus. Here they can understand the problems and complaints of passengers, sensitizing them before they meet the "real thing." Store and hotel openings are a classic example of role playing. On the days before the store opens to the public, other employees play the customer's role. This serves as interpersonal training for all concerned.

**Behavioral modeling** provides stereotypes with which an individual can categorize others and clues on how to handle the different categories. Consider the following example of how to deal with difficult customers. Customers are not always saints, and disruptive behavior impacts not only other customers, but service personnel as well. (For further insight into the realities of dealing with customers, visit customerssuck.com for a wide variety of often humorous and sometimes frightening provider stories about their customers—see E-Services in Action).

**technical training**
Training focused on teaching service providers their operational role in delivering the service.

**interpersonal training**
Training focused on teaching service providers how to deal with customers.

**behavioral modeling**
Categorizing customers to enable providers to more easily process them and remove stress.

technology
Interactions with customers

---

## E-SERVICES *IN ACTION*

### Where Employees Go Online to Sound Off!

We have all heard about customer complaint sites on the Internet. For example, unhappy United Airlines customers can voice their complaints on **www.untied.com** and unhappy students can register their dissatisfaction on **www.ratemyprofessor.com**, and many do just that! As of this writing, 558,559 professors from 4,596 schools have received over 3.5 million ratings with an additional 3,500 ratings or so being added everyday. It would seem that with this much feedback being handed out by customers, turnabout—where employees get their chance to sound off against problematic customers—should be fair play.

Despite the old adage that the customer is never wrong, **www.customerssuck.com** gives employees the chance to vent their frustrations with customers. To date, over 500,000 people have visited the site. Visitors can subscribe to "The Customers Suck! Newsletter," chat with fellow customer service reps on the site's message boards, and contribute to moderated sites such as:

- At the Movies
  Stories from the film industry
- Customer Service Definitions
  Terms that should be used for customers who do certain things

- Coffee Shop Blues
  Stories about dealing with customers before they get their daily dose of caffeine
- The Real Cellular Craze
  Stories from those in the cellular/phone industry
- Loving the Library
  Stories from Librarians
- Sick of Seniors
  The idea of a second childhood is apparently true
- Dealing with Drunks
  Customers are bad enough sober, but add a little alcohol...
- Customers Coming Clean
  Stories from customers who knew they screwed up
- Customers Being Bad to Other Customers
  When customers decided that for some reason they are the only customers who deserve respect in the store
- Disgruntled Employees Union!
  Other sites that deal with employees, customer service, etc.

Source: **http://www.customerssuck.com**, accessed 23 May 2005.

---

Five customer profiles have been developed, representing the worst that customers have to offer.[24] By categorizing unreasonable customers into one of the five profiles, contact personnel are more easily able to depersonalize the conflict and handle customer complaints more objectively. In reality, the worst customer of all is a little of all five types. The characteristics of each of the five "customers from hell" and suggestions for ways to deal with them are discussed below.

***Egocentric Edgar***   Egocentric Edgar is the guy Carly Simon had in mind when she wrote the song, "You're So Vain." Edgar doesn't believe he should stand in line for any reason. He'll push his way to the front and demand service on a variety of things that demand little immediate attention. If your company's creed is "we are here to serve," Edgar interprets that message as, "Your company exists to serve my needs and my needs alone, and right now!"

Another of Edgar's nasty characteristics is that he will walk over front-line employees to get to who he'll call "the man in charge." Edgar treats front-line employees like well-worn speed bumps that deserve just that much consideration. Once he gets to the top, Edgar uses the chance to belittle upper management and prove he knows how things should be done.

Dealing with Edgar is particularly troublesome for providers who are new on the job, unsure of their own abilities, and easily pushed around. The key to dealing with Edgar is to not let his ego destroy yours, while at the same time appealing to his ego. Because Edgar believes you are incapable of performing any function, take action that demonstrates your ability to solve his problem. This will surprise Edgar. In addition, never talk policy to Edgar. Edgar thinks he is special and that the rules that apply to everyone else should not apply to him. Policy should still apply to Edgar, but just don't let him know that you are restating policy. Phrases such as, "For you Edgar, I can do the following …." where "the following" is simply policy. This will appeal to Edgar's ego while still managing him within the policies of the organization.

**Bad-Mouth Betty**   Bad-Mouth Betty lets you know in no uncertain terms exactly what she thinks of you, your organization, and the heritage of both. If she cannot be right, she will be loud, vulgar, and insensitive. She is crude, not only to service employees, but also to other customers who are sharing her unpleasant experience.

Dealing with Betty consists of at least four options. First, since Betty is polluting the service environment with her foul mouth, attempt to move her "offstage" so as to not further contaminate the service environment of your other customers. Once isolated, one option is to ignore her foul language, listen to determine the core of the problem, and take appropriate action. This is a difficult option to undertake, particularly if her language is excessively abusive and personal in nature. A second option is to use selective agreement in an attempt to show Betty that you are listening and possibly on her side. Selective agreement involves agreeing with Betty on minor issues such as, "You're right, waiting 10 minutes for your Egg McMuffin is a long time." However, agreeing with Betty that your boss really is an "SOB" is not advisable, since Betty is likely to use this to her advantage at a later date. The last option that every good service firm should seriously consider is to "force the issue." In other words, let Betty know that you would be more than willing to help her solve her problem but you don't have to listen to her abusive language. If Betty continues to be crude, hang up, walk away, or do whatever is necessary to let her know she is on her own. In most cases, she will return the call or walk over and apologize, and let you get on with your job.

**Hysterical Harold**   Hysterical Harold is a screamer. If he doesn't get his way, his face will turn colors and veins will literally pop out from his neck. "Harold demonstrates the dark side … of the child inside all of us. He is the classic tantrum thrower, the adult embodiment of the terrible twos. Only louder. Much louder."

Dealing with Harold is much like dealing with Betty in many ways. These two occupy the "other customers" slot of the servuction model and negatively affect everyone else's service experience. Consequently, move Harold offstage and give your other customers a chance to enjoy the remainder of their encounter. When Harold has a problem, Harold has to vent. When offstage, let him vent and get it off his chest. This is when you can finally get to the heart of the matter and begin to take action. Finally, take responsibility for the problem. Do not blame the problem on fellow employees, upper management, or others who may ultimately be responsible. Offer an apology for what has occurred and, more importantly, a solution to Harold's problem.

**Dictatorial Dick**   Dictatorial Dick is claimed to be Egocentric Edgar's evil twin. Dick likes to tell everyone exactly how they are supposed to do their jobs because he has done it all before. Just so you don't get confused, Dick will provide you a written copy of his instructions, which is copied to your boss, your boss's boss, and his lawyer. Dick will most likely make you sign for your copy.

If his brilliant instructions do not produce the desired outcome, then it's your company's fault, or, more likely, your fault because you were too incompetent to fully understand Dick's brilliance. Or perhaps Dick's paranoia will set in, which makes him believe that you deliberately sabotaged his plan to make him look bad. You wouldn't do that, would you?

Dealing with Dick would test anyone's patience. The key is not to let him push you around. Employees should stick to their game plans and provide service in the manner they know is appropriate and equitable for all concerned. Since other customers are likely to be present, employees need to be consistent in how they deal with individual customers. Dick should not be treated as the "squeaky wheel" who always gets the grease. The best strategy for dealing with Dick is to tell him in a straightforward fashion exactly what you can do for him. If it's reasonable, fulfilling his request will break up Dick's game plan and resolve the conflict.

*Freeloading Freda*    Freeloading Freda wants it all for free. Give her an inch and she'll take the plates, the silverware, and everything else that's not nailed down. Freda will push your return policy to the limit. If her kid's shoes begin to wear out in a year or two, she'll return them for new ones. In need of a cocktail dress, Freda will buy one on Thursday and return it bright and early Monday morning, punch stains and all. Question her credibility, and Freda will scream bloody murder to anyone and everyone who will listen, including the news media and the Better Business Bureau.

Dealing with Freda, in many cases, involves biting your tongue and giving her what she wants. Despite popular beliefs, the Fredas of the world probably represent only 1 to 2 percent of your customers, if that. Most customers are honest and believe that they should pay for the goods and services they consume. Another possibility is to track Freda's actions and suggest possible legal action to persuade her to take her business elsewhere. Managers of competing firms often share information regarding the Fredas of the world to avoid their excessive abuses. Finally, recognize that Freda is the exception and not the common customer. Too often, new policies are developed for the sole purpose of defeating Freda and her comrades. These new policies add to the bureaucratization of the organization and penalize the customers who follow the rules. The filing of lengthy forms to return merchandise or invoke service guarantees is a common example of penalizing the majority of customers by treating them as suspected criminals rather than as valued customers.

*Hellish Thoughts*    When dealing with "customers from hell," it is difficult for employees not to take these sorts of confrontations personally. The consumer profiles introduced above should help employees prepare for the various types of difficult customers and provide strategies for minimizing the amount of conflict that actually occurs. Viewing customers as distinct profile types helps depersonalize the situation for the employee- "Oh, it's just Edgar again." This is not to say that each customer shouldn't be treated as an individual, but simply that customer complaints and behavior shouldn't be taken overly personally. In closing, one word of warning: Employees who truly master the art of dealing with difficult customers are rewarded by becoming these customers' favorite provider, the one they request by name time after time. No good deed goes unpunished!

## Controlling, Rewarding and Evaluating Service Providers

Employees behave as they do for many reasons. One of the most powerful is what they are told to do, what they are measured against, and what they are rewarded for. Unfortunately the very nature of services makes it difficult to send the consistent message so

"Mr Frimley, sir, can I have a word about the motivational artwork..."

Treating employees poorly and then asking them to treat customers like "Kings" is seldom an effective human resource strategy.

important to achieving a climate for service. The intangible nature of services means that performance is difficult for supervisors to monitor directly. Often employees must be trusted to monitor their own performance. The fact that customers are actively involved in the service production process means service providers must be sensitive to clients' needs and use the clues to guide their behaviors. Because of these characteristics of service jobs, service organizations should be more likely than manufacturers to include client input in the performance appraisal process.

Simultaneous production and consumption means that quality control cannot be achieved by the "inspect and correct" method typical in manufacturing. Instead, quality control has to occur at the point of delivery, and this changes the kinds of performance, control, and reward systems an organization can use.

Designing these HR systems is based on the required role that has previously been defined. At one extreme is the "industrialized model" typified by a fast food chain such as McDonald's. Here the employees' role is tightly constrained and the opportunities for empowerment limited. As we move away from the extreme, greater degrees of empowerment and enfranchisement are available and needed.

Let us start with the "fast food" model. Employees are given a tightly defined script in their training. As we saw, the script also programs much of the interpersonal interactions. The HR systems are built around this model. For example, evaluation includes mystery shoppers who visit stores as customers. They measure the "quality" against the same script and score the outlet on conformance. That score feeds into the performance evaluation system and to the rewards of the manager. Performance reviews for the service personnel are based on the script.

It is important to remember that rewards can be extrinsic (e.g., pay) or intrinsic such as enjoying the job itself, receiving recognition from coworkers and supervisors, and/or accomplishing challenging and meaningful goals. Fast food chains, like many service organizations, use intrinsic rewards such as "employee of the month" schemes and the "promotion" within the front-line jobs based on the star ranking system. These are predominantly recognition systems but often tied to a small financial reward. All of this is designed to reinforce the desired behaviors that are articulated in the script.

In general, effective reward systems pass the seven tests listed below. Interestingly, in many instances, pay alone does not pass these effectiveness tests.

*Availability*—Rewards must be available and substantial (relative to the role). Not having enough rewards—or large enough rewards—is likely to discourage desired behaviors rather than encourage them. There is nothing worse than the "Employee of the Month" who is disappointed by his or her prize.

*Flexibility*—Rewards should be flexible enough to be given to anyone at anytime. There is lots of evidence to show that behavior is reinforced more if the reward can be given immediately. "See something good and reward it." Think only of the house points scheme in the Harry Potter books; that is a classic intrinsic reward scheme.

*Reversibility*—If rewards are given to the wrong people for the wrong reasons, they should not be lifelong. Bonuses are better than pay increases that become lifetime annuities.

*Contingent*—Rewards should be directly tied to desired performance criteria – the desired behaviors. Only in this way are the rewards consistent with the service strategy being followed by the rest of the organization.

*Visibility*—Rewards should be visible, and their value should be understood by all employees. For example, pay is not visible and is often shrouded in secrecy, whereas recognition schemes are designed to be visible, which is why they work.

*Timeliness*—Not to say that employees are rats, but rats are trained to receive food pellets immediately following the execution of a desired behavior (e.g., pushing a bar). However, in this instance, employees are not that much different. Rewards should be given immediately following desired behaviors. If someone has been given a reward, don't wait until the end of the month to give it; it will have lost the power by then. Bonuses are best given in the form of cash or a check rather than through the payroll system—it takes too long.

*Durability*—The motivating effects of a reward should last for a long time. The motivational effects of plaques and medallions last longer than the short-term effects of pay.

A different kind of intrinsic reward can be given by redesigning the role of the service provider to enrich it. Enrichment comes from increasing the empowerment and enfranchisement of the employee. **Empowerment** means giving discretion to contact personnel to "turn the front-line loose." Empowerment is the reverse of "doing things by the book." **Enfranchisement** carries this logic even further by first empowering individuals and then coupling this with a reward system that recognizes people for their performance. In both cases the role is enriched by adding responsibility and autonomy, which builds an increased sense of accountability in the employee.

**empowerment** Giving discretion to front-line personnel to meet the needs of consumers creatively.

**enfranchisement** Empowerment coupled with a performance-based compensation method.

Empowerment clearly brings benefits. Empowered employees are more customer focused and quicker in responding to customer needs. They will customize the product or remix it in real time.[25] Empowered employees are more likely to respond in a positive manner to service failures and to engage in effective service recovery strategies.

Employees who are empowered tend to feel better about their jobs and themselves. This is automatically reflected in the way they interact with customers. They will be genuinely warmer and friendlier. Empowerment, therefore, not only can reduce unnecessary service recovery costs, but also can improve the quality of the product.

If close to the front line, an empowered employee is in a position continuously exposed to both the good and bad aspects of the service delivery system. This employee can be key to new service ideas and often a cheaper source of market research than going to the consumer directly.

***Levels of Empowerment***   As evidenced by the UPS and FedEx examples, high levels of empowerment are not for every firm. Firms can indeed be successful without fully empowering their employees. However, empowerment approaches vary by degree and include suggestion involvement, job involvement, and high involvement. Each of the

**FIG-9.4** The Continuum of Empowerment

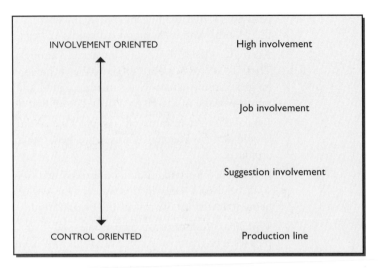

Source: Adapted from David E. Bowen and Edward E. Lawler III, "The Empowerment of Service Workers: What, Why, How, and When," *Sloan Management Review*, (Spring 1992), pp. 31–39.

**suggestion involvement** Low-level empowerment that allows employees to recommend suggestions for improvement of the firm's operations.

**quality circles** Empowerment involving small groups of employees from various departments in the firm, who use brainstorming sessions to generate additional improvement suggestions.

**job involvement** Allows employees to examine the content of their own jobs and to define their role within the organization.

**high involvement** Allows employees eventually to learn to manage themselves, utilizing extensive training and employee control of the reward allocation decisions.

three levels of empowerment fall along a continuum that ranges from control-oriented to involvement-oriented approaches (see Figure 9.4).[26]

**Suggestion involvement** falls near the control-oriented point of the empowerment continuum. Suggestion involvement empowers employees to recommend suggestions for improving the firm's operations. Employees are not empowered to implement suggestions themselves, but are encouraged to suggest improvements for formal review. Firms that utilize suggestion involvement typically maintain formal suggestion programs that proactively solicit employee suggestions. **Quality circles**, which often involve small groups of employees from various departments in the firm, are also utilized as brainstorming sessions to generate additional suggestions. Typical success stories of suggestion involvement programs include McDonald's, whose employees recommended the development of products such as the "Big Mac," "Egg McMuffin," and "McDLT." Even with narrowly defined roles, such as those in the fast food industry, this level of empowerment is possible. (See Sustainability and Services in Action for an example of using a green initiative to give suggestion involvement in the hotel industry.)

**Job involvement** typically falls in the middle of the empowerment continuum, between control-oriented and involvement-oriented approaches. Job involvement allows employees to examine the content of their own jobs and define their role within the organization. Firms engaged in job involvement use teams of employees extensively for the betterment of the firm's service delivery system. In contrast to suggestion involvement, employees engaged in job involvement use a variety of skills, have considerably more freedom, and receive extensive feedback from management, employees, and customers. However, higher level decisions and reward allocation decisions remain the responsibility of the firm's upper management.

**High involvement** falls at the involvement-oriented end of the empowerment continuum. Essentially, the goal of high involvement is to train people to manage themselves. Extensive training is utilized to develop skills in teamwork, problem solving, and business operations. Moreover, employees control the majority of the reward allocation decisions through profit sharing and employee ownership of the firm. In sum, virtually every aspect of a high-involvement firm is different from those of a control-oriented firm.

## SUSTAINABILITY AND SERVICES *IN ACTION*

### Florida's Green Lodging Program

The Florida Green Lodging Program encourages properties to preserve the state's natural resources. It was launched in 2004 to show the hospitality industry how they can reduce their energy use and water consumption, and manage their waste better.

Hotel management sees the program not only as a cost saving initiative, but as an added benefit to customers and staff. In 2004, Disney's Broadwalk Inn was the first hotel in Florida to receive green status. At the time, a Disney vice president of resort operations commented that, "For us, it's back to the heritage of the company and who we are."

A survey by Deloitte in late 2007 showed that about one-third of business travelers were concerned about green travel. Thirty-four percent said they seek out hotels that are environmentally friendly, and 38 percent have researched green facilities either online or through friends and relatives. Twenty-eight percent said they would be willing to pay 10 percent more to stay in a green facility.

To achieve green status the hotel must meet requirements in areas of communication, water conservation, energy efficiency, waste reduction and clean air. Top management must support the initiative, and the property must agree to form an active multi-disciplinary "Green Team."

Harris Rosen, who is president of the Rosen Group which manages three properties, began by educating his management team and held fun meetings to bring associates on board. One property held a scavenger hunt so that team members could learn about initiatives outside their departments. Rosen Hotels staff members also created a green character called Nesor, which accompanied Rosen and state officials on all hotel inspections. Nesor stickers placed under light switches and in other strategic areas remind employees to turn off lights or perform other conservation measures. The company held a rally to commemorate achieving green status.

As part of its green initiatives, the Rosen Shingle Creek property recycles its kitchen grease, converting it to biodiesel fuel to power its golf-course maintenance equipment. Guest rooms and public areas contain programmable thermostats to avoid heating or cooling empty spaces. Sensors control outdoor and back-of-house lighting. Anything viable left over by convention delegates, such as notebooks and pads of paper, is donated to local schools. Rosen also offers employees a payroll-deducted Lynx bus-pass program, as well as posting a directory of staff members interested in carpooling. The group also provides conference organizers with a green guide.

Source: **www.dep.state.fl.u/greenlodging**

*When to Empower and Enfranchise*    Unfortunately, empowerment and enfranchisement do carry costs. Empowerment increases the costs of the organization. A greater investment is needed in remuneration and recruitment to assure that the right people are empowered. A low-cost model of using inexpensive and/or part-time labor cannot cope with empowerment, so the basic labor costs of the organization will be higher.

Empowerment programs can quickly turn into disasters if the service providers are not given the appropriate work facilitation and interdepartmental support to do the empowered job. Empowerment must be accompanied by enablement. Technology is a great enabler of empowerment, but it comes with a cost. Junior banking staff can be empowered to give out loans but only when supported by sophisticated credit rating systems. These systems have to be integrated with the bank's infrastructure, be real time, and be available all the time.

Marketing implications also arise. By definition, an empowered employee will customize the product to a greater or lesser extent. This means that the service received will vary from one encounter to the next, depending on the employee. The delivery is also likely to be slower because the service is customized. Moreover, since customers are treated differently, other customers may perceive that some customers are receiving preferential treatment. Empowerment, therefore, has to be consistent with the service benefit concept.

Empowered employees, when attempting to satisfy customers, sometimes give away too much and make bad decisions. For example, a bellman who notices that a businessman forgot his briefcase at the front desk should make every attempt to return the briefcase to its owner. However, tracking the owner to the airport and hopping on the next available flight to the owner's destination is far beyond the call of duty and worlds beyond what is economically feasible. Empowerment has to have clearly defined boundaries.

A hidden cost may be that a new style of management may be needed. Empowered employees need different kinds of leadership. Theory Y managers, who coach and facilitate rather than control and manipulate, are needed to work with employees who have high growth needs and strong interpersonal skills—the needs and skills of empowered employees. In contrast, firms governed by Theory X managers believe that employees are working primarily to collect a paycheck. Theory X managers work best with employees who have low growth needs, low social needs, and weak interpersonal skills. Theory X managers fit best with control-oriented organizations.

The balance of empowerment and enfranchisement, therefore, comes down to the benefit concept of the organization and the resulting role definition of the service personnel. A branded organization that guarantees consistency of product and service dare not fully empower for fear of the inconsistency that would result. An organization that competes on the basis of value driven by a low cost base cannot afford to empower because of the costs involved. Equally, a high-cost service organization using a non-routine and complex technology almost certainly has to empower because its ability to use an industrial approach is severely limited. The decision on the degree of empowerment and enfranchisement, like the rest of the service HR strategy, depends upon the broad service strategy, the benefit concept, the technology, the servicescape, and the processes.

***Retaining the Service Providers***   One of the greatest problems facing service firms is staff turnover, often at levels of 20 percent to as high as 70 percent per year in many low-level subordinate service roles. The Sears Merchandise example quoted earlier highlights the direct costs of such turnover—the recruitment and training costs of new staff alone accounted for 17 percent of annual turnover.

It should be obvious from the rest of the chapter that there are even larger (but more difficult to quantify) hidden costs. When employees leave they are not replaced immediately, and when they are, the new people have lower levels of technical and interpersonal competencies. This means that the providers who stay are put under increased pressure, all of which threatens the overall service climate.

Retention can be managed directly or indirectly. Direct actions include the provision of benefits that are difficult to replace, or even the payment of retention bonuses. However most of the actions designed to engender a climate for service will have an indirect, positive effect on retention. A clearly defined role reduces the role conflict and ambiguity. Good recruitment and selection tied to the role demonstrably improve retention. A job that has the correct balance of intrinsic and extrinsic rewards will improve retention.

The Wegmans case history highlights other actions that can improve retention and the service climate at the same time. Cross-training employees for other jobs meets multiple objectives. It increases operational flexibility, since staff can cover for one another. It enriches the role of the employee and offers variety. Cross-training also enables employees to better understand the inter-dependencies in their role. A service provider is less likely to complain about another department letting them down when they have been trained to do that job and understand their problems.

Promotion from within, scholarship programs, and "store moves for new openings," all turn dead-end jobs into careers. Nothing is more de-motivating for front-line staff than to be given a new manager who needs training in the basics. It is better to promote from within. There is of course one caveat: promotion will often take someone away from customer contact. This may not motivate them, and certainly they have not been selected for a bigger role. Many firms re-introduce a formal selection process using tests and simulations to evaluate against this new role.

## The Role of Management

Our focus in this chapter has been on the first line service personnel. However they need to be supported by all levels of management. Starting at the very top, it is only the senior management that can ensure that the foundations are in place. It is they that have to invest in the core technology that allows the front-line team to do their work. Most importantly, it is the senior management that has to ensure that the different functions and departments are aligned behind the service benefit concept and do not lose focus on the customer. They can also have a direct impact on the service climate by "walking the talk." They must focus on the customers. Many firms formalize this by having specific days when management return to front-line roles to experience the customers again.

By the very nature of services there is always a day-to-day crisis. It is impossible given the simultaneous production, consumption, and people content, to run the service without failure. Middle management must, however, enable the front-line providers to focus on the customer and not be distracted. It is for them to manage the crisis and move the roadblocks to good service out of the way. It is for them to relieve pressure by doing some of the front-line work. Any restaurant manager can be seen clearing tables when things get busy.

## Information Technology and the Service Provider

Technology can be a great enabler for front-line staff, allow for empowerment, and free up time to focus on customers. However, some technological innovations have been viewed less favorably. The advent of customer relationship management systems, combined with the rollout of call centers throughout the world, has transformed the role of the service provider in large parts of the service sector. That transformation is for better or worse, but poses the same problems in a new setting when managing people. The jobs that deal with providing information, help, and to an extent, sales, will never be the same again. The technology has enabled the industrialization of large branches of services. Automated help lines now require that customers learn new scripts just to get to the correct recorded message. Email enquiries are answered miraculously from all over the world. It is, however, the call center with its sophisticated call management system that has become the visible symbol of the redesign.

It is now estimated that 4 percent of the total U.S. workforce is employed in a call center. That is without taking into account the booming outsourced called centers all over the world, but particularly in India (see Global Services in Action). All Fortune 500 companies have at least one call center and on average have 4500 customer service representatives (CSR's) in each. More than $300 billion is spent annually in the U.S. alone on call centers.

The logic described in the "Focus on Service Processes" chapter is amply demonstrated in a call center. By blueprinting the process of handling an enquiry, it is possible to identify the "points of contact" and realize that the majority are, or could be, done on the telephone. This, combined with two emerging software industries, caused the explosion. They are the sophisticated call handling technologies that can route calls based on rules tied to knowledge of the customer and the CRM systems.

## GLOBAL SERVICES *IN ACTION*

### Dell Offshore Tech Support: Lost in Translation

The interactions between a service firm's personnel and its customers define "moments of truth." Moments of truth represent the service firm's greatest opportunity for gains and losses. This is why employee selection and training are so important to service firms. One service firm that is currently struggling with this issue is Dell, Inc. of Austin, Texas.

To outsource tech support offshore or not, that is the question for Dell. What began as a means for the company to cut costs, the offshoring of Dell's tech support to India, has become somewhat of a political incident. During the tech recession, Dell laid off nearly 5,700 workers. Most of these employees were tech support personnel working in Texas. Since this time, most of the growth in Dell's workforce has occurred in overseas call centers based in India. To say the least, the average Texan is not too happy about this "motivated by cost savings" turn of events.

Dell is now faced with the decision about whether to recall some of these lost jobs to America. Dell customers have complained about the quality of support received from Indian-based call centers. Meanwhile, upset Indians are bristling at the thought that "their thick accents" and "scripted responses" have motivated Dell to move some of its tech support positions back to America. However, it does appear Dell has done just this particularly for its large-scale corporate clients. In fact, delivering customer support from North American-based locations appears to have become a major selling point for Dell's corporate clients.

The offshoring of customer tech support has become a thorny issue. On the one hand, India provides the cost savings that drive Dell's value proposition. On the other hand, more and more corporate customers are shopping tech firms based on the issue of the location of technical support. In the meantime, many industry observers are wondering whether the quality of technical support has really declined due to its India-based location or whether Dell has become the victim of well-organized email and bulletin board campaign that promotes protectionism. Commenting on Dell's dilemma, *The Economist* writes, "It may be its [Dell] customer service has become genuinely poorer as a result—though multi-regional, multi-racial America has its fair share of different accents, too. Which customers, after all, can claim happy experiences with Texan call-centers?"

Sources:
1. Patrick, Thibodeau, "Offshore Tech Support Still Stirs Controversy," *Computerworld* 39, 18, (May 2, 2005), p. 7.
2. "Lost in Translation," *The Economist*, 369, 8352, (November 29, 2003), p. 58.

## Customer Relationship Management

**customer relationship management (CRM)**
The process of identifying, attracting, differentiating, and retaining customers, where firms focus their efforts disproportionately on their most lucrative clients.

**Customer relationship management (CRM)** is the process of identifying, attracting, differentiating, and retaining customers. CRM allows the firm to focus its efforts disproportionately to its most lucrative clients. CRM is based on the old adage that 80 percent of a company's profits come from 20 percent of its customers; therefore, the 20 percent should receive better service than the 80 percent. For example, when a plastics manufacturer focused on its most profitable customers, it cut the company's customer base from 800 to 90 and increased revenue by 400 percent.[27]

The increased usage of CRM practices, where high-value customers are treated as superior to low-value customers, can be attributed to several external trends.[28] First, some believe that customers have done it to themselves by opting for price, choice, and convenience over high-quality service. Another reason CRM is currently fashionable is that labor costs have risen, yet competitive pressures have kept prices low. The end result is that gross margins have been reduced to 5 to 10 percent in many industries. With these kinds of margins, companies simply cannot afford to treat all their customers equally. Consider the plight of Fidelity Investments. Ten years ago the company received 97,000 calls a day. Half of those calls were handled by an automated telephone system. Today, Fidelity receives 700,000 calls and 550,000 website visits a day. Three-quarters of the calls are now handled by automated systems (telephone and website), which costs the company less than a dollar per call. The remaining calls are handled by live customer service personnel.

Finally, CRM is being increasingly implemented because markets are increasingly fragmented and promotional costs are on the rise. Bass Hotels & Resorts, the owners of Holiday Inn and Inter-Continental Hotels, have recently learned a valuable lesson by not treating customers equally. The company now only sends its promotional mailings to those who have "bit" on earlier mailings. The end result is that company has reduced mailing costs by 50 percent, meanwhile response rates have increased by 20 percent.

***CRM in Action***   At the heart of any CRM system is a customer database holding background information but most importantly sales and purchase patterns. The first stage in any CSR system is **coding**: Customers are graded based on how profitable their business is. CRM systems applied to sales organizations provide ranked opportunities to the sales teams. However, in a call center it is now possible to recognize the inbound telephone number, look up the client and provide background information and the coding to CSRs before the phone rings three times and they pick up. The CSRs are instructed to handle customers differently based on their category code. For example:

> **coding** Categorizing customers based on how profitable their business is.

- *A "platinum" customer of Starwood Hotels & Resorts Worldwide wants to propose to his girlfriend in India. Starwood arranges entry into the Taj Mahal after hours so that he can propose in private. Starwood also provides a horse-driven carriage, flowers, a special meal, and upgraded suite and a reception led by the hotel's general manager.*
- *Sears, Roebuck & Co's most profitable credit card customers get to choose a preferred two-hour time window for repair appointments. Ordinary customers are given a four-hour time window.*

The second use of the CRM system is in **routing** the call. Customers in profitable code categories get to speak to live customer service representatives. Less-profitable customers are inventoried in automated telephone queues. For example:

> **routing** Directing incoming customer calls to customer service representatives where more profitable customers are more likely to receive faster and better customer service.

- *Call this particular electric utility company and, depending on your status, you may have to stay on the line for quite awhile. The top 350 business clients are served by six people. The next tier, consisting of the next 700 most profitable customers, is handled by six more people. The next 30,000 customers are served by two customer service representatives. The final group, consisting of 300,000 customers, is routed to an automated telephone system.*
- *Charles Schwab Corp's top-rated "Signature" clients, consisting of customers who maintain $100,000 in assets or trade at least 12 times a year, never wait more than 15 seconds to have their calls personally answered by a customer service representative. Ordinary customers can wait up to 10 minutes or more.*

This systems are now sufficiently sophisticated that profitable customers can have fees waived and be **targeted** for special promotions in real time. Less profitable customers may never hear of the special deals. Examples include:

> **targeting** Offering the firm's most profitable customers special deals and incentives.

- *Centura Bank, Inc. of Raleigh, N.C., ranks its 2 million customers on a profitability scale from one to five. The most profitable customers are called several times a year for what the bank calls "friendly chats," and the CEO calls once a year to wish these same customers a "Happy Holiday!" Since the program was implemented, the retention rate of the most profitable group has increased by 50 percent. In comparison, the most unprofitable group has decreased from 27 to 21 percent.*

- *First Bank in Baltimore, Md., provides its most profitable customers a web option that its regular customers never see. The option allows its preferred customer to click a special icon that connects customers with live service agents for phone conversations.*
- *First Union codes its credit card customers with colored squares that flash on customer service representatives' screens. "Green squares" means the customer is profitable and should be granted fee waivers and given the "white-glove" treatment.*

**sharing** Making accessible key customer information to all parts of the organization.

The CRM record, augmented by input from the call center, can be used to **share** customer information with other parts of the organization. For example:

- *A United Airline's passenger was shocked when a ticketing agent told him: "Wow, somebody doesn't like you." Apparently the passenger was involved in an argument with another United employee several months earlier. The argument became part of the passenger's permanent record that follows him wherever he flies with United. The passenger, a Premier Executive account holder, feels that the airline has been less than accommodating following the incident.*
- *Continental Airlines has introduced a Customer Information System where every one of Continental's 43,000 gate, reservation, and service employees will have access to the history and value of each customer. The system also suggests specific service recovery remedies and perks such as coupons for delays and automatic upgrades. The system is proposed to provide more consistent staff behavior and service delivery.*

From a customer point of view there are limitations to CRM Practices: Finding out that there are different levels of service and you are not getting the best is upsetting. Other consumers worry about the privacy issues related to the databases underpinning these service models. Operationally, the CRM databases only measure historical purchases, although increasingly potential purchase criteria are being built in to the coding. Service discrimination also leads to some interesting ethical questions. Should only the wealthy be recipients of quality service? Is this a form of **red-lining**—the practice of identifying and avoiding unprofitable types of neighborhoods or types of people.

**red-lining** The practice of identifying and avoiding unprofitable types of neighborhoods or types of people.

Here, however, we should focus on the potential human resources problems. Call centers have been compared to the sweat shops of the late 19th century and the excesses of the industrial revolution. The inherent conflicts in the CSR role have been completely removed by automating which calls CSRs receive and, in some cases, scripting the conversation on the screen before the call is answered. The clarity of course comes with a price—boredom and tedium.

However the logic of the rest of this chapter is just as applicable. Enlightened firms are moving call centers to team working and enriching jobs by providing variety. The rigor of calls per hour is being tempered with measures of customer satisfaction. Cross-training is common, and creating career paths through supervisor roles is becoming more common. Selection criteria have been tightened and personality tests identified that can select individuals more likely to enjoy the call center environment.

## Summary

Successful service firms develop a seamless relationship between marketing, operations, and human resources, all based on the service benefit concept. This chapter has focused on some of the human resource issues that must be considered when marketing services. Much has been written about the fact that, for many service firms, personnel constitute the bulk of their product. It is thus important that the place of personnel within the organization be understood. By drawing on the concepts of organizational behavior and, in particular, the concepts of boundary-spanning roles, empowerment, enfranchisement, and reward and recognition, this chapter has provided a solid framework with which to execute the marketing implications of the benefit concept through personnel.

As boundary-spanners, service personnel perform the dual functions of interacting with both the firm's external environment and its internal organization and structure. Employees who occupy boundary-spanning roles are, by definition, placed in situations that produce conflict and stress. Marketing can help to reduce those stresses or increase them.

Nobody wants to give bad service. It is therefore necessary to mitigate those stresses and conflicts by creating an appropriate climate for service in order to set the service providers free. To understand how to achieve that climate, it is first necessary to define the role of the service provider in terms of the behaviors that must be displayed. Like a theatrical role, the role of the service provider must define what actions and behaviors take place at which point in the script. That role is based upon the marketing strategy, which is embodied in the service benefit concept.

Once the role is defined it can be used to ensure that the firm *recruits the right people; develops the competencies of service employees; controls, rewards and evaluates service employees* appropriately; and *retains the right people*. All of this feeds into ensuring that the firm has the appropriate climate for service.

## Key Terms

boundary-spanning roles, p. 239
subordinate service roles, p. 239
person/role conflict, p. 239
organization/client conflicts, p. 239
inter-client conflicts, p. 240
service sabotage, p. 240
work facilitation, p. 242
interdepartmental service support, p. 242
the service HR wheel, p. 243

climate for service, p. 244
employer brand, p. 245
technical training, p. 246
interpersonal training, p. 246
behavioral modeling, p. 246
empowerment, p. 251
enfranchisement, p. 251
suggestion involvement, p. 252
quality circles, p. 252
job involvement, p. 252

high involvement, p. 252
customer relationship management (CRM), p. 256
coding, p. 257
routing, p. 257
targeting, p. 257
sharing, p. 258
red-lining, p. 258

## Review Questions

1. Discuss the relevance of employee satisfaction as it relates to the service-profit chain.
2. What are boundary-spanning personnel? Discuss the types of conflict that they generally encounter.
3. From your own experience, give three examples of when you have been served badly and explain them in terms of the coping strategies.
4. How can marketing be utilized to reduce the amount of stress and conflict experienced by boundary-spanning personnel?
5. Suggest a company that has a good employer brand. What does the brand stand for, and how has the brand been created?

6. How does profiling disruptive customers assist customer contact personnel in dealing with "customers from hell"?
7. From a managerial point of view, what is the usefulness of websites such as **www.customer-suck.com?**
8. In what types of organizations would it be best to avoid empowerment approaches?
9. Discuss the various factors that would encourage employees not to leave an organization and how they can be turned in to a retention strategy.
10. Discuss the benefits and potential costs of consolidating a help desk into a call center.

## Notes

1. The first section of this chapter is based on Chapters 4 and 6 of John E. G. Bateson, *Managing* *of Services Marketing*, 3rd ed. (Fort Worth, TX: The Dryden Press, 1995).

2. James L. Heskett, Thomas O. Jones, Gary W. Loveman, W. Earl Sasser, Jr., and Leonard A. Schlesinger, "Putting the Service-Profit Chain to Work," *Harvard Business Review,* (March-April 1994), pp. 164–174.

3. Dave Ulrich et al., "Employee and Customer Attachment: Synergies for Competitive Advantage," *Human Resource Planning,* 14, 3, (1991), p. 89 (15).

4. Benjamin Schneider, Susan S. White and Michelle C. Paul, "Linking Service Climate and customer Perceptions of Service Quality: Test of a Causal Model," *Journal of Applied Psychology*, 83, 2, (1998), pp. 150–163. See also Benjamin Schneider, "The Service Organization: Climate Is Crucial," *Organizational Dynamics,* (Autumn 1980), pp. 52–65; and Benjamin Schneider and David E. Bowen, "The Service Organization: Human Resource Management is Crucial," *Organizational Dynamics,* (Spring 1993), pp. 39–52.

5. Cited in R. Rust and A. Zahorik, "Customer Staisfaction, customer retention and Market share," *Journal of Retailing,* 69, (1993), pp. 192–215; and M. Christopher, A. Payne and D. Ballantyne, *Relationship Marketing: Bringing Quality, Customer Service and Marketing Together* (London: Butterworth-Heinemann, 1991)

6. Leonard A. Schlesinger and James L Heskett, "The Service-Driven Service Company," *Harvard Business Review* (September-October, 1991), pp. 71–81.

7. Daine Brady, "Why Service Stinks?" *Business Week,* (October 23, 2000), pp. 118–128.

8. This idea was originally suggested in a slightly different form in W. Earl Sasser, P. Olsen, and D. Daryl Wycoff, *Management of Service Operations: Text, Cases, and Readings* (Boston: Allyn and Bacon, 1978).

9. Philip Kotler, *Marketing Management,* 8th ed. (Englewood Cliffs, NJ: Prentice-Hall, 1994), p. 303.

10. Ron Zemke and Kristen Anderson, "Customers from Hell," *Training* (February 1990), pp. 25–29.

11. J. D. Thompson, "Organization and Output Transactions," *American Journal of Sociology,* 68, (1967), pp. 309–324.

12. Boas Shamir, "Between Service and Servility: Role Conflict in Subordinate Service Roles," *Human Relations,* 33, 10, pp. 741–756.

13. See Arlie Hochshild, *The Managed Heart* (Berkeley, CA: University of California Press, 1983).

14. For example, see Jody D. Nyquist, Mary Jo Bitner, and Bernard Booms, "Identifying Difficulties in the Service Encounter: A Critical Incident Approach," in John Czepiel, Michael R. Solomon, and Carol F. Suprenant, eds., *The Service Encounter* (Lexington, MA: Heath, 1985), pp. 195–212.

15. Peter Klaus, "The Quality Epiphenomenon," in John Czepiel, Michael R. Solomon, and Carol F. Suprenant, eds., *The Service Encounter* (Lexington, MA: Heath, 1985), p. 15.

16. Charles T. Goodsell, "Bureaucratic Manipulation of Physical Symbols: An Empirical Investigation," *American Journal of Political Science,* XXI, (February 1977), pp. 79–91.

17. Lloyd C Harris and Emmanuel Ogbourne, "Exploring Service Sabotage: The Antecedents, Types and Consequences of Front-line, Deviant, Antiservice behaviors," *Journal of Service Research*, 4, 3, (2002), pp. 163–183.

18. Daniel Roth, "My Job at the Container Store," *Fortune* 141, 1, (January 10, 2000) pp. 74–78.

19. Adapted from Benjamin Schneider and David E. Bowen (1995), *Winning the Service Game*, (Boston, MA: Harvard Business School Press).

20. David E. Bowen and Edward E. Lawler, III, "The Empowerment of Service Workers: What, Why, How, and When," *Sloan Management Review* (Spring 1992), pp. 31–39.

21. See case histories on SHL.com website.

22. David Tansik, "Human Resource Issues for High Contact Service Personnel" in *Service Management Effectiveness*, David E Bowen, Richard B Chase and Thomas Cumming and Associates, eds. (San Francisco: Jossey-Bass Inc., 1990), pp. 152–174.

23. Ibid.

24. Ron Zemke and Kristen Anderson, "Customers from Hell," *Training* (February 1990), pp. 25–29.

25. Martin L. Bell, "Tactical Services Marketing and the Process of Remixing," in *Marketing of Services*, W. R. George and J. M. Donnelly, eds. (Chicago: American Marketing Association, 1986), pp. 162–165.

26. See reference 20.

27. Diane Brady, "Why Service Stinks," *Business Week*, (October 23 2000), pp. 118–128.

28. Ibid p. 122.

# Recruitment Cost Savings in the Gaming Industry

## The Background

One of the leading regional gaming and hospitality properties in the U.S. worked with SHL to get to the heart of its turnover challenges in the front of house, gaming, and back of house jobs. The company knew that employees that made it past the "magic 90-day" mark were substantially more likely to become reliable, long-term employees, and they needed an accurate method to predict this factor in the screening process.

## The Challenge

The HR Director for the properties worked with SHL to develop a predictive assessment that was statistically proven to identify candidates who would stay beyond the 90-day mark. The SHL assessment focused on measuring a trio of predictive factors based on in-depth analysis and company requirements:

- *Reliability: Measured aspects of stability, dependability, and lack of deviant behavior.*
- *Fit: Measured task, organizational, and reward expectations.*
- *Competencies: Measured attributes of communication, customer orientation, initiative and conscientiousness.*

The property also wanted a predictor that could go beyond the primary measures of tenure as they looked at longer-term performance goals.

## The Solution

SHL used a series of valid, well proven tools to create an assessment battery for each of the three job categories. The assessment results were linked to a proprietary job analysis process that ensured the reliability, fit, and competency measurements accurately represent elements of tenure and performance. Using that information as a foundation SHL screened more than 1,200 front of the house, 875 back of the house, and 900 gaming applicants and hires during the first phase of the program.

---

Source: Tracey, J. Bruce and Hinkin, Timothy R. *The Cost of Employee Turnover: Where the Devil is in the Details* (New York: School of Hotel Administration Center for Hospitality Research at Cornell University, 2006.).

"SHL" is a registered trademark of SHL Group Ltd.

# The Results

The results showed excellent predictability of tenure in all three job families. SHL developed a simplified scoring model that sorts candidates into three groups: Poor Fit, Marginal Fit, and Good Fit.

The SHL tools were particularly effective in predicting tenure of the gaming/cashier positions, jobs that include extra elements of risk and costs if a poor hire is made.

### Front of House Jobs

- *"Good Fit" candidates predicted by SHL were shown to stay on the job an average of 54 days longer than "Poor Fit" candidates.*
- *"Good fit" candidates consistently stayed on the job longer than the 90-day tenure mark, averaging 139 days.*

### Back of House Jobs

- *"Good Fit" candidates predicted by SHL were shown to stay on the job an average of 33 days longer than "Poor Fit" candidates.*
- *"Good Fit" candidates consistently stayed on the job longer than the 90-day tenure mark, averaging 137 days.*

### Gaming/Cashier Jobs

- *"Good Fit" candidates predicted by SHL were shown to stay on the job an average of 102 days longer than "Poor Fit" candidates.*
- *"Good Fit" candidates consistently stayed on the job longer than the 90-day tenure mark, with an average tenure of more than 6.5 months.*

# The Financial Impacts

Beyond the typical benefits seen from reduced turnover, including reduced recruitment costs, decreased time spent by hiring staff and decreased time to hire, the savings to the property are calculated in real dollars.

According to the School of Hotel and Administration, Center for Hospitality Research at Cornell University, the average turnover costs (based on job complexity) are between $5,693 and $9,932 per person.

The property did not consistently track turnover costs across all jobs, so the following classifications (based on job analysis data) are used to estimate the financial impact across the three positions:

- *Back of house: low complexity, $5,693.*
- *Front of House: Moderate complexity, $7,813.*
- *Gaming/Cashier: High Complexity, $9,932.*

### Front of House

For front of house positions, SHL predicted an average increase of tenure of 54 days per hire across a total of 401 hires (calendar year).

Converting the total savings in days based on the total hires per year, the savings result in:

- *$401 \times 54$ days $= 21,654$ days.*
- *$21,654$ days $\times 8$ hours per day $= 173,232$ hours.*
- *$173,232$ hrs/ $40$ hours $= 4331$ weeks.*

- *4331 weeks/ 48 weeks = 90 fewer hires.*
- *90 fewer hires × $7,813 = $703,170.*

**Front of House Turnover Savings: $703,170.**

# Back of House

Using the same method to calculate potential savings in each of the job categories:

- *Total hires: 374.*
- *Days saved/hire: 33.*
- *Turnover cost: $5,693.*

**Back of House Turnover Savings: $292,762**

# Gaming/Cashier

Using the same method to calculate potential savings in each of the other job categories:

- *Total hires: 359.*
- *Days saved/hire: 102.*
- *Turnover cost: $9,932.*

**Gaming/Cashier Turnover Savings: $1,515,375.**

# Total savings

Across the three job families, the potential annual savings for turnover reduction alone is approximately **$2.5 million.**

This compares to an investment cost for the entire assessment program of less than one 10$^{th}$ this cost per annum.

# Discussion Questions

1. How else could they quantify the benefits of better employees?
2. Are the savings more sensitive to the cost of turnover or to the tenure? Why is this important?
3. What costs should be included when calculating a "cost of turnover"?

## CHAPTER 10

# People as Strategy: Managing Service Consumers

*"If we could just get rid of these customers we could run a decent service."*

**Apocryphal**

## CHAPTER OBJECTIVES

After reading this chapter you should be able to:

- Understand the importance of the consumer in the production of a service and the impact consumer performance can have on both the operational efficiency of the business and customer satisfaction.

- Understand that there can be "novice" and "expert" consumers in their production role, and that the service firm has to cope simultaneously with both.

- Understand the steps management must take to manage service consumer performance rather than consumption.

- Understand how the inseparability of consumers can change the roles of marketing, operations and HR managers.

### HOW TO ORDER A WENDY'S HAMBURGER

When the Wendy's Hamburger Chain first appeared in Europe, customers were surprised to receive instructions on how to buy a burger. A leaflet was distributed to customers who had joined the line.

"At Wendy Restaurants we don't tell you how to have your hamburger. You tell us. The order-taker will want to know what size of hamburger you would like. A glance at the menu will help you to make up your mind. With cheese or without?

Then you've a choice of what goes on top. Mayonnaise, Ketchup, Pickle, Fresh Onion, Juicy Tomato, Crisp Lettuce, Mustard. Choose as many as you like – or have the lot – all at no extra charge…"

## Introduction

A study of weekend shopping at Blockbuster Video yielded an interesting finding. A number of customers entered the store and went directly to the returns bin instead of the shelves. They retrieved videos and moved directly to the checkout. What could they be doing?[1] Why would a retail customer not use the store in the way it was intended? What can we learn from these behaviors?

In this chapter we will first examine the unique role played by customers as they play their part in the delivery of their own service. Service customers are not only in the "factory" but have a role as a production worker. The more proficient they are as a service worker the better the service they will receive. One only has to look at the impact a "novice" service consumer can have. For example, a foreign tourist in an alien setting knows nothing of the process of which they are part. Their inexperience impacts the service for every other customer.

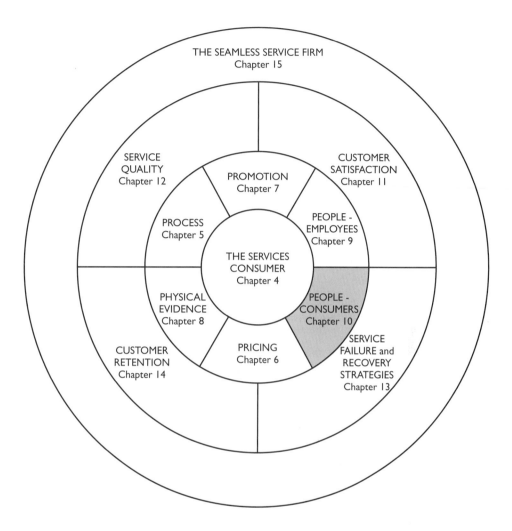

Customers can be involved at different levels and participate to a greater or lesser extent. For example, in providing information to the company delivering their tax return, they are a key part of the success of the whole service. In other cases their presence and conformance to the norms of the setting is all that is required. Watching a movie requires a little participation, but not following the rules, e.g., talking or walking about, will destroy the experience for everyone else.

Using some of the same ideas, we will go on to consider the management opportunities that arise because the consumer is still in the "environment, or factory, managed by the service firm during consumption." As well as influencing the customer as a "factory worker," it is possible to influence their perception of the service they receive. Consider two consumers experiencing exactly the same levels of physical density of people in a crowded setting such as a club or sporting event. One perceives the other people as an important part of the experience and something that adds excitement and fun. The other finds their fellow customers oppressive, restraining and even threatening. What could possibly explain the difference? Someone rang the fire alarm. This is an extreme example to illustrate that it is the consumers' perceptions that matter, and that they can differ significantly from an objective reality.

# Expert and Novice Consumers as Part of the Production Process

In essence, a service is a performance[2] in which consumers are often physically present and active participants. Consumers are assigned a specific set of tasks by the service organization and these tasks have to be performed by them. In restaurants, we queue up when asked to do so, order from a menu when asked, sometimes even clearing our own tables. At a doctor's surgery we provide the information necessary for the diagnosis. **Consumer performance**, our participation in the production process, needs to be managed for a service firm to be successful.[3]

**consumer performance** An individual's participation in the production of their own service.

Not all consumers are equally proficient in terms of performance. A service firm has to contend with "**novices**" and "**experts.**" A novice does not know what to do or how to perform. An expert, by comparison, knows how to be part of the production process and the role that they have to follow. An expert in Blockbuster would know how to use the store. They would understand how to make their own selection and check out. With even greater expertise, they would know how the different categories of titles are arranged and be efficient in their selection. A real Blockbuster expert learned a long time ago that the hottest new titles never stay on the shelves for long. The best place to look for them is in the returns bin before they are re-shelved.

**novice and expert performance** The spectrum of performance ability. Not all consumers are equally proficient. The novice does not know what to do and how to perform. An expert knows how to be part of the production process.

Compare that with the description of a dining experience provided to Customerssuck.com by a server. Is this a novice consumer?

*Server:* Hi, welcome to ****** how can I help you?

*Customer:* I'm hungry.

*Server:* Well, what would you like today?

*Customer:* I'm hungry ! Bring me food!

*Server:* Ma'am, unless you tell me what you would like, I can't really help you.

*Customer:* You're useless! I said I'm hungry! I just want FOOD!

*Server:* Ma'am, I'm asking what kind of food you would like.

*Customer:* Why are you asking me these stupid questions? I'm telling you everything you need to know!

**expert consumers** Individuals who have expertise in the purchase process for a particular good or service. Expert performers, by comparison, are expert in the service production process.

Expert consumer performance should not be confused with the concept of an "**expert consumer**," i.e., an individual who has expertise in the choice process of buying. They know how to buy well, but may be a novice when it comes to participating in the process of producing their own service.

# Consumer Performance and Operational Efficiency

For those in charge of the operations of a service business, customers are a source of many of their problems. The Apocryphal quote that opened this chapter has been attributed to operations managers in service business as diverse as bus companies and hotels. Since consumer performance is part of service operations, the diversity and unpredictability of consumers are a major source of uncertainty. Novice consumers in particular may disrupt the process by failing to comply with procedures.[4]

As discussed in Chapter 5, the extent to which the consumer is part of the process is regarded as the dominant constraint on the efficiency of the service system.[5,6] Logically, therefore, the efficiency of a service operation can be improved by limiting the extent of consumer performance in services.

This approach argues for the **buffering of the technical core**, or decoupling of production from environmental and customer disturbance. Raw material stocks are created to ensure a steady flow. Finished goods stocks are used to separate the manufacturing process from fluctuations in demand. The factory can therefore be isolated and optimized. Such models formed the foundation of modern manufacturing theory until the emergence of the idea of lean manufacturing.[7,8] Applied to services, this buffering approach argues for the minimization of the dependence on consumer performance and the "production-lining" of parts of the operation that can be isolated.[9,10,11]

Not all services are susceptible to such a low contact approach. In some cases the customer has to become part of the process, e.g., a hairdresser. In other cases the firm chooses to differentiate itself from competitors by offering "more personal service," i.e., higher contact. High contact systems can also be desirable when consumer actions can supplement or substitute for the labor and information provided by employees.

**High contact systems** depend for their efficiency on the management of the way the consumer behaves: consumer performance. **Low contact systems** can be isolated from the customer and are open to the use of more traditional manufacturing "production-line" approaches.

The impact of having performance expert consumers can be profound. In financial planning, for instance, planners log about five times as many hours on a first year client as they do on a repeat customer. Part of this is due to the time to create records and profiles. The rest of the time is taken by the client learning to communicate with the planner and the company. This collaborative learning between client and planner can create enormous productivity advantages.[12]

In the auto service business, expert customers are also cheaper to serve because they tend to call in advance for appointments, are more flexible on scheduling, and are better at describing the problem. New customers tend to drive in off the street at lunchtime, when bays are already fully utilized, and give vague descriptions of the problems with the car.[13]

A side benefit of expert consumers is their impact on the motivation of contact personnel. Because they are expert, they can recognize good service and praise employees. Equally, because they are expert, they understand the complexity of the system and can be more tolerant of failure.

One view is that the consumer is an enemy and a source of uncertainty. The alternative views the presence of the consumer in service operations as an opportunity to use the consumer as a resource—to increase the degree of consumer performance. This involves rethinking the service to transfer part of the current service production to the consumer.[14] The greater the consumer performance, the less labor input the service company needs to provide. Classic examples of shifting labor to the consumer are such things as self-service gasoline or the now universal habit of carrying baggage on to aircraft.

## Consumer Performance and Information Technology

The shifting of labor to the consumer or increasing the extent of consumer performance is increasingly being driven by IT and the web. Consider the complete transformation of the end-to-end process of taking an airline trip. This has been completely revolutionized by the productivity gains from IT and the web.

---

**buffering the technical core** The operations management concept of ensuring that the core of the production process is able to run as efficiently as possible. For manufacturing plants this is executed by creating buffers (stocks) of raw material input and buffers (stocks) of the outputs to ensure the factory itself can run uninterrupted.

**high and low contact systems** Service production processes arranged on a spectrum according to how much the consumer is part of the process. In a high contact system the consumer is an integral part of the process; in a low contact system, although present, the consumer has a smaller role to play.

The shifting of labor to the consumer or increasing the extent of consumer performance is increasingly being driven by IT and the web. Self-service check-in at many of the world's most busiest airports is a classic example.

The old model started with a retail service experience—a trip to the travel agent, airline office or airline ticket counters. In the interaction with a service provider the flight would be booked on a proprietary computer system and a multi-part ticket printed on a specialist printer. Part of the ticket was removed by the agent and sent back to the airline. At the airport, after queuing, the check-in involved the collection of all or part of the ticket, printing a new document—the boarding card—and the luggage check in.

Consider the new model as it exists today. The customer uses the Internet to locate a suitable ticket. They might use a web service to identify the best deals and an intermediary to make the booking. They might go directly to an airline site. They are then issued with an e-ticket. The e-ticket carries the same information as the paper version—it is just that the information is held in the airline's database. The record contains the date and time of travel, the origin and destination, and the class of travel.

The vast majority of airline tickets today are e-tickets. By December 2007, the International Air Transport Association (IATA) estimated that 92 percent of tickets were electronic globally, and 97 percent in the United States. Southwest Airlines is credited with issuing the first e-ticket in 1994. The switch has therefore been very rapid. It would have been completed sooner except for the restrictions imposed after the September 2001 tragedy.

More recently the focus has shifted to the rest of the process. Airlines can still use check-in agents to process e-tickets at the airports. Identification is checked and a boarding pass created. However, more than half of all check-ins are now done with self-service kiosks at the airport. These check identity with machine readable passports, credit cards or even frequent flyer cards. They are also able to print a boarding pass.

However even the kiosks are now being superseded. Passengers can print their own boarding passes at home, leaving the security check to the gate. Indeed passengers checking in at the airport are starting to find that the best seats have already gone. Lufthansa is going one step further, allowing customers to check in at home and sending an electronic boarding pass to their cell phone. The bar code on the phone is readable at the gate, where a single identity check is undertaken.

Without major advances in IT this transformation would not have been possible. Airline databases have had to be centralized and made available remotely anywhere in the world. The Internet booking systems have had to be integrated in realtime with the airline systems. The e-ticket databases have to be available to the hundreds of check-in points throughout the world and seamlessly integrated with the boarding card system. Historically, check-in agents retyped data from tickets into the boarding card system.

The benefits to consumers are enormous, as they are for the airlines. Automation collapses the need for lining up at ticket agents and check-in desks. E-tickets are impossible to lose, and for that reason hard to steal. All documents, such as itineraries, can be reprinted if necessary. E-tickets make it easier to change routes as journeys evolve due to such things as weather delays. In the latest systems, because records are electronic and linked to cell phones, passengers can be texted automatically when a delay happens.

IATA estimates that the migration to e-tickets alone has saved 50,000 mature trees a year, or the equivalent of three square miles of mature forest per year.

There have been huge productivity benefits for the airlines, as work which used to be performed done by ticket and check-in agents has moved to consumers. For example, a recent Forrester Research Report on self-service check-in at airports shows the scale of the potential benefits. The report estimated that self-service check-in costs the airline 16 cents a passenger, compared with $3.68 using ticket counter agents.[15] Given that Southwest Airlines, the largest U.S. carrier by passenger numbers, flew 52.3 million passengers in the first half of 2008, the savings to that one airline have been $184 million in six months.

Increasing consumer performance in this way, however, has changed completely the process for the consumer with implications for customer satisfaction.

www.CartoonStock.com

"If you hate being on hold and want to get on with your work, press 1 - if you want to be on hold for a long time so you can do the crossword, press 2."

The introduction of information technology to enhance service operations has produced mixed results.

# Consumer Satisfaction and Consumer Performance

If consumer performance is to be shifted or reduced or increased, what will be the impact on consumer satisfaction with the service? How can consumers be managed as part of the production process?

---

## E-SERVICES *IN ACTION*

### Mastering the Self-check-out Lane at the Grocery Store

I am standing in the self-check-out lane at the Albertson's, wondering what I am doing here. After all, the lines at the other check-out lanes with human grocery clerks are about the same length.

My ears are filling with the comforting drone of Muzak, thoughts straying to what I'm going to make for dinner, when I realize that I am not properly in line. There's a new red dotted line with arrows taped to the sparkling tile floor at my feet. It wasn't here the last time I shopped.

Someone's effort to enhance the ease-of-use of the self-check-out lane by Albertson's customers, no doubt.

But it's taken this apparently less than savvy user a good five minutes to get the message, and I and the woman who has fallen into line behind me in some kind of act of blind faith (perhaps I look like a bellwether who knows her way around the self-check-out kiosks) have to shuttle our wire carts back along the length of the dotted red line, following the arrows backwards, noting the several pairs of boots and shoes now ahead of us, instead of behind us, because of our misunderstanding of the line, until we are legally and officially at the end.

"I thought that we *were* in line," I whisper to her, not wanting to be overheard by the others.

"Me too." She shrugs, rolls her eyes, a fellow victim of technology.

The man in line in front of me who is wearing Teva sandals with brown wool socks and rock-climbing pants, cradling a loaf of wheat bread in his arms like a baby, casts a smart-alecky glance in my direction, as if I should know better.

"*Self-check-out lane elitist*," I think, and glue my eyes to the lighted boxes with the numbers above each self-check-out register, blood racing in my veins. I'm not going to make any errors tonight. No one will be able to grumble to themselves about that woman who doesn't know what she's doing and how she's slowing down the self-check-out line, which is supposed to be faster, to give us all a little control over our grocery

shopping experience in a world where that's in short supply. After all, I've had plenty of practice.

I scan in my Shopper Reward Code and proceed to fly through the process of scanning the barcodes of my items, although a pesky container of rice pudding gives me some trouble. Things go much smoother when I don't have my nine-year-old son around to perch his tired and lazy behind on the bagging area like it's some kind of park bench, making lights and whistles go off until the bored looking grocery store employee charged with overseeing all six self-check-out kiosks has to come and rescue me amid the annoyed looks of the other independent types around me who'd like to have me believe that they're infinitely more skilled at this game than I.

I even know where the barcode is on the low-fat mozzarella cheese. I glance up briefly to the regular, human manned check-out lanes and see that I'm way ahead of some folks who got into their lines about the same time as me. I successfully search for the codes for clementines and roast beef. I tell the machine that my bakery items are chocolate sprinkle covered donuts, not éclairs. I confirm that I'm done shopping and slide my credit card through the slot on the face of the machine. Get my receipt, and I'm outta here, ahead of the know-it-all fellow with the loaf of bread whose card has apparently been rejected, and who is now receiving independent and cross-armed expert consulting services from the omnipresent self-check-out manager.

I cannot resist smiling to myself.

I step out into the dark and the swirling snow, not exactly what the weatherman predicted, and head for my SUV, pushing my wire basket with its sticking wheels over the ice and drifts, a master of the self-check-out lane, a true woman of the 21$^{st}$ Century.

Source: Kimberly West, "Mastering the Self-checkout Lane at the Grocery Store," **http://www.associatedcontent.com/article/120918/mastering_the_selfcheckout_lane_at.html?cat=15**, (January 16, 2007).

**expected script** The script the consumer carries with them into the service setting; what they expect to happen and the benchmark against which they will evaluate the experience.

Chapter 11 covers the topic of consumer satisfaction in some detail; however, applying a simple logic it is clear that consumer performance can influence satisfaction in a number of ways. An expert consumer performer will enable the service firm to deliver an **expected script** and therefore meet expectations. Meeting expectations is one of the prime sources of consumer satisfaction. Moreover, the consumer will often have a sense of achievement in successfully navigating a service experience. Achievement is known to be a determinant of satisfaction. (See E-services in Action.) Successful performance will also give a consumer a sense of control of the situation, which has been shown to be motivational.[16]

A number of studies have also shown that a lack of consumer performance expertise can cause dissatisfaction. In a study of consumers' satisfaction with self-service technologies, researchers found that over one-third of incidents that caused dissatisfaction were due to "poor design." However further interpretation of what respondents were attributing to "poor design" showed what they actually meant was that they were novices and had not yet learned to participate in the service.[17]

**attribution** The allocation of responsibility to self and other people, or even chance.

Performance can also influence satisfaction through **attribution**. There is a proven tendency for individuals to claim more responsibility for success and less responsibility for failure in situations where the outcome is produced with others. The "self-serving bias" has been shown to be applicable to situations of co-production of service.[18] In studying self-service technology, it has also been shown that consumers tend to blame the technology when things go wrong, but take the credit themselves when the experience is satisfying.[19]

## The Theatrical Analogy

The key to managing consumer performance is an understanding of consumers' behavior during such service experiences. Such understanding provides insight into how to create experts and how to create systems to cope with novices and experts.

A useful metaphor for the service encounter is that of a theatrical drama.[20] The scene is set by the creation of the physical setting in which the performance is to be played. There are two kinds of actors: employees and consumers. Actors are assigned roles in which they have to play in the "production." The importance of roles for employees was discussed in the previous chapter, but the same logic can be just as easily applied to consumers. The performance is scripted with each actor receiving instructions (and dialogue), and works to the extent that all the actors "know their parts."

Interestingly, psychologists have for a long time suggested that knowledge about familiar, frequent situations of all kinds is stored in our minds as a coherent description of events expected to occur—the script. For example, a banking script assumes the presence of a cashier or teller, a branch, a counter, forms, and other customers.

**control and predictability** One of the primary motivational needs for an individual. Psychologists have agreed that all human beings like to feel in control of their environments. The source of that feeling of control is when the environment is predictable.

Like a theatrical script, psychologists suggest that scripts can be broken into subsets or scenes. Thus, an Internet retailing script may be composed of scenes relevant to logging-in, browsing, checking-out and paying. Scripts contain a set of actions related to the event. Researchers have shown that when respondents were asked to describe commonly occurring events, many actions were mentioned by more than half of the people.[21] Interestingly, scripts can be so strong that individuals will "fill in the gaps."[22] Experiments have shown that respondents, when shown a commonly occurring event and then asked to describe it, will often remember having seen actions that were not presented.[23] Experiments have also shown respondents reordering events that were presented to them to conform with what they could normally expect to find.

Scripts are extremely useful to individuals. We are continuously bombarded with events that have to be processed. Scripts enable us to recognize and categorize them, and to know what to do next.[24] Individuals have a deep-set need for **control and predictability**.[25] Scripts allow us to face new events and achieve predictability efficiently.

The theatrical analogy is clearly in use at Disney World. Employees are referred to as cast members who perform their roles for customers "on stage" and take breaks "off stage" out of sight of Mickey and Minnie fanatics.

### Defining "Novices" and "Experts" Using the Script Idea

Psychologists studying scripts for all kinds of settings can provide clues that help us define the expert and the novice at the service.[26,27,28]

A novice performer is an individual who uses more general scripts to handle situations that differ in quite significant ways: for example, using a "dining" script to cover a fine dining and family restaurant experience. Their script will tend to be relatively simple and have very few "if-then" branches within them. As a result, a novice is more likely to make mistakes in a specific setting, and less likely to cope with complex situations.

The expert performer, by comparison, will have rich and complicated scripts for the particular specific service. Having had multiple experiences of the service, they can cope with unexpected changes, and have plenty of "if-then" branches in their script. They have, for example, a fine dining script and can cope with different service personnel introducing variations or changes such as menu items not being available.

## Managing Consumer Performance Scripts

The theatrical analogy and, particularly, the idea of a script provide a way of tying together operational efficiency and consumer satisfaction. The service performance will be efficient to the extent that both the service provider and the consumer follow the script. Expert consumers are more able to adapt to the service provider's script and to optimize the efficiency of the operator.

If satisfaction comes when expectations are met or exceeded, if the service experience follows the expected script, then the consumer will be satisfied. If the performance unexpectedly exceeds the expectation, then the customer may well be delighted.[29] Aligning consumers' scripts with the service operation therefore has the double benefit of improving efficiency and increasing consumer satisfaction.

Applying the performance logic would suggest seven key tasks for management: audit your consumer performance expertise; increase your share of expert consumers; increase consumer loyalty; manage script changes carefully; create systems to cope with novices and experts; manage your customer and service mix; and use service provider strategies on your consumers.

## Audit Your Consumer Performance Expertise

**auditing consumer performance expertise** Measuring the current extent to which the consumer understands the script that the service system has been designed to deliver.

It is important to know what percentage of your consumers are expert performers. It is possible to measure the quality of an individual's script through market research. The simplest approaches require individuals merely to describe the relevant service experience in the form of a script.[30] Such an approach has been used in services and proved to be sufficiently sensitive to differentiate between scripts of the same general category, as for example between scripts for a fine dining restaurant and a fast food restaurant.[31] A score can then be computed comparing the company script with the elicited script.

An alternative approach relies on the reordering of events within the script. Respondents are presented with typical events in a jumbled fashion and asked to place them in the correct order. The individual's expertise can then be assessed by comparing their reordering with the correct order and computing a score.[32]

## Increasing the Share of Consumers Who Are Expert Performers

Can service organizations have a greater portion of experts? There are two generic approaches: Attract more existing experts; and help consumers become experts.

***Segmenting the Market to Attract Experts***    If consumer performance experts can be identified, it is then possible to see if any of the traditional segmentation measures of age and socio-economic group can be related to the expert segments. In the context of e-business, it is possible to measure consumer performance directly. By tracking consumers' behaviors on a website, it is possible to categorize them as experts objectively. One study of 20,000 users of a web service used the "speed of use" to define an expert. Analysis showed that experts did vary in terms of age, income, race, family status, and possibly region. More intriguingly, studying the same users over six months showed that expert consumers were also more loyal.[33]

***Creating Experts***    Is it possible to help consumers become experts by teaching them the script?

The psychologists suggest that scripts are built up from generalizations about experiences from early beginnings in life. As we grow up we learn by watching others and being taught how to behave by our parents. We may start off with a specific script for going out to, say, a Walmart, but soon learn that this is only part of a higher general experience called shopping.

When faced with a service experience which is new to us, we adopt a number of strategies. The first thing we do is to approximate using an analogous experience. In a study of consumer performance, an Internet banking system was created. Consumers were deliberately selected to have no experience of such a system. Some of the respondents were asked to move money between accounts and to check balances, without any additional instructions.

Because the system was electronic it was possible to measure their performance directly by measuring such things as transaction time and number of keystroke errors. Respondents also completed a questionnaire about related service experiences. The results clearly showed that the best prediction of a consumer's performance was their previous experience of banking, computers, and automatic teller machines.[34] Clearly the consumers were drawing on previous experience to create an approximate script. When creating a novel or new service, it is important to *give consumers clues about analogous services* so that they can create a script quickly.

The power of an analogous service as a model for consumers is shown in this quote from a service provider describing the problems her customers have with the in store ATM:

*Several customers have told me that we're the only store they know where the magnetic strip has to face the right. But that's why there is a neon orange sign on the machine saying, "Magnetic strip faces to the right". I mean, how much more simple can it get?*

*I can also understand it because usually you press one of the little gray buttons next to 'yes' or 'no' when it says, 'is such-and-such amount OK?' But again, there's a neon orange sign! It says "Enter = OK" .And it's not like it's some little ambiguous button, hiding in the corner of the machine. It's the biggest button on the thing! And it's bright green!*

*Even with these two signs taped to the machine, 95 percent of the customers swipe their cards upside down and backwards. Then when you try to give those simple instructions, like, "Flip your card the other way,", it's like their hands go into freaky frenzy, turning the card every OTHER way, and at a million miles an hour! I'm like, "Yes, that way – no, the—no, other side—YES! YOU'VE GOT IT!" Then when they finally get that part down pat, you hear them pushing every other button than the "Enter" button. I told one girl, "Push the green button," and she actually wiggled her finger and said, "Okay, green, green, green button …" She couldn't identify the color green.*

Source: "It's the Green Button," CustomersSuck website, July 9, 2007

The employee clearly blames the customers for being stupid. However the customers could reasonably ask why this store insists on having a "non-standard" machine. The script of the machine does not conform to the script stored in memory by the consumer under "ATM." Certainly, their dissatisfaction will be attributed to the store.

The second thing that consumers do is to *use the service experience itself to look for clues to a script.* Those clues can come from many different sources: from the physical environment, the service providers, or indeed other customers. Take something as prosaic as airline lavatories. Customer satisfaction depends upon the occupied signs being lit or unlit so that passengers can see the situation before leaving their seat. It is therefore important for passengers to lock the toilet door, hence triggering the occupied sign. How do the airlines ensure that this happens? They connect the door lock to the light switch. Some clues are less obvious, as in the strategic placement of tray return stands to ensure that consumers bus their own tables. Some electrical goods service organizations send all their customers checklists to be prepared before calling in a service report.

Some service businesses offer instructions for use. A hotel will provide a directory of services to guests on how to use the hotel. Novel experiences such as health farms or Club Med holidays will offer a formal orientation program at the beginning of the guest's stay. All are designed to increase the level of expertise of consumers' performance. Other orientation programs are less formal, but just as useful. Service employees can be instructed on how to recognize novice consumers and offer instructions. Bellboys will often ask if you are new to the hotel and, if you are, offer instructions on how to use your room and the different styles of restaurants within the hotel.

Airlines will place agents on the self-service check-in kiosks to catch novices and teach them the script.

The Internet banking study described earlier took another sample of consumers and allowed them to develop expert scripts by providing written instructions and screen-based practice sessions. The improvement in script compared to the novice group could be measured directly. Both the earlier novice and this expert group were offered a jumbled set of statements describing the Internet banking process and asked to place them in the correct order—in essence to reassemble the script. The expert group scored higher. They then made fewer mistakes when asked to use the system in earnest, and were much more satisfied with the experience.[35]

In another study of mammography exam screening, half of respondents received a detailed preview of what would happen and a short video illustrating the entire procedure. The other half of the sample received no such preview. After this, the respondents answered questions about their sense of control, their level of anxiety, and the accuracy of their expectations. All the women were then presented descriptions of three actual mammography experiences. One followed the preview exactly, one contained blunders by the provider, and the third described an enhanced service. The results showed that "teaching the script" through the preview generated more accurate expectations, considerably less anxiety, and higher levels of perceived control. Across all three scenarios those respondents with a preview were more satisfied with the described scenario.[36]

The final source of a script can be studying *the behavior of the other consumers.*[37] We learn from very young to look for other, expert, consumers and emulate their behavior. Tourists often adopt such a strategy. For example, they can be seen loitering outside Swiss banks learning how to use the complex security doors. There is a story, probably Apocryphal, of McDonald's having trouble when it first launched in the United Kingdom teaching consumers to clear their own tables. Their solution, allegedly, was to hire professional burger eaters who ate their food and, with exaggerated displays, emptied their trays into the bins and placed them on top of the receptacle.

***Increase Consumer Loyalty***    Research into why loyal customers are more profitable has suggested that there are many reasons related to such things as word of mouth and pricing. For services, an extra reason is added—that loyal customers can offer service businesses cost savings. It is suggested that loyal customers are also much more likely to be expert customers. An expert requires multiple exposures to a service experience in order to learn the script. Once the expert has been created, it is important for the firm to maintain that individual's loyalty. Expert customers are valuable and must be protected, whether through loyalty incentive programs, such as the airline's frequent flyer programs, or through recognition in the service experience.[38]

***Change Scripts Carefully***    In the drive for operational efficiency or product differentiation, service businesses are often keen to innovate in the way the service is delivered. To the extent that this involves a change of script, it needs to be managed carefully. Too big a change means that your expert consumers will have to renew their expertise. Expert consumers, with an existing script-based expectation, may see the new service as a service failure and be dissatisfied.

The Wendy's Hamburger "instruction book," described earlier, is a good example of a service business instinctively understanding the need to reprogram consumers' scripts. Wendy's followed McDonald's into the U.K. market. The most important thing for Wendy's, in terms of operational efficiency and customer satisfaction, was to reprogram customers. McDonalds, at that time, offered a very constrained menu and a tightly defined script. The customer script was therefore very different at Wendy's. This would inevitably reduce consumer performance, slow down service, and create dissatisfaction.

The revolution in the whole airline experience, described earlier, faces customers with a profoundly different role to play in the drama. They are expected to be Internet enabled and to be able to buy tickets electronically. They are expected to print their own itineraries and boarding pass. At the airport they must be capable of using the kiosk or knowing that they already have a boarding pass. The script is completely different, the consumer performance different, and the competencies required for the role very different.

As consumers we value predictability and control. We will therefore, in most cases, migrate towards a service experience where we know the script. We will look for props and signals in the way the stage is set in a service business, to judge whether this is a script with which we are familiar. This was precisely the problem faced by Citibank, many years ago, when it first introduced automatic teller machines into its New York branches. Regular customers would walk right past the empty ATMs to join the lines for the traditional tellers. In the end, the bank hired receptionists who intercepted clients and cajoled them to use the ATMs.[39]

The only exception to our desire for predictability seems to be when we deliberately look for something new. Foreign tourism automatically throws us into situations that are new; we become novices again and seem to enjoy the novelty of the experience. We may become exasperated by our inability to do the simplest of things—to withdraw money from the bank. We may, however, revert to familiar scripts to refresh ourselves by seeking out a familiar restaurant chain or staying in a branded multinational hotel. Such branded hotel chains offer us the predictability of a familiar script when we are in need of it. A Holiday Inn feels like a Holiday Inn whether it is in Atlanta, London, or Kuala Lumpur.

*Coping with Novices and Experts*    No matter how long a firm has been in operation, it will still have both old and new customers. A firm cannot only have experts because it grows by recruiting new customers, and these are likely to be novices. A service firm, therefore, will have to learn to manage two different segments at the same time: novices and experts. Operationally, this means that the system has to cope with two very different levels of consumer performance.[40]

Unfortunately novices and experts do not arrive with labels identifying the level of their consumer performance abilities. One of the few places where this does happen is in online retailing. Regular customers, when they log in, can be identified and the service experience customized to them. They receive fewer instructions and are flagged to use the short cuts within the system. Novice customers, by comparison, receive help boxes and guidance.

**self selection** Given the right clues about a service business, consumers will tend to choose for themselves the service that best fits their needs.

In the absence of an indication of performance expertise, all a service business can do is to allow users to **self-select**. The frequent traveler and user programs in the travel industry are good examples of this. The Hilton Honors "check-in" desk offers recognition to loyal customers. It also allows them to use their expertise to check in as efficiently as possible. The guests are often more proficient at the check-in script than the receptionists, and can be seen anticipating the next question or indeed prompting the receptionists. The same effect is often visible at frequent flyer check-ins, where expert passengers will answer the security questions even before they are asked.

Blockbuster did not hide the return bins from its expert customers. They were, after all, saving the staff time and effort. They were evidently advised instead to take some classic movies off the shelves and put them into the return bins. In this way their expert performers were rewarded by not having to search the shelves for these movies.

Unfortunately coping with experts and novices means that the firm has to manage their interaction with each other. Not only can a novice with an incomplete script interfere with an expert by virtue of their presence, but the scripts may be in direct conflict with each other. In a study of 330 service incidents, researchers looked at how the presence of others positively or negatively affected the service experience. Nearly half of the incidents described as satisfying or dissatisfying related to what were classified as "protocol." Many dissatisfying incidents referred to lining up when other customers clearly did not respect the protocol or script of acceptable behavior in a line.[41]

"At EPCOT there was a couple that was trying to cut in front of us...."

Equally, when there was agreement on the protocol or script, customers were satisfied. "There was no pushing or breaking in line to get ahead of others"

***Managing the Customer and Service Mix***    Because customers frequently interact with each other in the service setting, it is important to understand that different segments may have different scripts that may not be compatible. This can also put the service provider into the position of performing two scripts at the same time, something even the best actor would find difficult.

A hotel provides a classic example of the problem. On a given day it can be dealing with many difficult segments: individuals and couples staying in the hotel, groups staying in the hotel, a large conference occupying the ballroom, a board meeting in a small conference room, etc. Pity the staff in the restaurant serving guests with very different scripts from fine dining a la carte, to fixed menu groups, to conference buffet with a one and a half hour lunch break. Pity the other guests as they interact with their fellow diners who have very different scripts. Managing these multiple and often conflicting segments has been dubbed "**compatibility management.**"[42] Organizations will do their best to keep the different types of consumer separate and in homogeneous groups. They can use separate floors or rooms to do this, or even just simple signage.

Compatibility management can also include training consumers in the script or using codes of conduct (e.g., "please do not use the dining room before...."; "Please only use the buffet service," etc.). Finally, service personnel need to be trained and sensitized to watch for and manage the conflict between segments.

***Use Service Provider Strategies on Your Consumers***    Starting from a human resources perspective, consumers have been viewed as "**partial employees.**"[43] New employees are normally "socialized" into the organization and, logically, partial employees or customers should be socialized in the same way.[44] To be successful, new employees require a clear understanding of their role (role clarity), ability, and motivation. Clearly, the script idea relates heavily to the clarity of the role a consumer plays. It is also important, however, that the script a consumer is asked to perform is within their abilities. If a home Internet banking system requires too high a level of intelligence to be used, it will clearly alienate customers.[45]

If socialization can be achieved, then consumers will understand the policies of the organization and its values, if not the script. **Consumer Socialization** has been related to positive outcomes for the firm, including customer satisfaction, motivation and perceived quality.[46] See Figure 10.1.

# Managing Consumer Service Perceptions

Consumers will base their evaluation of the service they receive on their perceptions not reality. We will excuse poor service for good food and sometimes the other way around. Our perceptions are often influenced by our mood, something over which the service organization has no influence. Our past experiences or cultural background can influence our perceptions of the simplest service experiences (see Global Services in Action). However there are things that the service firm can do to influence our perceptions. Take for example, the whole problem of lines and waiting times.

Because production and consumption occur simultaneously, several customers often share a common service experience. As a result, demand often outpaces supply and lines

---

**compatibility management** The management of a diverse group of customers with different needs within the same service setting.

**partial employees** The operations management approach to consumer performance is to view the consumer as an employee (albeit only part of one) and to apply the same people logic to them as they would to an employee.

**consumer socialization** From a human resources management perspective, employees have to "on-board" successfully into the organization. They have to be taught their role, the places and procedures, and most importantly, "how we do things around here." That is the socialization process.

**FIG-10.1** Managing
Consumer Perfor-
mance Script

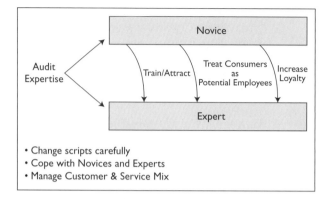

develop that must be effectively managed to minimize customer dissatisfaction. Due to the unpredictability of consumer demand inherent in many service operations, the only cases in which the supply of available service and consumer demand balance exactly *is by accident*. As a result, consumers of services often find themselves waiting for service.

Effectively managing consumer waits is particularly crucial due to the importance of first impressions on consumer perceptions of the service experience. First impressions are often long lasting, and can dramatically affect customer evaluations of the total experience, regardless of how good the service was after the wait. A dental patient waiting until 4 p.m. for an appointment that was supposed to begin at 2 p.m. will most likely care little about how friendly the staff and the dentist are by the time the appointment actually begins.

There is a real difference between actual and perceived waiting time for consumers and managers. Over the years, through trial and error, eight principles of waiting have developed to help service firms effectively manage consumer perceptions of waits..[47] In fact, in some instances, effective management of consumer waits has actually led to increased profit opportunities.

***Principle #1: Unoccupied Waits Feel Longer Than Occupied Waits***    Waiting around with nothing to do makes every minute seem so much longer. Successful service firms have learned to manage consumer waits by occupying the consumer's time. Restaurants can occupy consumer waits by offering to let the consumer wait in the lounge area, which also increases the profit-making opportunity for the firm. Similarly, golf courses offer driving ranges, and the medical community tends to offer reading materials. Ideally, tactics utilized to occupy consumers should be related to the ensuing service

A popular bar within a restaurant not only serves as an additional profit center for the restaurant but also provides an opportunity for customers to occupy their time while they wait to be seated.

encounter. Trivial attempts to occupy consumer waits, such as forcing the customer to listen to Muzak when placed on hold during a phone call, are sometimes met with customer resistance and frustration.

### Principle #2: Preprocess Waits Feel Longer Than Inprocess Waits—Postprocess Waits Feel Longest of All
The waiting period before the service starts feels longer to customers than waiting while the service is in process. For example, doctors often move waiting patients into empty examining rooms to convey the sense that the service has started. Realistically, the physician has simply changed the location of the wait. Effective techniques to manage preprocess waits include simply acknowledging the customer. For example, waitstaff are often too busy to serve customers as soon as they are seated. Phrases such as "I'll be with you as soon as I can," acknowledges the customer's presence and convey the message that the service has started. Other phrases, such as "your order is being processed," are also effective in keeping the customer informed of the status of the order.

Postprocess waits feel the longest of all waits. In many instances, the service has been delivered, and now the customer is simply waiting for the check or bill. It's baffling to customers to be subjected to delays when they simply want to give the service establishment money. Another example of customer impatience regarding postprocess waits can be experienced during deplaning procedures at the airport. On your next flight, listen to the sounds of passengers releasing their seatbelts as soon as (or before) the plane comes to a full stop. The door to the plane is not open, no one is leaving the plane, yet people are literally fighting for positions to get themselves off the plane as quickly as possible.

### Principle #3: Anxiety Makes the Wait Seem Longer
Have you ever noticed how much longer traffic lights take to change when you are in a hurry? This is because anxiety expands consumer perceptions of time. Effective service firms manage the anxiety levels of their customers by attempting to identify and then removing anxiety-producing components of the service encounter. The use of focus groups is particularly helpful in effectively identifying anxiety producers because many consumer fears may be irrational and/or overlooked by providers who fully understand the service delivery process. Often, information is one of the most effective tools in relieving consumer anxiety. For example, informing delayed airline passengers that connecting flights are being held for them, notifying waiting movie-goers that seats are available, and assisting new students in finding the right lines during registration will remove much of the anxiety felt by these consumer groups.

### Principle #4: Uncertain Waits Are Longer Than Known, Finite Waits
While waiting in a doctor's office, the wait "before" the stated appointment time passes much more quickly than the time spent waiting "beyond" the appointment time. Restaurants have learned this lesson the hard way. In the not-so-distant-past, it seemed that restaurants would purposely underestimate their wait times to encourage patrons not to leave the restaurant to dine at a competitor's establishment. This strategy resulted in angry, frustrated customers who felt they had been purposely misled and lied to for the sake of greed. By the time the customers were seated, they were so consumed with anger that the food, service, and atmosphere of the encounter became irrelevant, regardless of their quality. Moreover, many of these patrons would vow never to return. Today, it seems that restaurants overestimate their waits to provide consumers with a realistic timeframe from which to develop expectations. Other service providers simply make and keep appointments, which eliminates the customer's wait altogether. Even other providers, such as Disney, provide finite waiting times stated on signage which is strategically placed at certain points along the line (e.g., 10 minutes from this point).

***Principle #5: Unexplained Waits Are Longer Than Explained Waits***    It is human nature to want an explanation. You can almost see the disappointment in people's faces when the slow speed during a traffic jam on the highway resumes its normal pace without an explanation. Customers want to know why they have to wait, and the earlier the information is provided, the more understanding the consumer becomes, and the shorter the wait seems to take.

Due to the inseparability of services, customers sometimes have a difficult time understanding why all the service providers in the factory are not serving customers. Banks are a good example. Bank tellers must sometimes perform operational duties, such as balancing the cash drawer, which prohibits them from serving customers. However, since all bank teller stations are visible to the customers, customers often question why all the bank tellers are not actively serving the bank's customers.

Effective management may try to minimize this problem in one of two ways. First, management may consider educating consumers about the realities of the bank teller's duties, which extend beyond interactions with customers. Second, management may consider developing a physical facility where the teller is out of sight when performing non-customer related duties. This type of problem extends beyond the banking industry. Airlines, grocery stores, and other businesses that grant their employees rest breaks that are visible to the customer face similar challenges.

***Principle #6: Unfair Waits Are Longer Than Equitable Waits***    Effective consumer management should strive to provide a level playing field that is fair for all consumers. The majority of consumers are not unreasonable. Most restaurant consumers understand that larger parties will wait longer than smaller parties and that parties with reservations will be seated sooner than those who arrive unannounced. However, probably nothing will ignite a serious confrontation faster than consumers who feel they have been passed over by other customers who entered the service experience at a later time under the same set of circumstances.

Lines such as those found at McDonald's are classic examples of why consumers become frustrated. In each instance, the customer must pick the line he or she thinks will move fastest. Inevitably, the other lines move faster, and customers who entered the lines at a later time are served first, out of order. From a fairness perspective, methods that form a single line, such as those used at Wendy's, Burger King, and many banks, are preferable. Customers are served in the order in which they enter the service process.

Another classic example of unfair service is the priority that telephone calls receive over customers who are physically standing in line. The person on the telephone usually takes priority. This is the equivalent of that person walking up to the front of the line and bypassing all of the other customers whom have been patiently waiting for their turn. Management needs to consider the costs of having employees return phone calls at a more appropriate time versus the cost of alienating existing customers and placing employees in an awkward and often indefensible position.

***Principle #7: The More Valuable the Service, the Longer the Customer Will Wait***    Why else would you wait in a doctor's office for two hours? Is it any wonder that the word patient is a form of the word patience? The amount of time customers are willing to wait is often situational. When the service is considered valuable and few competitive alternatives exist, customers will be willing to wait much longer than if the reverse were true.

Perceived value of the service tends to increase with the title and status of the provider. Students will tend to wait longer for a full professor who is late for class than they will for an assistant professor; and they will wait for a dean or chancellor of the university even longer. Similarly, customers are willing to wait much longer for their meals at upscale restaurants than at fast food establishments. When managing consumer waits, the firm must understand the value its customers place on its services and the time they consider a reasonable wait because it does vary from sector to sector and within sectors.

***Principle #8: Solo Waits Are Longer Than Group Waits***    It is amusing to consider the amount of customer interaction typically displayed in a grocery store line. Generally, there is none at all, even though we are standing within inches of one another. However, note what happens when a delay occurs, such as a price check on an item or a customer who takes too long to fill out a check . . . the rest of the line quickly bonds like old friends! Group waits serve the function of occupying customers' time and reduce the perceived wait. When managing consumer waits, the practicality of actively encouraging consumers to interact may be considered.

Clearly many of these principles relate to the ideas introduced earlier in the chapter. The idea that customers like to feel in control of their environment underlies, for example, Principle #4. Information increases predictability and allows us to feel in control. Principle #6 suggests that we don't like an unfair wait, but this could just as easily be explained by the fact that we lose our sense of control and predictability when other consumers appear to have an alternative way through the process.

Operationally, the most important thing to understand is that applying these principles changes consumers perception of waiting time *without changing the actual time.* Organizations can spend large amounts of money and resources to reduce actual waiting time. The tradeoff is obviously between consumers' waiting and having spare resources. A bank teller line can be reduced by having more teller stations open. This costs money and leaves teller utilization low. Managing perceptions instead can often be more profitable.

Although we have focused here on managing the perceptions of waiting time, the ideas can be used to manage all the other aspects of the service experience as well. A supermarket will bake a small amount of fresh bread to allow the smell to permeate the whole store. This implies home cooking and freshness. Restaurants will manage the tempo of background music, slowing it down if the restaurant is empty and speeding it up if full. This has been shown to influence how long customers spend at the table. Everything in the servicescape can be used to help manage consumers' perceptions during the consumption of their service.

# Consumer Inseparability and the Role of Marketing and Operations

This section addresses the way managers from different functions need to change their thinking because of the consumer inseparability model.

Strategically, it is important to realize that the greater the extent of consumer participation in the production of their own service, the greater is the need to manage consumer performance. It is the only way to increase the productivity of such high contact services. Experts and novices are more than just partial employees of the service business. They are employees and consumers at the same time.[48] They can be accountable for their own satisfaction, and their perceived service can be managed.

Marketing managers need to broaden the scope of their thinking. Traditionally, marketing drives value for the business by focusing on how consumers make choices and what satisfies them. Understanding the choice process provides the clues to increase the firm's share of those choices. Satisfied customers can be retained.

When thinking about services, it is clear that the marketing toolkit can now be applied to improve the operational efficiency of the firm by creating expert performers. Experts can be created, scripts can be taught, and it will be seen as a benefit by the

## GLOBAL SERVICES *IN ACTION*

### Customer Service Expectations Vary Among Cultures

A European dining experience differs significantly from a Japanese dining experience. In Europe, dining is meant to be a slow-paced conversational event. Courses are deliberately spread out, and if you want your check, you will probably have to ask for it. A waiter who delivers an unrequested check to the table may be implicitly asking you to leave. Not so in Japan, says Misako Kamamoto, Chief Conductor of the Japan Travel Bureau. "When I take a group of Japanese tourists to a restaurant in Europe for the first time, I make a point to advise them…you must be resigned to the fact that it takes a good deal of time to have a meal in a European restaurant." Despite Kamamoto's warnings, the tourists still complain. "Why are European restaurants so slow in serving us? Please ask them to speed up the service. I don't want to wait for dessert and coffee. I can't stand a restaurant that gives such bad service."

Japanese tourists also feel treated shabbily in France where Paris retailers do not treat customers like "gods" as they are treated in Japan. Japanese customers are puzzled by the French attitude that they are "allowing the customer to buy" as opposed to being subservient to the customer. Many Japanese customers feel as though the French are acting like they are doing the customer a favor if the French retailer allows them to purchase merchandise from their shop.

Other customer service differences for the Japanese involve hotel bills and banking services. Hotel bills are assumed to be accurate and are paid on the spot. The Western habit of checking a hotel bill before offering payment would be considered rude in Japanese culture. Similarly, cashing a check in a bank would never involve double checking the amount the bank teller provides to the customer. Moreover, restaurant bills are always assumed to be accurate as well.

Finally, train stations also differ significantly between Eastern and Western cultures. Western train stations tend to be much quieter, and on the trains themselves peace and quiet is a valued environment. In contrast, Japanese train stations are noisy. Bells and loudspeakers announce the arrival and departures of trains, and on the trains, announcements regarding various types of topics are constant. At first blush, Japanese tourists truly enjoy the peace and quiet of the Western train experience; however, these feelings are quickly replaced by the anxiety caused by the perceived lack of information regarding their travel destinations. Effective service marketers must be aware and respond to the different customer service needs of its international customers.

Source: Jean-Claude Usunier and Julie Anne Lee, *Marketing Across Cultures,* 4th ed. (Harlow, England: Prentice Hall, 2005), 259.

customer. We are all motivated to learn by our need for control in our environment. Increasing the amount of consumer performance can, for some of us, increase that sense of predictability and control. For many of us, once we have learned the script, carrying our own bags onto the airline is an attractive proposition. What we fear is the novice flyer who argues that the locker above their seat is allocated to them!

Marketing can also be applied to managing the consumers' perceived rather than actual service. In this case the marketing expertise has to be applied through the design of the servicescape and the role of the service provider. A deep understanding of consumer psychology, however, can add value and save operations costs.

Operations' managers need to include the consumer in their planning. Starting from a more prescriptive point of view, it is important to be able to define an appropriate consumer script, given the nature of the service operation.[49,50] This again touches on the issue of scripts delivered through technology versus through people.[51]

Technology does impose tighter scripts on consumers. Service providers can be "empowered," as described in the previous chapter. Empowerment provides for the variation in the script to suit the particular consumer. Unfortunately, machines cannot be empowered. They can be programmed through "if-then" branches to categorize consumers and provide an appropriate script. Unfortunately, such programs are often self-defeating since they are regarded as tedious and boring by customers.

Operations managers also need to understand that it is consumers' perceptions that matter, and not just to focus on the operational statistics of the firm. Reducing actual waiting times by 25 percent would be an outstanding achievement, but the principles described earlier might mean that the perceived wait is perceived to be longer. If the changes made to reduce waits make consumers feel more inequitable, less certain, more anxious, etc., all the potential consumer value created by the operational changes can be lost by losing focus on consumer perception.

The concept of a script can just as easily be applied to the service provider.[52] They, too, have to cope with a frequently occurring service experience. Indeed, because they perform the script so often, they may be the ultimate experts. How provider and consumer scripts interact, what happens when an expert provider meets a novice consumer, and vice versa, are all key to designing satisfying experiences for consumers.

The human capital management systems need to be constructed to ensure that the service providers know and execute the correct script, which ensures that they are operationally efficient. The script can also influence how the consumers perceive the service. Frequently repeated scripts such as this have been shown to produce mindless or robotic performance.[53] Processes and systems have to be created to balance the needs of the service provider, the customer, and the firm. Service providers have to be experts, with scripts that can adapt to different levels of consumer performance expertise. Too much expertise may, however, create robot-like service.

Using the theatrical analogy, it is the script that ties together all the different actors in the play. Actors using a different script cannot deliver a successful performance. The service script needs to be learned by all the key players in the service experience. It is also

---

## SUSTAINABILITY AND SERVICES *IN ACTION*

### How Complicated Can it Be to Throw Garbage Away?

Imagine the poor foreigner coming to live in Germany. Without help from their neighbors, could they even throw away their garbage? Everybody automatically sorts their garbage into paper, glass, plastic and organized waste and puts the appropriate trash out on the appropriate day. The wrong trash in the wrong bin on the wrong day will not be collected. Toxic waste such as old batteries or unused pharmaceuticals has to be returned to the drugstore or supermarket. Similarly, larger electrical items like TVs have to be delivered to separate collection stations.

In Germany most plastic bottles have a deposit, and retailers who sell bottles and cans are required to take returns. Similarly, supermarkets are required to take back all types of packaging. Foreigners are often surprised to see other shoppers unwrap their purchases at the store and leave the packaging behind rather than sort and store it at home before leaving it our on the appropriate day in the month to be collected.

Now suppose we move elsewhere in Europe. In Northern Italy each household gets five bins for five different types of waste. They pay an annual fee, but are charged extra for the non-recyclable waste. In the United Kingdom and many parts of the United States the bins are now micro-chipped and weighed so customers can be charged for the type and weight of their waste.

the point on which the different functions in the service firm must converge: operations, marketing, human capital management. All the functions must be following the same script, and so must the consumers. However, in the end it will be the consumers' perception of the script and the experience that will determine the success of the firm.

## Summary

A service can be viewed as an experience in which the consumer is an active participant. This inseparability has two consequences for managers. Uniquely to services, consumers act to a greater or lesser extent as "partial employees" of the service firm. This chapter suggests that the best way to understand this consumer performance role is through a theatrical analogy with actors, roles and scripts. Consumers vary to the extent that they know the script and therefore to the extent to which they are experts and novices. The chapter suggests seven steps to managing performances using this expert and novice idea.

The consumers' perception of their service experience can still be influenced, since they are still part of the service system. Even objective things such as waiting time can be influenced by that environment. It is the customers' perceived service that matters to the organization.

The consumer as a partial employee and the need to manage perceptions change the role of operations, marketing and HR managers, making them much more inter-dependent than in the typical goods company.

## Key Terms

consumer performance, p. 266
novice and expert performance,
    p. 266
expert consumers, p. 266
buffering the technical core, p. 267
high and low contact systems,
    p. 267

expected script, p. 271
attribution, p. 271
control and predictability, p. 271
auditing consumer performance
    expertise, p. 273
self selection, p. 276

compatibility management,
    p. 277
consumer socialization, p. 277
partial employees, p. 277

## Review Questions

1. Discuss the pros and cons of increasing customer participation in the service delivery process.

2. An airline is planning to switch to self-service check-in using kiosks at the airport. Discuss alternative ways they can teach their customers the new script.

3. Describe a service experience in which you consider yourself an expert. Describe how you became an expert.

4. Describe a service situation in which a novice consumer performer reduces the satisfaction for an expert. Suggest management activities that could reduce the problem.

5. Describe a service environment in which the physical design, signage, layout, etc., makes it easy to understand the script. Describe another where the environment makes it very difficult to understand the role of and the script of the consumer.

6. Choose an example from your own experience of a service business that "changed the script" for their consumer. Suggest why they might have made the change and the problems it created.

7. From your own experiences as a service provider, describe how it feels to serve an expert and a novice consumer. Which would you prefer? And why?

8. Review the "Sustainability and Services in Action" description of garbage disposal. How would you suggest introducing changes to the services provided?

9. Despite the best attempts of many service firms to balance supply and demand, the only time the balance truly occurs may be by accident. Explain why this is so.

10. Select four of the eight "principles of waiting" and discuss their significance to managing the consumer's experience.

# Notes

The sections of this chapter about consumer performance are largely based on John E. G. Bateson, "Are your Customers Good Enough for your Service Business," *Academy of Management Executive*, 2002, 116, 4, pp. 110–114,

1. Paco Underhill, *Why We Buy*, Orion Books, 1999, p. 91.
2. J. M. Rathmell, "What is Meant by Service", *Journal of Marketing*, 30, 2966, (October, 1966), pp. 32–36.
3. John Bateson, "Do We Need Service Marketing?" in *Marketing Customer Services: New Insights*, eds Pierre Eiglier et al., (Cambridge MA: Marketing Services Institute, 1977), pp. 1–30.
4. R. B. Chase, "Where Does the Customer Fit in a Service Operation?" *Harvard Business Review*, 56, (November/ December, 1978), pp. 137–142.
5. R. B. Chase and David Tanzik, "The Customer Contact Model for Organizational Design," *Management Science*, 29, 9, (1983), pp. 1037–1105.
6. R. B. Chase, "The Customer Contact Approach to Services: Theoretical Base and Practical Extensions," *Operations Research*, 29, 4, (July-August, 1981), pp. 698–706.
7. J. F. Krafcik, "Triumph of the Lean Production System," *Sloan Management Review*, 30, 1, (1988), pp. 41–52.
8. J. P. Womak and D. T. Jones, *Lean Thinking: Banish Waste and Create Wealth in Your Corporation* (New York: Simon and Schuster, 1996).
9. See reference 4.
10. See reference 5.
11. R. B. Chase, G. B. Northcraft, and G. Wolf, "Designing High Contact Service Systems: Applications to Branches of a Savings and Loans," *Decision Sciences*, 15, (1984), pp. 542–556.
12. Frederick F. Riecheld *The Loyalty Effect*, (Boston: HBS Press, 1996), p. 45.
13. See reference 12.
14. C. H. Lovelock and R. F. Young, "Look to Consumers to Increase Productivity," *Harvard Business Review*, 57, 3, (1979), pp. 168–178.
15. B. Vroom, *Work and Motivation*, (New York: Wiley, 1964).
16. J. E. G. Bateson, "Perceived Control and the Service Encounter," J. A. Czepiel, M. R. Solomon, eds, *The Service Encounter* (Boston: Lexington Books, 1985), p. 67; J. E. G. Bateson, "Perceived Control and the Service Experience," *Handbook of Services Marketing and Management*, T. A. Swartz and D. Iacobucci eds., (Thousand Oaks, CA: Sage Publications, 2000), pp. 127–146.
17. Mathew L. Meuter, Amy L. Ostrom, Robert I. Rowntree and Mary Jo Bitner "Self Service Technologies; Understanding Customer Satisfaction with Technology-Based Service Encounters," *Journal of Marketing*, 64, (2000), pp. 50–64.
18. Neeli Bendepudi and Robert P. Leone (forthcoming), "Psychological Implications of Customer Participation in Co-production," *Journal of Marketing*
19. See reference 17.
20. J. E. G. Bateson, "Consumer Performance and Quality in Services," *Managing Service Quality*, 12, 4, (2002), pp. 1–7.
21. R. C. Shank, "The Structure of Episodes in Memory," *Representation and Understanding: Studies in Cognitive Science*, D. G. Bobrow and A. Collins, eds, (New York: Academic Press 1975), pp. 237–272; R. C. Shank and R. P. Abelson, "Scripts, Plans and Knowledge," *Advanced Papers of the Fourth International Joint Conference on Artificial Intelligence*, (USSR: Tbilisi, 1975), pp. 151–157.
22. G. H. Bower, J. B. Black and T. J. Turner, "Scripts in Memory for Text," *Cognitive Psychology*, 11, (1979), pp. 177–220.
23. C. Graesser, S. B. Woll, D. J. Kowalski and D. A. Smith, "Memory for Typical and Atypical Actions in Scripted Activities, *Journal of Experimental Psychology: Human Learning and Memory*, 6, (1980), pp. 503–515.
24. R. P. Abelson, "Script Processing in Attitude Formation and Decision Making," *Cognition and Social Behaviour*, eds J. S. Carroll and J. W. Payne, (Hillsdale, NJ: Earlbaum, 1976), pp. 33–45.
25. See reference 16.
26. These concepts were first applied to Service Provider Scripts in: Ronald Humphrey and Blake E. Ashforth "Cognitive Scripts and Prototypes in Service Encounters" in *Advances in Services Marketing and Management*, Teresa A. Swartz, David E. Bowen and Stephen W. Brown, eds. (JAI Press Inc., 1994), pp. 175–199.
27. S. M. Leong, P. S. Busch and D. R. John, "Knowledge Bases and Salesperson Effectiveness: A Script Theoretic Analysis," *Journal of Marketing Research*, 26, (May 1989), pp. 164–178.
28. D. R. John and J. C. Witney, Jr. "The Development of Consumer Knowledge in Children: A Cognitive

Structure Approach," *Journal of Consumer Research*, 12, (March 1986), pp. 406–417.

29. Ruth A. Smith and M. Houston, "Script-Based Evaluation of Satisfaction with Services," in L. Berry, G. L. Shostack and G. D. Upah, eds., *Emerging Perspectives on Services Marketing* (Chicago: American Marketing Association, 1982), pp. 59–62; Michael Hui and J. E. Bateson, "Perceived Control and the Effects of Crowding and Consumer Choice on the Service Experience," *Journal of Consumer Research*, 18, (September 1991), pp. 174–184; C. F. Surprenant and M. R. Solomon (1987) op. cit. For a discussion of customer delight see Richard L. Oliver, Roland T. Rust, and Sajeev Varki, "Customer delight : foundations, findings and managerial insight," *Journal of Retailing*, 73, 3, (1997), pp. 311–336.

30. G. H. Bower, J. B. Black and T. J. Turner, "Scripts in Memory for Text," *Cognitive Psychology*, 11, (1979), pp. 177–220.

31. G. J. and J. C. Whitney, "An Empirical Investigation of the Social Structure of Script," *An Assessment of Marketing Thought and Practice*, B. J. Walker et al., eds. (Chicago: AMA, 1982) pp. 75–79.

32. R. A. Smith and M. Houston, "A Psychometric Assessment of Measures of Scripts in Consumer Memory," *Journal of Consumer Research*, 12, (1985), pp. 214–224.

33. Mei Xue and Patrick T. Harker, "Customer Efficiency: Concept and Its Impact on E-Business Management," *Journal of Service Research*, 4, 4, (May 2002), pp. 253–267.

34. Gan Huat Tatt, "Cognitive Scripts in Computer Based Service Settings," Doctoral Thesis, London Business School, 1991. Bateson (2002) op. cit.

35. See reference 34.

36. Mary Jo Bitner, William T. Faranda, Amy R. Hubbert, Valerie A. Zeithaml, "Customer contributions and roles in Service Delivery," *International Journal of Service Industry Management*, 8, 3, (1997), pp. 193–205.

37. Cathy Goodwin, "I Can Do It Myself: Training the Service Consumer to Contribute to Service Productivity," *Journal of Services Marketing*, 2, 4, (Fall 1988), pp. 71–78.

38. See reference 11.

39. Eric Langeard, John E. G. Bateson, Christopher H. Lovelock and Pierre Eiglier, *Service Marketing: New Insights from Consumers and Managers* (Cambridge MA: Marketing Science Institute, 1981).

40. Charles L. Martin and Charles A. Pronter, "Compatibility Management: Customer to Customer Relationships in Service Environment," *Journal of Services Marketing*, 3, (Summer, 1989), pp. 6–15.

41. Stephen J. Grove and Raymond P. Fisk, "The Impact of Other Customers on Service Experiences: A Critical Incident Examination of 'Getting Along'" *Journal of Retailing*, 73, 1, (1997), pp. 63–85.

42. Charles I. Martin and Charles Practer, "Compatibility Management, Customer-to-Customer Relationships as a Service Production Strategy," *Academy of Management Review*, 8, 2, (1983) pp. 301–310.

43. D. Bowen, "Managing Customers as Human Resources in Service Organizations," *Human Resource Management*, 75, (1986), pp. 371–383; Peter K. Mills, "The Socialization of Clients as Partial Employees of Service Organizations," (1983) Working Paper: University of Santa Clara.

44. Peter K. Mills and Jamess H. Morris, "Clients as 'Partial' Employees of Service Organizations—Role Developments in Client Participation," *Academy of Management Review*, 11, 4, (1986), pp. 726–735; Cynthia A. Lengnick-Hall, "Customer Contributions to Quality: A Different View of the Customer-Orientated Firm," *Academy of Management Review*, 21, 3, (1996), pp. 791–824; Scott W. Kelley, James H. Donnelly and Steven J. Skinner, "Organizational Socialization of Service Customers," *Journal of Business Research*, 25, (1992), pp. 197–214.

45. Benjamin Schneider and David E. Bowen, *Winning the Service Game* (Boston: HBS Press, 1995), pp. 84–106.

46. Scott W. Kelley, Steven J. Skinner, and James H. Donnelly, "Organizational Socialization of Service Customers," *Journal of Business Research*, 25, (1992), pp. 197–214.

47. D. H. Maister, "The Psychology of Waiting in Lines," (Boston: Harvard Business School Note 9-684-064, Rev. May 1984), pp. 2–3.

48. David Bowen and B. Schneider, "Boundary Spanning Role Employees and the Service Encounter: Some Guidelines for Management and Research," *The Service Encounter*, ibid, pp. 127–147; J. E. G. Bateson, "The Self Service Consumer—Empirical Findings," *Emerging Perspectives on Services Marketing*, L Berry, G. L. Shostack, and G. D. Upah, eds. (Chicago: American Marketing Association, 1983) pp. 50–53.

49. Peter K. Mills, R. B. Chase and N. Marguiles, "Motivating the Client/Employee System as a Service Production Strategy," *Academy of Management Review*, 5, 2, (1983), pp. 301–310; Peter K. Mills and N. Marguiles, "Toward a Core Typology of Service Organizations," *Academy of Management Review*, 7, 3, (1982), pp. 467–478.

50. L. Argote, "Input uncertainty and organizational co-ordination in hospital emergency units," *Administrative Science Quarterly*, 27, (1982), pp. 420–434.

51. Rikard Larsson and David E. Bowen, "Organization and Customer: Managing Design and Co-ordination of Services," *Academy of Management Review*, 14, 2, (1989), pp. 213–233.

52. See reference 26.

53. E. J. Langer and L. G. Imber, "Why Practice makes Imperfect: Debilitating Effects of Over learning," *Journal of Personality and Social Psychology*, 37, 11, (1979), pp. 2014–2024.

# You Decide How Much Meals Are Worth, Restaurants Tell Customers

Nina Goswami

It sounds like a recipe for financial ruin: A restaurant that allows customers to pay what they think their meal is worth. Yet the business tactic is proving a success and "pay-what-you-like" restaurants are spreading across Britain.

The idea was spawned by Michael Vasos, the owner of Just Around The Corner, a French bistro in north London, where customers often spend two hours drinking fine wine and gorge themselves on salmon stuffed with crab. Afterwards, they must work out their own bill and most, surprisingly, leave a fair or generous amount.

Mr. Vasos's success is such that three other pay-what-you-like restaurants—Mju in Knightsbridge, central London, Lanes in east London, and Sweet Melinda's in Edinburgh—have copied the idea.

"If you give very good service and very good food, people leave a lot in tips," said Mr. Vasos. "So I thought why not just leave the whole bill to customers and they can pay what they think it's worth.

"As long as we gave a good show, I knew it would do well and we've been very successful from the beginning."

Mr. Vasos has stakes in four other restaurants, all with fixed-price menus. They, do not, however, take as much money as Just Around The Corner. "The other restaurants take about 60 percent profit a week; this one takes between 65 to 70 percent each week," he said.

Just Around The Corner's most generous customers were four Americans from the United States government who came in on Christmas Eve. "They had quite a few bottles of wine, champagne and ate three-course meals. They paid £600 and asked the waitress if it was enough. In a fixed-price restaurant they would have probably paid around £250. This is why the restaurant does better, as people are more generous," he said.

Mr. Vasos also has a foolproof way of ensuring that patrons do not underpay. "When people pay a silly amount, I give them their money back and make them feel very small so they realize that if they want to come back, they should really pay more."

He was amazed that pay-what-you-like restaurants were only just catching on as he has been running his business for 18 years. "I'm delighted that other restaurants have now taken the idea on board as it shows customers that others, not just me, can succeed," he said.

Margaret Coutts, with her son, David, and his girlfriend, Danielle Kronenberg, celebrated her 66th birthday with free-flowing champagne and a three-course meal, including lamb Wellington and supreme of chicken with tarragon and juniper berries. The decision on how much to pay was left to David who put down £70.

Mr. Coutts, 36, a carpenter from west London, said, "If you can order a glass of Coke or champagne and still give a reasonable amount at the end of the evening why not go for the champagne."

Mrs. Coutts, a chef visiting her son from Sydney, Australia, said, "Being able to choose your own price does put you under a little added pressure because you really have to think about what you've eaten; in a way you have to become a food critic. However, it's very clever because no one could ever complain."

Kevin O'Connor, who co-owns Sweet Melinda's seafood restaurant, was taken aback by the pay-what-you-like policy and "pinched" the idea for Tuesday nights. His business partner, Karen McLean, said, "People are normally bang on with their prices. They can be wary about the lack of prices, but it tends to be because they're worried that they haven't paid enough. The Brits being what they are, don't want to offend.

"It's very rare that we get people who take advantage. It does happen, and when it does you just have to smile at them and hope that they come back on another night.

"There were two boys who had a beer each and three courses each and left 50p for all the food—25p each. We are leaving ourselves open to exposure, so it serves us right when people take advantage, but generally people are nice and don't."

Mju, which offers contemporary European cuisine with an Asian twist also realized the potential of the pay-what-you-like policy after one member of staff visited Mr. Vasos's bistro.

Last year the restaurant decided to try the strategy out for the month of February and it proved so successful at bringing in new clientele that it is running it again for the next two weeks.

Jeremy Payne, Mju's sales director, said, "Our policy is slightly different as it is just on the food element of your bill, not for drinks."

## Discussion Questions

1. How much of a change in script does setting your own price constitute?
2. Would this be seen as a competitive advantage in the restaurant industry?
3. How dependent on the U.K. culture is the idea? Would it work in the US?

# Implementing Successful Service Strategies

Steve Vidler/Imagestate/PhotoLibrary

There is a little magic in every successful service strategy

Part III, Implementing Successful Service Strategies, focuses onassessing customer satisfaction and service quality, recovering from service complaints and minimizing future failures, building customer loyalty and retention, and developing a world-class service culture. Ideally, assessing and improving theservice delivery system will lead to "seamless" service—a service experience provided without interruption, confusion, or hassle to the customer.

# CHAPTER **11**
# The Essentials of Customer Satisfaction Measurement

## CHAPTER OBJECTIVES

After reading this chapter, you should be able to:

- Define customer satisfaction and understand the benefits associated with satisfied customers.

- Appreciate various methods for measuring customer satisfaction and discuss the limitations of customer satisfaction measurements.

- Discuss factors to consider when investing in customer satisfaction improvements.

- Understand the many factors that influence customer expectations.

The major objectives of this chapter are to introduce you to the importance and benefits of customer satisfaction and the important factors to consider when measuring customer satisfaction.

Image Copyright AVAVA. Used under license from Shutterstock

### RATEMYPROFESSOR. COM: AN OPPORTUNITY FOR STUDENTS TO VOICE THEIR SATISFACTION (OR LACK THEREOF)

**Ratemyprofessor.com** is an opportunity for students to turn the tables on their professors. Instead of professors grading students, **ratemyprofessor.com** provides the means for students to rate their satisfaction with their professors. Ultimately, the site allows students to take advantage of the knowledge gained from previous student experiences. Students can use this information to guide their instructor selections when alternatives are available. To date, ratemyprofessor.com contains over 10 million ratings of over 1 million instructors form 6,000 colleges and universities. New ratings are posted at the rate of over 3,000 to 4,000 a day.

In addition to its rating service, **ratemyprofessor.com** offers a number of other services to its users. One such service posted on its main menu is a collection of what the site designers call "Funny Ratings." These ratings are selected quotes from some very creative students who felt less than happy about their professors. So, here we go, the TOP 20 Funniest Ratings include:

- *You can't cheat in her class because no one knows the answers.*
- *His class was like milk, it was good for two weeks.*
- *Houston, we have a problem. Space cadet of a teacher, isn't quite attached to Earth.*
- *I would have been better off using the tuition money to heat my apartment last winter.*
- *Three of my friends got As in his class and my friends are dumb.*
- *Emotional scarring may fade away, but that big fat F on your transcript won't.*
- *Evil computing science teaching robot who crushes humans for pleasure.*

- *Miserable professor—I wish I could sum him up without foul language.*
- *Instant amnesia walking into this class. I swear he breathes sleeping gas.*
- *BORING! But I learned there are 137 tiles on the ceiling.*
- *Not only is the book a better teacher, it also has a better personality.*
- *Teaches well, invites questions and then insults you for 20 minutes.*
- *This teacher was a firecracker in a pond of slithery tadpoles.*
- *I learned how to hate a language I already know.*
- *Very good course, because I only went to one class.*
- *He will destroy you like an academic ninja.*
- *Bring a pillow.*
- *Your pillow will need a pillow.*
- *If I was tested on her family, I would have gotten an A.*
- *She hates you already.*

Sources:
1. **www.ratemyprofessor.com**, accessed 11 September, 2009.
2. **http://www.listafterlist.com/tabid/57/listid/8201/Education++History/Funniest+
Professor+Ratings+from+RateMyProfessorscom.aspx**, accessed 11 September, 2009.

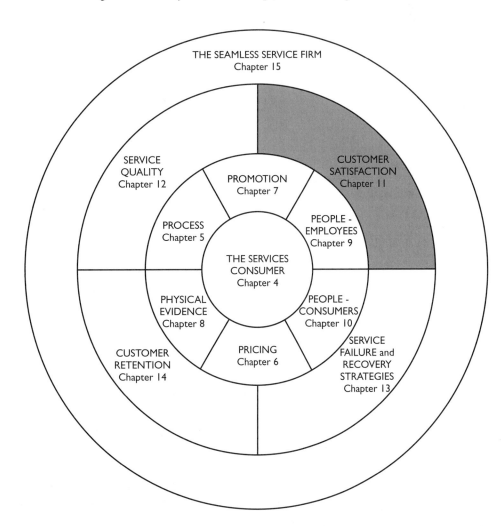

# Introduction

Customer satisfaction is one of the most studied areas in marketing.[1] From a historical perspective, a great deal of the work in the customer satisfaction area began in the 1970s, when consumerism was on the rise. The rise of the consumer movement was directly related to the decline in service felt by many consumers that could be attributed to a number of sources. First, skyrocketing inflation during the 1970s forced many firms to slash service in the effort to keep prices down. In other industries, deregulation led to fierce competition among firms that had never had to compete before. With no previous experience on how to compete, price competition quickly became the primary attempted means of differentiation, and price wars quickly broke out. Firms once again slashed costs associated with customer service to cut operating expenses.

As time went on, labor shortages also contributed to the decline in customer service. Service workers who were motivated were difficult to find, and who could blame them? The typical service job included low pay, no career path, no sense of pride, and no training in customer relations. Automation also contributed to the problem. Replacing human labor with machines (e.g., self-service gas pumps, ATMs, self check-outs at grocery stores, etc.) indeed increased the efficiency of many operating systems, but often at the expense of distancing customers from the firm and leaving customers to fend for themselves. Finally, over the years, customers have become tougher to please. They are more informed than ever, their expectations have certainly increased, and they are more particular about where they spend their discretionary dollars.

Forty years later, customer service is as much of a "hot" issue as ever. A tough economy, poor employment opportunities, fewer discretionary dollars, and an ever increasing educated workforce have set expectations for customer service to new levels. Customers believe that surely if they are going to spend their hard-earned dollars during tough economic times, service firms should appreciate the customers' business and deliver on their promises. Unfortunately, the reality is that the service firms of today struggle with providing customer satisfaction as much as their predecessors did 40 years ago.

# The Importance of Customer Satisfaction

The importance of customer satisfaction cannot be overstated. Without customers, the service firm has no reason to exist. Every service business needs to proactively define and measure customer satisfaction. Waiting for customers to complain in order to identify problems in the service delivery system or gauging the firm's progress in customer satisfaction based on the number of complaints received is naive. Consider the following figures gathered by the Technical Assistance Research Program (TARP):[2]

- *The average business does not hear from 96 percent of its unhappy customers.*
- *For every complaint received, 26 customers actually have the same problem.*
- *The average person with a problem tells nine or 10 people. Thirteen percent will tell more than 20.*
- *Customers who have their complaints satisfactorily resolved tell an average of five people about the treatment they received.*
- *Complainers are more likely to do business with you again than noncomplainers: 54-70 percent if resolved at all, and 95 percent if handled quickly.*

The TARP figures demonstrate that customers do not actively complain to service firms themselves. Instead, consumers voice their dissatisfaction with their feet, by defecting to competitors, and with their mouths by telling your existing and potential customers exactly how they were mistreated by your firm. Based on the TARP figures, a firm that serves 100 customers per week and boasts a 90 percent customer satisfaction rating will be the object of thousands of negative stories by the end of a year. For example, if 10 dissatisfied customers per week tell 10 of their friends of the poor service received, by the end of the year (52 weeks), 5,200 negative word-of-mouth communications will have been generated.

The TARP figures are not all bad news. Firms that effectively respond to customer complaints generate positive word-of-mouth communications. Although positive news travels at half the rate of negative news, the positive stories can ultimately translate into customer loyalty and new customers. Finally, a firm should also learn from the TARP figures that complainers are the firm's friends. Complainers are a free source of market information, and the complaints themselves should be viewed as opportunities for the firm to improve its delivery systems, not as a source of irritation.[3]

## What Is Customer Satisfaction/Dissatisfaction?

Although a variety of alternative definitions exist, the most popular definition of customer satisfaction/dissatisfaction is that it is a comparison of customer expectations to perceptions regarding the actual service encounter. (Alternative definitions are provided in Figure 11.1).[4] Comparing customer expectations with their perceptions is based on what marketers refer to as the **expectancy disconfirmation model**. Simply stated, if customer perceptions meet expectations, the expectations are said to be **confirmed** and the customer is satisfied. If perceptions and expectations are not equal, then the expectation is said to be **disconfirmed**.

Although the term disconfirmation sounds like a negative experience, it is not necessarily so. There are two types of disconfirmations. If actual perceptions were less than what was expected, the result is a **negative disconfirmation**, which results in customer dissatisfaction and may lead to negative word-of-mouth publicity and/or customer defection. In contrast, a **positive disconfirmation** exists when perceptions exceed expectations, thereby resulting in customer satisfaction, positive word-of-mouth publicity, and customer retention.

Every day, consumers utilize the disconfirmation paradigm by comparing their expectations with perceptions. While dining at a resort restaurant on the west coast of Florida, our waiter not only provided everything we requested but also was very good at anticipating needs. My three-year-old niece had had enough fun and sun for the day and was very tired. She crawled up into a vacant booth located directly behind our table and went to sleep. The waiter, noticing her absence from our table and on his own initiative, placed a white tablecloth over her to use as a blanket. This particular incident combined with others throughout the evening lead to a positive disconfirmation of our expectations. That evening's great service reinforced the notion that, with so much poor service all around, customers really do notice when the service is excellent.

**expectancy disconfirmation model** Model proposing that comparing customer expectations to their perceptions leads customers to have their expectations confirmed or disconfirmed.

**confirmed expectations** Customer expectations that match customer perception resulting in customer satisfaction.

**disconfirmed expectations** Customer expectations that do not match customer perceptions.

**negative disconfirmation** Customer perceptions that are lower than customer expectations resulting in customer dissatisfaction.

**positive disconfirmation** Customer perceptions that exceed customer expectations resulting in delighting customers.

**FIG-11.1** Alternative Satisfaction Dimensions

| Normative deficit definition | Compares actual outcomes to those that are culturally acceptable. |
| --- | --- |
| Equity definition | Compares gains in a social exchange—if the gains are unequal, the loser is dissatisfied. |
| Normative standard definition | Expectations are based on what the consumer believes he/she *should* receive—dissatisfaction occurs when the actual outcome is different from the standard expectation. |
| Procedural fairness definition | Satisfaction is a function of the consumer's belief that he/she was treated fairly. |

Source: Keith Hunt, "Consumer Satisfaction, Dissatisfaction, and Complaining Behavior." *Journal of Social Issues* 47, 1, (1991), 109–110.

Perceptions that fall short of expectation results in unhappy customers and lost business (not to mention wasted ketchup).

## The Benefits of Customer Satisfaction

Although some may argue that customers are unreasonable at times, little evidence can be found of extravagant customer expectations.[5] Consequently, satisfying customers is not an impossible task. In fact, meeting and exceeding customer expectations may reap several valuable benefits for the firm. Positive word-of-mouth generated from existing customers often translates into more new customers. For example, consider the positive publicity generated for the firms listed in the The 2009 Customer Service Hall of Fame provided in Figure 11.2. In comparison, as a potential employee, would you have any reservations about working for any of the firms listed in The 2009 Customer Service Hall of Shame (see Figure 11.3)? Satisfied current customers often purchase more products more frequently and are less likely to be lost to competitors than are dissatisfied customers.

Companies who command high customer satisfaction ratings also seem to have the ability to insulate themselves from competitive pressures, particularly price competition. In fact, customers are often willing to pay more and stay with a firm that meets their needs than to take the risk associated with moving to a lower priced service offering. Finally, firms that pride themselves on their customer satisfaction efforts generally provide better environments in which to work. Within these positive work environments,

Customer satisfaction is a two way street—benefitting customers and employees alike.

**FIG-11.2** The Customer Service Hall of Fame

When it comes to providing great service, some companies are just naturals at keeping their customers happy. Based on MSN Money's 2009 annual survey of the "10 Companies That Treat You Right," the following companies are legendary in their treatment of customers:

| THE 2009 CUSTOMER SERVICE HALL OF FAME | PERCENTAGE OF RESPONDENTS WHO RATED THE COMPANY'S SERVICE AS "*EXCELLENT.*" |
| --- | --- |
| 1. USAA (insurance provider) | 56.5% |
| 2. Trader Joes (food retailer) | 50.6% |
| 3. Netflix (movie retailer) | 45.8% |
| 4. Amazon (online retailer) | 43% |
| 5. Nordstrom (fashion retailer) | 42.2% |
| 6. Publix (food retailer) | 41.5% |
| 7. Whole Foods (food retailer) | 40.5% |
| 8. Apple (electronics retailer) | 39.6% |
| 9. Costco (general retailer) | 37.9% |
| 10. Southwest Airlines (air carrier) | 36.7% |

Source: **http://articles.moneycentral.msn.com/SmartSpending/ConsumerActionGuide/10-companies-that-treat-you-right.aspx?slide-number=10**, accessed 10 June, 2009.

**FIG-11.3** The Customer Service Hall of Shame

While some companies continuously deliver high levels of customer satisfaction, other firms just can't seem to get it right. In fact, based on MSN Money's 2009 annual survey of the "10 Companies Americans Love to Hate," nine of the top 10 were also on the 2008 list. Particularly disturbing about this list is that nine out of 10 of these firms are very service versus goods dominant. More specifically, the Hall of Shame includes four financial service companies, two cable companies, two phone companies, one online service provider, and one retailer. When it comes to providing poor service, the following companies lead the pack:

| THE 2009 CUSTOMER SERVICE HALL OF SHAME | PERCENTAGE OF RESPONDENTS WHO RATED THE COMPANY'S SERVICE AS "*POOR.*" |
| --- | --- |
| 1. AOL (online service provider) | 44.8% |
| 2. Comcast (cable provider) | 41.3% |
| 3. Sprint Nextel (phone company) | 40.5% |
| 4. Capital One (financial services) | 34.7% |
| 5. Time Warner Cable (cable provider) | 32.0% |
| 6. HSBC (financial services) | 31.8% |
| 7. Qwest (phone company) | 31.6% |
| 8. Abercrombie & Fitch (retailer) | 31.4% |
| 9. Bank of America (financial services) | 28.5% |
| 10. Citigroup (financial services) | 28.4% |

Source: **http://articles.moneycentral.msn.com/SmartSpending/ConsumerActionGuide/the-customer-service-hall-of-shame-2009.aspx**, accessed 10 June, 2009.

organizational cultures develop where employees are challenged to perform and rewarded for their efforts. Figure 11.4 provides an example of the types of attributes that are key in building great corporate reputations and the companies that excel at particular key attributes.

**FIG-11.4** Eight Key
Attributes of Reputation

| ATTRIBUTES | MOST ADMIRED COMPANIES |
|---|---|
| 1. Innovativeness | Charles Schwab, Herman Miler |
| 2. Quality of management | General Electric, Omnicom Corp. |
| 3. Employee talent | Goldman Sachs, Cisco Systems |
| 4. Financial soundness | Microsoft, Intel, Cisco Systems |
| 5. Use of corp. assets | Berkshire Hathaway, Cisco, General Electric |
| 6. Long-term investment value | Microsoft, Home Depot, Cisco Systems |
| 7. Social responsibility | McDonald's, DuPont, Herman Miller |
| 8. Quality of product/services | Omnicom Group, Philip Morris, UPS |

Source: Geoffrey Colvin, "America's Most Admired Companies, *Fortune,* 141, 4, (February 21, 2000), p. 110.

## The Benefits of Customer Satisfaction Surveys

In and of themselves, customer satisfaction surveys provide several worthwhile benefits. Such surveys provide a formal means for customer feedback to the firm, which may identify existing and potential problems. Satisfaction surveys also convey the message to customers that the firm cares about their wellbeing and values customer input concerning its operations.[6] However, the placement of customer feedback forms by some companies, such as Delta Airlines who inserts their survey near the back of their inflight magazines, makes customers wonder if they really want the feedback (see Figure 11.5).

Other benefits are derived directly from the results of the satisfaction surveys. Satisfaction results are often utilized in evaluating employee performance for merit and

87% OF THE 56% WHO COMPLETED MORE THAN 23% OF THE SURVEY THOUGHT IT WAS A WASTE OF TIME

When assessing customer satisfaction, careful consideration should be given to how long it takes the customer to complete the survey.

**FIG-11.5** Delta Customer Feedback Card

Source: Vicki Escarra, "We're Listening," *SKY,* (February, 2000), pp. 128–129.

compensation reviews and for sales management purposes, such as the development of sales training programs. Survey results are also useful for comparison purposes to determine how the firm stacks up against the competition. When ratings are favorable, many firms utilize the results in their corporate advertising.[7]

# Measuring Customer Satisfaction

**indirect measures**
Measures of customer satisfaction including tracking and monitoring sales records, profits, and customer complaints.

**direct measures**
Measures of satisfaction generally obtained directly from customers via customer satisfaction surveys.

Measures of customer satisfaction are derived via indirect and direct measures. **Indirect measures** of customer satisfaction include tracking and monitoring sales records, profits, and customer complaints. Firms that rely solely on indirect measures are taking a passive approach to determining whether customer perceptions are meeting or exceeding customer expectations. Moreover, if the average firm does not hear from 96 percent of its unhappy customers, it is losing a great many customers while waiting for the other 4 percent to speak their minds.

**Direct measures** of satisfaction are generally obtained via customer satisfaction surveys. However, to say the least, customer satisfaction surveys are not standardized among

Measuring customer satisfaction is often more difficult than it first appears.

firms. For example, the scales used to collect the data vary (e.g., 5-point to 100-point scales), questions asked of respondents vary (e.g., general to specific questions), and data collection methods vary (e.g., personal interviews to self-administered questionnaires). The following section focuses on the use of various scales.

## The Scale of 100 Approach

Some firms request customers to rate the firm's performance on a scale of 100. In essence, the firm is asking customers to give the firm a grade. However, the problems with this approach are readily apparent.

---

*On a scale that ranges from 1-100, how satisfied are with the service that you received today?*
   *Score:* _____

---

Let's say that the firm scores an average of 83. What does the 83 mean—the firm received a B-? Does an 83 mean the same thing to all customers? Not likely. More importantly, what should the firm do to improve its satisfaction rating? Although the score of 83 provides us with some general information, the 83 does not provide specific suggestions for improvements that would lead to an increased customer satisfaction rating.

## The "Very Dissatisfied/Very Satisfied" Approach

An improvement of the "Scale of 100" approach is the use of the "very dissatisfied/very satisfied" approach. This approach presents customers with a 5-point Likert scale, which is typically labeled utilizing the following format:

| How satisfied are you with the service you received today? | | | | |
|---|---|---|---|---|
| Very Dissatisfied | Somewhat Dissatisfied | Neutral | Somewhat Satisfied | Very Satisfied |
| 1 | 2 | 3 | 4 | 5 |

Firms utilizing this format generally combine the percentage of "somewhat satisfied" and "very satisfied" responses to arrive at a satisfaction rating. Similarly, firms that utilize a 10-point scale with anchor points of "very dissatisfied" and "very satisfied" define customer satisfaction as the percentage of customers rating their satisfaction higher than 6. Although this approach provides more meaning to the satisfaction rating itself, compared to the "Scale of 100" approach, it still lacks the diagnostic power to indicate specific areas of improvement. In other words, regardless of whether a firm uses a 100-point, 10-point, or 5-point scale, the interpretive value of the information is restricted by its quantitative nature. In addition to a quantitative score, firms truly seeking to improve their customer satisfaction should also collect qualitative information in order to highlight specific areas of improvement. This is exactly the problem Federal Express encountered when it set up its first customer satisfaction measurement program. Initially, customer satisfaction was measured on a 100-point scale and transaction success was defined as whether or not the package actually arrived the next day. Upon further qualitative examination, Federal Express determined that transaction success as defined by the customer was a much broader concept (see Figure 11.6). The company now proactively improves its customer satisfaction ratings by continually improving upon those activities that were identified by its customer base—termed "The Hierarchy of Horrors."

**FIG-11.6** FedEx's
Hierarchy of Horrors

1. Wrong Day Delivery (packaged delivered a day later than promised)
2. Right Day Late Delivery (packaged delivered on the promised day, but after the promised deadline)
3. Pick-up Not Made (failure to make a pick-up on the day requested)
4. Lost Package
5. Customer Misinformed by Federal Express (mistaken or inaccurate information on rates, schedules, etc.)
6. Billing and Paperwork Mistakes (invoice errors, overcharges, missed proof of delivery documents)
7. Employee Performance Failures (courtesy, responsiveness, etc.)
8. Damage Packages

Source: AMA Management Briefing, *Blueprints for Service Quality: The Federal Express Approach,* (New York: AMA Membership Publications Division, 1991).

## The Combined Approach

The combined approach utilizes the quantitative scores obtained by the "very dissatisfied/very satisfied" approach and adds a qualitative analysis of feedback obtained from respondents who indicated that they were less than "very satisfied." Customers who indicate that they are less than "very satisfied" are informing the firm that the delivery system is performing at levels lower than expected. By prompting customers to suggest how the firm could perform better, the firm can then categorize and prioritize the suggestions for continuous improvement efforts.

| *How satisfied are you with the service you received today?* | | | | |
|---|---|---|---|---|
| *Very Dissatisfied* | *Somewhat Dissatisfied* | *Neutral* | *Somewhat Satisfied* | *Very Satisfied* |
| *1* | *2* | *3* | *4* | *5* |
| *If less than very satisfied, what could the firm have done better?* | | | | |
| | | | | |
| | | | | |
| | | | | |

The combined approach provides two valuable pieces of information. The quantitative satisfaction rating provides a benchmark against which future satisfaction surveys should be compared (See Global Services in Action for more information pertaining to benchmarking). In addition, the quantitative rating provides the means of comparing the firm's performance against its competition. Complementing the quantitative rating, the qualitative data provides *diagnostic information* that pinpoints specific areas for improvement. Combining the qualitative and quantitative data outperforms either approach used alone.

## Understanding Customer Satisfaction Ratings

After a consultant conducted a customer satisfaction survey for a regional engineering firm, results revealed to upper management that the firm commanded an 85 percent customer satisfaction rating. Immediately, upper management wanted to know whether 85 percent was a "good" satisfaction rating or not. To effectively interpret and utilize

## GLOBAL SERVICES *IN ACTION*

### Benchmarking Customer Satisfaction Throughout the World

Ethos Consultancy, the United Arab Emirates' (UAE) leading service quality consultancy and measurement firm, recently announced its newest product—International Customer Satisfaction Benchmarking. Ethos plans to collect and benchmark UAE and Middle East satisfaction data with data from Canada, Australia, New Zealand, Singapore, the United Kingdom and the United States. Companies use benchmarking data to improve customer satisfaction which, in turn, drives customer loyalty and subsequently corporate profitability.

Tracking customer satisfaction in the United States has been conducted over the last 15 years through the joint efforts of the American Society for Quality, the University of Michigan's Business School, and CFI Group USA, LLC. The three groups have developed the American Customer Satisfaction Index (ACSI), which reports national customer satisfaction scores on a scale that ranges from zero to 100. The ACSI covers 10 economic sectors, 44 industries (including e-commerce and e-business), and more than 200 companies and federal or local government agencies. Companies included in the ACSI comprise 43 percent of the United States GDP. Key economic sectors include:

- Utilities
- Manufacturing/Durable goods
- Manufacturing/Nondurable goods
- Retail Trade
- Transportation & Warehousing
- Information
- Finance & Insurance
- Health Care & Social Assistance
- Accommodation & Food Services
- Public Administration and Government

The ACSI consists of 17 questions regarding issues such as consumer perceptions of service, quality, value, the performance of the product compared with expectations, how the product compares with an ideal product, and how willing consumers would be to pay more for the product. Consumer responses are gathered via telephone surveys of approximately 65,000 consumers. The products of each company included in the survey are assessed roughly 250 times. Economic sector sample sizes range from 2,500 to 18,000, and results for the various key economic sectors rotate on a quarterly basis.

Sources:
1. **http://www.theacsi.org/**, accessed 14 September, 2009.
2. **http://www.free-press-release.com/news/200901/1232980491.html**, accessed 14 September, 2009.

customer satisfaction ratings, it is necessary to understand the factors that may influence customer responses.

Despite the lack of standardization among data collection procedures and measures utilized for satisfaction studies, they share one common characteristic. "Virtually all self-reports of customer satisfaction possess a distribution in which a majority of the responses indicate that customers are satisfied and the distribution itself is negatively skewed"[8] (see Figure 11.7). Repeated findings such as these have led some researchers to conclude that "to feel above average is normal." Figure 11.8 displays a sample of customer satisfaction results across various industries. As can be viewed from the figure, it is not unusual to see results in the 80–90 percent range.

**FIG-11.7** Distribution of Satisfaction Measurements

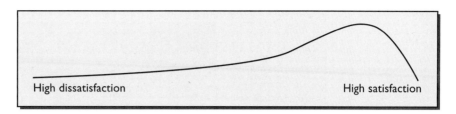

Source: Robert A. Peterson and William R. Wilson, "Measuring Customer Satisfaction: Fact and Artifact," *Journal of the Academy of Marketing Science* 20, 1, (1992), p. 61.

**FIG-11.8** Sampling of Satisfaction Results

| SAMPLE | PERCENTAGE SATISFIED |
|---|---|
| HMO enrollees | 92 |
| Buick (GM) | 88 |
| Google | 86 |
| British Airways customers | 85* |
| Sears' customers | 84* |
| Apple | 84 |
| FedEx | 84 |
| Medical care | 84* |
| Whirlpool | 83 |
| Shoes/students | 83* |
| Costco | 83 |
| Children's instructional programs/parents | 82* |
| Clothing/and white goods/adults | 82* |
| Southwest Airlines | 81 |
| Olive Garden | 81 |
| Nordstrom | 80 |
| Fidelity | 80 |

Sources:
1. Robert A. Peterson and William R. Wilson, "Measuring Customer Satisfaction: Fact and Artifact," *Journal of the Academy of Marketing Science* 20, 1, (1992), p. 61.
2. **http://www.theacsi.org/**, accessed 23 September, 2009.

## Factors Influencing Customer Satisfaction Ratings

Satisfaction ratings may be influenced by numerous factors that occur during the data collection process. The following section provides explanations for inflated satisfaction results and reinforces the notion that obtaining accurate measures of customer satisfaction is not an easily accomplished task.

***Customers Are Genuinely Satisfied***   One possible reason for high satisfaction scores is simply that customers are satisfied with the goods and services they typically purchase and consume—that's why they buy these products from the firm in the first place! For example, it would be totally expected that Internet companies that work to enhance the customer's online service experience such as Amazon.com would have truly satisfied customers (See E-services in Action). Intuitively, this makes good sense. If the majority of customers were neutral or dissatisfied, they would most likely defect to competitive offerings of goods and services. Of course, this explanation assumes that competitors in the market are better at providing goods and services than the original supplier.

Tim Pannell/Corbis/Jupiter Images

Personal methods of customer satisfaction data collection are likely to yield higher customer satisfaction ratings when compared to nonpersonal data collection methods.

**response bias** A bias in survey results because of responses being received from only a limited group among the total survey participants.

***Response Bias***    Another possible explanation for inflated satisfaction results may be **response bias**. Some experts argue that the reason ratings are so high is that companies hear from only satisfied customers. In contrast, dissatisfied customers do not believe that the firm's survey will do them any good or is worth their time to complete; therefore, the questionnaire is discarded.

Other experts discount this explanation. Their argument is that it makes more sense for highly dissatisfied customers to express their opinion than it does for highly satisfied customers to do so. This position is supported by prior research, which indicates that dissatisfaction itself is more action oriented and emotionally intense than satisfaction.[9] Others argue that it is possible that highly dissatisfied customers and highly satisfied customers are more likely to respond than are those who are more neutral. Although these additional explanations are intriguing, they fail to explain the traditional, negatively skewed response distribution depicted in Figure 11.7.

***Data Collection Method***    A third explanation for inflated satisfaction scores is the data collection method used to obtain results. Prior research suggests that higher levels of satisfaction are obtained via personal interviews and phone surveys compared with results from mail questionnaires and/or self-administered interviews. In fact, studies indicate that as much as a 10 percent difference exists between questionnaires administered orally and self-administered questionnaires. The reason is that respondents to personal interviews and phone surveys may feel awkward expressing negative statements to other "live" individuals as opposed to expressing them anonymously on a self-administered questionnaire.

Research on data collection modes' effects on satisfaction ratings has produced some interesting results. The data collection mode does indeed appear to influence the level of

---

## E-SERVICES *IN ACTION*

### Enhancing Online Customer Satisfaction

Strictly speaking, *e-service* pertains to customer service support provided on the net that is meant to enhance the customer's overall experience. E-service plays a critical role in the transformation of the customer's online experience that progresses over time from a basic functional experience to a more personalized experience. Ultimately, e-service attempts to humanize the net by providing various customer service activities while simultaneously reducing the online firm's operating costs. Consequently, when everything works as designed, it's a win-win for customers and businesses alike. Examples of e-service include:

- *Electronic Order Confirmation.* Noted as one of the easiest and most cost-effective methods to increase customer satisfaction, electronic order confirmation notifies customer within seconds that their order has been received by detailing the item purchased, quantity selected, cost of the item, shipping charges, and order availability.

- *Package Tracking Services.* Once an order has been placed, effective e-tailers also notify customers when their purchases have been shipped and provide an expected delivery date. In addition, the best companies also provide package tracking identification numbers so that customers can track the physical movement of their purchases through a shipper's website.

- *Electronic Wallets.* According to one study, two-thirds of all shopping carts are left at the virtual check-out counter. Checking out online can be a lengthy process as customers enter their credit card information, phone numbers, billing address, shipping address, etc. Electronic wallets have been designed for repeat customers where the customer's credit card and desired shipping preferences are stored on the company's server and automatically appear when the customer places an order.

- *Co-browsing.* In order to facilitate the social aspects on online shopping, e-tailers that offer co-browsing opportunities enable users to access the same website simultaneously from two

different locations. Live text boxes are also provided so that users can chat online while making their purchase decisions.

- *Live Text Chats and VoIP.* In addition to enabling customer-to-customer communications, live text chats and Voice over Internet Protocol (VoIP) are also facilitating customer-to-e-tailer communications as well. Innovative outsourcing firms, such as liveperson.com, staff a number of major e-tailers' live text chats and respond to customer inquiries online in often under 60 seconds.

- *Merchandise Return Services.* Twenty-five percent of all merchandise purchased online is returned, and the rate is higher in some industries, such as apparel. Today, many e-tailers include Supply Return Authorizations with their shipments to facilitate the return process. Other e-tailers outsource their return activities to the United States Postal Service's E-Merchandise Return Service, which enables customers to print return labels from the e-tailer's website and drop returns off at the post office.

- *Collaborative Filtering.* This software program facilitates suggestive selling by monitoring the purchasing behavior of like-minded customers online, and then suggesting (in real time) what other customers have purchased to individual users.

- *Utilizing Web 2.0 Technology.* This technology allows for more communication tools such as blogs, podcasting, and video-sharing capabilities.

- *Online FAQ and Troubleshooting Web Pages.* Offering web pages for frequently asked questions and troubleshooting provides customers with faster responses to their questions and reduces labor costs in the process.

Sources: **http://carolinanewswire.com/news/News.cgi?database= columns.db&command=viewone&id=369**, accessed 15 September, 2009; and Rafi A. Mohammed, Robert J. Fisher, Bernard J. Jaworski and Aileen Cahill. *Internet Marketing: Building Advantage in a Networked Economy*, (Boston, MA: McGraw-Hill Irwin, 2002). Ron Zemke and Tom Connellan, *E-Service: 24 Ways to Keep Your Customers—When the Comptetion is Just a Click Away*, (New York, NY: AMACOM).

---

**question form** The way a question is phrased, i.e., positively or negatively.

reported satisfaction; however, the negatively skewed distribution of the satisfaction ratings remains unchanged, regardless of the data collection mode.

*Question Form*   The way the question is asked on the questionnaire, or the **question form**, has also been posited as a possible explanation for inflated satisfaction ratings. It

**FIG-11.9** Responses by Question Form

| RESPONSE CATEGORY | "SATISFIED" | "DISSATISFIED" |
|---|---|---|
| Very satisfied | 57.4% | 53.4% |
| Somewhat satisfied | 33.6% | 28.7% |
| Somewhat dissatisfied | 5.0% | 8.5% |
| Very dissatisfied | 4.0% | 9.4% |

Source: Robert A. Peterson and William R. Wilson, "Measuring Customer Satisfaction: Fact and Artifact," *Journal of the Academy of Marketing Science* 20, 1, (1992), p. 65.

does appear that asking the question in positive form ("How satisfied are you?") as opposed to negative form ("how dissatisfied are you?") does have an impact on satisfaction ratings. Asking a question in the positive form appears to lead to greater reported levels of satisfaction than does posing the question in a negative form.

Figure 11.9 presents results from a study about the effects of stating the same question in two forms. In one version, the question asked respondents "how satisfied" they were, and in the other version, the question asked "how dissatisfied" they were. Results reveal that 91 percent of respondents reported feeling "very" or "somewhat satisfied" when the question was stated in its positive form but only 82 percent when stated in the negative form. Similarly, 9 percent of respondents expressed that they were "somewhat satisfied" or "very dissatisfied" when asked in the positive form, compared with nearly 18 percent when asked in the negative form.

**question context** The placement and tone of a question relative to the other questions asked.

*Context of the Question*    The **question context** may also affect the satisfaction rating. Question context effects pertain to the ordering of questions and whether questions asked earlier in a questionnaire influence answers to subsequent questions. For example, in a study concerning satisfaction with vehicles, asking a general satisfaction question (e.g., "In general, how satisfied are you with the products in your house?") prior to a specific vehicle satisfaction question (e.g., "How satisfied are you with your Toyota?") increased the tendency toward a "very satisfied" response for the specific question.

**question timing** The length of time after the date of purchase that questions are asked.

*Timing of the Question*    Satisfaction ratings may also be influenced by the **timing of the question** relative to the date of purchase. Customer satisfaction appears to be highest immediately after a purchase and then begins to decrease over time. Again, regarding automobile purchases, researchers have noted a 20 percent decline in satisfaction ratings over a 60-day period. It's not clear whether the initial ratings are inflated to compensate for feelings of cognitive dissonance or the latter ratings are deflated. Some consideration has been given that there may be different types of satisfaction measured at different points in time.

Another possible explanation is that satisfaction rates may decay over time as customers reflect upon their purchase decision. Prior research indicates that the influence of negative events, which are more memorable than positive events, carries more weight in satisfaction evaluations over time. Consequently, satisfaction surveys distributed longer after purchases provide respondents the opportunity to take retribution as they recall such negative events.

**social desirability bias** A bias in survey results because of respondents' tendencies to provide information they believe is socially appropriate.

*Social Desirability Bias*    **Social desirability bias** describes a respondent's tendency to provide information that the respondent believes is socially appropriate. For example, in some cultures children are taught by their parents the general rule-of-thumb, *"If you don't have anything nice to say, then don't say anything at all."* Consequently, with respect to satisfaction surveys, some researchers argue that respondents tend to withhold critical judgment because to do otherwise would be socially inappropriate. This would explain high satisfaction ratings and the shape of the distribution of results. Although the explanation is intriguing, widespread empirical support is lacking.

*Mood*   One final factor that could possibly influence customer satisfaction ratings is the mood of the customer while completing the survey. An abundance of research demonstrates the influence of positive mood states toward prosocial (positive) behaviors.[10] More specifically, prior research has shown that respondents in positive mood states make more positive judgments, rate products they own more favorably, tend to see the brighter side of things, and are more likely to rate strangers favorably. Hence, consumers in positive moods should give higher marks to service personnel and service firms than their neutral- or negative-mood counterparts. Firms that are able to positively influence the moods of customers through the creation of inviting servicescapes and friendly contact personnel may benefit in terms of higher customer satisfaction ratings.

### Are Customer Satisfaction Surveys Worth It?

Given the number of factors that may distort the "true" customer satisfaction ratings, one may wonder whether it's worth spending the time and money to measure satisfaction at all. Customer satisfaction ratings may fall under the category of the *Hawthorne effect*; that is, in and of themselves, satisfaction surveys might increase customer satisfaction regardless of the good or service being evaluated. Furthermore, due to the already high levels of customer satisfaction that already exist for most firms, it may not make sense to attempt to increase satisfaction levels across the board. However, two areas of satisfaction that do deserve special attention are (1) company attempts to maintain satisfaction over time to counter the decay effect (satisfaction tends to decline over time), and (2) concentration on the tail of the satisfaction distribution--those customers who are dissatisfied. In and of themselves, satisfaction ratings cannot be interpreted with much meaning. Consequently, **benchmarking** with past satisfaction measures and comparisons with competition provide more meaningful feedback to companies.

**benchmarking** Setting standards against which to compare future data collected.

All in all, despite all the possible complications and given the benefits derived from customer satisfaction, when firms use satisfaction surveys in conjunction with other measures, such as those described later in this chapter, the information provided is invaluable.

## Customer Satisfaction: How Good Is Good Enough?

How much satisfaction is enough? At 98 percent, a company that completes 1,000 transactions per week upsets 20 customers per week, who tell nine or 10 of their friends. Given this scenario, the bottom line translates into 200 negative stories per week and 10,400 negative stories per year. Although these numbers provide support for continuous improvements that enhance customer satisfaction ratings, we tend to forget that for every percentage of satisfaction improvement, very real investment costs are involved.

For example, if a firm currently boasts a 95 percent customer satisfaction rating, is it worth a $100,000 investment to improve satisfaction to 98 percent?[11] The answer is…"*It depends!*" Pete Babich, the quality manager for the San Diego division of Hewlett-Packard, was faced with this exact question. Hewlett-Packard defines customer satisfaction as the customer's willingness to refer Hewlett-Packard products to friends. Hewlett-Packard has found that 70 percent of its purchases are made because of previous positive experiences with the product or referrals from others.

Although Babich found an abundance of anecdotal evidence that retaining customers was much less expensive than seeking out new customers, this information failed to answer his original question…is it worth $100,000 investment to improve satisfaction to 98 percent? As a result, Babich proceeded to develop a customer satisfaction model that would predict market share changes over time as they related to customer satisfaction ratings.

**FIG-11.10** Customer Satisfaction Model: Three Scenarios

(a)

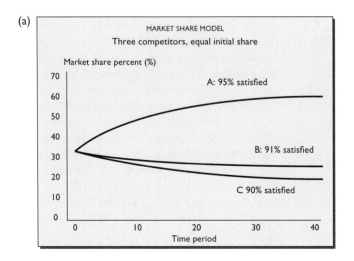

(b)

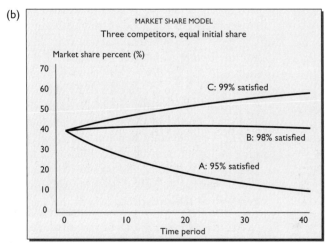

(c)

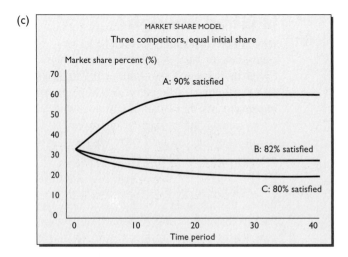

Source: Adapted from Peter Babich, "Customer Satisfaction: How Good Is Good Enough," *Quality Progress* (December 1992), pp. 65–67.

The Babich model is based on an algorithm that can easily be converted into a spreadsheet and is built upon a number of assumptions. First, in this particular example depicted in Figure 11.10, the model assumes a closed market of three firms that begin at period "zero" with equal market shares (i.e., 33.3%). The three firms offer comparable products and prices and compete for a growing customer base. Next, the model assumes that satisfied consumers will continue to buy from the same firm and that dissatisfied customers will defect to other firms in the market. For example, dissatisfied customers of Firm A will buy at Firm B or Firm C during the next time period. The length of the time period varies, depending on the product (e.g., eye exam versus lawn care).

The direction of customer defection depends upon the firm's market share. In other words, if Firm C's market share is higher than Firm B's market share, Firm C will obtain a higher share of Firm A's dissatisfied customers. This logic is based on the premise that dissatisfied customers will be more particular the next time around and will conduct more research and seek out referrals from others. In this case, due to Firm C's higher market share, Firm C would be the beneficiary of more positive referrals.

Results generated from the customer satisfaction model when given three different scenarios are also presented in Figure 11.10. Panel (a) illustrates the scenario of how a firm with a 95 percent customer satisfaction rating would stack up against firms commanding 90 percent and 91 percent customer satisfaction ratings. Clearly, the firm with 95 percent satisfaction dominates the market after 12 time periods. Panel (b) of the figure illustrates how that same firm with a 95 percent satisfaction rating would compete with firms commanding 98 percent and 99 percent ratings. In this scenario, the 95 percent firm controls less than 10 percent of the market after 24 time periods. This scenario dramatically illustrates the impact of the competition's satisfaction ratings.

Finally, Panel (c) illustrates the effect of customer satisfaction on market share at lower customer satisfaction levels. In this scenario, Firms A, B, and C command satisfaction ratings of 90 percent, 82 percent, and 80 percent, respectively. In essence, this panel illustrates the effect of increasing the dissatisfaction levels of Panel (a) by 2. In this scenario, Firm A once again achieves market dominance, but at a much faster rate.

What does Peter Babich's customer satisfaction model tell us? First, firms with higher customer satisfaction ratings make the firm more resistant to competitors' efforts to improve their market share. Secondly, if the firm knows what a 1 percent improvement in market share does for its bottom line, then comparing the 1 percent increase in market share to the investment needed to improve customer satisfaction gives the firm the necessary information to make a business decision. Finally, the model points out the necessity of knowing not only your own firm's satisfaction rating, but also your competitors'.

So, should a firm invest $100,000 to improve customer satisfaction ratings from 95 percent to 98 percent? It depends upon:

- *the satisfaction ratings of the firm's competitors;*
- *the dollar investment necessary to increase customer satisfaction relative to the impact of increasing the firm's market share;*
- *the number of time periods required to recoup the investment; and*
- *the opportunity costs associated with other uses of the $100,000.*

## Does Customer Satisfaction Translate into Customer Retention?

High satisfaction ratings do not necessarily mean that a firm is going to retain a customer forever.[12] In fact, according to one group of consultants, on average, 65 percent to 85 percent of customers who defect to competitors say they were "satisfied" or "very satisfied" with their former providers. Why is this so? Five criticisms of customer satisfaction research as they relate to customer retention provide insights into why firms with high satisfaction ratings may potentially lose customers. First, satisfaction research focuses on whether current needs are being met but fails to investigate customers' future needs. As customers' needs change, they will seek out a firm that best satisfies this new set of needs (See Sustainability & Services in Action). Consequently, the progressive service firm must proactively engage in assessing its customers' future needs.

A second criticism of customer satisfaction research is that it tends to focus on registered complaints. According to the TARP figures presented earlier, many customers who defect never relay their complaints to an employee or the firm's management. Consequently, satisfaction research that examines only registered complaints overlooks a great deal of information. In addition, limiting research to only registered complaints most likely also overlooks many of the problems that need to be remedied in order to lower defection rates.

A third criticism is that customer satisfaction research tends to focus on global attributes and ignores operational elements. For example, firms often phrase questions in their customer satisfaction questionnaires using broad, global statements such as, "The

---

## SUSTAINABILITY AND SERVICES *IN ACTION*

### TerraPass: Enhancing Satisfaction with Social Conscience

While many service providers such as banks, hospitals, restaurants, and hotels are working hard to become more environmentally friendly, an innovative service has been developed to help customers enhance their satisfaction with the goods and services they already own by offsetting their carbon footprint. TerraPass is a for-profit business entity that offers "a little piece of conscience" by investing in greenhouse gas reduction projects such as wind farms and methane digesters.

Here's how TerraPass works. Let's say that you just bought a new SUV and you're feeling the pressure to be more "green." Simply go to www.Terrapass.com where you can calculate your current carbon footprint. For example, a 2009 Buick Enclave driven 8,000 miles a year produces 8,237 lbs $CO_2$ per year. For $53.55 a year, TerraPass will invest your money in various green projects that will offset your vehicle's emissions. In addition, TerraPass will send you a bumper sticker to display proudly on your new automobile that visibly signals to your environmentally friendly peers that you do, in fact, have a social conscience. TerraPass also sells a Flight TerraPass to offset airplane emissions, a Home TerraPass to offset your home energy use, and a Wedding TerraPass for weddings and a variety of other events.

TerraPass is audited regularly to confirm that the company is, in fact, keeping its promise to customers, and that its investments are producing desired effects. TerraPass is particularly focused on investing in projects that will result in carbon offsets today. Consequently, the company shies away from investments that promise to yield results several years in the future or to help pay for reductions that happened years ago. Greenopia has named Terra-Pass as its Number 1 Carbon Offset Retailer, and *GOOD Magazine* boasts that "TerraPass has set the standard for transparency and user experience." The company also sells a limited array of environmentally friendly products such as gadgets and chargers, low-flow shower heads, toys and games, and a variety of gift ideas.

Sources:
1. **http://www.autoblog.com/2005/06/14/terrapass-offers-suv-drivers-a-piece-of-green/**, accessed 14 September, 2009.
2. **http://www.terrapass.com/**, accessed 14 September, 2009.

firm provides good service" and "The firm has good employees." Global statements such as these overlook the operational elements that make up these statements. Examples of operational elements that measure employee performance may include such things as eye contact, product knowledge, courteous actions, and credibility. Operational elements pertaining to good service might include the amount of time it takes to check in and check out at a hotel, the cleanliness of the facility, and the hours of operation. Utilizing global attributes instead of operational elements in surveys fails to provide the company with the information it needs for developing effective solutions to problems. Consider, for example, the operational usefulness of the Sheraton Hotels and Resorts Guest Satisfaction Survey conducted by J.D. Power and Associates, presented in Figure 11.11.

A fourth criticism of customer satisfaction research is that it often excludes the firm's employees from the survey process. Employee satisfaction drives customer loyalty. Employees' perceptions of the service delivery system need to be compared with customers' perceptions. This process provides feedback to employees about the firm's performance and assists in ensuring that employees and customers are on the same page. As internal customers, employees often contribute valuable suggestions for improving the firm's operations.

Finally, a fifth criticism is that some firms are convinced that customers may not know what they want and that sometimes ignoring the customer is the best strategy to follow, particularly when it comes to new product innovation.[13] Some believe that firms can go overboard listening to customers, thereby becoming slaves to demographics, market research, and focus groups. And, in fact, listening to customers often does discourage truly innovative products. As evidence, 90 percent of so-called new products are simply line extensions of existing products.

Listening to customers does have its faults. Customers often focus on current needs and have a difficult time projecting their needs into the future. In addition, consumers sometimes pick up cues from the person asking questions and attempt to answer questions in a direction that will please the interviewer. Other problems include the consumer's being in a hurry; not fully understanding what is being asked; not wanting to be rude and so cheerfully agreeing with whatever is being asked; and, most importantly, not making decisions using real money.

The list of products consumers initially rejected that went on to be huge successes is impressive. Products such as the Chrysler minivan, fax machines, VCRs, FedEx, CNN, Compaq PC servers, cellular phones, personal digital assistants, microwave ovens, and even Birdseye frozen foods were all rejected by customers during initial survey attempts. In contrast, products that surveyed customers indicated would be great successes, such as McDonald's McLean, KFC's skinless fried chicken, Pizza Hut's low-calorie pizza, and New Coke, among others, turned out to be flops.[14]

The problem is not so much listening to what customers have to say as it is companies' feeling paralyzed to make strategic moves without strong consumer support. Of course, customers should not be completely ignored. However, some marketers argue that the best consumer information is obtained through detached observation rather than through traditional survey techniques: "Ignore what your customers say; pay attention to what they do."[15]

## Customer Satisfaction: A Closer Look

So far, this chapter has provided a broad overview of customer satisfaction. The following section takes a closer look at customer expectations and how they relate to customer satisfaction and service quality assessments. This section of the chapter further defines

**FIG-11.11** Sheraton Hotels & Resorts Guest Satisfaction Survey

# SHERATON HOTELS & RESORTS GUEST SATISFACTION SURVEY

MAKE YOUR ANSWERS COUNT!    Correct Mark ☒ ☑

**1. How likely are you to...**

|  | Very Likely | Somewhat Likely | Somewhat Unlikely | Very Unlikely |
|---|---|---|---|---|
| Return to this hotel if you are in the same area again? | ☐ | ☐ | ☐ | ☐ |
| Recommend this hotel to a friend or colleague planning to visit the area? | ☐ | ☐ | ☐ | ☐ |
| Stay at a Sheraton hotel again? | ☐ | ☐ | ☐ | ☐ |

**2. How satisfied were you with...**

Outstanding ←————————————→ Unacceptable

| | | | | | | | | | |
|---|---|---|---|---|---|---|---|---|---|
| Your overall experience as a guest in this hotel | ☐ | ☐ | ☐ | ☐ | ☐ | ☐ | ☐ | ☐ | ☐ |
| The value for the price paid | ☐ | ☐ | ☐ | ☐ | ☐ | ☐ | ☐ | ☐ | ☐ |
| Cleanliness and maintenance of hotel | ☐ | ☐ | ☐ | ☐ | ☐ | ☐ | ☐ | ☐ | ☐ |
| Responsiveness of staff to your needs | ☐ | ☐ | ☐ | ☐ | ☐ | ☐ | ☐ | ☐ | ☐ |
| Knowledge of staff | ☐ | ☐ | ☐ | ☐ | ☐ | ☐ | ☐ | ☐ | ☐ |

**Check-In**

| | | | | | | | | | |
|---|---|---|---|---|---|---|---|---|---|
| Accuracy of reservation | ☐ | ☐ | ☐ | ☐ | ☐ | ☐ | ☐ | ☐ | ☐ |
| Speed/efficiency of check-in | ☐ | ☐ | ☐ | ☐ | ☐ | ☐ | ☐ | ☐ | ☐ |
| Staff friendliness at check-in | ☐ | ☐ | ☐ | ☐ | ☐ | ☐ | ☐ | ☐ | ☐ |

**Guest Room**

| | | | | | | | | | |
|---|---|---|---|---|---|---|---|---|---|
| Size of room | ☐ | ☐ | ☐ | ☐ | ☐ | ☐ | ☐ | ☐ | ☐ |
| Comfort of bed | ☐ | ☐ | ☐ | ☐ | ☐ | ☐ | ☐ | ☐ | ☐ |
| Room décor/furnishings | ☐ | ☐ | ☐ | ☐ | ☐ | ☐ | ☐ | ☐ | ☐ |
| Ability to work in guest room | ☐ | ☐ | ☐ | ☐ | ☐ | ☐ | ☐ | ☐ | ☐ |
| Cleanliness of guest room | ☐ | ☐ | ☐ | ☐ | ☐ | ☐ | ☐ | ☐ | ☐ |
| Maintenance of guest room | ☐ | ☐ | ☐ | ☐ | ☐ | ☐ | ☐ | ☐ | ☐ |
| Cleanliness of bathroom | ☐ | ☐ | ☐ | ☐ | ☐ | ☐ | ☐ | ☐ | ☐ |
| Bath/shower water pressure | ☐ | ☐ | ☐ | ☐ | ☐ | ☐ | ☐ | ☐ | ☐ |

**Hotel Services (If Used)**

| | | | | | | | | | | |
|---|---|---|---|---|---|---|---|---|---|---|
| Helpfulness of bell staff | ☐ | ☐ | ☐ | ☐ | ☐ | ☐ | ☐ | ☐ | ☐ | ☐ N/A |
| Hotel safety/security | ☐ | ☐ | ☐ | ☐ | ☐ | ☐ | ☐ | ☐ | ☐ | ☐ N/A |

**Food and Dining (If Used)**

| | | | | | | | | | | |
|---|---|---|---|---|---|---|---|---|---|---|
| Food quality | ☐ | ☐ | ☐ | ☐ | ☐ | ☐ | ☐ | ☐ | ☐ | ☐ N/A |
| Speed/efficiency of service | ☐ | ☐ | ☐ | ☐ | ☐ | ☐ | ☐ | ☐ | ☐ | ☐ N/A |
| Room service speed/efficiency | ☐ | ☐ | ☐ | ☐ | ☐ | ☐ | ☐ | ☐ | ☐ | ☐ N/A |

**Check-Out**

| | | | | | | | | | |
|---|---|---|---|---|---|---|---|---|---|
| Speed/efficiency of check-out process | ☐ | ☐ | ☐ | ☐ | ☐ | ☐ | ☐ | ☐ | ☐ |
| Accuracy of billing | ☐ | ☐ | ☐ | ☐ | ☐ | ☐ | ☐ | ☐ | ☐ |

**3. Please rate...**

| | | | | | | | | | |
|---|---|---|---|---|---|---|---|---|---|
| Delivery of Sheraton promise "I'll take care of you" | ☐ | ☐ | ☐ | ☐ | ☐ | ☐ | ☐ | ☐ | ☐ |
| This experience compared to other Sheraton hotels | ☐ | ☐ | ☐ | ☐ | ☐ | ☐ | ☐ | ☐ | ☐ |

**4. Are you a member of the Starwood Preferred Guest Program?**    ☐ Yes    ☐ No

**5. If you are a member of the Starwood Preferred Guest Program, how satisfied were you with the benefits you received during your stay?**

☐ ☐ ☐ ☐ ☐ ☐ ☐ ☐ ☐    ☐ N/A

**6. Please mark any problem you experienced during your stay. (MARK ALL THAT APPLY)**

| | | | |
|---|---|---|---|
| ☐ Air conditioner/heater | ☐ Hotel maintenance | ☐ Reservation date | ☐ Room maintenance |
| ☐ Bathroom cleanliness | ☐ Noise | ☐ Reservation rate | ☐ Room readiness |
| ☐ Check-in | ☐ No reservation | ☐ Responsiveness of staff | ☐ Sink/tub/toilet |
| ☐ Guest room cleanliness | ☐ Number of towels | ☐ Room assignment | ☐ Other |

**7. Did you contact anyone in the hotel to resolve the problem?**    ☐ Yes    ☐ No

**8. Was the problem resolved to your satisfaction?**    ☐ Yes    ☐ No

**9. Which of the following best describes the reason for your stay?**    ☐ Business    ☐ Both Business/Leisure    ☐ Leisure    ☐ Meeting/Conference

**10. Your gender:**    ☐ Female    ☐ Male

Please write in your e-mail address: |__|__|__|__|__|__|__|__|__|__|__|__|__|__|__|__|__|__|__|__|__|__|__|__|__|

Additional comments: _____

Please return in the enclosed envelope to: J.D. Power and Associates, 30401 Agoura Road, Suite 200, Agoura Hills, CA 91301

Source: J.D. Power and Associates, Agoura Hills, CA 91301.

the facets of customer satisfaction more specifically and provides the transition into the next chapter, which focuses solely on service quality issues.

## Types of Customer Expectations

**predicted service** The level of service quality a consumer believes is likely to occur.

**desired service** The level of service quality a customer actually wants from a service encounter.

**perceived service superiority** A measure of service quality derived by comparing desired service expectations and perceived service received.

**adequate service** The level of service quality a customer is willing to accept.

**perceived service adequacy** A measure of service quality derived by comparing adequate service and perceived service.

At first glance, comparing expectations with perceptions when developing customer satisfaction evaluations sounds fairly straightforward. Expectations serve as benchmarks against which present and future service encounters are compared. However, this relatively simple scenario becomes a bit more confusing when you realize that there exist at least three different types of expectations.[16]

**Predicted service** is a probability expectation that reflects the level of service customers believe is likely to occur. For example, bank customers tend to conduct their banking business at the same location. Customers become accustomed to dealing with the same bank personnel and, over time, begin to anticipate certain performance levels. It is generally agreed that customer satisfaction evaluations are developed by comparing predicted service to perceived service received (see Figure 11.12).

In contrast, **desired service** is an ideal expectation that reflects what customers actually want compared with predicted service, which is what is likely to occur. Hence, in most instances, desired service reflects a higher expectation than predicted service. For example, our bank customer's desired service is that he not only receive his predicted service but that the tellers call him by his first name and enthusiastically greet him as he enters the bank. Comparing desired service expectations to perceived service received results in a measure of **perceived service superiority** (see Figure 11.12).

Finally, **adequate service** is a minimum tolerable expectation and reflects the level of service the customer is willing to accept. Adequate service is based on experiences or norms that develop over time. For example, most adult consumers have dined at hundreds, if not thousands, of restaurants throughout their lives. Through these experiences, norms develop that consumers expect to occur. Hence, one factor that influences adequate service is predicted service. Encounters that fall below expected norms fall below adequate service expectations. Comparing adequate service with perceived service produces a measure of **perceived service adequacy** (see Figure 11.12).

**FIG-11.12** Comparison between Customer Evaluation of Service Quality and Customer Satisfaction

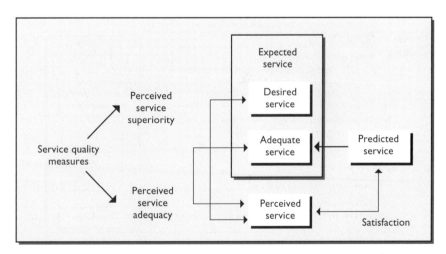

Source: Adapted from Valerie A. Zeithaml, Leonard L. Berry, and A. Parasuraman, "The Nature and Determinants of Customer Expectations of Service," *Journal of the Academy of Marketing Science*, 21, 1, (1993), pp. 1–12. Reprinted with kind permission from Springer Science and Business Media.

**zone of tolerance** Level of quality ranging from high to low and reflecting the difference between desired service and adequate service; expands and contracts across customers and within the same customer, depending on the service and the conditions under which it is provided.

**enduring service intensifiers** Personal factors that are stable over time and increase a customer's sensitivity to how a service should be best provided.

**derived expectations** Expectations appropriated from and based on the expectations of others.

**personal service philosophies** A customer's own internal views of the meaning of service and the manner in which service providers should conduct themselves.

## The Zone of Tolerance

Due to the heterogeneity of services provided, consumers learn to expect variation in service delivery from one location to the next and even in the same provider from one day to the next. Consumers who accept this variation develop a **zone of tolerance**, which reflects the difference between desired service and adequate service (see Figure 11.13). The zone of tolerance expands and contracts across customers and within the same customer depending on the service and the conditions under which the service is provided. Other factors, such as price, for example, may influence the zone of tolerance. Typically, as the price increases, the customer's zone of tolerance decreases as desired service needs begin to dominate, and the customer becomes less forgiving for sloppy service.

Another interesting characteristic of the zone of tolerance is that desired service is less subject to change than adequate service. One way to picture the zone of tolerance is to compare it with a projection screen located at the top of a blackboard. The metal canister bolted to the wall that holds the screen represents the desired service level. The desired service level represents what the customer believes the ideal service firm should provide to its customers. Because it is bolted to the wall, the metal canister's movement is less subject to change than the rest of the screen. The screen itself represents the zone of tolerance, and the metal piece with the handle at the bottom of the screen represents the adequate service level. Adequate service fluctuates based on circumstances surrounding the service delivery process and changes the size of the zone of tolerance accordingly.

## Factors Influencing Service Expectations: Desired Service

Desired service expectations are developed as a result of six different sources (see Figure 11.14). The first source, **enduring service intensifiers**, are personal factors that are stable over time and that increase a customer's sensitivity to how the service should be best provided. Two types of enduring service intensifiers include the customer's **derived expectations** and **personal service philosophies**. Derived expectations are created from the expectations of others. For example, if your boss requests that you find someone to pressure-wash the office building, your expectations of the provider performing the job will most likely be higher than if you had hired the provider on your own initiative. In

**FIG-11.13** The Zone of Tolerance

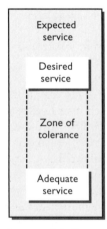

Source: Valerie A. Zeithaml, Leonard L. Berry, and A. Parasuraman, "The Nature and Determinants of Customer Expectations of Service," *Journal of the Academy of Marketing Science* 21, 1, (1993), pp. 1–12. Reprinted with kind permission from Springer Science and Business Media.

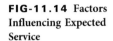

**FIG-11.14** Factors Influencing Expected Service

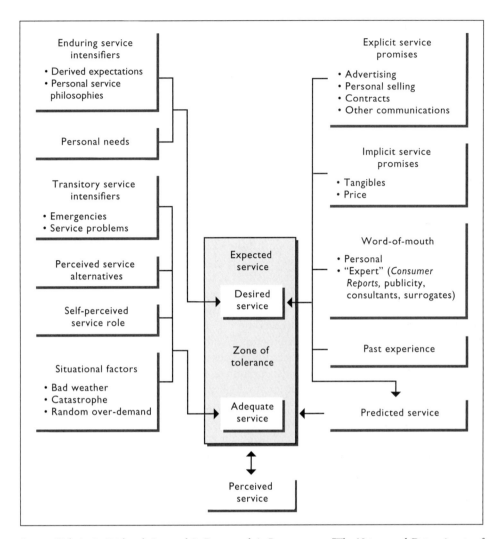

Source: Valerie A. Zeithaml, Leonard L. Berry, and A. Parasuraman, "The Nature and Determinants of Customer Expectations of Service," *Journal of the Academy of Marketing Science* 21, 1, (1993), pp. 1–12. Reprinted with kind permission from Springer Science and Business Media.

the attempt to satisfy your boss's expectations, your sensitivity to the caliber of service significantly increases.

Similarly, the customer's personal service philosophies, or personal views of the meaning of service and the manner in which service providers should conduct themselves, will also heighten his or her sensitivities. Customers who work in the service sector are particularly sensitive to the caliber of service provided. These customers hold their own views regarding exactly how service should be provided—they want to be treated the way they believe they treat their customers.

**personal needs** A customer's physical, social, and psychological needs.

The second factor influencing desired service expectations is the customer's own **personal needs**, including physical, social, and psychological needs. Simply stated, some customers have more needs and are "higher maintenance" than others. Some customers are very particular about where they are seated in a restaurant, while others are happy to sit nearly anywhere. In a hotel, some customers are very interested in the hotel's amenities, such as the pool, sauna, dining room, and other forms of available entertainment, while others are simply looking for a clean room. This is one of the reasons that managing a service firm is particularly challenging. Customers have a variety of needs, and no two customers are alike in every way.

## Factors Influencing Service Expectations: Desired Service and Predicted Service

The other four factors that influence desired service expectations also influence predicted service expectations and include (1) explicit service promises; (2) implicit service promises; (3) word-of-mouth communications; and (4) past experience (see Figure 11.14).

**explicit service promises** Obligations to which the firm commits itself via its advertising, personal selling, contracts, and other forms of communication.

**Explicit service promises** encompass the firm's advertising, personal selling, contracts, and other forms of communication. Due to the lack of a tangible product, consumers of services base their evaluations of the service on various forms of information available. The more ambiguous the service, the more customers rely on the firm's advertising when forming expectations. If a hotel stresses modern and clean rooms, customers expect the rooms to be exactly the way they were pictured in the advertisement. Similarly, if a builder states that a customer's new house will be completed in December, the customer takes this as the builder's promise, and the standard is established on which the customer will base subsequent evaluations.

**implicit service promises** Obligations to which the firm commits itself via the tangibles surrounding the service and the price of the service.

**Implicit service promises** also influence desired service and predicted service. The tangibles surrounding the service and the price of the service are common types of implicit service promises. As the price increases, customers expect the firm to deliver higher quality services. In the absence of a tangible product, the price becomes an indicator of quality to most consumers. For example, customers would probably have higher expectations for service at a higher priced hair salon than they would for "Cheap Charley's Barber Shop." Similarly, if the tangibles surrounding a service are luxurious, customers interpret those tangibles as a sign of quality. In general, the nicer the furnishings of the service establishment, the higher customer expectations become.

**word-of-mouth communications** Unbiased information from someone who has been through the service experience, such as friends, family, or consultants.

**Word-of-mouth communications** also play an important role in forming customer expectations. As discussed in Chapter 3 on Unique Discrepancies between Goods and Services, customers tend to rely more on personal sources of information than on non-personal ones when choosing among service alternatives. Since services cannot be evaluated fully before purchase, customers view word-of-mouth information as unbiased information from someone who has been through the service experience. Sources of word-of-mouth information range from friends and family to consultants to product review publications such as *Consumer Reports.*

**past experience** The previous service encounters a consumer has had with a service provider.

Finally, **past experience** also contributes to customer expectations of desired and predicted service. Service evaluations are often based on a comparison of the current service encounter to other encounters with the same provider, other providers in the industry, and other providers in other industries. In the education system, student-desired and student-predicted service expectations of instructors are likely to be based on past experience in other classes with the same instructor, and on other classes with other instructors.

## Factors Influencing Service Expectations: Adequate Service

Adequate service reflects the level of service the consumer is willing to accept and is influenced by five factors: (1) transitory service intensifiers; (2) perceived service alternatives; (3) customer self-perceived service roles; (4) situation factors; and (5) predicted service (see Figure 11.14).

**transitory service intensifiers** Personal, short-term factors that heighten a customer's sensitivity to service.

***Transitory Service Intensifiers***    In contrast to enduring service intensifiers, **transitory service intensifiers** are individualized, short-term factors that heighten the customer's sensitivity to service. For example, customers who have had service problems in the past with specific types of providers are more sensitive to the quality of service delivered during subsequent encounters. Another example is the need for service under personal emergency situations. Typically, consumers are willing to wait their turn to see a physician. However, under personal emergency conditions, consumers are less willing to be patient and expect a higher level of service in a shorter period of time. Hence, the level of adequate service increases, and the zone of tolerance becomes more narrow.

**perceived service alternatives** Comparable services customers believe they can obtain elsewhere and/or produce themselves.

*Perceived Service Alternatives*    The level of adequate service is also affected by the customer's **perceived service alternatives**. The larger the number of perceived service alternatives, the higher the level of adequate service expectations, and the more narrow the zone of tolerance. Customers who believe that they can obtain comparable services elsewhere and/or that they can produce the service themselves expect higher levels of adequate service than those customers who believe they are not able to receive sufficiently better service from another provider.

**self-perceived service role** The input a customer believes he or she is required to present in order to produce a satisfactory service encounter.

*Self-perceived Service Role*    As has been discussed on numerous occasions, the service customer is often involved in the production process and can directly influence the outcome of the service delivery system. When customers have a strong **self-perceived service role**, that is, when they believe that they are doing their part, their adequate service expectations are increased. However, if customers willingly admit that they have failed to complete forms or provide the necessary information to produce a superior service outcome, then their adequate service expectations decrease, and the zone of tolerance increases.

**situational factors** Circumstances that lower the service quality but that are beyond the control of the service provider.

*Situational Factors*    As a group, customers are not unreasonable. They understand that from time to time **situational factors** beyond the control of the service provider will lower the quality of service. If the power goes out in one part of town around dinner time, restaurants in other parts of town will be overrun by hungry patrons. As a result, lengthy waits will develop as the service delivery system becomes backed up. Similarly, after a hurricane, tornado, or other natural disaster occurs, the customer's insurance agent may not be as responsive as under normal circumstances. When circumstances occur beyond the control of the provider and the customer has knowledge of those circumstances, adequate service expectations are lowered, and the zone of tolerance becomes wider.

*Predicted Service*    The level of service consumers believe is likely to occur is the fifth and final factor that influences adequate service expectations. Predicted service is a function of the firm's explicit and implicit service promises, word-of-mouth communications, and the customer's own past experiences. Taking these factors into consideration, customers form judgments regarding the predicted service that is likely to occur and set adequate service expectations simultaneously.

## The Link between Expectations, Customer Satisfaction, and Service Quality

Now that we have introduced the concepts of predicted, adequate, and desired service, you may wonder what all the fuss is about. It is actually simple and straightforward. When evaluating the service experience, consumers compare the three types of expectations (predicted service, adequate service, and desired service) to the perceived service delivered. Customer satisfaction is calculated by comparing predicted service and perceived service. Perceived service adequacy, which compares adequate service and perceived service, and perceived service superiority, which compares desired service and perceived service, are measures of service quality (refer to Figure 11.12). Other major differences between service quality and customer satisfaction, as well as issues related to service quality measurement, are discussed in greater detail in Chapter 12.

## Summary

Customer satisfaction research is one of the fastest growing areas in market research today. Defined as a comparison of perceptions and predicted service expectations, customer satisfaction has been associated with such benefits as repeat sales, more frequent sales, increased sales per transaction, positive word-of-mouth communications, insulation from price competition, and pleasant work environments for employees. Customer satisfaction questionnaires send the signal to consumers that the firm cares about its customers and wants their input. In addition, data collected from questionnaires facilitates the development of employee training programs, identifies strengths and weaknesses in the firm's service delivery process, and provides information to be used in employee performance reviews and compensation decisions.

Firms use a variety of methods to track customer satisfaction. Moreover, a number of factors can dramatically increase or decrease the firm's satisfaction ratings. The main lessons to be learned are that (1) customer satisfaction surveys that collect qualitative and quantitative data are better than those that collect either qualitative or quantitative data alone; and (2) regardless of the methods used, such as the timing of the questions, the context of the questions, the data collection method, and a variety of other research issues, the service firm must be consistent in its approach in order to make benchmark comparisons over time meaningful. Overall, customer satisfaction ratings tend to be negatively skewed, indicating that above-average performance tends to be the norm.

Despite its challenges, the assessment of customer satisfaction is a valuable management exercise. However, firms should not attempt to increase their satisfaction ratings without carefully considering (1) the satisfaction ratings of competing firms; (2) the cost of an investment in increasing market share relative to the impact on the firm's bottom line; (3) the number of time periods it takes to recoup such an investment; and (4) the opportunity costs associated with the use of the firm's funds. Finally, among the key driving forces behind customer satisfaction are customer expectations. Three types of expectations and the factors influencing each type were presented. The three types of expectations form the bases for both customer satisfaction and service quality assessments, which are discussed in Chapter 12.

## Key Terms

expectancy disconfirmation model, p. 295
confirmed expectations, p. 295
disconfirmed expectations, p. 295
negative disconfirmation, p. 295
positive disconfirmation, p. 295
indirect measures, p. 299
direct measures, p. 299
response bias, p. 304
question form, p. 305
question context, p. 306
question timing, p. 306

social desirability bias, p. 306
benchmarking, p. 307
predicted service, p. 313
desired service, p. 313
perceived service superiority, p. 313
adequate service, p. 313
perceived service adequacy, p. 313
zone of tolerance, p. 314
enduring service intensifiers, p. 314
derived expectations, p. 314
personal service philosophies, p. 314

personal needs, p. 315
explicit service promises, p. 316
implicit service promises, p. 316
word-of-mouth communications, p. 316
past experience, p. 316
transitory service intensifiers, p. 316
perceived service alternatives, p. 317
self-perceived service role, p. 317
situational factors, p. 317

## Review Questions

1. Discuss the differences among a *confirmation,* a *positive disconfirmation,* and a *negative disconfirmation.*

2. What is meant by the description that most satisfaction scores are *negatively skewed*? Why does this score distribution occur?

3. Discuss how the *form of a question* may influence satisfaction scores.

4. Should a company always attempt to achieve 100 percent customer satisfaction? Please explain.

5. Discuss the relationship between *customer satisfaction* and *customer retention.*

6. What are the drawbacks of listening to customers and assessing customer satisfaction?

7. Define and explain the relevance of the *zone of tolerance.*

8. What are the major factors that influence customer expectations for *adequate service*?

9. What are the major factors that influence customer expectations for *desired service*?

10. Go to http://www.theacsi.org/ and click on "ACSI Scores & Commentary." Next, click on "ACSI Quarterly Scores." Based on the four quarters of information available, develop a "Top Ten" list for those firms that score highest in customer satisfaction. In addition, develop a "Bottom Ten" list for those firms that score lowest in customer satisfaction. Compare the two lists and comment on the major differences between the firms in the "Top Ten" list and the "Bottom Ten" list. Discuss why you think this difference exists.

## Notes

1. Robert A. Peterson and William R. Wilson, "Measuring Customer Satisfaction: Fact and Artifact," *Journal of the Academy of Marketing Science* 20, 1, (1992), p. 61.

2. Karl Albrecht and Ron Zemke, *Service America! Doing Business in the New Economy* (Homewood, IL: Business One Irwin, 1985), p. 6.

3. Janelle Barlow and Claus Moller, *A Complaint is a Gift* (San Francisco: Berrett- Koehler Publishers, Inc., 2008).

4. Keith Hunt, "Consumer Satisfaction, Dissatisfaction, and Complaining Behavior," *Journal of Social Issues* 47, 1, (1991), pp. 109–110.

5. Leonard L. Berry, A. Parasuraman, and Valerie A. Zeithaml, "Improving Service Quality in America: Lessons Learned," *Academy of Management Executive* 8, 2, (1994), p. 36.

6. Peterson and Wilson, "Measuring Customer Satisfaction," p. 61.

7. Peterson and Wilson, "Measuring Customer Satisfaction," p. 61.

8. Peterson and Wilson, "Measuring Customer Satisfaction," p. 62.

9. Marsha L. Richins, "Negative Word-of-Mouth by Dissatisfied Consumers: A Pilot Study," *Journal of Marketing,* 47, (Winter 1983), pp. 68–78.

10. K. Douglas Hoffman, "A Conceptual Framework of the Influence of Positive Mood States on Service Exchange Relationships," *Marketing Theory and Applications,* Chris T. Allen, et al., eds. (San Antonio, TX: American Marketing Association Winter Educator's Conference), p. 147.

11. Adapted from Peter Babich, "Customer Satisfaction: How Good Is Good Enough," *Quality Progress,* (December 1992), pp. 65–67.

12. Adapted from Michael W. Lowenstein, "The Voice of the Customer," *Small Business Reports,* (December 1993), pp. 57–61.

13. Justin Martin, "Ignore Your Customer," *Fortune,* (May 1, 1995), pp. 121–126.

14. Ibid.

15. Ibid, p. 126.

16. This section adapted from Valerie A. Zeithaml, Leonard L. Berry, and A. Parasuraman, "The Nature and Determinants of Customer Expectations of Service," *Journal of the Academy of Marketing Science* 21, 1, (1993), pp. 1–12.

# The Crestwood Inn

Christy Kelley moved from Boston, Massachusetts, to take over as the general manager of The Crestwood Inn located in Lexington, Kentucky. Previous to her new job at The Crestwood, Christy had been the assistant general manager of a large chain hotel in the downtown area of Boston. She had grown tired of the harsh winters and fast pace of the Northeast, and felt it would be a welcome change to move to a warmer climate and a much more relaxed atmosphere. Christy had worked for the large chain for several years, starting in the management training program and working her way up eventually to assistant general manager to her new position as general manager of the inn.

The Crestwood Inn is one of the oldest properties in the area, but it has been renovated periodically over the years. The inn is owned by a group of independent investors and has 116 rooms with basic amenities. There is no restaurant or pool, but there are some restaurants in the local area. The inn's room rate is at the low end for the market, which consists mainly of upscale properties. The Crestwood Inn's primary strategic advantages included its price and location, which was convenient to local horse racing venues.

Upon starting her new position as general manager, Christy realized that there were major differences between working for a large chain and working at a small, independent motel. The large chain hotels had sophisticated computer systems for reservations, sales, catering, and revenue management. In addition, customer information was systematically gathered through surveys and comment cards. The surveys and comment cards provided managers with valuable information that could be used to make important decisions about hotels rates and services. Unfortunately, The Crestwood Inn had a very simple reservations system and no additional information except for some historical figures on past rates and occupancy. As Christy took over as general manager, the average room rate was $100 and the occupancy rate was around 70 percent.

Christy understood the value of gathering customer information, and personally developed a comment card to be placed in every room. Customers were asked to complete the comment card and leave it in the room for housekeeping to collect. The purpose of the comment card was to determine how guests staying at the motel felt about the property and its services. Christy wanted to make sure that all her guests were satisfied. At the end of the first year, she received a total of 169 completed comment cards.

After compiling the information contained on the comment cards, Christy looked at guest responses pertaining to their overall customer satisfaction:

*Which of the following best describes your experience at The Crestwood Inn?*

| | |
|---|---|
| The motel exceeded my expectations. | 18.7 percent |
| The motel met my expectations. | 56.8 percent |
| The motel failed to meet my expectations. | 24.5 percent |

The percentages indicate the guests' responses to the question—nearly 75 percent of guests indicated that the inn met or exceeded their expectations. Christy was pleased that that this year's results could serve as a benchmark for future years, but was concerned that The Crestwood Inn failed to meet the expectations for approximately one-fourth of its guests. Next, Christy looked at the guests' ratings of the motel's facilities and services on a four-point scale (1 = poor, 2 = fair, 3 = neutral, 4 = good, and 5 = excellent).

| HOTEL SERVICES | MEAN |
|---|---|
| Reservations | 4.46 |
| Front desk/check-in | 4.52 |
| Front desk/checkout | 4.34 |
| Front desk/guest service | 4.50 |
| GUEST ROOM | |
| Comfort | 4.18 |
| Bedroom lighting | 3.90 |
| Cleanliness | 4.31 |
| Furnishings | 4.10 |
| Adequacy of supplies | 4.21 |
| Heating/air-conditioning | 3.89 |
| Overall quality | 4.15 |
| Price/room rate | 4.12 |

## Discussion Questions

1. Discuss the pros and cons of Christy's development of the comment card.
2. Describe the potential problems associated with involving the housekeeping staff to collect the comment cards.
3. With regards to three expectation questions that address the guest's experience: (1) What information can Christy learn from these three questions; (2) what additional information would be helpful to improve the level of service provided by the hotel; and (3) how can this additional information be collected?
4. Christy also collected information pertaining to the hotel's services and guest rooms. (1) What information can Christy learn from these questions; (2) what additional information would be helpful to improve the level of service provided by the hotel; and (3) how can this additional information be collected?

"It's just the little touches after the average man would quit that makes the master's fame."

*Orison Swett Marden,*
*Founder,* Success
*magazine*

## CHAPTER 12

# Service Quality: Identifying and Rectifying the Gaps

## CHAPTER OBJECTIVES

After completing this chapter, you should be able to:

- Discuss the differences and the similarities between service quality and customer satisfaction.

- Identify the gaps that influence consumer perceptions of service quality and discuss factors that influence the size of each of the service quality gaps.

- Understand the basic concepts of the SERVQUAL measurement scale and how "gap scores" are calculated.

- Describe the variety of customer and noncustomer research approaches a service firm can utilize to construct a service quality information system.

The major objectives of this chapter are to introduce you to the concepts of service quality, service quality measurement, and service quality information systems.

### THE MALCOLM BALDRIGE NATIONAL QUALITY AWARD

The most prestigious quality award in the United Sates is the Malcolm Baldrige National Qual-

Peter Yates/Time Life Pictures/Getty Images

ity Award. The award is named for Malcolm Baldrige, who served as Secretary of Commerce during the Reagan administration for the period 1981 to 1987. Malcolm Baldrige was an innovator. Dur-ing his seven-year tenure as Sec-retary of Commerce, Baldrige developed and implemented groundbreaking Administration trade policy with China, India, and the Soviet Union. In addition, he was recognized for his exceptional managerial excellence in improving the efficiency and effectiveness of government. Tragically, Baldrige was killed in a rodeo accident in 1987.

In honor of Baldrige, the Malcolm Baldrige National Quality Award was signed into law on August 27, 1987, as Public Law 100-107. The Award is given to three enterprises in each of five business sectors that exhibit overall excellence in the areas of leadership, strategic planning, customer and market focus, information and analysis, human resource development, management and business results. The five sectors include manufacturing, service, small business, education, and health care. More specifically, the fundamental reasons behind the Malcolm Baldrige National Quality Award can be found within the Findings and Purposes Section of Public Law 100-107 which state:

1. The leadership of the United States in product and process quality has been challenged strongly (and sometimes successfully) by foreign competition, and our Nation's productivity growth has improved less than our competitors' over the last two decades.

2. American business and industry are beginning to understand that poor quality costs companies as much as 20 percent of sales revenues nationally and that improved quality of goods and services goes hand in hand with improved productivity, lower costs, and increased profitability.

3. Strategic planning for quality and quality improvement programs, through a commitment to excellence in manufacturing and services, are becoming more and more essential to the well-being of our Nation's economy and our ability to compete effectively in the global marketplace.

4. Improved management understanding of the factory floor, worker involvement in quality, and greater emphasis on statistical process control can lead to dramatic improvements in the cost and quality of manufactured products.

5. The concept of quality improvement is directly applicable to small companies as well as large, to service industries as well as manufacturing, and to the public sector as well as private enterprise.

6. In order to be successful, quality improvement programs must be management-led and customer-oriented, and this may require fundamental changes in the way companies and agencies do business.

7. Several major industrial nations have successfully coupled rigorous private-sector quality audits with national awards giving special recognition to those enterprises the audits identify as the very best; and

8. A national quality award program of this kind in the United States would help improve quality and productivity by:

   a. helping to stimulate American companies to improve quality and productivity for the pride of recognition while obtaining a competitive edge through increased profits;

   b. recognizing the achievements of those companies that improve the quality of their goods and services and providing an example to others;

   c. establishing guidelines and criteria that can be used by business, industrial, governmental, and other organizations in evaluating their own quality improvement efforts; and

   d. providing specific guidance for other American organizations that wish to learn how to manage for high quality by making available detailed information on how winning organizations were able to change their cultures and achieve eminence.

In the end, applicants for the award are thrilled to win the Malcolm Baldrige National Quality Award; however, win or lose, they find high value in the review process itself. Some organizations, such as Motorola, Inc., apply for the award with no real intent of actually winning. Says Bob Barnett, Executive Vice President of Motorola, Inc.: "We applied for the Award, not with the idea of winning, but with the goal of receiving the evaluation of the Baldrige Examiners. That [Baldrige] evaluation was comprehensive, professional, and insightful … making it perhaps the most cost-effective, value-added business consultation available anywhere in the world today."

Sources:
1. "The Malcolm Baldrige National Quality Improvement Act of 1987 – Public Law 100-107," **http://www. baldrige.nist.gov/Improvement_Act.htm**, accessed 31 August, 2009.

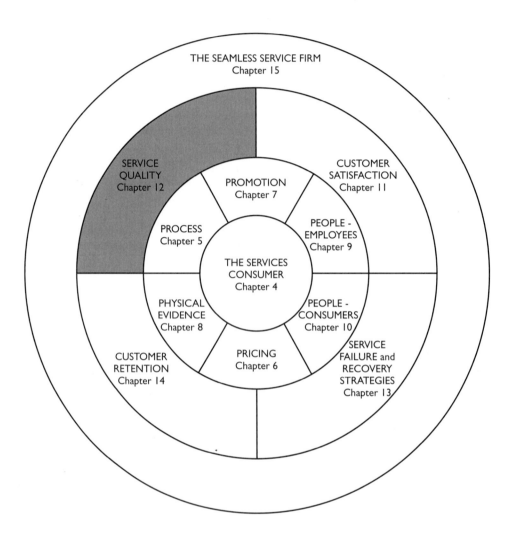

2. "Biography of Malcolm Baldrige," **http://www.baldrige.nist.gov/Biography.htm**, accessed 2 September, 2009.

## Introduction

One of the few issues on which service quality researchers agree is that service quality is an elusive and abstract concept that is difficult to define and measure.[1] This particular problem is challenging for academicians and practitioners alike. Case in point, traditional measures of productivity such as Gross Domestic Product (GDP) do not account for increases in service quality delivered. In fact, providing poor quality can actually increase the country's GDP![2] If a mail-order company sends you the wrong product, the dollars spent on phone calls and return mailings to correct the mistake will actually add to the country's GDP.

Other governmental institutions, such as the Bureau of Labor Statistics (BLS), have attempted to account for increases in quality by adjusting the consumer price index. For example, if a car costs more this year than last but includes quality improvements such as an air bag, better gas mileage, and cleaner emissions, the BLS will subtract the estimated retail value of the improvements before calculating the consumer price index. However, the BLS does this for only a few industries and without the help of customers—the true evaluators of quality improvements. Efficiency measures are also of no help. A retail store, which stocks lots of merchandise, may please more customers and make more money while decreasing the firm's efficiency rating.

As further evidence of the complexities involved in measuring service quality enhancements, the productivity of education and government services is notoriously difficult to measure. Increases in quality, such as improving the quality of education and training governmental employees to be more pleasant throughout their daily interactions with the pubic, do not show up in productivity measures. Moreover, a university can increase the quality of its faculty and educational instruction; however, at the end of the day it's the number of graduates (quality or not) that often defines the university's performance. Despite its elusiveness, it is readily apparent that increases in quality can have a dramatic impact on a firm's or industry's survival. As evidence, Japan did not simply bulldoze its way into U.S. markets by offering lower prices alone—superior quality relative to the competition at that time ultimately won customers over.

## What Is Service Quality?

**service quality** An attitude formed by a long-term, overall evaluation of a firm's performance.

Perhaps the best way to begin a discussion of service quality is to attempt first to distinguish **service quality** from customer satisfaction. Most experts agree that customer satisfaction is a short-term, transaction-specific measure, whereas service quality is an attitude formed by a long-term, overall evaluation of a performance.

Without a doubt, the two concepts of customer satisfaction and service quality are intertwined. However, the relationship between these two concepts is unclear. Some believe that customer satisfaction leads to perceived service quality, while others believe that service quality leads to customer satisfaction. In addition, the relationship between customer satisfaction and service quality and the way these two concepts relate to purchasing behavior remains largely unexplained.[3]

One plausible explanation is that satisfaction assists consumers in revising service quality perceptions.[4] The logic for this position consists of the following:

1. Consumer perceptions of the service quality of a firm with which he or she has no prior experience is based on the consumer's expectations.
2. Subsequent encounters with the firm lead the consumer through the disconfirmation process (where perceptions and expectations are compared), and revised perceptions of service quality are formed.
3. Each additional encounter with the firm further revises or reinforces service quality perceptions. In other words, if we added up a customer's satisfaction over time with a single firm, this would equate to the customer's service quality perception (e.g., $Sat_1 + Sat_2 + Sat_3 + Sat_4 + Sat_n = $ Service Quality).
4. In turn, revised service quality perceptions modify future consumer purchase intentions toward the firm.

To deliver a consistent set of satisfying experiences that can build into an evaluation of high quality requires the entire organization to be focused on the task. The needs of the consumer must be understood in detail, as must the constraints under which the service firm operates. Service providers must be focused on quality, and the system must be designed to support that mission by being controlled correctly and delivering services as it was designed to do.

### The Difference in Quality Perspectives between Goods and Services

Service quality offers a way of achieving success among competing services.[5] Particularly, where a small number of firms that offer nearly identical services are competing within a small area (e.g., a dry cleaner, local banks, restaurants, insurance agents). In fact, establishing service quality may be the only way of differentiating oneself. For example, some restaurants are finding that "going green" has enhanced their reputations for service quality (see Sustainability and Services in Action). Service quality differentiation can generate increased market share and ultimately mean the difference between financial success and failure.

Ample evidence suggests that the provision of quality can deliver repeat purchases as well as new customers. The value of retaining existing customers is discussed in much greater detail in Chapter 14. Briefly, repeat customers yield many benefits to the service

## SUSTAINABILITY AND SERVICES *IN ACTION*

### Certifed 'Green': Enhancing Perceptions of Service Quality

Seeking the blessing of the ecologically aware, restaurants are finding that becoming a "certified green restaurant" enhances the customer's perception of their overall service quality and differentiates them from the competition. The financial motivation to embrace "green" initiatives is clear. Based on a survey conducted by the National Restaurant Association, 62 percent of respondents indicated that their restaurant choice would likely be influenced by the restaurant's environmental friendliness.

Apparently, when it comes to going "green" the restaurant industry has lots of room for improvement. Figures provided by the Boston-based Green Restaurant Association (GRA) indicate that of all the energy that is used by U.S. retail businesses, the U.S. restaurant industry accounts for one-third! In fact, the GRA further reports that the restaurant industry uses 500 percent more energy than other retail businesses—including lodging! Perhaps just as surprising, it is estimated that for every restaurant meal served, an average of 1.5 pounds of trash is produced. When one considers that the average American eats out 4.2 times a week multiplied by a population of approximately 310 million, the amount of trash is staggering.

Examples of "green" restaurant practices include:

- Constructing dining rooms and tables out of reclaimed wood
- Utilizing nontoxic and non-polluting cleaning products
- Providing customers with to-go cups made of corn and spoons using potato starch that disintegrate in 30–60 days in a commercial compost site as opposed to a landfill
- Purchasing from local suppliers to reduce the amount of fossil fuels used in transportation
- Cooking with organic ingredients
- Utilizing recycled paper and soy-based inks for menus
- Composting food waste
- Purchasing energy efficient lighting
- Avoiding the use of fresh flowers that have been sprayed with pesticides

Going "green" is not cheap. According to one restaurant owner, using organic ingredients increases her costs by 20 percent, and her labor costs are also 20 percent higher than comparable competitors—"Someone has to haul the compost. Everything adds up." However, the benefits offset the cost. Green restaurants are "in." "My business is better than ever, because more and more people are aware and concerned about healthy eating and the environment." Customers that try to live "green" can now come to restaurants that share the mutual goal of engaging in environmentally friendly behaviors.

Source: Walter Nichols, "A Tall Order of Green," *washingtonpost.com*, (Wednesday, January 16, 2008), p. 4. Can also be found at **http://www.washingtonpost.com/wp-dyn/content/article/2008/01/15/ AR200 8011500755.html**, accessed 9 February, 2009.

organization. The cost of marketing to them is lower than that of marketing to new customers. Once customers have become regulars of the service, they know the appropriate behavioral script from pervious interactions with the firm, and are efficient users of existing service systems (e.g., a customer using its banks ATM for the 30th time). As they gain trust in the organization, the customer's level of perceived risk is reduced, and they are more likely to consolidate their business with the firm. For example, insurance customers tend to move existing policies to and purchase new policies from the one provider they feel best serves their needs, whether those needs are financial and/or emotional.

Goods manufacturers have already learned this lesson over the past decade, and have made producing quality goods a priority issue. Improving the quality of manufactured goods has become a major strategy for both establishing efficient, smoothly running operations and increasing consumer market share in an atmosphere in which customers are consistently demanding higher and higher quality. Goods quality improvement measures have focused largely on the quality of the products themselves, and specifically on eliminating product failure. Initially, these measures were based on rigorous checking of all finished products before they came into contact with the customer. More recently, quality control has focused on the principle of ensuring quality during the manufacturing process, on "getting it right the first time," and on reducing end-of-production-line failures to zero. The final evolution in goods manufacturing has been to define quality as delivering the right product to the right customer at the right time, thus extending quality beyond the good itself and using external as well as internal measures to assess overall quality.

However, service quality cannot be understood in quite the same way. The service firm depends on the customer as a participant in the production process, and normal quality control measures that depend on eliminating defects before the consumer sees the product are not available. Consequently, service quality is not a specific goal or program that can be achieved or completed, but must be an ongoing part of all management and service production on a daily basis. In the end, service quality is as much an art as it is science.

## Diagnosing Failure Gaps in Service Quality

Implementing and evaluating service quality is a difficult task. In the first place, perceptions of quality tend to rely on a repeated comparison of the customer's expectation about a particular service. If a service, no matter how good, fails repeatedly to meet a customer's expectations, the customer will perceive the service to be of poor quality. Second, unlike goods marketing, where customers evaluate the finished product alone, in services, the customer evaluates the *process* of the service as well as its *outcome*. A customer visiting a physician, for example, will evaluate service not only on the basis of whether he or she experienced a positive outcome (e.g., feeling better), but also on whether the physician was friendly, competent, and caring.

In the hopes of better understanding how a firm can improve its overall service quality, the service quality process can be examined in terms of five gaps between expectations and perceptions on the part of management, employees, and customers (see Figure 12.1).[6] The most important gap, the **service gap** (for our purposes also known as Gap 5), describes the distance between customers' expectations of service and their perception of the service actually delivered. Ultimately, the goal of the service firm is to close the service gap, or at least narrow it as much as possible. Consequently, examining service quality gaps is much like the disconfirmation of expectations model discussed in Chapter 11. However, remember that service quality focuses on the customer's cumulative satisfaction toward the firm, which is collected by the consumer from a number of successful or unsuccessful service experiences.

**service gap** The distance between a customer's expectation of a service and perception of the service actually delivered.

Image copyright Phil Date. Used under license from Shutterstock.com

When employees follow the standards set by management to deliver excellent service, the delivery gap is nonexistent.

**knowledge gap** The difference between what consumers expect of a service and what management perceives the consumers to expect.

**standards gap** The difference between what management perceives consumers to expect and the quality specifications set for service delivery.

**delivery gap** The difference between the quality standards set for service delivery and the actual quality of service delivery.

**communications gap** The difference between the actual quality of service delivered and the quality of service described in the firm's external communications.

Before the firm can close the service gap, it must close or attempt to narrow four other gaps:

Gap 1: The **knowledge gap**—the difference between what consumers do expect of a service and what management perceives that consumers expect.

Gap 2: The **standards gap**—the difference between what management perceives that consumers expect and the quality specifications set for service delivery.

Gap 3: The **delivery gap**—the difference between the quality specifications set for service delivery and the actual quality of service delivered. For example, do employees perform the service as they were trained?

Gap 4: The **communications gap**—the difference between the actual quality of service delivered and the quality of service described in the firm's external communications (e.g., advertising, point-of-purchase materials, and personal selling efforts).

Hence, the service gap is a function of the knowledge gap, the specifications gap, the delivery gap, and the communications gap. In other words, Gap 5 = f(Gap 1 + Gap 2+ Gap 3 + Gap 4). As each of these gaps increases or decreases, the service gap responds in a similar manner.

## The Knowledge Gap (Gap 1)

The most immediate and obvious gap is usually between what customers want and what managers think customers want. Briefly, many managers think they know what their customers want but are, in fact, sometimes mistaken. For example, airlines might

**FIG-12.1** Conceptual Model of Service Quality

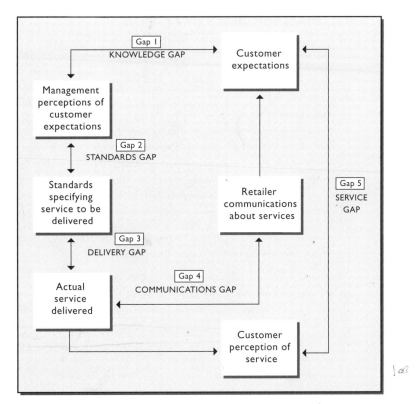

Source: Adapted from A. Parasuraman, Valerie Zeithaml, and Leonard Berry, "A Conceptual Model of Service Quality and Its Implications for Service Quality Research," *Journal of Marketing*, 49, (Fall 1985), pp. 41–50.

mistakenly believe that customers have the same expectations and perceptions regarding airline travel around the world (see Global Services in Action). As another example, banking customers may prefer security to a good interest rate. Some restaurant customers may prefer the quality and taste of food over an attractive arrangement of the tables or a good view from the window. A hotel may feel that its customers prefer comfortable rooms, when, in fact, the majority of them spend little time in their rooms and are more interested in on-site amenities, such as the exercise facilities, pools, and spa.

When a knowledge gap occurs, a variety of other mistakes tend to follow. The wrong facilities may be provided, the wrong staff may be hired, and the wrong training may be undertaken. Services may be provided that customers have no use for, while the services they do desire are not offered. Closing this gap requires minutely detailed knowledge of what customers desire, and then building that response into the service operating system.

***Factors Influencing the Knowledge Gap***   Three main factors influence the size of the knowledge gap. First, the firm's **research orientation**, which reflects its attitude toward conducting customer research, can dramatically influence the size of the gap. Information obtained from customer research defines consumer expectations. As the firm's research orientation increases and the firm learns more about the needs and wants of its customers, the size of the knowledge gap should decrease. The amount of **upward communication** is a second factor that influences the size of the knowledge gap. Upward communication refers to the flow of information from front-line personnel to upper levels of the organization. In other words, does upper management listen to and value the

---

**research orientation** A firm's attitude toward conducting consumer research.

**upward communication** The flow of information from front-line personnel to upper levels of the organization.

## GLOBAL SERVICES *IN ACTION*

### American versus European Expectations and Perceptions of Airline Service Quality

Based on a study of nearly 1,200 European and U.S. airline passengers, the SERVQUAL measurement instrument was put to the test to find: (1) if SERVQUAL could be effectively used in international settings with multiple languages; and (2) if expectations and perceptions of airline service quality varied between U.S. and European airline passengers. With respect to airline travel as measured by SERVQUAL, findings revealed the following:

■ Although expectations and perceptions vary, the SERVQUAL measurement instrument was found to be a reliable measurement instrument that can be used in a variety of international settings with multiple languages.

■ Although all SERVQUAL dimensions are important, American and Europeans agreed on the relative importance of the five SERVQUAL dimensions in the following order (1 = most important; 5 = least important).

1. Reliability

■ "When a customer has a problem, an excellent airline shows a sincere interest in solving it." (This was rated as the highest SERVQUAL expectation item for all dimensions for both groups.

2. Responsiveness
3. Assurance
4. Empathy
5. Tangibles

■ "Excellent airlines will have modern looking aircraft." (This was rated as the lowest SEVQUAL expectation item for all dimensions for both groups.)

■ Americans reported a higher expectation for tangibles, specifically for items such as the appearance of the airline office, terminal, and gate.

■ Americans also had a greater expectation for airline personnel appearance.

■ U.S. and European airlines were perceived by both Americans and Europeans as *not* meeting expectations. In other words, gap scores were negative for all five dimensions.

■ Americans perceived service quality to be higher on 20 of 22 service quality statements for both U.S. and European airlines. In other words, Europeans are generally more critical of specific service quality issues and general overall airline service quality.

Findings from this study are useful for companies wishing to expand their business into international markets. Business should carefully take into consideration the differences in nationally based expectations and perceptions when formulating the customer's service experience. What may be acceptable service in one country may be unacceptable in another.

Source: Fareena Sultan and Merlin C. Simpson, Jr., "International Service Variants: Airline Passenger Expectations and Perceptions of Service Quality," *Journal of Services Marketing*, 14, 3, (2000), pp. 188–216.

---

**levels of management**
The complexity of the organizational hierarchy and the number of levels between top management and the customers.

feedback provided by its front-line personnel? Front-line personnel interact with customers on a frequent basis, so they are often more in touch with customer needs than top management. Consequently, as the flow of upward communication increases through the organization, the knowledge gap should become smaller. Finally, the **levels of management** in the organization can also influence the size of the knowledge gap. As the organizational hierarchy becomes more complex and more levels of management are added, higher levels of management tend to become more distant from customers and the day-to-day activities of the organization. As a result, when the levels of management increase, the size of the knowledge gap tends to increase.

## The Standards Gap (Gap 2)

Even if customer expectations have been accurately determined, the standards gap may open between management's perception of customer expectations and the actual standards set for service delivery. A simple analogy would be to consider an exchange of ideas between an architect and a home buyer. The home buyer communicates ideas to the architect for the construction of their dream home; moreover, let's assume that the architect clearly understands the home buyer's wishes. In this case, a knowledge gap does not exist. Once the architect understands the home buyer's wishes, blueprints are created that set the exact specifications for a builder to follow. If the architect is unable to convert the home buyer's wishes to blueprint specifications, a standards gap is created.

When developing standards, the firm should use a flowchart of its operations to identify all points of contact between the firm and its customers. Detailed standards can be written for: (1) the way the system should operate and (2) the behavior of contact personnel at each point in the system. For example, specifications can be written for restaurant waitstaff personnel to greet customers, provide glasses of water, take drink orders for those wanting something other than water, deliver drinks, take food orders, and deliver food all within specific timeframes. Essentially, specifications provide a guidebook for employees to follow with the goal of meeting or exceeding customer expectations.

*Factors Influencing the Standards Gap* In many cases, management does not believe it can or should meet customer requirements for service. For example, overnight delivery of mail used to be thought of as an absurd possibility before Fred Smith and FedEx proved that, in fact, it could be done. Another factor that influences the size of the standards gap is management's commitment to the delivery of service quality. Corporate leadership may set other priorities that interfere with setting standards that lead to good service. For example, a company's orientation toward implementing cost-reduction strategies that maximize short-term profits is often cited as a misguided priority that impedes the firm's progress in delivering quality services. Personal computer companies whose automated service hotlines reduce the number of customer service representatives employed are typical examples. In some instances, customers in need of service have been forced to remain on hold for hours before they could actually speak to a "real person." Hotlines were originally named to reflect the speed with which the customer could talk to the manufacturer. Now the name more appropriately reflects the customer's temper by the time he or she talks to someone who can actually help.

Other factors influencing the size of the standards gap include: (1) sometimes there is simply no culture for service quality and management genuinely fails to understand the issues involved; (2) management may wish to meet customer requirements but feels hampered by insufficient methods of measuring quality or by converting those measurements into standards; and (3) because of the difficulties in attempting to write specifications for particular employee behaviors, some managers feel that quality measurement is not worth the effort.

## The Delivery Gap (Gap 3)

The delivery gap occurs between the actual performance of a service and the standards set by management. The existence of the delivery gap depends on both the willingness and the ability of employees to provide the service according to specification. Continuing our home buyer analogy, if the home builder does not follow the standards set by the architect's blueprints, a delivery gap is created. Similarly, if a restaurant's waitstaff does not execute the standards developed in their training manual, a delivery gap is formed.

### Factors Influencing the Delivery Gap

One factor that influences the size of the delivery gap is the employee's **willingness to perform** the service. Obviously, employees' willingness to provide a service can vary greatly from employee to employee and in the same employee over time. Many employees who start off working to their full potential often become less willing to do so over time because of frustration and dissatisfaction with the organization. Furthermore, a considerable range exists between what the employee is actually capable of accomplishing and the minimum the employee must do in order to keep his/her job. Most service managers find it difficult to keep employees working at their full potential all the time.

Other employees, no matter how willing, may simply not be able to perform the service to specification. Hence, a second factor that influences the size of the delivery gap is the **employee-job fit**. Individuals may have been hired for jobs they are not qualified to handle or to which they are temperamentally unsuited, or they may not have been provided with sufficient training for the roles expected of them. Generally, employees who are not capable of performing assigned roles are less willing to keep trying.

Another common factor influencing the size of the delivery gap is **role conflict**. Whether or not the knowledge gap has been closed, service providers may still see an inconsistency between what the service manager expects employees to provide and the service their customers actually want. A waiter who is expected to promote various items on the menu may alienate some customers who prefer to make their own choices undisturbed. In more formal settings, persistent waiters may find customers retaliating by not leaving a tip. In other cases, the service provider may be expected to do too many kinds of work, such as simultaneously answering telephones and dealing with customers face to face in a busy office. If this kind of conflict continues to occur, employees become frustrated, gradually lose their commitment to providing the best service they can, and/or simply quit altogether.

Yet another cause of the delivery gap is **role ambiguity**. Role ambiguity results when employees, due to poor employee-job fit or inadequate training, do not understand the roles of their jobs or what their jobs are intended to accomplish. Sometimes they are even unfamiliar with the service firm and its goals. Consequently, as role ambiguity increases, the delivery gap widens.

A further complication for employees is the **dispersion of control**, the situation in which control over the nature of the service being provided is removed from employees' hands. When employees are not allowed to make independent decisions about individual cases without first conferring with a manager, they may feel marginalized, alienated from the service firm, and less committed to their job. Furthermore, when control over certain aspects of the service is moved to a different location, such as control over credit being removed from individual bank branches, employee alienation is bound to increase. Eventually, employees experience **learned helplessness** and feel unable to respond to customer requests for help. Consequently, as the dispersion of control increases, the delivery gap becomes wider.

Finally, the delivery gap may also suffer due to **inadequate support**, such as not receiving personal training and/or technological and other resources necessary for employees to perform their jobs in the best possible manner. Even the best employees can be discouraged if they are forced to work with out-of-date or faulty equipment, especially if the employees of competing firms have superior resources and are able to provide the same or superior levels of service with far less effort. Failure to properly support employees leads to a lot of wasted effort, poor employee productivity, unsatisfied customers, and an increase in the size of the delivery gap.

**willingness to perform**
An employee's desire to perform to his/her full potential in a service encounter.

**employee-job fit** The degree to which employees are able to perform a service to specifications.

**role conflict** An inconsistency in service providers' minds between what the service manager expects them to provide and the service they think their customers actually want.

**role ambiguity** Uncertainty of employees' roles in their jobs and poor understanding of the purpose of their jobs.

**dispersion of control** The situation in which control over the nature of the service being provided is removed from employees' hands.

**learned helplessness** The condition of employees who, through repeated dispersion of control, feel themselves unable to perform a service adequately.

**inadequate support** A management failure to give employees personal training and/or technological and other resources necessary for them to perform their jobs in the best possible manner.

### The Communications Gap (Gap 4)

The communications gap is the difference between the service the firm promises it will deliver through its external communications and the service it actually delivers to its customers. If advertising or sales promotions promise one kind of service and the consumer receives a different kind of service, the communications gap becomes wider and wider. All firms need to understand that all external communications are essentially promises the firm makes to its customers, thereby increasing customer expectations. When the communications gap is wide, the firm has broken its promises, resulting in a lack of future customer trust. A customer who orders a bottle of wine from a menu only to be told it is out of stock may feel that the offer held out on the menu has not been fulfilled. A customer who is promised delivery in three days who then has to wait two weeks will perceive service quality to be far lower than expected.

***Factors Influencing the Communications Gap***    The communications gap is often influenced primarily by two factors. The first, the propensity of the firm to **overpromise**, occurs in highly competitive business environments as firms try to outdo one another in the name of recruiting new customers. The second factor pertains to the flow of **horizontal communication** within the firm. In other words, "Does the left hand know what the right hand is doing?" All too often, communications are developed at the firm's headquarters without conferring with decentralized regional and local service operations in the field. In some instances, new service programs are announced to the public by corporate headquarters before the local service firms are aware that the new programs exist. A lack of horizontal communication places an unsuspecting service provider in an awkward position when a customer requests the service promised and the provider has no idea what the customer is talking about.

**overpromising** A firm's promise of more than it can deliver.

**horizontal communication** The flow of internal communication between a firm's headquarters and its service firms in the field.

## Measuring Service Quality: The SERVQUAL Measurement Scale

Although measurements of customer satisfaction and service quality are both obtained by comparing perceptions to expectations, differences between the two concepts are seen in their operational definitions. While satisfaction compares consumer perceptions to what consumers *would* normally expect, service quality compares perceptions to what

"Sure, we can spend all day nitpicking specifics but aren't sweeping generalities so much more satisfying?"

The five SERVQUAL dimensions allow companies to take a much more in-depth look at what is driving customer satisfaction and dissatisfaction.

**SERVQUAL** A 44-item scale that measures customer expectations and perceptions regarding five service quality dimensions.

a consumer *should* expect from a firm that delivers high-quality services. Given these definitions, service quality appears to measure a *higher standard* of service delivery.

A frequently used and highly debated measure of service quality is the **SERVQUAL** scale.[7] According to its developers, SERVQUAL is a diagnostic tool that uncovers a firm's broad weaknesses and strengths in the area of service quality. The SERVQUAL measurement scale is based on five service quality dimensions that were obtained through extensive focus group interviews with consumers. The five dimensions include *tangibles, reliability, responsiveness, assurance, and empathy*, and they provide the basic "skeleton" underlying service quality.

The SERVQUAL measurement scale consists of two sections of questions. The first section is comprised of 22 questions that ask respondents to record their *expectations* of excellent firms in the specific service industry. The second section of questions is comprised of 22 matching questions that assess consumer *perceptions* of a particular company in that service industry. For example, the tangibles dimension of SERQUAL is addressed by comparing the mean of four expectation questions to the mean of four perception questions. When the mean expectation score is subtracted from the mean perception score (e.g., P − E), a "gap score" is created. Positive gap scores reflect situations where perceptions exceed expectations and customers are happy. Negative gap scores where perceptions are less than expectations reflect unsatisfactory situations and customer unhappiness. When the gap score equals zero, customer perceptions have met customer expectations and customers are satisfied. The purpose of the SERVQUAL measurement scale is to compare mean perceptions and mean expectations to arrive at "gap scores" for each of the five dimensions.

Customer expectations are measured on a seven-point scale with the anchor labels of "not at all essential" and "absolutely essential."[8] Similarly, customer perceptions are measured on another seven-point scale with anchor labels of "strongly agree" and "strongly disagree." Hence, SERVQUAL is a 44-item scale that measures customer expectations and perceptions regarding five service quality dimensions. The remainder of this section of the chapter discusses each of the five SERQUAL dimensions, as well as some final thoughts about the SERQUAL measurement instrument itself.

### The Tangibles Dimension

**tangibles dimension** The SERVQUAL assessment of a firm's ability to manage its tangibles.

Because of the absence of a physical product, consumers often rely on the tangible evidence that surrounds the service in forming evaluations. The **tangibles dimension** of SERVQUAL compares consumer expectations to consumer perceptions regarding the firm's ability to manage its tangibles. A firm's tangibles consist of a wide variety of objects such as architecture, design, layout, carpeting, desks, lighting, wall colors, brochures, daily correspondence, and the appearance of the firm's personnel. Consequently, the tangibles component in SERVQUAL is two-dimensional—one dimension focuses on equipment and facilities, the other dimension focuses on personnel and communications materials.

The tangibles dimension of SERVQUAL is assessed via four expectations questions (E1–E4) and four perception questions (P1–P4). Keep in mind that the expectation questions apply to excellent firms within a particular industry, while the perception questions apply to the specific firm under investigation. Comparing the perception scores to the expectation scores provides a numerical variable that indicates the tangibles gap. The smaller the number, the smaller the gap, and the closer consumer perceptions are to their expectations. The questions that pertain to the tangibles dimension are as follows:[9]

### Tangibles Expectations:

E1. Excellent companies will have modern looking equipment.

E2. The physical facilities at excellent companies will be visually appealing.

E3. Employees of excellent companies will be neat in appearance.

E4. Materials associated with the service (such as pamphlets or statements) will be visually appealing in an excellent company.

### Tangibles Perceptions:

P1. XYZ has modern-looking equipment.

P2. XYZ's physical facilities are visually appealing.

P3. XYZ's employees are neat in appearance.

P4. Materials associated with the service (such as pamphlets or statements) are visually appealing at XYZ.

## The Reliability Dimension

**reliability dimension**
The SERVQUAL assessment of a firm's consistency and dependability in service performance.

In general, the **reliability dimension** reflects the consistency and dependability of a firm's performance. Does the firm provide the same level of service time after time, or does quality dramatically vary with each encounter? Does the firm keep its promises, bill its customers accurately, keep accurate records, and perform the service correctly the first time? Nothing can be more frustrating for customers than unreliable service providers.

The number of businesses that fail to keep their promises is disturbing. In many instances, the consumer is ready to spend money if only the service provider will show up and conduct the transaction as promised. As students, you may have experienced the reliability gap while attempting to have the local cable company install its services in your new apartment. Typically, the cable company will approximate the time at which the installer will come to your apartment in four-hour increments (e.g., morning or afternoon). In many cases, you may miss class or work waiting for the cable installer to arrive. All too often, the installer fails to show up during this time period and you must reschedule... missing yet more classes and/or time at work. Further aggravating this process is that you, the customer, must initiate the rescheduling process. Often the cable company offers no apology and provides little explanation other than, "Our installers are very busy."

Based on the findings of numerous studies that have used SERVQUAL, consumers rate the reliability dimension to be the most important of the five SERVQUAL dimensions. Ultimately, little else matters if the service is unreliable. The questions used to assess the reliability gap are as follows:

### Reliability Expectations:

E5. When excellent companies promise to do something by a certain time, they will do so.

Little else matters when the service is unreliable.

E6. When customers have a problem, excellent companies will show a sincere interest in solving it.

E7. Excellent companies will perform the service right the first time.

E8. Excellent companies will provide their services at the time they promise to do so.

E9. Excellent companies will insist on error-free records.

### Reliability Perceptions:

P5. When XYZ promises to do something by a certain time, it does so.

P6. When you have a problem, XYZ shows a sincere interest in solving it.

P7. XYZ performs the service right the first time.

P8. XYZ provides its services at the time it promises to do so.

P9. XYZ insists on error-free records.

## The Responsiveness Dimension

**responsiveness dimension** The SERVQUAL assessment of a firm's commitment to providing its services in a timely manner.

Responsiveness reflects a service firm's commitment to provide its services in a timely manner. As such, the **responsiveness dimension** of SERVQUAL concerns the willingness and/or readiness of employees to provide a service. Occasionally, customers may encounter a situation in which employees are engaged in their own conversations with one another while ignoring the needs of the customer. Obviously, this is an example of unresponsiveness.

Responsiveness also reflects the preparedness of the firm to provide the service. Typically, new restaurants do not advertise their "opening night" so that the service delivery system can be fine-tuned and prepared to handle larger crowds, thereby minimizing service failures and subsequent customer complaints. The SERVQUAL expectation and perception items that address the responsiveness gap are as follows:

### Responsiveness Expectations:

E10. Employees of excellent companies will tell customers exactly when services will be performed.

E11. Employees of excellent companies will give prompt service to customers.

E12. Employees of excellent companies will always be willing to help customers.

E13. Employees of excellent companies will never be too busy to respond to customer requests.

### Responsiveness Perceptions:

P10. Employees of XYZ tell you exactly when service will be performed.

P11. Employees of XYZ give you prompt service.

P12. Employees of XYZ are always willing to help you.

P13. Employees of XYZ are never too busy to respond to your requests.

## The Assurance Dimension

**assurance dimension** The SERVQUAL assessment of a firm's competence, courtesy to its customers, and security of its operations.

SERVQUAL's **assurance dimension** addresses the competence of the firm, the courtesy it extends to its customers, and the security of its operations. Competence pertains to the firm's knowledge and skill in performing its service. Does the firm possess the required skills to complete the service on a professional basis?

Courtesy refers to how the firm's personnel interact with the customer and the customer's possessions. As such, courtesy reflects politeness, friendliness, and consideration for the customer's property (e.g., a mechanic who places paper floor mats in a customer's car to avoid soiling the car's carpet).

Security is also an important component of the assurance dimension. Security reflects a customer's feelings that he or she is free from danger, risk, and doubt. Recent robberies at ATM locations provide ample evidence of the possible harm that may arise at service locations. In addition to physical danger, the security component of the assurance dimension also reflects financial risk issues (e.g., will the bank fail?) and confidentiality issues (e.g., are my medical records at the school's health center kept private?). The SERVQUAL items utilized to address the assurance gap are as follows:

## Assurance Expectations:

E14. The behavior of employees of excellent companies will instill confidence in customers.

E15. Customers of excellent companies will feel safe in their transactions.

E16. Employees of excellent companies will be consistently courteous with customers.

E17. Employees of excellent companies will have the knowledge to answer customer questions.

## Assurance Perceptions:

P14. The behavior of employees of XYZ instills confidence in customers.

P15. You feel safe in your transactions with XYZ.

P16. Employees of XYZ are consistently courteous with you.

P17. Employees of XYZ have the knowledge to answer your questions.

## The Empathy Dimension

**empathy dimension** The SERVQUAL assessment of a firm's ability to put itself in its customers' place.

Empathy is the ability to experience another's feelings as one's own. Empathetic firms have not lost touch of what it is like to be a customer of their own firm. As such, empathetic firms understand their customers' needs and make their services accessible to their customers. In contrast, firms that do not provide their customers individualized attention when requested and offer operating hours convenient for the firm and not its customers fail to demonstrate empathetic behaviors. The SERVQUAL **empathy dimension** addresses the empathy gap as follows:

## Empathy Expectations:

E18. Excellent companies will give customers individual attention.

E19. Excellent companies will have operating hours convenient for all their customers.

E20. Excellent companies will have employees who give customers personal attention.

E21. Excellent companies will have the customer's best interest at heart.

E22. The employees of excellent companies will understand the specific needs of their customers.

## Empathy Perceptions:

P18. XYZ gives you individual attention.

P19. XYZ has operating hours convenient to all its customers.

P20. XYZ has employees who give you personal attention.

P21. XYZ has your best interests at heart.

P22. Employees of XYZ understand your specific needs.

## Determining the Importance of Each of the Five Dimensions

Managers of service firms who utilize SERVQUAL to assess gaps in service quality should also understand the importance that customers place on each of the service quality dimensions. This information is important in prioritizing where the firm should allocate its resources when faced with service quality improvements. For example, if a manager calculates identical gap scores for a firm's tangibles and empathy, which dimension should receive the firm's most immediate attention?

An easy method to ascertain customer perceptions of each dimension's importance is to simply ask SERVQUAL respondents to allocate 100 points among each of the five dimensions. For example, a typical allocation of 100 points may look like the following:

| | |
|---|---|
| Reliability | 30 |
| Responsiveness | 20 |
| Tangibles | 10 |
| Assurance | 20 |
| Empathy | 20 |
| | 100 |

The mean importance rating for each dimension can then be determined, providing management with additional insight into customer needs and wants and how these wishes should impact resource allocation decisions. As reported earlier, the reliability dimension is consistently reported as the most important of the five dimensions. In contrast, the tangibles dimension is consistently reported as the least important. Please note that this does not mean that tangibles are unimportant; simply of the five SERVQUAL dimensions, customers believe that the other dimensions are more pressing. Consequently, a service firm that is getting ready to spend a great amount of resources on building a new facility may first want to look at how it is performing on the other service quality dimensions. A nice new facility that provides unreliable service will likely soon become a nice new facility for someone else's business venture!

## Criticisms of SERVQUAL

Since the development of the SERVQUAL instrument, it has received its share of criticism.[10] The major criticisms of the instrument involve the length of the questionnaire and the validity of the five service quality dimensions. The following discussion focuses on each of these issues and their respective importance to interpreting SERVQUAL results.

***Length of the Questionnaire***    Combining the expectation and perception items of SERVQUAL results in a 44-item survey instrument. Opponents of the SERVQUAL instrument argue that the 44 items are highly repetitive and unnecessarily increase the questionnaire's length. Opponents further argue that the expectations section of the instrument is of no real value, and that the perceptions (actual performance) section should be utilized alone to assess service quality.[11]

In response, the developers of SERVQUAL effectively argue that including the expectations section enhances the managerial usefulness of the scale as a diagnostic tool due to the gap scores developed for each dimension. Perception scores alone merely rate whether the respondent agrees or disagrees with each question. For example, Figure 12.2 provides a set of perception scores and SERVQUAL scores for a hypothetical firm. Utilizing this information for diagnostic purposes, perception scores alone would suggest placing an equal emphasis on improving the reliability and empathy dimensions. Incorporating expectations into the SERVQUAL score indicates that improving the reliability dimension should be the firm's top priority. Given that implementing service quality improvements requires a financial investment from the firm, maintaining the expectation section becomes valuable.

**FIG-12.2** The
Diagnostic Advantage
of SERVQUAL Scores

| DIMENSION | PERCEPTION SCORES | SERVQUAL SCORES |
|---|---|---|
| Tangibles | 5.3 | 0.0 |
| Reliability | 4.8 | −1.7 |
| Responsiveness | 5.1 | −1.0 |
| Assurance | 5.4 | −1.5 |
| Empathy | 4.8 | −1.1 |

   Creative suggestions have been made for maintaining the expectations component while at the same time reducing the questionnaire's length by 22 questions. Three approaches have been suggested: (1) On a single scale, ask respondents where they would rate a high-quality company and then where they would rate the firm under investigation; (2) utilize the scale's midpoint as the expected level of service from a high-quality company, and then rate the specific firm in relation to the midpoint—above expectation or below; and (3) utilize the end point (e.g., 7 on a 7-point scale) as the expected level of a high-quality company, and rate the specific company relative to the high-quality company on the same scale. All three approaches provide alternatives for assessing customer perceptions and expectations while reducing the questionnaire's length.

*The Validity of the Five Dimensions*    Another frequent criticism of the SERVQUAL instrument is that the five proposed dimensions of service quality—reliability, responsiveness, assurance, empathy, and tangibles—do not hold up under statistical scrutiny. Consequently, opponents of SERVQUAL question the validity of the specific dimensions in the measurement instrument.

   SERVQUAL's developers argue that although the five dimensions represent conceptually distinct facets of service quality, they are interrelated. Hence, some overlap may exist (as measured by correlations) among items that measure specific dimensions. In particular, the distinction among the responsiveness, assurance, and reliability dimensions tends to blur under statistical scrutiny. However, when respondents are asked to assign importance weights to each dimension, results indicate that consumers do indeed distinguish among the five dimensions, as exhibited in Figure 12.3. According to the developers of SERVQUAL, this ranking provides additional evidence of the dimensions' distinctiveness. For the statistical enthusiast, a variety of articles offering additional evidence and rationale supporting the viability of the five-dimensional framework is cited in the "Notes" section located at the end of the chapter.[12]

**FIG-12.3** Relative
Importance of
SERVQUAL
Dimensions as
Reported by
Consumers

| SERVQUAL DIMENSION | IMPORTANCE (%)* |
|---|---|
| Reliability | 32 |
| Responsiveness | 22 |
| Assurance | 19 |
| Empathy | 16 |
| Tangibles | 11 |

*Consumers were asked to allocate 100 points among the five dimensions. The Importance (%) reflects the mean point allocation for each dimension.

Source: Leonard L. Berry, A. Parasuraman, and Valerie A. Zeithaml, "Improving Service Quality in America: Lessons Learned," *Academy of Management Executive*, 8, 2, (1994), pp. 32–52.

### SERVQUAL: Some Final Thoughts

***The Importance of Contact Personnel***   SERVQUAL highlights several points that service providers should consider when examining service quality. First, customer perceptions of service are heavily dependent on the attitudes and performance of contact personnel. Of the five dimensions measured, responsiveness, empathy, and assurance directly reflect the interaction between customers and staff. Even the assessment of the tangibles dimension depends partly on the appearance, dress, and hygiene of the service staff.

***Process Is as Important as Outcome***   The manner in which customers judge a service depends as much on the service *process* as on the *outcome*. How the service is delivered is as important as the frequency and nature of the service. Consequently, customer satisfaction depends on the production of services as well as their consumption.

Viewing services as a process raises considerable difficulties for management when trying to write service quality standards. Standards can be examined either from the perspective of the consumer or from that of the operating system. Thus, a specification can be written based on consumers' ratings of the responsiveness of the organization. Unfortunately, although this is a quantitative measure, it does little to guide the behavior of operations managers and contact personnel.

***Consumer Perceptions Are Unpredictable***   Ratings of service quality dimensions may be influenced by factors outside the control of the organization that may not be readily apparent to managers. For example, consumer moods and attitudes may influence ratings. Studies have shown that, when rating services, consumers use a diverse variety of clues. A recent study shows that, even if a service firm generates a negative outcome for a consumer, it may not be judged as delivering a poor level of satisfaction. Since they are part of the process, consumers may attribute failures to themselves or to factors outside the control of the firm. Such attributions are shown to depend on the physical characteristics of the service firm. For example, a tidy office setting leads negative attributions for poor service away from the firm and the blame is placed on other factors beyond the control of the firm. On the other hand, a messy office generates attributions of dissatisfaction toward the firm regardless of where the real blame should fall.[13]

***Assessing the Criticisms of SERVQUAL***   Despite its opponents, SERVQUAL remains a frequently utilized instrument to assess service quality and is currently being modified to address service quality issues in e-business (see E-Services in Action). From the beginning, its developers have claimed that SERVQUAL is a useful starting point for measuring service quality and was never presented as "the final answer." The developers of SERVQUAL further contend that when used in conjunction with other forms of measurement, both quantitative and qualitative, SERVQUAL provides a valuable diagnostic tool for evaluating the firm's service quality performance. Overall, as was the case with satisfaction measures, SERVQUAL is most valuable when compared with a firm's own past service quality trends and with measures of competitive service quality performance.

## Service Quality Information Systems

**service quality information system** An ongoing research process that provides relevant data on a timely basis to managers, who use the data in decision making.

Firms that are serious about improving their service quality utilize a number of approaches that combine to form a **service quality information system** to understand consumer perceptions and expectations. A service quality information system is a continuous process that provides relevant data on a timely basis to managers, who then utilize the data for decision-making purposes.[14] More specifically, service quality information systems utilize service quality and customer satisfaction measures in conjunction with other measures

## E-SERVICES *IN ACTION*

### The Seven Dimensions of E-QUAL

The importance of service quality in improving customer satisfaction and loyalty in traditional business settings has been established via SERVQUAL. Recommendations are given below for how consumers might evaluate online business via E-QUAL

Accessibility — Is the site easily found? The number of search engines and directories that a site is registered and links to related sites.

Navigation — How easy is it to move around the site? A good rule-of-thumb is to be within 3-clicks of the information that is most desired by customers.

Design and Presentation — What is the image projected from the site? Design elements include colors, layout, clarity, and originality.

Content and Purpose — The substance (breadth) and richness (depth) of the site. Currency and accuracy are important aspects of the "content" dimension. Strategic purposes include developing the site for an Internet presence (informational purpose) and online store fronts (revenue-producing purpose).

Responsiveness — The company's propensity to respond to email messages. The collection of visitor information (i.e., cookies, guest book, contests, chat rooms, clubs, storybooks, auto-email, and options to speak to customer representatives), and what the company does with this information.

Interactivity, Customization, and Personalization — The high-touch level of service provided. Interactivity, customization, and personalization relate to the empathy dimension of service quality. Amazon.com, for example, provides the quality of interaction and personalization that rivals traditional brick-and-mortar businesses.

Reputation and Security — Related to the assurance dimension of service quality, reputation and security pertain to consumer confidence issues. Consumer confidence is being built via proven encryption technologies.

Source:
Shohreh A. Kaynama, "A Conceptual Model to Measure Service Quality of Online Companies: E-qual, in Developments in Marketing Science," Harlan E. Spotts and H. Lee Meadow, eds., *Proceedings of the Academy of Marketing Science*, 22, (2000), pp. 46–51.

---

obtained at various points to assess the firm's overall performance. Components of a service quality information system include:

**customer research**
Research that examines the customer's perspective of a firm's strengths and weaknesses.

1. reports on solicitation of customer complaints,
2. after-sales surveys,
3. customer focus group interviews,
4. mystery shopping results,
5. employee surveys, and
6. total market service quality surveys.

**noncustomer research**
Research that examines how competitors perform on service and how employees view the firm's strengths and weaknesses.

In general, service quality information systems focus on two types of research: customer research and noncustomer research. **Customer research** examines the customer's perspective of a firm's strengths and weaknesses and includes such measures as customer complaints, after-sales surveys, focus group interviews, and service quality surveys. In contrast, **noncustomer research** focuses on employee perspectives of the firm's strengths and weaknesses and employee performance (e.g., employee surveys and mystery shopping). In addition, noncustomer research examines how competitors perform on service aspects (via total market service quality surveys) and serves as a basis for comparison.

## Solicitation of Customer Complaints

The primary objectives of soliciting customer complaints are twofold. First, customer complaints identify unhappy customers. The firm's follow-up efforts may enable it to retain many of these customers before they defect to competitors. The second objective of soliciting customer complaints is to identify weaknesses in the firm's service delivery system and take the corrective actions necessary to minimize future occurrences of the same problem. Customer complaints should be solicited on a continuous basis.

The value of continuous customer feedback cannot be understated. Unfortunately, many firms address one complaint at a time and fail to analyze the content of the complaints as a group. The Chicago Marriott took 15 years to figure out that 66 percent of the calls to its customer service line concerned requests for an iron or ironing board.[15] As a result of learning this, the hotel redesignated $20,000 that had been earmarked for color televisions in guest bathrooms to purchase irons and ironing boards for the hotel. Interestingly, few, if any, customers had ever complained about the black-and-white televisions in the bathrooms. If the color televisions had been installed, we would have seen a classic example of a firm defining service quality on its own as opposed to listening to the voice of the customer. Chapter 13 takes an in-depth look at analyzing customer complaints and developing effective recovery strategies for use when service failures do occur.

## After-Sales Surveys

**after-sales surveys**
A type of satisfaction survey that addresses customer satisfaction while the service encounter is still fresh in the customer's mind.

As part of the service quality information system, **after-sales surveys** should also be conducted on a continuous basis. Since after-sales surveys pertain to discrete transactions, they are a type of satisfaction survey and, as such, are subject to the advantages and disadvantages of all customer satisfaction surveys discussed in Chapter 11. For example, after-sales surveys address customer satisfaction while the service encounter is still fresh in the customer's mind. Consequently, the information reflects the firm's recent performance but may be biased by the customer's inadvertent attempt to minimize cognitive dissonance.

Although after-sales surveys can also identify areas for improvement, after-sales surveys are a more proactive approach to assessing customer satisfaction than soliciting customer complaints. Many firms wait for customers to complain and then take action based on those complaints. Given the average customer's reluctance to complain, waiting for customer complaints does not provide the firm a "true" picture of its performance. The after-sales survey attempts to contact every customer and take corrective action if a customer is less than satisfied with his or her purchase decision.

## Customer Focus Group Interviews

**focus group interviews**
Informal discussions with eight to 12 customers that are usually guided by a trained moderator; used to identify areas of information to be collected in subsequent survey research.

Another important component of the service quality information system involves customer **focus group interviews**.[16] Focus group interviews are informal discussions with eight to 12 customers that are usually guided by a trained moderator. Participants in the group are encouraged to express their views and comment on the suggestions made by others in the group. Because of the group interaction, customers tend to feel more comfortable, which motivates them to talk more openly and honestly. Consequently, researchers feel that the information obtained via focus group interviews is richer than data that reflects the opinions of a single individual.

One of the major benefits of utilizing focus groups to assess service quality is that the thoughts of others in the group often spark new ideas that were never considered before.

Focus groups are probably the most widely used market research method. However, their primary purpose is to identify areas of information to be collected in subsequent survey research. Although the information provided by the group is considered very valuable, other forms of research are generally necessary to confirm that the groups' ideas reflect the feelings of the broader segment of customers. Advocates of service quality information systems believe that customer focus groups should be conducted on a monthly basis.

## Mystery Shopping

**mystery shopping**
A form of noncustomer research that consists of trained personnel who pose as customers, shop at the firm unannounced, and evaluate employees.

**Mystery shopping** is a form of noncustomer research that measures individual employee service behavior. As the name indicates, *mystery* shoppers are generally trained personnel who pose as customers and shop at the firm unannounced. The idea is to evaluate an individual employee during an actual service encounter. Mystery shoppers evaluate employees on a number of characteristics, such as: the time it takes for the employee to acknowledge the customer, eye contact, appearance, and numerous other specific customer service and sales techniques promoted by the firm.

Mystery shopping is a form of observation research that is recommended to be conducted on a quarterly basis. Results obtained from mystery shoppers are used as constructive employee feedback. Consequently, mystery shopping aids the firm in coaching, training, evaluating, and formally recognizing its employees. For example, waitstaff at the Texas Roadhouse, a popular restaurant in the United States, are rewarded with a $100 bonus every time they receive a perfect evaluation from a mystery shopper. The bonus not only rewards the employee but reinforces the positive service behaviors desired by management in the process.

## Employee Surveys

**employee surveys**
Internal measures of service quality concerning employee morale, attitudes, and perceived obstacles to the provision of quality services.

Another vital component of the service quality information system is employee research. When the product is a performance, it is essential that the company listen to the performers. Too often, employees are forgotten in the quest for customer satisfaction. However, the reality is that employee satisfaction with the firm directly corresponds with customer satisfaction. Hence, the lesson to be learned by service firms is that if they want the needs of their customers to come first, they cannot place the needs of their employees last.

Conducted quarterly, **employee surveys** provide an internal measure of service quality concerning employee morale, attitudes, and perceived obstacles to the provision of quality services. Often employees would like to provide a higher level of quality service, but feel that their hands are tied by internal regulations and policies. Employee surveys provide the means to uncover these obstacles so that they can be removed when appropriate. Moreover, employees are customers of internal services and assess internal service quality daily. Because of their direct involvement in providing service delivery, employee complaints serve as an early warning system; that is, employees often see the system breaking down before customers do.

## Total Market Service Quality Surveys

**total market service quality surveys**
Surveys that measure the service quality of the firm sponsoring the survey and the service quality of the firm's competitors.

**Total market service quality surveys** not only measure the service quality of the firm sponsoring the survey but also assess the perceived service quality of the firm's competitors. When service quality measures such as SERVQUAL are used in conjunction with other measures, a firm can evaluate its own performance compared with previous time periods and with its competitors. Service quality surveys provide a firm with information about needed improvements in the service delivery system and measure the progress the firm has been making in previously identified needed improvements.

Advocates of the service quality information system recommend that total market service quality surveys be conducted three times a year. However, as is the case with all the components of the service quality information system, the recommended frequencies depend on the size of the customer base. Too frequent contact with the same customers can be an annoyance to them. On the other hand, conducting surveys too infrequently may ultimately cost the business its existence.

Overall, the service quality information system provides a comprehensive look at the firm's performance and overcomes many of the shortcomings of individual measures used in isolation. As with all measures, the information system's true value lies in the information it gives managers and front-line employees to help in their decision making. The measures should serve as a support system for decisions but should not be the only inputs into the decision process. Managerial expertise and intuition remain critical components of every business decision. Ultimately, the key components that need to be built into every service quality system include:[17]

*Listening*: Quality is defined by the customer. Conformance to company specifications is not quality; conformance to customers' specifications is. Spending wisely to improve service comes from continuous learning about expectations and perceptions of customers (see Figure 12.4).

*Reliability*: Reliability is the core of service quality. Little else matters to a customer when the service is unreliable.

*Basic Service*: Forget the frills if you cannot deliver the basics. American service customers want the basics; they expect fundamentals, not fanciness, performance, or empty promises.

*Service Design*: Reliably delivering the basic service that customers expect depends, in part, on how well various elements function together in a service system. Design flaws in any part of a service system can reduce the perception of quality.

*Recovery*: Research shows that companies consistently receive the most unfavorable service quality scores from customers whose problems were not resolved satisfactorily. In effect, companies that do not respond effectively to customer complaints compound the service failure, thereby failing twice.

*Surprising Customers*: Exceeding customers' expectations requires the element of surprise. If service organizations can not only be reliable in output, but also surprise the customer in the way the service is delivered, then they are truly excellent.

**FIG-12.4** Quality Improvements Need Focus, Not Just $$$

Although adequate resource support is directly related to the successful implementation of service delivery systems, providing support without direction can be a huge waste of resources. For example, the United States leads the world in healthcare expenditures per capita. Yet, the United States ranks 37th in terms of the quality of care provided to its citizens. The United States Devotes 10 to 14 percent of national income to health care, with an average per capita expenditure of $3,724; meanwhile, other countries such as England spend 6 percent and are ranked 18th in the world.

## The most doesn't mean the best

A study of world health systems has found that the United States spends the most per person but ranked 37th for quality of service. Here are the top rankings for overall performance and spending.

**\* Indicates G-7 country, the seven richest countries in the world**

| Overall performance | Total spending, per capita | |
|---|---|---|
| 1. France* | 1. **United States*** | $3,724 |
| 2. Italy* | 2. Switzerland | $2,644 |
| 3. San Marino | 3. Germany* | $2,365 |
| 4. Andorra | 4. France* | $2,125 |
| 5. Malta | 5. Luxembourg | $1,985 |
| 6. Singapore | 6. Austria | $1,960 |
| 7. Spain | 7. Sweden | $1,943 |
| 8. Oman | 8. Denmark | $1,940 |
| 9. Austria | 9. Netherlands | $1,911 |
| 10. Japan* | 10. Canada* | $1,836 |
| 18. United Kingdom* | 11. Italy* | $1,824 |
| 25. Germany* | 13. Japan* | $1,759 |
| 30. Canada* | 26. United Kingdom* | $1,193 |
| 37. **United States*** | | |

Source: World Health Report 2000                                         AP

Source: Robert Cooke "U.S. Leads in Health-Care Spending, but Not Quality," *Fort Collins Coloradoan*, (Wednesday, June 21, 2000), B1.

*Fair Play*: Customers expect service companies to treat them fairly and become resentful and mistrustful when they perceive they are being treated otherwise.

*Teamwork*: The presence of "teammates" is an important dynamic in sustaining a server's motivation to serve. Service team building should not be left to chance.

*Employee Research*: Employee research is as important to service improvement as customer research.

*Servant Leadership*: Delivering excellent service requires a special form of leadership. Leadership must serve the servers—inspiring, coaching, and enabling them to achieve.

# Summary

This chapter has focused on defining and measuring service quality. The concepts of service quality and customer satisfaction are intertwined. In general, customer satisfaction can be defined as a short-term, transaction-specific measure. In turn, service quality is a long-term, overall measure. Another difference is that satisfaction compares perceptions to what customers *would* normally expect. In comparison, service quality compares perceptions to what customers *should* expect from a high-quality firm. Customer satisfaction and service quality assessments compliment each other. Satisfaction evaluations made after each service transaction help revise customers' overall service quality evaluations of the firm's performance.

Firms that excel in service quality do so by avoiding potential quality gaps in their delivery systems. Service quality gaps discussed in this chapter include *knowledge, standards, delivery,* and *communications*. Numerous managerial, marketing, and operational factors influence the size of each of these gaps. Ultimately, the goal of every firm is to minimize the service gap—the difference between customer perceptions and expectations. The *service gap* is a function of the knowledge, standards, delivery, and communications gaps, and responds accordingly in the combined direction of the four gaps.

One popular method for assessing service quality is the SERVQUAL measurement scale. The original SERVQUAL survey instrument consists of 44 questions that compare consumers' expectations to perceptions along five service quality dimensions—*tangibles, responsiveness, reliability, assurance,* and *empathy*. Gap scores for each of the five dimensions can be calculated by comparing consumers' mean expectations and mean perception ratings. The SERVQUAL gaps indicate specific areas in need of improvement and assist the service firm in its continuous improvement efforts.

SERVQUAL is only one method to assess a firm's service quality. A service quality information system utilizes a variety of continuous measures to assess the firm's overall performance. The major components of such a system collect information about both customer and noncustomer research. Customer research methods include analyzing customer complaints, after-sales surveys, focus group interviews, and service quality surveys. Noncustomer research methods include employee surveys and mystery shopping.

In closing, service quality offers a means of achieving success among competing firms that offer similar products. The potential benefits associated with service quality include increases in market share, repeat purchases, and improved profitability. Ultimately, the keys to delivering service quality are a detailed understanding of the needs of the consumer, service providers who are focused on providing quality, and service delivery systems that are designed to support the firm's overall quality mission.

## Key Terms

service quality, p. 325
service gap, p. 327
knowledge gap, p. 328
standards gap, p. 328
delivery gap, p. 328
communications gap, p. 328
research orientation, p. 329
upward communication, p. 329
levels of management, p. 330
willingness to perform, p. 332
employee-job fit, p. 332
role conflict, p. 332

role ambiguity, p. 332
dispersion of control, p. 332
learned helplessness, p. 332
inadequate support, p. 332
overpromising, p. 333
horizontal communication, p. 333
SERVQUAL, p. 334
tangibles dimension, p. 334
reliability dimension, p. 335
responsiveness dimension, p. 336
assurance dimension, p. 336
empathy dimension, p. 337

service quality information system, p. 340
customer research, p. 341
noncustomer research, p. 341
after-sales surveys, p. 342
focus group interviews, p. 342
mystery shopping, p. 343
employee surveys, p. 343
total market service quality surveys, p. 344

## Review Questions

1. What are the basic differences between customer satisfaction and service quality?
2. Explain how a manager might use the conceptual model of service quality to improve the quality of his/her own firm.
3. Discuss the knowledge gap and what factors contribute to the size of the knowledge gap?
4. Interview a member of a restaurant's waitstaff. Provide five standards that are provided to them by management pertaining to greeting and serving their customers.

5. How does the communications gap relate to success in e-business (see E-Services in Action)?
6. Discuss the basics of the SERVQUAL measurement instrument in terms of how "gap scores" are calculated for each of the five service quality dimensions.
7. Why would a manager want to know the importance customers place on each of the five service quality dimensions?
8. Discuss the most and least important of the five service quality dimensions. Why do you believe

that most customers rank these two service quality dimensions in this particular order?

9. What are the criticisms of SERVQUAL? What is the limitation of only using the 22 perception questions?

10. You have been hired by a firm to develop the firm's service quality information system. What are the components of this system?

# Notes

1. J. Joseph Cronin, Jr., and Steven A. Taylor, "Measuring Service Quality: A Reexamination and Extension," *Journal of Marketing*, 56, (July 1992), p. 55.
2. Thomas A. Stewart, "After All You've Done for Your Customers, Why Are They Still Not Happy?" *Fortune*, (December 11, 1995), pp. 178–182.
3. Cronin, Jr., and Taylor, "Measuring Service Quality," pp. 60–63.
4. Ibid.
5. This section was adapted from John E. G. Bateson, *Managing Services Marketing*, 3rd ed. (Fort Worth, TX: The Dryden Press, 1995) pp. 558–565.
6. A. Parasuraman, Valerie A. Zeithaml, and Leonard L. Berry, "A Conceptual Model of Service Quality and Its Implications for Future Research," *Journal of Marketing*, 49, (Fall 1985), pp. 41–50.
7. A. Parasuraman, Leonard L. Berry, and Valerie A. Zeithaml, "SERVQUAL: A Multiple-Item Scale for Measuring Customer Perceptions of Service Quality," *Journal of Retailing*, 64, 1, (1988), pp. 12–40.
8. Parasuraman, Zeithaml, and Berry, "A Conceptual Model."
9. Scale items from A. Parasuraman, Leonard L. Berry, and Valerie A. Zeithaml, "Refinement and Reassessment of the SERVQUAL Scale," *Journal of Retailing*, 67, (Winter 1991), pp. 420–450.
10. Cronin, Jr., and Taylor, "Measuring Service Quality," pp. 60–63.
11. A. Parasuraman, Valerie A. Zeithaml, and Leonard L. Berry, "Reassessment of Expectations as a Comparison Standard in Measuring Service Quality: Implications for Future Research," *Journal of Marketing*, 58, (January 1994), pp. 111–124.
12. See A. Parasuraman, Leonard L. Berry, and Valerie A. Zeithaml, "Refinement and Reassessment of the SERVQUAL Scale," *Journal of Retailing*, pp. 420–450; A. Parasuraman, Leonard L. Berry, and Valerie A. Zeithaml, "More on Improving Service Quality Measurement," *Journal of Retailing*, 69, 1 (Spring 1993), p. 1401; and A. Parasuraman, Valerie A. Zeithaml, and Leonard L. Berry, "Reassessment of Expectations as a Comparison Standard in Measuring Service Quality: Implications for Future Research," *Journal of Marketing*, 58, (January 1994), pp. 111–124.
13. Mary Jo Bitner, "Evaluating Service Encounters: The Effects of Physical Surroundings and Employee Responses," *Journal of Marketing*, (April 1990), pp. 42–50.
14. Leonard L. Berry, A. Parasuraman, and Valerie A. Zeithaml, "Improving Service Quality in America: Lessons Learned," *Academy of Management Executive*, 8, 2 (1994), pp. 32–52.
15. Ibid., p. 33.
16. **http://managementhelp.org/evaluatn/focusgrp.htm**, accessed 4 September, 2009.
17. Berry, Parasuraman, and Zeithaml, "Improving Service Quality," pp. 32–52.

# Service Quality at the Libertador Hotel

## Day One

Maria Martin had recently transferred to the Libertador Hotel to improve the level of service quality. She had been with the company for five years and had been quite successful in improving the level of service quality at the two previous Chilean hotels to which she had been assigned. Maria knew that the Libertador was going to be a real challenge. The mix of business was 60 percent individual transient guests, due to its proximity to the airport, and 40 percent group business. Of this group business, about one-third was motor coach tour groups.

On her first day on the job, Maria Martin witnessed quite a sight. There was a line of about 20 guests waiting to check in when two motor coaches arrived and more than 80 additional guests and guides walked into the lobby to check in. Needless to say, the two front desk agents had a look of terror in their eyes as they worked diligently to process the registrations for those waiting to check in. Some 40 minutes later, everyone had been checked in, but the general manager said to Maria, "I'm glad that you are here; we need to work out a better system. Let's meet for lunch tomorrow to discuss your initial ideas." Maria had just picked up a pen to start brainstorming ideas to present to the general manager when a guest approached her desk.

"Hello, my name is Juan Diaz , and I stayed at your hotel last night with my family. We really did not have a good experience, and I want to tell you about it. I want to make sure that this does not happen again, to me or anyone else." Mr. Diaz then proceeded to tell Maria his account of the events. "I was traveling with my wife and our son, who is four years old. Our LAN connecting flight was delayed, so we did not arrive at our final destination until 10 p.m. The Libertador had an advertised check-in facility at the airport, and I assumed that I would be able to secure my room while waiting for the luggage. When I approached the employee at the hotel's airport facility, I was told that check-in service was not available at that time of the day. I found this to be surprising, since this was the very type of situation in which an airport facility would be beneficial.

"Next, my family took a shuttle van from the airport to the hotel, where we were given directions to the front desk. Two front desk clerks were on duty when the passengers from the airport shuttle arrived a little before 11 p.m. However, one of the front desk clerks was apparently going off duty at 11, and she proceeded to close her drawer at that exact moment. This left a line of approximately 10 or 12 guests to be checked in by one clerk. Needless to say, it took some time to process all of the guests, and we had to wait 20 or 30 minutes for our turn. We were assigned to a room, but at this point we had a few bags and my son was fast asleep and had to be carried. When I asked for assistance with our luggage, I was told that no one was available at that time of night. The hotel was large, having over and the rooms were spread out among several adjacent buildings. Our room was two buildings away from the lobby area. My wife and I struggled to carry the luggage and our son to the room. We arrived there about 11:30 and attempted to enter the room. The key unlocked the door, but the door would not open. After a couple of attempts, we heard a woman's voice in the room. Obviously, the room had been double-booked and the woman woken from her sleep. I used the house phone to call the front desk and explain the predicament. The front desk manager offered a quick apology and said that she would send someone with a key to a nearby room. About ten minutes later, a housekeeper happened to be going through the hallway, and she let my family into the room that I had been given over the phone. However, the housekeeper had no idea what was going on and took my word. After we had been in the room for ten minutes, the phone rang and I spoke with the front desk manager. She acted as though she had sent the housekeeper to open the room, but she still needed to send someone with the room keys. She apologized one last time and told me to call the front desk if I had any other problems." Maria went home that night and began to think about all the challenges the Libertador was currently facing.

## Day Two

When Maria met with the General Manager the next day, Maria was presented with a set of service quality data that was collected earlier in the year. Hotel guests participating in the survey were asked to record their perceptions pertaining to the hotel's service quality on all five service quality dimensions. Respondents were asked to rate the hotel on a 1 to 7 likert scale ranging from 1 (strongly disagree) to 7 (strongly agree). Typically, the higher the number guests' recorded, the more favorable the perception of the hotel's service quality on each dimension. Guests were asked to rate the hotel on their perception of the hotel's tangibles (rooms, dining facilities, lounges, etc.), reliability, responsiveness, empathy, and assurance. Results were presented as follows:

|                | Customer Perceptions |
|----------------|----------------------|
| Tangibles      | 6.2                  |
| Reliability    | 5.8                  |
| Responsiveness | 6.1                  |
| Empathy        | 5.3                  |
| Assurance      | 5.0                  |

## Discussion Questions

1. Based on Maria's Day 1 observations and conversation with Mr. Diaz, provide examples of the service quality gaps (e.g., knowledge, standards, delivery, communication, and service) that are evident at the Liberator Hotel.

2. Given the customer perception information that was provided by the General Manager on Day 2, which <u>one</u> dimension of service quality should Maria attempt to improve first? Please explain your answer.

3.  After further reviewing files left by her predecessor, Maria found that customer expectation data was also collected and yielded the information provided below. How does this impact the decision you made in answering question #2 above?

|  | Customer Expectations |
|---|---|
| Tangibles | 6.4 |
| Reliability | 6.5 |
| Responsiveness | 6.8 |
| Empathy | 5.5 |
| Assurance | 5.0 |

4.  What other piece of information does Maria need to make sure that her efforts to improve the service quality of the Libertador have gotten off to a good start?

CHAPTER **13**

# Managing Service Failures and Implementing Effective Recovery Strategies

## CHAPTER OBJECTIVES

After reading this chapter, you should be able to:

- Discuss the psychology of complaining behavior, including the types of complainers and the types of complaints.

- Explain customer complaining behavior with regards to the reasons customers do or do not complain, and the outcomes associated with customer complaints.

- Describe the organic and mechanistic steps involved in developing a service recovery management program.

- Understand the value of tracking and monitoring service failures and employee recovery efforts.

- Discuss the basic rules of thumb of the art of service recovery.

The major objectives of this chapter are to introduce the concepts pertaining to complaint and service recovery management.

Image Source/Jupiter Images

### HELL NOW HATH NO FURY LIKE A CUSTOMER SCORNED!

Despite a service firm's improvements in service quality, service firms will inevitably make mistakes resulting in unhappy customers. It is the nature of the service business: Simply stated, humans provide the majority of services, and humans are not always perfect, nor are the customers who are the recipients of the services. As a result, the traditional manufacturing mantra of "zero defects"(no mistakes) is likely an impossible goal. In its place, the art of appropriately handling customer complaints that result in "zero defections" (successfully recovering from mistakes and retaining customers) becomes the service firm's primary objective. There are countless examples of situations where customers received poor customer service and the firm's inadequate response actually exacerbated the failure situation. In recent cases, the customer has taken justice into their own hands and become a consumer activist. This type of situation has become so common that *BusinessWeek* devoted a recent cover story to *Consumer Vigilantes* with the tagline: "*Memo to Corporate America: Hell now hath no fury like a customer scorned.*"

Consider the case of Mona Shaw, a 76-year-old retired nurse and AARP secretary, from Manassas, Virginia. Mona had requested that Comcast, her local cable company, install cable service in her home. Apparently, the cable provider did not install the service properly. As a response, Mona personally visited the local Comcast office to ask for some assistance. The cable company had her wait in a hallway on a bench for two hours to see a manager. After the two hours had elapsed and still no manager showed, Mona quietly left the office, went home, and returned to the office with a hammer. Asking the front office personnel, "Do I now have your attention?" Mona proceeded to smash a computer keyboard and telephone. Shortly thereafter, Mona was arrested and fined $345 for her actions. On the flip side, Mona became a media sensation who was adored by the public and Comcast was portrayed as the villain. Obviously, the public could relate to Mona's desire to smash the cable company! Comcast's response—"We apologize for any customer service issues that Ms. Shaw experienced."

Equally enraged with his treatment by Apple, Michael Whitford uploaded a video on YouTube ("Macbook Destruction") where he smashes his nonworking Macbook to smithereens with a sledgehammer. Apple had declined to fix the Macbook under warranty due to damage from a spilled liquid. Whitford claimed that no such event with a spilled liquid ever took place and that Apple should have fixed the Macbook under warranty. After Michael explained his situation to an Apple supervisor, the supervisor suggested that Michael should purchase his next computer from another provider. As of the writing of this text, the video has been seen by nearly a half a million people. Apple has since capitulated and provided Michael with a new laptop. Says Michael, "I'm very happy now, and Apple has regained my loyalty." Nevertheless, the video remains on YouTube.

These are just two of many examples of how improperly handling customer complaints cost the company much more in bad publicity than would fixing the original problem in the first place. The original *BusinessWeek* article sparked several other articles that sent a clear message to corporate America—customers are fed up and are not going to sit quietly accepting subpar solutions to service failures. Consequently, service firms need to listen to customer complaints, resolve failure situations, and minimize future occurrences by developing and implementing effective service recovery management systems.

Source: **http://www.businessweek.com/magazine/content/08_09/b4073038437662.htm**, accessed 7 April, 2010.

# Introduction

Despite a service firm's best efforts, unhappy customers are inevitable. Planes are sometimes late, restaurant meals are not always cooked to perfection, and hotel employees are occasionally inattentive. On the flip side, some customers are just plain unreasonable and will never be pleased. Don't give up! Developing an indifferent attitude or accepting unhappy customers as a part of everyday business can be "the kiss of death." Customers are quick to reward their loyalty to companies that genuinely care about their concerns; and they are equally quick to punish unresponsive companies. Given the availability of YouTube and other forms of electronic communication, customers can spread the news of their discontent which can snowball quickly as other unhappy customers join in and publicly voice their unhappiness with the offending firm. For example, one unhappy United Airlines customer created his own website called Untied.com that is purely dedicated to customer and employee unhappiness with this specific airline. Unfortunately for United, Untied.com is now a fairly well-known website. Ultimately, the secrets to win over unhappy customers are to take a proactive stance to reduce the occurrence of **service failures** and equip employees with a set of effective **service recovery** tools to repair the service experience when failures do occur.

The reasons failures are inherent events in the service encounter are directly related to the unique characteristics that distinguish services from goods described in Chapter 3. Due to intangibility, customer comparison of perceptions to expectations is a highly

**service failures** Breakdowns in the delivery of service; service that does not meet customer expectations.

**service recovery** A firm's reaction to a complaint that results in customer satisfaction and goodwill.

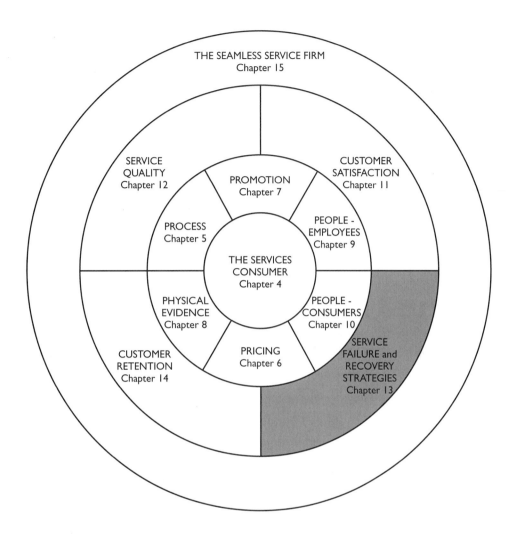

subjective evaluation; consequently, not all customers are going to be satisfied given their individual expectations and the individual perceptions of the world around them. Due to heterogeneity, variations in the service delivery process are going to occur, and not every service encounter is going to be identical to the last. As a result, customers openly wonder why their past experiences with a firm are not quite the same as their current experiences. The unique service characteristic of perishability provides another source of potential problems. Due to perishability, supply and demand problems are a common occurrence within service firms, which in turn cause customers to wait for service. When the wait becomes excessive, customers become unhappy, as in the story about Mona Shaw in the opening vignette. Finally, the unique service characteristic of inseparability often places the service provider in a face-to-face interaction with the customer, which provides a Pandora's Box of service failure possibilities. In fact, service providers' face-to-face contacts with customers has been termed "critical incidents" or "moments of truth," highlighting the importance of the possible gains and losses that may result due to this interaction. Research indicates that nearly two-thirds of all customers who defect from a service firm do so because of an interaction gone wrong with one of the firm's employees.[1] The Apple supervisor who encouraged Michael Whitford to purchase his next computer from another provider may well have provided Michael the added motivation to take a sledgehammer to his beloved Apple laptop.

# The Psychology of Customer Complaining Behavior

In a striking example of the impact of service failures, consumers were asked: "Have you ever been so upset at an employee or firm that you said, 'I'll never go into that store or buy that brand again,' and you haven't?" Researchers found that they had to limit respondents to relating only three incidents to keep the interview time reasonable. The oldest incident had happened more than 25 years ago, and 86 percent of the incidents were more than five years old. Apparently customers are not prone to "forgive and forget" when it comes to customer service failures!

The consequences of service failures can be dramatic. The vast majority of respondents in the survey (87 percent) indicated that they were still somewhat or very emotionally upset, and were more upset about the treatment they received from employees than about the store or product performance. More than three-quarters of respondents indicated that they had engaged in negative word-of-mouth communications regarding the incident (46 percent claimed that they had told "lots of people"). Finally, true to form in what is typical consumer complaint behavior today, only 53 percent had voiced their complaint to the store, even though 100 percent defected to other firms.[2]

Most companies cringe at the thought of customers who complain, while other companies look at complaints as a necessary evil in conducting business. The truth of the matter is that every company should encourage its customers to complain. Complainers are telling the firm that it has some operational or managerial problems that need to be corrected. Hence, complainers are offering the company a free gift; that is, they act as consultants and diagnose the firm's problems—at no fee.[3] Moreover, complainers provide the firm with the chance to reestablish a customer's satisfaction. Most importantly, complainers are more likely to do business with the firm again than are noncomplainers. Consequently, successful firms view complaints as an opportunity to satisfy unhappy customers and prevent defections as well as unfavorable word-of-mouth communications.[4]

It's not the complainers the company should worry about, it's the noncomplainers! Customers who do not express their complaints to the service firm are already gone or ready to leave for the competition at any moment. In fact, 63 percent of dissatisfied customers who do not complain and who have purchased goods or services costing $1 to $5 will defect to a competitor. Even more disturbing, as purchases exceed $100, the defection rate approaches 91 percent.[5] Of the countless books and articles that have been written about handling customer complaints (a recent Google search yielded over 2,770,000 results), the common theme of actively soliciting customer complaints becomes of paramount importance. Although many customers may complain to friends, family, and other acquaintances, complaining directly to the offending business happens far less often than one would think. Furthermore, customer complaining behavior and recovery expectations may differ depending on the customer's culture, as is the case with Chinese customers who are seeking "junzi" while maintaining the states of "lian" and "mianzi" (see Global Services in Action).

## Types of Complaints

In general, complaining is often defined as "expressing discontent, dissatisfaction, protest, resentment, or regret."[6] Complaining is different from criticism. Complaining expresses a dissatisfaction within the complainer, while criticism may be an objective and dispassionate observation about a person or object. Based on past research in consumer

## GLOBAL SERVICES *IN ACTION*

### Service Failures and Recovery Strategies: A Chinese Perspective

Effective service failure and recovery management practices need to be culturally relevant. This is particularly true in the hospitality sector where there is a high level of human interaction among hotel staff and guests with diverse cultural backgrounds. Ultimately, effective service recovery involves restoring the balance between customer expectations and perceptions. Consequently, understanding the influence of cultural background on expectations and perceptions is vital. Past studies have reported cultural differences in evaluating service quality, complaint behavior, and perceptions of service failure and service recovery effectiveness.

The Chinese are a prime example of how cultural differences impact expectations and perceptions pertaining to service failures and recovery strategies. For example, people in many eastern cultures (including China) may attribute the cause of a service failure to external forces such as luck or fate rather than accuse a service provider directly. Such an attribution would maintain a harmonious relationship and avoid conflict. More specifically, the Chinese appear to rely on five key value themes when evaluating the effectiveness of service recovery strategies.

1. Face Protection—the protection of one's own or other people's reputations. Face protection is comprised of *lian* (an individual's moral reputation) and *mianzi* (honor individuals may claim from their achievements and success). The value theme of face protection illustrates the heightened importance of interactional justice for Chinese customers. Service firms need to address negative situations in a very sensitive manner.

2. Equity—the desire to be treated fairly. Similar to western cultures, the Chinese compare the service received with the costs involved. If there is an imbalance, customers expect to be compensated for their loss. The value theme of equity illustrates the importance of distributive justice.

3. Valued Customers—to be respected as valued customers in service exchange relationships. A valued customer feels accepted, regardless of racial and economic background. When failures occur, valued customers receive an apology, providers are polite and courteous, and providers expend effort to recover. In addition, customers are made to feel they have a genuine concern, are treated with honesty, and their rights are respected.

4. Junzi Aspiration—to strive to live with the values of compassion, kindness, and other benevolent qualities. For example, a customer with a junzi behavior believes that "respect is gained by not being too aggressive towards others." In other words, in service failure situations, Chinese customers may behave in a nonconfrontational manner in order to preserve their junzi image.

5. Social Harmony—the desire to relate in a harmonious manner when disputes occur. Harmony is obtained by both sides of a dispute displaying goodwill, diplomacy, patience, understanding, and tolerance toward one another.

When the five values are considered together, four of the five demonstrate the importance of interactional justice to the Chinese culture. Hospitality firms that serve Chinese clientele should emphasize the interactional component of service recovery when service failures occur.

Source: **http://jht.sagepub.com/cgi/reprint/31/4/504**, accessed 2 March, 2009.

**instrumental complaints** Complaints expressed for the purpose of altering an undesirable state of affairs.

psychology, it becomes quickly apparent that all complaints are not created equally. For example, complaints can be instrumental or noninstrumental.[7] **Instrumental complaints** are expressed for the purpose of altering an undesirable state of affairs. For instance, complaining to a waiter about an undercooked steak is an instrumental complaint. In

A consumer voicing a complaint to an employee is most likely making an ostensive and instrumental complaint.

such a case, the complainer fully expects the waiter to take action in order to correct the situation. Interestingly, and perhaps sadly, research indicates that instrumental complaints make up only a very small number of the millions of complaints that are voiced every day.

In contrast, **noninstrumental complaints** are voiced without any expectation that the undesirable state will be altered. These kinds of complaints are voiced much more often than are instrumental complaints. For example, complaints about the weather such as, "It's too hot!" are voiced without any real expectation that conditions will change. Another type of noninstrumental complaint is an instrumental complaint that is voiced to a second party, and not to the offending source. For example, complaining to a friend about the poor condition of a hotel room is a noninstrumental complaint. The friend is most likely not going to take it upon him/herself to fix the condition of the room, nor does the person who voiced the complaint expect the friend to do so.

Types of complaints also vary based on who the complainer believes is the source of the problem. Accordingly, complaints can be categorized as ostensive or reflexive. **Ostensive complaints** are directed at someone or something outside the realm of the complainer. In other words, the source of the problem is perceived as someone other than the complainer. In contrast, **reflexive complaints** are directed at some inner aspect of the complainer. In contrast to ostensive complainers, reflexive complainers blame themselves as the primary source of the problem. Perhaps not surprisingly, most customers voice ostensive complaints. Research indicates that this phenomenon occurs for two reasons. First, people generally avoid making negative comments about themselves so as not to reinforce negative self-esteem. Second, people seldom want to convey negative attributes about themselves to others. Stew Leonard of Stew Leonard's Dairy learned this lesson long ago when he first opened his legendary grocery store. The store has been deemed by Ripley's Believe It or Not as "The World's Largest Dairy" and *Fortune Magazine* has selected the business as one of the top "100 Businesses to Work For." Customers entering the store see a large three-ton boulder just outside the store engraved with two simple rules: Rule #1: The Customer is Always Right! and Rule #2: If the Customer is Ever Wrong, Reread Rule #1. Stew Leonard learned that when customers are unhappy about a situation (even if the customer is mistaken) what really matters is who the customer perceives is the source of the problem. The bottom line is that most complainers live in an ostensive world, and service providers should be grateful when customers voice instrumental complaints!

**noninstrumental complaints** Complaints expressed without expectation that an undesirable state will be altered.

**ostensive complaints** Complaints directed at someone or something outside the realm of the complainer.

**reflexive complaints** Complaints directed at some inner aspect of the complainer.

## Types of Complainers

Before we launch into a discussion about "Why Do" and "Why Don't" customers complain, it is worthwhile to understand that there are different types of complainers in the world. According to one of the most recent exposés on the topic, at least five types of complainers can be identified.[8]

- *The Meek Customer*—a customer who generally never complains. The primary strategy for responding to meek customers is to actively solicit comments from the customer and act appropriately to resolve the complaint. The customer may not be saying anything negative, but trained service providers typically can recognize the nonverbal signs of dissatisfaction when something is wrong.

- *The Aggressive Customer*—the alter ego of the meek customer. This customer complains on a regular basis, often at length and often loudly enough for everyone else to hear. Response recommendations for this customer include listening completely to everything he or she has to say, agreeing that indeed a problem does exist, providing no excuses, indicating what will be done to resolve the problem and when it will be resolved, and asking "what else?" This indicates that the firm is ready to go the extra mile to satisfy the customer. Given the loudness factor of the aggressive customer, providers may also consider inviting aggressive customers "off stage" away from other customers to avoid negatively impacting the experience of others.

- *The High-Roller Customer*—a customer who expects the best and is willing to pay for it. Unless this customer is a hybrid of the aggressive customer with money, high-roller customers typically complain in a reasonable manner. The appropriate responses to the complaints of a high-roller are very similar to the response recommendations for the aggressive customer—listen carefully, no excuses, ask questions to determine the real cause of the problem, and respond appropriately. There is typically no need to isolate this customer from others, since this customer complains in a reasonable manner.

- *The Rip-Off Customer*—a customer who wants more than they're entitled to receive. The rip-off customer typically can be quickly identified with a constant and repetitive response of "not good enough" for any solution that the service firm offers to resolve the problem. Appropriate responses for this customer can range from letting the customer walk away unhappy to allowing the customer to dictate the appropriate recovery effort. Simply asking the customer, "What can we do to make things right?" places the recovery solution in their hands.

- *The Chronic Complainer Customer*—a customer who is never satisfied yet continues to return. The chronic complainer customer will test the patience of any service provider, but they should not be ignored. The chronic complainer will accept an apology and appreciate any efforts to correct the situation. Chronic complainers are often looking for a sympathetic ear, and will spread positive word-of-mouth referrals when problems are resolved.

The types of complainers listed above are general in nature and may very well cut across the various service sectors. However, some industries have created their own "Types of Complainers." For example, the hotel industry has identified seven types of complainers, including "People with Ruined Dreams," "Face-savers," "Freebie-lovers," "Wounded-warriors," "Martyrs/passive-aggressives," "The Loyal Customers," and "The Truly Injured."[9] It should also be noted at this time that customers should not always be kept happy regardless of the cost. Truly, some customers are more important than others and the service firm needs to decide which customers should be retained and which should be allowed to take their business elsewhere. Guidelines pertaining to which customers to retain and which to turn loose are provided within Chapter 14, which focuses on customer retention issues and strategies.

## Why Do Customers Complain?

The reasons customers complain are directly related to the type of complaint voiced. In the case of the instrumental complaint, the reason a customer complains is pretty clear. The complainer wants the undesirable situation to be corrected. For example, consider TreeHugger's complaint about Delta Airlines (see Sustainability and Services in Action). Delta's likely to not be very happy about TreeHugger's observations; however, the comments provide feedback to Delta so that they never make the same mistake again and make future improvements.

In contrast, the reasons customers complain are not as obvious when it comes to noninstrumental complaints. Psychological experts believe that noninstrumental complaints

---

### SUSTAINABILITY AND SERVICES *IN ACTION*

#### TreeHugger Has Issues with Delta Sky: The Green Issue

Over the last several years, Delta airlines has led the airline industry in promoting eco-friendly business practices such as launching the first comprehensive in-flight recycling program in the United States. Delta has also partnered with The Conservation Fund—a non-profit organization that allows passengers to offset their air-travel carbon emissions. In addition, Delta's *Sky Magazine* is certified by the Sustainable Forestry Initiative, indicating that the airline is buying paper products from well-managed forests.

Despite Delta's past success in positioning itself as an environmentally friendly airline, there have been a few hiccups along the way. TreeHugger, the leading media outlet dedicated to driving sustainability mainstream, recently took aim at Delta Airlines' celebration of the launch of its in-flight magazine's environmentally themed March 2008 issue. The celebration took place at the airline's Sky 360° lounge in Manhattan, where guests were served large quantities of Vodka 360—alledgedly the world's first eco-luxury vodka brand. TreeHugger admitted that no one was complaining about the vodka; however, eco-minded details about the airline were few and far between. TreeHugger representatives were particularly confused by the environmentally unfriendly contents of the "goodie bags" that were distributed to invited guests. According to TreeHugger, the "goodie bag" itself was made of recyclable polypropylene from China, and its contents included:

1. A Sky360° T-shirt, sized large, conventional cotton
2. A Delta amenities bag (contents all made in China)
3. A Heineken face towel, conventional cotton
4. A copy of Greenopia's San Francisco guide, plus a coupon for a free copy of the New York City guide when it's released
5. A SkyMall keychain, plus a 10 percent SkyMall discount voucher
6. A compact fluorescent bulb (OK, this we get)
7. A Vodka 360 martini glass
8. A tiny bottle of Stirring's Simple Apple Martini mixer (non-organic, as far as we can tell)

In other words, Delta's "goodie bag" was a gigantic failure in the eyes of its eco-friendly guests. One Delta employee chimed in on TreeHuggers' blog that they were embarrassed that the airline could not find at least one natural or organic gift, and suggested that the airline should do its homework before jumping on the green bandwagon. Adding additional insult to injury, another blogger who was an invited freelance writer that had RSVP'd for the event was turned away at the door by a staff member who was described as rude and obnoxious. The writer felt that the whole event was more about promoting the airline and its magazine, and far less about Delta's green ideas and concepts.

Source: **http://www.treehugger.com/files/2008/02/delta_green.php**, accessed 2 March, 2009.

occur for several reasons. First, complaining serves a function much like the release of a pressure valve—it provides the complainer an emotional release from frustration. In essence, complaints provide people with a mechanism for venting their feelings.

Complaining behavior is also seen as related to control. More specifically, complaining serves as a mechanism for the complainer's desire to regain some measure of control. Control is reestablished if the complainer is able to influence other people's evaluations of the source of the complaint. For example, negative word of mouth spread by the complainer for the purpose of taking revenge on an offending business gives the complainer some measure of control through indirect retribution.

A third and fourth reason people complain to others (noninstrumental complaints) is to solicit sympathy and test for consensus of the complaint, thereby validating the complainer's subjective evaluation of the events that led to the complaint in the first place. In other words, the complainer wants to know whether others would feel the same way under similar circumstances. If they would, the complainer then feels justified in having voiced the complaint.

Finally, complainers may complain simply to create an impression. As strange as it may seem, complainers are often considered to be more intelligent and discerning than noncomplainers (e.g., Simon Cowell, the most critical judge on "American Idol").[10] The implication is that the complainer's standards and expectations are higher than those of noncomplainers. For example, most have friends who are particularly prone to complain more than others. Although, we may grow weary of their constant complaining behavior, we do take notice when these chronic complainers actually voice happiness with a service provider or firm. As a result, the recommendations of chronic complainers tend to carry more weight than the average person. Service firms may actively solicit complaints from chronic complainers given the value of the word-of-mouth these individuals may generate.

## Why Don't Customers Complain?

We know that a great percentage of customers never complain to the offending party, but why is this so? Moreover, service customers are less likely to complain than

"Contrary to popular opinion, most people's opinons aren't so popular."

Although a firm may never hear from unhappy customers and foolishly believe everything is fine, a great number of customers may actually be unhappy.

**FIG-13.1** Why Customers "Do" and "Don't" Complain

| WHY CUSTOMERS "DO" COMPLAIN | WHY CUSTOMERS "DON'T" COMPLAIN |
|---|---|
| To correct an undesirable situation | Don't think it will change anything |
| An emotional release from frustration | Don't know whom to complain |
| To regain some measure of control | May accept part of the blame themselves |
| Solicit sympathy | Doubt their own subjective evaluation |
| Test for consensus | May lack technical or specialized expertise |
| To create an impression of being more intelligent or discerning | May feel uncomfortable about complaining in a face-to-face exchange |

customers of goods. A greater percentage of services' problems than goods' problems are not voiced "because potential complainers do not know what to do or think that it wouldn't do any good."[11] This situation is directly attributable to the intangibility and inseparability inherent in the provision of services. Due to intangibility, evaluation of the service delivery process is primarily subjective. Consequently, consumers often lack the security of making an objective observation and may doubt their own subjective evaluations. For example, customers of home remodeling services often have a difficult time assessing the competence and quality of work completed by service providers such as painters, electricians, and hardwood floor installers.

Due to inseparability, customers often provide inputs into the process. Hence, given an undesirable outcome, customers may place much of the blame upon themselves for failing to convey to the service provider a satisfactory description of the level and type of service desired. In addition, inseparability encompasses the often face-to-face interaction between the customer and the service provider, where the customer may feel uncomfortable about complaining because of the physical presence of the provider. A classic example would involve the interaction between a customer and a hair stylist. The customer attempted to convey directions to the new hair stylist, but in the end the customer was not happy with the result. The customer may blame themselves for not accurately articulating their needs and wants, and may shy away from having a direct confrontation with the stylist.

Finally, many services are technical and specialized. Customers may not feel adequately qualified to voice a complaint for fear that they lack the expertise to evaluate the quality of the service. For example, most customers feel they lack the technical expertise to evaluate the competence of their physicians, accountants, lawyers, and/or auto mechanics. A summary of why customers "Do" and "Don't" complain is provided in Figure 13.1.

## Complaining Outcomes

**voice** A complaining outcome in which the consumer verbally communicates dissatisfaction with the store or the product.

**exit** A complaining outcome in which the consumer stops patronizing the store or using the product.

In general, complaining behavior results in three outcomes: voice, exit, and retaliation.[12] **Voice** refers to an outcome in which the consumer verbally communicates dissatisfaction with a specific service provider or providing firm. *High voice* means that the communication is expressed to the manager or someone higher in the organizational hierarchy than the actual provider. *Medium voice* occurs when the consumer communicates the problem to the person providing the service. *Low voice* occurs when the consumer does not communicate the problem to anyone associated with the providing firm, but may be relaying the problem to others outside the store—a classic case of noninstrumental complaining.

**Exit**, the second type of complaining outcome, describes the situation in which a consumer stops patronizing the service firm. *High exit* occurs when the consumer makes a

**retaliation** A complaining outcome in which the consumer takes action deliberately designed to damage the physical operation or hurt future business.

conscious decision never to purchase from the firm or buy the product again. *Medium exit* reflects a consumer's conscious decision to try not to use the service firm again if at all possible. In other words, customers will seek out and purchase from alternative providers whenever available. *Low exit* means that the consumer does not change his or her purchasing behavior and continues to purchase the firm's services as usual.

The third type of complaint outcome is **retaliation**, the situation in which a consumer takes action deliberately designed to either damage the physical operation or hurt future business. *High retaliation* involves the situation where the consumer physically injures the service provider or damages the firm, or goes out of his or her way to communicate negative aspects about the business to others. The two customers featured in the opening vignette are classic examples of high retaliation. In *medium retaliation*, the consumer creates minor inconveniences for the firm or perhaps tells only a few people about the incident. *Low retaliation* involves no retaliation at all against the provider or firm, and perhaps consists of only minor negative word of mouth.

Interestingly, the three complaining outcomes are not mutually exclusive and can be considered as three aspects of one behavior that may occur simultaneously. Experiencing high levels of all three outcomes simultaneously can result in explosive behavior. For example, "In one high-high-high example, the customer shouted his dissatisfaction at the clerk and the store manager, vowed never to buy at the store again, went out of the store, got in his car, and crashed through the front doors of the store, through the checkout counter and between two lines of shelving, destroying everything in its path."[13] In contrast, a consumer who displays high-voice, low-exit, and low-retaliation behavior would typify the chronic complainer who nevertheless continues to purchase from the firm as usual.

## Developing a Service Recovery Management Program

Service managers and personnel are facing intensive customer service pressures now more than ever. Customers are more informed, their expectations for quality service are high, and the state of the economy has heightened their sensitivity to poor service. When a service failure does occur, the service provider's reaction can either reinforce a strong customer bond or change a seemingly minor distraction into a major incident. Consequently,

An effective service recovery management program focuses the organization's strategic priorities on reestablishing customer satisfaction once a failure has occurred.

**FIG-13.2** Developing a Service Recovery Management Program

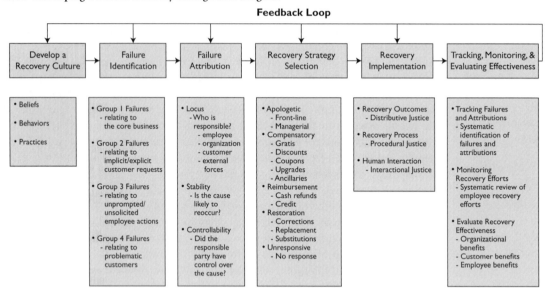

it is imperative that managers have an established service recovery management program in place to overcome possible service failures.

By formalizing a service recovery management program (see Figure 13.2) firms can develop a step-by-step process consisting of both "**mechanistic**" and "**organic**" components that assist the firm in efficiently and effectively recovering from service failures.[14] Mechanistic approaches to service recovery pertain to formalized step-by-step processes that are developed to facilitate the firm's failure analysis and service recovery efforts. In contrast, organic approaches to service recovery are informal sets of values and beliefs that comprise the firm's service recovery culture.

## Developing a Positive Internal Recovery Culture

The first step in developing an effective service recovery management program is instilling a **service recovery culture** throughout the firm.[15] Developing a recovery culture can be described as an organic approach to service recovery. Organic recovery cultures are not formalized or systematized, they are simply an informal set of beliefs, behaviors, and practices that set the tone for how the firm wishes to address customer complaints. A positive internal recovery culture reflects the supportiveness of the firm's internal environment with respect to complaint handling. A negative recovery culture dooms service recovery efforts before they ever get off the ground. Case in point, Japan's Mitsubishi Motors. For decades, Mitsubishi employees have apparently been going to great lengths to hide consumer complaints. Letters have been hidden in boxes, in changing rooms, behind lockers, and stashed in secret computer files. The primary reason for the cover-up appears to be cultural. Eventually, the company's president stood before the world press, took a deep sigh and an even deeper bow of apology as he confessed to the company's systematic and deliberate attempts to avoid the recall of over 800,000 of its defective vehicles. "We were ashamed of reporting recalls," said the company's president, Katsuhiko Kawasoe. The cost of the recall to the company was estimated to be in the tens of millions; however, the damage to its reputation and brand name was much worse.[16]

**mechanistic processes** Formalized step-by-step processes that are developed to facilitate the firm's failure analysis and service recovery efforts.

**organic processes** Informal sets of values and beliefs that comprise the firm's service recovery culture.

**service recovery culture** An informal set of beliefs, behaviors, and practices that set the tone for how the firm wishes to address customer complaints.

Great service recovery cultures start at the top with the firm's upper management. The firm's leadership must "walk the talk" and facilitate as opposed to hindering the firm's service recovery efforts. A positive recovery culture consists of top managers recognizing that service failures do occasionally occur, providing the training and tools necessary for service personnel to recover effectively from service failures, and making service recovery a top priority for the firm. Traditional new employee training programs focus on how to deliver service right the first time. It's almost as if the trainers believe that "failure is not an option." Service firms need to recognize that the occasional service failure is a distinct possibility, and that simply ignoring this fact is likely to make failure situations even worse. Firms that develop a positive internal recovery culture recognize the need to openly discuss the possibility of service failures and the company's desire to retain customers through effective service recovery strategies.

## Service Failure Identification

Service firms with positive internal recovery cultures (organic approach) are likely to develop formalized processes (mechanistic approach) for analyzing and learning from past service failures to minimize their future occurrence. Consequently, the second step in implementing a service recovery management program is failure identification. Although a firm may receive hundreds of customer complaints pertaining to perceived service failures throughout a year, ultimately these complaints can be systematically categorized into employee responses to one of four main groups: (1) core service delivery system failures, (2) failures relating to customer needs and requests, (3) failures relating to unprompted and unsolicited employee actions, and (4) failures relating to problematic customers (see Figure 13.3).[17]

**core service failures**
Failures in the core service offering of the firm including unavailable service, unreasonably slow service, and other core service failures.

*Core Service Delivery System Failures*   **Core service failures** are failures that relate directly to the fundamental service offering. For example, airlines that do not depart on time, hotels that do not adequately clean their guest rooms, and insurance firms that do

**FIG-13.3** The Four Types of Service Failure Identification

| PRIMARY FAILURE TYPE | FAILURE SUBGROUPS |
|---|---|
| *Service Delivery System Failures* | Unavailable Service<br>Unreasonably Slow Service<br>Other Core Service Failures |
| *Customer Needs and Requests* | "Special Needs" Customers<br>Customer Preferences<br>Admitted Customer Error<br>Disruptive Others |
| *Unprompted/Unsolicited Employee Actions* | Level of Attention<br>Unusual Action<br>Cultural Norms<br>Gestalt |
| *Problematic Customers* | Drunkenness<br>Verbal and Physical Abuse<br>Breaking Company Policies<br>Uncooperative Customers |

Sources: Adapted from Mary Jo Bitner, Bernard H. Booms, and Mary Stanfield Tetreault, "The Service Encounter: Diagnosing Favorable and Unfavorable Incidents," *Journal of Marketing*, (January 1990), pp. 71–84; Mary Jo Bitner, Bernard H. Booms and Lois A. Mohr, "Critical Service Encounters: The Employee's Viewpoint," *Journal of Marketing*, 58, (October 1994) pp. 95–106.

not process their claims in a timely manner are all guilty of core service delivery system failures. In general, core service delivery system failures consist of employee responses to three types of failures: (1) unavailable service, (2) unreasonably slow service, and (3) other core service failures. *Unavailable service* refers to services normally available that are lacking or absent. *Unreasonably slow service* concerns services or employees that customers perceive as being extraordinary slow in fulfilling their function. Finally, *other core service failures* encompass all other core service failures. This category is deliberately broad to reflect the various core services offered by different industries, such as financial services, health care, insurance, travel and tourism, retail, and so on. Each industry contains its own unique set of core service issues. For example, core service failures that pertain to the "other" category relating to the restaurant industry may include cooking issues, facility problems, unclear company policies, and out of stock conditions.

***Failures Relating to Customer Needs and Requests***    The second type of failure category, **customer needs and requests**, pertains to employee responses to individual consumer needs and special requests. Consumer needs can be implicit or explicit. *Implicit needs* are not requested. For example, a disabled customer seated in a wheelchair should not be led to an elevated booth in a restaurant. In contrast, *explicit requests* are overtly requested. A customer who asks for her or his steak to be cooked medium-rare and who would like to substitute mashed potatoes for the baked potato listed on the menu is making explicit requests.

In general, customer needs and requests consist of employee responses to four types of possible failures: (1) special needs, (2) customer preferences, (3) customer errors, and (4) disruptive others. Employee responses to *special needs* involve complying with requests based on a customer's special medical, dietary, psychological, language, or sociological difficulties. Preparing a meal for a vegetarian would fulfill a "special request." Employee responses to *customer preferences* require the employee to modify the service delivery system in some way that meets the preferred needs of the customer. A customer request for a substitution at a restaurant is a typical example of a customer preference. An employee response to a *customer error* involves a scenario in which the failure is initiated by an admitted customer mistake (e.g., lost tickets, lost hotel key, forgot to tell the waitress to "hold the tomato"). Finally, employee responses to *disruptive others* require employees to settle disputes between customers, such as requesting patrons to be quiet in movie theaters or asking that smoking customers not smoke in nonsmoking sections of a restaurant.

***Unprompted/Unsolicited Employee Actions***    The third type of service failure, **unprompted and unsolicited employee actions**, pertains to events and employee behaviors that are totally unexpected by the customer. These actions are not initiated by the customer via a request, nor are they part of the core delivery system. Subcategories in this group include: (1) level of attention, (2) unusual action, (3) cultural norms, (4) gestalt, and (5) adverse condition.

Within the failure group of unprompted or unsolicited employee action, the subcategory of *level of attention* refers to employees who have poor attitudes, employees who ignore a customer, and employees who exhibit behaviors consistent with an indifferent attitude. Level of attention failures can also occur when employees pay too much attention to the customer to the point that the customer feels uncomfortable. Examples of too much attention might include an employee who flirts with the customer or an employee "stalks" a customer, mistakenly believing that customer is a potential shoplifter.

The *unusual action* subcategory can also reflect positive and negative events. For example, a Domino's employee happened to see a family searching through the burnt-out remains of their house while making a delivery to another customer in the area. The

**failures relating to customer needs and requests** Service failures relating to the implicit and explicit needs of customers including special needs, customer preferences, customer errors, and disruptive others.

**failures relating to unprompted/ unsolicited employee actions** Failures relating to level of attention, unusual employee actions, violations of cultural norms, gestalt, and responses to adverse conditions.

employee reported the event to the manager, and the two immediately prepared and delivered pizzas for the family free of charge. The family was stunned by the action and never forgot the kindness that was extended toward them during their time of need. Unfortunately, an unusual action can also be a negative event. Employee actions such as rudeness, abusiveness, and inappropriate physical contact would qualify equally as unusual actions.

The *cultural norms* subcategory refers to actions that either positively reinforce cultural norms such as equality, fairness, and honesty, or violate the cultural norms of society. Violations would include discriminatory behavior, acts of dishonesty such as lying, cheating, and stealing, and other activities considered unfair by customers. Infringing on a customer's personal space as a result of cultural norms would also qualify.

The *gestalt* subcategory refers to customer evaluations that are made holistically; that is, the customer does not describe the service encounter as discrete events but uses general phrases such as "the whole experience was terrible." A comment such as, "It is almost unbelievable how poorly we were treated by the employees of your airline, almost a perfect negative case study in customer service," would be a classic example of a gestalt failure.

Finally, the *adverse conditions* subcategory covers positive and negative employee actions under stressful conditions. If an employee takes effective control of a situation when all others around him or her are "losing their heads," customers are impressed by the employee's performance under those adverse conditions. In contrast, if the captain and crew of a sinking ship board the lifeboats before the passengers, this obviously would be remembered as a negative action under adverse conditions.

*Group 4: Problematic Customers*   The fourth and final service failure type involves instances where neither the employee nor the service firm is at fault for the service failure. In these situations, the cause of the service failure lies with the customer's own misbehavior. Service failures involving **problematic customers** include: (1) drunkenness, (2) verbal and physical abuse, (3) breaking company policies, and (4) uncooperative customers. Problematic customer behavior involving *drunkenness* occurs when the intoxicated customer's behavior adversely affects other customers, service employees, or the service environment in general. In one incident, numerous members of a company sales group became intoxicated and began to expose themselves to other customers. The captain quickly cut off liquor sales, but the group continued to drink by opening their own personal bottles of liquor that they had purchased at the duty-free shop before boarding.[18] *Verbal and physical abuse* causes problems when the customer verbally or physically abuses either the employee or other customers. For example, if a lovers' quarrel breaks out in the middle of a restaurant and the couple begins screaming and/or hitting one another, this situation would qualify as verbal and physical abuse. A customer who *breaks company policies* refuses to comply with policies employees are attempting to enforce. For example, a queuing policy or a no substitution policy that is ignored by a customer would create a problematic situation. Finally, an *uncooperative customer* is one who is generally rude, uncooperative, and unreasonably demanding. Regardless of how the service employee attempts to appease this customer, the effort is typically futile. The customer simply will not be pleased.

**failures relating to problematic customers** Failures relating to the customer's own misbehavior, including drunkenness, verbal and physical abuse, violations of company policies, and uncooperative customers.

## Service Failure Attribution: Indentifying the Root Cause

The third step in developing a service recovery management program is failure attribution. In order to learn more from the types of failures identified, service firms that excel at recovery efforts also systematically determine the source or attribution of the failure. Hence, failure attribution becomes our second mechanistic approach to service recovery. Understanding customer attributions of failures assists the firm in tracking the perceived sources of failures, and facilitates subsequent steps in the service recovery management program such as what to offer customers and how to offer it to them. Attributions for failure situations are typically broken down into locus, stability, and controllability assessments.

- *Locus*—Who is responsible for the failure? Is the source of the failure the service provider, the service firm, the customer, or some external force?
- *Stability*—Is the cause of the failure likely to recur? Is this a one-time incident (unstable), or is the cause of the failure likely to recur (stable)?
- *Controllability*—Did the responsible party have control over the cause of the failure?

**locus** A service failure attribution pertaining to the possible source of the failure including the service provider, the firm, the customer, or external forces.

**Locus** pertains directly to the source of the failure. For example, typical sources for service failures may include the service provider (e.g., rude, apathetic, incompetent), the service firm itself (e.g., unfriendly policies, negative internal recovery culture), the customer (e.g., failed to make a reservation, failed to follow directions) or external forces (e.g., natural forces such as bad weather, or economic forces such as a recession). It should be noted that the service firm's locus of a failure situation may be quite different from the customer's perceived locus of the problem. The firm's own diagnosis of the problem helps the firm to minimize future occurrences of the problem if possible. Ultimately, the customer's perception of who's to blame dictates their reaction to the failure and sets their recovery expectations. For example, online customers are more likely to

---

## E-SERVICES *IN ACTION*

### Who Done It? Customer Attributions for Online Service Failures

As do-it-yourself online services continue to grow (e.g., airline and hotel reservations), and as service firms attempt to turn more and more of their customers into partial employees by directing customers to websites to fulfill their requests, service providers need to be aware of how to recover appropriately from online service failures. As we all know, all customers are not created equally when conducting business online, and mistakes will occur. Equally apparent is that all online service firms are not created equally, and some online environments are much more customer friendly than others. Consequently, online service failures are inevitable. The main questions, then, are: (1) do customers have different attributions when failures occur online versus offline; and (2) do customers have different recovery expectations for online versus offline failures?

According to one study that investigated offline and online customers of banks and airlines, online customers tend to blame themselves more for service failures than offline customers. Moreover, online customers who blame themselves also expect less of a recovery solution, and may be willing to pay additional charges to resolve the situation. Furthermore, online customers are also more willing to resolve the situation on their own if given the opportunity. In contrast, offline customers are more likely to blame the service

firm for the service failure and have higher expectations for recovery.

The managerial implications of these findings are twofold. First, since online customers have a lower recovery expectation, the cost of recovering from online failures should be less than offline failures. In fact, the recovery costs of online customers can be further minimized by implementing self-service recovery options. On the other hand, since online customers have a lower recovery expectation, exceeding customer expectations for recovery and delighting the customer should be easier if the service firm chooses to do so. Second, front-line service employees should be trained to deal with offline customers who tend to blame the firm more for service failures. Customers who attribute the service failure to the firm are expecting a higher level of recovery. Consequently, service personnel should be trained to listen to online and offline customer attributions for failure situations and respond appropriately. The cost and the manner in which a service firm recovers are dictated by whom the customer blames for the failure.

Source: **http://www.emeraldinsight.com/Insight/viewContentItem.do?contentId=1576503&contentType=Article**, accessed 7 April, 2010.

attribute the source of the problem to their own performance, whereas customers of "brick and mortar" stores are more likely to blame the store or employees for their service problems (see E-Services in Action). Research reports that customers who perceive that contact personnel are the source of the failure increase their registered complaints to the firm, engage in negative word-of-mouth about the firm to others, suffer from decreased customer satisfaction, and maintain higher recovery expectations.[19]

**stability** A service failure attribution pertaining to the likelihood the service failure will recur.

**Stability** attributions pertain to the likelihood that the service failure will recur. From the firm's point of view, if the service failure is diagnosed as a rare event, the firm is not likely to invest a lot of time and resources to fix the source of the problem. On the other hand, service failures that are likely to recur on frequent basis should receive immediate attention. From the customer's perspective, the perceived stability of the failure situation influences their recovery expectations. In cases where the customer believes the cause of the failure is likely to recur, customers prefer refunds rather than exchanges believing that accepting an exchange will just result in another failure. When they believe the failure is a random one-time event, customers readily accept an exchange as a solution to the failure situation in anticipation of future satisfaction.[20]

**controllability** A service failure attribution pertaining to whether or not the firm had control over the cause of the failure.

**Controllability** attributions address whether the firm had control over the cause of the failure situation. Much like stability assessments, the time and effort the firm is willing to invest in correcting the source of the failure is based on whether the firm believes it can control future outcomes. For example, if the cause of the failure situation was a weather event that caused a power outage in a restaurant on busy night, there may be little the restaurant can do to ensure that the situation never happens again. Once again, customer perceptions of the controllability issue may differ from the firm's assessment. Customers who experience a service failure that they believe is preventable (controllable) tend to be angrier, have lower repurchase intentions, and have a greater desire to actively voice their dissatisfaction.[21] Upon watching Michael Whitford's video on YouTube discussed in the opening vignette of this chapter, it is clear this customer felt that Apple had control over whether it wanted to repair his laptop. Customer attributions of failures greatly influence their recovery expectations. Service recovery training should highlight the importance of understanding customer attributions along the three principle dimensions of locus, stability, and controllability and their relevance to recovery strategy selection and implementation.

## Recovery Strategy Selection: What Should the Customer Receive to Offset the Failure?

The fourth step in developing a service recovery management program pertains to recovery strategy selection.[22] Service firms that systematically track the attributions of service failures are also likely to identify formally the types of recovery strategies that are available to the service organization. As a result, recovery strategy selection is another mechanistic approach to a firm's recovery efforts, along with the steps of service failure identification and failure attribution. Recovery strategies involve the actions service providers take in response to failure situations. For example, a restaurant may quickly replace a customer's meal if the original meal was cooked incorrectly, or a bank may recoup service charges for ATM withdrawals if the customer was misinformed. Recovery tactics generally fall within five broad recovery strategy categories—*compensatory, restoration, apologetic, replacement*, and *unresponsive*.

Although each tactic contains subtle differences from the next, customer evaluations of the effectiveness of the tactic may vary widely. For example, compensatory and restoration recovery tactics tend to solve the customer's original product need. In contrast, apologetic, reimbursement, and unresponsive tactics result in the original customer's

Offering an airline customer a free upgrade from coach class to business class is often a welcome compensation to recover from a service failure.

need remaining unfulfilled. It is also important to note that recovery tactics can be used in isolation or in combination. A listing and description of each type of recovery strategy and tactic is provided below:

**compensatory strategies** A set of recovery strategies that compensate the customers to offset the costs of the service failure.

**Compensatory strategies** compensate the customer to offset the costs (e.g., emotional, monetary, time lost ) of the service failure. Typically, customers get to keep the good or service provided and the compensation provides added value.

- *Gratis* (e.g., customer is provided with free good/service)
- *Discount* (e.g., customer receives an immediate discount)
- *Coupon* (e.g., coupon is redeemable at a later date and tied to a future purchase)
- *Free Upgrade* (e.g., upgrade from economy rental car to luxury rental car to compensate for a failure)
- *Free Ancillary Product* (e.g., free dinner to compensate a hotel guest for problems associated with their room)

**restoration strategies** A set of recovery strategies offered to offset the current failure situation by providing an identical offering, corrections to the original offering, or by offering a substitute.

**Restoration strategies** are offered to customers to offset the current failure situation by providing a new identical product, corrections to the original product, or by offering a substitute product.

- *Total replacement* (e.g., defective product is replaced with new product)
- *Correction* (e.g., defective product is repaired and returned to customer)
- *Substitution* (e.g., defective product is unwanted/unavailable and a substitute product is provided)

**apologetic strategies** A set of verbal recovery strategies involving apologies from front-line providers and/or upper-level management.

**Apologetic Strategies** indicate to the customer that the firm is truly sorry for the service failure. Apologies can come from front-line providers and/or managers. Front-line apologies are typically a faster response to the failure situation; however, managerial responses are more valued by customers. When apologies are made from managers, customers feel that their complaints have been heard by personnel of importance and are justified.

- *Front-line apology* (e.g., service provider apologizes to customer)
- *Upper-management apology* (e.g., upper-management apologizes to customer)

**reimbursement strategies** A set of recovery strategies that provide the customer with a refund or store credit.

**Reimbursement Strategies** differ from compensatory strategies in that customers typically return the product provided (if possible) and receive restitution in the form of refunds or store credits. As a result of the return requirement, the customer's original needs and/or wants remain unfulfilled. The customer must then restart their search for another provider.

- *Refund* (e.g., customer is refunded the purchase price of product in cash/credit card)
- *Store Credit* (e.g., customer is refunded the purchase price of product in store credit)

**Unresponsive Strategies** describe the situation where the providing firm simply does not respond to customer complaints about service failures. Perhaps the firm has no internal service recovery culture and/or has decided that the firm has a constant stream of new customers to offset the losses of unhappy customers.

- *No Response* (e.g., no response to customer complaint)

Formal training efforts pertaining to recovery strategy selection should involve discussion concerning the broad differences among the five recovery strategies and the subtle but significant differences among recovery tactics within each recovery strategy category. Additional training should include the service firm's preference for which recovery tactics are acceptable to both the firm and the customer. Further discussion might include whether certain recovery tactics are more applicable to certain types of failure situations and/or certain types of customers. Clearly, the idea here is that the firm doesn't always have to give away their goods or services for free. There are many other viable options that exist that not only meet or exceed the customer's recovery expectation, but also allow the firm to maintain its profit margins.[23]

## Recovery Strategy Implementation: How Should the Recovery Strategy Be Presented to the Customer?

Once an appropriate recovery strategy has been selected, the fifth step of an effective service recovery management program involves the systematic (mechanistic) delivery of the service recovery strategy to the customer. Firms that formally acknowledge the service recovery strategies that are available to them also address the manner in which they are presented to the customer. Ultimately, regaining customer satisfaction is about reestablishing the balance between customer inputs and outputs and making the customer feel that they have received some form of justice.[24] Typical customer inputs into the failure situation include the costs such as monetary, time, and energy. The outputs the customer receives include the value the customer places on the recovery strategy itself, the process the customer experiences to receive the recovery, and the interpersonal nature of the service recovery exchange. Accordingly, **perceived justice** consists of three components: distributive justice, procedural justice, and interactional justice.

**Distributive justice** focuses on the specific outcome of the firm's recovery effort. In other words, what specifically did the offending firm offer the customer to recover from the service failure, and did this outcome (output) offset the costs (inputs) of the service failure? Distributive outcomes consists of the five recovery strategies—*compensatory, restoration, apologetic, replacement,* and *unresponsive.*

**Procedural justice** examines the process that is undertaken to arrive at the final outcome. Hence, even though a customer may be satisfied with the type of recovery strategy offered, recovery evaluation may be poor, due to the process endured to obtain the recovery outcome. For example, research has indicated that when implementing identical recovery strategies, those that are implemented "promptly" are much more likely to be associated with higher recovery effectiveness ratings and retention rates than their "delayed" counterparts.

**Interactional justice** refers to the interpersonal manner in which the service recovery process is implemented and how recovery outcomes are presented. In other words,

---

**unresponsive strategy** A recovery strategy in which the firm purposely decides not to respond to customer complaints.

**perceived justice** The process where customers weigh their inputs against their outputs when forming recovery evaluations.

**distributive justice** A component of perceived justice that refers to the outcomes (e.g., compensation) associated with the service recovery process.

**procedural justice** A component of perceived justice that refers to the process (e.g., time) the customer endures during the service recovery process.

**interactional justice** A component of perceived justice that refers to human content (e.g., empathy, friendliness) that is demonstrated by service personnel during the service recovery process.

interactional justice involves the courtesy and politeness exhibited by personnel, empathy extended, and effort observed in resolving the situation. Customers are frustrated by service failures; consequently, the interpersonal nature in which the failure is addressed makes a big impact on how the firm's service recovery efforts are received.

The three components of distributed, procedural, and interactional justice must be taken into consideration when formulating effective service recovery strategies. Deploying recovery efforts that satisfy distributive justice needs without consideration of customer procedural and interactional justice needs may still result in customer defections. Service firms that are truly committed to the recovery process and retaining customers for life formally address all three aspects of justice dimensions into their service recovery management programs.

### Providing Feedback to Employees

**role conflict** A situation where the employee is caught between the opposing wishes of the firm's customers and the firm's management.

**role ambiguity** A situation where the employee does not know how to perform their job.

Most service providers are not naturals at service recovery. When faced with service failures, many employees feel trapped between the customer's expectations for service and the company's goals of cost containment. Effective recovery strategies often require service personnel to make decisions and to occasionally break company rules—the types of behaviors that many firms prohibit their employees from initiating. The end result is a classic case of **role conflict** where employees are frustrated by company rules and regulations that tie their hands and often prevent them from effectively addressing customer needs. Moreover, due to the lack of training in recovery efforts exhibited by most firms, many employees simply do not know how to recover from service failures, resulting in **role ambiguity**. Given this scenario, the likely outcome is a poor response or no response at all to customer complaints.

Providing formalized feedback to employees regarding the types of service failures and failure attributions that are likely to happen prepares employees for failure situations before they actually occur. This type of feedback sensitizes employees so they are not caught off guard when faced with unhappy customers. Similarly, providing feedback to employees regarding the types of recovery strategies available to them and the manner in which they should be offered should reduce the stressfulness and ambiguous nature of the situation. The value of providing feedback to employees cannot be overstated. Recent studies suggest that nearly half the responses to customer complaints actually reinforce a customer's negative feeling toward a firm.[25] Finally, providing feedback to employees should reinforce the firm's positive service recovery culture. By providing constructive feedback, the firm's leadership is symbolically signaling to employees that service recovery is a valued and important dimension of the firm's overall culture.

# The Art of Service Recovery: Basic Rules of Thumb

While some companies are great at delivering service until something goes wrong, other companies thrive on recovering from service failures and impressing customers in the process. Customers of service organizations often allow the firm one mistake.[26] Consequently, when a failure occurs, the customer generally provides the business with an opportunity to make amends. Unfortunately, many companies still drop the ball, and further aggravate the customer by failing to take the opportunity to recover.

When the service delivery system fails, it is the responsibility of contact personnel to react to the complaint. The content and form of the contact personnel's response determines the customer's perceived satisfaction or dissatisfaction with the service encounter.[27] Ironically, customers will remember a service encounter favorably if the contact personnel respond in a positive manner to the service failure. Hence, even though the service encounter included a service failure, the customer recalls the encounter as a

**service recovery paradox** A situation in which the customer rates performance higher if a failure occurs and the contact personnel successfully recovers from it than if the service had been delivered correctly the first time.

positive event. In fact, a customer may rate a service performance higher if a failure occurs and the employee successfully recovers from the failure than if the service were delivered correctly the first time. This phenomena has been termed the **service recovery paradox**. As firms seek to improve their service recovery efforts, the following rules of thumb should be considered.

## Measure the Costs

The costs of losing and the benefits of keeping existing customers as opposed to chasing new customers are substantial. In short, the costs of obtaining new customers are three to five times greater than those of keeping existing customers. Current customers are more receptive to the firm's marketing efforts and are, therefore, an important source of profit for the firm. In addition, existing customers ask fewer questions, are more familiar with the firm's procedures and employees, and are willing to pay more for services.

## Actively Encourage Complaints

Experts assert that actively encouraging complaints is a good way to "break the silence." Remember that complainers who actually voice their complaints to the source of the problem are the exception—most customers don't speak up. In fact, research indicates that the average company does not hear from 96 percent of its unhappy customers.[28] This doesn't mean that customers don't complain—only that they complain to friends and family rather than to the company. The average unhappy customer voices displeasure with a firm to 11 other people. If these 11 tell five other people, the firm has potentially lost 67 customers.[29] Strategies to encourage complaints include customer surveys, focus groups, and actively monitoring the service delivery process to ensure customer satisfaction throughout the encounter—before a customer leaves the premises.

## Anticipate Needs for Recovery

Every service encounter is made up of a series of critical incidents, the points in the system where the customer and the firm interact. Firms that are effective in service recovery anticipate in advance the areas in their service delivery process where failures are most likely to occur. Of course, these firms take every step possible to minimize the occurrence of the failure in the first place, but they are prepared for recovery if delivery goes awry. Experts believe that firms should pay special attention to areas in which employee turnover is high. Many high-turnover positions are low-paying customer contact positions, and employees often lack motivation and/or are inexperienced in effective recovery techniques.

## Train Employees

Expecting employees to be naturals at service recovery is unrealistic. Most employees don't know what to do when a failure occurs, and many others find making on-the-spot decisions a difficult task. Employee training in service recovery should take place on two levels. First, the firm must work at creating an awareness of customer concerns in the employee. Placing an employee in the shoes of the customer is often enlightening for an employee who has forgotten what it's like to be a customer of their own firm. For example, hospitals have made interns and staff dress in hospital gowns and had them rolled around on gurneys to experience some of the hospitals' processes firsthand.

The second level of employee training, beyond developing an appreciation for customer needs, is defining management's expectation toward recovery efforts. What are acceptable recovery strategies from management's perspective? Effective recovery often means that management has to let go and allow employees to take risks, a transition that frequently leads to the empowerment of front-line employees.

### Empower the Front Line

Effective recovery often means that the employee has to bend the firm's rules and regulations—the exact type of activity that employees are trained not to do at any cost. Often the rules and regulations of the firm tie the hands of employees when it comes to effective recovery efforts, particularly in the area of prompt response. In many instances, firms require managerial approval before any effort to compensate a customer is undertaken. However, the manager is often engaged in other duties, which delays the response and adds to frustration for both the customer and employee. For example, Ritz Carlton employees are empowered to spend up to $2,000 on recovery efforts when necessary.

### Respond Quickly

When a service failure does occur, the faster the company responds, the more likely that the recovery effort will result in a successful outcome. In fact, past studies have indicated that if the complaint is handled promptly, the company will retain 95 percent of its unhappy customers. In contrast, if the complaint is resolved at all, the firm retains only 64 percent of unhappy customers.[30] Time is of the essence. The faster the firm responds to the problem, the better the message the firm sends to customers about the value it places on pleasing them. Why not give customers what they want, when they want it? Is it really worth it to the firm for employees to actively argue with customers?

One firm that learned this lesson the hard way was a bank in Spokane, Washington. A customer who had millions of dollars in the bank's checking, investment, and trust accounts was denied having his parking validated because he "only" cashed a check as opposed to making a deposit. The customer was at a branch of the bank that was not his normal branch. After explaining the situation to the teller, who was unimpressed, and more loudly voicing his opinion to the branch manager, the customer drove to his usual branch of the bank and threatened to close his accounts if he did not receive a response from the bank's upper management by the end of the day. As incredible as it may seem, the call never came, and the customer withdrew $1 million the first thing next morning. This action did get the bank's attention, and the bank has been trying to recover ever since.[31]

### Close the Loop

Finally, one of the most important activities in service recovery is providing feedback to the customer about how that customer's complaint made a difference. Customer-oriented firms that have a sound recovery strategy solve the customer's problem. However, firms that excel at recovery go the extra mile and reestablish contact with the customer for the purpose of informing the customer how their complaint made a difference. Incorporating the customer's complaint during a training session or developing new procedures to minimize future occurrences of the failure based on the customer's complaint closes the loop and wins a customer for life!

## Summary

Many of today's service firms are great as long as the service delivery system is operating smoothly. However, once kinks develop in the system, many firms are unprepared to face unhappy customers who are looking for solutions to their problems. As evidence, nearly half the responses to customer complaints reinforce customers' negative feelings toward a firm. Consequently, firms that truly excel in customer service equip employees with a set of recovery tools to repair the service encounter when failures occur and customer complaints are voiced.

Customer complaints should be viewed as opportunities to improve the service delivery system and ensure that the customer is satisfied before the service encounter ends. This chapter discussed five types of complainers and four broad types of complaints—instrumental, noninstrumental, ostensive, and reflexive. Customers voice complaints for a number of reasons including: to have the problem resolved; to gain an emotional release from frustration; to regain some measure of control by influencing other people's evaluation of the source of the complaint; to solicit sympathy or test the consensus of the complaint; or to create an impression of intelligence.

However, it's not the complainers about whom service firms should worry; it's the people who leave without saying a word, who never intend on returning, and who inform others, thereby generating negative word-of-mouth information. A number of reasons explain why many consumers do not complain. Most simply, customers of services often do not know to whom they should complain and/or do not think complaining will do any good. Other reasons consumers fail to complain are: (1) consumer evaluation of services is highly subjective; (2) consumers tend to shift some of the blame to themselves for not clearly specifying to the service

provider their exact needs; (3) many services are technical and specialized, so many consumers do not feel qualified to voice their complaints; and (4) due to the inseparability of services, consumers may feel that a complaint is too confrontational. Regardless of whether the customer openly complains or not, the outcomes associated with poor customer experiences include voice, exit, and retaliation.

Firms that excel at service recovery often have a formalized service recovery management program consisting of a positive internal service recovery culture, failure identification, failure attribution, recovery strategy selection, recovery strategy implementation, and providing feedback to employees. Service recovery management programs consist of organic and mechanistic components. Mechanistic approaches to service recovery pertain to formal step-by-step processes that are developed to facilitate the firm's failure analysis and service recovery efforts. In contrast, organic approaches to service recovery are informal sets of values and beliefs that comprise the firm's service recovery culture.

Finally, in practical terms, firms that excel at service recovery measure the cost, actively encourage customers to complain, anticipate the need for service recovery, train employees, empower the front line, respond quickly, and close the loop. Successful service recovery efforts such as these play an important role in developing customer loyalty and retention—the featured topic of the next chapter.

# Key Terms

service failures, p. 352
service recovery, p. 352
instrumental complaints, p. 355
noninstrumental complaints, p. 356
ostensive complaints, p. 356
reflexive complaints, p. 356
voice, p. 360
exit, p. 360
retaliation, p. 361
mechanistic processes, p. 362
organic processes, p. 362

recovery culture, p. 362
core service failures, p. 363
customer needs and requests, p. 364
unprompted/unsolicited employee actions, p. 364
problematic customers, p. 365
locus, p. 366
stability, p. 367
controllability, p. 367
compensatory strategies, p. 368

restoration strategies, p. 368
apologetic strategies, p. 368
reimbursement strategies, p. 368
unresponsive strategy, p. 369
perceived justice, p. 369
distributive justice, p. 369
procedural justice, p. 369
interactional justice, p. 369
role conflict, p. 370
role ambiguity, p. 370
service recovery paradox, p. 371

# Review Questions

1. Discuss the following types of complaints: instrumental, noninstrumental, ostensive, and

reflexive. Which types of complaints are voiced the most?

**2.** Previous research has found that 96 percent of unhappy customers do not complain. Why is this so?

**3.** Which type of company is more likely to hear from unhappy customers—a company that produces goods or a company that provides services? Please explain.

**4.** Discuss the following types of failure outcomes: voice, exit, and retaliation.

**5.** Describe the basic differences between organic and mechanistic approaches to service recovery.

**6.** A national restaurant chain has hired you to categorize customer complaints. Discuss the basic differences between the four main failure identification categories, and provide restaurant-related examples of each.

**7.** Define and discuss the subclass failures associated with the implicit/explicit request failure category.

**8.** What is the service recovery paradox? What should managers learn from the service recovery paradox?

**9.** Define perceived justice. How is perceived justice used to evaluate a firm's service recovery efforts.

**10.** After a customer voices a complaint to an employee or a manager, what does it mean to "close the loop?" Why is this particular step important in handling complaints?

# Notes

1. Christopher W. L. Hart, James L. Heskett, and W. Earl Sasser, "The Profitable Art of Service Recovery," *Harvard Business Review*, (July-August 1990), pp. 148–156.

2. H. Keith Hunt, "Consumer Satisfaction, Dissatisfaction, and Complaining Behavior," *Journal of Social Issues*, 47, 1, (1991), p. 116.

3. Janelle Barlow and Claus Moller, *A Complaint Is a Gift* (San Francisco: Berrett-Koehler Publishers, Inc., 2008).

4. Mary C. Gilly, William B. Stevenson, and Laura J. Yale, "Dynamics of Complaint Management in the Service Organization," *The Journal of Consumer Affairs*, 25, 2, (1991), p. 296.

5. Oren Harari, "Thank Heaven for Complainers," *Management Review*, (January 1992), p. 60.

6. **http://www.merriam-webster.com/cgi-bin/ mwwod.pl**, accessed 29 August, 2009.

7. Mark D. Alicke, et al., "Complaining Behavior in Social Interaction," *Personality and Social Psychology Bulletin*, (June 1992), p. 286.

8. **http://www.sutherlinoptical.com/index.php? option=com_fireboard&Itemid=703&func=rules**, accessed 5 March, 2009.

9. **http://edis.ifas.ufl.edu/HR005**, accessed 5 March, 2009.

10. T. M. Amabile, "Brilliant but Cruel: Perceptions of Negative Evaluators," *Journal of Experimental Social Psychology*, 19, (1983), pp. 146–156.

11. Gilly, Stevenson, and Yale, "Dynamics of Complaint Management," p. 297.

12. Hunt, "Consumer Satisfaction," p. 114.

13. Hunt, "Consumer Satisfaction," p. 115.

14. C. Homburg and A. Fürst, "How Organizational Complaint Handling Drives Customer Loyalty: An Analysis of the Mechanistic and Organic Approach," *Journal of Marketing*, 69, (July 2005), pp. 95–114.

15. G. R. Gonzalez, K. D. Hoffman, and T. N. Ingram, "Improving Relationship Selling through Failure Analysis and Recovery Efforts: A Framework and Call to Action," *Journal of Personal Selling and Sales Management*, 25, 1, (2005), pp. 57–65.

16. Mark Magnier and John O'Dell, "Mitsubishi Admits to Complaint Cover-up," *Coloradoan*, (August 23, 2000), pp. A1–A2.

17. Mary Jo Bitner, Bernard H. Booms, and Mary Stanfield Tetreault, "The Service Encounter: Diagnosing Favorable and Unfavorable Incidents," *Journal of Marketing*, (January 1990), pp. 71–84; Mary Jo Bitner, Bernard H. Booms, and Lois A. Mohr, "Critical Service Encounters: The Employee's Viewpoint," *Journal of Marketing*, 58, (October 1994), pp. 95–106.

18. Asra Q. Nomani, "In the Skies Today, A Weird New Worry: Sexual Misconduct," *Wall Street Journal*, (June 10, 1998), p. A1; Frances Fiorino, "Passengers Who Carry, Surly Bonds of Earth' Aloft," *Aviation Week and Space Technology*, 149, 5, (December 28, 1998), p. 123.

19. S. R. Swanson and Kelley, S. W., "Service Recovery Attributions and Word-of-Mouth Intentions," *European Journal of Marketing*, 35, 1/2, (2001), pp. 194–211.

20. Ibid.

21. Valerie S. Folkes, "Consumer Reactions to Product Failure: An Attributional Approach," *Journal of Consumer Research*, 10, (March 1984), pp. 398–409.

22. Scott W. Kelley, K. Douglas Hoffman, and Mark A. Davis, "A Typology of Retail Failures and Recoveries," *Journal of Retailing*, (Winter 1993), pp. 429–445.

23. Adapted from K. Douglas Hoffman, Scott W. Kelley, and Holly M. Rotalsky, "Tracking Service Failures and Employee Recovery Efforts," *Journal of Services Marketing*, 9, 2, (1995), pp. 49–61.

24. This section adapted from K. Douglas Hoffman and Scott W. Kelley, "Perceived Justice Needs and Recovery Evaluation: A Contingency Approach," *European Journal of Marketing*, 34, 3/4, (2000), pp. 418–432.

25. Adapted from Christopher W. L. Hart, James L. Heskett, and W. Earl Sasser, "The Profitable Art of Service Recovery," *Harvard Business Review*, (July-August 1990), pp. 148–156.

26. James L. Heskett, et al., "Putting the Service-Profit Chain to Work," *Harvard Business Review*, (March-April 1994), p. 172.

27. Bitner, Booms, and Tetreault, *"The Service Encounter,"* p. 321.

28. Karl Albrecht and Ron Zemke, *Services America* (Homewood, IL: Dow-Jones Irwin, 1985) p. 6.

29. Donna Partow, "Turn Gripes into Gold," *Home Office Computing*, (September 1993), p. 24.

30. Albrecht and Zemke, *Services America*, p. 6.

31. Hart, Heskett, and Sasser, "The Profitable Art," p. 150.

# Part I: Is This Any Way
# to Run an Airline?

The following letters are detailed accounts of an actual service encounter that involved numerous service failures and the company's response. Read Part I of the letter first, which presents the customer's letter to the airlines. Answer the discussion questions listed at the end of Part I. Next, read Part II, the airline's response, and address the questions at the end of Part II.

July 23, 2010

Dear Customer Service Manager:

Through the Carolina Motor Club, my wife and I booked round-trip, first-class and clipper-class seats on the following World Airlines flights on the dates indicated:

1 July World Airlines 3072 Charlotte to Kennedy

1 July World Airlines 86 Kennedy to Munich

21 July World Airlines 87 Munich to Kennedy

21 July World Airlines 3073 Kennedy to Charlotte

We additionally booked connecting flights to and from Wilmington and Charlotte on Trans Air flights 263 (on 1 July) and 2208 (on 21 July).

The outbound flights 3072 and 86 seemed pleasant enough, especially since World Airlines had upgraded our clipper-class seats on flight 86 to first class. However, mid-flight on 86 we discovered that we had been food poisoned on flight 3072, apparently by the seafood salad that was served in first class that day (it seemed warm to us and we hesitated to eat it, but unfortunately did so anyway). My wife was so ill that, trying to get to the restroom to throw up, she passed out cold, hitting her head, and, we discovered over the next few days, apparently damaging her back. The flight attendants were very concerned and immediately tried to help her, but there was nothing they could do except help her clean herself up and get the food off her from the food trays she hit. In addition to the nausea and diarrhea, she had a large knot on her head and headaches for several days. Her lower back has been in constant pain ever since. I, too, was very ill for several days. A nice start for a vacation! But it gets worse.

During the long layover between flights at Kennedy, there was a tremendous rainstorm, and our baggage apparently was left out in it; a situation that we discovered when we arrived at our first night's lodging and discovered ALL of our clothing was

Source: Richard A. Engdahl and K. Douglas Hoffman, "World Airlines: A Customer Service Air Disaster," in Carol A. Anderson, ed., *Retailing: Concepts, Strategy, and Information* (Minneapolis/St. Paul: West, 1993) pp. 215–218.

literally wringing wet. In addition, four art prints we were bringing as gifts for friends were ruined.

The return flights were better only in that we did not get poisoned; instead we did not get fed! Flight 87 out of Munich was apparently shorthanded and, due to our seating location, the flight attendant who had to do double duty always got to us last. We had to ask for drinks; there were no hot towels left for us; the meals ran out and we were given no choice but an overdone piece of gray meat with tomato sauce on it. We tasted it, but it was odd tasting and, given our experience on flight 3072, we were afraid to eat it.

Flight 87 was delayed in boarding due to the slowness in cleaning the aircraft (according to an announcement made) and also due to the late arrival of the crew. In addition, the flight was further delayed due to a heavy rainstorm, which backed up traffic for takeoff. However, had the flight boarded on time it would not have lost its takeoff priority and could likely have taken off two hours sooner than it did. We might have been able to make our connection in Charlotte. Onboard the flight, the plane was the dirtiest and in the most disrepair of any aircraft I have ever flown on—peeling wall coverings, litter on the floor, overhead bins taped shut with duct tape, etc. As a first-class passenger I asked for some cold beer while we were waiting for the rest of the passengers to board; it was warm. We were quite hungry, having not eaten much in the past 12 hours, and asked for some peanuts; there were none—the plane had not been stocked. I asked for a pillow and blanket for my wife—there was none. What a great first-class section! There were only three flight attendants for the whole plane, and I felt sorry for the pregnant one who had to do double duty in first class and the rear cabin. She was very sympathetic to the poor conditions. I don't see how you keep employees when they are treated like that.

Due to the excess delay at Kennedy, Flight 87 was very late and we could not make our connection from Charlotte to Wilmington. As it turned out, we would have barely been able to make it if the flight had been on time, because World Airlines had changed not only the flight numbers, but also the flight times on the Kennedy-Charlotte leg of our journey—AND WE WERE NEVER NOTIFIED OF THIS CHANGE UNTIL WE ARRIVED AT THE AIRPORT! I deplaned in Raleigh to try to alert the people meeting us in Wilmington that we would not be in that night; however, it was too late and they had already gone to the airport. The gate attendant at Raleigh assured me that World Airlines would put us up for the night in Charlotte, so I returned to the plane. However, when we arrived in Charlotte, the World Airlines representative refused to take care of us, stating that, since we had not booked the Wilmington-Charlotte portion of our trip through World Airlines, "it is not our problem." Furthermore, he tried to wash his hands of it, saying we had an "illegal connection" due to the times between flights, and that he wouldn't provide lodging and meals. After I pointed out to him at least three times that the connection was not illegal when booked and World Airlines changed its flight times without notifying us, and further made it clear that not only was I not going to go away, but that there was going to be a lot more said about the matter, he finally capitulated and gave us a voucher.

After traveling for 24 hours, receiving lousy service, poor food, no amenities, it is a real pleasure to run into an argumentative SOB like your agent in Charlotte. He should be fired!!! As first-class passengers we have been treated like cattle! But, it does not end here.

Upon arriving in Wilmington the next morning, only two of our four bags arrived with us. We had to initiate a baggage trace action. Our missing bags were finally delivered to our house around 3 p.m. on July 23rd. And, SURPRISE, they were left out in the rain at Kennedy again and EVERYTHING was so wet that water poured out of the pockets. I poured water out of the hairdryer. All of our paper purchases, maps, guidebooks, photos, souvenir brochures, etc., are ruined. I don't know yet if the dryer, radio, electric toothbrush, voltage converters, etc., will work—they are drying out as this is being written. In addition, my brand new bag now has a hole in the bottom of a corner where it was obvious that World Airline baggage handlers dragged it on the tarmac (obviously a water-logged duffle bag-size piece of luggage is too heavy to lift).

As near as I can figure, we have lost at least a roll of color prints (irreplaceable); approximately $100 in travel guides and tour books, many souvenir booklets, brochures, menus, etc.; $100 in art prints; $50 in damage to luggage; an unknown amount in electronics that may not work; a lot of enjoyment due to pain and suffering resulting from illness and injury (bill for x-rays enclosed); and all sense of humor and patience for such inexcusable treatment by an airline.

If there is to be any compensation for what we have suffered, it should be in monetary form. There is no recapturing the lost time and pleasure on the vacation. The art, books, etc. (except for the photos) can be replaced...assuming we should make such a trip again. But if we do, you can be assured we would not choose World Airlines.

In closing, I am particularly angry and adamant about this whole fiasco as we wanted this vacation to be special and treated ourselves to the luxury of first-class treatment... which we got everywhere except on World Airlines...it is almost unbelievable how poorly we were treated by your airline, almost a perfect negative case study in customer service. I have purposely tried to mention every little nitpicky thing I can recall because I want you to realize just how totally bad this whole experience has been!

In disgust,

J. Q. Customer

---

# Part I: Discussion Questions

1. In general, is the above complaint letter: (1) instrumental or noninstrumental; and (2) ostensive or reflexive? Please explain your answer.
2. Identify the service failures that occurred and classify each failure according to the four main failure categories presented in Figure 13.3.
3. Select three of the service failures identified above and discuss the possible attributions for these failures in terms of locus, stability, and controllability.
4. Discuss the recovery strategy or strategies you would recommend to offset the customer's complaint.

# CASE 13

# Part II: World Airline's Response

The following is World Airline's actual response to the customer's letter. The first letter was written by the Claims Manager, and the second by the Customer Relations Manager.

September 25, 2010

Dear Mr. and Mrs. Customer:

This letter confirms the settlement agreed upon during our phone conversation just concluded.

Accordingly, we have prepared and enclosed (in duplicate) a General Release for $2,000. Both you and your wife should sign in the presence of a Notary Public, have your signatures notarized, and return the Original to this office, keeping the copy for your records. As soon as we receive the notarized Release, we will forward our draft for $2,000.

Again, our sincerest apologies to Mrs. Customer. It will be most helpful for our Customer Relations staff if you included with the Release copies of all available travel documents.

Very truly yours,

Claims Manager

October 12, 2010

Dear Mr. Customer:

Let me begin by apologizing for this delayed response and all of the unfortunate incidents that you described in your letter. Although we try to make our flights as enjoyable as possible, we obviously failed on this occasion.

Our claims manager informs me that you have worked out a potential settlement for the matter regarding the food poisoning. We regret you were not able to enjoy the food service on the other flights on your itinerary because of it. I assure you that such incidents are a rare occurrence, and that much time and effort is expended to ensure that our catering is of the finest quality.

Fewer things can be more irritating than faulty baggage handling. Only in an ideal world could we say that baggage will never again be damaged. Still, we are striving to ensure baggage is handled in such a way that if damage should occur, it will be minimized.

Flight disruptions caused by weather conditions can be particularly frustrating since, despite advanced technology, accurate forecasts for resumption of full operations cannot always be obtained as rapidly as one would wish. These disruptions are, of course, beyond the airlines' control. Safety is paramount in such situations and we sincerely regret the inconvenience caused.

We make every reasonable effort to lessen the inconvenience to passengers who are affected by schedule changes. Our practice is, in fact, to advise passengers of such changes when we have a local contact for them and time permits. We also try to obtain satisfactory alternative reservations. We are reviewing our schedule change requirements with all personnel concerned and will take whatever corrective measures are necessary to ensure that a similar problem does not arise in the future.

You made it clear in your letter that the interior of our aircraft was not attractive. We know that aircraft appearance is a reflection of our professionalism. We regret that our airplane did not measure up to our standards, since we place great emphasis on cabin maintenance and cleanliness. Please be assured that this particular matter is being investigated by the responsible management, and corrective action will be taken.

As tangible evidence of our concern over your unpleasant trip, I have enclosed two travel vouchers, which may be exchanged for two first-class tickets anywhere that World Airlines flies. Once again, please accept our humble apology. We hope for the opportunity to restore your faith in World Airlines by providing you with completely carefree travel.

Sincerely,
Customer Relations Manager

---

## Part II: Discussion Questions

1. Describe the recovery strategies that were offered by the company to offset the customer's complaint. Classify the recovery strategies based on the recovery strategy categories provided in this chapter.
2. Discuss the adequacy of the recovery strategies offered in terms of meeting the customer's distributive, procedural, and interactional justice needs.
3. Explain what the company and its employees can learn from this complaint letter.

CHAPTER **14**

# Strategies for Facilitating Customer Loyalty and Retention

## CHAPTER OBJECTIVES

After reading this chapter, you should be able to:

- Understand the differences between the service marketing concepts of loyalty and retention and the relationship between the two.

- Discuss why the concept of customer retention has become increasingly important.

- Master successful tactics for retaining existing customers.

- Describe emerging customer retention programs.

- Explain defection management.

The major objective of this chapter is to introduce you to the concept of customer retention.

### HARRAH'S LOOKS BEYOND GAMBLERS FOR NEW LOYALTY PROGRAMS

Customer loyalty and retention are important service goals for many industries, but perhaps no company has taken it more seriously than Harrah's Entertainment, Inc. With nearly 80 casino resorts on four continents with brand names such as Harrah's, Paris, Bally's, Caesars Palace, Horseshoe, the Flamingo, and the World Series of Poker, Harrah's Entertainment

AP Photo/Isaac Brekken

is the world's largest provider of branded casino entertainment. Clearly, Harrah's wants your business and wants you to return time and time again. According to the company's website, "Harrah's Entertainment is focused on building loyalty and value with its customers through a unique combination of great service, excellent products, unsurpassed distribution, operational excellence and technology leadership."

Harrah's was one of the first companies in the gaming industry to use its loyalty program, Total Rewards, to identify its best and most loyal customers, and to reward these customers in ways they had never been rewarded before. After enrolling in the Total Rewards program, customers simply swipe/insert their Total Rewards card each time they play at a slot machine or visit a gaming table. Regular points are allocated to the rewards card based on the amount of the bet. After a certain number of regular points have been accumulated, bonus points are then added to the customer's card which can qualify them for Gold, Platinum, or Diamond Club membership. Club membership and reward points can be redeemed for perks such as speedy check-ins, free rooms, free food, spa treatments, and show tickets. Consequently, the Total Rewards program enables customers not only to win money at the casino, but also to win other perks through their involvement with Harrah's loyalty program.

The Total Rewards Program has been a huge success for Harrah's. The program has over 40 million members with over 6 million active customers who have used their cards in the last year. Harrah's estimates that over 75 percent of its gaming revenues are now tracked by the card. The loyalty program has also increased cross-market play—the amount of gambling revenue generated by customers outside of their home markets. For example, customers who typically gamble at Harrah's in Las Vegas may also visit Harrah's locations in Atlantic City. Customers stay loyal to Harrah's since points continue to accumulate on their cards wherever the customer gambles. Since implementing the loyalty program, Harrah's has also seen a big increase in high-roller business as the company experienced double-digit increases in Platinum and Diamond club memberships. Data obtained from the loyalty cards also allowed Harrah's to better understand its low-roller customers that make up nearly 40 percent of Harrah's revenues. Many other casino loyalty programs simply overlook the low-roller segment of their business. Harrah's redesigned its casino floors to include more lower denomination slot machines and video poker games, which netted a 12 percent increase in slot revenues.

More recently, Harrah's has expanded its loyalty program and now offers reward points to non-gamblers who spend money on entertainment, restaurants, and other services. Harrah's generates approximately 20 percent of its revenues from non-gambling sources, and is serious about expanding its non-gambling offerings as the U.S. economy struggles and gambling revenues decline. In comparison, MGM Mirage, Inc. generates nearly 58 percent of its total revenues from non-gambling sources. Overall, the success of Harrah's loyalty program compared to the competition has been attributed to the company's recognition that different customers have different needs and desires. Clearly, gamblers and non-gamblers have different expectations of the gaming industry. As a result, the perks provided by the Total Rewards program offer customers, whatever their folly, what they truly value. In turn, customers, gamblers and non-gamblers alike, reward Harrah's with their loyalty.

Sources:
1. **http://www.cioinsight.com/c/a/Past-News/Make-Every-Customer-More-Profitable-Harrahs-Entertainment-Inc/**, accessed 31 March, 2009.
2. **http://www.eweek.com/c/a/IT-Management/Harrahs-Bets-on-IT/**, accessed 31 March, 2009.
3. **http://www.harrahs.com/**, accessed 31 March, 2009.

# Introduction

This chapter focuses on the important service concepts of customer loyalty and retention. Customer loyalty and retention are key strategies in today's leading-edge service firms as both concepts reflect a more futuristic outlook than does the concept of

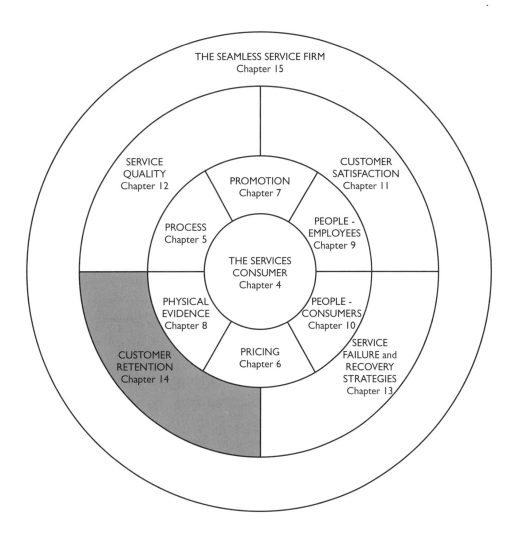

customer satisfaction. As discussed in Chapter 11, customer satisfaction measures assess the customer's current state of evaluation but fail to tap into the customer's set of changing needs. Consequently, additional measures that assess the customer's commitment to the service firm, evolving customer expectations, the probability of future purchases with the firm, and the customer's willingness to conduct business with competitive firms are necessary in order to truly assess the firm's customer loyalty and retention efforts.

## What Is Customer loyalty?

**customer loyalty**
Reflects an emotional attachment as well as a business attachment to the service firm.

Although many business people may use the terms loyalty and retention interchangeably, for our purposes **customer loyalty** reflects an emotional attachment as well as a business attachment to the service firm. As one Harvard service guru explains, "It's not enough to have [customer satisfaction]. You need the hearts and minds of the customer to close the loyalty gap."[1] My father built and managed a golf course in northeastern Ohio for nearly 40 years and many of our customers were loyal customers for decades. We knew their families, they knew my family, and every spring was an extended family reunion as the golf course opened for each new season. Looking back, I can now actually say these were "loyal" customers as opposed to "retained" customers because there was a lot of

"My family? Hell no, those are my clients!"

Although many business people may use the terms loyalty and retention interchangeably, customer loyalty reflects an emotional attachment as well as a business attachment to the firm.

competition in the area. When a service firm has no competition, loyalty matters less since customers have nowhere else to go. However, as competition enters the marketplace, establishing and maintaining customer loyalty is essential to keeping customers from defecting to the competition.

Ultimately, customer loyalty is a deeper conviction to the firm than pure retention alone. It is intuitively appealing to believe that customer satisfaction leads to customer loyalty which leads to customer retention. The truth is that without loyalty, customer satisfaction may or may not lead to customer retention, and retained customers may not be loyal customers. The bottom line is that the service firm cannot simply assume that retained customers are loyal customers. Consequently, service firms wishing to build their business and nurture strong customer relationships need to understand the added strategic value of customer loyalty over customer retention.

## You're Great, but It's Over!

Although intuitively higher levels of customer satisfaction would be expected to be associated with higher levels of customer retention, the relationship does not always necessarily exist.[2] Based on a survey of 767 business executives who purchase pensions and health insurance products for their firms, customer satisfaction is not necessarily the "holy grail" of customer retention. Although 75 percent of the executives claimed to be satisfied with their current financial service supplier, 66 percent reported that they were planning to find an alternative source for their financial services needs. According to industry experts, what seems to be lacking are the personal relationships that bind suppliers and customers. Other clues indicating that a break-up may be imminent include that only 49 percent of purchasers thought their suppliers were highly ethical; and only 28 percent believed that the supplier treated their own customers well. Even among their own members, less than 50 percent of financial service companies claimed to be loyal to their providers.

The shaky link between customer satisfaction and customer retention also exists in B2C markets. Consider the following cases where: (1) customers are not satisfied, yet they are retained; and (2) customers are satisfied, yet they defect to competitive offerings.

Low Satisfaction/High Retention

- *Regulated monopoly or few substitutes (e.g., hospitals, airlines)*
- *Dominant brand equity (e.g., Microsoft)*
- *High cost of switching (e.g., physicians, financial institutions)*
- *Proprietary technology (e.g., Microsoft)*

High Satisfaction/Low Retention

- *Commodity products or little or no differentiation (e.g., rental cars)*
- *Consumer indifference (low involvement) (e.g., car wash, drycleaner)*
- *Many substitutes (e.g., lawn care service)*
- *Low costs of switching (e.g., trash collection services)*

## Strategies for Cultivating Customer Loyalty

There is an old adage that states "It's just the little touches after the average man would quit, that makes the master's fame." These are well chosen words that reflect the relational aspects that can be cultivated with both customers and employees that enhance customer loyalty. The services marketing literature is full of suggestions to build customer loyalty. These common themes include:

- *Developing a Proper Perspective*—Managers and employees of service firms need to remember that the company exists to meet the needs and wants of its consumers. Processing customers like raw materials on an assembly line or being rude to customers is incredibly shortsighted. Companies such as USAir employ slogans such as, *"The U in USAir starts with you, the passenger."* Credos such as this affect customer expectations and reinforce to employees exactly where the firm's priorities lie. Interacting with the public is not an easy task, and, unfortunately, employees occasionally fail to maintain the proper perspective. The same questions may have to be asked over and over, and not every customer is polite. Maintaining the proper perspective involves a customer-oriented frame of mind and an attitude for service. Employees need to remember that every customer has his or her own personal set of needs, and that the customer's, not the employee's, expectations define performance.
- *Staying in Touch*—Contacting customers between service encounters is a useful approach in building relationships with the service firm. The key is making customer contact sincere and personal. Typical approaches include sending birthday, get-well, and/or anniversary cards; writing personal notes congratulating customers for their personal successes; and keeping in touch with consumers concerning the performance of past services rendered and offering assistance if necessary. The goal of this tactic is to communicate to customers that the firm genuinely cares for their wellbeing.
- *Providing Discretionary Effort*—Discretionary effort is behavior beyond the call of duty. It is the Proctor & Gamble salesperson who voluntarily bags groceries at the grand opening of a new grocery store. It is the hotel that sends items misplaced by its customers to their homes at no charge. It is the oil company that recognizes the special needs of its customers during difficult times such as a natural disaster (see Figure 14.1). Discretionary effort involves countless personal touches—the little things that distinguish a discrete business transaction from an ongoing relationship (see E-Services in Action).

## E-SERVICES *IN ACTION*

### I Heart Zappos

As this online shoe retailer's website proudly boasts, "If you are looking for the best service and the best selection of shoes, clothes, and handbags, shop at Zappos.com!" Thousands of customers would agree, and have subsequently pledged their loyalty to this popular e-tailer. Much of Zappos' success has come from customer referrals that have been posted on blogs and picked up by authors of popular trade books such as *A Complaint is Gift*.

One such story involves a woman who purchased seven pairs of shoes from Zappos for her mother who was terminally ill. The mother had lost a lot of weight throughout her illness and the daughter was no longer sure of the correct shoe size. When placing the order, the daughter ordered different sizes of the same shoes so that the correct size would be included in the order. The mother died shortly after the shoes arrived, and the daughter (occupied by more important thoughts) missed out on Zappos' 15-day free return policy. A thoughtful Zappos's customer service representative, remembering the daughter's order and that the shoe size was a guess, contacted the customer and asked her if she would like to return any of the shoes. After learning of the customer's mother's death, the representative made arrangements with UPS to go to the women's house and return the shoes free of charge. In addition, Zappos sent the customer a huge flower arrangement the following day. Overcome with the company's kindness, the daughter immediately posted a message online that read, "I burst into tears. I'm a sucker for kindness, and if that isn't one of the nicest things I've ever had happen to me, I don't know what is. So...IF YOU BY SHOES ONLINE, GET THEM FROM ZAPPOS. With hearts like theirs, you know they're good to do business with."

Online or offline, companies that have a heart are rewarded with consumer loyalty. The woman's comment has been linked with thousands of other websites, and discussed in hundreds of blogs by people referring to Zappos heart. It's a great story and exemplifies how online service providers can connect with their customers through simple acts of human kindness.

Source: Jane Barlow and Claus Moller, *A Complaint Is a Gift* (San Francisco, CA: Berrett Koehler Publishers, Inc., 2008) pp. 33–34.

- *Leading through top-down loyalty*—Upper management that is loyal to its employees create a service culture where employees pass that loyalty onto their customers. Employee loyalty drives customer loyalty.
- *Training and empowering employees*—Convey to employees the expectation for great service delivery and provide them with the tools, training, and autonomy necessary to deliver it.
- *Providing incentives*—Although you may already have the hearts and minds of your customers, they love you more when you love them back. Incentives are a nice value-added feature that both cultivate and maintain loyalty.
- *Remembering your customers' purchases*—A good memory about past customer purchases signals to the customer that they are important individuals and not part of a mass known only as "the customer." Remembering past purchases not only builds loyalty, but also helps sell goods and services that complement their original purchase.
- *Building trust through reliability*—Trust is defined as a firm belief or confidence in the honesty, integrity, and reliability of another person. In the service environment, three major components of trust are: (1) the service provider's expertise, (2) the service provider's reliability, and (3) the service provider's concern for the customer. Generally speaking, strategies for building trust include:

  - *Protecting confidential information;*
  - *Telling customers the truth, even when it hurts;*

**FIG-14.1** An Example of Discretionary Effort

```
BP OIL COMPANY                                              [BP]
101 PROSPECT AVENUE, WEST
CLEVELAND OH 44115

September 18, 1996

K DOUGLAS HOFFMAN
WILMINGTON NC 28409

RE: 04122

Dear K DOUGLAS HOFFMAN:

We are very concerned about the devastation from the recent hurricane in your
area. We hope you have not been personally affected.

If you have, we know how disruptive and financially burdensome such a loss of
property is. We'll be happy to give you additional time to pay any balance that may
be due on your credit card account with no finance charges or late fees.

Just write a short note at the bottom of this letter to let us know how you wish
to extend payment over the next few months. Or, you may call us toll free at
1-800-883-5527 to work out an arrangement.

We realize this is a small gesture but we wanted to offer a helping hand to you as
one of our valued customers.


BP Oil Company

Credit Card Account Number: 04122

Payment Plan:
_____
_____
_____
_____
_____
_____
_____
_____
_____
```

- *Providing customers with full information*—the pros and the cons; and
- *Being dependable, courteous, and considerate with customer.*

- *Flexibility*—Nothing depersonalizes a service faster than referring to a company policy. *"Excuses*—such as 'That's our policy'—will lose more customers than setting the store on fire."[3]
- *Replace technology with humans*—*"Your call is important to us!"* voiced by an automated telephone system does little to cultivate customer loyalty. For many, technology is viewed as yet another tactic the firm implements to distance itself from its customers.
- *Be great with names*—Nothing personalizes a relationship faster than calling the customer by name. Great service hotels, such as The Fullerton in Singapore, have mastered the art of greeting the customer by name, even if the customer has never been there before. Employees know who is checking in each day and the use of the web often provides staff information and photos of guests before they arrive—talk about going the extra distance and making a great first impression!
- *Being available when you're needed the most*—When a customer has a problem is not the time to crawl under a rock and hide. Every service firm should stand behind what it sells and ensure that every transaction is handled to the customer's satisfaction. Most customers are realistic and understanding. Many times customers are simply looking for advice and alternative solutions to problems, and are not looking

for *someone to blame.* Expressing a sincere concern for the customer's situation reinforces the firm's customer retention efforts.

Ultimately, customer loyalty leads to customer retention and all of its associated benefits. The discussion that follows outlines the continued importance and benefits of customer retention, emerging customer retention programs, and guidelines for developing a defection management program.

## What Is Customer Retention?

**customer retention**
Focusing the firm's marketing efforts toward the existing customer base.

Simply stated, **customer retention** refers to focusing the firm's marketing efforts toward the existing customer base. More specifically, in contrast to seeking new customers, firms engaged in customer retention efforts work to satisfy existing customers with the intent of developing long-term relationships between the firm and its current clientele for the purpose of growing its business (see Figure 14.2).

Many examples of successful customer retention efforts are based on the firm's ability to redefine its existing business. Companies are challenging themselves, now more than ever before, to look at what their goods and services really provide to their customers. Understanding consumer uses of goods and services and the steps required by consumers to obtain the product often leads to ideas that assist the firm in differentiating itself from its competition. Providing value-added services to the consumer reshapes the traditional and often confrontational supplier–customer relationship into more of a partnership.

**FIG-14.2** Cost of
New vs. Old Customers:
**The Leaky Bucket**

The leaky bucket depicted below portrays two companies. Each company is working hard to generate new customers each year and has managed to generate 10 percent more new customers per year, perhaps by developing new services or targeting new segments. However, not all of the customers acquired by the firm in a given year stay with the firm. The retention rate is not 100 percent; there is a "hole in the bucket." For company A, the "hole" is small, and the company loses only 5 percent of its customers each year. As a result, after 14 years company A has doubled the number of its customers. Company B has a bigger problem, because retention is 90 percent and the "hole in the bucket" is 10 percent. As a result, company B loses and gains customers at the same rate.

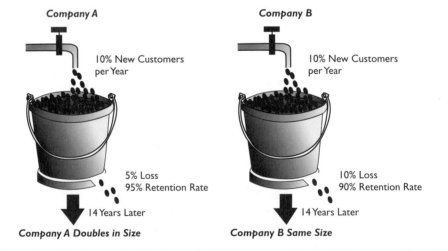

Note: Adapted from Frederick F. Reichheld and W. Earl Sasser, Jr., "Zero Defections: Quality Comes to Services," *Harvard Business Review,* (September–October 1990), pp. 106–107.

Source: John E.G. Bateson and K. Douglas Hoffman, *Managing Services Marketing,* 4th ed. (Fort Worth, TX: Dryden Publishers, 1999).

After rethinking its business, British Airways no longer viewed itself solely as a provider of air transportation.[4] As a result, the airline has revised its focus on first-class transatlantic customers to include improved services on the ground, as well as in the air. Realizing that many of its customers would like to sleep through the night rather than eat huge meals followed by lavish desserts, accompanied with an endless supply of alcohol and bad movies, British Airways now provides its first-class passengers with the option of having dinner on the ground in its first-class lounge. Once on board, passengers are provided British Airway pajamas, real pillows, and a duvet to curl up in.

Once the plane has landed, and after a good night's sleep, passengers are provided with breakfast on the ground, as well as a shower and dressing room so that they can be fresh for the day's events. British Airways will even have passengers' clothes pressed while they are enjoying their breakfasts. With value-added services such as these, it is not surprising to learn that British Airway's profits have steadily increased.

## The Trend toward Customer Retention

Today's market is totally different than the ones global marketers have experienced in the past. Competition is intense, and differentiation among competitors is minimal.[5] Let's face it, there is no great deal of difference today among many services, be they insurance companies, banks, or eye exams. Due to the relative parity among brand choices, consumer risk associated with switching brands has been drastically minimized. For example, consumers may be indifferent about the firm that holds their car insurance policy. Consequently, many consumers have forgone brand loyalty and selected the product that offers the best value—the best product at the best price.

Unfortunately, the majority of marketers today have reacted to this new environment of "brand parity" and "nonbrand loyalty" by constantly chasing new customers. Firms that are constantly seeking new customers are engaged in **conquest marketing**. Typical conquest marketing techniques include offering discounts and markdowns and developing promotions that encourage new business. Results obtained from conquest marketing are generally successful in the short run due to customers' lack of brand loyalty. The firm engaged in conquest marketing may even get a repeat purchase or two. However, as soon as the competition offers another "discount special," the firm loses many of the customers it previously obtained.

To this day, many companies spend the bulk of their marketing efforts on attracting new customers instead of on keeping the customers they already have. If you find this hard to believe, consider how many promotional pieces of mail you receive from financial institutions pertaining to credit cards. Who do you hear from more—your current bank, or new banks that want your business? If you are like many of us, new banks are constantly filling your mailbox with promotional offers. The long-term profitability of firms that solely rely on conquest marketing techniques is highly questionable. When one considers the cost of a sales promotion to attract customers, along with the financial incentives to lure in new business, profits are minimized.

Even when conquest marketing techniques are successful, they sometimes lead to the demise of the firm. All too often, businesses are tempted to grow as fast as they can in order to increase their sales volume. However, because of the inseparability inherent in services, extensive growth of many service firms is commonly associated with a decrease in the quality of service provided. Consider the plight that Starbucks found itself in after years of phenomenal growth. The coffee giant is now shrinking the size of its operation to return to basics and recapture the loyalty of its customers.

Considering the costs associated with winning new customers, the only way to make a profit and avoid the continuous cycle of price discounts is to increase the lifetime

**conquest marketing** A marketing strategy for constantly seeking new customers by offering discounts and markdowns and developing promotions that encourage new business.

spending of existing customers. Customer retention is, therefore, far more important than customer attraction. Given today's marketing environment, coddling existing clients makes good economic sense.

## The Importance of Customer Retention

Customer retention has become increasingly important because of several changes in the marketing environment. First, many consumer markets throughout the world are stagnant. The once vibrant global economy has been rocked to its core. Although the situation varies throughout the world, in many places population growth has slowed. Consequently, there are not as many new customers as there once were, and those customers who do exist are spending less.

Another reason customer retention has become important to today's marketers is the increase in competition. Factors contributing to increased competition include the relative parity and lack of differential advantage of goods and services on the market; deregulated industries that now must compete for customers in an open market; the growth of online alternatives; and accessible market information that is available to more firms, thereby minimizing informational advantages among competing firms. As a result of the increase in competition and the predominant use of conquest marketing techniques, firms are finding that retaining their current customer base is now more challenging than ever.

Customer retention is also becoming increasingly important because of the rising costs of marketing. In particular, the cost of mass marketing advertising, the primary tool of conquest marketers, has substantially increased. For example, the cost of a 30-second television spot in 1965 was $19,700. In contrast, the average cost of producing a 30-second national television commercial in 2009 is approximately $350,000.[6] Coupled with the increased cost of advertising has been the loss of the advertiser's "share of voice." Due to the shorter time period now allotted for individual commercials (the average length of commercials has decreased from 60 seconds, to 30 seconds, to 15 seconds), the number of commercials has increased by approximately 25 percent over the past 10 years. Hence, firms are competing for attention in a medium that is constantly expanding. In addition, new forms of advertising have evolved such as Facebook and YouTube; consequently, consumer markets have become more fragmented, which

"We have to develop a new way to build our customer base. Antispam software has put a dent in our marketing strategy."

As conquest marketing techniques have become more expensive and more complicated to deploy, marketing activities aimed at retaining customers have become increasingly important.

further dilutes the chances of an advertiser's message reaching its intended target audience.

Interestingly, the recent growth of direct mail marketing is directly attributed to the high costs of mass marketing and subsequent heightened importance of customer retention efforts. Marketers became more selective about how and where their advertising dollars were spent. As a result, the databases built for direct marketing provided the means to identify current customers and track purchases. Subsequently, advertising to current customers became much more efficient than mass marketing in reaching the firm's target market.

Changes in the channels of distribution utilized in today's markets are also having an impact on customer retention. In many cases, the physical distance between producer and consumer is increasing. The continued growth of nonstore retailing such as the Internet and direct mail catalogs are prime examples of how the physical distance between the provider of products and the customer is changing. Transactions can be conducted by phone, mail order, or over the Internet, thereby limiting the physical contact between the provider and the customer. Firms engaged in customer retention efforts should be aware of the old adage, "Out of sight, out of mind," and realize that separation from the customer does not diminish their obligation to the customer.

Another change in the channel of distribution is the increasing use of market intermediaries, or "third parties," that assist in the transaction between provider and customer. In this scenario, the marketing intermediary becomes a surrogate provider and, as such, represents the service firm that produces the product. Although the use of third parties and other market intermediaries increases the firm's market coverage, it can also adversely affect customer retention rates. For example, a travel agent who sells an airline's service may misrepresent the airline (e.g., flight times, seating arrangements, and so on) and damage the relationship between the customer and the airline. Again, firms engaged in customer retention efforts must recognize that the physical distance between themselves and their customers does not minimize their responsibility.

Customer retention has also become increasingly important to firms because today's customers have changed. Typical consumers today compared with past generations are more informed about purchasing decisions, command more discretionary income, and are increasingly skeptical about the average firm's concern for their business. Consequently, firms that engage in customer retention practices are usually noticed by today's consumers and rewarded for their efforts via repeat sales.

## The Benefits of Customer Retention

Some experts believe that customer retention has a more powerful effect on profits than market share, scale economies, and other variables commonly associated with competitive advantage. In fact, studies have indicated that as much as 95 percent of profits come from long-term customers via profits derived from sales, referrals, and reduced operating costs (see Figure 14.3).[7]

### Profits Derived from Sales

One of the key benefits of customer retention is repeat sales (see Figure 14.4). In addition to the base profit derived from sales, profits are also acquired from increased purchase frequency and interest rates applied to higher balances on charge accounts (for firms that offer credit services). An added bonus of retaining existing customers is that existing customers are willing to pay more for a firm's offering. This occurs because customers become accustomed to the firm, its employees, and the manner in which the service is delivered. Subsequently, a relationship develops that lowers the customer's risk. In

**FIG-14.3** Why Customers Are More Profitable over Time

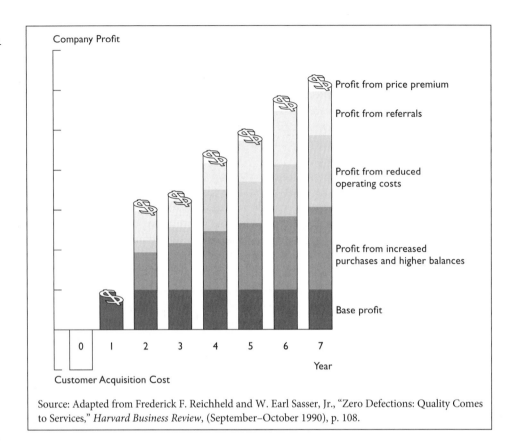

Source: Adapted from Frederick F. Reichheld and W. Earl Sasser, Jr., "Zero Defections: Quality Comes to Services," *Harvard Business Review*, (September–October 1990), p. 108.

**FIG-14.4** Why E-Shoppers Come Back

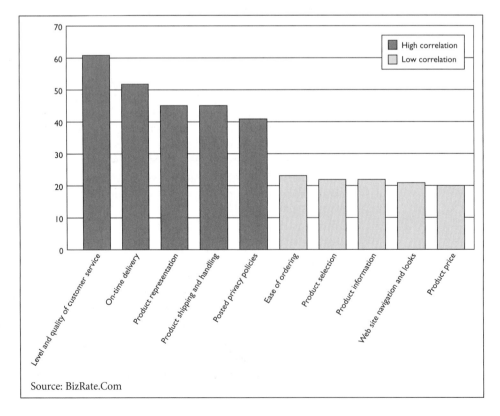

Source: BizRate.Com

essence, repeat customers are willing to pay more for purchases and purchase more frequently in situations where the uncertainty of the outcome is lessened or removed. For example, credit card companies encourage their existing customers to use their credit cards when shopping online and protect them from fraud in the process.

Increasing customer retention rates can have a profound effect on a firm's profitability. For example, past studies have shown that a 5 percent increase in retention rate can translate into 85 percent higher profits for a branch bank, 50 percent higher profits for an insurance broker, and 30 percent higher profits for an auto-service chain.[8]

## Profits from Reduced Operating Costs

Past research has indicated that it costs three to five times less to keep a customer than to get a new one.[9] The trusting relationship that develops between customers and the firm makes existing customers more receptive to the firm's marketing efforts and, therefore, easier to sell new services to. This, in turn, lowers the cost of the firm's marketing efforts.

Overall, long-term customers tend to have lower maintenance costs. Existing customers become accustomed to the company, employees, and procedures; therefore, they ask fewer questions and have fewer problems and require less attention. Over the years, airline price wars presented a few unintended consequences for the airlines. On one hand, the lower prices achieved their desired effect—increasing sales. Many of these sales, however, were to passengers who had never or rarely flown before, and who were unfamiliar with ticketing practices, check-in processes, baggage restrictions and handling, and typical airline behavior. Even common services such as complimentary beverages had to be explained to new passengers who were unfamiliar with the term "complimentary." In one particularly disturbing instance, a passenger requested instructions on how to "roll down her window." The end result of adding new customers to the mix was stressed-out and overworked flight attendants and lower than average quality service to existing customers.

## Profits from Referrals

Another major benefit of customer retention is the positive word-of-mouth advertising generated by satisfied customers. Existing customers are necessary for a firm to develop a reputation that attracts new business. Satisfied customers often refer businesses to their friends and family, which, in turn, reinforces their own decision. Personal sources of information are particularly important to service consumers because of intangibility and the perception of increased risk associated with service purchases. New business attributed to current customer referrals can be dramatic. For example, one leading home builder in the United States has found that 60 percent of its business is based on referrals from past customers.[10]

## Clarifying the Benefits of Customer Retention

It seems like a company's best customers would be its most loyal customers, but are they really the best?[11] New research has found that the link between retention and profitability may be much weaker than most think. In a study of four companies' customer databases, there was little to no evidence that customers who purchased on a regular basis were less expensive to serve, less sensitive to prices, or referred the companies' services more than other customers. In fact, in some cases, just the opposite was found. For example, in the high-tech industry, high volume customers understand their worth to the selling company and tend to demand extra service and lower prices.

Evaluating the worth of a customer has been traditionally measured through techniques such as RFM which stands for recency, frequency, and monetary value. Recency captures the time period since the last purchase, such as within the last three months, in the past three to six months, or between six months and one year ago. Customers who have made more recent purchases are given a higher score. Frequency measures the number of times a customer has made a purchase within each of these time periods (e.g., once, twice, four purchases, etc.). The higher the frequency of customer purchases, the higher the score assigned to the customer. Scores obtained from recency and frequency assessments are then added together, and the monetary value of these purchases is taken into consideration. This research indicates that companies must look beyond customer retention percentages alone and link retention to profitability to determine which customers are truly the best.

## Determining the Lifetime Value of a Customer

**lifetime value (LTV) of a customer** The average dollar amount per sale multiplied by the average number of times customers reorder (discounted to the present).

Another useful method for determining the real value of customer retention is to determine the average **lifetime value (LTV) of a customer**[12] The idea here is that a customer is worth much more than their one time purchase. As the firm's customers return time after time, the LTV of its customer base increases. Consequently, the true value of customers is the value of all the purchases they have made plus the value of all the purchases they are likely to make in the future (discounted to the present). Service firms wishing to calculate the LTV can do so by multiplying their average sales by the average number of times that customers return to make a purchase.

Hence, to estimate the lifetime value of an average customer:

$$\text{Average Lifetime Value} = (\text{Average Sale}) \times (\text{Estimated Number of Times Customers Reorder})$$

**lifetime profit (LTP) of a customer** The average profit per sale multiplied by the average number of times customers reorder (discounted to the present).

Firms wishing to determine how much they can spend to acquire customers can do so by first calculating the average **lifetime profit (LTP) of a customer**. To determine LTP, average profit per sale is multiplied by the estimated number of times customers reorder. Ultimately, LTP provides the average amount of profit the firm expects to receive from each customer.

$$\text{Average Lifetime Profit} = (\text{Average Profit Per Sale}) \times (\text{Estimated Number of Times Customers Reorder})$$

Once the firm's LTP has been calculated, it can then be used to determine how much money a firm can spend to acquire customers and still make profits in the long run. This figure is simply calculated by adding the average customer acquisition cost to the LTP figure. In other words:

$$\text{Break-Even Customer Acquisition Cost} = (\text{Average Lifetime Profit}) + (\text{Average Customer Acquisition Cost})$$

**customer acquisition cost** The monetary amount spent on marketing and other activities to acquire a new customer.

The end result is how much money the firm can spend to acquire each new customer and break even. Firms that spend less than this amount to acquire each new customer will turn a profit. The lesson to learn here is that firms can spend more than LTP to acquire each new customer and should spend less than LTP plus the average **customer acquisition cost** to make a profit. Students wishing for a more in-depth description of LTV and LTP, particularly with respect to discounting present values, can find a multitude of examples on the Internet.[13]

## Is It Always Worthwhile to Keep a Customer?

Although saving every customer at any cost is a controversial topic and opinions are divided, many experts now believe that every customer is not always worth retaining.

In fact, it is totally acceptable in some instances to "fire" the customer. Guidelines for severing relationships with customers include the following conditions:[14]

- *The account is no longer profitable.*
- *Conditions specified in the sales contract are no longer being met.*
- *Customers are abusive to the point that it lowers employee morale.*
- *Customer demands are beyond reasonable, and fulfilling those demands would result in poor service for the remaining customer base.*
- *The customer's reputation is so poor that associating with the customer tarnishes the image and reputation of the selling firm.*

Other experts believe that, although these criteria are valid, a more appropriate strategy is to retreat but keep the lines of communication open. Overall, retention efforts should focus on retaining the most profitable customers. Although zero defections to competitors is an admirable goal worth pursuing, the investment in customer retention and service recovery programs may not be economically justified in every case. Moreover, it is argued that focusing too heavily on customer retention efforts can harm the firm in the long run if customer acquisition and development efforts are completely overlooked in the process.[15]

## Customer Retention Programs

Over the years, several marketing programs have surfaced that typify the recent interest in customer retention strategies such as frequency marketing, relationship marketing, aftermarketing, and service guarantees. Each of these programs exemplifies the effort firms are willing to extend to build customer retention.

### Frequency Marketing

**frequency marketing**
Marketing technique that strives to make existing customers purchase more often from the same provider.

The primary goal of **frequency marketing** is to make existing customers more productive.[16] In short, customers become more productive as they increase the frequency of their purchases with the same provider. For example, service customers may attend more shows at the local theater, purchase more or increase the values of existing policies from their insurance agent, or dine out more often at their favorite restaurant.

To begin, the first step in implementing a frequency marketing program is to collect data on the firm's best customers and to determine their level of relationship with the firm. The level of relationship pertains to the number of different services the customer purchases. For example, bank customers may have a relationship with their bank not only through checking accounts, but also through savings accounts, car loans, investments, or a home mortgage. The next step in establishing a frequency marketing program is to

An airline's frequent flyer program is a classic example of an effective frequency marketing strategy.

communicate with customers on a personal level. Communications need to be *interactive* to the point that customers can ask questions and establish a relationship with the firm and *action-oriented* in that the firm's communications incite customers to respond. Personal communications demonstrate to customers that the firm recognizes the importance of their patronage. When reward programs are developed that prompt customers to act within a certain time frame, the communications become action-oriented. Perhaps the most successful frequency marketing programs of all time are the frequent-flyer programs. Airlines throughout the globe have developed frequent-flyer programs designed to reward passengers for flying with one airline or a network of airlines that share the same frequency marketing program. For example, the Star Alliance network shared by United, Thai, and Lufthansa as well as nearly 20 other airlines previously was voted the Best Airline Alliance at the Business Traveler Awards.[17] Passenger loyalty is rewarded with credit for "miles," which can be redeemed for discounted fares, free flights, upgraded seating, and a variety of other goods and services.

In addition to appealing to the pleasure traveler, frequent-flyer programs are the easiest way for airlines to compete for business travelers who often travel 10 to 12 times a year or more. Due to the nature of their activities, business travelers often book flights at the last minute and pay higher fares than pleasure travelers. To attract the more profitable business flyer segment, most airlines now assign their best customers, customers who fly more than 25,000 to 30,000 miles a year, to premium memberships that include reservation hotlines, early boarding, bonus mileage, and frequent upgrade privileges.[18]

The frequent-flyer programs have become so popular that they are now referred to as the "Green Stamps of the 1990s." In addition to redeeming miles for airline associated discounts, miles are increasingly redeemed for things other than flights, such as free nights at hotels, savings bonds, restaurant meals, cruises, and merchandise from a variety of retailers. This new way to redeem miles has been accompanied with new ways to earn the miles as well. Other businesses, such as credit card and telephone companies, have signed on with the airlines and typically pay an airline 2 cents per mile to help retain their own customers as well as attract new ones. Travel experts report that frequent-flyer program members earn, on average, 40 percent of their miles without flying and redeem 10 percent of their miles for things other than free trips.[19]

## Relationship Marketing

**relationship marketing**
Marketing technique based on developing long-term relationships with customers.

Another marketing approach that typifies the newfound interest in customer retention efforts is relationship marketing. **Relationship marketing** is the union of customer service, quality, and marketing. More specifically, the relationship marketing perspective takes place on two levels: macro and micro.[20] At the macro level, firms engaged in relationship marketing recognize that the marketing activity impacts customer markets, employee markets, supplier markets, internal markets, and influencer markets (such as financial and government markets). Simultaneously, at the micro level, relationship marketing recognizes that the focus of marketing is changing from completing the single transaction and other conquest marketing practices to building a long-term relationship with existing customers (see Sustainability and Services in Action).

Proponents of relationship marketing believe that their firm's products will come and go; consequently, the real unit of value is the long-term relationship with the customer. For example, construction and agricultural equipment manufacturer John Deere & Co. measures its success in terms of generations of farming families that have used its products. Baxter International, a $9 billion healthcare products and services company, has also embraced the relationship marketing concept.[21] Baxter International actually offers to share the business risk with some of its customers by jointly setting sales and cost reduction targets and sharing the savings or extra expenses.[22]

## SUSTAINABILITY AND SERVICES *IN ACTION*

### Being "Green" Increases Loyalty in Banking

According to a Javelin Strategy & Research report, 687,000 tons of paper could be saved on an annual basis if bank consumers would opt for paperless alternatives. That's enough paper to circle the Earth 239 times!

Corporate motives to engage in green banking extend beyond the ecological mission of saving the world's resources to establishing a more personal bond with customers. According to a recent study, customers are rewarding "green banks" with their loyalty. When asked about "the importance of green banking," customers have indicated by a 6-to-1 margin that they are more likely to be loyal to financial institutions that engage in environmentally-friendly practices. Perhaps then it comes as no surprise that companies like Washing Mutual have recently donated $1 million to The National Arbor Day Foundation to celebrate its one million customers that have switched to paperless statements. Additional findings among green banks reveal:

- 34 percent of customers who have switched to electronic banking have done so to minimize their impact on the environment.
- 43 percent of customers stated that they prefer to conduct business with companies that they perceive to be green.
- 60 percent of consumers who engage in green banking or have indicated that environmentally friendly business practices are "extremely important" to their banking decisions are women.
- 64 percent of consumers who have indicated that they are "very less likely" to be more committed to their bank because of green practices are men.

It should further be noted that, although most customers have indicated an interest in adopting green banking behaviors, three out of four customers continue to receive paper statements. However, as banks are providing easy-to-adopt green options, the future looks bright. Seventy-six percent of U.S. households are expected to bank online by 2011.

Source: **http://www.environmentalleader.com/2008/06/04/customers-more-loyal-to-green-banks/**, accessed 30 March, 2009.

Overall, relationship marketing emphasizes the importance of customer retention and a concern for quality that transcends departmental boundaries. Relationship marketing broadens the definition of the customer from final consumer to all the groups (e.g., suppliers, employees, influencer markets, etc.) that are integral components in bringing the good or service to the marketplace. Efforts to retain the relationship with all these types of customers are at the core of the relationship marketing concept.

### Aftermarketing

**aftermarketing**
Marketing technique that emphasizes marketing after the initial sale has been made.

A third marketing program that embraces customer retention efforts is aftermarketing.[23] **Aftermarketing** emphasizes the importance of marketing efforts after the initial sale has been made. An example of aftermarketing would be a physician that calls the patient to check on the patient's progress several days after an initial visit for an illness. Can you imagine the loyalty and retention that would be established by this simple effort? Aftermarketing techniques include the following:

- *Identifying customers and building a customer database so that customers can be easily contacted after the sale has been completed.*

- *Measuring customer satisfaction and continuously making improvements based on customer feedback.*
- *Establishing formal customer communication programs, such as newsletters that convey information on how the company is using customer feedback in its continuous improvement efforts.*
- *Creating an aftermarketing culture throughout the firm that reinforces the importance of maintaining a relationship with the customer after the initial sale.*

The automobile industry has made some of the biggest strides in aftermarketing. Customers are frequently contacted by sales and service personnel after a vehicle has been purchased or after service has been completed on a vehicle. Generally, customers have been very impressed by the dealer's concern in an industry that has historically focused on the quick sell.

Weyerhaeuser, the paper giant, has taken aftermarketing even farther by requiring some of its employees to actually work at their clients' operations sites for a week. One aftermarketing success story involved the placement of a bar code on newsprint rolls the company regularly shipped to its consumers. Weyerhaeuser employees in the field noticed that the bar code would regularly stick to its customers' high-speed presses. The problem was solved by merely moving the bar code a few inches. Weyerhaeuser later found that other customers had experienced similar problems but never complained. Placing employees in the field to see personally how customers use the company's products has been beneficial for both Weyerhaeuser and its customers.[24]

## Service Guarantees

One of the most innovative and intriguing customer retention strategies to be developed in recent years is the service guarantee.[25] Although guarantees in and of themselves are not particularly new, they are very new with respect to services—particularly professional services. Overall, service guarantees appear to facilitate three worthwhile goals:

- *reinforce customer loyalty,*
- *build market share, and*
- *motivate the firm offering the guarantee to improve its overall service quality.*

In general, successful guarantees are unrestrictive, stated in specific and clear terms, meaningful, hassle free when invoked, and quick to be paid out. On the other hand, mistakes to avoid when constructing a guarantee include: (1) promising something that is trivial and normally expected, (2) specifying an inordinate number of conditions as part of the guarantee, and (3) making the guarantee so mild that it is never invoked.

***Types of Guarantees***   In general, there are three types of guarantees: (1) the unconditional guarantee, (2) the specific result guarantee, and (3) the implicit guarantee. An **unconditional guarantee** is the most powerful of the three types of guarantees. The unconditional guarantee "in its pure form promises complete customer satisfaction, and, at a minimum, a full refund or complete, no-cost problem resolution for the payout."[26] In general, offering unconditional guarantees benefits the firm in two ways. First, the firm benefits from the influence that the guarantee has on customers. More specifically, customer-directed benefits associated with unconditional guarantees include the following:

- *Customers perceive they are getting a better value.*
- *The perceived risk associated with the purchase is lower.*
- *The consumer perceives the firm to be more reliable.*
- *The guarantee helps consumers decide when comparing competing choices; consequently, the guarantee serves as a differential advantage.*

**unconditional guarantee** A guarantee that promises complete customer satisfaction and, at a minimum, a full refund or complete, no-cost problem resolution.

- *The guarantee helps in overcoming customer resistance toward making the purchase.*
- *The guarantee reinforces customer loyalty, increases sales, and builds market share.*
- *A good guarantee can overcome negative word-of-mouth advertising.*
- *The guarantee can lead to brand recognition and differentiation; consequently, a higher price can be commanded.*

The second benefit of the unconditional guarantee is directed at the organization itself. A necessary condition for a firm to offer an unconditional guarantee is that it must first have its own operations in order. If not, the payouts associated with an unconditional guarantee will eventually bankrupt the firm. Organization-directed benefits of offering unconditional guarantees include the following:

- *The guarantee forces the firm to focus on the customer's definition of good service as opposed to the firm's own definition.*
- *In and of itself, the guarantee states a clear performance goal that is communicated to employees and customers.*
- *Guarantees that are invoked provide a measurable means of tracking poor service.*
- *Offering the guarantee forces the firm to examine its entire service delivery system for failure points.*
- *The guarantee can be a source of pride and provide a motive for team building within the firm.*

As with the other types of guarantees, a number of risks worth discussing are associated with unconditional guarantees. First, guarantees may send a negative message to some customers, thereby tarnishing the image of a firm that offers one. Some customers may wonder why the firm needs to offer the guarantee in the first place. For example, customers may consider whether the guarantee is because of failures in the past or out of desperation for new business. The second drawback to unconditional guarantees involves the actual payout when the guarantee is invoked. Customers may be too embarrassed to invoke the guarantee; consequently, the guarantee may actually motivate customers not to complain. Other potential problems associated with the payout involve the amount of documentation the firm requires to invoke the guarantee and the time it takes for the actual payout to be completed.

**specific result guarantee** A guarantee that applies only to specific steps or outputs in the service delivery process.

The second type of guarantee is a specific result guarantee. A **specific result guarantee** is considered milder than an explicit unconditional guarantee as "the conditions for triggering the guarantee are narrower and well defined, and the payouts are less traumatic."[27] In contrast to an unconditional guarantee, which covers every aspect of the service delivery process, a specific result guarantee applies only to specific steps or outputs.

On the positive side, specific result guarantees are most easily applied to quantitative results. For example, FedEx guarantees overnight delivery. Moreover, by guaranteeing a specific result as opposed to an overall guarantee, the firm may be able to state its commitment to a particular goal more powerfully. On the negative side, a specific result guarantee may appear weak compared with an unconditional guarantee, and customers may perceive this as the firm's lack of confidence in its own abilities.

**implicit guarantee** An unwritten, unspoken guarantee that establishes an understanding between the firm and its customers.

The **implicit guarantee** is essentially an unwritten, unspoken guarantee that establishes an understanding between the firm and its customers. Although the guarantee is not specified, customers of firms that offer implicit guarantees are ensured that the firm is dedicated to complete customer satisfaction. Consequently, a partnership spirit develops between the firm and its customers based on mutual trust and respect.

The tradeoffs associated with an implicit guarantee strategy are intriguing. On the positive side, because the guarantee is implicit, no explicit specifications state exactly what the firm will do should the guarantee need to be invoked. Consequently, the service firm can tailor the payout of the guarantee to fit the magnitude of the service failure. Hence, an implicit guarantee may not result in an all-or-nothing type of arrangement. Other benefits associated with the implicit guarantee strategy are that: (1) it avoids the appearance of a tacky marketing ploy compared with an explicit guarantee; and (2) it avoids stating publicly the possibility that the firm on occasion may not fulfill its promises. In sum, an implicit guarantee is thought to be the "classy" way of pursuing a guarantee strategy.

An implicit guarantee also has its drawbacks. Since an implicit guarantee is unspoken and unwritten, "a firm pursuing an implicit guarantee strategy has to earn its reputation by repeated acts of goodwill communicated to potential clients via word of mouth, a time-consuming process."[28] Hence, an implicit guarantee does little to differentiate a firm early in its business life cycle. In addition, because the guarantee is implicit, new customers may be unaware of the firm's stance on customer satisfaction and may not bring problems to the firm's attention.

***Professional Service Guarantees*** As a final note, guarantees as they relate to professional services deserve special consideration.[29] Experts in the area of guarantees believe that guarantees are most effective for professional service providers under the following conditions:

- *Prices are high*—Professional service prices easily approach the five- and six-figure range. Guarantees may alleviate some of the risk associated with such costly decisions.
- *The costs of a negative outcome are high*—Simply stated, the more important the decision and the more disastrous a negative outcome, the more powerful the guarantee.
- *The service is customized*—As opposed to standardized services, where outcomes are fairly certain, customized services are accompanied by a degree of uncertainty. The guarantee helps to alleviate some of the risks associated with the uncertainty.
- *Brand recognition is difficult to achieve*—It is difficult to successfully differentiate professional services. For example, an eye exam or dental services are fairly consistent from one provider to the next. In cases like these, the unconditional service guarantee may successfully differentiate the service from the competition.
- *Buyer resistance is high*—Due to the expense of many professional services and the uncertainty of the outcome, buyers of professional services are highly cautious. An unconditional guarantee may help in overcoming customer reservations and making the sale.

# Defection Management: Developing a Zero Defection Culture

Another strategy for increasing the customer retention rate is to reduce customer defections. The concept of defection management has its roots in the total quality management (TQM) movement. **Defection management** is a systematic process that actively attempts to retain customers before they defect. Defection management involves tracking the reasons that customers defect and using this information to continuously improve the service delivery system. The motivation for establishing an effective defection management program is clear—cutting defections in half doubles the average company's growth rate. Moreover, reducing the defection rate by even 5 percent can boost profits 25 percent to 85 percent, depending on the industry (see Figure 14.5).[30]

## Zero Defects versus Zero Defections

Since the acceptance of total quality management by the manufacturing sector, the guide to follow has been the **zero defects model**. Although appropriate within the

**defection management** A systematic process that actively attempts to retain customers before they defect.

**zero defects model** A model used in manufacturing that strives for no defects in goods produced.

**FIG-14.5** Reducing Defections 5 Percent Boosts Profits 25 Percent to 85 Percent

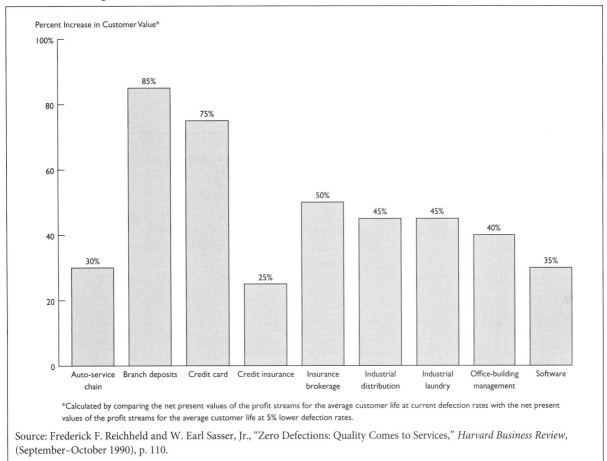

Source: Frederick F. Reichheld and W. Earl Sasser, Jr., "Zero Defections: Quality Comes to Services," *Harvard Business Review*, (September–October 1990), p. 110.

manufacturing sector, where specifications can be identified well ahead of production, the zero defects model does not work well in the service sector.[31]

Service customers carry specifications in their minds and can only approximate their desires to a service provider. For example, customers often show hairstylists pictures of a desired hairstyle and request a similar style for themselves. The picture is an approximation of a desired result—it does not specify exact lengths to be cut nor specific degree of curve for curls.

Another obstacle to applying the zero defects model in the service sector is that each consumer has his or her own set of expectations and corresponding specifications. As one hairstylist stated, "They [some consumers] come in here with two spoonfuls of hair and expect to leave here looking like Diana Ross!" Consequently, specifications that are available in the service sector frequently cannot be standardized for all customers. As a result, the service provider must be able to adapt to each set of expectations on the spot.

Because of the unique properties of the service delivery system, namely the unique service characteristic of heterogeneity, the zero defects model used in the manufacturing sector is out of touch with the realities of the service sector. A more appropriate philosophy for service firms would be **zero defections**. In contrast to the "defect pile" of unsellable goods for the manufacturing sector, the "defect pile" in the service sector consists of customers who will likely never come back.

**zero defections** A model used by service providers that strives for no customer defections to competitors.

**FIG-14.6** A Credit Card Company's Defection Curve

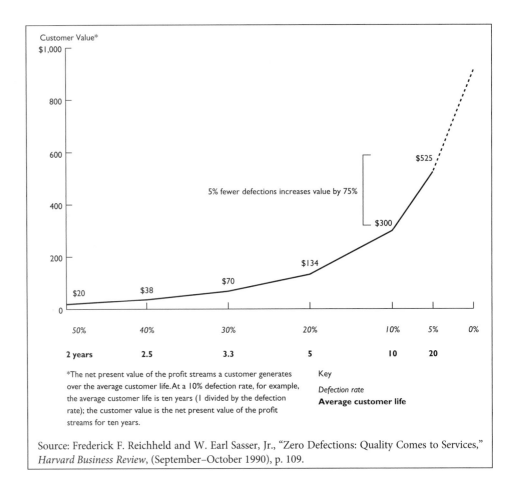

*The net present value of the profit streams a customer generates over the average customer life. At a 10% defection rate, for example, the average customer life is ten years (1 divided by the defection rate); the customer value is the net present value of the profit streams for ten years.

Key

*Defection rate*
**Average customer life**

Source: Frederick F. Reichheld and W. Earl Sasser, Jr., "Zero Defections: Quality Comes to Services," *Harvard Business Review*, (September–October 1990), p. 109.

## The Importance of Defection Management

Businesses commonly lose 15 percent to 20 percent of their customers each year.[32] In some industries, the rate is much higher. For example, the cable television industry loses in excess of 50 percent each year,[33] the cellular phone industry experiences turnover at a rate of 30 percent to 45 percent per year,[34] and customer defections in the pager industry range from 40 percent to 70 percent annually.[35] Reducing customer defections is associated with immediate payoffs. In the credit card industry, for example, a 2 percent decrease in defections has the same net effect on the bottom line as a 10 percent decrease in cost (see Figure 14.6).[36]

Another reason that monitoring customer defections is important is the disturbing findings discussed earlier that customer defection rates are not necessarily directly associated with customer satisfaction ratings.[37] One would think that satisfied customers would be easily retained. Although the idea is intuitively appealing, receiving high satisfaction marks from current customers does not necessarily translate into undying customer loyalty. On average, 65 to 85 percent of defectors say they were satisfied or very satisfied with their former provider.[38] Why, then, do customers defect?

**price defectors** Customers who switch to competitors for lower-priced goods and services.

## Defector Types

Customers defect for a variety of reasons.[39] **Price defectors** switch to competitors for lower-priced goods and services and are probably the least loyal of any customer type. Many businesses that pursue a customer retention philosophy are willing to sacrifice

## GLOBAL SERVICES *IN ACTION*

### Singapore Airlines Experiences Rare Backlash from Customers

Loyalty programs such as frequent-buyer programs, frequent-flyer programs, frequent-player cards, and frequent-dining coupons are common throughout the world. Today, nearly 75 percent of U.S. shoppers now belong to at least one loyalty program. At their core, the main idea behind loyalty programs was to track customer's shopping habits, identify the most profitable customers, and to target these customers with special deals and promotions.

Loyalty programs were originally developed by the airlines in the 1970s with the industry's invention of frequent-flyer miles. Frequent-flyer programs often lock in customers, particularly frequent and business travelers, to one airline even though less expensive flights and more favorable connections may be available on competing airlines. Customers are willing to pay a little extra in exchange for frequent-flyer rewards such as free or discounted flights, increased baggage allowances, and/or better seating arrangements.

More than ever, customers now feel entitled to special treatment due to their memberships in loyalty programs. According to one industry observer, "the airlines broke what was a one-price-fits-all standard and introduced a some-people-are-more-special-than-others psyche that has changed the American, and global, marketplace forever." Consequently, what was once thought as a great idea to track data has now become the price of doing business. Moreover, loyalty programs have created a marketplace psychology that has become not only uncomfortable but unsustainable for companies like Singapore Airlines.

Singapore Airlines recently attempted to withdraw some its benefits offered to its highest level PPS Club members. In addition to the usual perks, PPS Club members were originally offered a lifetime membership once they reached a certain level. Stating that the program offer was unsustainable, the airline withdrew the lifetime membership provision and further claimed that the terms of its loyalty program entitled it to make changes. Customer reaction to the announced changes was swift. A group of "high-profile businessmen and professionals" threatened the airline with a class-action lawsuit. Singapore Airlines is now faced with the situation of alienating some its most powerful and loyal customers.

Sources:
1. **http://www.reuters.com/article/tnBasicIndustries-SP/idUSSIN11878720070327**, accessed 30 March, 2009.
2. **http://www.cioinsight.com/c/a/Special-Reports/Trends-Loyalty-Programs/**, accessed 30 March, 2009.

price defectors to avoid constantly discounting their own products and services. In particular, firms that differentiate themselves from competitors based on factors such as reliability, responsiveness, empathy, assurance, and the effective management of the tangible evidence that surrounds the service are generally able to retain customers without constantly discounting their products.

**product defectors**
Customers who switch to competitors who offer superior goods and services.

**Product defectors** switch to competitors who offer superior goods and services. As such, product defectors are the most difficult to bring back to the fold once they leave. For example, it is difficult to imagine returning to a provider of inferior service once a superior provider is found. The secret to minimizing product defectors is to not become complacent with today's successes and ignore the changing needs of customers. Innovations and continuous improvement are critical in the battle of retaining product defectors.

**service defectors** Customers who defect due to poor customer service.

**Service defectors** defect due to poor customer service (see Global Services in Action). Contrary to other defector types, firms that are plagued by service defectors are actually

Two-thirds of customers who defect from companies do so due to the unhelpfulness of service employees.

providing existing customers with reasons to take their business elsewhere. Inadequately informed personnel, unfulfilled promises, and unacceptable employee behavior are typical reasons customers flee to the competition. Service failures like these combined with inadequate employee responses to those failures can lead to service defections. While other defector types are primarily externally driven, service defectors leave as a result of problems with the internal operations of the firm.

**market defectors** Customers who exit the market due to relocation or business failure.

**Market defectors** exit the market for relocation or business failure reasons. Customers, both individuals and businesses, who move out of the market area would be considered market defectors. Similarly, companies that go out of business and are no longer in the market for goods and services are market defectors.

**technological defectors** Customers who switch to products outside the industry.

**Technological defectors** switch to products outside the industry. Typical examples of technological defections include the switch from lamp oil to electricity and from rail to air transportation. As is the case with product defections, technological defections may occur due to the complacency of the firm. Successful firms are often lulled into a false sense of security and fail to react to technological developments outside their own industry. For example, the manufacturers of vinyl albums who were caught off guard by the development and consumer acceptance of the compact disk lost much of their business through technological defections. Of course, compact disk sales are now being replaced by online downloads of music, as technological innovations continue to change traditional industry models.

**organizational defectors** Customers who leave due to political considerations inside the firm, such as reciprocal buying arrangements.

**Organizational defectors** result from political considerations inside the firm. In some instances, organizational defections will occur due to reciprocal buying arrangements. For example, an engineering firm may switch its paper products purchasing to a firm that sells the brand of paper products marketed by the pulp and paper mill that retains the engineering firm's services. In other instances, organizational defections may occur as the result of friendships or business relationships that develop through civic clubs, country clubs, and a variety of other social and business gatherings.

## The Defection Management Process

Although customer defections are frustrating for many firms, defection rates are measurable and manageable.[40] Defections indicate where profits are heading as well as specific reasons that customers are leaving. Information obtained by analyzing defections can assist firms in reaching the goal of continuous improvement.

The key to defection management is the creation of a zero defections culture within the firm. Everyone in the firm must understand that zero defection is a primary goal of the organization. To establish this goal, the firm's first step in the defection management process is communicating to its employees the importance of retaining current customers and the benefits obtained by reducing defections. The earlier discussions in this chapter outline the importance and benefits of customer retention that should be conveyed to all employees. The zero defections goal communicated to employees must have supporters at all levels, starting at the top of the organization. It is critical that upper management lead by example and managers "walk the talk." Managers who talk about the need and importance of customer service in employee meetings and then bad-mouth customers in the backroom will never successfully implement a zero defections culture within their firm.

The second step in creating a zero defections culture is to train employees in defection management. Defection management involves:

1. Gather customer information—who are our customers, what do they purchase, how much do they purchase, and how frequently do they place orders?
2. Provide specific instructions to employees about what to do with the information—acknowledge the customer by name, cross-sell other goods and services, and recognize the importance of the customer to the long-run success of the firm.
3. Instruct employees in how to react to the information—all customers are not created equally and some get more special treatment than others.
4. Encourage employees to respond to the information.

The third and perhaps most critical step in the defection management process is to tie incentives to defection rates. Simply stated, if the firm truly values reducing defections, the reward structure should reinforce customer retention efforts. Firms such as MBNA are dedicated to customer retention and have developed reward systems consistent with their customer retention efforts. It is MBNA's policy to talk with every customer who wishes to drop its services. MBNA's employees earn up to 20 percent of their salaries in bonuses associated with customer retention efforts. As a result of the reward structure and these extra communication efforts with customers, MBNA retains 50 percent of customers who call intending to end the relationship.[41] How do MBNA's customer retention efforts affect the bottom line? MBNA's overall customer retention rate is 95 percent, and MBNA keeps its customers twice as long as industry averages. In fact, MBNA's retention rate of profitable customers—those who revolve their balances—is 98 percent. In addition, MBNA's credit losses due to bad debt are one-third to one-half lower than those of other companies. Moreover, MBNA customers use their cards more often and maintain higher balances—$2,500 compared with the industry average of $1,600. Another great example is State Farm Insurance. State Farm agents receive the same commission for securing renewals as they do for signing up new customers.[42] As a company, State Farm recognizes the value of customer retention and rewards employees for their customer retention efforts.

Finally, firms successful in defection management also carefully consider creating switching barriers that discourage defections.[43] A customer switching banks is subjected to the time-consuming task of closing one account at the old bank, opening a new account at the new bank, and sometimes paying for new checks to be printed. Switching to a new dentist may require the cost of new x-rays, and switching to a new physician may translate into completing extensive patient information forms and enduring an extensive physical exam. The key to successfully implementing switching barriers is to develop low entry barriers and nonmanipulative, yet high exit barriers.

Overall, the key to defection management is the realization that customer defections are measurable and manageable. Too often, firms simply write off customers who no longer request their services. Defection management focuses on retaining customers before they defect and determining the reasons for defections when they do occur. In sum, defectors are a valuable source of information regarding the firm's operations, its employees, and its future.

# Summary

Due to stagnant markets, increased competition, the rising costs of marketing, changes in channels of distribution, and the ever-changing needs of consumers, the concepts of customer loyalty and retention have increased in importance. Customer loyalty reflects attempts by the service firm to build an emotional attachment as well as a business attachment to the service firm. Customers that are retained by the service firm may be loyal customers or customers that simply continue to patronize the firm for other reasons, such as high switching costs that constrain their attempts to leave or lack of substitutes.

Strategies for cultivating loyalty include ongoing communications, providing great customer service, leaders who lead by example, training and empowering employees, remembering past customer purchases, focusing on reliability, flexibility in dealings with customers, balancing technology with high-touch, and being fantastic at remembering customer names.

Ultimately, customer retention refers to focusing the firm's marketing efforts toward its existing customer base. Firms engaged in customer retention efforts work to satisfy existing customers in the hope of further developing the customer—provider relationship. Customer retention is associated with a wide variety of benefits, including the profits derived from initial and repeat sales, the profits from reduced operating costs, and the profits from referrals. Typically, existing customers make more efficient use of the supply of service available, and often prefer to stay with one provider over long periods of time to reduce the risk associated with service purchases.

Despite the importance of customer retention, not all customers may be worth keeping. Service firms should seriously consider releasing customers who are no longer profitable, do not follow contract conditions, are abusive to employees, make unreasonable demands, and have developed such a poor reputation that it tarnishes the reputation of those that conduct business with them.

Firms focusing their efforts on customer retention often engage in programming efforts such as frequency marketing, relationship marketing, aftermarketing, and service guarantees. Service firms that have implemented these types of programs have found their efforts to be worthwhile and profitable.

In addition to attracting customers and building loyalty, service firms also benefit by proactively developing a defection management program. The motivation for establishing an effective defection management program is clear—cutting defections in half doubles the average company's growth rate. Customers defect to competitors for a number of reasons and can be described by defector type—price, product, service, market, technology, and organizational. The key to building an effective defection management program is instituting a zero defections culture throughout the firm. This is accomplished by employing leadership that lead by example, training employees in defection management, tying incentives to defection rates, and developing nonmanipulative switching barriers that discourage customer defections.

# Key Terms

## Review Questions

1. Define the concepts and explain the relationship between customer loyalty and customer retention.
2. Why has conquest marketing become an acceptable form of business for many of today's firms?
3. Discuss the problems associated with conquest marketing.
4. Is it always worthwhile to retain a customer?
5. Discuss the steps associated with frequency marketing as they relate to frequent-flyer programs.
6. How have changes within service distribution channels had an impact on customer retention?
7. Discuss the distinction between zero defects and zero defections.
8. How do service defectors differ from other defector types?
9. Discuss the characteristics of successful guarantees.
10. What are the tradeoffs associated with utilizing implicit guarantees?

## Notes

1. **http://www.cioinsight.com/c/a/Special-Reports/ Trends-Loyalty-Programs/**, accessed 12 August, 2009.
2. Pallavi Gogoi and Ira Sager, "I Love You—But I'm Leaving You," *Business Week*, (July 21, 2003), p. 10; K. Douglas Hoffman and John E. G. Bateson, *Essentials of Services Marketing*, 3842, 2nd ed, (Mason, Ohio: South-Western Publishers, 2001).
3. Frederick F. Reichheld and W. Earl Sasser, Jr., "Zero Defections: Quality Comes to Services," *Harvard Business Review*, (September–October 1990), pp. 105–111; and **http://www.allbusiness.com/sales/ customer-service/1961-1.html**, accessed 27 March, 2009.
4. Rahul Jacob, "Why Some Customers Are More Equal than Others," *Fortune*, (September 19, 1994), pp. 218, 220.
5. Terry G. Vavra, *Aftermarketing: How to Keep Customers for Life through Relationship Marketing* (Homewood, IL: Business One Irwin, 1992) pp. 2–6.
6. **http://www.gaebler.com/Television-Advertising-Costs.htm**, accessed 21 August, 2009.
7. Michael W. Lowenstein, "The Voice of the Customer," *Small Business Reports*, (December 1993), pp. 57–61.
8. Frederick F. Reichheld and W. Earl Sasser, Jr., "Zero Defections: Quality Comes to Services," *Harvard Business Review*, (September–October 1990), pp. 105–111.
9. Barry Farber and Joyce Wycoff, "Customer Service: Evolution and Revolution," *Sales and Marketing Management*, (May 1991), pp. 44–51.
10. Frederick F. Reichheld and W. Earl Sasser, Jr., "Zero Defections: Quality Comes to Services," p. 107.
11. **http://strikeachord.wordpress.com/2009/06/18/ customer-loyalty-profitability-and-mythology/**, accessed 24 August, 2009.
12. **http://www.zeromillion.com/marketing/determining-lifetimevalue.html#ixzz0OxTj0PNE**, accessed 22 August, 2009.
13. **http://www.dbmarketing.com/articles/Art251a. htm**, accessed 22 August, 2009.
14. "Is Customer Retention Worth the Time, Effort and Expense," *Sales and Marketing Management*, 143, 15 (December 1991), pp. 21–22; and **http:// www.businessweek.com/magazine/content/ 07_44/b4056431.htm**, accessed 20 August, 2009.
15. Robert E. Wayland and Paul M. Cole, "Turn Customer Service into Customer Profitability," *Management Review*, (July 1994), pp. 22–24.
16. Richard Barlow, "Building Customer Loyalty through Frequency Marketing," *The Bankers Magazine*, (May/June 1990), pp. 73–76.
17. **http://www.staralliance.com/en/meta/airlines/**, accessed 22 August, 2009.
18. Jim Ellis, "Frill-Seeking in the Clouds," *Business Week*, (September 13, 1993), pp. 104–105.
19. Adam Bryant, "Airlines' Frequent-Flier Miles Not Just for Flying Anymore," *Sunday Star-News*, (August 21, 1994), p. 10A.
20. Martin Christopher, Adrian Payne, and David Ballantyne, *Relationship Marketing* (Oxford: Butterworth-Heinemann, 1991).
21. Jacob, "Why Some Customers," p. 222.
22. Ibid., p. 215.
23. Vavra, *Aftermarketing*, p. 1.
24. Jacob, "Why Some Customers," p. 222.
25. Adapted from Christopher W. L. Hart, Leonard A. Schlesinger, and Don Maher, "Guarantees Come to

Professional Service Firms," *Sloan Management Review*, (Spring 1992), pp. 19–29.

26. Hart, Schlesinger, and Maher, "Guarantees Come," p. 20.

27. Ibid., p. 28.

28. Ibid., p. 29.

29. Ibid., p. 20.

30. Reichheld and Sasser, "Zero Defections," p. 110.

31. Ron Zemke, "The Emerging Art of Service Management," *Training*, (January 1992), pp. 37–42.

32. Reichheld and Sasser, "Zero Defections," p. 108.

33. "How Five Companies Targeted Their Best Prospects," *Marketing News*, (February 18, 1991), p. 22.

34. *The Cellular Telephone Industry: Personal Communication* (Silver Spring, MD: Herschel Shostack Assoc., 1992) p. 122.

35. The Pager Industry: ProNet Annual Report, 1989.

36. Reichheld and Sasser, "Zero Defections," p. 108.

37. Lowenstein, "The Voice," p. 57.

38. Patricia Sellers, "Keeping the Buyers," *Fortune*, (Autumn/Winter 1993), pp. 56–58.

39. Glenn DeSouza, "Designing a Customer Retention Plan," *The Journal of Business Strategy*, (March/April 1992), pp. 24–28.

40. Reichheld and Sasser, "Zero Defections," p. 105.

41. Larry Armstrong, "Beyond May I Help You?," *Business Week/Quality*, (1991), pp. 100–103.

42. Sellers, "Keeping the Buyers," p. 58.

43. DeSouza, "Designing," p. 27.

# The Mandalay Bay Conundrum

## Background

Mandalay Bay Resort and Casino in Las Vegas, Nevada promotes itself as a 39-story luxury hotel offering unmatched luxury, fine dining, renowned entertainment, and personal service. The main hotel boasts over 3,300 rooms, a 135,000 square foot casino, a variety of water attractions including a wave pool and a lazy river, nongaming entertainment options such as the House of Blues, and 24 restaurants and cafes. Mandalay Bay is owned by MGM Mirage and is connected by a free tram service to its sister properties, Excalibur and Luxor. Professor Taylor (ironically, a services marketing professor) and his wife were looking forward to spending four nights at the resort and casino and spending some time with his sister and brother and their respective spouses who live across the country—a mini-family reunion was the purpose of the trip.

Professor Taylor's brother, Ted, had received a direct mail piece from Mandalay Bay months earlier that offered a promotional rate of $69.99 a night (a discount of $30 a night off the regular room rate). After contacting his siblings and agreeing on a date, Ted immediately booked three rooms for each of the three couples, and the mini-family reunion was set.

On checking into the hotel in August, Ted and his brother-in-law, Bill, renegotiated all three couples' accommodations. The deal resulted in a double upgraded room for each couple consisting of a 765 square foot mini-suite, a Jacuzzi bathtub, and views of the Vegas strip. The additional cost for these upgrades was $25 a night—a price everyone agreed was a very good deal.

Professor Taylor and his wife arrived at the hotel a day later than the other two couples who had rooms on the 10th floor. Due to availability constraints, the professor and his wife were given a room on the penthouse level (floors 35-39) of the hotel that are uniquely numbered as floors 60-64. This room was the same size as the other two couples' rooms; however, the penthouse floors came with the added advantages of an express elevator and enhanced views of the Vegas strip due to being placed at a higher elevation.

Everyone was very pleased with their rooms and all the accommodations available at the Mandalay Bay Resort and Casino. The couples attended shows, laid out by the pools, walked the strip, enjoyed dining together, and dabbled in the various hotels' casinos—many of which are owned by the MGM Mirage. The days passed quickly, and the couples often found themselves returning to their hotel rooms around 3 a.m. each night.

# The Situation

On the second night of their stay at Mandalay Bay, the professor and his wife returned to their room, 60201, and noticed a slightly foul smell present in their room that had not been there earlier in the day. The couple went to sleep that night and never thought about it the next day because the smell was no longer present in the morning. Upon returning to their room at around 3 a.m. on the third night, the foul smell had returned. By 3:30 a.m. the smell had so greatly intensified, the couple was nearly overcome with nausea and called security to investigate. A young security employee noted that the smell was not present anywhere else in the hallway except for directly outside of Room 60201. Not sure what to do, the young security employee, covering her nose (the smell was really bad), called her manager to help investigate further.

The security manager, with finger under nose, entered the room and immediately called for the hotel's engineering staff (maintenance). The security manager briefly apologized, then called the front desk to arrange for another room for the professor and his wife. Engineering entered the room with spray deodorizers in hand and attempted at least to mask the odor. Engineering believed that a gas bubble had built up in the hotel's sanitation system, and the smell was the result of a "burp" that was directly venting into Room 60201. A new room was provided for the couple, and a bellman helped pack up their belongings around 3:45 to 4 a.m. Other security guards were now present in the hallway, with hands covering their noses and mouths as they attempted to get "upwind" (their words) of "the smell."

The new accommodations for the professor and his wife were located one floor above their existing room (still on the penthouse floors) and were quite nice. In fact, the room was no longer a room—it was now a five-room suite. The new accommodation was approximately 1,700 to 2,000 square feet, consisting of a full dining room, wet bar, living room, entertainment options including a large plasma television and enhanced audio capabilities such as docking station for an iPod with speakers located throughout, a four poster bed, electronic curtains, two bathrooms (including a steam room), etc. The regular price for the room ranged from $350 to $500 per night (the professor and his wife were not charged the additional price). The professor and his wife spent their last two nights at Mandalay Bay in this suite. No one from the hotel initiated contact with the couple after they were placed in their new accommodations.

## Other Notable Considerations

- *Although nice Las Vegas hotel rooms can be obtained at reasonable rates, guests spend the majority of their "Vegas budget" on airfare, child and/or pet care, meals, entertainment (including gambling and show tickets), car rental and/or taxi fees, and retail shopping. The vast majority of meal and entertainment dollars are spent on property. It would not be unreasonable to assume that a couple could easily spend $1,500 to $2,000 for a five day/four night stay.*
- *The professor and his wife vacation in Las Vegas approximately once or twice every five years.*
- *The professor's brother-in-law talked to the manager on duty the next morning who had no idea the situation had taken place. The manager advised that the guests affected should file a formal report with security. Security was contacted, and took a formal report, but were visibly confused as to why they were involved.*
- *The professor's wife complained of nausea and a headache that lasted for approximately 12 hours after the incident.*
- *The professor's wife called the front desk to inquire about the cause of the foul odor and was instructed to contact the Risk Management Office. Risk Management offered*

*to compensate the couple with two free nights at Mandalay Bay that could be used anytime in the next two years. When asked if they could provide accommodations that were similar to the couple's original room (765 square feet), the Risk Management Office noted that they could not guarantee similar accommodations.*

- *Mandalay Bay was to send the vouchers for the two-night stay to the home of the professor and his wife. Several weeks have past, and the couple received no mail from Mandalay Bay.*

## Discussion Questions

1. Should Mandalay Bay Resort and Casino and other Vegas hotel destinations be concerned with service marketing concepts such as customer loyalty and retention? Please explain your answer.

2. As a guest of Mandalay Bay that experienced this situation, what would be a reasonable expectation for the hotel's service recovery efforts?

3. Evaluate Mandalay Bay's service recovery efforts from the perspectives of distributive justice, procedural justice, and interactional justice.

4. What recommendations would you provide the management of Mandalay Bay to handle future situations such as the one described in this case?

# CHAPTER **15**

# Pulling the Pieces Together: Creating a World-Class Service Culture

## LEARNING OBJECTIVES

After reading this chapter, you should be able to:

- Compare and contrast the concept of service seamlessness to departmentalization and functionalism.

- Describe how a service firm's internal logics impacts its service culture.

- Understand the fundamental differences between the industrial management approach versus the market-focused management approach.

- Describe observational and indirect questioning approaches for assessing the organization's current culture.

- Explain the basic components of a service audit.

- Discuss four fundamental strategies that facilitate cultural change.

## GOOGLE'S GOOGLE-Y CULTURE

How would you like to have the rare job title of Chief Culture Officer for a company that has been recognized as the "Best Place to Work in America," operates the most popular website in the world, and where the company name is now a verb in the dictionary! As Google's CCO, Stacy Savides Sullivan works hard to maintain

Stephen Brashear/Getty Images

Google's core values—sustaining a flat organization and facilitating a collaborative work environment. Hiring the right employees that are Google-y is the key to maintaining and growing the company's culture. Google-y employees are described as flexible, adaptable, not focused on job titles and hierarchy, and able to get stuff done. Consequently, beyond skill sets, academic background, experience, and credentials, potential new hires are screened for their fit with the company's culture and collaborative work ethic.

Employee perks set the tone for Google's culture and differentiate the company from its competition. Results from employee happiness surveys revealed that employee happiness is not based on salary and stock options alone. As a result, the company has spent a lot of effort on developing programs and activities centered around employee career development and growth. In addition, although Google facilities around the world differ in their offerings, employees fortunate enough to work at Google's world headquarters known as the "Googleplex" located in Mountain View, California, enjoy a multitude of unique benefits.

The Googleplex lobby consists of a piano, lava lamps, and live information pertaining to search queries from around the world. Throughout the building, bicycles and large rubber exercise balls are readily available for anyone feeling the need to work off a little steam. Bulletin boards, located virtually everywhere throughout the facility, exhibit Google-related press clippings from around the world. Offices are purposely cohabitated with three to four employees and furnished with couches to improve information flow, save on heating bills, and improve server setup effectiveness. Dogs are welcome guests in the Googleplex. Recreation facilities within the Googleplex offer workout rooms equipped with exercise equipment, locker rooms complete with washers and dryers, a massage room, video games, Foosball, pool table, ping pong, and a baby grand piano. Roller hockey is even available twice a week in the parking lot.

One of the most valued employee perks is food. Employees don't have to leave the Google campus to eat; the food provided is great, and employees have the option of healthy food selections. Stations within the Google Café include "Vegheads," "Back to Albuquerque," "East Meets West," and "Charlie's Grill." Snack Rooms stocked with cereal, Gummi bears, M&Ms, nuts, yogurt, fresh fruit and a variety of other choices are common in every Google facility. Drinks are also available, including sodas, fresh juice, and a make-your-own-cappuccino station.

Ultimately, a firm's culture is based on its values and beliefs. Google not only instills its core values through employee selection and training, the company also uses its servicescape to reinforce the firm's culture through the use of physical evidence. Space allocation, office composition and location, bulletin boards and displays, and cafés and snack rooms all reinforce Google's core values of a flat organization, a lack of hierarchy, and working within a collaborative environment. Organizations that provide excellent service set themselves up for success, and Google is a prime example of a company that takes its service culture seriously.

Sources:

1. **http://www.google.com/corporate/culture.html**, accessed 9 April, 2009; and
2. **http://news.cnet.com/Meet-Googles-culture-czar/2008-1023_3-6179897.html**, accessed 9 April, 2009.

# Introduction

The purpose of this chapter is to tie together the information presented in this text in a meaningful manner. In order to provide service excellence, the individual components of the service firm must act in unison to create a "seamless" service culture. Creating a **seamless service** organization means providing services without interruption, confusion, or hassle to the customer.[1] Seamless service firms manage to simultaneously provide reliable, responsive, competent, and empathetic services, and have the personnel, facilities, and resources necessary to get the job done (see E-Services in Action). Seamlessness thrives on tightly connected interrelated parts within the service delivery system that foster a service culture throughout the organization. In contrast, the firm will not act as one if it chooses to embrace the traditional *industrial management model* notions of departmentalization and **functionalism** that serve as obstacles to creating a world-class service culture.

Creating and supporting a market-focused organizational culture that centers on the customer and the employees who support the customer is critical. For example, the Ritz-Carlton's Gold Standards consisting of its *Credo*, *Motto*, *The Three Steps of Service*, *Service Values*, *The 6th Diamond*, and *The Employee Promise* clearly articulate the Ritz-Carlton's dedication not only to its guests, but also to its own personnel (www.ritzcarlton.com). Before an organization can change its culture, it must first understand its current culture. By assessing the firm's current culture, a seamless service culture is

**seamless service** Services that occur without interruption, confusion, or hassle to the customer.

**functionalism** The belief that the function of something rather than the experience it creates should determine its design.

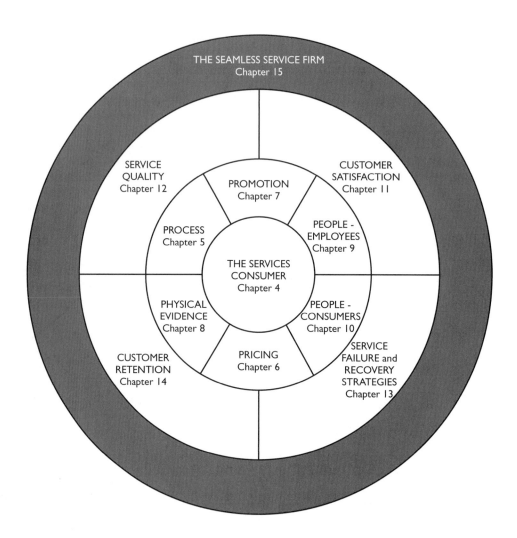

fostered as personnel throughout the organization come to appreciate the challenges faced and the contributions made by everyone involved in the firm's final effort to deliver world-class service.

## Obstacles to World-Class Service: Departmentalization and Functionalism

Traditional industrial-based organizational models based on the foundations of functionalism and departmentalization kill seamlessness. For example, consider the following three memos sent to a young manager of a branch bank on the same day:[2]

From the marketing department:

*We shortly will be launching a new advertising campaign based on the friendliness of our staff. This is in direct response to the increasingly competitive marketplace we face. Please ensure that your staff members deliver the promises we are making.*

From the operations department:

*As you are aware, we are facing an increasingly competitive marketplace and, as a result, our profits have come under pressure. It is crucial, therefore, that we minimize*

---

## E-SERVICES *IN ACTION*

### Zappos' Core Values that Drive Its Service Culture

Zappos is ranked high on Fortune magazine's list of "The 100 Best Companies to Work For," placing 23rd in 2009. The online shoe retailer is touted for many reasons, prompting industry experts to delve into the firm's culture of superior service and excellent treatment of its employees. Zappos embraces 10 core values known as "The 10 Commandments of Zappos" that help shape the organization's culture.

1. "Deliver Wow through service"—Known for its excellent customer service, Zappos also provides its suppliers with the same access to inventory and sales data as the company's executives.
2. "Embrace and drive change"—The CEO embraces the idea that as the company grows most of the new ideas will bubble up from the bottom of the organization. Every idea is valued regardless of its origin.
3. "Create fun and a little weirdness"—Zappos gets the job done but has fun along the way. Interviewees may be asked about their favorite superhero; training is often communicated through Saturday Night Live-style skits; and it's not uncommon for employees to sing, laugh, have parades, wear blue hair, or have nose rings. What more could one possibly say?
4. "Be adventurous, creative, and open-minded"—Zappos is willing to take risks and make mistakes. Managers are encouraged to interact with team members outside the office on fun "field trips" to create stronger bonds; and call center employees are encouraged to try new approaches to delighting customers.
5. "Pursue growth and learning"—Zapponians, the name given to the company's employees, are encouraged to learn by the company's offering classes and providing free books that enable

employees to advance upward through the company's ranks.
6. "Build open and honest relationships with communication"—Zappos prides itself on running a transparent operation where everything is out in the open. For employees desiring direction, Zappos provides full-time life coaches and career advice for employees wishing to move up or on to other choices.
7. "Build a positive team and family spirit"—Employees are encouraged to think of each other as extended family members. By doing so, the company actually takes "the concept of work/life balance off the table" as employees work together, play together and have meals together.
8. "Do more with less"—After training "bonding sessions" that used to cost $3,000 at the local bar have been substituted with an in-house ice cream social that costs $110. The net effect is the same, and the company is saving money during down economic times.
9. "Be passionate and determined"—Employees are encouraged to be passionate about their jobs and to share their outside passions with others within the organization. Says recruiting manager Christa Foley, "If you're passionate about running a marathon and want to get the company involved, do it. Don't wait for someone else."
10. "Be humble"—Humility underlies every behavior at Zappos. Despite all the recognition the company and its CEO have received, the company always recognizes that there is more to learn and other ways to do a better job.

Source: **http://money.cnn.com/2009/01/15/news/companies/Zappos_best_companies_obrien.fortune/index.htm**, accessed 8 April, 2009.

---

*waste to keep our costs under control. From today, therefore, no recruitment whatsoever will be allowed.*

From the personnel department:

*Our staff members are becoming increasingly militant. This is due, in large part, to the availability of alternative employment with our new competitors. We currently are involved in a particularly delicate set of negotiations and would be grateful if you could minimize any disruptions at the local level.*

These instructions from the three different departments obviously conflict with one another. To obey the operations department means no recruitment and, therefore, an increase in the work load for contact personnel. The increased work load will most likely be a hot topic during labor negotiations, and could be disastrous for the personnel department. Finally, the increased work load, in all probability, will have a negative effect on staff morale. Given the inseparability of the service, the staff's low morale will be visible to customers and negatively affect subsequent customer satisfaction levels.

If this particular branch bank is marketing-oriented, the young manager will attempt to trade off the three sets of instructions, giving added weight to the marketing department's instructions. It should be stressed that, in service firms, it is nearly impossible to be totally marketing-oriented. Customers cannot be given everything they want because of the constraints imposed by the firm's service delivery system. For example, in a restaurant setting, every customer cannot be seated by the window with the scenic view and served immediately upon arrival due to seating and available service (personnel) constraints.

If this branch is operations-oriented, added weight will be given to the operations department's set of instructions. The young manager may relay marketing's request to the vice-president of operations and ask for clarification. The operations vice-president, in turn, may fire off an abusive memo to her counterpart in marketing. The memo may ask why marketing was sending memos directly to the branches at all and suggest that, in the future, all other requests made by marketing should be cleared by operations.

Firms that continue to cling to functional and departmental mindsets are often besieged by internal conflict as departments compete against one another for resources instead of pulling together to provide exceptional service. The conflict that often occurs between marketing, operations, and human resources is not personal.[3] It is a result of the different cultures which are functions of each department's goals, planning horizons, departmental structure, people-management systems, and the specific individuals in each department.

## Overcoming the Silo Mentality: Understanding Internal logics

One of the primary challenges of creating a service culture that embraces a seamless service experience is to get the various departments within the firm to work with one common goal in mind—serving the customer. Before attempting to integrate the various departments of the firm, it is important to understand that each is driven by its own **internal logic**—implicit and explicit principles that drive organizational performance.[4] Each department's logic is internally focused on its own departmental needs and creates seams in the service delivery process. This silo mentality isolates the department from the rest of the organization as it pursues self-interested goals in the forms of **departmentalization** and functionalism. For example, consider the logic behind each of the following functions that drive the service experience: operations management, marketing, and human resources.

**Operations logic** is driven by the goal of reducing or containing costs through mass production or the use of advanced technologies. Operations and marketing are often in conflict with each other, which creates seams in service delivery. While marketing is concerned with identifying and understanding customer needs and providing goods and services that meet those needs, operations is concerned with how these products and services will be produced and delivered. In essence, marketing is concerned with the management of demand, while operations is concerned with the management of supply. Marketing attempts to focus on meeting demand in the most effective manner in terms of product form, location, price, and promotions; while operations is primarily concerned with meeting demand in the most cost-effective manner. Typical goals of operations management and marketing concerns regarding these goals are displayed in Figure 15.1.

**internal logic** Implicit and explicit principles of individual departments that drive organizational performance.

**departmentalization** The act of dividing an organization into departments that focus on their own set of activities.

**operations logic** The reasoning that stresses cost containment/ reduction through mass production.

**FIG-15.1** Operations and Marketing Perspectives on Operational Issues

| OPERATIONAL ISSUES | TYPICAL OPERATION GOALS | COMMON MARKETING CONCERNS |
|---|---|---|
| Productivity improvement | Reduce unit cost of production. | Strategies may cause decline in service quality. |
| Make-versus-buy decisions | Trade off control against comparative advantage and cost savings. | "Make" decisions may result in lower quality and lack of market coverage; "buy" decisions may transfer control to unresponsive suppliers and hurt the firm's image. |
| Facilities location | Reduce costs; provide convenient access for suppliers and employees. | Customers may find location unattractive and inaccessible. |
| Standardization | Keep costs low and quality consistent; simplify operations tasks; recruit low-cost employees. | Consumers may seek variety, prefer customization to match segmented needs. |
| Batch-versus-unit processing | Seek economies of scale, consistency, efficient use of capacity. | Customers may be forced to wait, feel "one of a crowd," be turned off by other customers. |
| Facilities layout and design | Control costs; improve efficiency by ensuring proximity of operationally related tasks; enhance safety and security. | Customers may be confused, shunted around unnecessarily, find facility unattractive and inconvenient. |
| Job design | Minimize error, waste, and fraud; make efficient use of technology; simplify tasks for standardization. | Operationally oriented employees with narrow roles may be unresponsive to customer needs. |
| Learning curves | Apply experience to reduce time and costs per unit of output. | Faster service is not necessarily better service; cost saving may not be passed on as lower prices. |
| Management of capacity | Keep costs down by avoiding wasteful under-utilization of resources. | Service may be unavailable when needed; quality may be compromised during high-demand periods. |
| Quality control | Ensure that service execution conforms to predefined standards. | Operational definitions of quality may not reflect customer needs, preferences. |
| Management of queues | Optimize use of available capacity by planning for average throughput; maintain customer order, discipline. | Customers may be bored and frustrated during wait, see firm as unresponsive. |

Source: ©1989 by Christopher H. Lovelock. Reprinted with permission from Christopher H. Lovelock. Christopher H. Lovelock, "Managing Interactions between Operations and Marketing and Their Impact on Customers," Bowen et al., eds., *Service Management Effectiveness* (San Francisco: Jossey Bass, 1990) p. 362.

The major challenge for operations function in a service setting is the involvement of customers in the production process. Compared with raw materials in a pure manufacturing setting, customers are unpredictable and decrease the efficiency of the delivery system. Operations would like to remove the customer from the production process as much as possible, while marketing promotes the importance of the customer in the production process. Consequently, operations and marketing must establish a point of equilibrium between the variety and depth of products that marketing would like to offer and the cost effectiveness of meeting that demand through efficient operations.

# SUSTAINABILITY AND SERVICES *IN ACTION*

## Developing a "Green" Culture: Sustainable Business Practices for Hotels

It's one thing to value and talk about the ideals associated with "green lodging," but it's quite another for hotels to engage in effective behaviors that help to sustain the environment. Global Stewards provide the following tips and sustainable solutions for hotels that wish to pursue green culture initiatives.

| | |
|---|---|
| 1. Start a reuse program for towels and sheets. | 17. Use paper dollies to protect cups instead of wrapping cups in plastic. |
| 2. Use low-flow showerheads and sink aerators. | 18. Install skylights if possible. |
| 3. Install low-flow toilets. | 19. Consider obtaining green certification for restaurant and kitchen areas. |
| 4. Utilize compact fluorescent light bulbs and sensors/timers to reduce electrical use. | 20. Use drought resistant plants in landscaping. Replaced mowed areas with native ground cover. |
| 5. Switch to refillable hair and skin care dispensers. | 21. Switch to LED exit signs. |
| 6. When rooms are unoccupied, turn off lights, pull drapes, and turn down the heating/air conditioning. | 22. Regularly maintain filters, coils and thermostats. |
| 7. Install window film. | 23. Utilize an Energy Management System to reduce heating/cooling costs. |
| 8. Provide guest room recycle baskets. | 24. Provide staff incentives to participate and improve environmentally friendly practices. |
| 9. Provide recycle baskets throughout the property. | 25. Switch to energy efficient insulation and reflective roofing materials. |
| 10. Purchase office and guest products that contain recycled materials. | 26. Contact the U.S. Green Building Council for ideas on construction and remodeling. |
| 11. Purchase organic, fair trade, and cruelty-free guest products. | 27. When replacing major components of existing systems, evaluate the performance of the total system and search out green alternatives. |
| 12. Switch to recycled paper products and use soy-based inks. | 28. Switch to heat pumps and geothermal technologies. |
| 13. Use nontoxic or low toxic cleaners and pesticides. | 29. Donate old furniture, appliances, and guest supplies to charities. |
| 14. Switch to "Energy Star" Products. | 30. Conduct an energy audit. |
| 15. Install a solar water heating system. | 31. Purchase fair trade products to be sold in the gift shop. |
| 16. Use reusable items such as cloth napkins and glass cups. | 32. Provide discounted room rates to organizations that champion sustainable living. |

Source: **http://www.globalstewards.org/hotel.htm**, accessed 8 April, 2009.

**marketing logic** The reasoning that stresses providing customers with options that better enable the service offering to meet individual needs.

While operations management is internally focused, marketing focuses externally on meeting the expectations and needs of consumers. For example, hotels may want to meet the needs of their guests by going "green (see Sustainability and Services in Action)." Ideally, the **marketing logic** is to provide customers with options that better enable the service offering to meet individual consumer needs. Although ideal for customers, providing numerous options leads to serious cost inefficiencies in a firm's operations.

In addition to often being in conflict with operations, marketing may also find itself in conflict with human resources, creating additional seams in service delivery. For example, marketing would like to staff all personnel positions with individuals who, in addition to being technically competent, possess strong interpersonal skills that enable the organization to better communicate with its customers. Marketing would argue that hiring personnel who possess well-developed interpersonal skills (in addition to being technically competent) is free. In contrast, human resources would argue that obtaining and keeping highly trained and personable personnel is much more expensive than hiring people who simply adequately perform their roles in the organization. Furthermore, human resources will point out that certain market segments can be served by personnel who are simply civil with customers and who perform their duties adequately. This point is valid. Does the customer really want a restaurant's waitstaff employee to engage the customer in a lengthy conversation about the weather, community happenings, and family matters, or would the customer rather have a simply civil employee take the order and deliver the food in a speedy manner? Moreover, the food is more likely to be less expensive when provided by adequate as opposed to superior personnel because of the savings in labor costs.

**human resources logic** The reasoning that stresses recruiting personnel and developing training to enhance the performance of existing personnel.

**Human resources logic** is to recruit personnel and develop training that enhances the performance of existing personnel. In the service encounter, operations, marketing, and human resources are inextricably linked. Figure 15.2 depicts the link between operations and human resources. This figure, which compares the degree of customer contact with production efficiency, reveals that no such person as the perfect service employee exists. Characteristics of the "right employee" depend on the characteristics of the particular job in question. Some employees will need to be people oriented, while others will need to be more task oriented to process "things" instead of "people."

The importance of service firm personnel as they interact with customers throughout the service delivery process highlights the link between human resources and marketing. Within a service firm, human resources is one of the few sources of quality control. Consequently, the hiring, training, and reward structures developed by human resources will ultimately play a major role in how employees interact with the firm's customers.

Despite the opportunity to make major contributions to the firm's overall service effort, human resources departments are often stuck in their own production-oriented silo mentality. Human resources' production-oriented activities include mistakes such as: using the same employee evaluation forms for everyone in the firm, even though the jobs may be very different; conducting canned employee training programs that never change from year to year; and utilizing generic employee selection procedures for a

**FIG-15.2** The Three-Cornered Fight for Control

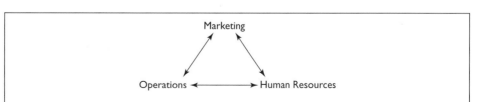

Source: John E. G. Bateson, *Managing Services Marketing: Text and Readings*, 3rd ed. (Fort Worth, TX: The Dryden Press, 1995).

variety of jobs that actually require different skill sets. In contrast, service-oriented human resources programs would be co-designed and co-taught with relevant managers, and evaluation forms would be thought of as coaching and evaluating devices rather than as rating forms used solely for compensation decisions. Overall, the service-oriented human resources department would work much more closely with its customers—the firm's employees—and form an ongoing, interactive, long-term relationship in pursuit of supporting those who serve the firm's final consumers.

**service logic** Promotes seamlessness by balancing the internal logics of marketing, operations, and human resources.

Ultimately, the firm's **service logic** stitches the departmental and functional seams together in order to help provide flawless service. Seamlessness can be referred to as "tooth-to-tail" performance—a term commonly used in the armed forces. "The personnel out front in the trenches need to be backed up with coordinated supplies, information resources, personnel reinforcements, and so on."[5] Similarly, when developing a service culture, the primary efforts of the service firm should equally focus on the customer (marketing logic), service delivery process (operations logic), and on the personnel providing customer services (human resources logic). However, before this can happen, firms must first understand the business philosophies that drive their current cultures.

## Business philosophies: The Industrial Versus Market-Focused Management Models

In the effort to create an excellent service culture, the firm should first consider its current philosophical approach to running the organization. Two models of management presently dominate the manner in which service firms operate, thereby directly influencing the development of the firm's service culture—the industrial management model and the market-focused management model. The *industrial management model* approach is more traditional and based on past schools of thought. Despite its outdated methods, the industrial management approach is alive and well in many service organizations today—traditions and bad habits are hard to break. Before an organization can transform itself into a world-class service operation, it must first understand the roots of its current business philosophy and all its unintended consequences.

## The Industrial Management Model

**industrial management model** An approach to organizing a firm that focuses on revenues and operating costs and ignores the roles personnel play in generating customer satisfaction and sustainable profits.

The industrial management model, which has its roots in the manufacturing sector, is still employed today by many service organizations.[6] Organizations that follow the **industrial management model** believe that: (1) location strategies, sales promotions, and advertising drive sales revenue; and that (2) labor and other operating costs should be kept as low as possible. In sum, the industrial management model focuses on revenues and operating costs, and ignores (or at least forgets) the role personnel play in generating customer satisfaction and sustainable profits. Given the role that employees play throughout the service encounter, it is sadly ironic how the industrial management model continues to be embraced by many of today's companies. For example, a general manager of a local internationally known hotel brand recently told a group of services marketing students that the keys to the hotel's success were quite simple—maximize daily room rates and minimize daily labor costs. This philosophical attitude is a classic industrial management model approach to business. Absent from the general manager's keys to success were employee and guest satisfaction among other factors, including employee and customer retention, goals relating to service quality and service recovery, and many other worthy objectives that lead to providing seamless service to guests.

In general, followers of the industrial management model believe that good employees are difficult to find and support the notion that "all things being equal, it is better to rely on technology, machines, and systems than to depend on human beings."[7] In addition, advocates of the industrial approach further believe that most employees are indifferent, unskilled, and incapable of fulfilling any duties beyond performing simple tasks. Consequently, jobs under the industrial model are intentionally narrowly defined to leave little room for employees to exercise judgment. As a result, employees are held to low job performance expectations, their wages are kept as low as possible, and few opportunities exist for advancement. As opposed to valuing front-line employees, the industrial model places a higher value on upper and middle managers while viewing the people who deliver service to the customer as the "bottom of the barrel." The industrial approach assumes that only managers can solve problems; consequently, resolving customer problems quickly becomes almost impossible as additional steps are built into the service delivery process.

### Consequences of the Industrial Management Model

The industrial model by definition guarantees a cycle of failure, as service failures are designed directly into the service delivery system. Due to its lack of support for front-line personnel, the industrial approach, albeit unintentionally, actually encourages front-line employees to be indifferent to customer special requests and problems. In essence, the system prohibits the front-line employee from taking any action even if the employee wants to assist in meeting customer requests or correcting the problem. Customer reactions to employee indifference are not surprising. Two-thirds of customers who now defect from their former suppliers do so not because of the product, but because of the indifference and unhelpfulness of the person providing the service.[8]

In further attempts to reduce operating costs, many firms that embrace the industrial model have replaced their full-time personnel with less-experienced and less-committed part-time personnel. These individuals are paid less than full-time personnel and receive few, if any, company benefits. In some instances, companies routinely release workers before mandatory raises and other benefits begin, in an attempt to keep operating costs down. Managerial practices such as this have created a new class of migrant worker in the United States—millions of employees now travel from one short-term job to another. Consequently, the industrial management model flies directly in the face of the position advocated by the proponents of the service-profit chain. Employees are not valued, internal service quality is not a priority, and employee retention and subsequent productivity are not an issue. How can firms that operate under the industrial management model continue to hold the expectation that customers will experience external value and return to enhance the firm's profitability?

The consequences associated with the industrial model in regard to service organizations have been self-destructive. The industrial model has produced dead-end front-line jobs, poor pay, superficial training, no opportunity for advancement, and little, if any, access to company benefits. Moreover, the industrial approach has led to customer dissatisfaction, flat or declining sales revenues, high employee turnover, and little or no growth in overall service productivity. In sum, many believe that the industrial approach is bad for customers, employees, shareholders, and even the quality of life for the countries in which this organizational philosophy continues to be embraced. Yet, the industrial management model continues to operate because the lessons of the past have not been effectively communicated to the business leaders of tomorrow. Clearly, it is time to break with tradition and adopt a business philosophy that promotes a service-oriented culture and balances the needs of employees, customers, and company operations.

**market-focused management model**
A new organizational model that focuses on the components of the firm that facilitate the firm's service delivery system.

### The Market-Focused Management Model

In contrast to the industrial management model, proponents of the **market-focused management model** believe that the number one purpose of the firm is to serve the

Among the six service triangle relationships, the customer/service provider interaction, also known as "critical incidents" or "moments of truth," is perhaps the most important relationship of them all.

customer.[9] Consequently, logic suggests that *although the purpose of the firm is to serve the customer, the firm should be organized internally in a manner that supports the people who serve the customer.* By following this approach, service delivery becomes the focus of the system and the overall differential advantage in terms of competitive strategy. In essence, the market-focused management approach promotes a service-oriented culture that benefits customers, employees, and the organization itself.

The Services Triangle framework presented in Figure 15.3[10] visually depicts six key relationships that comprise the market-focused management approach. First, the firm's service strategy must be communicated to its customers. If superior service is the focus of the firm and the key point of differentiation on which it distinguishes itself from competitors, customers need to be made aware of the firm's commitment to service excellence. For example, The Ritz-Carlton's Gold Standards discussed earlier explicitly state the company's commitment to service excellence. However, it is important to note, the firm must have an effective service delivery system in place before it announces to the world that superior service is its primary objective.

Second, the firm's service strategy (commitment to service excellence) needs to be communicated to the firm's employees. Good service starts at the top, and management

**FIG-15.3** The Service Triangle

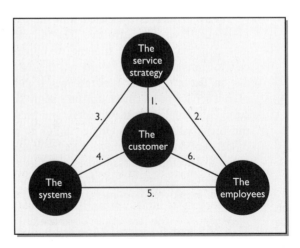

Source: Adapted from Karl Albrecht and Ron Zemke, *Service America* (Homewood, IL: Dow Jones-Irwin, 1985) pp. 31–47.

must lead by example. If top management is not committed to processes that facilitate service excellence, front-line employees who interact with the firm's customers will be ineffective at best. Front-line employees who interact with customers emulate the firm's leadership. Leadership that values customers and processes that deliver customer and employees satisfaction will yield employees who share the same values. The opposite is true as well. Managers who despise their customers create a toxic service culture for employees and customers alike.

The third relationship depicted within the service triangle focuses on the consistency of the service strategy with the systems that are developed to run the day-to-day operations. In other words, the firm's service delivery systems should flow logically from the service strategy and enhance the service encounter for all involved. For example, online banking systems are an extension of the bank's interaction with its customers. If the bank publicly states that service is a priority, then its online systems should be exceptional as well. This third relationship of the services triangle seems so straightforward, but apparently it is difficult to implement. How many companies tout the importance of customer service, yet queue their customers in endless automated telephone loops or route their calls to outsourced call centers where, even when connected, language barriers prevent customers from communicating effectively with the firm's employees? Adding to the frustration is the firm's voice recorded message that repeatedly boasts, "Your call is important to us!" Given the inept systems that are set up by firms to handle customer calls, how important can the calls really be?

The fourth relationship illustrated in the service triangle involves the impact of organizational systems upon the customer's service experience. Interactions with the firm's systems should enhance the customer's service experience. For example, if the firm touts service excellence as its primary strategy, systems such as check-out procedures, delivery systems, and return policies should be excellent as well. Service firms should avoid designing defensive systems developed for the sole purpose of keeping a small minority of customers from taking advantage of the company. Systems such as rigid return policies may weed out a few bad customers at the expense of honest customers, who are forced to suffer through systems and policies that treat them as suspects instead of valued assets.

The fifth relationship within the services triangle pinpoints the importance of organizational systems and employee efforts. Organizational rules and regulations should not be obstacles in the way of employees wishing to provide great service. For example, wheelchair attendants at Denver's International Airport are only allowed to transport passengers with disabilities to the curb of the terminal building. Proceeding into the covered parking garage 50 feet away from the terminal is not permissible (apparently for liability reasons). As a result, family members who have greeted the disabled passenger inside the terminal to help with luggage, must exit the parking garage, pay the parking toll, and return to passenger arrivals to receive their family member. This extra step in the process can easily add 15 to 20 minutes to actually getting the disabled family member in their family's vehicle.

Finally, the sixth and last relationship depicted in the service triangle is perhaps the most important of them all—the customer/service provider interaction. Also known as "critical incidents" or "moments of truth," the importance of the interaction between service providers and customers cannot be overstated.

Service providers must be more flexible, communicative, able to deal with stress, and willing to take initiative than their manufacturing counterparts. To the customer, service providers are the face of the organization and occupy a two-way communication role— from the organization to the customer, and from the customer back to the organization. Service firms that successfully navigate the customer/service provider interaction do so by avoiding the "human resources trap." This trap makes the fatal flaw in judgment of placing the full burden of "moments of truth" upon the service provider. The firm's non-personal services—such as the physical facility, the accuracy and timeliness of billing, and all the behind-the-scenes support staff who enable service providers to perform their jobs—must be in place and working together for the firm to provide seamless service. Ultimately, service providers are only as good as the service delivery systems and service culture that supports their efforts.

Ultimately, the market-focused management model is based on the belief that the purpose of the firm is to serve the customer. As a result, this approach promotes the stance that the firm should be organized in such a way to help serve the people who serve the customer. In many ways, the market-focused management approach is consistent with the service-profit chain's emphasis on internal service quality and employee satisfaction. The market-focused management approach believes employees want to do good work and experience individual career growth. Hence, advocates of this approach are much more optimistic regarding their faith in human nature than their industrial management counterparts.

# Developing a Service Culture

**culture** The shared values and beliefs that drive an organization's overall service philosophy.

A service firm's **culture** reflects the shared values and beliefs that drive the organization—the formally written, the unwritten, and actual occurrences that help employees understand the norms for behavior in the organization (see Global Services in Action). In short, organizational culture establishes the "dos and don'ts" of employee behavior, and provides the basis on which various employee behaviors can coalesce.[11] For example, consider Southwest Airlines, 11 Primary Attitudes depicted in Figure 15.4 that guide employee behavior.

## Assessing the Current Culture of the Service Firm: Observation and Indirect Questioning Techniques

Before an organization can change its culture, it must first understand its current culture. Assessing the firm's current culture can be accomplished via informal (observational and indirect questioning techniques) and formal approaches, such as conducting a formal

**FIG-15.4** Southwest's 11 Primary Attitudes

"We are not an airline with great customer service. We are a great customer service organization that happens to be in the airline business."

*Colleen Barrett*

*Southwest Executive*

1. Employees are number one. The way you treat your employees is the way they will treat your customer.
2. Think small to grow big.
3. Manage in the good times for the bad times.
4. Irreverence is okay.
5. It's okay to be yourself.
6. Have fun at work.
7. Take the competition seriously, but not yourself.
8. It's difficult to change someone's attitude, so hire for attitude and train for skill.
9. Think of the company as a service organization that happens to be in the airline business.
10. Do whatever it takes.
11. Always practice the Golden Rule, internally and externally.

Source: Kevin Freiberg and Jackie Freiberg, *Nuts! Southwest Airlines' Crazy Recipe for Business and Personal Success* (Bard Press: Austin, TX, 1996).

## GLOBAL SERVICES *IN ACTION*

### International Considerations for Service Cultures

What may be a great service culture in one country may be considered socially unacceptable in another; consequently, when conducting business with customers from abroad, international cultural differences must be taken into consideration. Consider, for example, the nuances of the simple handshake. In general, it is typically acceptable for a man to extend a hand to another man to initiate a handshake. However, the rules of this typical greeting may change when a man greets a woman, a woman greets a man, or when a woman greats another woman. In addition, even when a handshake is a common greeting, the acceptable firmness and length of the handshake varies from one culture to the next. Thankfully, author Kimberley Roberts has provided the following international success tips to clarify this important first step of saying hello.

| | |
|---|---|
| Germany and the United States | Both countries typically have firm handshakes, but the length of the greeting varies. The German handshake is very brief. In contrast, the U.S. handshake typically lasts three to four seconds. |
| France, Guatemala, and Japan | All three countries prefer a less firm handshake. In fact, the handshake in these three countries has been described as limp. Some Japanese prefer a traditional bow in lieu of a handshake. |
| Singapore | A typical handshake in Singapore may last 10 seconds or longer. |
| New Zealand, Singapore, South Korea, and Taiwan | Culture dictates that women should take the lead when a handshake is offered. |
| South Korea | Additional respect is shown by cupping the left hand under the right forearm when shaking with the right hand. |
| China, Hong Kong, and Japan | A traditional bow is the preferred greeting. Japan may vary between handshakes and the traditional bow. |
| India | The traditional greeting is "namaste," which involves placing palms together in a praying position with fingers just beneath the chin, bowing, and saying "Namaste." |
| Thailand | The traditional greeting in Thailand involves placing the hands together in a praying position just in front of the chin, bowing the head to touch the top of the fingers, and saying "Sawasdee." Women actually say "Sawasdee Ka" and men respond by saying "Sawasdee Kab." "Sawasdee" means good luck. |
| Chile, Costa Rica, El Salvador, Honduras, Mexico, Nicaragua, and Panama | Women in these countries greet each other by patting the right forearm or shoulder. |
| Hindus and Muslims | When following religious customs, men are forbidden public contact with women. It is best to follow cues from the host to determine if religious customs will be followed. If Western culture is to be followed, Hindu and Muslim women should wait for the man to offer his hand first. |

Source: **http://www.international-business-center.com/international_success_tips.html**, accessed 10 April, 2009.

service audit. Informal approaches such as the observational techniques provided below often provide keen insights into the values and beliefs of the organization.[12]

1. Observe the current culture as an impartial observer—if you were an observer who had never seen this group of employees interact before, what would you learn from their conversations and actions?

2. Gauge employee emotions—what are employees passionate about? What do people inside the organization get excited about and about what do they argue? Individuals only get excited or argue about issues that are truly important to them.

3. Observe objects and artifacts—what is hanging on office walls and what do employees display on their desks? Cartoons about the incompetence of management (e.g., Dilbert) or the stupidity of customers are typical indicators of the values and beliefs held by the firm's employees.

4. Observe what is missing—what should be visible that is not? Some employee offices look like a home away from home, while other offices are barely decorated. The former approach may indicate that the employee views their job as an integral part of their life, while the latter may indicate that the employee's primary motivation for work is a paycheck.

5. Go for a culture walk—take a walk around the firm and look for the physical signs of culture. Experts advise to observe:
   a. Space allocation and office location—who gets the most space, the best offices, and who is separated from whom?
   b. Bulletin boards and displays—conduct a content analysis of what is being posted and what it says about the organization.
   c. Common areas—what are the common areas used for and for whom?
   d. Memos and emails—what is the content, what is the tone, and do people primarily communicate verbally or through written communications?
   e. Employee interaction—is there any employee interaction and is there emotion displayed?

6. Conduct culture interviews and surveys—In addition to observational techniques, indirect questions such as the following can also provide key insights into a current culture.
   a. What would employees tell their friends about working at this organization?
   b. What is the one thing employees would like to change?
   c. Who are the company heroes? Why these persons?
   d. What is the employee's favorite characteristic of the company?
   e. What kinds of people would fail in this organization?
   f. What is your favorite question to ask a job candidate?

Assessing the current culture of a firm via observational and indirect questioning techniques can be very enlightening and challenging. By determining the current culture, the firm's leadership gains a better understanding of how to move the firm forward to its new set of values and beliefs.

### Assessing the Current Culture of the Service Firm: Conducting a Service Audit[13]

**service audit** A series of questions that force the firm to think about what drives its profits and suggests strategies for competitive differentiation and long-term profitability.

Another useful approach in assessing the firm's current culture involves conducting a service audit. The **service audit** asks direct questions of front-line and top management personnel, and requires the firm to think about the forces that drive its current profits. Moreover, the active involvement of front-line and top management personnel in conducting the audit facilitates the change in culture if necessary. The audit consists of 22 questions that address nine components: profit and growth, customer satisfaction,

Eros Hoagland/Redux

Before an organization can change its culture, it must first understand its current culture. Observational techniques often provide keen insights into the values and beliefs of the organization. What do you believe is the culture of this organization?

external service value, employee productivity, employee loyalty, employee satisfaction, internal service quality, leadership, and the relationships between these measurements.

## The Service Audit: The Profit and Growth Component

*1. How Does the Firm Define Customer Loyalty?*    Traditional measures of customer loyalty involve repeat sales, purchase frequency, and increases in amounts purchased. The firm also needs to consider the depth of the relationship. For example, the depth of a customer's banking relationship would be defined by types of transactions and accounts, such as savings, checking, certificates of deposit, car loans, home mortgages, savings bond programs, safety deposit box rentals, and so on.

*2. Does the Firm Measure Profits from Referrals?*    Customer loyalty and satisfaction should also be measured in terms of the customers' willingness to refer the firm to friends, family, and colleagues. Given the importance consumers place upon personal sources of information when selecting from among competing services, encouraging referrals, or at least creating an atmosphere where customers freely inform others of the firm's services is crucial.

*3. What Proportion of the Firm's Development Funds Are Spent on Retaining Customers as Opposed to Attracting New Ones?*    As discussed in Chapter 14 the benefits of customer retention are clear. Current customers generate referrals, are less expensive to market to, purchase more services more frequently, are knowledgeable about the firm's operating system and, therefore, are more efficient users of the system, and are a great source of information about how the firm can better serve its targeted markets. Unfortunately, under traditional models of management, firms spend the majority of their resources on obtaining new customers while neglecting their existing customers.

*4. When Customers Do Not Return, Do We Know Why?*    Service firms that excel pursue the bad news as well as the good. Traditionally, customer satisfaction assessments are obtained from current customers, who tend to rate the firm toward the more positive end of the scale. Uncovering the reasons customers defect reveals potentially fatal flaws in the firm's service delivery system that other customers have yet to discover and of which the firm may have been unaware. Consequently, contacting customers who have defected provides the firm with the opportunity to make improvements. Moreover, contacting customers who defect makes a positive impression that the firm cares about its customers, and may actually lead to recapturing some lost customers.

## The Service Audit: The Customer Satisfaction Component

*5. Is Customer Satisfaction Data Collected in a Systematic Manner?*   In chapters 11 and 12, we discussed a number of methods for assessing customer satisfaction and service quality. The key to successful measurement is consistency so that current assessments can be compared with past benchmarks. Satisfaction measurement should also occur on a regular basis, and not only when problems arise. Catching minor problems early through periodic customer satisfaction surveys enables the firm to adjust the service delivery system before major gaps in service occur.

*6. What Methods Are Utilized to Obtain Customer Feedback?*   The service quality information system discussed in Chapter 12 reveals a number of important methods for obtaining customer feedback on a variety of issues. The active solicitation of customer complaints, after-sale surveys, customer focus group interviews, mystery shopping, and total market service quality surveys should be used in conjunction with employee surveys. Too often, employees are left out of traditional customer feedback loops, even though they are exposed to vast amounts of information about customers' daily interactions with the firm.

*7. How Is Customer Satisfaction Data Used?*   Is the information used at all, or is it stuffed in the bottom drawer of a manager's desk? Customer satisfaction data needs to be shared with employees who provide the service. Front-line employees should feel they are an active part of the firm's overall goals and take pride in improvements in customer satisfaction scores. The data should reveal company strengths that can be used for promotional purposes and weaknesses that can be corrected through training programs or by redesigning the service system itself.

## The Service Audit: The External Service Value Component

*8. How Does the Firm Measure Value?*   One key to providing superior customer service is to define service value from the customer's perspective. Traditional approaches define value internally and frequently miss what is really important to customers. Remember, buyers' perceptions of value represent a tradeoff between the perceived benefits of the service to be purchased and the perceived sacrifice in terms of the total costs to be paid.

*9. How Is Information On Customer Perceptions of the Firm's Value Shared within the Company?*   Keeping customer information in the hands of top management does little to improve the service effort on the front line. By sharing information about customer perceptions with the front line, the employees become sensitized to the behaviors and outcomes that are really important to customers. Improvements made in these specific areas should increase customer satisfaction scores. Similarly, sharing the information with operations, marketing, and human resources personnel should assist each area in understanding the customer's perception of the entire service delivery process.

*10. Does the Firm Actively Measure the Gap between Customer Expectations and Perceptions of Services Delivered?*   Once customer perceptions are obtained, a comparison with customer expectations is vital in assessing customer satisfaction. Customer perceptions alone do not tell the full story. This point was made particularly clear in Chapter 12 regarding the SERVQUAL scale. Perception scores alone merely reflect whether customers agree with the statement, not whether what they are evaluating is really important to them. Including expectation measures increases the managerial usefulness of the information. Given that making improvements often involves a financial investment, comparing expectations to perceptions assists the firm in allocating resources to the most appropriate areas.

**11. Is Service Recovery an Active Strategy Discussed among Management and Employees?**   Although many firms will spend vast amounts of time and effort to deliver the service right the first time, little discussion centers on appropriate courses of action for employees to take when things do not go according to plan. Consequently, employees are left to fend for themselves while dealing with unhappy customers, and it is apparent that employees often do a poor job in service recovery efforts. Chapter 13 stresses the benefits of both service failure and service recovery analysis. Actively tracking failures and recoveries identifies failure points in the system, and allows the firm to minimize their occurrence by training employees in service recovery techniques.

## The Service Audit: The Employee Productivity Component

**12. How Does the Firm Measure Employee Productivity?**   If the firm does not measure what it really believes is important, employees will never pay attention to it. In addition, if productivity is measured simply in terms of output and outcomes and not by the behaviors used to achieve these outcomes, the firm may actually be rewarding employees for anticustomer-oriented activities. For example, the employee may be very curt with one customer so that a quick sale can be transacted with another customer who already knows what he or she wants. Service productivity measures such as timeliness, accuracy, and responsiveness need to be developed to reinforce these types of customer-oriented behaviors.

## The Service Audit: The Employee Loyalty Component

**13. Does the Firm Actively Pursue Strategies to Promote Employee loyalty?**  Employee loyalty to the organization is often visible to customers and directly influences customer evaluations of the firm. When employees feel more positive about the firm, customers feel more positive about the services the firm delivers. Preaching that employees are the firm's most important asset and then laying off employees in large numbers during periods of downsizing sends a hypocritical message to both employees and customers.

**14. Does the Firm Set Employee Retention Goals?**   Although rarely is 100 percent the correct level, employee retention saves the firm funds in terms of recruiting and training costs. Additionally, customers prefer the continuity of interacting with the same personnel over time so much that the firm's personnel may be its key differential advantage over competitors. When service personnel do leave, their regular customers often seek them out at their new places of employment.

## The Service Audit: The Employee Satisfaction Component

**15. Are Employee Satisfaction Measures Linked to Customer Satisfaction Measures?**   Employee satisfaction is linked to increases in productivity and external service value. External service value is linked to customer satisfaction and the additional benefit of customer loyalty. The net effects of customer loyalty are increased revenues and profitability for the firm. The outcomes associated with employee satisfaction—external service values, customer satisfaction, customer loyalty, revenue growth, and increased profitability—provide feedback and reinforce the company's internal service quality and employee satisfaction.

*16. Are Customer and Organizational Needs Considered When Hiring?*    Southwest Airlines invites panels of customers to help select flight attendants. Customers are so sold on the idea that some take off time from their own work schedules to be on the selection team. Hiring people with good job skills is important in manufacturing. Hiring people with good job skills and good interpersonal skills is vital in services.

*17. Are Employee Reward Programs Tied to Customer Satisfaction, Customer Loyalty, and Quality of Employee Performance?*    Service firms wishing to enhance the customer focus of their employees must implement behavior-based reward systems that monitor employee activities and evaluate employees on the aspects of their job over which they have control. Traditional, outcome-based reward systems often discourage the development of long-term relationships with the firm's customers in pursuit of short-term profitability.

## The Service Audit: The Internal Service Quality Component

*18. Are Employees Aware of Internal and External Customers?*    The ideal service firm should work seamlessly as a team. Each member of the team should understand fully how individual performance affects the performance of other team members as they provide superior service to external customers. Consequently, employees need to understand that the firm's external customers are not the only ones who are depending on their efforts.

*19. Do Employees Have the Support Necessary to Do Their Jobs?*    Does the firm just talk about providing superior service, or does it talk about it and back up it with the support necessary to get the job done right? Over the past few years, Taco Bell, a fast food franchise, has emerged as a firm with some fairly progressive service strategies. Personnel are supported by the latest advances in information technology, self-managing team training, effective food service equipment, and work scheduling that enhances employee performance.

## The Service Audit: The Firm's Leadership Component

*20. Does the Firm's Leadership Help or Hinder the Service Delivery Process?*    Service personnel frequently find that, even though they want to provide good service,

In order to be an effective leader within a service organization, management must "walk the talk" which in this case—it's not happening!

their hands are tied by overbearing, conservative, upper management types. Frequently, upper management is far removed from the front line of the operation and has lost touch with the realities associated with daily service interactions. The leaders of successful firms act as enablers, coaches, and facilitators; and they are participatory managers who listen to employees and encourage creative approaches to solving old problems.

***21. Is the Firm's Leadership Creating a Corporate Culture that Helps Employees as They Interact with Customers?*** Top management sets the tone and provides the resources that support personnel who interact with customers. The links in the service-profit chain discussed in Chapter 9 reveal that employee satisfaction and customer satisfaction are directly related. Top management's job is, therefore, to create an organization culture in which employees thrive.

### The Service Audit: The Measurement Relationship Component
***22. How Do the Preceding Measures of Service Performance in the Service Audit Relate to the Firm's Overall Profitability?*** The preceding components of the audit provide strategic measures that aid the provision of superior service. Ideally, the contribution of each measure should be related to the firm's bottom line. Relating these measures to the firm's overall profitability provides a resounding message throughout the company that service and quality pay!

## Strategies that Facilitate Cultural Change

Upon assessing the service firm's current culture, the firm's leadership may wish to cultivate new cultural beliefs and values. Figure 15.5 presents a simple framework for considering the options available when implementing cultural change in the service organization.[14] The figure suggests that culture is internally linked to and partly an outcome of three organizational components: structure, systems, and people. **Structure** relates to the formal reporting channels normally represented in an organizational chart (such as front-line employees reporting to middle managers, who report to regional managers, who report to national managers, who report to the chief executive officer).

The **systems** component of the framework refers to the people-management systems utilized for control, evaluation, promotion, and recognition. Evaluation and promotion systems include both formal and informal components. For example, management by objectives would be a formal component, while "What do I really have to do around here to get noticed?" would be an informal part of the system. Recognition systems focus on formal and informal rewards as well, ranging from formal rewards such as company trips to informal "pats on the back," such as lunch with the boss.

**structure** The formal reporting hierarchy normally represented in an organizational chart.

**systems** People-management systems of control, evaluation, promotion, and recognition.

**FIG-15.5** Cultural Framework

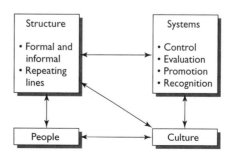

Source: John E. G. Bateson, *Managing Services Marketing: Text and Readings* (Fort Worth, TX: The Dryden Press, 1995).

The other two major components of the culture framework are the people who work in the organization and the firm's current culture. Creating a more customer-focused organization can be accomplished by altering any one of the four components: structure, systems, people, and culture, individually or together.

## Changing Culture through Structure

The organization's culture is a function of its structure. Changing culture through structure, however, is a slow process, because, in many instances, it takes years to successfully implement an organizational change in structure. In the effort to create a more customer-focused organization, two approaches to changing the culture through structure have been tried: (1) utilizing the marketing department as a change agent; and (2) restructuring the firm around the customer's experience.

*Marketing Department as Change Agents*    Marketing departments can be created simply to change the current orientation of the firm by creating a customer advocate within the organization. In its 99th year of existence, State Farm Insurance, the largest insurer of homes and automobiles in the United States, was attempting to make a radical transformation within its corporate culture. For almost 100 years the company had been operating with a sales culture where it attempted to sell insurance products that the company had already developed. As the company approached its 100th year of operation, State Farm's management team recognized the importance of strategic and marketing planning in achieving its future growth objectives. By switching from a sales-oriented to a marketing-oriented culture, the firm was essentially transforming its business philosophy from "selling what we make" to "making what we can sell." The transformation to a marketing culture was accomplished on a number of fronts including changing the structure of the company. Changing the structure of the company was completed by creating a marketing department within State Farm. As amazing as it may seem, the company had not had a formal marketing department throughout its previous 99-year history. By creating a marketing department, the corporate level of State Farm was signaling to its employees and agents that "marketing" and enhancing the customer experience had taken on a new sense of importance within the State Farm family.

Despite the effectiveness of utilizing the marketing department as a change agent, some pro-customer experts are wary about this particular strategy. Some feel that once the marketing department has been created, other departments may quickly transfer the complete responsibility for customer satisfaction to the marketing department.[15] Moreover, this transfer is likely to create open warfare among departments in the organization.[16] Consider again the logic of the operations and the marketing departments. Operations departments, by their very nature, tend to be cost-driven. Their focus is on evaluating the operation to find costs to save and procedures to simplify. This outlook tends to have a short time horizon. Marketing, by comparison, is looking for product enhancements in order to create a competitive advantage. The creation of such an advantage is not something that firms can expect to achieve in the short run.

The coordination of conflicting departments such as marketing and operations often requires the use of unconventional management techniques. To mesh the logics of the different groups and to allow them to understand one another, a number of strategies have been suggested by organizational-behavior theory. **Interfunctional task forces** are a classic way of forcing individuals with diverse viewpoints to work together and develop a better understanding of one another's perspectives. In the same way, **interfunctional transfers** can create informal networks of individuals from different departments who understand and trust one another. For example, operations managers who are promoted to run a marketing department will face initial problems. Their orientation is toward

**interfunctional task force** Problem-solving group in which individuals with diverse viewpoints work together and develop a better understanding of one another's perspectives.

**interfunctional transfers** Moving, via promotion or transfer, an employee from one organizational department to another to foster informal networks among departments.

operations, but their new roles require a marketing perspective. If such a transfer can be achieved successfully, the result is usually a general manager who makes rational and clear tradeoffs between operations and marketing. Moreover, it also creates a marketing person who has direct contacts in the operations group and who can overcome many of the traditional barriers to change.

***Restructuring around the Customer Experience***    As discussed much earlier in this text, the servuction model outlined the major forces that ultimately impact the customer's overall service experience. In response, a number of service firms have explicitly or implicitly restructured their organization based upon the customer's experience. For example, one major airline has all departments that have direct customer contact report to the head of marketing. Only engineering and the flight crew (pilots) report to the head of operations. Combining all customer-contact departments with the marketing group has reversed the arguments from, "It will cost too much; it is inefficient," to, "The customer needs this; how can we make it happen?" Still other firms have gone as far as creating the key leadership position of Vice President of the Customer Experience, and have restructured lines of reporting accordingly.

## Changing Culture through Systems

The firm's culture is also a function of the *systems* put into place that control, evaluate, promote, and recognize the firm's personnel. A number of approaches have been used to change culture through these systems. Some firms, for example, have started to give bonuses to managers at all levels based upon the firm's customer satisfaction scores. The firm's overall research effort can be tailored to measure satisfaction down to the branch level, and managers can be rewarded for improved scores. Unfortunately, the problem with this approach is that only part of the customer's satisfaction is under the control of management. The customer's expectations can be raised by competitive offerings, and satisfaction scores can drop as a consequence.

Another approach has been to introduce revenue into branch manager targets. A major New York bank wanted to change the retail branch manager orientation from one of considering only costs and security to one of considering customers first. The bank introduced a revenue-based performance evaluation system. For the first time, managers had to worry about where the customers came from and stop thinking of them as "people who made a mess of my branch." Early successes by a few managers produced interesting results. Up to 20 percent of managers left the company, claiming that this was not what they were hired to do. The balance of the managers woke up the bank's sleeping central marketing department to demand help in getting more customers. The long-term result of the change in the system was an increase in customers as well as in bad debt. The managers had discovered that money is an easy product to sell, and the bank had discovered it needed to revamp its credit control function.

Planning systems can also be used to change the orientation of companies. Formal marketing planning can drive organizations through the logic of marketing and can force them to develop an understanding of consumers' needs. For example, in addition to creating a marketing department, State Farm also facilitated its cultural transformation by putting new reward systems in place that would speed the adoption of the new marketing culture. State Farm wanted its agents to develop marketing plans for each agency. However, State Farm's current contract with its agents did not specifically require this activity. Consequently, State Farm created its "Select Agent" program as a special designation for those agents who participated in marketing planning. One of the major perks of being a "Select Agent" was the inclusion of the agent's name at the end of State Farm's corporate television advertising. Hence, even though numerous agents may be available in a given area, only "Select Agents" would be listed at the conclusion of any State Farm regional television advertisements. By modifying existing systems, in this case the reward system, State Farm was effectively able to facilitate the behavior change in culture desired.

### Changing Culture through People

Outsiders increasingly are being brought into the marketing departments of service firms to try to change the orientation. One strategy is the creation of key leadership positions within the organization to champion the marketing effort. Thus far, we have learned that State Farm transformed its culture by changing the structure of the company (introducing a marketing department) and by implementing new systems (providing incentives that modified the existing reward system). In addition to these efforts, State Farm created a highly visible management position within the organization to lead the corporate marketing department—Vice President of Marketing. Moreover, the Vice President of Marketing was given the same power and influence as all the other vice presidents in the company. The creation of this highly visible position, occurring concurrently with the change in structure and systems, once again signaled the importance of marketing's new role throughout the entire organization.

### Changing Culture Directly

In addition to changing culture through structure, systems, and people, culture-change can also be facilitated by changing the culture directly via the development of training programs inside the service firm. State Farm furthered its culture-change initiative by providing corporate-wide marketing training programs so that all employees truly understood the difference between a sales orientation and a marketing orientation. By implementing all four culture-change initiatives simultaneously (structure, systems, people, and directly through programming), State Farm substantially increased the rate of culture transformation and dramatically increased its odds of success.

Culture-change programs are becoming increasingly popular. These programs range from broad-scale educational activities to highly empowering personnel in order to re-engineer the firm's entire service delivery process around the customer. Figure 15.6 provides a simple way to categorize such activities. Along one axis is the nature of the

In addition to changing culture through structure, systems, and people, culture change can also be facilitated by changing the culture directly via the development of training programs inside the service firm.

**FIG-15.6**
**Categorizing Culture-Change Initiatives**

| EMPOWERMENT | GROUP | |
| --- | --- | --- |
| | MIXED | FAMILY |
| Low | "Putting the Customer First" | "Orientation Change" |
| High | "Change the Way You Work" | "Change the Way We Work" |

Source: John E. G. Bateson, *Managing Services Marketing: Text and Readings*, 3rd ed. (Fort Worth, TX: The Dryden Press, 1995).

groups used. Mixed groups are cross-sectional or interdepartmental; family groups can be a department or a naturally occurring group based on process, such as all the individuals involved in loading a particular flight with passengers. The second axis deals with the level of empowerment given to employees. Low levels of empowerment imply that individuals will change their behavior, but that the group will have no authority to change the processes and systems of the organization. High-level empowerment implies an ability to change the organization during the event or series of events. The slogans in the cells represent the hypothetical titles of such change programs, which often involve one or more meetings.

The top left cell refers to "**putting the customer first**" programs that take place in mixed groups within the organization. Seated together in sessions, personnel are lectured to and motivated to put the customer first. Through role playing, they are encouraged to recognize the importance of customers and change their behavior accordingly.

These types of programs can be very successful. To be successful, however, the new behavior needs to be reinforced on the job. If management and front-line personnel do not share the same level of enthusiasm and dedication toward the goal of creating a customer-oriented organization, the value of the lessons learned can be wiped out within hours. Without commitment to change, the new behaviors learned will be trivialized by colleagues, the old behaviors will be reinstated quickly, and the value of the program will be a total loss.

The top right cell, "**orientation change**," overcomes these problems by processing personnel by family groups whose members can reinforce one another on the job. Both cells, however, focus on changing attitudes and individual behaviors. Changing organizational processes and systems are not part of these programs. This potentially produces role conflict as desired individual behaviors are stopped by organizational constraints such as the physical environment or the current operating system.

"**Change the way you work**," in the lower left cell, draws on the empowerment ideas described in detail in Chapter 9. It implies active empowerment of the personnel attending the program. Personnel are allowed to break the rules in the context of serving their customers. Because of the mixed group, however, this type of initiative is focused on the individual rather than on process-level empowerment.

The lower right cell, "**change the way we work**," refers to initiatives that draw on many of the ideas in this book. Groups are in families and can be asked to flowchart their activities. They can then be asked to re-engineer the process to better serve their customers. The level of excitement in such groups is matched only by the anxiety of their bosses. Empowerment at this level really does place the boss in the role of coach and facilitator, and that is exactly what the boss's role should be. In creating a seamless organization, it is not management's job to force or dictate to employees to deliver service excellence. "Management's job is to put together a system that actually makes it possible to deliver quality service."[17]

**"putting the customer first"** The element of the culture-change initiative that teaches personnel to put the customer first.

**"orientation change"** The element of the culture-change initiative that teaches "families" of personnel to reinforce one another on the job.

**"change the way you work"** The element of the culture-change initiative that allows personnel to break the rules in the context of serving their customers.

**"change the way we work"** The element of the culture-change initiative that teaches personnel to flowchart their activities and to re-engineer the process to better serve their customers.

# Summary

In pursuit of creating a world-class service culture, the individual departments and functions of a service firm must act in unison to create a seamless organization. The firm will not act as one if the current focus of the organization is on departmental and functional needs. Before attempting to integrate the various departments of the firm, it is important to understand that each department is driven by its own internal logics—implicit and explicit principles that drive organizational performance. Ultimately, the firm's service logic stitches the departmental and functional seams together created by marketing, operations, and human resources in order to help provide flawless service. However, before this can happen, service firms must first understand the industrial management and market-focused management business philosophies that drive their current cultures.

Creating and supporting a market-focused organizational culture is critical when developing a seamless operation. The firm's culture drives employee behavior and directly influences the quality of the firm's service delivery system and subsequent consumer evaluations of the firm's service effort. Before an organization can change its culture, it must first understand its current culture. Assessing the firm's current culture can be accomplished via informal (observational and indirect questioning techniques) and direct questioning approaches such as conducting a formal service audit. By conducting a service audit, a seamless service culture is fostered as organizational personnel throughout the organization come to appreciate the challenges faced and the contributions made by everyone involved in the firm's final service delivery effort. The service audit deals directly with such issues as profit and growth, customer satisfaction, external service value, employee productivity, employee loyalty, employee satisfaction, internal service quality, leadership, and measures that assess the impact of each of these issues on the firm's bottom line.

Service firms wishing to transform their current cultures can facilitate the process by changing the firm's structure, systems, key personnel, or they can change the culture directly through broad-based educational programming. By implementing all four culture-change initiatives simultaneously, service firms can substantially speed the rate of culture transformation and dramatically increase their odds of success.

In closing, we hope that this book has helped develop your understanding of the special challenges involved in the marketing and management of service operations. With challenge comes opportunity, and, as you well know, plenty of opportunities exist in our current business environment to make the service encounter a more productive and pleasant experience for everyone involved—customers and employees alike. While many service firms are endlessly chasing the next big "out-of-the-box" idea, the service firms that truly succeed are the ones that focus "inside the box" itself. The "box" reflects the basic ideas of managing the four forces that impact the customer's experience— contact personnel, other customers, the servicescape, and the behind-the-scenes activities driving organizational systems that ultimately impact the customer's experience. Service firms that excel at "inside-the-box" activities thrive on providing internal service quality for their employees and produce the external service values of reliability, responsiveness, assurance, empathy; and they manage the tangible aspects of their service firms in a manner that meets or exceeds the expectations of their target markets. The time has come to make a difference...and we look forward to writing about the differences you make in future editions of this text.

# Key Terms

seamless service, p. 413
functionalism, p. 413
internal logic, p. 416
departmentalization, p. 416
operations logic, p. 416
marketing logic, p. 419
human resources logic, p. 419
service logic, p. 420

industrial management model, p. 420
market-focused management model, p. 421
culture, p. 424
service audit, p. 426
structure, p. 431
systems, p. 431

interfunctional task force, p. 432
interfunctional transfers, p. 432
"putting the customer first", p. 435
"orientation change", p. 435
"change the way you work", p. 435
"change the way we work", p. 435

## Review Questions

1. Discuss seamlessness as it relates to "tooth-to-tail" performance. Does departmentalization and functionalism facilitate or hinder seamlessness?

2. Discuss the fight for control among marketing, operations, and human resources personnel and how it impacts a service firm's culture.

3. Describe the major philosophical differences between the industrial management approach and the market-focused management approach.

4. Briefly discuss the six key relationships depicted in the "services triangle."

5. What is organizational culture? Why is it important?

6. Discuss four observations that may provide insight into a service firm's current culture.

7. What are the key components of a service audit?

8. Explain the relevance of interfunctional task forces and interfunctional transfers as they relate to corporate culture.

9. Discuss the four approaches to directly changing culture as presented in the text.

10. Briefly describe what you believe to be the Top 10 characteristics of a service firm that exhibits a world-class service culture.

## Notes

1. Benjamin Schneider and David E. Bowen, *Winning the Service Game* (Boston: Harvard Business School Press, 1995) pp. 1–16.

2. This section was adapted from John E. G. Bateson, *Managing Services Marketing*, 3rd ed. (Fort Worth, TX: The Dryden Press, 1995) pp. 636–645.

3. Bateson, *Managing Services Marketing*, pp. 636–645.

4. Jane Kingman-Brundage, William R. George, and David E. Bowen, "Service Logic-Achieving Service System Integration," *International Journal of Service Industry Management*, (1995), pp. 20–39.

5. Schneider and Bowen, *Winning the Service Game*, p. 199.

6. Leonard A. Schlesinger and James L. Heskett, "The Service-Driven Service Company," *Harvard Business Review*, (September-October 1991), pp. 71–75.

7. Ibid, p. 74.

8. Ibid, p. 71.

9. Ibid, p. 77.

10. Karl Albrecht and Ron Zemke, *Service America* (Homewood, IL: Dow Jones-Irwin, 1985) pp. 31–47.

11. Cynthia Webster, "What Kind of Marketing Culture Exists in Your Service Firm? An Audit," *The Journal of Services Marketing*, 6, 2, (Spring 1992), pp. 54–67.

12. **http://humanresources.about.com/od/organizationalculture/a/culture_create.htm**, accessed 8 April, 2009.

13. This section was adapted from James L. Heskett, Thomas O. Jones, Gary W. Loveman, W. Earl Sasser, Jr., and Leonard A. Schlesinger, "Putting the Service-Profit Chain to Work," *Harvard Business Review*, (March-April 1994), pp. 165–174.

14. Bateson, *Managing Services Marketing*, pp. 636–645.

15. Gronroos, "Designing a Long-Range Marketing Strategy," p. 36.

16. C. H. Lovelock, E. Langeard, J. E. G. Bateson, and P. Eiglier, "Some Organizational Problems Facing Marketing in the Service Sector," in J. Donnelly and W. George, eds., *Marketing of Services* (Chicago: American Marketing Association, 1981) pp. 148–153.

17. Schneider and Bowen, *Winning the Service Game*, p. 8.

# Assessing Your College's Culture: Go for a Culture Walk

Given that this is the last chapter of the text, students should now have a solid under-standing of what it takes to deliver an exceptional service experience. Moreover, since education is a service setting and many of the concepts and strategies presented in this text can certainly apply to higher education, students can utilize their new found knowl-edge to assess their current surroundings. The purpose of this live case is for students to conduct a culture walk within their own college, or perhaps assess the culture of another college on campus.

Before an organization can change its culture, it must first understand its current cul-ture. The culture walk exercise is one strategy for assessing an organization's current culture. Students should observe the college's culture as impartial observers. In other words, students should observe the college's culture as if they were new to the college and had never before interacted with its faculty, staff, and students. Typical assessments conducted during a culture walk include observation and interpretation of:

- *Space allocation and office location*—who gets the most space, the best offices, and who is separated from whom? What does space allocation and office location signify?
- *Bulletin boards and displays*—conduct a content analysis of posted and displayed materials. What does it say about the organization?
- *Common areas*—what are the common areas used for, and by whom?
- *Memos, emails, and other communication methods*—what is the content of these communications, what is the tone, and do people primarily communicate orally or through written communications?
- *Employee interaction*—do employees interact with one another, and is there any emotion displayed during these interactions?
- *Student interaction*—do students interact with one another, and is there any emo-tion displayed during these interactions?
- *Employee/student interaction*—do employees/students interact with one another, and is there any emotion displayed during these interactions?
- *Further assessment of the college's culture can be accomplished through culture inter-views and surveys with faculty, staff, and students. Thought provoking questions that provide insight into the college's culture may include:*
  - *What would faculty, staff, and students tell their friends about working at or attending this college?*
  - *What is the one thing faculty, staff, and students would like to change?*
  - *Who are the college heroes? Why these people?*

Source: **http://humanresources.about.com/od/organizationalculture/a/culture_create.htm**, accessed 8 April, 2009.

- *What are the faculty, staff, and students' favorite characteristics of the college?*
- *What kinds of faculty, staff, and students would fail at this college?*
- *What would be the faculty, staff, and students' favorite question to ask individuals who were considering working or attending this college?*

## Discussion Questions

1. Assessing the current culture of a firm can be very enlightening and challenging. By determining the current culture, the college's leadership gains a better understanding of how to move the college forward, if desired, to a new set of values and beliefs. Upon the collection and evaluation of the above information, students should report on what they consider are the core values and beliefs that make up the college's current culture. Define the core values and beliefs of the college and provide justification for why you believe these core values exist.
2. Provide a discussion on whether you believe the college's core values are appropriate.
3. Make recommendations for how the college's current culture should be changed. What strategies could you use to change the college's culture?

# Glossary

## A

**activity-based costing (ABC)**   Costing method that breaks down the organization into a set of activities, and activities into tasks, which convert materials, labor, and technology into outputs.

**activity time**   The time required to perform one activity at one station.

**adequate service**   The level of service quality a customer is willing to accept.

**aftermarketing**   Marketing technique that emphasizes marketing after the initial sale has been made.

**after-sales surveys**   A type of satisfaction survey that addresses customer satisfaction while the service encounter is still fresh in the customer's mind.

**ambient conditions**   The distinctive atmosphere of the service setting that includes lighting, air quality, noise, music, and so on.

**anticipating**   Mitigating the worst effects of supply and demand fluctuations by planning for them.

**apathetic customers**   Consumers who seek convenience over price and personal attention.

**apologetic strategies**   A set of verbal recovery strategies involving apologies from front-line providers and/or upper-level management.

**approach/avoidance behaviors**   Consumer responses to the set of environmental stimuli that are characterized by a desire to stay or leave an establishment, explore/interact with the service environment or ignore it, or feel satisfaction or disappointment with the service experience.

**arousal-nonarousal**   The emotional state that reflects the degree to which consumers and employees feel excited and stimulated.

**assurance dimension**   The SERVQUAL assessment of a firm's competence, courtesy to its customers, and security of its operations.

**attribution**   The allocation of responsibility to self and other people, or even chance.

**auditing consumer performance expertise**   Measuring the current extent to which the consumer understands the script that the service system has been designed to deliver.

**awareness set**   The set of alternatives of which a consumer is aware.

## B

**behavioral modeling**   Categorizing customers to enable providers to more easily process them and remove stress.

**beliefs**   Consumers' opinions about the provider's ability to perform the service.

**benchmarking**   Setting standards against which to compare future data collected.

**benefit concept**   The encapsulation of the benefits of a product in the consumer's mind.

**benefit-driven pricing**   A pricing strategy that charges customers for services actually used as opposed to overall "membership" fees.

**blueprinting**   The flowcharting of a service operation.

**bottlenecks**   Points in the system at which consumers wait the longest periods of time.

**boundary-spanning personnel**   Personnel who provide their services outside the firm's physical facilities.

**boundary-spanning roles**   The various parts played by contact personnel who perform dual functions of interacting with the firm's external environment and internal organization.

**buffering**   Surrounding the technical core with input and output components to buffer environmental influences.

**buffering the technical core**   The operations management concept of ensuring that the core of the production process is able to run as efficiently as possible. For manufacturing plants this is executed by creating buffers (stocks) of raw material input and buffers (stocks) of the outputs to ensure the factory itself can run uninterrupted.

**business ethics**   The principles of moral conduct that guide behavior in the business world.

# C

**capacity sharing**   Strategy to increase the supply of service by forming a type of co-op among service providers that permits co-op members to expand their supply or service as a whole.

**categorization**   The process of categorizing servicescapes based on previous experiences.

**"change the way we work"**   The element of the culture change initiative that teaches personnel to flowchart their activities and to re-engineer the process to better serve their customers.

**"change the way you work"**   The element of the culture change initiative that allows personnel to break the rules in the context of serving their customers.

**climate for service**   The shared perception of the service practices, procedures, and kind of behaviors that get reward.

**code of ethics**   Formal standards of conduct that assist in defining proper organizational behavior.

**coding**   Categorizing customers based on how profitable their business is.

**cognitive dissonance**   Doubt in the consumer's mind regarding the correctness of the purchase decision.

**commercial cue**   An event or motivation that provides a stimulus to the consumer and is a promotional effort on the part of the company.

**communication mix**   The array of communications tools available to marketers including advertising, personal selling, publicity, sales promotions, and sponsorships.

**communication strategy**   Communicates the firm's positioning strategy to its target markets, including consumers, employees, stockholders, and suppliers for the purpose of achieving organizational objectives.

**communications gap**   The difference between the actual quality of service delivered and the quality of service described in the firm's external communications.

**compatibility management**   The management of a diverse group of customers with different needs within the same service setting.

**compensatory strategies**   A set of recovery strategies that compensate the customers to offset the costs of the service failure.

**complements**   The effect of cross-price elasticity in which an increase in the price of Product A decreases the demand for Product B.

**complexity**   A measure of the number and intricacy of the steps and sequences that constitute a process.

**complimentary services**   Services provided for consumers to minimize their perceived waiting time, such as driving ranges at golf courses, arcades at movie theaters, or reading materials in doctors' offices.

**confirmed expectations**   Customer expectations that match customer perception resulting in customer satisfaction.

**conflict of interest**   The situation in which a service provider feels torn between the organization, the customer, and/or the service provider's own personal interest.

**conquest marketing**   A marketing strategy for constantly seeking new customers by offering discounts and markdowns and developing promotions that encourage new business.

**consideration set** Of the brands in the evoked set, those considered unfit (e.g., too expensive, too far away, and so on) are eliminated right away. The remaining alternatives are termed the consideration set.

**consumer decision process** The three-step process consumers use to make purchase decisions; includes the prepurchase stage, the consumption stage, and the postpurchase evaluation stage.

**consumer management** A strategy service personnel can implement that minimizes the impact of "other customers" on each individual customer's service experience (e.g., separating smokers from nonsmokers in a restaurant).

**consumer performance** An individual's participation in the production of their own service.

**consumer socialization** The process by which the consumer as an individual adapts to the values, norms, and required behavior patterns of an organization.

**consumption process** The activities of buying, using, and disposing of a product.

**contact personnel** Employees other than the primary service provider who briefly interact with the customer.

**contrast/clash** Visual effects associated with exciting, cheerful, and informal business settings.

**control and predictability** One of the primary motivational needs for an individual. Psychologists have agreed that all human beings like to feel in control of their environments. The source of that feeling of control is when the environment is predictable.

**controllability** A service failure attribution pertaining to whether or not the firm had control over the cause of the failure.

**convergent scripts** Employee/consumer scripts that are mutually agreeable and enhance the probability of customer satisfaction.

**copy** The content of the firm's communication message.

**core service failures** Failures in the core service offering of the firm including unavailable service, unreasonably slow service, and other core service failures.

**corrective control** The use of rewards and punishments to enforce a firm's code of ethics.

**creative pricing** Pricing strategies often used by service firms to help smooth demand fluctuations, such as offering "matinee" prices or "early bird specials" to shift demand from peak to nonpeak periods.

**credence attributes** Product attributes that cannot be evaluated confidently even immediately after receipt of the good or the service.

**critical incident** A specific interaction between a customer and a service provider.

**cross-price elasticity** A measure of the responsiveness of demand for a service relative to a change in price for another service.

**culture** The shared values and beliefs that drive an organization's overall service philosophy.

**customer acquisition cost** The monetary amount spent on marketing and other activities to acquire a new customer.

**customer loyalty** Reflects an emotional attachment as well as a business attachment to the service firm.

**customer participation** A supply strategy that increases the supply of service by having the customer perform part of the service, such as providing a salad bar or dessert bar in a restaurant.

**customer relationship management (CRM)** The process of identifying, attracting, differentiating, and retaining customers, where firms focus their efforts disproportionately on their most lucrative clients.

**customer research** Research that examines the customer's perspective of a firm's strengths and weaknesses.

**customer retention** Focusing the firm's marketing efforts toward the existing customer base.

**customization** Taking advantage of the variation inherent in each service encounter by developing services that meet each customer's exact specifications.

# D

**decoupling** Disassociating the technical core from the servuction system.

**defection management** A systematic process that actively attempts to retain customers before they defect.

**delivery gap** The difference between the quality standards set for service delivery and the actual quality of service delivery.

**departmentalization** The act of dividing an organization into departments that focus on their own set of activities.

**derived expectations** Expectations appropriated from and based on the expectations of others.

**desired service** The level of service quality a customer actually wants from a service encounter.

**dichotomization of wealth** The rich get richer and poor get poorer.

**direct measures** Measures of satisfaction generally obtained directly from customers via customer satisfaction surveys.

**disconfirmed expectations** Customer expectations that do not match customer perceptions.

**dispersion of control** The situation in which control over the nature of the service being provided is removed from employees' hands.

**distributive justice** A component of perceived justice that refers to the outcomes (e.g., compensation) associated with the service recovery process.

**divergence** A measure of the degrees of freedom service personnel are allowed when providing a service.

**divergent scripts** Employee/consumer scripts that "mismatch" and point to areas in which consumer expectations are not being met.

**dominance-submissiveness** The emotional state that reflects the degree to which consumers and employees feel in control and able to act freely within the service environment.

**dual entitlement** Cost-driven price increases are perceived as fair, whereas demand-driven price increases are viewed as unfair.

## E

**economic customers** Consumers who make purchase decisions based primarily on price.

**economies of scale** Based on the idea of the more you produce, the cheaper it is to produce it…the cheaper it is to produce it, the cheaper it can be sold…the cheaper it can be sold, the more it is sold… the more it is sold, the more it can be produced (and so on and so forth).

**efficiency pricing** Pricing strategies that appeal to economically minded consumers by delivering the best and most cost-effective service for the price.

**emotional responses** Feelings that are a result of the servicescape.

**empathy dimension** The SERVQUAL assessment of a firm's ability to put itself in its customers' place.

**employee-job fit** The degree to which employees are able to perform a service to specifications.

**employee socialization** The process through which an individual adapts and comes to appreciate the values, norms, and required behavior patterns of an organization.

**employee surveys** Internal measures of service quality concerning employee morale, attitudes, and perceived obstacles to the provision of quality services.

**employer brand** The brand that is created in the market for staff, which is analogous to the brand in the customer market.

**empowerment** Giving discretion to front-line personnel to meet the needs of consumers creatively.

**enduring service intensifiers** Personal factors that are stable over time and increase a customer's sensitivity to how a service should be best provided.

**energy costs** The physical energy spent by the customer to acquire the service.

**enfranchisement** Empowerment coupled with a performance-based compensation method.

**environmental psychology** The use of physical evidence to create service environments and its influence on the perceptions and behaviors of individuals.

**e-service** An electronic service available via the net that completes tasks, solves problems, or conducts transactions.

**ethical customers** Consumers who support smaller or local firms as opposed to larger or national service providers.

**ethical vigilance** Paying close attention to whether one's actions are "right" or "wrong," and if ethically "wrong," asking why you are behaving in that manner.

**ethics**   A branch of philosophy dealing with what is good and bad and with moral duty and obligations; the principles of moral conduct governing an individual or group.

**evaluation of alternatives**   The phase of the prepurchase stage in which the consumer places a value or "rank" on each alternative.

**evoked set**   Alternatives that the consumer actually remembers at the time of decision making.

**exit**   A complaining outcome in which the consumer stops patronizing the store or using the product.

**expansion preparation**   Planning for future expansion in advance and taking a long-term orientation to physical facilities and growth.

**expectancy disconfirmation model**   Model proposing that comparing customer expectations to their perceptions leads customers to have their expectations confirmed or disconfirmed.

**expected script**   The script the consumer carries with them into the service setting; what they expect to happen and the benchmark against which they will evaluate the experience.

**experience attributes**   Product attributes that can be evaluated only during and after the production process.

**expert consumers**   Individuals who have expertise in the purchase process for a particular good or service. Expert performers, by comparison, are expert in the service production process.

**explicit service promises**   Obligations to which the firm commits itself via its advertising, personal selling, contracts, and other forms of communication.

**external search**   A proactive approach to gathering information in which the consumer collects new information from sources outside the consumer's own experience.

# F

**facility exterior**   The physical exterior of the service facility; includes the exterior design, signage, parking, landscaping, and the surrounding environment.

**facility interior**   The physical interior of the service facility; includes the interior design, equipment used to serve customers, signage, layout, air quality, and temperature.

**factories in the field**   Another name for multisite locations.

**fail points**   Points in the system at which the potential for malfunction is high and at which a failure would be visible to the customer and regarded as significant.

**failures relating to customer needs and requests**   Service failures relating to the implicit and explicit needs of customers including special needs, customer preferences, customer errors, and disruptive others.

**failures relating to problematic customers**   Failures relating to the customer's own misbehavior, including drunkenness, verbal and physical abuse, violations of company policies, and uncooperative customers.

**failures relating to unprompted/unsolicited actions**   Failures relating to level of attention, unusual employee actions, violations of cultural norms, gestalt, and responses to adverse conditions.

**financial risk**   The possibility of a monetary loss if the purchase goes wrong or fails to operate correctly.

**fixed costs**   Costs that are planned and accrued during the operating period regardless of the level of production and sales.

**flat-rate pricing**   A pricing strategy in which the customer pays a fixed price and the provider assumes the risk of price increases and cost overruns.

**focus group interviews**   Informal discussions with eight to 12 customers that are usually guided by a trained moderator; used to identify areas of information to be collected in subsequent survey research.

**focused factory**   An operation that concentrates on performing one particular task in one particular part of the plant; used for promoting experience and effectiveness through repetition and concentration on one task necessary for success.

**forward buying**   When retailers purchase enough product on deal to carry over until the product is being sold on deal again.

**frequency marketing**   Marketing technique that strives to make existing customers purchase more often from the same provider.

**functionalism** The belief that the function of something rather than the experience it creates should determine its design.

# G

**goods** Objects, devices, or things.

# H

**halo effect** An overall favorable or unfavorable impression based on early stages of the service encounter.

**hard technologies** Hardware that facilitates the production of a standardized product.

**harmony** Visual agreement associated with quieter, plusher, and more formal business settings.

**heterogeneity** A distinguishing characteristic of services that reflects the variation in consistency from one service transaction to the next.

**high and low contact systems** Service production processes arranged on a spectrum according to how much the consumer is part of the process. In a high contact system the consumer is an integral part of the process; in a low contact system, although present, the consumer has a smaller role to play.

**high involvement** Allows employees eventually to learn to manage themselves, utilizing extensive training and employee control of the reward allocation decisions.

**holistic environment** Overall perceptions of the servicescape formed by employees and customers based on the physical environmental dimensions.

**horizontal communication** The flow of internal communication between a firm's headquarters and its service firms in the field.

**hue** The actual color, such as red, blue, yellow, or green.

**human resources logic** The reasoning that stresses recruiting personnel and developing training to enhance the performance of existing personnel.

# I

**image value** The worth assigned to the image of the service or service provider by the customer.

**implicit guarantee** An unwritten, unspoken guarantee that establishes an understanding between the firm and its customers.

**implicit service promises** Obligations to which the firm commits itself via the tangibles surrounding the service and the price of the service.

**inadequate support** A management failure to give employees personal training and/or technological and other resources necessary for them to perform their jobs in the best possible manner.

**indirect measures** Measures of customer satisfaction including tracking and monitoring sales records, profits, and customer complaints.

**individual behaviors** Responses to the servicescape that are typically described as approach and avoidance behaviors.

**industrial management model** An approach to organizing a firm that focuses on revenues and operating costs and ignores the roles personnel play in generating customer satisfaction and sustainable profits.

**inelastic demand** The type of market demand when a change in price of service is greater than a change in quantity demanded.

**information search** The phase in the prepurchase stage in which the consumer collects information on possible alternatives.

**inseparability** A distinguishing characteristic of services that reflects the interconnections among the service provider, the customer involved in receiving the service, and other customers sharing the service experience.

**instrumental complaints** Complaints expressed for the purpose of altering an undesirable state of affairs.

**intangibility** A distinguishing characteristic of services that makes them unable to be touched or sensed in the same manner as physical goods.

**intangible dominant** Services that lack the physical properties that can be sensed by consumers prior to the purchase decision.

**intensity** The brightness or the dullness of the colors.

**interactional justice** A component of perceived justice that refers to human content (e.g., empathy, friendliness) that is demonstrated by service personnel during the service recovery process.

**inter-client conflicts** Disagreements between clients that arise because of the number of clients who influence one another's experience.

**interdepartmental service support**   The support provided by other departments in the service organization that allow service providers to do their job.

**interfunctional task force**   Problem-solving group in which individuals with diverse viewpoints work together and develop a better understanding of one another's perspectives.

**interfunctional transfers**   Moving, via promotion or transfer, an employee from one organizational department to another to foster informal networks among departments.

**internal logic**   Implicit and explicit principles of individual departments that drive organizational performance.

**internal response moderators**   The three basic emotional states of the SOR model that mediate the reaction between the perceived servicescape and customers' and employees' responses to the service environment.

**internal search**   A passive approach to gathering information in which the consumer's own memory is the main source of information about a product.

**interpersonal services**   Service environments in which customers and providers interact.

**interpersonal training**   Training focused on teaching service providers how to deal with customers.

**invisible organization and systems**   That part of a firm that reflects the rules, regulations, and processes upon which the organization is based.

## J

**job involvement**   Allows employees to examine the content of their own jobs and to define their role within the organization.

## K

**knowledge gap**   The difference between what consumers expect of a service and what management perceives the consumers to expect.

## L

**lagged effect**   When demand for the service is infrequent, and therefore the success of the communication strategy may not be realized until a later point in time.

**learned helplessness**   The condition of employees who, through repeated dispersion of control, feel themselves unable to perform a service adequately.

**levels of management**   The complexity of the organizational hierarchy and the number of levels between top management and the customers.

**lexicographic approach**   A systematic model that proposes that the consumer make a decision by examining each attribute, starting with the most important, to rule out alternatives.

**lifetime profit (LTP) of a customer**   The average profit per sale multiplied by the average number of times customers reorder (discounted to the present).

**lifetime value (LTV) of a customer**   The average dollar amount per sale multiplied by the average number of times customers reorder (discounted to the present).

**linear compensatory approach**   A systematic model that proposes that the consumer creates a global score for each brand by multiplying the rating of the brand on each attribute by the importance attached to the attribute and adding the scores together.

**locus**   A service failure attribution pertaining to the possible source of the failure including the service provider, the firm, the customer, or external forces.

## M

**market defectors**   Customers who exit the market due to relocation or business failure.

**market-focused management model**   A new organizational model that focuses on the components of the firm that facilitate the firm's service delivery system.

**marketing logic**   The reasoning that stresses providing customers with options that better enable the service offering to meet individual needs.

**materialismo snobbery**   Belief that without manufacturing there will be less for people to service and so more people available to do less work.

**maximum output per hour**   The number of people that can be processed at each station in one hour.

**mechanistic processes**   Formalized step-by-step processes that are developed to facilitate the firm's failure analysis and service recovery efforts.

**mistargeted communications**   Occurs when the same communication message appeals to two diverse market segments.

**mixed bundling**   Price-bundling technique that allows consumers to either buy Service A and Service B together or purchase one service separately.

**molecular model**   A conceptual model of the relationship between the tangible and intangible components of a firm's operations.

**monetary cost**   The actual dollar price paid by the consumer for a product.

**multisite locations**   A way service firms that mass produce combat inseparability, involving multiple locations to limit the distance the consumers have to travel and staffing each location differently to serve a local market.

**mystery shopping**   A form of noncustomer research that consists of trained personnel who pose as customers, shop at the firm unannounced, and evaluate employees.

## N

**negative disconfirmation**   Customer perceptions that are lower than customer expectations resulting in customer dissatisfaction.

**niche positioning strategy**   A positioning strategy that increases divergence in an operation to tailor the service experience to each customer.

**noncustomer research**   Research that examines how competitors perform on service and how employees view the firm's strengths and weaknesses.

**noninstrumental complaints**   Complaints expressed without expectation that an undesirable state will be altered.

**nonpeak demand development**   A strategy in which service providers use their downtime to prepare in advance for peak periods or by marketing to different target markets that follow different demand pattern than the firm's traditional market segment.

**nonsystematic evaluation**   Choosing among alternatives in a random fashion or by a "gut-level feeling" approach.

**novice and expert performance**   The spectrum of performance ability. Not all consumers are equally proficient. The novice does not know what to do and how to perform. An expert knows how to be part of the production process.

## O

**one-sided blueprint**   An unbalanced blueprint based on management's perception of how the sequence of events *should* occur.

**operations logic**   The reasoning that stresses cost containment/reduction through mass production.

**organic processes**   Informal sets of values and beliefs that comprise the firm's service recovery culture.

**organism**   The recipients of the set of stimuli in the service encounter; includes employees and customers.

**organization/client conflicts**   Disagreements that arise when a customer requests services that violate the rules of the organization.

**organizational defectors**   Customers who leave due to political considerations inside the firm, such as reciprocal buying arrangements.

**organizational relationships**   Working relationships formed between service providers and various role partners such as customers, suppliers, peers, subordinates, supervisors, and others.

**"orientation change"**   The element of the culture change initiative that teaches "families" of personnel to reinforce one another on the job.

**ostensive complaints**   Complaints directed at someone or something outside the realm of the complainer.

**"other customers"**   The term used to describe customers that share a service experience with the primary customer.

**other tangibles**   Other items that are part of the firm's physical evidence, such as business cards, stationery, billing statements, reports, employee appearance, uniforms, and brochures.

**overpromising**   A firm's promise of more than it can deliver.

## P

**partial employees**   The operations management approach to consumer performance is to view the consumer as an employee (albeit only part of one) and to apply the same people logic to them as they would to an employee.

**past experience**   The previous service encounters a consumer has had with a service provider.

**penetration strategy**   A positioning strategy that increases complexity by adding more services and/or enhancing current services to capture more of a market.

**perceived justice**   The process where customers weigh their inputs against their outputs when forming recovery evaluations.

**perceived service adequacy**   A measure of service quality derived by comparing adequate service and perceived service.

**perceived service alternatives**   Comparable services customers believe they can obtain elsewhere and/or produce themselves.

**perceived service superiority**   A measure of service quality derived by comparing desired service expectations and perceived service received.

**perceived servicescape**   A composite of mental images of the service firm's physical facilities.

**perceived-control perspective**   A model in which consumers evaluate services by the amount of control they have over the perceived situation.

**perfect-world model**   J. D. Thompson's model of organizations proposing that operations' "perfect" efficiency is possible only if inputs, outputs, and quality happen at a constant rate and remain known and certain.

**performance risk**   The possibility that the item or service purchased will not perform the task for which it was purchased.

**perishability**   A distinguishing characteristic of services in that they cannot be saved, their unused capacity cannot be reserved, and they cannot be inventoried.

**person/role conflict**   A bad fit between an individual's self-perception and the specific role the person must play in an organization.

**personal needs**   A customer's physical, social, and psychological needs.

**personal service philosophies**   A customer's own internal views of the meaning of service and the manner in which service providers should conduct themselves.

**personal sources of information**   Sources such as friends, family, and other opinion leaders that consumers use to gather information about a service.

**personalized customers**   Consumers who desire to be pampered and attended to and who are much less price sensitive.

**personnel value**   The worth assigned to the service-providing personnel by the customer.

**physical cue**   A motivation, such as thirst, hunger, or another biological cue that provides a stimulus to the consumer.

**physical evidence/tangible clues**   The physical characteristics that surround a service to assist consumers in making service evaluations, such as the quality of furnishings, the appearance of personnel, or the quality of paper stock used to produce the firm's brochure.

**physical risk**   The possibility that if something does go wrong, injury could be inflicted on the purchaser.

**physiological responses**   Responses to the firm's physical environment based on pain or comfort.

**plant-within-a-plant (PWP)**   The strategy of breaking up large, unfocused plants into smaller units buffered from one another so that each can be focused separately.

**pleasure-displeasure**   The emotional state that reflects the degree to which consumers and employees feel satisfied with the service experience.

**positioning strategy**   How the firm is viewed by consumers relative to its competitors. Positioning strategy speaks to the firm's differential advantage.

**positive disconfirmation**   Customer perceptions that exceed customer expectations resulting in delighting customers.

**predicted service**   The level of service quality a consumer believes is likely to occur.

**price bundling**   The practice of marketing two or more products and/or services in a single package at a single price.

**price defectors**   Customers who switch to competitors for lower-priced goods and services.

**price discrimination**   The practice of charging different customers different prices for essentially the same service.

**problem awareness**   The second phase of the pre-purchase stage, in which the consumer determines whether a need exists for the product.

**procedural justice**   A component of perceived justice that refers to the process (e.g., time) the customer endures during the service recovery process.

**process time**   Calculated by dividing the activity time by the number of locations at which the activity is performed.

**product**   Either a good or a service.

**product defectors**   Customers who switch to competitors who offer superior goods and services.

**product-line pricing**   The practice of pricing multiple versions of the same core product or grouping similar products together.

**product value**   The worth assigned to the product by the customer.

**production-line approach**   The application of hard and soft technologies to a service operation in order to produce a standardized service product.

**psychic costs**   The mental energy spent by the customer to acquire the service.

**psychological risk**   The possibility that a purchase will affect an individual's self-esteem.

**"putting the customer first"**   The element of the culture change initiative that teaches personnel to put the customer first.

## Q

**quality circles**   Empowerment involving small groups of employees from various departments in the firm who use brainstorming sessions to generate additional improvement suggestions.

**question context**   The placement and tone of a question relative to the other questions asked.

**question form**   The way a question is phrased, i.e., positively or negatively.

**question timing**   The length of time after the date of purchase that questions are asked.

## R

**rationing**   Direct allocations of inputs and outputs when the demands placed on a system by the environment exceed the system's ability to handle them.

**red-lining**   The practice of identifying and avoiding unprofitable types of neighborhoods or types of people.

**reflexive complaints**   Complaints directed at some inner aspect of the complainer.

**reimbursement strategies**   A set of recovery strategies that provides the customer with a refund or store credit.

**relationship marketing**   Marketing technique based on developing long-term relationships with customers.

**relationship pricing**   Pricing strategies that encourage the customer to expand his or her dealings with the service provider.

**reliability dimension**   The SERVQUAL assessment of a firm's consistency and dependability in service performance.

**remote services**   Services in which employees are physically present while customer involvement in the service production process is at arm's length.

**research orientation**   A firm's attitude toward conducting consumer research.

**reservation price**   The price a consumer considers to capture the value he or she places on the benefits.

**reservation system**   A strategy to help smooth demand fluctuations in which consumers ultimately request a portion of the firm's services for a particular time slot.

**response bias**   A bias in survey results because of responses being received from only a limited group among the total survey participants.

**responses (outcomes)**   Consumers' reaction or behavior in response to stimuli.

**responsiveness dimension**   The SERVQUAL assessment of a firm's commitment to providing its services in a timely manner.

**restoration strategies**   A set of recovery strategies offered to offset the current failure situation by providing an identical offering, corrections to the original offering, or by offering a substitute.

**retaliation**   A complaining outcome in which the consumer takes action deliberately designed to damage the physical operation or hurt future business.

**role ambiguity**   Uncertainty of employees' roles in their jobs and poor understanding of the purpose of their jobs.

**role conflict**   An inconsistency in service providers' minds between what the service manager expects them to provide and the service they think their customers actually want.

**routing**   Directing incoming customer calls to customer service representatives where more profitable customers are more likely to receive faster and better customer service.

# S

**satisfaction-based pricing**   Pricing strategies that are designed to reduce the amount of perceived risk associated with a purchase.

**scale of market entities**   The scale that displays a range of products along a continuum based on their tangibility ranging from tangible dominant to intangible dominant.

**script congruence**   Occurs when the actual scripts performed by customers and staff are consistent with the expected scripts.

**script norms**   Proposed scripts developed by grouping together events commonly mentioned by both employees and customers, and then ordering those events in their sequence of occurrence.

**script perspective**   Argues that rules, mostly determined by social and cultural variables, exist to facilitate interactions in daily repetitive events, including a variety of service experiences.

**seamless service**   Services that occur without interruption, confusion, or hassle to the customer.

**search attributes**   Product attributes that can be determined prior to purchase.

**self-perceived service role**   The input a customer believes he or she is required to present in order to produce a satisfactory service encounter.

**self selection**   Given the right clues about a service business, consumers will tend to choose for themselves the service that best fits their needs.

**self-service technologies**   Technologically based services that help customers help themselves.

**self-services**   Service environments that are dominated by the customer's physical presence, such as ATMs or postal kiosks.

**service audit**   A series of questions that force the firm to think about what drives its profits and suggests strategies for competitive differentiation and long-term profitability.

**service cost per meal**   The labor costs associated with providing a meal on a per-meal basis (total labor costs/maximum output per hour).

**service defectors**   Customers who defect due to poor customer service.

**service-dominant logic**   Philosophical viewpoint that the primary role of marketers is to deliver service. Consequently, goods are simply a means of rendering a service to the customer.

**service economy**   Includes the "soft parts" of the economy consisting of nine industry supersectors.

**service failures**   Breakdowns in the delivery of service; service that does not meet customer expectations.

**service gap**   The distance between a customer's expectation of a service and perception of the service actually delivered.

**service imperative**   Reflects the view that the intangible aspects of products are becoming the key features that differentiate products in the marketplace.

**service logic**   Promotes seamlessness by balancing the internal logics of marketing, operations, and human resources.

**service marketing myopia**   Condition of firms that produce tangible products and overlook the service aspects of their products.

**service providers**   The primary providers of a core service, such as a waiter or waitress, dentist, physician, or college instructor.

**service quality**   An attitude formed by a long-term, overall evaluation of a firm's performance.

**service quality information system**   An ongoing research process that provides relevant data on a timely basis to managers, who use the data in decision making.

**service recovery**   A firm's reaction to a complaint that results in customer satisfaction and goodwill.

**service recovery culture**   An informal set of beliefs, behaviors, and practices that set the tone for how the firm wishes to address customer complaints.

**service recovery paradox**   A situation in which the customer rates performance higher if a failure occurs and the contact personnel successfully recovers from it than if the service had been delivered correctly the first time.

**service sabotage**   Willful and malicious acts by service providers designed to ruin the service.

**service value**   The worth assigned to the service by the customer.

**services**   Deeds, efforts, or performances.

**servicescapes**   The use of physical evidence to design service environments.

**SERVQUAL**   A 44-item scale that measures customer expectations and perceptions regarding five service quality dimensions.

**servuction model**   A model used to illustrate the four factors that influence the service experience, including those that are visible to the consumer and those that are not.

**shades**   Darker values.

**sharing**   Making accessible key customer information to all parts of the organization.

**shortage**   The need for a product or service due to the consumer's not having that particular product or service.

**signpost items**   Items that customers frequently purchase and are very well aware of typical prices.

**signs, symbols, artifacts**   Environmental physical evidence that includes signage to direct the flow of the service process, personal artifacts to personalize the facility, and the style of decor.

**situational factors**   Circumstances that lower the service quality but that are beyond the control of the service provider.

**size/shape/colors**   The three primary visual stimuli that appeal to consumers on a basic level.

**SMART**   When setting objectives, objectives should be SMART—specific, measurable, achievable, relevant, and time-bound.

**smoothing**   Managing the environment to reduce fluctuations in supply and/or demand.

**social cue**   An event or motivation that provides a stimulus to the consumer, obtained from the individual's peer group or from significant others.

**social desirability bias**   A bias in survey results because of respondents' tendencies to provide information they believe is socially appropriate.

**social risk**   The possibility of a loss in personal social status associated with a particular purchase.

**socialization**   The process by which an individual adapts to the values, norms, and required behavior patterns of an organization.

**soft technologies**   Rules, regulations, and procedures that facilitate the production of a standardized product.

**space/function**   Environmental dimensions that include the layout of the facility, the equipment, and the firm's furnishings.

**specialization positioning strategy**   A positioning strategy that reduces complexity by unbundling the different services offered.

**specific result guarantee**   A guarantee that applies only to specific steps or outputs in the service delivery process.

**stability**   A service failure attribution pertaining to the likelihood the service failure will recur.

**standardization**   The goal of standardization is to produce a consistent service product from one transaction to the next.

**standards gap**   The difference between what management perceives consumers to expect and the quality specifications set for service delivery.

**stations**   A location at which an activity is performed within a service blueprint.

**stimuli**   The various elements of the firm's physical evidence.

**stimulus**   The thought, action, or motivation that incites a person to consider a purchase.

**stimulus-organism-response (SOR) model**   A model developed by environmental psychologists to help explain the effects of the service environment on consumer behavior; describes environmental stimuli, emotional states, and responses to those states.

**structure** The formal reporting hierarchy normally represented in an organizational chart.

**subordinate service roles** The jobs within service organizations where the customers' decisions are entirely discretionary such as waitresses, porters.

**substitutes** The effect of cross-price elasticity in which an increase in the Price of Product A increases the demand for Product B.

**suggestion involvement** Low-level empowerment that allows employees to recommend suggestions for improvement of the firm's operations.

**sustainability** The ability to meet current needs without hindering the ability to meet the needs of future generations in terms of economic, environmental, and social challenges.

**switching costs** Costs that can accrue when changing one service provider to another.

**symbolic meaning** Meaning inferred from the firm's use of physical evidence.

**systematic evaluation** Choosing among alternatives by using a set of formalized steps to arrive at a decision.

**systems** People-management systems of control, evaluation, promotion, and recognition.

## T

**tangible dominant** Goods that possess physical properties that can be felt, tasted, and seen prior to the consumer's purchase decision.

**tangibles dimension** The SERVQUAL assessment of a firm's ability to manage its tangibles.

**target markets** The market segment that becomes the focus of a firm's marketing efforts.

**targeting** Offering the firm's most profitable customers special deals and incentives.

**technical core** The place within an organization where its primary operations are conducted.

**technical training** Training focused on teaching service providers their operational role in delivering the service.

**technological defectors** Customers who switch to products outside the industry.

**the service HR wheel** The HR functions that together support the creation of a climate for service.

**third parties** A supply strategy in which a service firm uses an outside party to service customers and thereby save on costs, personnel, etc.

**time costs** The time the customer has to spend to acquire the service.

**tints** Lighter values.

**total market service quality surveys** Surveys that measure the service quality of the firm sponsoring the survey and the service quality of the firm's competitors.

**transitory service intensifiers** Personal, short-term factors that heighten a customer's sensitivity to service.

**two-sided blueprint** A blueprint that takes into account both employee and customer perceptions of how the sequence of events actually occurs.

**type 1 service staff** Service staff who are required to deal with customers quickly and effectively in "once only" situations where large numbers of customers are present.

**type 2 service staff** Service staff who deal with numerous, often repeat customers in restricted interactions of somewhat longer duration.

**type 3 service staff** Service staff required to have more highly developed communication skills because of more extended and complex interactions with customers.

## U

**unbundling** Divesting an operation of different services and concentrating on providing only one or a few services in order to pursue a specialization positioning strategy.

**unconditional guarantee** A guarantee that promises complete customer satisfaction and, at a minimum, a full refund or complete, no-cost problem resolution.

**unfulfilled desire** The need for a product or service due to a consumer's dissatisfaction with a current product or service.

**unresponsive strategy** A recovery strategy in which the firm purposely decides not to respond to customer complaints.

**upward communication** The flow of information from front-line personnel to upper levels of the organization.

# V

**value**   The lightness and darkness of the colors.

**variable costs**   Costs that are directly associated with increases in production and sales.

**visual pathway**   Printed materials through which the professional image of the firm can be consistently transmitted, including firm brochures, letterhead, envelopes, and business cards.

**voice**   A complaining outcome in which the consumer verbally communicates dissatisfaction with the store or the product.

**volume-oriented positioning strategy**   A positioning strategy that reduces divergence to create product uniformity and reduce costs.

# W

**willingness to perform**   An employee's desire to perform to his/her full potential in a service encounter.

**word-of-mouth communications**   Unbiased information from someone who has been through the service experience, such as friends, family, or consultants.

**work facilitation**   The provision of the basic infrastructure and technology to enable service providers to deliver the desired service.

# Z

**zero defections**   A model used by service providers that strives for no customer defections to competitors.

**zero defects model**   A model used in manufacturing that strives for no defects in goods produced.

**zone of tolerance**   Level of quality ranging from high to low and reflecting the difference between desired service and adequate service; expands and contracts across customers and within the same customer, depending on the service and the conditions under which it is provided.

# Index